Indian History

Class 6-12 (Old+New)

Authors
Amibh Ranjan
Mudit Sharma

Series Editor
Santosh Dutt Pandey

ARIHANT PUBLICATIONS (INDIA) LIMITED

卐 Administrative & Production Offices

Regd. Office
'Ramchhaya' 4577/15, Agarwal Road, Darya Ganj, New Delhi -110002
Tele: 011- 47630600, 43518550

Head Office
Kalindi, TP Nagar, Meerut (UP) - 250002
Tel: 0121-7156203, 7156204

卐 Sales & Support Offices
Agra, Ahmedabad, Bengaluru, Bareilly, Chennai, Delhi, Guwahati, Hyderabad, Jaipur, Jhansi, Kolkata, Lucknow, Nagpur & Pune.

卐 PRICE ₹310.00

卐 PO No. : TXT-59-T066306-08-25

Published by Arihant Publications (India) Ltd.

For further information about the books published by Arihant, log on to www.arihantbooks.com or e-mail at info@arihantbooks.com

Follow us on   

Few Words

NCERTs are the Foundation in the Journey of IAS...

Civil Service Examinations are the most prestigious, tough and challenging examinations in India.

Being the toughest exam, it automatically consists of a vast and a detailed syllabus. Aspirants often find it difficult to cover the entire syllabus and lack a right direction for a proper and a systematic study for the exam.

The most important aspect of this preparation journey are the NCERT books. Every year approximately **35-40 questions** directly or indirectly asked from NCERT books.

NCERT books also play a key role in understanding the Basic Concepts; so that aspirants can easily form the basic foundation of the entire syllabus. But due to the demand for many NCERT books which are required for study, it becomes exhausting to cover each and every NCERT book.

NCERT MCQs series presented by Arihant Publications covers MCQs from Class 6th to 12th NCERT books (both Old & New) in a comprehensive manner.

Features of Revised Edition

- Each and Every Question is designed as per Latest Pattern of UPSC and State PCS.
- The chapter-wise questions given in the sequential form in the series along with the source of the questions.
- 100% Error free and detailed explanations will make the preparation easy and convenient.
- Additional coverage of Tamil Nadu Board and NIOS Books.
- 3 Practice Sets also provided for overall practice related to subject.

The book is adorned with questions prepared by a team of experts along with a vital role played by the Project Management team with members: Mona Yadav (Project Manager), Manshi Gupta (Project Coordinator), Seema Saini (Proof Reading TL), Pradeep Chaudhary (DTP TL), Bilal and Ankit Tyagi (Cover and Inner designer).

We hope this book will help the aspirants to achieve their goals of clearing UPSC as well as State PCS exams. Your valuable suggestions have always inspired us to strive for useful, authentic and more trustworthy publications.

Your inputs and suggestions are welcomed for subsequent editions.

We wish you all the very best for your preparation and journey!!

Authors

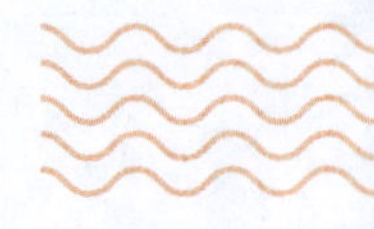

CONTENTS

ANCIENT HISTORY

ART AND CULTURE

Sources of Ancient Indian History

Sources of Ancient Indian History

Archaeological Sources

Coins
- **Study of coins** Numismatics
- **Earliest coins** Punch marked coins
- Largest number of coins- post Mauryan age
- Largest number of gold coins- Gupta age

Inscriptions

Study of Inscriptions- Epigraphy
- Carved out on seals, stone pillars, rocks, copper plates
- Earliest- Harappan (not been deciphered so far)
- Oldest deciphered Brahmi Script engraved by Ashoka (deciphered by James Princep)

Languages Used
- Prakrit, Greek and Dramaic

Scriptes Used
- Brahmi and Kharoshti Greek and Aramaic- Ashoka's inscription in Afghanistan

Literary Sources

Manuscript
- Hand-written on palm leaves or on the specially prepared bark of a tree

Vedic Literature
- Rigveda compiled between 1500-1000 BC
- Samaveda, Yajurveda and Atharvaveda, Brahmanas and Upanishad, compiled between 1000-500 BC

Religious Literature
- **Puranas** total 18 giving genealogical records of rulers
- **Mahabharata** compiled by Ved Vyas, oldest epic of the world
- **Ramayana** compiled by Valmiki, originally 6000 verses which were raised to 12,000 AD finally raised to 2400 verses
- **Buddhist** first composed in Pali; Jain Literatures composed in Prakrit language
- **Dharmashastra** compiled in 500-200 BC describes duties of different varnas

Books	Authors
Ashtadhyayi	Panini
Arthashastra	Kautilya
Mahabhashya (commentary on Ashtadhyayi)	Patanjali
Harshacharita	Banabhatta
Rajatarangini	Kalhana
Ramacharitam	Sandhyakar Nandi

Foreign Accounts

Greek and Roman Sources
- **Indica by Megasthenes** information about Mauryan administration and social and cultural life during the age of Chandragupta Maurya
- Periplus of the Erythrean Sea by unknown writer and Ptolemy's Geography : information about ancient geography and commerce Periplus of the Erythrean Sea was translated from Greek language to English by William H. Schoff in 1912

Chinese Sources
- Fa-Hien (5th century AD): Socio-economic life during Gupta age
- Hiuen Tsang (7th century AD): Socio-economic life during reign of Harsha

Arab Sources
- Earliest Arab writer: Sulaiman wrote Silsilat al-Tawarikh
- Al-Biruni (contemporary of Mahmud Ghaznavi) wrote Tahqiq-i-Hind

SOURCE ***New NCERT Class VI*** *(What Books and Burials Tell Us),* ***Old NCERT Class XI*** *(The Importance of Ancient Indian History),* ***Old NCERT Class XI*** *(Modern Historians of Ancient India),* ***Old NCERT Class XI*** *(Types of Sources and Historical Construction),* ***New NCERT Class XII*** *(Bricks, Beads and Bones),* ***New NCERT Class XII*** *(Kings, Farmers and Towns)* ***Tamil Nadu Board Class XI*** *(Early India)*

Archaeological Excavations

1 **Archaeological evidence of a bead-making industry in the Sangam Era, using precious and semi-precious stones, has been found in Kodumanal. It is located in which of the following present day states of India?** *(Chap 2, Class-XII, New NCERT)*

(a) Andhra Pradesh (b) Karnataka
(c) Tamil Nadu (d) Kerala

Ans. (c)

Exp. Archaeological evidence of a bead-making industry, using precious and semi-precious stones, has been found in Kodumanal.

Presently located in Tamil Nadu.

The site is located on North bank of river Noyyal. It was an important ancient trade city belonging to the Sangam Era.

2 **With reference to the methodology of excavation of mound, which among the following statements is/are correct?** *(Chap 3, Class-XI, Old NCERT)*

1. Vertical excavations results in uncovering the period-wise sequence of cultures.
2. Horizontal excavation is generally confined to entire or part of a particular site.

Codes

(a) Only 1
(b) Only 2
(c) Both 1 and 2
(d) Neither 1 nor 2

Ans. (c)

Exp. Both the statements (1) and (2) are correct with reference to the methodology of excavation of mound.

A mound can be excavated vertically or horizontally.

Vertical excavation is done by doing lengthwise digging to uncover the period-wise sequence of cultures; it is usually limited to a part of the site.

Horizontal excavation means digging the mound's most of the part or entirely. This method enables the excavator to get a complete idea of the site culture in a particular period.

3 **With reference dating in archaeology consider the following statements.** *(Chap 2, Class-XII, New NCERT)*

1. History of vegetation is known through pollen analysis.
2. Examination of animal bone cannot suggest whether the animal was domesticated or not.
3. Carbon dating has suggested that agriculture was practiced in Kashmir in 6000 BC.

How many of the statements given above is/are correct?

(a) Only one (b) Only two
(c) All three (d) None of these

Ans. (b)

Exp. Only two statements i.e., (1) and (3) are correct with reference to dating in archaeology.

The history of climate and vegetation of plant residue is known through an examination of plant residue and especially through pollen analysis.

The dates of material remains are fixed according to the Radiocarbon Method (Carbon 14 dating). Carbon dating has suggested that agriculture was practiced in Rajasthan and Kashmir as tax back as 6000 BC.

Statement (2) is incorrect as an examination of the animal bones enables us to find out whether the animals were domesticated and for finding out their use.

4 **Consider the following statements.** *(Unit 3, Class-XI, Tamil Nadu Board)*

Statement-I Archaeological excavation of the various sites of ancient India revealed some of the urban features.

Statement-II Presence of ring wells and Northern Black Polished Ware gives evidence of urban features.

Which of the following is correct in respect of the above statements?

(a) Both Statement-I and Statement-II are correct and Statement-II is the correct explanation for Statement-I.
(b) Both Statement-I and Statement-II are correct but Statement-II is not the correct explanation for Statement-I.
(c) Statement-I is correct but Statement-II is incorrect.
(d) Statement-I is incorrect but Statement-II is correct.

Ans. (a)

Exp. Both Statement-I and Statement-II are correct and Statement-II is the correct explanation for Statement-I.

As archaeological excavation of the various cities revealed urban feature of these sites and these urban feature is evidence by following

(i) Northern Black Polished Ware (NBPW) considered luxury, ware and 'Urban hallmark' have been excavated.
(ii) Facilities such as drains, ring wells and soak-pit are found contfirming the second urbanisation in the Gangetic plains.
(iii) Houses were built with mud bricks and in some case with burnt brick.

5 **With reference to John Marshall's stint as Director-General of Archaeological Survey of India, which of the following statements are correct?** *(Chap 1, Class-XII, New NCERT)*

1. During his stint, the Indus Valley Civilisation was excavated.
2. He recognised while excavating that it was necessary to follow stratigraphy of the site.
3. He brought his experience of working in Greece and Crete to India.

Codes

(a) 1 and 2 (b) 2 and 3 (c) 1 and 3 (d) 1, 2 and 3

Ans. (c)

Exp. Statements (1) and (3) are correct with reference to John Marshall's stint as Director-General of Archaeological Survey of India (ASI).

John Marshall as Director-General of the ASI worked in the excavations of Indus Valley Civilisation. He was the first professional archaeologist to work in India who brought his experience of working in Greece and Crete to the field of archaeology. He was interested in spectacular findings and was equally keen to look for patterns of everyday life.

Statement (2) is incorrect because Marshall usually excavated along regular horizontal units, measured uniformly throughout the mound, ignoring the stratigraphy of the site.

6 Which of the following statements is incorrect with reference to archaeological sources? *(Chap 1, Class-VI, New NCERT)*

(a) Ring wells were usually found in individual houses.
(b) Megalithic burials sets in South India provides evidence of iron tools.
(c) Archaeological sites of Sulaiman hills suggest that the wheat began to grow there 8000 years ago.
(d) Use of iron tools did not begin in India until 2000 years ago.

Ans. (d)

Exp. Statement (d) is incorrect with reference to archaeological sources. Use of iron began in Indian sub-continent around 3000 years ago.

Around 2500 years ago, there are evidence of ample use of iron tools, which include iron axes for clearing forests and the iron ploughshare. Some of the largest collection of iron tools and weapons were found in the Megalithic burials excavated in South India.

Coins

7 With reference to the coins issued in ancient India, which of the following statements is/are incorrect? *(Chap 3, Class-XI, Old NCERT)*

1. Ancient coins are made up of metals such as copper, silver, gold and lead.
2. Coin moulds of burnt clay have been discovered in large numbers in India.
3. The coin moulds belonging to the post-Gupta period has been discovered in largest number.

Codes

(a) 1 and 2
(b) Only 2
(c) Only 3
(d) 1, 2 and 3

Ans. (c)

Exp. Statement (3) is incorrect with reference to the coins issued in ancient India as most of the discovered coin moulds belong to the Kushan period between the first to third century AD.

8 Consider the following statements regarding coins in ancient India. *(Chap 3, Class-XI, Old NCERT)*

1. The coins mentioned the names of kings, gods or dates.
2. Coins were issued by the guilds of merchants and goldsmiths with the permission of ruler.
3. Coins of major dynasties have been catalogued and preserved in various museums in India.
4. Coins belonging to the Harappa Civilisation carried symbol of humped bull.

Which of the statements given above are correct?

(a) 1, 2 and 4
(b) 2, 3 and 4
(c) 1, 2 and 3
(d) All of these

Ans. (c)

Exp. Statements (1), (2) and (3) are correct regarding coins of ancient India.

Earliest coins of ancient India's have a few symbols, but the later coins have the names of kings, gods or dates. The areas where they are found indicate the region of their circulation. Some coins were issued by the guilds of merchants and gold smiths with the permission of the rulers. This shows that crafts and commerce had become important.

Coins helped transactions on a large scale and contributed to trade. Coins of the major dynasties have been catalogued and published most notably in Indian Museum at Kolkata and British Museum at London.

Statement (4) is incorrect as coins belonging to the Harappa Civilisation have not been discovered yet. The trade and commerce in Harappa Civilisation was done through barter and humped bull is found on a seal not on coins.

9 Which of the following pairs is/are correctly matched? *(Chap 3, Class-XI, Old NCERT)*

	Ingredients of the Coins		Historical Reconstruction
(a)	Names of kings and dates	–	Flourishing trade and commerce.
(b)	More circulation of gold coins	–	Ruling dynasties and their extent
(c)	Religious symbols and gods	–	Socio-economic aspect of history

(d) None of the above

Ans. (d)

Exp. None of the given pairs are correctly matched.

Names of kings, gods and dates on coins help in finding the area of their circulation and about ruling dynasties at that time. It had helped in reconstruction of history of tribal republic of Yaudheyas based in Haryana and Punjab between first to second century AD.

More circulation of gold coins indicates flourishing trade and communication as it helped in large scale of transactions and helped commerce in the areas. For instance, the large circulation of gold coins in Gupta era attested the flourishing trade with Roman Empire.

Religious symbols and gods help us understand the people's culture and religious traditions. It also portrayed their artistic sense. The portrayal of god and goddesses helps in figuring out the religion patronised by the ruling adynasty.

10 **In the history of Indian Coinage, Punch Marked Coins (PMC) have a special place which of the following are true with reference to Punch Marked Coins?** *(Chap 2, Class-XII, New NCERT)*

1. They are the earliest coinage in India.
2. They were not in circulation in South India.
3. We can notice symbols on one or both sides of these coins.
4. These coins are made of silver.

Codes

(a) 1 and 4 (b) 1 and 3 (c) 1, 2, 3 and 4 (d) 1, 3 and 4

Ans. (d)

Exp. Statements (1), (3) and (4) are correct. The earliest coins were called Punch-Marked Coins. They were generally rectangular or sometimes square in shape.

We can notice symbols on one or both sides of these coins. They contain a few symbols but later coins mention the names of kings, gods or dates of issuance. The coins were not inscribed but were stamped with symbols using dies or punches. Hence, they are called Punch-Marked Coins.

Punch Marked Coins were largely made of silver. Ancient coins were made of various metals like copper, silver gold or lead.

Statement (2) is incorrect because Punch-marked coins were in circulation in South India. These coins are found over most part of the sub-continent and remained in circulation (from 7th to 6th centuries BC and 1st century AD).

11 **With reference to coinage in ancient India, consider the following statements.** *(Class-XI, Old NCERT)*

1. Varaha were the gold coins issued by the Vijaynagar empire.
2. Gold coins of the Vijaynagar empire contain the King's name in Nagari script.
3. Royal ladies of Chalukya dynasty issued gold coins in some instances.

How many of the statements given above is/are incorrect?

(a) Only one
(b) Only two
(c) All three
(d) None of these

Ans. (d)

Exp. None of the statements are incorrect with respect to coinage system in ancient India.

Chalukya dynasty of Jayasimha I appointed royal ladies as provincial governors. They also used gold coins in some instances.

Varaha were the gold coins issued by the Vijaynagar empire. The gold coins have image of various Hindu deities and animal like the bull, the elephant. Gold coins of the Vijaynagar empire contains the king's name in the Nagari script or Kanada script.

12 **Boghazkoi inscription is important because** *(Chap 3, Class-XI Old NCERT) (WBCS Pre 2020)*

(a) it is known as significant trading centre between Central Asia and Tibet.
(b) the original text of the Vedas was composed there.
(c) inscription found here mention the names of Vedic Gods and Goddesses.
(d) None of the above

Ans. (c)

Exp. Boghazkoi inscription found in Asia Minor mentions the name of Vedic Gods and Goddesses like Mitra, Varuna, Indra and Nasatya. The Boghazkoi inscription which recorded a treaty between the Hittites and another kingdom in 13th century BC was discovered in 1906-07 at the site of Hittite capital Boghazkoi, in present-day, written in the Hittite language.

13 **Consider the following pairs.** *(Chap 2, Class-XII, New NCRET)* *(Chap 2, Class-VII, New NCERT)*

Inscriptions		Significance
1. Uttaramerur	–	First inscription in pure Sanskrit
2. Eran	–	Earliest evidence of Sati found in India here
3. Aihole	–	Eulogy of Chalukya king Pulakeshin-II

How many pairs given above is/are matched incorrectly?

(a) Only one (b) Only tow
(c) All three (d) None of these

Ans. (a)

Exp. Only one pair i.e., (1) is incorrectly matched because Uttaramerur inscription is located in Chengalpattu district of South of Chennai. It is noted for its temple inscriptions that describe a self-governance system existing around 7th to 9th century AD.

14 **With reference to ancient Indian History, consider the following pairs.** *(Class-XI, Old NCERT)*

Inscription		Associated dynasty/kingdom
1. Banskhera copper plate inscription	–	Vardhana dynasty
2. Mandagappattu inscription	–	Chola kingdom
3. Pugalur inscription	–	Chera kingdom
4. Paharpur copper plate inscription	–	Gupta dynasty

How many of the pairs given above is/are incorrectly matched?

(a) Only one (b) Only two (c) Only three (d) All four

Ans. (a)

Exp. Only one pair i.e., (2) is incorrectly matched. Mandagappattu inscription is associated with Pallava dynasty Mahendravarman claims in his Mandagappattu inscription that his shrine to Brahma, Isvara and Vishnu were made without using traditional such as brick, timber, metal and mortar.

15 The office of Chief Epigraphist of India which contains the largest number of inscriptions is located at which of the following places? *(Chap 3, Class-XI, Old NCERT)*

(a) Kolkata (b) New Delhi (c) Chennai (d) Mysore

Ans. (d)

Exp. The largest number of inscriptions are found in the office of the Chief Epigraphist at Mysore.
It was established in 1886 in Bangalore with Dr. E Hultzsch as the head of the office.

16 With reference to the cultural history of India, what is the significance of 'Corpus Inscriptionum Indicarum'? *(Chap 3, Class-XI, Old NCERT)*

(a) It is a series of collection containing inscriptions belonging to Maurya, Post-Maurya and Gupta times.
(b) It is a collection of inscription containing history of ancient and medieval India.
(c) It is a series of collection containing inscriptions belonging to the Mauryan Emperor Ashoka.
(d) It is a museum in London dedicated to the inscriptions containing history of India.

Ans. (a)

Exp. 'Corpus Inscriptionum Indicarum' is a published series of collection. It has records on the history of Mauryan, Post-Mauryan and Gupta times. No such compilation is available for Post-Gupta times. Written by Alexander Cunningham.

17 Consider the following statements. *(Chap 3, Class-XI, Old NCERT)*

1. An epigraphist can decipher most inscription of the country up to about 7th century AD, if he had carefully learnt Brahmi script.
2. Kharosthi script was written from left to right and was prevalent in North-Western part of Indian subcontinent.

Which of the statements given above is/are correct?

(a) Only 1 (b) Only 2
(c) Both 1 and 2 (d) Neither 1 nor 2

Ans. (a)

Exp. Statement (1) is correct as knowledge of Brahmi script is essential for an epigraphist to decipher most inscription of the country up to about 7th century AD. This script was used by rulers of major dynasties including Ashoka for engraving their inscriptions in Indian subcontinent. After the 7th century AD, there were strong regional variations in the script.
Statement (2) is incorrect because Kharosthi script was written from right to left. This script was used by Ashoka to engrave his inscriptions in North-Western part of Indian subcontinent. Later, it was also used by rulers of Indo-Greeks and Kushans.

18 Consider the following statements regarding inscriptions in India. *(Chap 3, Class-XI, Old NCERT)*

1. The earliest inscriptions are found on the seals of Harappa belonging to about 2500 BC.
2. Ashokan inscriptions were engraved in the Brahmi script, which was written from left to right.
3. The oldest inscriptions deciphered so far were issued by Harappans in India.

Which of the statements given above are correct?

(a) 1 and 2 (b) 2 and 3
(c) 1 and 3 (d) 1, 2 and 3

Ans. (a)

Exp. Statements (1) and (2) are correct regarding inscriptions in India.
The earliest inscriptions are found on the seals of Harappa belonging to about 2500 BC. They have not been deciphered so far. They are written in pictographic form.
Ashokan inscriptions were written in Brahmi script, which is written from left to right. Though some of them were also written in Kharosthi script which is written from right to left.
Statement (3) is incorrect because the oldest inscriptions deciphered so far were issued by Ashoka in the third century BC.

19 The Girnar rock inscription states that repair of Sudarshana lake was undertaken by the rulers of various dynasties of ancient India. The kings of which among the following dynasties were associated with Girnar rock inscriptions? *(Chap 2, Class-XII, New NCERT)*

1. Mauryan Empire 2. Saka Empire
3. Gupta Empire 4. Kushan Dynasty

Codes

(a) 1, 2 and 3 (b) 2, 3 and 4
(c) 1, 2 and 4 (d) All of these

Ans. (a)

Exp. The Kings of Mauryan Empire, Saka Empire and Gupta Empire are associated with the Girnar inscription. This inscription mentions that Sudarshana lake, with embankments and water channels, was built by a local governor during the rule of the Mauryas. However, a terrible storm broke the embankments and water gushed out of the lake.
Then, Saka ruler Rudradaman, who was then ruling in the area, got the lake repaired using his own resources, without imposing any tax on his subjects. Another inscription on the same rock (Circa fifth century) mentions how one of the rulers of the Gupta dynasty got the lake repaired once again.
Kushan dynasty was associated with the Rabatak inscription.

20 **The Allahabad Pillar Inscriptions helped in historical reconstruction of which of the following Kingdoms/ Empires of ancient and medieval India?**

(Chap 7, Class-VI, New NCERT) (UP RO/ARO Pre 2016)

1. Maurya Empire
2. Gupta Empire
3. Delhi Sultanate
4. Mughal Empire

Codes

(a) 1, 2 and 3 (b) 2, 3 and 4
(c) 1, 2 and 4 (d) All of these

Ans. (c)

Exp. Allahabad Pillar Inscription helped in historical reconstruction of Maurya Empire, Gupta Empire and Mughal Empire.

This inscription also known as Prayag Prashasti. It was commissioned during the reign of Ashoka. It also has eulogy about Samudragupta and his exploits as king. It also had writings about Mughal Emperor Jahangir.

21 **Match the following lists correctly and choose the correct code.** *(Chap 2, Class-XII, New NCERT)*

List I (Types of Inscriptions)		List II (Characteristics)
A. Votive	1.	Highlights the achievements of conquerors and rulers
B. Royal	2.	Gifts of money and cattle by artisans and merchants
C. Eulogy	3.	Gifts made to religious institutions
D. Donative	4.	Decree issued by the Kings and Princes

Codes

	A	B	C	D
(a)	1	2	3	4
(b)	2	3	1	4
(c)	2	1	4	3
(d)	3	4	1	2

Ans. (d)

Exp. The correct matching is A-3, B-4, C-1, D-2.

Votive in the second century BC, short votive inscriptions were found. These mention the name of the donor, and sometimes specify his/ her occupation as well. They tell us about people who lived in towns i.e., weavers, scribes, carpenters, potters, goldsmiths, blacksmiths, officials, religious teachers, merchants and kings.

Royal inscriptions as evident from the name were the orders and decree which were issued in the form of inscription.

Eulogy was written in praise of kings and warriors in inscription form. It was usually written in exaggeration and tells about the exploits of the King.

Donative inscriptions had records of donations made by women and men to religious institutions. These people were mostly merchants and traders.

22 **With reference to limitations of inscriptions as a source of historical reconstruction, which of the following statements is/are correct?**

(Chap 2, Class-XII, New NCERT)

1. The content of the inscriptions only projects the perspective of the person(s) who commissioned them.
2. History regarding socio-cultural life of the common people is often missing in the inscriptions.
3. As all of them are recorded on perishable materials which provides scope for alteration.

Codes

(a) 1 and 2 (b) 2 and 3 (c) 1 and 3 (d) 1, 2 and 3

Ans. (a)

Exp. Statements (1) and (2) are correct with reference to limitations of inscriptions as a source of historical reconstruction. Inscriptions were commissioned by people who were kings or in power and usually contain what they wanted to show or perspective of the ruling elites. The history regarding socio-cultural life of people is often missing in the sculptures.

Statement (3) is incorrect because some of the inscriptions were also recorded on non-perishable materials such as stones and metals.

Literary Sources

23 **The ancient manuscripts of India were written on which of the following materials?**

(Chap 3, Class-XI, Old NCERT)

(a) Wooden tablets (b) Copper plate
(c) Sheep leather (d) Birch bark

Ans. (d)

Exp. The ancient manuscripts of India were written on birch bark. Although the ancient Indians knew writing as early as 2500 BC, most ancient manuscripts, not older than the fourth century AD have been found in Central Asia. In India, they were written on birch bark and palm leaves, but in Central Asia, where the Prakrit language had spread from India, manuscripts were also written on sheep leather and wooden tablets.

24 **In which of the following texts the list of the sixteen great states (Shodasa Mahajanapadas) of ancient India occur?** *(Chap 2, Class-XI, Old NCERT) (RAS/RTS 2016)*

1. Arthashastra
2. Anguttara Nikaya
3. Digha Nikaya
4. Bhagavati Sutra

Codes

(a) 2 and 3 (b) 2, 3 and 4 (c) 1 and 4 (d) 1, 2 and 3

Ans. (b)

Exp. Among the given options, the Buddhist text, *Anguttara Nikaya* and *Digha Nikaya* give the list of sixteen great states (Shodasa Mahajanapadas) of ancient India. These sixteen Mahajanapadas occured around 600 BC and is referred as the period of second urbanisation in India. The list of sixteen Mahajanapadas is also found in Jaina text *Bhagavati Sutra*.

Arthashastra is treatise on statecraft written by Kautilya. It gives information regarding the state of polity prevalent in Mauryan Empire.

25 Consider the following statements regarding Ramayana. *(Chap 3, Class-XI, Old NCERT)*

1. It was composed by the sage Valmiki and originally consisted of 6000 verses.
2. Contrary to Mahabharata, it contains only narrative portion.
3. Its composition was started in the fifth century BC and since then it passed through five stages.

Which of the statements given above are correct?

(a) 1 and 2 (b) 2 and 3 (c) 1 and 3 (d) 1, 2 and 3

Ans. (c)

Exp. Statements (1) and (3) are correct regarding Ramayana.

Ramayana, composed by Valmiki originally consisted of 6,000 verses and its final compilation contains 24,000 verses. The Ramayana composition started in 5th century BC and since then it is passed through five stages, and the fifth stage is as late as the 12th century AD.

Statement (2) is incorrect as Ramayana also had its own didactic portions which were added to it later.

26 With reference to the earliest Buddhist texts, which of the following statements are correct? *(Chap 3, Class-XI, Old NCERT)*

1. They helps in historical reconstruction of the Magadha, North Bihar and Eastern Uttar Pradesh.
2. They were written in Pali language and were finally compiled in the second century BC in Sri Lanka.
3. The Buddhist canonical literature, Jataka throws invaluable light on social and economic conditions ranging from the fifth to second century BC.

Codes

(a) 1 and 2 (b) 2 and 3 (c) 1 and 3 (d) 1, 2 and 3

Ans. (a)

Exp. Statements (1) and (2) are correct with reference to earliest Buddhist text.

The earliest Buddhist texts tell us not only about the life of the Buddha but also about some of his royal contemporaries who ruled over Magadha, North Bihar and Eastern Uttar Pradesh.

They were written in the Pali language, which was spoken in Magadha or South Bihar. They were finally compiled in the second century BC in Sri Lanka.

Statement (3) is incorrect because the most important and interesting portion of the 'non-canonical' literature is provided by the stories of the previous births of Gautama Buddha. Each birth story is called a Jataka which is a folk tale. These Jatakas throw invaluable light on social and economic conditions.

27 With reference to earliest Jaina literature, which of the following statements are correct? *(Chap 3, Class-XI, Old NCERT)*

1. They were written in Prakrit and were finally compiled in the sixth century AD in Shravanabelagola in Karnataka.
2. They help in reconstructing the political history of Eastern Uttar Pradesh and Bihar in the age of Mahavira.
3. It also throws light on the state of trade and crafts and repeatedly refers to trade and traders.

Codes

(a) 1 and 2 (b) 2 and 3
(c) 1 and 3 (d) 1, 2 and 3

Ans. (b)

Exp. Statements (2) and (3) are correct with reference to earliest Jaina literature.

The Jaina texts contain political history of Eastern Uttar Pradesh and Bihar in the age of Mahavira.

It also has details and information which provides valuable data about trade, crafts, and about traders.

Statement (1) is incorrect because the Jaina texts were written in Prakrit and were compiled in Vallabhi, Gujarat, in sixth century AD.

28 Which of the following pairs is/are not matched correctly? *(Chap 3, Class-XI, Old NCERT)*

	Biographical Accounts		Authors
(a)	Harshacharita	–	Sandhyakara Nandi
(b)	Vikramanakadevacharita	–	Bilhana
(c)	Mushika Vamsha	–	Atula
(d)	All of the above		

Ans. (c)

Exp. (a) Only pair (a) is not matched correctly.

Harshacharita is a biographical account of Harshavardhana. It was written by his court poet Banabhatta in 7th century AD.

29 Match the following lists correctly and choose the correct code. *(Chap 3, Class-XI, Old NCERT)*

List I (Ancient Literature)	List II (Characteristics)
A. Srautasutras	1. Domestic rituals
B. Grihyasutras	2. Philosophical speculations
C. Shulbasutras	3. Royal coronation ceremonies
D. Upanishada	4. Measurements for construction of sacrificial altars

Codes

	A	B	C	D		A	B	C	D
(a)	1	2	3	4	(b)	2	3	1	4
(c)	2	1	4	3	(d)	3	1	4	2

Ans. (d)

Exp. The correct matching is A-3, B-1, C-4, D-2.

Srautasutras provide for many pompous royal coronation ceremonies. They mention that it big public sacrifices meant for princes.

Grihyasutras listed out domestic rituals related to birth, naming, marriage, funerals etc.

Shulbasutras prescribed various kinds of measurements for construction of sacrificial platforms.

Upanishada had philosophical speculation about the nature of the world and social realities.

30 With reference to literary work, consider the following statements. *(Unit 9, Class-XI, Tamil Nadu Board)*

1. Mahavamsa written in Prakrit is a Buddhist source which provides information on the cultural development during Pallava period.
2. Panniru Tirumurai is canonised version of Saiva literature.
3. Mattavilasa Prahasana written by Mahendravarman I is an important source for the Pallava period.

How many of the statements given above is are correct?

(a) Only one (b) Only two
(c) All three (d) None of these

Ans. (b)

Exp. Only two statements i.e., (2) and (3) are correct. The Saiva literatare was canonised as the Panniru Tirumurai. While the poems of Vaishnavite orch wars were compiled as the Nalayira Divya Prabhandam. The Mattavilasa Prahasana written by Mahendravarman I in Sanskrit, is an important source for the Pallava period.

Statement (1) is incorrect because Buddhist sources such as Deepvansa and Mahavamsa, written in Pali give us details about the socio-religious and cultural conditions of the Pallava times.

31 With reference to the Sangam literature as a source of history, consider the following statements. *(Class-XI, Old NCERT)*

1. Sangam corpus is the extant Tamil grammatical text dealing with poetry, society and culture of times.
2. Women did not contribute to the corpus of Sangam poetry.
3. Thirumurugatrupatai is one of the eight anthologies of classical Sangam corpus.

How many of the statements given above is/are correct?

(a) Only one (b) Only two
(c) All three (d) None of these

Ans. (a)

Exp. Only one statement i.e., (1) is correct as the classical Sangam corpus consists of Tholkappiyam, the eight anthologies (Ettu thogai) ten idylls (Path thupattu) in which Tholkappiyam is the earliest extant Tamil grammatical text dealing not only with poetry but also the society and culture of times.

Statements (2) and (3) are incorrect. Over 450 poets who contributed to the corpus of Sangam poetry among 30 of them are women. They composed more than 150 poems. The most prominent and prolific among them was Avvaiyar.

Thirumungatrupatai is one of ten idylls of the classical Sangam corpus. Other Paththupatu (ten idylls) includes Perunaratrupatai and Sirupanatruppatai, etc.

Foreign Account

32 Match the following lists correctly and choose the correct code. *(Chap 3, Class-XI, Old NCERT)*

List I (Foreign Travellers/ Writers)	List II (Historical Reconstruction)
A. Megasthenes	1. Trade between India and Roman Empire
B. Ptolemy	2. India in fourth century BC
C. Fa-Hien	3. India in fourth and fifth century AD
D. Hiuen Tsang	4. India in seventh century AD

Codes

	A	B	C	D
(a)	1	2	3	4
(b)	2	1	3	4
(c)	2	1	4	3
(d)	3	1	4	2

Ans. (b)

Exp. The correct matching is A-2, B-1, C-3, D-4.

Megasthenes's Indica tells about Maurya rule in the time of Chandragupta Maurya in the fourth century and helps reconstruct the history of the period.

Ptolemy's Geography was written in Greek and provides information about ancient geography and commerce between India and the Roman empire around 150 AD.

Fa-Hien a Chinese traveller/pilgrim came in the age of Guptas in fifth century AD and describes the social, religious and economic situations.

His writing inspired other Buddhist scholars and travellers from China to visit India in subsequent years.

Hiuen Tsang came to India in the seventh century AD. He gave an elaborate account of state of polity, society, economy and culture of India during the reign of Harshavardhana.

33 The Chinese traveller Yuan Chwang (Hiuen Tsang) who visited India recorded the general condition and culture of India at that time. In this context which of the following statement(s) is/are correct?

(Chap 3, Class-XI, Old NCERT)

1. The roads and river - routes were completely immune from robbery.
2. As regards punishment for offences, ordeals by fire, water and poison were the instruments for determining the innocence or guilt of a person.
3. The tradesman had to pay duties at ferries and barrier stations.

Select the correct answer by using the codes given below.

(a) Only 1
(b) 2 and 3
(c) 1 and 3
(d) 1, 2 and 3

Ans. (b)

Exp. Statements (2) and (3) are correct in context of record of Chinese traveller Yuan Chwang about India. Yuan Chwang mentions that ordeals by fire, water and poison were used as a means of determining the guilt or innocence of a person.

He mentions that tradesman had to pay a duty at ferries and barrier stations in order to pass through. This duty was used to maintain the roads and bridges.

Statement (1) is not correct because road was not immune from robbery. He described government was liberal in the case of tax and revenue collection.

34 Consider the following statements.

(Chap 3, Class-XI, Old NCERT)

1. Fa-Hien was a Chinese pilgrim who visited India during the reign of Harsha.
2. Hiuen Tsang was a Chinese Buddhist monk who visited India during the reign of Chandragupta II.

Which of the above statements is/are correct?

(a) Only 1
(b) Only 2
(c) Both 1 and 2
(d) None of the above

Ans. (d)

Exp. None of the above statements are correct.

Fa-Hien was a Chinese pilgrim who visited India during the reign of Chandragupta II. He left a detailed account of the reign of Chandragupta II. He provided detailed information about Pataliputra. According to him Pataliputra was given utmost important during reign of Chandragupta II.

Hiuen Tsang, Chinese Buddhist monk, who visited India during the reign of Harsha. He wrote about the Fourth Buddhist Council and studied with various monks which include 14 months with Vinita Prabha.

Historians of Ancient India

35 Which among the following authors is credited with the first systematic history of Ancient India?

(Chap 2, Class-XI, Old NCERT)

(a) Vincent Arthur Smith
(b) William Hawkins
(c) Max Mueller
(d) William Jones

Ans. (a)

Exp. Vincent Arthur Smith is credited with the first systematic history of Ancient India. He has prepared the first systematic history of ancient India in 1904. His book which was based on a deep study of the available sources gave primacy to political history. It served as a text book for nearly fifty years and is still used by scholars.

36 With reference to the contributions of Max Mueller in Indian historiography, which of the following statements is/are correct? *(Chap 2, Class-XI, Old NCERT)*

1. Under his editorship ancient Indian scriptures were translated on the massive scale and were published under the Sacred Books of the East Series.
2. He opposed the popular belief that ancient Indian lacked a sense of chronology and were accustomed to the despotic rule.

Codes

(a) Only 1
(b) Only 2
(c) Both 1 and 2
(d) Neither 1 nor 2

Ans. (a)

Exp. Statement (1) is correct with reference to the contributions of Max Mueller in the Indian historiography. The greatest push to Indological or Indian studies was given by the German-born scholar F. Max Mueller (1823-1902) who spent most of his time in England.

Ancient scriptures were translated on a massive scale under the editorship of Max Mueller. Altogether fifty volumes, some in several parts were published under the Sacred Books of the East Series.

Statement (2) is incorrect because he didn't oppose but put down the popular belief that ancient Indians lacked a sense of chronology and were accustomed to despotic rule.

37 With reference to the colonial school of historiography, which of the following statements are correct?

(Chap 2, Class-XI, Old NCERT)

1. It believed that India did not experienced political modern unity until the establishment of British rule in India.
2. It made generalisation to serve as propaganda material for perpetuation of the despotic British rule in India.
3. It didn't write about the prevalence of caste system in early Indian society.

Codes

(a) 1 and 2 (b) 2 and 3

(c) 1 and 3 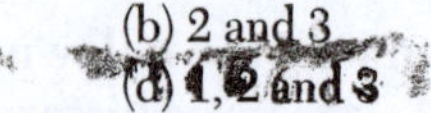 (d) 1, 2 and 3

Ans. (a)

Exp. Statements (1) and (2) are correct with reference to the colonial school of historiography.

British colonial historians stated that the ancient Indians lacked a sense of history especially of the factor of time and chronology. They added that the Indians were accustomed to despotic rule.

The Western scholars stressed that the Indians had neither experienced feelings of nationhood nor any kind of self-government. So, they justified the British rule over India.

Statement (3) is incorrect because they wrote about caste systems, and considered it as worst form of discrimination.

38 Which of the following pair is/are matched correctly? *(Chap 2, Class-XI, Old NCERT)*

	Scholars related with Nationalist School of Historiography		Books
(a)	R G Bhandarkar	–	Political history of Deccan under Satavahanas
(b)	V K Rajwade	–	Indo-Aryans
(c)	Pandurang Vaman Kane	–	History of the Dharamasastra
(d)	Both a and c		

Ans. (d)

Exp. Both pairs (a) and (c) are matched correctly.

RG Bhandarkar (1837-1925) reconstructed the political history of the Deccan under Satavahanas and History of Vaishnavism and other sects.

Pandurang Vaman Kane (1880-1972) wrote 'History of Dharamasastra' for which he received Bharat Ratna in 1963. It is 6500 pages research work conducted in 40 years.

While pair (b) is not matched correctly because VK Rajwade (1869-1926) wrote a book named 'History of Institutions of Marriage'.

39 With reference to the source of history, consider the following statements. *(Class-XI, Old NCERT)*

Statement-I Plays altest to the significance of oral traditions which are now accepted as an additional source of history.

Statement-II Play Mudrarakshasa by Visakhadatta detailing the Samundragupta's accession to the throne is considered as corroborative source of Gupta period.

Which one of the following is correct in respect of the above statements?

(a) Both Statement-I and Statement-II are correct and Statement-II is the correct explanation for Statement-I.

(b) Both Statement-I and Statement-II are correct but Statement-II is not correct explanation for Statement-I.

(c) Statement-I is correct but Statement-II is incorrect.

(d) Statement-I is incorrect but Statement-II is correct.

Ans. (c)

Exp. Statement-I is correct but Statement-II is incorrect. Plays as a literary work altest to the significance of oral traditions, which are now accepted as an additional valid source of history. Play Mudrarakshasa by Visakhadatta was written during the Gupta period, sometimes after the 4th century CE. It narrates Chandragupta's accession to the throne of the Magadha empire. This play is often cited as a corroborative source since it supports the information gathered from other contemporary sources about Chandragupta.

Chapter 02

Pre-Historic Cultures

Pre-Historic Cultures

Paleolithic Age

Introduction

- No written records available
- Studied by archaeological evidences only; First director of the Archaeological Survey of India: Sir Alexander Cunningham
- Father of Indian Pre History: Robert Bruce Foote
- Humans were not Civilised
- Divided into

Paleolithic Age

- Old-stone age; The term Palaeolithic coined by John Lubbock; Covered time-period from 2 million years ago to about 12,000 years ago; Hunting and gathering were the main occupation of the people stone tools used; Divided into three periods
- **Lower Paleolithic** (5,00,000 BC-50,000 BC) Main tools- handaxes, cleavers and choppers
- Important sites- Sohan valley, Bhimbetka, Belan valley and Didwana
- **Middle Paleolithic** (50,000 BC-40,000 BC) Main tools- based on flakes technology, blades, points, borers and scrapers
- Important sites-Sohan and Narmada valley
- **Upper Paleolithic** (40,000 BC-10,000 BC) Appearance of Homo-sapiens; Main tools- massive flakes, blades, burins and scrapers; **Important sites**- Bhimbetka and Gujarat dunes

Mesolithic and Neolithic Age

- **Mesolithic Age** Transitional phase between Paleolithic and Neolithic age
- Main tools- microliths; Subsistence pattern- people lived on hunting, fishing and food-gathering
- **Important Sites** Adamgarh, Bagor, Chhota Nagpur plateau and

Neolithic Age

- Earliest farming communities; Domesticated animals and started living in permanent settlements; Used tools and implements of polished stones; Cultivated crops-rice, wheat, barley, ragi and horse gram; Used wheel made pottery
- **Society** Division of labour between men and women
- Rudimentary political organisation
- **Religious** Worshipped Sky-God and Earth-Goddess
- **Important Sites**
  - **North**- Mehargarh,Burzahom, Gufkral, Chirand
  - **South**- Maski, Hallur, Brahmagiri, Paiyampalli
  - **East**- Garo hills, Daojali Hading

Chalcolithic Age and Other Culture

Chalcolithic Age

- First metal copper was used; Mixed with zinc and lead- Bronze age; Development of different types of potteries; Domesticated- cow, sheep, goat, pig and buffalo
- **Cultivated** Barley; Wheat and lentil (Western India) and Rice (Southern and Eastern region)
- **Religion** Terracotta figurines of women and bull

Neolithic Age

- **Aahar culture** (Rajasthan) Black and Red ware
- **Kayatha culture** (Madhya Pradesh) Red slipped ware
- **Malwa culture** (Gujarat)- Red or Black ware
- **Savalda culture** (Maharashtra)- Non- Harappan culture
- **Prabhas and Rangpur** (Gujarat)- Polished Red Ware

Copper Age in India

- The period covered by the ochre-coloured pottery culture is roughly placed between 2000 BC and 1800 BC
- The people of Copper Hoard Culture were contemporaries of Harappans
- Hoards of copper objects have been found in a wide area ranging from the Chhota Nagpur plateau to the upper Gangetic basin

SOURCE New NCERT Class VI (From Hunting-Gathering to Growing Food), Old NCERT Class VI (Early Man), Old NCERT Class IX (Life in Prehistoric Times), New NCERT Class XI (The Dawn of History in the Deep South), Old NCERT Class XI (The Geographical Setting), Old NCERT Class XI (The Stone Age : The Early Man), Old NCERT Class XI (Chalcolithic Farming Cultures), New NCERT Class XII (Kings, Farmers and Towns) Tamil Nadu Board Class XI (Early India)

1 With reference to cultural evolution of man, consider the following statements.

(Chap 1, Class-IX, Old NCERT)

1. Stone age started during pleistocene period of ice age.
2. Hand axes, choppers and flake implements are associated with Mesolithic phase of human cultural evolution.
3. Lower paleolithic age is characterised by glaciation.

How many of the statements given above is/are correct?

(a) Only one (b) Only two
(c) All three (d) None of these

Ans. (b)

Exp. Only two statements i.e., (1) and (3) are correct.

Stone age started during Pleistocene period of ice age. The old stone age is known as Paleolithic age. In India, it is divided into three phases according to the nature of the stone tools used by the people and also according to the nature of change in climate.

Lower Paleolithic in India is characterised by glaciations and covered greater part of ice age. During this phase, rock shelters served as seasonal camps for human life, for instance Belan sites contain caves and rock shelters which could have served as seasonal camps.

Statement (2) is incorrect because Hand axes, choppers and flake implements are associated with paleolithic phase of human cultural evolution.

Lower Paleolithic sites are found in the valley of river Soan or Sohan in Punjab (now in Pakistan) other sites were found at Hunsgi, Karnataka.

2 The Upper Palaeolithic phase of Andhra Pradesh and Karnataka gives evidences of which of the following types of tools? *(Chap 5, Class-XI, Old NCERT)*

(a) Blades and burins (b) Hand axes and cleavers
(c) Microliths (d) Borers and burins

Ans. (a)

Exp. Upper Palaeolithic phase in Andhra Pradesh and Karnataka has evidence of use of blades and burins. These tools have also been found in upper levels of Gujarat dunes.

Caves and rock shelters of this age have been discovered at Bhimbetka near Bhopal. Homo sapiens also mark their presence in upper Palaeolithic age.

3 Consider the following statement with reference to cultural phase of Upper Palaeolithic in India.

(Chap 5, Class-XI, Old NCERT)

1. It coincided with last phase of the Ice age when climate became comparatively warm.
2. Caves and rock shelters used by early human beings in the Upper Palaeolithic phase have been discovered at Bhimbetka.
3. Most of the sites belonging to the Upper Palaeolithic phase have been discovered in alluvial plains of the Indus and the Ganga.

Which of the statements given above is/are incorrect?

(a) 1 and 2 (b) 2 and 3
(c) Only 1 (d) Only 3

Ans. (d)

Exp. Statement (3) is incorrect with reference to cultural phase of Upper Palaeolithic in India as the sites belonging to the Upper Palaeolithic phase are absent in alluvial plains of the Indus and the Ganga.

4 With reference to the pre-historic art, which of the following statements is/are correct?

(Chap 5, Class-XI, Old NCERT)

1. The early men practised rock paintings which depicted different facets of hunting-gathering economy.
2. Bhimbetka situated in Maharashtra contains more than 500 painted rock shelters.

Codes

(a) Only 1
(b) Only 2
(c) Both 1 and 2
(d) Neither 1 nor 2

Ans. (a)

Exp. Statement (1) is correct with reference to the Pre-historic art. The people of Palaeolithic and Mesolithic ages used painting which shows they were hunters and food gatherers. Prehistoric art appears at several places, but Bhimbetka in Madhya Pradesh contains richest specimen of Prehistoric art. It is situated in the Vindhyan range, 45 km South of Bhopal. It has more than 500 painted rock shelters, distributed in an area of 10 sq km.

Statement (2) is incorrect as Bhimbetka is in Madhya Pradesh.

5 Consider the following statements.

(Unit 1, Class-XI, Tamil Nadu Board)

Statement-I Around 12,000 years ago, people started herding and rearing animals that survived on grass.

Statement-II Climate of the world shifted to relatively warm conditions which led to the development of grassland.

Which one of the following is correct in respect of the above statements?

(a) Both Statement-I and Statement-II are correct and Statement-II is the correct explanation for Statement-I.
(b) Both Statement-I and Statement-II are correct and Statement-II is the correct explanation for Statement-I.
(c) Statement-I is correct but Statement-II is incorrect.
(d) Statement-I is incorrect but Statement-II is correct.

Ans. (a)

Exp. Both Statement-I and Statement-II are correct and Statement-II is the correct explanation of Statement-I as around 12,000 years ago, people started to think about herding and rearing of the animals that survived on grass and this was made parable by development of grassland preceded by shift in the climate.

Around 12,000 years ago, there was a major change in the climate of the world, with a shift to a relatively warm conditions. In many areas, this led to development of grasslands. This in turn led to increase in the number of deer, antelope, goat, sheep and cattle that survived on grass. This helped people to recar these animals.

6 Consider the following pre-historic site of ancient India. *(Chap 5, Class-XI, Old NCERT)*

1. Birbhanpur
2. Tirunelveli
3. Balu
4. Manda

Which among the given sites were associated with the Mesolithic age?

(a) 1 and 2 (b) 2 and 3 (c) 1 and 3 (d) 2, 3 and 4

Ans. (a)

Exp. Among the given options, Birbhanpur and Tirunelveli are the pre-historic sites associated with the Mesolithic Age in India. Birbhanpur is located in present day state of West Bengal whereas Tirunelveli is located in present day state of Tamil Nadu. From both of these sites, microliths belonging to the Mesolithic period had been excavated. Balu and Manda are the sites associated with the Indus Valley Civilisation, are located in Haryana and Jammu and Kashmir respectively.

7 With reference to the tools used in Paleolithic age, consider the following statements. *(Class-XI, Old NCERT)*

1. Upper Paleolithic is characterised by the appearance of flint industries.
2. Middle Paleolithic industries are mainly based upon flakes.
3. Lower Paleolithic age is characterised by the absence of habitation-cum factory sites.

How many of the statements given above is/are incorrect?

(a) Only one (b) Only two
(c) All three (d) None of these

Ans. (d)

Exp. None of the statements are incorrect with reference to the stone tools used by the people of Paleolithic age.

Upper Paleolithic age is marked by the appearance of new flint industries and modern men. This phase was characterised by massive flakes, blades, burins and scrapers, which have been found in the upper level of Gujarat dunes.

Middle Paleolithic industries are mainly based upon flakes which are found in different parts of India and show regional variations.

The principal tool are varities of blades, points, berers and scrapers made of flakes.

Lower Paleolithic age is marked by the presence of habitation-cum factory sites where people lived for longer time. At such sites, large number of tools are found.

8 With reference to the sources of pre-historic India, consider the following statements. *(Class-XI, Old NCERT)*

1. Phytoliths helps us to gain knowledge of farming practiced by stone age people.
2. The mitochondrial DNA (mt-DNA) studies provide information on pre-historic migration.
3. Study of the evolution of language families cannot be considered as source of pre-historic India.

How many of the statements given above is/are incorrect?

(a) Only one (b) Only two
(b) All three (d) None of these

Ans. (a)

Exp. Only one statement i.e., (3) is incorrect because language families are important source of pre-historic India. Indo-Aryan, Dravidian, Austro-Asiatic and Tibeto Burman language families have flourished in India. These languages developed and evolved during the various phases of migrations in Indian history.

9 With reference to cultural phase of Mesolithic in India, which of the following statements are correct? *(Chap 5, Class-XI, Old NCERT)*

1. Stone tools found during this period are smaller in size, and are called microliths.
2. It intervened as a transitional phase between the Old and New Stone age.
3. This phase of cultural evolution flourished between the 18,000 BC to 10,000 BC in India.

Codes

(a) 1 and 2
(b) 2 and 3
(c) 1 and 3
(d) 1, 2 and 3

Ans. (a)

Exp. Statements (1) and (2) are correct with reference to cultural phase of Mesolithic in India.

The characteristic tools of the Mesolithic Age were microliths. They were smaller in size and were distinctively different from lower Palaeolithic period's axes, choppers and cleavers.

This phase was a phase of change between Upper Palaeolithic period and Neolithic period, people changed from hunting, fishing and food gathering to domesticating animals and pastoralism.

Statement (3) is incorrect as flourishing time period for Mesolithic phase was from 9000 BC to 4000 BC.

10 With reference to pre-history culture, consider the following pairs. *(Class-XI, Old NCERT)*

Pre-historic sites		Evidence found
1. Kurnool	–	evidence of rectangular houses
2. Belan Valley	–	evidence of circular pit house
3. Adamgarh	–	earliest evidence of domestication of animal
4. Mehrgarh	–	evidence of growing of barley for first time

How many of the pairs given above is/are correctly matched?

(a) Only one
(b) Only two
(c) Only three
(d) All four

Ans. (b)

Exp. Only two pairs i.e., (3) and (4) are correctly matched. Adamgarh is a mesolithic age site in Madhya Pradesh which provide the earliest evidence for the domestication of animals. Bager in Rajasthan provides evidence for the same.

Mehrgarh was the earliest neolithic settlement where people learnt to grow barley and wheat for the first time. Mehrgarh is located in a fertile plain near the Belan Pass at Baluchistan (Pakistan). It is probably one of the places were people reared sheep and goat for first time.

While pairs (1) and (2) are not correctly matched. Evidence of remains of square or rectangular houses were found at Mehrgarh and not Kurnool. Kurnool is a Palaeolithic site where discovery of fire is evidence by the traces of fire. It is located in Andhra Pradesh.

Evidence of circular pit house have been discovered in Inamgaon which is chalcolithic sites. Animal remains were found on Belan valley which provides evidence of domestication around 25,000 BC.

11 Match the following lists correctly and choose the correct code. *(Chap 5, Class-XI, Old NCERT)*

List I (Mesolithic Sites)	List II (Present day states)
A. Bagor	1. Uttar Pradesh
B. Adamgarh	2. Tamil Nadu
C. Belan Valley	3. Rajasthan
D. Theni	4. Madhya Pradesh

Codes

	A	B	C	D		A	B	C	D
(a)	1	2	3	4	(b)	2	3	1	4
(c)	2	1	4	3	(d)	3	4	1	2

Ans. (d)

Exp. The correct matching is A-3, B-4, C-1, D-2.

Bagor is presently in Bhilwara district in Rajasthan. It had a microlith industry and inhabitants lived pastoral lives and hunted animals.

Adamgarh is in Madhya Pradesh. This site is placed around 5000 BC and is characterised by domestication of animals. It is presently in Hoshangabad district.

Belan Valley is in Uttar Pradesh at the Northern side of Vindhyan ranges. It has evidence of all three phases of Palaeolithic, and also of Mesolithic and Neolithic age.

Theni is located in Tirunelveli district of Tamil Nadu, here microliths tools of Mesolithic age have been found.

12 With reference to pre-historic India, consider the following statements. *(Class-XI, Old NCERT)*

1. The Acheulian tools tradition is prominent in Western Ghats, North-Eastern India.
2. Acheulian and Sohanian are now considered as two distinct cultural traditions.
3. Hunsgi valley in Karnataka is the paleolithic site where the Acheulian tools are found.

How many of the statements given above is/are correct?

(a) Only one
(b) Only two
(c) All three
(d) None of these

Ans. (a)

Exp. Only one statement i.e., (3) is correct as Hunsgi valley in Karnataka is the paleolethic site where the Acheulian tools are found.

Athirampakkam, Pallavaram and Gudiyam, near Chennai, Isampur in Karnataka and Bhimbetka in Madhya Pradesh are some other important sites where the Acheulian tools are found.

Statements (1) and (2) are incorrect because the Acheulian tools tradition is absent in the Western Ghats, Coastal areas and North-Eastern India. Heavy rainfall is attributed to its absence. Acheulian tool sites are found more in Central India and in South-Eastern part of India. Acheulian and Sohanian cultural traditions are not considered distinct any longer. Recent studies argue that there was no independent Sohan tradition as Acheulian tools are found in the Sohan industry as well.

13 Which among the following ancient pre-historic site contains archaeological evidences of all the three phases of Paleolithic followed by the Mesolithic and Neolithic cultural phase? *(Chap 5, Class-XI, Old NCERT)*

(a) Belan Valley in Uttar Pradesh
(b) Bagor in Rajasthan
(c) Mehargarh in Pakistan
(d) Inamgaon in Maharashtra

Ans. (a)

Exp. On the Northern spurs of the Vindhyas in the Belan valley in Uttar Pradesh, all the three phases of the Palaeolithic followed by the Mesolithic and then by the Neolithic have been found in a sequence, and same is the case with the middle part of the Narmada valley.

The Pre-historic sites of Belan valley include Mahgara, Chopani Mando and Koldihwa in Belan valley have provided earliest evidence of rice cultivation.

14 With reference to the Mesolithic age, consider the following statements. ***(Class-XI, Old NCERT)***

1. Human groups became highly mobile in the Mesolithic age with the advent of global warming.
2. Agriculture was not practiced in the early stages of the Mesolithic age.
3. Circular huts are seen in the rock paintings of the Mesolithic age.
4. Mesolithic people didn't bury their dead.

How many of the statements given above is/are correct?

(a) Only one (b) Only two (c) Only three (d) All four

Ans. (c)

Exp. Only three statements i.e., (1), (2) and (3) are correct with reference to the Mesolithic age. After the ice age, with the advent of global warming, human groups became highly mobile and began to occupy various eco-zones.

The Mesolithic people were highly mobile. Agriculture was not practiced in the early stages of the Mesolithic age. Hunting wild animals and gathering plant food and fishing were people's main occupation during this age. Circular huts are seen in rock paintings. Traces of oval and circular huts and possible wattle daub are found in Chopani Mando and Damdama in Uttar Pradesh and Bagor and Tilwara in Rajasthan.

Statement (4) is incorrect because the Mesolithic people buried the dead, which suggests their belief and humane relationship. At Mahadaha, a man and a woman were buried together. One burial had an ivory pendant as the grave good.

15 Consider the following statements. ***(Unit 1, Class-XI, Tamil Nadu Board)***

Statement-I Neolithic culture began earlier in North-Western part of India as compared to North-Eastern India.

Statement-II The Neolithic cultures of India flourished in different time periods.

Which one of the following is correct in respect of the above statements?

(a) Both Statement-I and Statement-II are correct and Statement-II is the correct explanation for Statement-I.

(b) Both Statement-I and Statement-II are correct but Statement-II is not the correct explanation for Statement-I.

(c) Statement-I is correct but Statement-II is incorrect.

(d) Statement-I is incorrect but Statement-II is correct .

Ans. (a)

Exp. Both Statement-I and Statement-II are correct and Statement-II is the correct explanation for Statement-I. Neolithic culture began earlier in North-Western part of India as compared to North-Eastern India. The Neolithic cultures of India are divided into various regional cultures and they flourished in different time periods. In North-Western part of India and Pakistan, it began at a very early date. In North-Eastern India, Neolithic cultures appeared at a very late date, around the early historic time.

16 The Neolithic sites of South India are distinguished on the basis of tools used. They were ***(Chap 5, Class-XI, Old NCERT)***

(a) axes with oval sides and pointed butt
(b) rectangular axes with curved cutting edge
(c) polished stone axes with rectangular butt
(d) polished stone axes with triangular butt

Ans. (a)

Exp. The Neolithic sites of South India are distinguished on the basis of axes with oval sides and pointed butt. Based on the types of axes used by Neolithic settlers, there are three important areas of Neolithic settlements; North-Western, North-Eastern and Southern.

The Southern group is distinguished by axes with oval sides and pointed butt. The North-Western group of Neolithic tools represents rectangular axes with curved cutting edges. The North-Eastern group shows polished stone axes with rectangular butt and has occasional shouldered hoes.

17 Consider the following statements with reference to the Neolithic age in South India. ***(Chap 5, Class-XI, Old NCERT)***

1. People of this age usually settled on the top of Granite hills or on plateaus near the river banks.
2. They used rubbing stone querns, which shows that they were acquainted with the art of producing cereals.

Which of the statements given above is/are correct?

(a) Only 1 (b) Only 2
(c) Both 1 and 2 (d) Neither 1 nor 2

Ans. (c)

Exp. Both the statements (1) and (2) are correct with reference to the Neolithic age in South India.

A group of Neolithic people lived in South India, South of the Godavari river. They usually settled on the tops of Granite hills or on plateaus near the river banks. They used stone axes and also some kind of stone blades.

Fire-baked earthen figurines suggest that they kept a large number of cattle. They possessed cattle, sheep and goats. They used rubbing stone querns, which shows that they were acquainted with the art of producing cereals.

18 With reference to the Neolithic site of 'Piklihal', which of the following statements are correct? ***(Chap 5, Class-XI, Old NCERT)***

1. It is located in the present day state of Andhra Pradesh of India.
2. Both ash mounds and habitation sites have been found at Piklihal.
3. People living in this site set-up seasonal camps surrounded by cowpens made with posts and stakes.

Codes

(a) 1 and 2 (b) 2 and 3 (c) 1 and 3 (d) 1, 2 and 3

Ans. (b)

Exp. Statements (2) and (3) are correct with reference to the Neolithic site of 'Piklihal'. The Neolithic inhabitants in Piklihal were cattle-herders. They domesticated cattle, sheep, goats, etc. and set up camps surrounded by cowpens made with posts and stakes.

In these enclosures, they accumulated dung. Then the entire camping ground was put to fire and cleared for camping in the next session. Both ash mounds and habitation sites have been found in Piklihal.

Statement (1) is incorrect because Piklihal is located in Karnataka.

19 Which among the following innovations started in the Neolithic age is still used by the people of India? *(Chap 2, Class-VI, New NCERT)*

1. Mortars and pestles for grinding grain.
2. Earthen pots for cooking and storing grains.
3. Needles for weaving clothes.

Codes

(a) 1 and 2 (b) 2 and 3 (c) 1 and 3 (d) 1, 2 and 3

Ans. (d)

Exp. All the Neolithic innovations mentioned in the question are still used by the people of India.

Mortars and pestles for grinding grain, earthen pots for cooking and storing grains and needles for weaving clothes, all three techniques of Neolithic age are still used in different forms, by people of India.

20 Identify the Neolithic site with the help of statements given below. *(Chap 5, Class-XI, Old NCERT)*

1. It has yielded considerable amount of bone implement made up of horns of deer.
2. It is situated on the bank of confluence of three rivers– Ganga, Gandak and Ghaghra.
3. It is marked by the paucity of stone tools.

Codes

(a) Chirand (b) Mahagara
(c) Koldihwa (d) Sarai Nahar Rai

Ans. (a)

Exp. Chirand is the Neolithic site mentioned in the question. This site has yielded considerable bone implement in India. It is situated 40 km West of Patna on the Northern side of the Ganga. Made of antlers (horns of deer), these implements have been found in a late Neolithic set in an area which received about 100 cm of rainfall. The settlement became possible because of the open land available on account of the joining together of the three rivers-Ganga, Gandak and Ghaghra at this place. It is marked by the paucity of stone tools.

21 With reference to Neolithic age in India, consider the following statements. *(Class-XI, Old NCERT)*

1. The Neolithic revolution is marked by generation of surplus grains.
2. The Neolithic site of Mehrgarh has not produced evidence of the use of pottery.
3. Burzahom and Mehrgarh were contemporary to the Harappan civilisation.

How many of the statements given above is/are incorrect?

(a) Only one (b) Only two
(c) All three (d) None of these

Ans. (a)

Exp. Only one statement i.e., (2) is incorrect with reference to Neolithic age in India as second, cultural period of Neolithic age (5500 to 4800 BC) at Mehrgarh has produced evidence of the use of pottery however first cultural period of the Neolithic age (7000 to 5500 BC) at Mehrgarh has not produced evidence of the use of pottery by the people.

22 With reference to Neolithic culture of India, consider the following statements. *(Class-XI, Old NCERT)*

1. The Neolithic culture of Kashmir had established contact with South-East Asia.
2. Neolithic culture of Eastern India shows similarities with the Neolithic complexes of East and South-East Asia.
3. The Neolithic culture of North-Eastern India is marked by the presence of Austro-Asiatic languages.

How many of the statements given above is/are incorrect?

(a) Only one (b) Only two
(c) All three (d) None of these

Ans. (a)

Exp. Only one statement i.e., (1) is incorrect because Neolithic culture of Kashmir had established contacts with Central Asia and this was evidenced by the use of lentils.

23 Match the following lists correctly and choose the correct code. *(Chap 2, Class-VI, New NCERT)*

List I (Neolithic Sites)	List II (Present day states)
A. Brahmagiri	1. Uttar Pradesh
B. Koldihwa	2. Assam
C. Chirand	3. Bihar
D. Daojali Hading	4. Karnataka

Codes

	A	B	C	D		A	B	C	D
(a)	1	2	3	4	(b)	2	3	1	4
(c)	4	1	3	2	(d)	3	1	4	2

Ans. (c)

Exp. The correct matching is A-4, B-1, C-3, D-2.

Brahmagiri is a Neolithic site located in Southern India in the state of Karnataka. Maski, Hallur, Kodekal, Sanganakallu, T. Narasipura and Takkalakota are other Neolithic sites of Karnataka.

Koldihwa is located in Vindhyan range in Uttar Pradesh. Here archaeological evidences suggesting prevalence of agriculture and animal domestication had been excavated.

Chirand is located 40 km West of Patna in Bihar, it is at the Northern side of the Ganga river. Here considerable amounts of bone implements have been found.

Daojali Hading is in Assam where Neolithic tools have been discovered. They are also found in range of Garo hills in Meghalaya.

24 With reference to the Neolithic settlements of South India, which of the following statements is/are correct? *(Chap 5, Class-XI, Old NCERT)*

1. The settlements were formed on the top of Granite hills or on plateaus near the river banks.
2. The people lived settled life and were primarily involved in agriculture.

Codes

(a) Only 1
(b) Only 2
(c) Both 1 and 2
(d) Neither 1 nor 2

Ans. (c)

Exp. Both the statements (1) and (2) are correct with reference Neolithic settlements of South India. The Neolithic people of South India usually settled on the tops of Granite hills or on plateaus near the river banks. They used stone axes and also some kind of stone blades. The Neolithic settler of this region lived settled life and were primarily involved in agriculture. They constructed circular or rectangular houses made of mud and reed.

25 Consider the following Assertion (A) and Reason (R) and choose the correct code. *(Chap 5, Class-XI, Old NCERT)*

Assertion (A) People of Stone Age could not found settlements far away from the hilly areas.

Reason (R) They had to depend almost entirely on tools and weapons made of stone.

Codes

(a) Both A and R are true and R is the correct explanation of A.
(b) Both A and R are true, but R is not the correct explanation of A.
(c) A is true, but R is false.
(d) A is false, but R is true.

Ans. (a)

Exp. Both Assertion (A) and Reason (R) are true and Reason (R) is the correct explanation of Assertion (A).

The people of the Stone Age had one great limitation as they had to depend almost entirely on tools and weapons made of stone.

They could not settle far away from the hilly areas. They settled down only on the slopes of hills, rock shelters and hilly river valleys.

26 Consider the following statements with reference to Chalcolithic culture of Ahar and Gilund. *(Chap 6, Class-XI, Old NCERT)*

1. This culture flourished in the dry zones of Amravati river in Andhra Pradesh.
2. At Ahar, Stone axes or blades are completely absent.
3. At Gilund, archaeological evidences regarding stone blade industry have been excavated.

Which of the statements given above is/are incorrect?

(a) 1 and 2 (b) Only 1 (c) Only 3 (d) 2 and 3

Ans. (b)

Exp. Statement (1) is incorrect regarding Chalcolithic culture of Ahar and Gilund because both of these culture flourished in the dry zones of Banas river in Rajasthan.

27 With reference to Chalcolithic culture of India, consider the following statements. *(Class-XI, Old NCERT)*

1. People in the Chalcolithic period domesticated goats, cows and horses.
2. There is evidence that the settlements at Eran and Inamgaon were fortified.
3. Chalcolithic communities of South India were specialised in the production of lentils.
4. Navdatoli is a rural Chalcolithic site in Uttar Pradesh excavated by archeologist HD Sankalia.

How many of the statements given above is/are correct?

(a) Only one
(b) Only two
(c) Only three
(d) All four

Ans. (a)

Exp. Only one statement i.e, (2) is correct as archeological evidence excavated from the Chalcolithic sites of Eran in Madhya Pradesh and Inamgaon in Maharashtra suggests fortification of the houses. These settlements were also surrounded by moats. At Inamgaon, large mud houses with ovens and circular pit houses, have been discovered.

Statements (1), (3) and (4) are incorrect because people in the Chalcolithic period domesticated cattle, sheep, goats, cows and camels. Horse was not known to Indians in this period and it came to be used later in the Rig Vedic period.

The Chalcolithic communities of South India were specialised in the production of rice and not Lentils. People of Western India cultivated barley, wheat, and lentils.

Navdatoli is the rural Chalcolithic site located in Madhya Pradesh excavated by HD Sankalia.

It is the most extensively studied rural Chalcolithic site of India.

28 **Consider the following statements with reference to the Chalcolithic phase of cultural development.** *(Chap 6, Class-XI, Old NCERT)*

1. All the sites related with Chalcolithic age appeared before the Indus Valley Civilisation.
2. They were primarily rural communities spread over in hilly and riverine areas of the country.
3. Besides copper, they also occasionally used low-grade bronze.

Which of the statements given above is/are incorrect?

(a) 1 and 2 (b) 2 and 3 (c) Only 1 (d) Only 3

Ans. (c)

Exp. Statement (1) is incorrect with reference to Chalcolithic phase of cultural development as though the Chalcolithic stage applied usually to the Pre-Harappan, but in various parts of the country the Chalcolithic cultures appear after the end of the bronze Harappan culture. Such cultures appear in the later part of the mature Harappan culture or after its end.

29 **Consider the following statements with reference to difference between Harappan Civilisation and Chalcolithic age.** *(Chap 6, Class-XI, Old NCERT)*

1. People in Harappan Civilisation used bronze as a predominant metal whereas copper was the main metal in Chalcolithic age.
2. The Harappan Civilisation was characterised by urbanisation whereas people in Chalcolithic age mostly lived in villages.
3. Wheat, barley and cotton were the main crops in Harappan Civilisation whereas it was not known to the people in Chalcolithic age.

Which of the statements given above are correct?

(a) 1 and 2 (b) 2 and 3 (c) 1 and 3 (d) 1, 2 and 3

Ans. (a)

Exp. Statements (1) and (2) are correct with reference to difference between Harappan Civilisation and Chalcolithic Age.

People of Harappan Age used mainly bronze, while copper was the main metal used in Chalcolithic Age. The nature of settlement also differed in these two ages. The Harappan Civilisation was characterised by urbanisation whereas people in Chalcolithic Age used to live in villages.

Statement (3) is incorrect because Chalcolithic people also produced barley, cotton, ragi, rice, wheat, etc.

30 **Consider the following statements with reference to the state of art and crafts in the Chalcolithic age.** *(Chap 6, Class-XI, Old NCERT)*

1. People in Chalcolithic age were skilled artisans, they manufactured beads of semi-precious stones such as carnelian, steatite and quartz crystal.
2. They were also well acquainted with manufacture of tools and weapons from copper, bronze and iron.
3. People knew the art of spinning and weaving because spindle whorls have been discovered at Malwa.

Which of the statements given above are correct?

(a) 1 and 2 (b) 2 and 3 (c) 1 and 3 (d) 1, 2 and 3

Ans. (c)

Exp. Statements (1) and (3) are correct with reference to the state of art and crafts in the Chalcolithic age.

Chalcolithic artisans were expert coppersmiths and also good workers in stone. Tools, weapons and bangles of copper were found at different sites. They manufactured beads of semi-precious stones such as carnelian, steatite, and quartz crystal.

People knew the art of spinning and weaving because spindle whorls have been discovered in Malwa. Cotton, flax and silk threads made of cotton silk of semal (silk cotton tree) have been found in Maharashtra.

Statement (2) is incorrect as iron was not known to Chalcolithic age people.

31 **Consider the following statements with reference to Ochre Coloured Pottery (OCP) sites in India.** *(Chap 6, Class-XI, Old NCERT)*

1. Most Ochre coloured Pottery sites are found in the Western Uttar Pradesh.
2. On the basis of a series of eight scientific dating, it is roughly placed between 2500 BC and 2000 BC.
3. Jodhpura on the borders of Haryana and Rajasthan shows the thickest OCP deposits accounting for 1.1 metre.

Which of the statements given above is/are incorrect?

(a) 1 and 2 (b) 2 and 3 (c) Only 2 (d) Only 1

Ans. (c)

Exp. Statement (2) is incorrect with reference to Ochre Coloured Pottery (OCP) sites in India as on the basis of a series of eight scientific dating, it is roughly placed between 2000 BC and 1500 BC.

32 **Consider the following statements with reference to limitation of Chalcolithic cultures in India.** *(Chap 6, Class-XI, Old NCERT)*

1. Absence of plough or hoe suggests that they didn't practised agriculture at extensive scale.
2. Inspite it being a food producing economy, the rate of infant mortality was high.
3. They didn't carried internal trade among themselves and were unaware of cultural change in other contemporary habitations.
4. People didn't knew the art of mixing tin with copper to make much stronger and useful metal called bronze.

Which of the statements given above are correct?

(a) 1, 2 and 3 (b) 2, 3 and 4
(c) 1, 3 and 4 (d) 1, 2 and 4

Ans. (d)

Exp. Statements (1), (2) and (4) are correct with reference to limitation of Chalcolithic cultures in India. Chalcolithic people living in the black cotton soil area of Central and Western India did not practise cultivation on any intensive or extensive scale. Neither plough nor hoe has been found at chalcolithic sites.

Another weakness of Chalcolithic cultures is evident from the burials found in a large number of children. In spite of a food-producing economy, the rate of infant mortality was very high. They also didn't not knew much about metal and they didn't knew mixing tin and copper which produced stronger metal, the bronze.

Statement (3) is incorrect because they carried trade among themselves.

33 With reference to Chalcolithic cultures in India, consider the following statements. *(Chap 6, Class-IX, Old NCERT)*

1. Distinctive feature of Ahara culture is black and red ware.
2. Malwa culture was located along the Narmada river.
3. Polished red ware is the hallmark of Prabhas and Rangpur culture.

How many of the statements given above is/are correct?

(a) Only one (b) Only two
(c) All three (d) None of these

Ans. (c)

Exp. All three statements i.e., (1), (2) and (3) are correct with reference to Chalcolithic cultures in India. Ahara culture is a Chalcolithic site located in Rajasthan. The distinctive feature is black and red ware, decorated with the white designs. Malwa culture is a Chalcolithic site situated along the Narmada river and its tributaries in Gujarat. Malwa culture is one of the largest Chalcolithic settlements. Prabhas and Rangpur culture are located in Gujarat.

The polished red ware is the hallmark of this culture both of them are derived from the Harappan culture.

34 Which of the following pair is/are matched correctly? *(Chap 6, Class-XI, Old NCERT)*

Chalcolithic Sites		Present day States
(a) Hanumangarh	–	Uttar Pradesh
(b) Khairadih	–	Rajasthan
(c) Pandu Rajar Dhibi	–	Gujarat

(d) None of the above

Ans. (d)

Exp. None of the given pairs are matched correctly. Hanumangarh is in Rajasthan. It is situated on the banks of river Ghaghar.

Khairadih is in Ballia district of Eastern Uttar Pradesh.

Pandu Rajar Dhibi is in Burdwan district of West Bengal.

Rangpur is in Saurashtra region of Gujarat. It lies in Surendranagar district.

35 Consider the following pairs. *(Chap 6, Class-XI, Old NCERT)*

Chalcolithic sites		River system
1. Amri	–	Ganga
2. Kaushambi	–	Indus
3. Nagda	–	Chambal
4. Navdatoli	–	Narmada

How many of the pairs given above is/are matched incorrectly?

(a) Only one (b) Only two
(c) Only three (d) All four

Ans. (b)

Exp. Only two pairs i.e., (1) and (2) are matched incorrectly.

Amri is Chalcolithic site located near the bank of Indus river. Other site located near the bank of this river include Ropar and Hanumangarh.

Kaushambi is the Chalcolithic site, located near the basin of Ganga river. Alamgir in Uttar Pradesh is another site located near basin of Ganga River.

36 Consider the following Assertion (A) and Reason (R) and choose the correct code. *(Chap 5, Class-XI, Old NCERT)*

Assertion (A) Some of the Chalcolithic habitations in Western and Central India were contemporary with Indus Valley Civilisation.

Reason (R) In the context of art and architecture, art of writing and Urbanisation, they benefitted immensely from the Indus Valley Civilisation.

Codes

(a) Both A and R are true and R is the correct explanation of A.
(b) Both A and R are true, but R is not the correct explanation of A.
(c) A is true, but R is false.
(d) A is false, but R is true.

Ans. (c)

Exp. Assertion (A) is true, but Reason (R) is false. Some of the Chalcolithic settlements in Western and Central India existed at the same time as with the Indus Valley Civilisation, though in art of writing and Urbanisation, they didn't benefit from the Indus Valley Civilisation.

37 Consider the following statements. *(Chap 4, Class-VI, New NCERT)*

1. The Megalith phase of the history of South India was associated with the metal iron.
2. Stone circles or boulders placed on the surface served as signposts to find burial site.

Which of the statements given above is/are correct?

(a) Only 1 (b) Only 2
(c) Both 1 and 2 (d) Neither 1 nor 2

Ans. (c)

Exp. Both the statements (1) and (2) are correct regarding Megalith phase of the history of South India. In this phase, arrowheads, spearheads, hoes and sickles made of iron were found.

While some Megaliths can be seen on the surface, other Megalithic burials are often underground. Stone circles or boulders placed on the surface served as signposts to find burial site.

38 With reference to the 'Megalith' culture, which of the following statements is/are incorrect?
(Chap 18, Class-XI, Old NCERT)

1. The practice of building Megalith began around 3000 years ago and was prevalent in South India only.
2. The Megalith people of Southern Tamil Nadu buried the skeletons of dead in urns made of red pottery in pits.
3. The Megalith people did not practice an advanced type of agriculture.

Codes

(a) Only 1 (b) Only 2 (c) Only 3 (d) None of these

Ans. (a)

Exp. Statement (1) is incorrect with reference to the 'Megalith' culture. The practice of building Megalith began around 1000 BC. It was also found in the Peninsular region, but was concentrated in Andhra and Tamil Nadu.

39 Consider the following statements with reference to the cultural advancement of the 'Megalith' builders.
(Chap 18, Class-XI, Old NCERT)

1. They used the iron to make arrowheads, spearheads, hoes and sickles.
2. The produced paddy and ragi.
3. They domesticated horses and were acquainted with ornaments made up of stone and gold.

Which of the statements given above are correct?

(a) 1 and 2 (b) 2 and 3
(c) 1 and 3 (d) 1, 2 and 3

Ans. (d)

Exp. All the statements (1), (2) and (3) are correct with reference to the cultural advancement of the 'Megalith' builders.

Megalithic people used iron tools in the form of arrowheads, spearheads, hoes and sickles. They produced paddy and ragi but the area used for cultivation was limited.

They domesticated horses and were acquainted with ornaments made up of stone and gold as bones and these ornaments have been found with dead bodies in graves of megaliths.

40 With reference to evolution of man, arrange the following hominids species in correct chronological order. *(Chap 1, Class-IX, Old NCERT)*

1. Australopithecus
2. Sinanthropus
3. Neanderthal
4. Cro-Magnon

Codes

(a) 1, 2, 3, 4 (b) 2, 3, 1, 4
(c) 3, 1, 4, 2 (d) 4, 1, 3, 2

Ans. (a)

Exp. The correct chronological order of hominids species with reference to evolution of man is 1, 2, 3, 4 i.e., Australopithecus, Sinanthropus, Neanderthal, Cro-Magnon.

Australopithecus existed in Africa and remains of Sinanthropus have been found in China. Neanderthal were inhabitants of Eurasian region and Cro-Magnon were the early Homo sapiens who came in upper Palaeolithic phase.

Chapter 03

Indus Valley Civilisation

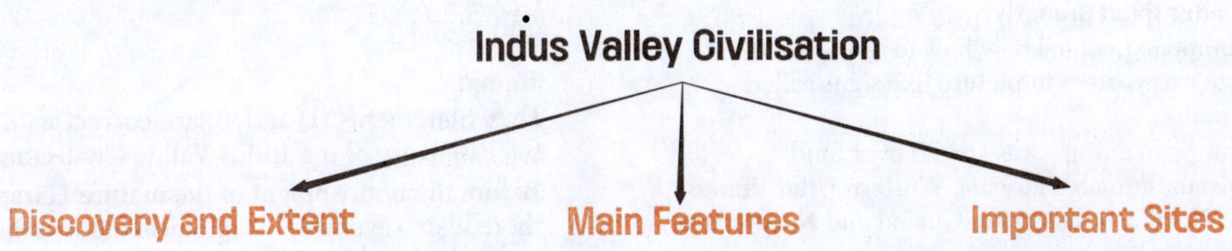

Discovery and Extent

Other Names
- Bronze age civilisation
- Proto-historic culture
- First urban civilisation

Discovery
- In 1875 by Alexander Cunningham
- In 1921 by Dayaram Sahni (Harappa)
- In 1922 by Rakhaldas Banerjee Mohenjodaro

Territorial Extent
- Triangular (12,99,600 km.sq.) area
- Manda in North (Jammu and Kashmir)
- Sutkagendor in West (Baluchistan)
- Alamgirpur in East (Uttar Pradesh)
- Daimabad in South (Maharashtra)

Contemporary Civilisation
- Egypt (on bank of Nile)
- Mesopotamia (on bank of Euphrates and Tigris)
- Hwang Ho (on bank of Hwang Ho)

Other Evidence
- According to Piaget, Harappa and Mohenjodaro were twin capitals of the Indus valley

Contemporary Civilisations

Civilisation	Banks of River
Egypt	Nile river
Mesopotamia (Modern Iraq)	Euphrates and Tigris rivers
Hwang Ho (China)	Hwang Ho river

Main Features

Urban Planning
- Drainage system
- Use of baked brick
- Rectangular Tank
- Public building

Social Lives
- Society Matriarchal in nature
- Possibly ruled by class of merchants
- Social stratification
- Hair dressing by both men and women

Economic Condition
- People followed diverse profession such as priests
- Warrior class
- Peasants
- Traders
- Greeks called cotton as Sindhun
- Prominence of agriculture

Religious lives
- No evidence of religious place and temple
- Evidence of fire worship
- Worshipped mother Goddess and Pashupati Mahadeva

Art and Culture
- Bronze and copper seal
- Acquainted with the knowledge of lost-wax technique
- Bead maker shop

Script
- Pictographic script
- Written from right to left and from left to right in alternate lines
- Around 250 to 400 pictographs are found

Important Sites

Harappa
Discovered by Dayaram Sahni in 1921; on the bank of Ravi; Important discoveries- Granary stone symbol of lingam

Mohenjo-Daro
- Discovered by Rakhaldas Banerjee in 1922; On the bank of Indus; Important discoveries- great bath, Unicorn seals, dancing girl statue

Chanhudaro
- Discovered by NG Majumdar; On the bank of Ghaggar river
- Important discoveries- bangle factory, inkpot, bead-maker shop

Kalibangan
- Discovered by Amlanand Ghosh
- On the bank of Ghaggar river; Important discoveries- Ploughed field, evidence of earthquake, wooden plough

Lothal
- Discovered by Rangnath Rao; On the bank of Bhogavo river
- Important discoveries- bead making factory, rice husk

Alamgirpur
- Discovered by YD Sharma; On the bank of Hindon river
- Important discoveries-pottery, animal bones, plant fossils, copper tools

Banawali
- Discovered by RS Bisht; On the banks of Saraswati river; Important discoveries- oval shaped settlement

SOURCE **Old NCERT Class-VI** *(Man Takes to City Life)*, **Old NCERT Class-XI** *(Harappa Civilisation : Bronze Age Civilisation)*, **New NCERT Class-XII** *(Bricks, Beads and Bones : The Harappan Civilisation)* **Tamil Nadu Board Class XI** *(Early India)* **NIOS Module** *(The Harappan Civilisation)*

Sources of Indus Valley Civilisation

1 Which among the following statements do not entails that the Harappan culture was a civilisation?

(Chap 2, Class-VI, Old NCERT)

(a) People were living a more advanced life than those of the previous primitive ages.
(b) The cities were well planned and great care was taken to look after them properly.
(c) The Harappan people knew how to write and their language was written in picture like signs called 'pictographs'.
(d) The Harappan culture was spread over Sind, Baluchistan, Punjab, Haryana, Western Uttar Pradesh, Jammu, Northern Rajasthan, Gujarat and Northern Maharashtra.

Ans. (d)

Exp. Statement (d) do not entails that the Harappan culture was a civilisation. It only tells about the geographical extent of this cultivation that the Harappan culture was spread over the whole of Sind, Baluchistan, Punjab, Northern Rajasthan, Kathiawar, and Gujarat but not in Northern Maharashtra. The presence of advanced life-style, planned urbanisation and prevalent of writing are some of the features that show that Harappan culture was a civilisation.

2 With reference to the Pre-Harappan culture, which of the following statements is/are correct?

(Chap 6, Class-XI, Old NCERT)

1. The central zone of Pre-Harappan culture was located in Sindh.
2. It is older yet more developed than Chalcolithic culture.

Codes

(a) Only 1 (b) Only 2
(c) Both 1 and 2 (d) Neither 1 nor 2

Ans. (c)

Exp. Both the statements (1) and (2) are correct regarding Pre-Harappan culture. The Central zone of Pre-Harappan culture was located in Sindh. As many as 52 sites belonging to Pre-Harappa culture has been discovered from Sindh Province of Pakistan. Amri, Damb Sadat and Kot Diji are some of the more prominent Harappan site. Some of the pre as well as mature Harappan sites are older than Chalcolithic sites such as Daimabad, Inamgaon etc but owing to its advanced town planning and well-developed system of writing, it was more advanced than the Chalcolithic culture.

3 Consider the following statements with reference to the discovery of the Indus Valley Civilisation.

(Chap 6, Class-XI, Old NCERT)

1. There were several archaeological cultures in Punjab and Sindh region prior to the mature Harappan culture.
2. It originated in the North-Eastern part of the Indian sub-continent.
3. The civilisation was first discovered in 1921 at the site of Harappa.

Which of the statements given above are correct?

(a) 1 and 2
(b) 2 and 3
(c) 1 and 3
(d) 1, 2 and 3

Ans. (c)

Exp. Statements (1) and (3) are correct with reference to the discovery of the Indus Valley Civilisation.

Before the flourishment of the mature Harappan site there were several archaeological cultures in the Sindh and Punjab region. These cultures were associated with distinctive pottery, evidence of agriculture and Pastoralism. It is called Harappan because this civilisation was first discovered in 1921 at the modern site of Harappa in West Punjab in Pakistan.

Statement (2) is incorrect because the Indus Valley Civilisation arose in the North-Western part of the Indian sub-continent.

4 With reference to discovery of Harappan culture, consider the following statements.

(Class-XI, Old NCERT)

1. Tenure of Sir John Marshan as director General of ASI was marked by the beginning of extensive research at the site of Harappa.
2. Archaeologist Daya Ram Sahni is associated with excavations at Dholavira.
3. Pakistan is left with no Harappan sites after partition of India in 1947.

How many of the statements given above is/are correct?

(a) Only one (b) Only two
(c) All three (d) None of these

Ans. (a)

Exp. Only one statement i.e., (1) is correct as tenure of Sir John Marshan as the director of ASI was marked by the beginning of extensive research at the Indus site of Harappa. The significance of these sites were not realised completely until he took over as the director of ASI. Sir John Marshan played an important role in the development of archaeology in India.

Statements (2) and (3) are incorrect. Archaeologist Daya Ram Sahni is associated with the excavations at the site of Harappa, while excavations at Dholavira began under archeologist RS Bisht. Many of the Harappan sites such has Harappa (Punjab, Pakistan), Mohenjodaro (Sindh, Pakistan) became part of Pakistan after the partition of India in 1947. Indian sites of Harappan civilisation include Lothal and Surkotada (Gujarat, India), Kalibangan (Rajasthan, India) and Banawali and Rakhigarhi (Haryana, India).

5 With reference to Indus culture, consider the following statements. *(Class-XI, Old NCERT)*

1. It was contemporary to some Mesolithic cultures prevailing in other parts of India.
2. The central zone of Pre-Harappan Culture was located in Sindh.
3. It was older and less developed than Chalcolithic culture.

How many of the statements given above is/are correct?

(a) Only one (b) Only two
(c) All three (d) None of these

Ans. (b)

Exp. Only two statements i.e., (1) and (2) are correct with reference Indus culture. Indus civilisation was contemporary to some Mesolithic cultures prevailing in other parts of India. While the Indus civilisation was at its peak, several cultures, namely, Mesolithic and Neolithic cultures prevailed in other parts of India. The central zone of Pre-Harappan Culture was located in Sindh. As many 52 sites belonging to Pre-Harappan Culture has been discovered from Sindh province of Pakistan.

Statement (3) is incorrect because some of the pre as well as mature Harappan sites are older than Chalcolithic sites such as Daimabad, Inamgaon, etc., but it was more advanced than Chalcolithic culture. This is due to the advanced town planning and well-developed system of writing of Indus culture as compared to Chalcolithic cultures.

6 With reference to Indus valley site, consider the following statements. *(Unit 1, Class-XI, Tamil Nadu Board)*

1. Burnt bricks were used in construction in Harappan and Egyptian civilisation and not in Mesopotamian civilisation.
2. In some Indus towns brick platforms were used as granaries.
3. Building structure of Indus towns shows that they had concern for privacy.

How many of the statements given above is/are correct?

(a) Only one (b) Only two
(c) All three (d) None of these

Ans. (b)

Exp. Only two statements i.e., (2) and (3) are correct with reference to Indus valley site. In some Indus towns brick platforms were used as granaries. For instance, in Kalibangan, in Rajasthan the brick platforms have been found, which indicates they have been used for granaries. Building structure of Indus town shows they had concern for privacy and this has attested by the fact that there are no windows in the walls along the main road.

Statement (1) is incorrect because both Harappan and Mesopotamian civilisation used burnt bricks. In Mesopotamia burnt bricks was used on a smaller scale as compared to Harappan civilisation. While in Egypt mainly dried bricks were used.

7 With reference to the citadel, consider the following statements. *(Chap 6, Class-XI, Old NCERT)*

1. The citadel was located in the West to the city which was smaller and higher.
2. The citadel had a distinctive structure called Warehouse.
3. The Great Bath was also located in the citadel.

How many of the statements given above is/are correct?

(a) Only one
(b) Only two
(c) All three
(d) None of the above

Ans. (c)

Exp. All three statements i.e., (1), (2) and (3) are correct with reference to the citadel discovered from the cities of Indus valley civilisation. The Harappan cities were usually divided into two parts. The upper town (known as citadel) and the lower town.

The citadel occupied Western end of the site and served as the habitation site for the member of ruling class. It was constructed on the raised platform and was smaller than the lower part of the town. Structures having public importance such as granary, Great Bath, warehouse, etc were situated on the citadel. The warehouse was also one of the distinctive structures on the citadel. It was a massive structure of which the lower brick portion remains, while the upper portion, probably made of wood, decayed long ago.

8 With reference to Indus Valley Civilisation, consider the statements. *(Class-XI, Old NCERT)*

1. Kalibangan in Rajasthan was the first site to be excavated after independence.
2. Kot Diji in Pakistan represents the phase leading up to Mature Harappan Site.
3. Indus, Jhukar and Jhangar represent cultural layers of Harappan civilisation.
4. The Citadel of the Chaundaro includes a multi-pillared assembly hall.

How many of the statements given above is/are correct?

(a) Only one (b) Only two
(c) Only three (d) All four

Ans. (b)

Exp. Only two statements i.e., (2) and (3) are correct. Kot diji, located in Khairpur (Sindh, Pakistan) represents the phase leading up to the Mature Harappan phase. It represents the early Harappan phase (3300 to 2600 BC). It is located on the river Indus. It was excavated in 1935 and figurines of ox, steatite seal are the major findings from this site. Kalibangan is located in Rajasthan where three different layers i.e., Indus, Jhukar and Jhangar can be seen. It was excavated in 1953. Granary, ploughed field, wooden drainage, evidence of earthquake are the major findings of this site.

Statements (1) and (4) are incorrect because Ropar in Punjab was the first site to be excavated after independence of India in 1953. It is located in Punjab on the bank of river Sutlej. Five-fold sequence of culture is the major finding of Ropar.
Chaundaro didn't have a citadel and is the only Indus city without a citadel. The citadel area had important residential structures that were either used by the public or selected residents.

9 Consider the following pairs.

(Chap 6, Class-XI, Old NCERT)

Harappan sites		Present day location
1. Rojdi	–	Gujarat
2. Banawali	–	Haryana
3. Rangpur	–	Rajasthan
4. Alamgirpur	–	Uttar Pradesh

Which of the pairs given above is/are correctly matched?

(a) 1 and 2 (b) 2 and 3 (c) 1 and 3 (d) 1, 2 and 4

Ans. (d)

Exp. Pairs (1), (2) and (4) are correctly matched.
Rojdi is a later phase Harappan site in Kathiawar Peninsula in Gujarat.
Banawali is a Harappan site in Fatehabad district of Haryana. It saw two cultural phases- pre-Harappan and Harappan similar to Kalibangan in Rajasthan.
Alamgirpur is a Harappan site in Meerut district of Uttar Pradesh. It is considered as the Eastern most site of the civilisation.

While pair (3) is incorrectly matched because as Rangpur is an Indus valley city in Gujarat. Here, a later Harappan culture was found.

10 With reference to the Indus Valley Civilisation, consider the following statements.

(Chap 6, Class-XI, Old NCERT)

1. The spread of Harappan civilisation was eastward and southward from Sindh and Punjab.
2. Surkotada was the coastal city characterised by the early phase of Harappan civilisation.
3. Lothal has been perceived by the historians to be an outpost for sea-trade with contemporary west asian societies.
4. Evidence of Oval-shaped settlement is found only from Banawali.

How many of the statements given above is/are incorrect?

(a) Only one (b) Only two
(c) Only three (d) None of these

Ans. (d)

Exp. None of the statements are incorrect as with reference to Indus Valley Civilisation. The spread of Harappan civilisation was eastward and southwards from Sindh and Punjab. The central zone of mature Harappan culture was in Sindh and Punjab. From here, it spreads southwards and eastwards.

Surkotada was the coastal city characterised by the early phase of Harappan Civilisation. It was excavated in 1964. Evidence of bones of horses, beads, stone covered beads are found here.
Lothal has been perceived by historians to be an outpost for sea-trade with contemporary West-Asian societies, particularly Oman. Banawali is the only Harappan city with oval shaped settlement, radial streets and lack of systematic drainage pattern.

11 With reference to the Indus Valley Civilisation, consider the following statements.

(Chap 6, Class-XI, Old NCERT)

1. The Harappan culture extended from Jammu in the North to Narmada in South, and from Makaran coast of Baluchistan in the West to Meerut in the North-East.
2. The spread of Harappan civilisation was eastwards and Southwards from the Sind and Punjab.

Which of the statements given above is/are correct?

(a) Only 1 (b) Only 2
(c) Both 1 and 2 (d) Neither 1 nor 2

Ans. (c)

Exp. Both the statements (1) and (2) are correct with reference to the Indus Valley Civilisation.
As Harappan culture developed and matured into an urban civilisation, which emerged in Sind and Punjab. The Central zone of mature Harappan culture was in Sindh and Punjab.
From here, it spreads Southwards and Eastwards. It extended from Jammu in the North to the Narmada estuary in the South.
In this way Harappan culture covered parts of Punjab, Haryana, Sindh, Baluchistan, Gujarat, Rajasthan and the fringes of Western Uttar Pradesh.

Town Planning and Structure

12 Indus Valley Civilisation, which was placed on the banks of, which of the following rivers?

(Chap 6, Class-XI, Old NCERT) (UPPSC Pre 2009)

1. Sindhu 2. Chenab
3. Jhelum 4. Ganga

Codes

(a) 1 and 2 (b) 1, 2 and 3
(c) 2, 3 and 4 (d) All of these

Ans. (b)

Exp. Indus Valley Civilisation was placed on the bank of Indus (Sindhu), Chenab and Jhelum river.
The prominent site of this civilisation such as Chanhudaro and Mohenjodaro was situated on the bank of Indus river and Harappa was situated on the bank of Ravi river.
The Indus Valley sites in Jammu and Kashmir and Punjab were also situated on the bank of Jhelum and Chenab rivers.

Besides these other sites such as Kalibangan and Lothal was situated on the bank of Ghaggar- Hakra (Saraswati) and Bhogva river respectively.

Ganga river became the cradle of civilisation only after 1000 BC when Mahajanapadas and Magadha Empire was established.

13 Which among the following statements is not true with respect to town planning of Harappan culture?

(Chap 3, Class-VI, New NCERT)

(a) The Harappan cities were divided into two or more parts.
(b) The part to the East of city was smaller and represented citadel.
(c) The part to the East of city was larger and represented lower town.
(d) The part to the West of city was smaller but higher.

Ans. (b)

Exp. Statement (b) is not true with respect to town planning of Harappan culture because generally the part to the East was larger but lower. This is called the lower town. Many of Harappan cities were divided into two or more parts and usually, the part to the West was smaller but higher. Archaeologists describe this as the citadel.

14 Which one of the following ancient towns is well-known for its elaborate system of water harvesting and management by building a series of dams and channelising water into connected reservoirs?

(Class-XI, Old NCERT), (IAS Pre 2022)

(a) Dholavira
(b) Kalibangan
(c) Rakhigarhi
(d) Ropar

Ans. (a)

Exp. Dholavira is well-known for its elaborate system of water harvesting and management by building a series of dams and channelising water into connected reservoirs. Dholavira dates from the third to the mid-second millennium BC. The site was discovered in 1968 and its distinctive features includes its elaborate stone construction, multi-layered defensive mechanisms, water management system, and unique burial structures.

Its intricate system gathers and stores precipitation within multiple reservoirs. Planners in the ancient city of Dholavira had conceptualised an amazing system of drains, dams and tanks to manage water.

15 Which of the following is incorrect in the context of the Great Bath at Mohenjodaro?

(Unit 1, Class-XI, Tamil Nadu Board)

(a) The Great Bath was a special tank that was lined with bricks, coated with plaster.
(b) The Great Bath was made watertight with the use of natural tar.
(c) There were steps leading down to the Great Bath from two sides and there were rooms on all sides.
(d) Water was probably brought in from rivers and drained out after the use.

Ans. (d)

Exp. Statement (d) is incorrect with reference to the Great Bath at Mohenjodaro, because water was brought in from a well and drained out after use.

According to archaeologists, the Great Bath was a massive structure used by wealthy and prominent people for ritualised bathing. It was a large rectangular tank in a courtyard surrounded by a corridor on all four sides.

16 Consider the following statements with reference to the Indus Valley Civilisation.

(Chap 6, Class-XI, Old NCERT)

1. The houses in the Harappan culture were arranged in a grid system.
2. The roads cut across one another at right angles and the city was divided into several blocks.
3. The lower town was made up of brick houses, which were inhabited by ruling class.

Which of the statements given above are correct?

(a) 1 and 2
(b) 2 and 3
(c) 1 and 3
(d) 1, 2 and 3

Ans. (a)

Exp. Statements (1) and (2) are correct with reference to the Indus Valley Civilisation because Harappan city had remarkable arrangement of houses in grid system. Under this system, roads cut across one another almost at right angles, and the city was divided into so many blocks. This was true of almost all Indus settlements regardless of size.

Statement (3) is incorrect because the lower town was inhabited by the common people. The ruling class lived in citadel or acropolis.

17 Consider the following statements with reference to the town planning and structures of the Indus Valley Civilisation. *(Chap 6, Class-XI, Old NCERT)*

1. The largest granary is found in Mohenjodaro which measures 45.71 metre in length and 15.23 metre in width.
2. The combined floor space of 1200 square metre of granaries at Harappa is much larger than the Great Granary at Mohenjodaro.
3. The circular brick platforms to the South of granaries at Harappa served as working floors and were meant for threshing grains.

Which of the statements given above is/are incorrect?

(a) 1 and 2
(b) Only 1
(c) Only 2
(d) 1, 2 and 3

Ans. (c)

Exp. Statement (2) is incorrect with reference to the town planning and structures of the Indus Valley Civilisation as the combined floor space of Harappa granaries is 838 square metres, which is approximately same to the area of Great Granary of Mohenjodaro.

18 **With reference to the citadel, consider the following statements.** *(Chap 1, Class-XII, New NCERT)*

1. The citadel was located in the West to the city, which was smaller and higher.
2. The citadel had a distinctive structure called warehouse.
3. The Great Bath was also located in the citadel.

Which of the statements given above are correct?

(a) 1 and 2 (b) 2 and 3
(c) 1 and 3 (d) 1, 2 and 3

Ans. (d)

Exp. All the statements (1), (2) and (3) are correct regarding citadel discovered from the cities of Indus Valley Civilisation. The Harappan cities were usually divided into two parts. The upper town (known as citadel) and the lower town. The citadel occupied Western end of the site and served as the habitation site for the member of ruling class. It was constructed on the raised platform and was smaller than the lower part of the town.

Structures having public importance such as granary, great bath, warehouse, etc were situated on the citadel.

19 **The burnt bricks were used in construction of buildings in which of the following civilisations?** *(Chap 6, Class-XI, Old NCERT)*

1. Harappa 2. Egypt 3. Mesopotamia

Codes

(a) 1 and 2 (b) 2 and 3 (c) 1 and 3 (d) 1, 2 and 3

Ans. (c)

Exp. The burnt bricks were used in construction of building in Harappa and Mesopotamia civilisations.

In Mesopotamia burnt bricks have been used but in smaller scale than that of Harappa. While in Egypt mainly dried bricks were used.

20 **Consider the following statements with reference to the drainage pattern of Harappan cities.** *(Chap 6, Class-XI, Old NCERT)*

1. Most of the houses big or small had its own courtyard and bathroom.
2. Water flowed from the house to streets, which did not have drains.
3. The remains of streets and drains have also been found at Banawali.

Which of the statements given above is/are incorrect?

(a) 1 and 2 (b) Only 2
(c) Only 3 (d) 1, 2 and 3

Ans. (b)

Exp. Statement (2) is incorrect with reference to the drainage pattern of Harappan cities as water flowed from the house to the streets which had drains. Sometimes these drains were covered with bricks and sometimes with stone slabs. The street drains were equipped with manholes.

Agriculture and Domestication of Animals

21 **With reference to Indus Valley Civilisation,consider the following statements.** *(Class-XI, Old NCERT)*

1. Most of the Harappan sites were located in semi-arid lands.
2. Wells and canals were used for irrigation purposes.
3. Shortughai in Afghanistan have produced evidence of canals.

How many of the statements given above is/are incorrect?

(a) Only one (b) Only two
(c) All three (d) None of these

Ans (d)

Exp. None of the statements are incorrect with reference to the Indus Valley Civilisation.

Most Harappan sites were located in semi-arid lands where irrigation was required for agriculture.

Archeological evidence suggested that canals, wells and water reservoirs were used for irrigation purposes.

Traces of canals have been found at the Harappan site of Shortughai in Afghanistan, but not in Punjab or Sindh.

Water reservoir found in Dholavira (Gujarat) may have been used to store water for agriculture.

22 **With reference to the subsistence pattern of Harappan civilisation, consider the following statements.** *(Class-XI, Old NCERT)*

1. Excavated evidence suggests that they ploughed the land and then sowed the seeds.
2. Zebu was a tool used by Harappan for ploughing.
3. It was characterised by surplus in agricultural production.
4. People of Harappan didn't adopt the double cropping system.

How many of the statements given above is/are correct?

(a) Only one (b) Only two (c) Only three (d) All four

Ans (b)

Exp. Only two statement i.e., (1) and (3) are correct with reference to subsistence pattern of Harappan civilisation excavated evidence at Kalibangan (Rajasthan) suggests that they ploughed the land and then sowed the seeds. Ploughed fields have been found at Kalibangan. They also used both canal and well irrigation.

Agriculture surplus in Harappan civilisation was an important stimulus for a number of developments. Agriculture was an important source of subsistence for the Harappans.

Statements (2) and (4) are incorrect because the Harappan cattle are called Zebu. It is a large breed, often represented in their seals. People of Harappan civilisation adopted a double cropping system.

23 Among, which of the following sites, the terracotta models of plough has been found?

(Chap 1, Class-XII, New NCERT)

1. Chanhudaro
2. Cholistan
3. Banawali
4. Rakhigarhi

Codes

(a) 1 and 2 (b) 2 and 3 (c) 1 and 3 (d) 1, 2 and 3

Ans. (b)

Exp. Codes (2) and (3) are correct regarding tervacotta models of plough in Harappan civilisation. The terracotta models of plough has been found Cholistan and Banawali. Cholistan is the portion of Thar desert found in Pakistan. Banawali is located in Harayana. This along with terracotta model of bull discovered from other Harappan sites suggest prevalence of flourishing agriculture in the Harappa civilisation. Archaeologist have also found evidence of ploughed field at Kalibangan.

Chanhudaro located in Sindh Region of Pakistan was almost exclusively devoted to the craft production.

Rakhigarhi situated in Haryana is the largest Harappan site of India.

24 Evidences suggest that the irrigation was probably required for the agriculture in Harappan civilisation. Which among the following sources of water were used for irrigation purposes?

(Chap 1, Class-XII, New NCERT)

1. Canals
2. Wells
3. Water reservoirs

Codes

(a) 1 and 2 (b) 2 and 3 (c) 1 and 3 (d) 1, 2 and 3

Ans. (d)

Exp. Codes (1), (2) and (3) are correct regarding sources of water for irrigation purpose in Harappan civilisation. Evidences suggested that canals, wells and water reservoirs were used for irrigation purposes.

Canals have been found at the Harappan site of Shortughai in Afghanistan, but not in Punjab or Sind. It is possible that ancient canals silted up long ago. Water drawn from wells was used for irrigation. Wells are found in many houses in Harappan settlements.

Water reservoirs are found in Dholavira, Gujarat, which might have been used to store water for agriculture.

25 Consider the following animals. *(Class-XI, Old NCERT)*

1. Elephants
2. Rhinoceros
3. Camels
4. Lions

How many of the above animals were known to Harappans?

(a) Only one (b) Only two (c) Only three (d) All four

Ans. (c)

Exp. Only three animals i.e., elephants, rhinoceros and camels were known to Harappan people. These animals are found on seals, pictographs, etc of that period.

Besides these animals, oxen, buffaloes, goats, sheep and pigs were domesticated by the Harappans from the very beginning.

26 Consider the following statements.

(Class-XI, Old NCERT)

Statement-I People of Harappan civilisation used to grow two different crops together.

Statement-II Excavation at some Harappan sites has produced evidence of a ploughed field which had two sets of furrows at right angles to each other.

Which one of the following is correct in respect of the above statements?

(a) Both Statement-I and Statement-II are correct and Statement-II is the correct explanation for Statement-I.

(b) Both Statement-I and Statement-II are correct but Statement-II is not the correct explanation for Statement-I.

(c) Statement-I is correct but Statement-II is incorrect.

(d) Statement-I is incorrect but Statement-II is correct.

Ans. (a)

Exp. Both Statement-I and Statement-II are correct and Statement-II is the correct explanation for Statement-I. Archeological evidence found at the early Harappan site of Kalibangan suggests the existence of a ploughed field. The field had two sets of furrows at right angles to each other, suggesting that two different crops were grown together. Happran perhaps ploughed the land and then sowed the seeds.

Trade, Technology and Crafts

27 With reference to the Indus Valley civilisation, consider the following statements.

(Class-XI, Old NCERT)

1. People of Harappan civilisation belonged to the Bronze age but were equipped to make copper tools.
2. Rohrichert was used for making stone blades and tools.
3. Tools made of iron were in use during mature Indus Valley civlisation.

How many of the statements given above is/are correct?

(a) Only one (b) Only two
(c) All three (d) None of these

Ans. (a)

Exp. Only one statement i.e., (2) is correct with reference to the Indus Valley civilisation as people of Harappan civilisation used the Chert, a fine grained sedimentary rock, for making stone blades and tools. The chert, was found in the region of Rohri in Pakistan.

Statements (1) and (3) are incorrect because the Harappan civilisation belongs to the bronze age civilisation and Harappans knew how to make copper and bronze tools. As per the archeological evidence, people of Harappan civilisation didn't have the knowledge of iron. The Harappans used chert blades, copper objects and bone and ivory tools.

28 **Which among the following pair is incorrectly matched?** *(Chap 6, Class-XI, Old NCERT)*

Minerals Sourced by Harappans		Regions
(a) Gold	–	South India
(b) Lapis Lazuli	–	Afghanistan
(c) Tin	–	Jammu and Kashmir
(d) Copper	–	Baluchistan

Ans. (c)

Exp. Pair (c) is incorrectly matched as tin was sourced by Harappans from Afghanistan. It was used for making bronze, by mixing it with copper. Gold was brought from the South India and Lapis Lazuli from the mines of Afghanistan. They sourced copper from the Baluchistan region.

29 **Consider the following statements with respect to existence of huge brick structures in Harappan culture.** *(Chap 6, Class-XI, Old NCERT)*

1. Brick laying was an important craft.
2. The class of masons existed during the Harappan culture.

Which of the statements given above is/are correct?

(a) Only 1 (b) Only 2
(c) Both 1 and 2 (d) Neither 1 nor 2

Ans. (c)

Exp. Both the statements (1) are (2) correct with respect to existence of huge brick structures in Harappan culture. The Harappan sites have huge brick structures. They suggest that brick laying was an important craft. The brick structures are evidence of this craft. So, according to historians there existed a class of masons.

30 **Consider the following in context of import of metals.** *(Chap 6, Class-XI, Old NCERT)*

1. Copper was obtained from Rajasthan and Baluchistan.
2. Tin was imported from Afghanistan.

Which of the statements given above is/are correct?

(a) Only 1 (b) Only 2
(c) Both 1 and 2 (d) Neither 1 nor 2

Ans. (c)

Exp. Both the statements (1) and (2) are correct in context of import of metals.

The Harappan culture is known as Bronze age civilisation because it exist during the Bronze age, which occured between 3000 BC and 1000 BC. Impurities of ores found show they are from Khetri mines (Rajasthan) and could also have been brought from Baluchistan.

Tin was sourced from the mines located in Afghanistan it was also found in Hazaribagh and Bastar region of Eastern and Central India respectively. However, no conclusive evidence suggesting its import to Harappan civilisation has been discovered.

31 **Which among the following evidence suggest the importance of trade in lives of Harappans?** *(Chap 6, Class-XI, Old NCERT)*

1. Presence of granaries
2. Presence of seals
3. Uniform script
4. Regulated weights and measures

Codes

(a) 1 and 2 (b) 2 and 3
(c) 1, 2 and 3 (d) 1, 2, 3 and 4

Ans. (d)

Exp. All the given evidences suggests that trade was important in the lives of Harappans.

The people of Harappa Civilisation were indulged in both internal as well as external trade.

The presence of granaries highlights the practise of storage and transportation of grains. It was also used for exchange of finished goods. The presence of seals as far as in Mesopotamia, Bahrain and Oman highlights the long-distance trade carried out by Harappans.

Uniform scripts and regulated weight and measures projects that there was centralised administrative authority supporting trade and commerce in the territory.

32 **Consider the following statements with reference to the cultural contact between the people of Harappa and the Mesopotamia.** *(Chap 6, Class-XI, Old NCERT)*

1. In Mesopotamian texts, the Indus Valley has been referred as Meluhha.
2. The inspiration behind efficient town planning of Harappa Civilisation was the cities of Mesopotamia Civilisation.

Which of the statements given above is/are incorrect?

(a) Only 1
(b) Only 2
(c) Both 1 and 2
(d) Neither 1 nor 2

Ans. (b)

Exp. Statement (2) is incorrect regarding the cultural contact between the people of Harappa and the Mesopotamia as town planning in Harappan cities was for more superior than that of Mesopotamia.

Harappans planned its town with chess-board system, streets, drainage pipes and cess pits. On the other hand, the Mesopotamian cities show a haphazard growth.

33 **With reference to Indus Valley Civilisation, consider the following statements.** *(Class-XI, Old NCERT)*

1. Harappan civilisation maintained a trade relation with various regions of India.
2. Meluhha in the cuneiform inscription refers to the Indus region.
3. Sumerian sites have produced evidence of Harappan seals.
4. A Harappan jar has been found in Iraq.

How many of the statements given above is/are correct?

(a) Only one (b) Only two (c) Only three (d) All four

Ans (c)

Exp. Only three statements i.e., (1), (2) and 3 are correct. Harappans had close trade contacts with various cultures of India. This can be inferred by the fact that the Harappans who had knowledge of water crafts might have had connection and interaction with South India. Also, Harappans also interacted with various regions of India and acquired raw materials and processed them.
Harappans had close trade contact with the Mesopotamians. The cuneiform inscription mentions the trade contacts between Mesopotamians and Harappans.
Harappans seals and materials have been found in the sumerians sites in Oman, Bahrain, Iraq and Iran.
Statement (4) is incorrect because a Harappan jar has been found in Oman.

34 Which among the following is an incorrectly matched for the regions mentioned in Mesopotamian texts and their present day location? *(Chap 1, Class-XII, New NCERT)*

(a) Dilmun – Iran
(b) Magan – Oman
(c) Uruq – Iraq
(d) Meluhha – India and Pakistan

Ans. (a)

Exp. Pair (a) is an incorrectly matched because Dilmun is now in present day island of Bahrain. It is located in Persian Gulf and served as intermediate trading station. Due to its strategic position in the Gulf, this civilisation was able to develop as a trade center.

35 Which among the following products have been mentioned in Mesopotamian texts? *(Chap 1, Class-XII, New NCERT)*

1. Carnelian 2. Lapis Lazuli
3. Copper 4. Gold

Codes

(a) 1 and 2 (b) 3 and 4
(c) 1, 2 and 3 (d) 1, 2, 3 and 4

Ans. (d)

Exp. All the options i.e., carnelian, lapis lazuli, copper, and gold are mentioned in Mesopotamian texts.
This texts also mentions the name of Dilmun (island of Barhain), Meluhha, and Magan (Oman), from where there trade was done.

36 Chanhudaro, a tiny settlement in Indus Valley Civilisation was best-known for *(Chap 1, Class-XII, New NCERT)*

1. Bead-making 2. Shell-cutting
3. Metal-working 4. Seal-making
5. Weight-making

Codes

(a) 1, 2 and 3 (b) 1, 2 and 5
(c) 1, 2 , 3 and 5 (d) 1, 2, 3, 4 and 5

Ans. (d)

Exp. Chanhudaro (Sind, Pakistan) is a tiny settlement (less than 7 hectares) as compared to Mohenjodaro (125 hectares), almost exclusively devoted to craft production i.e., bead-making, shell-cutting, metal-working, seal-making and weight-making.

37 Which among the following evidences suggests that Harappan cities were also centres for craft production? *(Chap 1, Class-XII, New NCERT)*

1. Stone nodules 2. Whole shells
3. Copper ore 4. Tools
5. Rejects and waste materials

Codes

(a) 1, 2, 3 and 4 (b) 1, 2, 3 and 5
(c) 1, 2 , 4 and 5 (d) 1, 2, 3, 4 and 5

Ans. (d)

Exp. All the given evidences i.e., (1), (2), (3), (4) and (5) suggest that Harappan cities were also centres for craft production.
Regarding craft production, archaeologists usually look for the raw material such as stone nodules, whole shells, copper ore; tools, unfinished objects, rejects and waste material. In fact, waste is one of the best indicators of craft work.

38 Consider the following Assertion (A) and Reason (R) and choose the correct codes. *(Chap 1, Class-XII, New NCERT)*

Assertion (A) Nageshwar and Balakot were specialised centres for making shell objects including bangles, ladles and inlays.

Reason (R) Nageshwar and Balakot are present near the coast.

Codes

(a) Both A and R are true and R is the correct explanation of A.
(b) Both A and R are true, but R is not the correct explanation of A.
(c) A is true, but R is false.
(d) A is false, but R is true.

Ans. (a)

Exp. Both Assertion (A) and Reason (R) are true and Reason (R) is the correct explanation of Assertion (A).
The Harappans procured materials for craft production in various ways. For instance, they established settlements such as Nageshwar and Balakot in areas where shell was available.
Nageshwar in Gujarat near Gulf of Kutch, while Balakot is in Pakistan near Arabian sea coast. So, both places had abundance of shells.

39 **Consider the following statements with respect to bead-making process in Harappan culture.**

(Chap 1, Class-XII, New NCERT)

1. The variety of materials like carnelian, jasper, crystal, quartz and steatite, metals (such as copper, bronze and gold), shell, faience and terracotta or burnt clay were used to make beads.
2. The red colour of carnelian was obtained by firing the yellowish raw material and beads at various stages of production.
3. Specialised drills used in bead-making process have been found at Harappan sites of Chanhudaro, Lothal and more recently at Dholavira.

Which of the statements given above are correct?

(a) 1 and 2 (b) 2 and 3 (c) 1 and 3 (d) 1, 2 and 3

Ans. (d)

Exp. All the statements (1), (2) and (3) are correct with respect to bead-making process in Harappan culture.

At Harappan sites, materials used to make beads is remarkable. Stones like carnelian (of a beautiful red colour), jasper, crystal, quartz and steatite; metals like copper, bronze and gold; and shell, faience and terracotta or burnt clay have been used. Some beads were made of two or more stones, cemented together, some of stone with gold caps.

At Harappan site, archaeologists' excavations have revealed that the red colour of carnelian was obtained by firing the yellowish raw material and beads at various stages of production. Nodules were chipped into rough shapes, and then finely flaked into the final form. Grinding, polishing and drilling completed the process.

Specialised drills have been found at Chanhudaro (Pakistan), Lothal (Gujarat) and more recently at Dholavira (Gujarat).

40 **Consider the following statements with respect to trade and commerce in Harappan culture.**

(Chap 6, Class-XI, Old NCERT)

1. Harappans carried out trade in stone, metal, shells etc., within the Indus culture zone and these exchanges were carried out through barter.
2. Harappans knew the use of wheels, carts and practiced navigation on the coast of the Arabian Sea.
3. The Harappans had commercial relation with Mesopotamia, however, they failed to establish trading relations with Afghanistan and Iran.

Which of the statements given above is/are incorrect?

(a) 1 and 2 (b) Only 3 (c) Only 2 (d) 1, 2 and 3

Ans. (b)

Exp. Statement (3) is incorrect with respect to trade and commerce in Harappan culture as besides Mesopotamia, Harappans also established trade relations with Afghanistan and Iran. There were no use of coins or any money. It happened on exchange of materials, which is called Barter System.

Political Organisation

41 **Which among the following statements indicates that there might have been existence of central authority in Harappan society?**

(Chap 1, Class-XII, New NCERT)

1. The extraordinary cultural homogeneity in Harappan society as evident from uniformity in Harappan artefacts across different sites.
2. Settlements were strategically set up in specific locations such as near the sources of raw material.
3. Labour force was mobilised for making bricks and for the construction of massive walls and platforms.

Codes

(a) 1 and 2 (b) 2 and 3
(c) 1 and 3 (d) 1, 2 and 3

Ans. (d)

Exp. All the given statements indicate that there might have been existence of central authority in Harappan society.

Indications of complex decisions being taken and implemented in Harappan society are many. For example, the extraordinary uniformity of Harappan artefacts as evident in pottery, seals, weights and bricks. Bricks were of a uniform ratio throughout the region, from Jammu to Gujarat.

Settlements were set up at particular locations for easy reach to raw material and according to people's work. It shows that everything was made carefully. Labour was used for constructions of Harappan high platforms and brick walls.

42 **Which among following is likely to be true regarding political organisation of Harappan society?**

(Chap 6, Class-XI, Old NCERT)

1. It was ruled by King and their kins.
2. There was existence of a single state.
3. Harappa was possibly ruled by a class of merchants.

Codes

(a) 1 and 2 (b) 2 and 3
(c) 1 and 3 (d) 1, 2 and 3

Ans. (b)

Exp. Statements (2) and (3) are true regarding political organisation of Harappan society.

Harappan culture shows uniformity in planning and same structures through cities, which indicates a single state. There was cultural homogeneity in Indus Valley Civilisation. There was focus on commerce and there were no weapons, which show it was possibly a class of merchants who ruled Harappa.

Statement (1) is not true as there is no evidence of prevalence of monarchial authority or presence of kings Harappan civilisation.

Religious Practices

43 Consider the following statements regarding the Indus Valley Civilisation.

(Chap 1, Class-XII, New NCERT) (IAS Pre 2011)

1. It was predominantly a secular civilisation and the religious element, though present did not dominate the scene.
2. During this period, cotton was used for manufacturing textiles in India.

Which of the statements given above is/are correct?

(a) Only 1
(b) Only 2
(c) Both 1 and 2
(d) Neither 1 nor 2

Ans. (c)

Exp. Both the statements (1) and (2) are correct regarding Indus Valley Civilisation. Absence of religious structures and no conclusive evidence of presence of priestly class highlights that Indus Valley Civilisation was predominantly a secular civilisation. Religious elements such as figurines of Mother- Goddess, Pashupati etc did not dominated the scene. The Indus people were the earliest people to produce cotton, it was used for manufacturing textiles.

44 With reference to the Chalcolithic culture and Indus Valley Civilisation, consider the following statements. *(Class-XI, Old NCERT)*

1. Both of them venerated the mother goddess.
2. There is an absence of belief in the afterlife in the Chalcolithic period but this belief had gradually developed in the Indus Valley Civilisation people.
3. Both of them depict the presence of social inequalities.

How many of the statements given above is/are correct?

(a) Only one (b) Only two
(c) All three (d) None of these

Ans. (b)

Exp. Only two statements i.e., (1) and (3) are correct with reference to the Chalcolithic culture and Indus Valley Civilisation.

Terracotta figures of women from the Chalcolithic period suggest that the Chalcolithic people venerated the mother goddess. Similar terracotta figures of the mother goddess have also been found from the Indus Valley Civilisation.

Both the settlement pattern and burial practices suggest the beginning of social inequalities in the Chalcolithic society. Some settlements in Jorwe are as large as twenty hectares but others are only five hectares and even less. This suggests that the large settlements dominated the smaller ones. In the Indus Valley Civilisation, the citadel and the lower town were depiction of social inequalities.

Statement (2) is incorrect because both people of Chalcolithic and Harappan civilisation had belief in the afterlife. The people of the Chalcolithic period used to deposit pots and some copper objects in the graves for the use of the dead in the next world. This shows their belief in the afterlife.

Similarly, Harappan people also buried pottery and ornaments, indicating a belief that these could be used in the afterlife.

45 Consider the following statements with reference to Pashupati in Harappan civilisation.

(Chap 6, Class-XI, Old NCERT)

1. He is a male deity represented on a seal.
2. The God has a two-horned heads.
3. He is represented in a sitting posture of a yogi.

Which of the statements given above are correct?

(a) 1 and 2 (b) 2 and 3 (c) 1 and 3 (d) 1, 2 and 3

Ans. (c)

Exp. Statements (1) and (3) are correct with reference to *Pashupati*. The male deity is represented on a seal. He is shown sitting in a Yogi posture, placing one leg on the other. This God is *Pashupati*, though identification is doubtful as other civilisations also depict horned Gods. Statement (2) is incorrect as the Pashupati seal has three horned heads.

46 With reference to Indus Valley Civilisation, consider the following statements.

(Chap 6, Class-XI, Old NCERT)

1. Harappans didn't have belief in the afterlife.
2. Harappan believed in ghosts and evil forces and therefore used amulets against them.
3. One horned unicorn was one of the important animals worshiped in Harappan culture.

How many of the statements given above is/are incorrect?

(a) Only one (b) Only two
(c) All three (d) None of these

Ans (a)

Exp. Only one statement i.e., (1) is incorrect with reference to Indus valley civilisation.

Harappans had believed in an afterlife. This is suggested by Harappan burials having pottery, ornaments, jewellery, copper mirrors and beads. Burials were made elaborately and evidence of cremation is also reported.

Statements (2) and (3) are correct. A large number of amulets have been found in Harappan. They believed ghosts and evil spirits can harm them, so wore amulets as protection from them.

One horned unicorn was one of the important animals worshiped in Harappan culture. Animals were worshiped in Harappan culture and they were usually represented on seals. On one seal a one horned unicorn is represented, which is taken to be rhinoceros.

Art and Culture: Scripts, Pottery and Terracotta Figurines

47 Consider the following statements with reference to Harappan scripts. *(Chap 1, Class-XII, New NCERT)*

1. The signs in Harappan scripts ranges from 375 to 400.
2. The longest Harappan inscription contains about 26 signs.
3. The script was written from left to right.

Which of the statements given above is/are incorrect?

(a) Only 1 (b) 2 and 3 (c) 1 and 3 (d) Only 3

Ans. (d)

Exp. Statement (3) is incorrect with reference to Harappan scripts as it is apparent that the script was written from right to left as some seals show a wider spacing on the right and cramping on the left, as if the engraver began working from the right and then ran out of space.

48 With reference to weights and measurements in Harappan culture, consider the following statements. *(Chap 1, Class-XII, New NCERT)*

1. Exchanges were regulated by a precise system of weights, usually made of a stone called chert and generally cubical with no markings.
2. The lower denominations of weights were binary while the higher denominations followed the decimal system.

Which of the statements given above is/are correct?

(a) Only 1 (b) Only 2
(c) Both 1 and 2 (d) Neither 1 nor 2

Ans. (c)

Exp. Both the statements (1) and (2) are correct with reference to weights and measurements in Harappan culture.

Economic exchanges as well as trade and commerce were managed with an accurate system of weights, usually made of a stone called chert and generally cubical with no markings.

The lower denominations of weights were binary (1, 2, 4, 8, 16, 32, etc. up to 12,800), while the higher denominations followed the decimal system. The smaller weights were probably used for weighing jewellery and beads.

49 With reference to Harappan pottery, consider the following statements. *(Chap 6, Class-XI, Old NCERT)*

1. Harappan pots were generally decorated with design of trees, men and circles.
2. The Harappans did not have knowledge of potter's wheel.

Which of the statements given above is/are incorrect?

(a) Only 1 (b) Only 2
(c) Both 1 and 2 (d) Neither 1 nor 2

Ans. (b)

Exp. Statement (2) is incorrect with reference to Harappan pottery.

The Harappan people were great experts in the use of potter's wheel. There have been many finds of pots painted in various designs. These pots were usually decorated with designs of trees and circles. Images of men have also been found on some pottery fragments.

50 With reference to Harappan seal, consider the following statements. *(Chap 6, Class-XI, Old NCERT)*

1. Harappan seal featured only one horned bull, buffalo and goat.
2. The seal of Pashupati contains depiction of oxen and tiger.

Which of the statements given above is/are incorrect?

(a) Only 1 (b) Only 2
(c) Both 1 and 2 (d) Neither 1 nor 2

Ans. (c)

Exp. Both the statements (1) and (2) are incorrect with reference to Harappan seal. Almost 2000 Harappan seals have been found and they carry inscriptions with pictures of the one-horned bull, tiger, buffalo. rhinoceros, elephant and goat. There is no oxen on the seal of Pashupati. The seal of Pashupati is surrounded by elephant, a tiger, a rhinoceros and has a buffalo and two deer below his throne.

51 Consider the following with respect to seals used in Harappan Culture. *(Chap 1, Class-XII, New NCERT)*

1. It used to facilitate long distance communication.
2. The sealing on the bag was used to prevent the bag of good from tampering.
3. The sealing also conveyed the identity of the sender.

Which of the statements given above are correct?

(a) 1 and 2 (b) 2 and 3
(c) 1 and 3 (d) 1, 2 and 3

Ans. (d)

Exp. All the statements (1), (2) and (3) are correct with respect to seals used in Harappan Culture.

Seals and sealings of Harappa were used to facilitate long-distance communication by pictures on them. Mouth of bag was tied with rope and on the knot was affixed some wet clay on, which one or more seals were pressed, leaving an impression. If the bag reached with its sealing intact, it meant that it had not been tampered with. This sealing also conveyed the identity of the sender.

52 Consider the following with respect to Harappan terracotta figurines. *(Chap 6, Class-XI, Old NCERT)*

1. Terracotta figurines were made up of fire-baked earthen clay.
2. The terracotta figurines exhibit the sophisticated artistic works.
3. These were used by members of upper class.

Which of the statements given above is/are incorrect?
(a) Only 1 (b) Only 3 (c) 2 and 3 (d) 1, 2 and 3

Ans. (b)

Exp. Statement (3) is incorrect regarding Harappan terracotta figurines. When compared to the artefacts made up of precious metals, the Harappan terracotta figurines were more numerous and was used by both the rich and common person alike. In Harappa, numerous terracotta figurines of women have been found. It were made up of fire-baked earthen clay and exhibited the sophisticated artistic works.

End of Harappan Civilisation

53 **Which among the following suggests for the end of Harappan Civilisation?** *(Chap 1, Class-XII, New NCERT)*

1. Disappearance of seals, and the script.
2. Disappearance of distinctive beads and pottery.
3. Shift from a standardised weight system to the use of local weights.
4. The decline and abandonment of cities.

Codes
(a) 1 and 2 (b) 3 and 4
(c) 1, 2 and 3 (d) 1, 2, 3 and 4

Ans. (d)

Exp. All the given statements are correct regarding end of Harappan Civilisation.

In the few Harappan sites, that continued to be occupied after 1900 BC, there seems to have been a transformation of material culture, marked by the disappearance of the distinctive artefacts of the civilisation – weights, seals, special beads, etc.

Long distance trade and craft specialisation disappeared which lead to a shift from standard weights to local weights.

House construction techniques deteriorated and large public structures were no longer constructed. The settlements like of Cholistan were abandoned and population moved towards Gujarat, Haryana and Western Uttar Pradesh.

54 **Which among the following could be the cause of decline of Harappan Civilisation?** *(Chap 6, Class-XI, Old NCERT)*

1. Decrease in rainfall
2. Increased salinity and desertation
3. Flood due to subsidence or upliftment of land

Codes
(a) 1 and 2 (b) 2 and 3 (c) 1, 2 and 3 (d) 1 and 3

Ans. (c)

Exp. All the reasons given in the question could be the cause of decline of Harappan Civilisation.

It is found that amount of rainfall had decreased, which affected agriculture and stockbreeding.

It also led to increased salinity, which was caused by desertification of nearby areas.

According to the studies conducted by archaeologists and geologists, the sudden subsidence or upliftment of land caused flood.

55 **Consider the following with respect to post-urban phase of Harappan Culture.** *(Chap 6, Class-XI, Old NCERT)*

1. The post-urban phase of Harappan culture is also called Sub-Indus Culture.
2. The post-urban phase broadly covers the period from 1500 to 500 BC.

Which of the statements given above is/are incorrect?
(a) Only 1 (b) Only 2
(c) Both 1 and 2 (d) Neither 1 nor 2

Ans. (b)

Exp. Statement (2) is incorrect with respect to post-urban phase of Harappan Culture. The post-urban phase covers the period from 1900 to 1200 BC. This phase was known as Sub-Indus culture and now is popularly called late Harappan culture.

56 **Which among the following is/are correct match for post-urban settlements and their present-day location?** *(Chap 6, Class-XI, Old NCERT)*

Post-urban settlements	Present day location
1. Patan	– Gujarat
2. Ahar	Uttar Pradesh
3. Gilund	– Rajasthan
4. Bhagwanpura	– Punjab

Codes
(a) 1 and 2 (b) 2 and 4 (c) 1 and 3 (d) 1 and 4

Ans. (c)

Exp. Pairs (1) and (3) are matched correctly.

Prabhas, Patan and Rangpur in Gujarat are direct descendant of Harappan culture.

Gilund is a village and an archaeological site located in Rajsamand district of Rajasthan state.

While pairs (2) and (4) are matched incorrectly because Ahar is located in Udaipur, Rajasthan. They mostly used technology based on copper. Bhagwanpura is in Haryana. Here the burnt brick were found in late Harappan phase.

57 **Consider the following statements.** *(Chap 6, Class-XI, Old NCERT)*

1. At several sites in Punjab and Haryana, Grey ware associated with Vedic people have been found in conjunction with late Harappan pottery dated around 2000 to 1200 BC.
2. The intrusion by Vedic people was solely responsible for decline of Indus Valley Civilisation in Sind and Punjab region.

Which of the statements given above is/are incorrect?
(a) Only 1 (b) Only 2
(c) Both 1 and 2 (d) Neither 1 nor 2

Ans. (b)

Exp. Statement (2) is incorrect because there is no evidences suggesting that intrusion of Vedic people from North-West was solely responsible for decline of Indus Valley Civilisation in Sind and Pakistan.

58 Consider the following pairs.

(Chap 6, Class-XI, Old NCERT)

Post-urban settlements		Description
1. Gilund	–	Regional centre of Ahar culture
2. Daimabad	–	Largest Jorwe settlement
3. Swat valley	–	Southernmost outpost of late Harappan culture

Which of the pairs given above are correctly matched?

(a) 1 and 2 (b) 2 and 3
(c) 1 and 3 (d) 1, 2 and 3

Ans. (a)

Exp. Pairs (1) and (2) are correctly matched.
Gilund in Rajasthan is a regional centre of Ahar culture, near Udaipur. It has brick structures.
Numerous Jorwe sites are found in valley of Tapi, Godavari and Bhima. Largest Jorwe site is Daimabad in Maharashtra.
While pair (3) is incorrectly matched because Swat valley located in Northernmost outpost of late Harappan culture.

59 With reference to the people of Indus Valley civilisation, consider the following statements.

(Chap 6, Class-XI, Old NCERT)

1. They possessed great palaces and temples.
2. They worshiped, both male and female deities.
3. They employed horse-drawn chariots in warfare.

How many of the above statements are the characteristics of the people of the Indus Civilisation?

(a) Only one
(b) Only two
(c) All three
(d) None of the above

Ans. (a)

Exp. Only one statement i.e., (2) is correct with reference to the people of Indus Valley Civilisation. They worshiped both male and female deities. In Harappa, numerous terracotta figurines of women have been found. In one figurine a plant is shown growing out of the embryo of a woman, probably it represents the goddess of Earth. So it is evident that they probably worshiped the mother goddess. The male deity is represented on a seal. This god has three-horned heads. The depicted god is identified as Pashupati.
Statements (1) and (3) are not correct because characteristics of people of Harappan society as archaeological remains of temples have not been discovered from any of the cities of Indus civilisation. The use of horse- drawn chariots, started with the advent of Indo-Aryans in 1500 BC.

60 With reference to decline of Harappan civilisation, consider the following statements.

(Chap 1, Class-XII, New NCERT)

1. It's one of the consequences was disappearance of distinctive artefacts.
2. Ecological imbalance theory by Walter Fair servies suggest of abrupt end of the civilisation.
3. Decline of the civilisation is followed by the shifting of people to Western and Northern regions.

How many of the statements given above is/are correct?

(a) Only one (b) Only two
(c) All three (d) None of these.

Ans. (a)

Exp. Only one statement i.e., (1) is correct with reference to the decline of the Harappan civilisation. The disappearance of distinctive i.e., weights, seals, special beads was one of the consequences of the decline which amounted to transformation of material culture after 1900 BC. Those Harappan sites which continued to be occupied after 1900 BC, witnessed this transformation of material culture.
Statements (2) and (3) are incorrect because ecological imbalance theory was propounded by Walter Fairservies which didn't suggest abrupt end of the civilisation rather gradual end.

Chapter 04

The Vedic Age

The Vedic Age

Vedic Literature

Rigveda
- Oldest veda; Contains 1028 hymns; divided into 10 Mandalas
- **Samaveda** – Vedas of chants; Provided with musical notations
- **Yajurveda** Deals with Procedures for the performance of sacrifices
- **Atharvaveda** Classified into 20 books, 730 hymnsad 6,000 mantras
- **Brahmanas** Prose texts explaining hymns in the Vedas; Each Veda has one or more of its own Brahmanas
- **Aranyakas** Philosophies written mainly for the forest-dwelling hermits
- **Upanishads** Total 108 Upanishads; Explained concepts of Atman and Brahman
- **Vedangas** Limbs of Vedas written for how to chant Vedas properly; Total 6 Vedangas
- **Upaveda** 4 Upavedas- Ayurveda (life), Gandharvaveda (music), Shilpaveda (architecture) and Dhanurveda (archery and warfare)
- **Sutra Sahitya** Upneaeavol period of social, political and religions thought There are six sutra;
- **Kalpa Sutra** It contains the sacrificial practice and systematic sutras
- **Srautasutras** It contains teaching of the performance of the great sacrifices
- **Sulvasutras** It is related to geometry and mathematics
- **Gruhasutras** It contains rules of domestic life

Vedic Age (1500-1000 BC)

Geographical Extent
- Eastern Afghanistan; North- West frontier Province Punjab and parts of Western Uttar Pradesh

Vedic Polity
- Hereditary post of tribal chief (Rajan) Presence of tribal or the clan-based assemblies such as Sabha, Samiti, Vidhata and Gana; Army chiefs- Senani; Head of families- Kulapas

Vedic Society
- Kinship based society; Tribes referred as Vris/ Jana; patriarchal society; provided the identity rk for the social order
- Varna term used for colour; Women given opportunities for spiritual and intellectual development; Widow remarriage; No

Vedic Economy
- Pastoralist economy; Most important animal- cow;
- Mentions artisans such as carpenter, chariot-maker, weaver etc; People knew about sowing, harvesting and threshing

Vedic Religion
- Personified natural forces; Worshipping through recitation of prayers and offering of sacrifices; Worshipping gods for material benefits

Important Vedic Gods
- The most important divinity in the Rig Veda is Indra
- The second position is held by Agni
- The third important position is occupied by Varuna
- Soma was considered to be the God of plants
- Maruts was considered as the God of the storm; Some female divinities such as Aditi and Usha

Later Vedic Age (1000-600 BC)

Geographical Extent
- Second phase of Vedic expansion
- Migrated to Ganga-Yamuna doab
- They lived between the saraswati and the Drishadvati rivers
- Set up their capital at Hastinapur

Later Vedic Polity
- Rigvedic popular assemblies lost importance and royal power increased
- Formation of bigger kingdom made kings more powerful
- Kings performed sacrifices such as Rajasuya, Ashvamedha yajna and Vajapeya

Later Vedic Society
- Divided into 4 varnas-Brahmanas (priests), Kshatriya (warriors), Vaishyas (agriculturalist and traders) were entitled to Upanayana and shodras (to serve the other varnas)
- Discrimination began with shudras Women were given lower positions

Later Vedic Economy
- Chief occupation- agriculture; Chief crops- barley, wheat and rice; Accquainted with four types of pottery- black and red ware, black-slipped ware, painted grey ware and red ware

Later Vedic Religion
- Brahmanical influence increased
- Rigvedic gods Indra and Agni lost their importance
- Gods such as Prajapati, Rudra and Vishnu became prominent

SOURCE **New NCERT Class VI** *(What Books and Burials Tell us)*, **Old NCERT Class VI** *(Life in the Vedic Age)*, **Old NCERT Class IX** *(Early Iron-Age Civilisation)*, **Old NCERT Class XI** *(The Advent of Aryans and Age of Rigveda)*, **Old NCERT Class XI** *(Transition to State and Social Formation)* **Tamil Nadu Board Class XI** *(Early India)* **NIOS Module-1** *(The Vedic Age)*

Advent of Aryans

1 **With reference to the advent of Indo-Aryans in India, which of the following statements is/are correct?** *(Chap 3, Class-IX, Old NCERT)*

1. They entered the Indian subcontinent from the North-West.
2. Punjab was the first permanent home of the Indo-Aryans in India.

Codes
(a) Only 1 (b) Only 2
(c) Both 1 and 2 (d) Neither 1 nor 2

Ans. (c)

Exp. Both the statements (1) and (2) are correct regarding the advent of Indo-Aryans in India. According to the prominent scholars, they migrated from area around Caspian sea and entered the Indian sub continent from the North-West. After their arrival, they first settled in land of seven rivers, the Sapt Sindhu. It is now identified with modern day territories of Punjab.

2 **Which among the following is the common link between Indo-Aryans and their contemporary tribes living in Europe and Asia?** *(Chap 3, Class-IX, Old NCERT)*

(a) Pottery (b) Predominance of agriculture
(c) Religion (d) Language

Ans. (d)

Exp. Language is the common link between Indo-Aryans and their contemporary tribes living in Europe and Asia. Aryans were of different tribes and their culture was more or less same. But they were distinguished by their language, Indo-European, which is now spread in different forms over Europe, Iran, and part of Indian subcontinent.

3 **Consider the following Assertion (A) and Reason (R) and choose the correct code.** *(Chap 3, Class-IX, Old NCERT)*

Assertion (A) Vedic hymns is the most important source of reconstruction of history of Aryans in India.

Reason (R) Vedic hymns were poems composed for Gods, recited and passed on from generation to generation.

Codes
(a) Both A and R are true and R is the correct explanation of A.
(b) Both A and R are true, but R is not the correct explanation of A.
(c) A is true, but R is false.
(d) A is false, but R is true.

Ans. (b)

Exp. Both Assertion (A) and Reason (R) are true, but Reason (R) is not the correct explanation of Assertion (A). The history of Aryans is dated back to around 1500 BC. Vedic hymns composed by Indo-Aryans in Sapt Sindhu area is the most important source for historical reconstruction of Aryans in India. This hymns were poems composed for Gods, recited and passed on from generation to generation.

It gives significant information regarding society, polity and Geography of India in the first millennium BC.

4 **An inscription of 14th century BC which describes the Vedic gods has been found in** *(Chap 8, Class-XI, Old NCERT) (UPPSC Mains 2016)*

(a) Ecbatana (b) Boghazkoi
(c) Babylon (d) Bisotun

Ans. (b)

Exp. Boghazkoi inscription of 14th century BC describes the Vedic gods namely Indra, Varuna, Mitra and Nasatyas. This inscription helps in establishing link between the movement and original homeland of the Aryans.

5 **With reference to the Aryans in India, consider the following statements.** *(Chap 8, Class-XI, Old NCERT)*

1. They created Rigveda, the earliest specimen of Indo-European language.
2. Agriculture was the most important occupation of Indo-Aryans.
3. Their name appears in Mitanni inscriptions of Iraq.

How many of the statements given above is/are correct?
(a) Only one (b) Only two
(c) All three (d) None of these

Ans. (a)

Exp. Only one statement i.e., (1) is correct with reference to Aryans in India as Aryans are credited with creating Rigveda which is the earliest specimen of Indo-European language. After settlement in the Sapta Sindhu region of modern day Punjab they compiled Rigveda. Rigveda contains hymns and poems mostly recited and dictated to people.

Statements (2) and (3) are incorrect because Agriculture was not the most important occupation of Indo-Aryans rather it was pastoralism.

Mitanni inscriptions do contain the name of Aryans however it is in Syria and not in Iraq. Kassite inscriptions from Iraq and Mitanni inscriptions from Iraq mention the name of Aryans.

6 **With reference to Indian history (2000BC to 600BC), consider the following statements.** *(Unit 2, Class-XI, Tamil Nadu Board)*

1. Decline of the Indus Valley is characterised by semi-sedentary and sedentary agro-pastoral communities.
2. Early Vedic culture is correlated with the Painted Grey ware culture of the Iron Age.
3. Zend Avesta has reference to the Eastern and South-Western parts of India.

How many of the statements given above is/are incorrect?

(a) Only one (b) Only two
(c) All three (d) None of these

Ans. (b)

Exp. Only two statements i.e., (2) and (3) are incorrect with reference to Indian history (2000BC to 600BC), as Early Vedic culture is correlated with some of the Chalcolithic cultures of India, while the Later Vedic culture is correlated with the Painted Grey Ware culture of Iron Age in North India. Zend Avesta, a Persian/ Iranian text of Zoroastrainism, has reference to the regions of Northern and North-Western parts of India.

7 With reference to the difference between the culture of Rigvedic Aryans and Indus Valley people, which of the following statements is/are correct? *(Class XI, Old NCERT) (UPSC Pre 2017)*

1. Rigvedic Aryans used the coat of mail and helmet in warfare whereas the people of Indus Valley Civilisation did not leave any evidence of using them.
2. Rigvedic Aryans knew gold, silver and copper whereas Indus Valley people knew only copper and iron.
3. Rigvedic Aryans had domesticated the horse whereas there is no evidence of Indus Valley people having been aware of horse.

How many of the statements given above is/are correct?

(a) Only one (b) Only two
(c) All three (d) None of these

Ans. (b)

Exp. Only two statements i.e., (1) and (3) are correct with reference to the difference between the culture of Rigvedic Aryans and Indus Valley people.

Rig Vedic Aryans used the cost of mail and helmet in warfare whereas the people of Indus Valley Civilisation did not leave any evidence of using them. There is also evidence of swords, arrows, bows used during Rigvedic Aryans. Rigvedic Aryans had domesticated the horse whereas there is no evidence of Indus Valley people having been aware of horse.

Statement (2) is incorrect. Rigvedic Aryans know gold, silver, copper, iron whereas Indus valley people knew gold, copper, bronze but they did not know iron.

8 With reference to Aryans, consider the following statements. *(Class XI, Old NCERT)*

1. Aryans were not acquainted with the domestication of horses and use of chariots.
2. Use of Soma drinks were prevalent among the speakers of the Indo- Aryan languages.
3. The Bactria-Margina Archaeological complex is closely related to Aryan culture dated to 1900BC-1500BC.

How many of the statements given above is/are incorrect?

(a) Only one (b) Only two
(c) All three (d) None of these

Ans.(a)

Exp. Only one statement i.e., (1) is incorrect with reference to Aryans because from the Vedas it is evident that Aryans used domesticated horses and chariots. Their chariots had spoked wheels and they used bows and arrows.

9 With reference to Vedic Literature, consider the following statements. *(Class XI, Old NCERT)*

1. Samhitas are ritualistic texts.
2. Samhitas are the added text of Brahmanas which have commentaries on the hymns and rituals.
3. Aranyakas contains mystical instructions for the sages.

How many of the statements given above is/are correct?

(a) Only one (b) Only two
(c) All three (d) None of these

Ans. (c)

Exp. All three statements i.e., (1), (2) and (3) are correct with reference to vedic literature. Samhitas are ritualistic texts and they explain the social and religious importance of rituals. Each Samhita has added texts called Brahmanas which have commentaries on the hymns and rituals. Each Brahmanas has an Aranyakas containing mystical ritual instructions to be undertaken in secret by the sages who live in the forests.

10 With reference to Rigvedic age, consider the following statements. *(Class XI, Old NCERT)*

1. Dasyus came in conflict with Aryans when they moved into India.
2. There are significant traces of the urban way of life in the Rigveda as evident from Anatolian inscriptions of 1900-1700(BC).
3. Rigveda mentions the term horse(Ashva) and bull (Vrishabha).

How many of the statements given above is/are correct?

(a) Only one (b) Only two
(c) All three (d) None of these

Ans. (a)

Exp. Only one statement i.e., (3) is correct with reference to Rigvedic age. In Rigveda, the term Ashva (horse) occurs 215 times and Vrishabha(bull) 170 times. The term Asva and several other terms in Rigveda have common roots in various Indo-Aryan languages.

Statements (1) and (2) are incorrect. When Rigvedic people moved into India they came into conflict with people whom they referred to as Dasyus and Dasas. There are no traces of the urban way of life in the Rigveda.

11 With reference to Vedic literature, consider the following statements. *(Class XI, Old NCERT)*

1. Brahamanas literature provides scientific knowledge of observational astronomy.
2. Each veda has one only Brahamanas as prose texts that explain the hymns in the Vedas.
3. Taittiriya and Aitareya are Brahamanas to Rigveda and Yajur Veda respectively.

How many of the statements given above is/are correct?

(a) Only one (b) Only two
(c) All three (d) None of these

Ans. (b)

Exp. Only two statements i.e., (1) and (3) are correct with reference to Vedic literature. Brahamana literature also provides scientific knowledge of the vedic period, including observational astronomy, construction and geometry. They also explain the symbolism and meaning to the Samhitas. Taittiriya and Jaiminiya are Brahamanas to Yajurveda and Aitareya or Kaushitaki Brahamanas were alloted to the Rigveda.

Political Organisation

12 With reference to the Political organisation of the vedic age, consider the following statements. *(Chap 4, Module-1, NIOS)*

1. The chiefship was hereditary in the early Vedic phase while in later phase they got elected by tribe.
2. Nature of the Sena (army) remained the same in both early and late Vedic phases.
3. Tribal assemblies levied mandatory tax on the people, known as Bali.

How many of the statements given above is/are correct?

(a) Only one (b) Only two
(c) All three (d) None of these

Ans. (d)

Exp. None of the statements are correct with reference to Political organisation of the Vedic age.

The post of the chief was not hereditary in the Vedic age while in the later Vedic phase it became hereditary.

Nature of Sena(army) was different in both the phases. In the early phase the Sena or army was not a permanent fighting group while in Later Vedic phase a rudimentary army emerged as an important element of the political structure.

Bali was not a mandatory tax, it was just a voluntary contribution made by the ordinary tribesmen on special occasions.

13 Among the tribal assemblies of the Rigvedic Aryans, which was most accessible to the common people? *(Chap 3, Class-VI, Old NCERT)*

(a) Sabha (b) Samiti (c) Vidhata (d) Gana

Ans. (b)

Exp. Among the tribal assemblies of the Rigvedic Aryans, *Samiti* was the most accessible to common people. In *Samiti*, everyone was allowed to speak their and draw the attention of others towards their grievances.

Tribal assemblies were divided into two i.e., *Samiti* and *Sabha*, which was smaller group of selected people.

14 Match the following lists correctly and choose the correct code. *(Chap 3, Class-VI, Old NCERT)*

List I	List II
A. Vrajapati	1. Head of the family
B. Gramanis	2. Head of the fighting hordes
C. Senani	3. Head of the Army
D. Kulapa	4. Head of the pasture grounds

Codes

	A	B	C	D		A	B	C	D
(a)	1	2	3	4	(b)	2	3	4	1
(c)	4	2	3	1	(d)	3	1	4	2

Ans. (c)

Exp. The correct matching is A-4, B-2, C-3, D-1.

Vrajapati in Vedic period was the head of the pasture grounds. He supported the king in the wake of war and tribal raids.

Gramanis were the heads of fighting hordes. In the beginning, the *gramani* was just the head of a small tribal fighting unit.

Senani were the head of Army. They were the second most important functionary after *purohit*.

Kulapas were head of families. Generally, eldest males were the head of families.

15 With reference to the administrative machinery of the Rig Vedic Aryans, consider the following statements. *(Class XI, Old NCERT)*

1. There is no evidence of tax collecting officers in the Rigveda.
2. There is no reference to an officer entrusted with administration of Justice in the Rigveda.
3. Vrajapati was the officer who controlled the territory in the Vedic phase.

How many of the statements given above is/are correct?

(a) Only one (b) Only two
(c) All three (d) None of these

Ans. (c)

Exp. All three statements i.e., (1), (2) and (3) are correct with reference to administrative machinery of the Rigvedic Aryans.

Rigveda mention different functionaries for tasks, but there is no mention of any officer for judicial administration or tax collection. Perhaps people made a voluntary contribution called Bali to the king.

The officer who controlled the territory was called Vrajapati. He helped the heads of fighting groups called gramini. Gramini was the head of villages and fighting unit.

16 **With reference to tribal polity of the Indo-Aryan, consider the following statements.** *(Class XI, Old NCERT)*

1. Rigveda mentions the victory of Divodasa of Bharata clan.
2. There is no reference to the sea (samundra) and boats(nau) in the Rigveda.
3. People of the Vedic age had no knowledge of gold.

How many of the statements given above is/are correct?

(a) Only one (b) Only two
(c) All three (d) None of these

Ans. (a)

Exp. Only one statement i.e., (1) is correct with reference to tribal polity of the Indo-Aryan.

The Rigveda mentions the defeat of a chief called Sambara by Divodasa of the Bharata clan.

Statements (2) and (3) are incorrect because there are references to the sea (samundra) and boats (nau) in the Rigveda. Boats driven by 100 oars are mentioned.

People of Vedic age had knowledge of gold. Apart from copper, bronze and gold, Later Vedic texts also mention tin, lead and silver.

17 **What was the main function performed by the officer called Sangrihti in Later Vedic Ages?** *(Chap 3, Class-IX, Old NCERT)*

(a) Collection of taxes and tributes.
(b) Maintaining law and order in the districts.
(c) Establishment and maintenance of irrigation sources.
(d) Record keeping of all the irrigated lands.

Ans. (a)

Exp. In later Vedic ages, collection of taxes and tributes had become a common practice and an officer appointed to that was called *Sangrihti*.

18 **With reference to Vedic age, consider the following pairs.** *(Class XI, Old NCERT)*

1. Rajasuya-Conferred supreme power to the king
2. Ashvarmedha-Unquestionable control over the area where horse ran interruped
3. Vajapeya-Blessed king with a male child.

How many of the pairs given above is/are correctly matched?

(a) Only one (b) Only two
(c) All three (d) None of these

Ans. (b)

Exp. Only two pairs i.e., (1) and (2) are correctly matched with reference to Vedic age.

These ritual, Rajasuya, Ashvamedha and Vajapeya increased kings prestige and influence over people. It also increased the material wealth of the Brahmana who were rewarded with the gifts for conducting these rituals.

While pair (3) is incorrectly matched because Vajapeya was a chariot race, in which a royal chariot was run and was supposed to win against his kinsmen.

19 **Consider the following statements regarding changes in political organisation during Later Vedic age.** *(Chap 8, Class-XI, Old NCERT)*

1. Women were no longer allowed to participate in the Sabha and it was dominated by Princess and rich nobles.
2. The king started to possess long standing armies for protection of their territories.
3. The dominant tribes became identical to the territories in which they resided.

Which of the statements given above is/are incorrect?

(a) 1 and 2 (b) 2 and 3 (c) Only 2 (d) Only 3

Ans. (c)

Exp. Statement (2) is incorrect regarding changes in political organisation during Later Vedic ages as even in Later Vedic period king did not possess standing armies, but called upon tribal units in times of war.

Society

20 **Which among the following factor played the most important role in creation of social divisions during the Rigvedic age?** *(Chap 3, Class-IX, Old NCERT)*

(a) Technological superiority
(b) Agricultural landholding
(c) Conquest of the indigenous inhabitants by the Aryans
(d) Occupation

Ans. (c)

Exp. The conquest of indigenous inhabitants by the Aryans was the most important factor of social division in Rigvedic age. The *Dasas* and *Dasyus* were conquered and treated as slaves and Shudras.

21 **With reference to Vedic society, consider the following statements.** *(Class XI, Old NCERT)*

1. Women were denied Upanayana in the Later Vedic age.
2. Later Vedic age witnessed the emergence of the idea of Gotra.
3. Concept of private property in land emerged in the early Vedic phase.
4. Polygyny was prevalent in the Later Vedic age.

How many of the statements given above is/are correct?

(a) Only one (b) Only two
(c) Only three (d) All four

Ans. (c)

Exp. Only three statements i.e., (1), (2) and (4) are correct with reference to society of Vedic age.

Women were denied Upanayana(sacred thread) and Gayatri Mantra. Upanayana was limited to the upper section of the society.

The idea of Gotra emerged in the Later Vedic period. Gotra literally meant 'cowpen' and it referred to a group of people from a common ancestor. Polygyny was prevalent in the Later Vedic age. The practice of levirate and widow marriage was prevalent in the Later Vedic phase.

Statement (3) is incorrect. There was no private property on land. Donations to the priest were mainly cows and women slaves but not land.

22 Consider the following statements regarding state of religion during the Rigvedic period. *(Chap 8, Class-XI, Old NCERT)*

1. Large temples were constructed for the worship of Gods.
2. Dominate mode of worship of Gods was through recitation of prayers and offering of sacrifices.
3. Every tribe or clan was the votary of the special God.

Which of the statements given above are correct?

(a) 1 and 2 (b) 2 and 3 (c) 1 and 3 (d) 1, 2 and 3

Ans. (b)

Exp. Statements (2) and (3) are correct regarding state of religion during the Rigvedic period.

The dominant mode of worshipping the gods was through the recitation of prayers and offering of sacrifices.

Prayers played an important part in Rigvedic times. Both collective and individual prayers were offered.

Originally every tribe or clan was the votary of a special god. Prayers were offered to Gods in chorus by the members of a whole tribe.

Statement (1) is incorrect because there is no finding of any large temple of Rigvedic times.

23 With reference to vedic society consider the following statements. *(Class XI, Old NCERT)*

1. Vedic society was largely egalitarian in the initial period.
2. Shudras as a category of people at the end of Rig vedic period.

Which of the statements given above is/are incorrect?

(a) Only 1 (b) Only 2
(c) Both 1 and 2 (d) Neither 1 nor 2

Ans. (d)

Exp. Neither statements (1) nor (2) are incorrect with reference to the Vedic society.

Vedic society was largely egalitarian and social destination emerged later.

Shudras as a category of people appeared at the end of the Rigvedic period. These social divisions are considered to have aruen towards the end of the early Vedic period.

24 Which of the following pairs is/are matched incorrectly? *(Chap 8, Class-XI, Old NCERT)*

Functionaries		Responsibilities
(a) Upanayana	–	Fourfold division of society
(b) Varna	–	Decent from the common ancestors
(c) Ashrama	–	Sacred thread ceremony
(d) All of the above		

Ans. (c)

Exp. All the given pairs are matched incorrectly.

Upanayana was sacred thread ceremony for which all three higher caste were entitled but not *Shudras*.

Varna was the fourfold division system of Rigvedic times.

Ashrama was the four stages of life. They were Brahmacharya or student, *Grihastha* or householder, Vanaprastha or hermit and *sanyasin* or ascetic.

Gotra, appeared in later Vedic times. It signified descent from a common ancestor.

25 Which among the following changes was/were observed in the state of religion during Later Vedic phase? *(Chap 8, Class-XI, Old NCERT)*

1. Prominent Rigvedic God Indra and Agni lost their importance.
2. People began to worship idols.
3. Brahmanas lost their ritual dominance.

Codes

(a) 1 and 2 (b) 2 and 3 (c) 1 and 3 (d) 1, 2 and 3

Ans. (a)

Exp. Changes mentioned in statements (1) and (2) were observed in the state of religion. During Later Vedic phase as in this period the most important Gods of Rigvedic period the Indra and Agni lost their importance and Prajapati the creator came to occupy the supreme position. Some objects began to be worshipped as symbols of divinity, signs of idolatry appear in later Vedic times.

Change mentioned in statement (3) was not observed as more the rituals and practice of sacrifice increased, the prominence of Brahmana increased simultaneously.

26 Consider the following Assertion (A) and Reason (R) and choose the correct code. *(Chap 3, Class-IX, Old NCERT)*

Assertion (A) During the Later Vedic age, the growing cult of sacrifices enormously added to the power and privileges of Brahmanas.

Reason (R) They conducted rituals and sacrifices for their clients and officiated at the festivals associated with agricultural operations.

Codes

(a) Both A and R are true and R is the correct explanation of A.
(b) Both A and R are true, but R is not the correct explanation of A.
(c) A is true, but R is false.
(d) A is false, but R is true.

Ans. (a)

Exp. Both Assertion (A) and Reason (R) are true and Reason (R) is the correct explanation of (A).

As mode of worship changed during Later Vedic period, sacrifices became far more important and they assumed both public and private character. Sacrifices were carried on with a formulas which had to be pronounced correctly. These sacrifices and formulas were made and performed by Brahmanas. They conducted rituals and *yajna* for kings and people. Priestly knowledge and expertise became their monopoly of Brahmanas and this increased their power and privileges.

27 Consider the following statements. *(Class XI, Old NCERT)*

Statement-I There is no evidence of child marriage in early Vedic period.

Statement-II Women had been excluded from rituals in the later Vedic period.

Which one of the following is correct in respect of the above statements?

(a) Both Statement-I and Statement-II are correct and Statement-II is the correct explanation for Statement-I.
(b) Both Statement-I and Statement-II are correct and Statement-II is not the correct explanation for Statement-1.
(c) Statement-I is correct but Statement-II is incorrect.
(d) Statement-I is incorrect but Statement-II is correct.

Ans. (b)

Exp. Both Statement-I and Statement-II are correct and Statement-II is not the correct explanation for Statement-I. Vedic period shows no prevalence of child marriage. In the Later Vedic period women were excluded from rituals. The status of women declined as the society became more structured and the patriarchal family became more important.

28 Consider the following statements regarding position of women in the Later Vedic era. *(Chap 11, Class-XI, Old NCERT)*

1. Women were thought to be inferior and subordinate to the men.
2. They were barred from participating in activities related with Sabha.

Which of the statements given above is/are correct?

(a) Only 1 (b) Only 2
(c) Both 1 and 2 (d) Neither 1 nor 2

Ans. (c)

Exp. Both the statements (1) and (2) are correct regarding the position of women in Later Vedic era. The families started to be dominated by father and it became patriarchal. Women were generally given lower position.

As the importance and character of tribal assemblies changed. The women were no longer allowed to take part in *Sabha*. It came to be dominated by nobles and princes.

Economy

29 Which was the main source of copper for the Indo-Aryans? *(Chap 11, Class-XI, Old NCERT)*

(a) Zawar mines of Gujarat
(b) Khetri mines of Rajasthan
(c) Chhota Nagpur Plateau
(d) Punjab

Ans. (b)

Exp. The Khetri mines of Rajasthan was the main source of copper for the Indo-Aryans.

Tools and artefacts belonging to 1500-1000 BC have been discovered from many parts of North India. Among these, tools made up of copper has also been discovered. It was one of the first metal used by Indo-Aryans for making tools, utensils and ornaments.

30 Consider the following statements. *(Chap 7, Class-XI, Old NCERT)*

1. Hunting and gathering was the chief occupation of Indo-Aryans.
2. In later Vedic period, rice and wheat became the chief crops.
3. Wooden ploughshare were used by the farmers in later Vedic period.

Which of the statements given above is/are incorrect?

(a) Only 1 (b) 2 and 3 (c) 1 and 3 (d) Only 3

Ans. (a)

Exp. Statement (1) is incorrect because the Pastoralism was the chief occupation of the Indo-Aryans. Hunting and gathering is usually associated with the tribes living in forest areas.

31 With reference to Vedic age, consider the following statements. *(Class XI, Old NCERT)*

1. The term Ayas and Syama denotes iron and copper respectively.
2. Vrihi in Vedic text refers to Barley.

Which of the statements given above is/are correct?

(a) Only 1 (b) Only 2
(c) Both 1 and 2 (d) Neither 1 nor 2

Ans. (d)

Exp. Neither statements (1) nor (2) are correct with reference to the Vedic age.

In Vedic text, the terms Ayas and Syama denotes copper and iron respectively. The term Ayas used for copper or bronze shows that metal-work was known towards the end of Vedic period. Knowledge of Iron implements spread in Eastern Uttar Pradesh.

Earliest iron implements discovered in this area belong to the seventh century BC and the metal is called Shyama or Krishna Ayas.

Rice is referred by the term 'Virhi' in Vedic text. Its remains have been found in Hastinapur belonging to eighth century BC.

32 With reference to Vedic age, consider the following statements. *(Chap 8, Class-XI, Old NCERT)*

1. Only Black and red ware is associated with archaeological sites of Indo-Aryans.
2. They used ploughshare made up of wood for agriculture.
3. They were acquainted with sowing, harvesting and threshing and knew about different seasons.

How many of the statements given above is/are incorrect?

(a) Only one (b) Only two
(c) All three (d) None of these

Ans. (a)

Exp. Only one statement i.e., (1) is incorrect with reference to Vedic age.

Painted Grey Ware (PGW) and Black and Red Ware (BRW) are associated with the archaeological sites of Indo-Aryans. Later Vedic period people were acquainted with four types of pottery- black and red ware, painted grey ware, black slipped ware and red ware.

33 Consider the following statements. *(Chap 9, Class-XI, Old NCERT)*

1. Agriculture and various crafts enabled the Later Vedic people to live a settled life.
2. They gave up the pastoralist and semi-nomadic lives practiced in Rigvedic era.
3. Iron was the first metal used by the Vedic people.

Which of the statements given above is/are incorrect?

(a) 1 and 2 (b) Only 1 (c) 1 and 3 (d) Only 3

Ans. (d)

Exp. Statement (3) is incorrect as iron was used by people of Later Vedic period, earlier Rigvedic people used metals such as copper, tin, gold and silver.

Thus, the people of Later Vedic period gave up the pastoralist way of life practised in Rigvedic period.

34 Consider the following statements. *(Chap 9, Class-XI, Old NCERT)*

1. Besides agriculture, cattle rearing, fishing, metal work and carpentry were the main occupation of the people in later Vedic phase.
2. The use of iron axe – heads helped in the clearing heavy forests in the Ganga Valley.
3. All persons in the same families were strictly advised to follow same occupations.

Which of the statements given above is/are incorrect?

(a) Only 1 (b) 2 and 3 (c) 1 and 3 (d) Only 3

Ans. (d)

Exp. Statement (3) is incorrect because there is no such restrictions on following any particular occupation on family members.

Statements (1) and (2) are correct. Later Vedic people had primarily became agriculturist. But the knowledge of metals like iron and copper gave rise to crafts.

With knowledge of iron, Vedic people defeated the adversaries in Doab region. Excavations show weapons made up of iron at that time. The iron axe may have helped them clear the forests of Gangetic regions.

Miscellaneous

35 Which one of the following Vedic literature talks about Salvation? *(Chap 3, Class-IX, Old NCERT) (UPPSC Mains 2003)*

(a) Rigveda (b) Later Samhitas
(c) Brahmanas (d) Upanishads

Ans. (d)

Exp. Among the given options, Vedic literature Upanishads talks about Salvation. They were compiled around 600 BC and criticised the rituals and laid stress on the value of right belief and knowledge. Upanishads further emphasised that the knowledge of the self or atman should be acquired and the relation of atman with Brahma should be properly understood.

36 The famous battle of 'Ten Kings' as described in the Rigveda was fought on the bank of *(Chap 8, Class-XI, Old NCERT) (UPPSC Mains 2008)*

(a) Parushni (b) Saraswati (c) Vipasa (d) Askini

Ans. (a)

Exp. The famous battle of 'Ten Kings' as described in the Rigveda was fought on the bank of Parushni river. This river is identical with the modern-day Ravi river. This battle was fought between the Bharatas on the one hand and host of ten chiefs on the other. In this battle, Sudas emerged victorious and established the supremacy of Bharatas.

37 Which of the following rivers among the following referred as *Matetama, Devitama* and *Naditama* in the Rigveda? *(Chap 8, Class-XI, Old NCERT) (UPPSC Spl, Mains 2008)*

(a) Sindhu (b) Saraswati (c) Vitasta (d) Yamuna

Ans. (b)

Exp. In the Rigveda, the Saraswati river was referred as *Matetama*, *Devitama* and *Naditama*. It was considered the most pious river of all and is identified with the Ghaggar-Hakra Channel in Harayana and Rajasthan.

38 Which of the following rivers mentioned in the Rigveda indicates the relations of Aryans with Afghanistan? *(Chap 8, Class-XI, Old NCERT) (UPPSC Pre 2010)*

(a) Askini (b) Parushni
(c) Kubha, Kramu (d) Vipasha, Shutudri

Ans. (c)

Exp. Among the given rivers, Kubha and Kramu mentioned in Rigveda indicates the relations of Aryans with Afghanistan. The earliest Aryans lived in the geographical area covered by Eastern Afghanistan. Kubha river is identified with modern day Kabul river of Afghanistan.

Chapter 05

Religious Movements

Religious Movements

Jainism

Origin

- Rishabhanatha (born in Ayodhya), Parshvanatha (born in Varanasi) and Vardhaman Mahavira (born in Kundagrama, Vaishali) are 1st , 23rd and 24th Tirthankara respectively

Doctrine

- **5 doctrines** Do not commit violence; Do not speak a lie; Do not steal; Do not possess any property and observe celibacy

Philosophy

- Believed in theory of Syadvada (relativity of knowledge); 2 categories of living- conscious being (Jiva) and non-living being (Ajiva)

Sects

- 2 main sects Digambara- (ardent followers), Shwetambara- (adopted various changes to face famine in Magadha)

Literature

- Divided into 2 categories- 1) Agama- sacred literature 2) Non-Agama- commentaries and explanation of Agama by scholars

Architecture

- Cave architecture at Udayagiri, Khandagiri, Ellora; Temples at Dilwara, Khajuraho and Ranakpur; Statue of Gomateshwara

Decline

- Lacked royal patronage; Easy living by monks; Jaina philosophy of austerity and division in Jainism

Buddhism

Origin

- Started in 6th century BC by Gautama Buddha after enlightenment; Gautama Buddha born in 563 BC at Lumbini in royal family
- Attained enlightenment at Bodh Gaya and gave first sermon at Sarnath; Attained Mahaparinirvana at Kushinagar

Doctrine

- Four noble truths- world is full of sorrows; Desire is root cause of sorrows; Nirvana can be attained by conquering desires and there is path for cessation of sorrows

Philosophy

- Buddha, Dhamma and Sangha are three jewels; Preached madhyam marga for attainment of nirvana; Asked followers to follow the eight-fold path

Sects

1) Theravada 2) Sarvastivadina
3) Mahasanghika 4) Hinayana
5) Mahayana 6) Vajrayana

Significance

- Promoted equality; Elimination of poverty; Simplistic way of living and equal status to women and Shudras

Decline

- Hostility of rulers; Undue emphasis on rituals and laxity by monks resulted in decline of Buddhism in 11th and 12th century AD

Other Religious Movement

Ajivika

- Propounded by Makkhali Gosala
- Believed in fate and destiny
- Popular during the time of Bindusara of Mauryan Dynasty

Unchedvadi

- Propounded by Ajita Kesakambali;
- Promoted materialism and professed no life after death

Bhagwatism

- Emerged in post-Mauryan period - Worship of incarnation of Vishnu - Emphasised on Bhakti, Karma and Jnana marg to attain Moksha; Believed in idol worship

Sects of Bhagwatism

- Vishishtadvaita- Ramanuja
- Dvaita-Madhavacharya
- Shuddhadvaita- Vallabhacharya
- Achintya Bheda Abheda- Chaitanya Mahaprabhu
- Ten Avtars of Vishnu Matsya (fish), Kurma(Tortoise),Varaha (bour), Narasimha (Man-lion), Vaman (dwarf), Parashurama, Rama, Krishna, Buddha and Kalki

Islam

- Emerged in Arabia in 7th century AD
- Muhammad was the Prophet
- After Arab conquest of Sindh, Islam gained its followers in India
- Muhammad believed that there was only one God
- They kept their political control over Sind

SOURCE ***Old NCERT Class VI*** *(India from 600 BC to 400 BC),* ***Old NCERT Class IX*** *(Early Iron-Age Civilisation),* ***Old NCERT Class XI*** *(Jainism and Buddhism),* ***Old NCERT Class XI*** *(State and Varna at the Age of Buddha),* ***New NCERT Class XII*** *(Thinkers, Beliefs and Buildings),* ***New NCERT Class XII*** *(Kinship, Caste and Class)* ***Tamil Nadu Board XI*** *(Rise of Territorial Kingdoms and New Religious Sect)*

Causes of Origin of Buddhism and Jainism

1 Consider the following statements with reference to Indian society of the sixth century BC.
(Chap 10, Class-XI, Old NCERT)

1. The Status of Dvija was manifestation of rigidity of varna society.
2. A general reluctance for animal sacrifice is associated with the exigency of a new agrarian economy.
3. Desire for upliftment in the social hierarchy made Vaishya look for new religious denominations.

How many of the statements given above is/are correct?

(a) Only one (b) Only two (c) All three (d) None

Ans. (c)

Exp. All three statements i.e., (1), (2) and (3) are correct with reference to the Indian society of the sixth century. Vaishya enjoyed the status of Dvija along with Brahamanas and Kshatriyas and only they were allowed to study vedas and undergo sacred thread ceremony.

There was general reluctance to the practice of animal sacrifice associated with the exigency of the new agrarian economy.

The new agrarian economy characterised by the use of iron ploughs was preceded by the vedic practice of killing cattle and this practice slowly diminished the livestock population. In order to make the new economy stable, the practice of animal sacrifice needed to be stopped.

The Vaishyas and trader class made generous support to Vardhamana Mahavira and Gautama Buddha as Vaishya gained prominence economically and this created a desire in them for the upliftment in the social hierarchy.

2 Consider the following statements regarding origin of Buddhism and Jainism in the sixth century BC.
(Chap 9, Class-XI, Old NCERT)

1. Introduction of new agricultural economy was the main cause of origin of Buddhism and Jainism in the sixth century BC.
2. These religions emerged in the areas surrounding the Indus Valley in the North-Western India.
3. The third varna of the Indian society, Vaishyas generously supported the new emerging religions in India.

Which of the statements given above is/are incorrect?

(a) 1 and 2 (b) 2 and 3
(c) Only 2 (d) Only 3

Ans. (c)

Exp. Statement (2) is incorrect regarding the origin of Buddhism and Jainism in the sixth century BC because both of these religions emerged in North-Eastern India including the modern day territories of Bihar and Eastern Uttar Pradesh. It coincided with the emergence of the first Empire (Magadha) in India.

3 Which of the following pairs is incorrectly matched?
(Chap 4, Class-XII, New NCERT)

Thinkers		Countries
(a) Kong Zi	–	India
(b) Zarathustra	–	Greece
(c) Socrates	–	Iran

(d) All of the above

Ans. (d)

Exp. All of the given pairs are incorrectly matched.

Kong Zi (also known as Confucius) was a Chinese philosopher and thinker in the fifth century BC. Through his teachings, he laid stress on the importance of personal ethics and the morality.

Zarathustra was an Iranian spiritual leader and thinker in seventh and sixth centuries BC. He founded the Zoroastrianism religion.

Socrates was a Greek philosopher and thinker in the fourth century BC. He is credited as the founder of Western Philosophy.

4 The rise of Buddhism and Jainism in the sixth century BC resulted in *(Chap 9, Class-XI, Old NCERT)*

(a) strengthening of the rigidity of the caste system.
(b) emancipation of women and Shudras.
(c) compilation of Upanishads.
(d) development of classical Sanskrit.

Ans. (b)

Exp. The rise of Buddhism and Jainism in the sixth century BC resulted in emancipation of women and Shudras.

Both Buddhism and Jainism allowed women in their orders and also didn't give much importance to Varna system of Vedic religion, which led to their upliftment. The Vedic era (between 1500-500 BC) led to the strengthening of the rigidity of the caste system, compilation of Upanishads and Mahakavyas besides veda and development of classical Sanskrit.

5 Consider the following statements regarding differences between Buddhism and Jainism.
(Chap 9, Class-XI, Old NCERT)

1. Buddha taught that a person should avoid excess of both luxuries and austerity whereas Mahavira emphasised on living an austere life.
2. Jainism prohibited the practice of agriculture as it involves killing of living beings whereas Buddha supported the expansion of agriculture.
3. Buddhism recognises the Vedic concept of karma, soul and rebirth whereas Jainism rejected them.

Which of the statements given above is/are incorrect?

(a) 1 and 2
(b) 2 and 3
(c) Only 2
(d) Only 3

Ans. (d)

Exp. Statements (3) is incorrect regarding differences between Buddhism and Jainism because Buddhism rejected Vedic concept of karma, soul and rebirth.

Buddha said to follow the middle path, while Mahavira added the fourth code in Jainism doctrine of Jainas, of observing continence, which was an extreme measure.

6 With reference to the history of Ancient India, which of the following was/were common to both Buddhism and Jainism? *(Chap 9, Class-XI, Old NCERT) (IAS Pre 2012)*

1. Avoidance of extremities of penance and enjoyment.
2. Indifference to the authority of Vedas.
3. Denial of the efficacy of rituals.

Codes

(a) Only 1 (b) 2 and 3
(c) 1 and 3 (d) 1,2 and 3

Ans. (b)

Exp. Principle of indifferences to the authority of Vedas and Denial of the efficacy of rituals were common to both Buddhism and Jainism. They believed that true knowledge and liberation could be attained through personal experience and introspection, rather than relying on external scriptures.

Both Buddhism and Jainism rejected the efficacy of rituals and sacrifices in attaining spiritual liberation.They believed that true liberation could be attained through inner purity and detachment from worldly desires.

While, both Buddhism and Jainism believed that extreme practices could not lead to spiritual liberation. Both Buddhism and Jainism emphasised the middle path between extreme self-mortification and indulgence in worldly pleasures.

Jainism

7 With reference to Jainism, consider the following statements. *(Unit 3, Class-XI, Tamil Nadu Board)*

1. Rishabhanatha was referred to as Nigantha Nataputta in the Buddhist text.
2. There is no mention of Tirthankaras in the Vedas.
3. Ajitanatha was one of the Tirthankaras of Jainism.

How many of the statements given above is/are correct?

(a) Only one (b) Only two
(c) All three (d) None of these

Ans. (a)

Exp. Only one statement i.e., (3) is correct with reference to Jainism.

Ajitanatha was the second Tirthankaras of Jainism with whom Elephant as a symbol is associated.

Statements (1) and (2) are incorrect.

Vardhamana Mahavira was referred to as Nigantha Nataputta by Buddhist text.

Mahavira was known as Jina (conqueror) of the soul and hence his sect came to be known as Jainism.

Yajurveda mentions three of the Tirthankaras viz., Rishabhanatha, Ajitanatha and Aristanemi.

8 With reference to Vardhamana Mahavira, consider the following statements. *(Chap 4, Class-XI, Old NCERT)*

1. Lion was the symbol associated with the last Tirthankara.
2. He preached his doctrine in the common man's language of that time.
3. He attained Kaivalya which liberation from pain and grief.

How many of the statements given above is/are incorrect?

(a) Only one (b) Only two (c) All three (d) None of these

Ans. (d)

Exp. None of the statements given above are incorrect with reference to Vardhamana Mahavira.

The symbol associated with Vardhamana Mahavira is Lion. He was born in 540 BC in Kundagram, Vaishali.

Mahavira taught the simple doctrine of 'Ahimsa'(non-violence) in Prakrit language which was a common man's language at that time. Through Kaivalya, Mahavira conquered misery and happiness,

9 In the context of the religious history of India, the term 'Basadi' refers to *(Chap 9, Class-XI, Old NCERT)*

(a) monastic establishments of Jaina monks.
(b) educational institutions specialising in theology.
(c) buildings were sacred relics of Jaina Tirthankara were kept.
(d) yearly congregation of Jaina monks.

Ans. (a)

Exp. In the context of the religious history of India, the term 'Basadi' refers to monastic establishments of Jaina monks. After the spread of Jainism in South around third century AD, it sprang up in Karnataka and were granted land by the king for their support.

10 With reference to religious history of Jainism, consider the following statements. *(Chap 4, Class-XII, New NCERT (Chap 6, Class-VI, New NCERT)*

1. Sthulabhadra is credited with carrying Jainism in South India.
2. Out of the five doctrines of Jainism, don't acquire property was added by the last the tirthankara.
3. Rejection of infallibility of Vedas makes Jainism an unorthodox religion.

How many of the statements given above is/are correct?

(a) Only one (b) Only two
(c) All three (d) None of these

Ans. (a)

Exp. Only one statement i.e., (3) is correct with reference to the religious history of Jainism in India. Rejection of infallibility of vedas makes Jainism an unorthodox religion. Mahavira rejected Vedic authority. Hence, Jainism is an unorthodox religion. According to Jainism, the world has no beginning or end.

Statements (1) and (2) are incorrect because the Jaina monk Bhadrabahu is given credit for carrying Jainism in South India. The Jain monks in order to survive the famine of Magadha went to the South under the leadership of Bhadrabahu.

Mahavira added only the fifth doctrine Mahavira i.e., observe continence.

11 The Jainas believe that Jainism is the outcome of the teachings of twenty-four Tirthankaras. In the light of given context, which one among the following is correct about Vardhamana Mahavira?

(Chap 9, Class-XI, Old NCERT)

(a) He was the first Tirthankara and the founder of Jainism.
(b) He was contemporary of the Mauryan emperor, Chandragupta Maurya.
(c) He propagated Jainism for 10 years in Magadha, Vaishali and Koshala only .
(d) Jainism mainly aims at the attainment of freedom from wordly bonds.

Ans. (d)

Exp. In the light of given context, statement (d) is correct about Vardhamana Mahavira.

Mahavira was 24th and the last *Tirthankara* of Jainism. He was contemporary of the Magadha King, Ajatashatru. He propagated his religion and teachings for 30 years, and went Koshala, Champa, Mithila etc.

Jainism mainly aimed at the attainment of freedom from worldly bonds. No rituals is required for acquiring such liberation it can be obtained through right knowledge, right faith and right action.

12 Which of the following statements about Jainism is/are correct? *(Chap 9, Class-XI, Old NCERT)*

1. It didn't recognised the existence of God.
2. Asceticism and penance are required to free oneself from the cycle of Karma.

Codes

(a) Only 1 (b) Only 2
(c) Both 1 and 2 (d) Neither 1 nor 2

Ans. (b)

Exp. Statement (2) is correct regarding Jainism.

Similar to the Vedic philosophy Jainism also believed in the doctrine of *Karma*. It preached that the asceticism and penance are required to free onself from the cycle of Karma.

Statement (1) is incorrect because Jainism recognised the existence of God. But it placed them lower than Jina. It didn't condemn the Varna system.

13 With reference to Jainism, consider the following statements. *(Chap 6, Class-VI, New NCERT)*

Statement-I The earliest Jain Literature compiled in the sixth century AD was in Ardha-Magadhi language which was a branch of Prakrit.

Statement-II Choice of language by early Jainas was an extension of their stand against the dominance of Brahminism in the way of life.

Which one of the following is correct in respect of the above statements?

(a) Both Statement-I and Statement-II are correct and Statement-II is the correct explanation for Statement-I.
(b) Both Statement-I and Statement-II are correct and Statement-II is not the correct explanation for Statement-I.
(c) Statement-I is correct, but Statement-II is incorrect.
(d) Statement-I is incorrect, but Statement-II is correct.

Ans. (a)

Exp. Both Statement-I and Statement-II are correct and Statement-II is the correct explanation for Statement-I. The earlier Jain Literature compiled in the sixth century AD, was Ardha-Magadhi language. It was a branch of Prakrit language.

Choice of language of common man's at that time was an extension of their stand against the dominance of Brahminism in the way of life because Sanskrit was the language of Brahmanas and they were against the fact that Hinduism had become rigid and orthodox with complex rituals and dominance of Brahmins. And therefore they adopted the Prakrit language of the common people.

14 Which of the following statements is/are applicable to Jaina doctrine?

(Chap 9, Class-XI, Old NCERT) (IAS Pre 2013)

1. The surest way of annihilating Karma is to practise penance.
2. Every object, even the smallest particle has a soul.
3. Karma is the bane of the soul and must be ended.

Codes

(a) Only 1 (b) 2 and 3 (c) 1 and 2 (d) 1, 2 and 3

Ans. (d)

Exp. All the given statements (1), (2) and (3) are applicable to Jaina doctrine. The doctrine of Karma is integral to Jainism and according to Mahavira, the surest way of annihilating Karma is to practise penance. He further preached that, 'a person is born in a high or in lower *Varna*' in consequences of the sins or virtues acquired by him in the previous birth.

Jainism further believed that the entire world is animated. It means every object, even the smallest particle has a soul.

This is the reason why in Jainism utmost importance is given to *ahimsa* or 'non-injury.' *Triratna* of Jainism helps in eliminating the impact of *Karma*, which is considered bane of the soul.

15 **With reference to the religious philosophy of Jainism, consider the following statements.** *(Class XI, Old NCERT)*

1. It postulates that the world has no beginning or end.
2. It advocates monism.
3. Endless cycle of birth and rebirth is created by the coming together of soul and matter.
4. In Jainism only monks could achieve liberation from the cycle of birth and rebirth.

How many of the statements given above is/are incorrect?

(a) Only one
(b) Only two
(c) Only three
(d) All four

Ans. (a)

Exp. Only one statement i.e., (2) is incorrect with reference to the religious philosophy of Jainism.

Jainism advocates dualism, that is, the world is made of soul(jiva) and matter (ajiva), which are eternal creates Karma which leads to and endless cycle of birth and rebirth. In Jainism only monks could achieve liberation from the cycle of birth and rebirth.

16 **With reference to religious doctrine of Jainism, consider the following statements.** *(Unit 3, Class XI, Tamil Nadu Board)*

1. Samyag-darshana, Samyag-jnana and Samyad-mahavrata are considered essential for attaining liberation from the cycle of Karma and rebirth.
2. Jains could not practice any craft that involved injury to living organisms.
3. Women were neither admitted to monastic order nor they could attain salvation.

How many of the statements given above is/are correct?

(a) Only one (b) Only two
(c) All three (d) None of these

Ans. (b)

Exp. Only two statements i.e., (1) and (2) are correct with reference to religious doctrine of Jainism.

Samyag-darshana, Samyag-jnana and Samyad-mahavrata are considered essential for attaining liberation from the cycle of Karma and rebirth.

These are the three principles called Triratnas or Three Gems. Jains could not practice agriculture or other crafts that involve killing or injury to living organisms.

Statement (3) is not correct because women were admitted into monastic order. However, as a woman one can't attain salvation. By accumulating merit by good deeds, a woman could be reborn as a man and then strive to attain salvation.

17 **With reference to the doctrines of Jainism, consider the following statements.** *(Chap 9, Class-XI, Old NCERT)*

1. Jainism recognised the existence of God but placed them below jina.
2. Jainism vehemently condemned the Varna system.

Which of the statements given above is/are incorrect?

(a) Only 1 (b) Only 2
(c) Both 1 and 2 (d) Neither 1 nor 2.

Ans. (b)

Exp. Only statement (2) is incorrect with reference to the doctrine of Jainism.

Jainism does not condemn the Varna System while Buddhism does. According to Mahavira, a person is born in a high or in a lower varna in consequence of the sins or the virtues acquired by him in the previous birth.

18 **With reference to spread of Jainism, consider the following statements.** *(Chap 9, Class-XI, Old NCERT)*

1. For propagating his religion, Mahavira organised order of followers, which included both men and women.
2. The first Jaina Council was organised in Pataliputra.
3. As it did not clearly mark itself out from the Brahmanical religion, it failed to attract the masses.

Which of the statements given above is/are correct?

(a) 1 and 2 (b) 2 and 3 (c) 1 and 3 (d) 1, 2 and 3

Ans. (d)

Exp. All the statements (1), (2) and (3) are correct regarding the spread of Jainism.

In order to spread the teachings of Jainism, Mahavira organised an order of his followers, which admitted both men and women. It is said that his followers counted 14,000.

In order to sort out the differences between two sects– Svetambara and Digambara, and compile the main teachings of Mahavira, first Jaina Council was convened at Pataliputra (Patna). Jainism did not clearly marked itself out from the Brahmanical religion, it failed to attract the masses.

19 **With reference to sects of Jainism, consider the following statements.** *(Chap 9, Class-XI, Old NCERT)*

1. After Jaina Council at Pataliputra, it was divided into two sects-Digambaras and Shvetambaras.
2. Bhadrabahu was the leader of Shvetambaras sects of Jainism and his followers were always dressed in white.
3. Digambaras sect was founded by the ascetics who went to South India to protect themselves from the great famine.

Which of the statements given above is/are incorrect?

(a) 1 and 2 (b) 2 and 3 (c) Only 2 (d) Only 3

Ans. (c)

Exp. Statement (2) is incorrect regarding the sects of Jainism as Sthulabhadra was the leader of Shvetambaras not Bhadrabahu. His followers wear white dresses. Svetambara monks follow the tradition of Acharya Sthulabhadra.

20 Identify the Tirthankara of Jainism based on the statements given below. *(Chap 9, Class-XI, Old NCERT)*

1. He was born in Varanasi and gave up royal life to become an ascetic.
2. According to the Jaina traditions, he lived two hundred years before Mahavira.
3. Many teachings of Jainism are attributed to him.

Codes

(a) Mahavira (b) Parshvanatha
(c) Mallinatha (d) Sthalabahu

Ans. (b)

Exp. All the given statements (1), (2) and (3) are correctly related to twenty third *Tirthankara* Parshvanath. According to the Jaina tradition, most of the early Tirthankaras were born in Ganga basin and attained Nirvana in Bihar.

He was born in Varanasi and gave up royal life and became an ascetic.

21 With reference to the spread of Jainism, consider the following statements. *(Chap 9, Class-XI, Old NCERT)*

1. Kalinga King Kharavela patronised Jainism in the first century BC.
2. Jainism penetrated to Malwa and Gujarat.
3. State patronage received by Jainism was significantly much higher than Buddhism.

How many statements given above is/are correct?

(a) Only one (b) Only two
(c) All three (d) None of these

Ans. (b)

Exp. Only two statements i.e., (1) and (2) are correct with reference to the spread of Jainism.

Jainism spread to Kalinga in Orissa in the fourth century BC and in the first century BC, it enjoyed the patronage of the Kalinga king Kharavela. Jainism penetrated Malwa, Gujarat and Rajasthan.

Statement (3) is incorrect because Jainism didn't win as much state patronage as Buddhism did and didn't spread very fast in early times.

22 Which of the following statements is/are incorrect regarding contribution of Jainism ? *(Chap 9, Class-XI, Old NCERT)*

1. It played an important role in development of regional languages such as Marathi and Kannada.
2. It helped in exporting the Indian culture in the countries of South Asia.
3. It contributed substantially to art and architecture in medieval times.

Codes

(a) 1 and 2 (b) 2 and 3 (c) Only 2 (d) Only 3

Ans. (c)

Exp. Statement (2) is incorrect regarding contribution of Jainism as Buddhism (not Jainism) helped in exporting the Indian culture in the countries of South Asia. Jainism as a religion was confined to few Indian states only.

23 With reference to Jaina literature, consider the following statements. *(Class XI, Old NCERT)*

1. Canon of Jain literature compiled at the Great Council in Pataliputra consists of 24 angas.
2. 12 Upangas were added in the Great Council of Valabhi in the 5th century CE.
3. Jain monks wrote only religious literature and not any secular literature.

How many statements given above is/are correct?

(a) Only one (b) Only two
(c) All three (d) None of these

Ans. (a)

Exp. Only one statement i.e., (2) are correct with reference to Jaina literature, at the great Council, held at Valabhi Gujarat in the fifth century CE, 12 Upangas were added.

Statements (1) and (3) are incorrect because it considered of 12 (not of 24) Angas (limbs). On the death of Bhadrabahu, Shulabhadra held a great Council at Pataliputra, which compiled the Jain canon. The Jain monks not only wrote religious treaties but also promoted secular literature.

24 Consider the following statements as Assertion (A) and Reason (R) and choose the correct code. *(Chap 9, Class-XI, Old NCERT)*

Assertion (A) Jainism believed in the vedic concept of Karma.

Reason (R) According to Mahavira, a person is born in a high or in a lower varna in consequences of sins and virtues acquired by him in the previous birth.

Codes

(a) Both A and R are true and R is the correct explanation of A.
(b) Both A and R are true, but R is not the correct explanation A.
(c) A is true, but R is false.
(d) A is false, but R is true.

Ans. (a)

Exp. Both Assertion (A) and Reason (R) are true and Reason (R) is the correct explanation of Assertion (A).

According to Mahavira, one can attain freedom from cycle of birth and death by good deeds and not doing wrong (Karma).

According to him, a person was born in a varna in consequence of the sins or the virtues of his previous birth. And by living a pure and meritorious life, a person from lower caste can also attain salvation.

Buddhism

25 The first human statue worshipped in India was of *(Chap 9, Class-XI, Old NCERT), (RAS, RTS Pre 2010)*

(a) Brahma (b) Vishnu
(c) Buddha (d) Shiva

Ans. (c)

Exp. The first human statue worshipped in India was of Buddha. The Mahayana sect of Buddhism, which emerged during first century AD emphasised on worship of Buddha through idols. The faithful devotees portrayed the various events in life of Buddha in stone.

26 Consider the following statements regarding traditions of debate and discussion in the sixth century BC. *(Chap 4, Class-XII, New NCERT)*

1. During this phase, teachers travelled from place to place, trying to convince one another as well as laypersons, about the validity of their philosophy.
2. Debates took place in the Kutagarashala, which was a hut with a pointed roof where travelling mendicants halted.

Which of the statements given above is/are correct?

(a) Only 1 (b) Only 2
(c) Both 1 and 2 (d) Neither 1 nor 2

Ans. (c)

Exp. Both the statements (1) and (2) are correct regarding traditions of debate and discussion in the sixth century BC.

A glimpse of lively discussions and debates is shown from Buddhist texts, which mention as many as 64 sects or schools of thought. Teachers travelled from place to place, trying to convince one another as well as laypersons, about the validity of their philosophy or the way they understood the world.

Debates took place in the Kutagarashala – literally, a hut with a pointed roof – or in groves where travelling mendicants halted.

27 With reference to Buddhist teaching, which of the following statements is/are incorrect? *(Chap 4, Class-XII, New NCERT)*

1. Gautama Buddha regarded the social world as the creation of humans rather than of divine origins.
2. For attaining liberation, the participation and guidance of Buddhist Sangha is essential.

Codes

(a) Only 1 (b) Only 2
(c) Both 1 and 2 (d) Neither 1 nor 2

Ans. (b)

Exp. Statement (2) is incorrect regarding Buddhist teaching as the participation in Sangha was not mandatory. According to Buddhism, there were different paths of liberation. Individual effort was expected to transform social relations. The Buddha emphasised individual agency and righteous action as the means to escape from the cycle of rebirth and attain self-realisation and nibbana, literally the extinguishing of the ego and desire – and thus end the cycle of suffering for those who renounced the world.

28 In, which one of the following aspects, there is similarity between the Vedic philosophy and Buddhist teaching? *(Chap 4, Class-XII, New NCERT)*

(a) Both agreed on the authority of the Veda.
(b) Both accepted the social division based on the caste system.
(c) Both believed in the doctrine of Karma.
(d) Both encouraged animal sacrifices.

Ans. (c)

Exp. The similarity between the Buddhist and the Vedic philosophy is that they both believed in the doctrine of Karma. Vedic philosophy placed value on Karma as according to it people were born into different Varna and rebirth was accordingly.

Buddha also believed in right actions and Karma. This was almost common to all religions. His eight codes of conduct are similar to Karma. There was a conversation between Buddha and Ajatashatru about Karma. And how it helps to regain humans get free from cycle of birth and death.

29 With reference to the Buddhism, consider the following statements. *(Chap 4, Class-XII, New NCERT) (Chap 9, Class-XI, Old NCERT)*

1. In Buddhism the word Sangha denoted a place where Buddhist monk meditated.
2. Debtors, women and slaves were not allowed to be members of Sangha.
3. The earliest Buddhist literature was written in Pali.

How many of the statements given above is/are correct?

(a) Only one (b) Only two
(c) All three (d) None of these

Ans. (a)

Exp. Only one statement i.e., (3) is correct. The earliest Buddhist literatures were written in Pali language. It was also used by the Buddha to preach the masses.

Statements (1) and (2) are incorrect because Sangha is a Buddhist community not a place of meditation for Buddhists monk.

Debtors and slaves were not allowed to be members of Sangha. However, women were allowed to be part of Sangha.

30 In, which one of the following states, the Buddhist monasteries of Karle and Bedsa has been discovered? *(Chap 4, Class-VI, Old NCERT)*

(a) Maharashtra (b) Madhya Pradesh
(c) Bihar (d) Karnataka

Ans. (a)

Exp. The Buddhist monasteries of Karle and Bedsa caves has been discovered in Western Ghats near Pune, Maharashtra. They are Buddhist monasteries built for monks to live, called chaitya. They are built by Satavahana rulers. They were built by cutting rocks and were also decorated by sculptures.

31 Which one of the following statements regarding the doctrine of middle path is incorrect? *(Chap 9, Class-XI, Old NCERT)*

(a) It was preached by the Gautama Buddha.
(b) According to this doctrine, a person should avoid excess of both luxury and austerity.
(c) This concept was borrowed from the Jaina philosophy.
(d) It can be followed by monks as well as by the laypersons.

Ans. (c)

Exp. Statement (c) is incorrect regarding the doctrine of middle path because this concept was exclusively propounded by Lord Buddha and was not borrowed from Jaina philosophy.

Lord Buddha was a practical reformer and through the concept of middle path he taught that a person should avoid the excess of both luxury and austerstity. It can be followed by monks as well as by the laypersons.

32 Which one of the following define the concept of Nirvana in Buddhism? *(Chap 9, Class-XI, Old NCERT)*

(a) Freedom from the cycle of death and birth.
(b) The complete annihilation of self.
(c) State of complete blissfulness.
(d) Freedom from the sorrow and happiness.

Ans. (a)

Exp. Statement (a) define the concept of Nirvana in Buddhism. Buddha was a practical reformer. He said that world is full of sorrows and people suffer on account of desires. If desires are conquered, Niravana will be attained, i.e., man/woman will be free from the cycle of death and birth.

Doctrine of Buddhism

33 With reference to Buddhist doctrine, consider the following statements. *(Class XI, Old NCERT)*

1. Gautama Buddha neither accepted nor denied the existence of God.
2. It promoted trade and capitalism.
3. Pratitya Samudpada is the continuous cycle of birth and rebirth.

How many statements given above is/are incorrect?

(a) Only one (b) Only two
(c) All three (d) None of these

Ans. (d)

Exp. None of the statements given above are incorrect with reference to Buddhist doctrine. Buddha did not mention or talk about God. He neither accepted nor denied the existence of God.

It promoted trade and capitalism as it was against waste and advocated frugality. Pratitya Samudpada is the continuous cycle of birth and rebirth. Its root cause is ignorance.

34 Which among the following statements is correct regarding Buddhism? *(Chap 9, Class-XI, Old NCERT)*

(a) The Buddha's followers came from upper caste only.
(b) The Buddhist text Abhidhamma Pitaka contains teaching of Buddha.
(c) Buddhism in starting was involved in meta physical realities and ignored the worldly problems.
(d) Buddha in his lifetime tried to fight, evil by goodness and hatred by love.

Ans. (d)

Exp. Statement (d) is correct regarding Buddhism. The personality of the Buddha and the method adopted by him to preach his religion helped the spread of Buddhism. He tried to fight evil by goodness and hatred by love. He refused to be provoked by slander and abuse. He used his presence of mind and wit.

Statements (a) (b) and (c) are incorrect because Buddha's followers came from lower and different sections also. *Abhidhamma Pitaka* contains philosophical doctrines. Buddhism wasn't concerned with metaphysical realities, it dealt with worldly issues and sufferings.

35 '*Anda, harmika, yashti* and *chhatri*' are integral part of, which one of the following Buddhist monuments? *(Chap 4, Class-XII, New NCERT)*

(a) Chaityas (b) Viharas
(c) Stupas (d) Basadis

Ans. (c)

Exp. '*Anda, harmika, yashti* and *chhatri*' are integral part of stupas.

Stupas were a simple semi-circular mound of Earth, later called *Anda*. Gradually, it evolved into a more complex structure, balancing round and square shapes. Above the *Anda* was the *Harmika*, balcony-like structure that represented the abode of the gods. Arising from the *harmika* was a mast called the *yashti*, often surmounted by a *Chhatri* or umbrella. Around the mound was a railing, separating the sacred space from the secular world.

36 With reference to inclusion of women in the Buddhist Sangha, which of the following statements is/are correct? *(Chap 4, Class-XII, New NCERT)*

1. On the mediation of Ananda, Buddha allowed women into the Sangha.
2. The foster mother of Buddha, Mahapajapati Gautami was the first women to be ordained as a bhikkhuni.

Codes

(a) Only 1 (b) Only 2
(c) Both 1 and 2 (d) Neither 1 nor 2

Ans. (c)

Exp. Both the statements (1) and (2) are correct regarding inclusion of women in the Buddhist *Sangha*. Initially, only men were allowed into the Sangha, but later women also came to be admitted.

According to Buddhist texts, this was made possible through the mediation of Ananda, one of the Buddha's dearest disciples, who persuaded him to allow women into the Sangha. The Buddha's foster mother, Mahapajapati Gautami was the first woman to be ordained as a *bhikkhuni*.

37 The followers of, which one of the following religious sects created a new hybrid Sanskrit by mixing Pali with Sanskrit? *(Chap 9, Class-XI, Old NCERT)*

(a) Hinduism (b) Jainism
(c) Buddhism (d) Ajivika

Ans. (c)

Exp. The followers of Buddhism created a new hybrid Sanskrit by mixing Pali with Sanskrit. In the first three centuries of the Christian Era, by mixing Pali with Sanskrit, the Buddhists created a new language, which is called Hybrid Sanskrit.

38 Consider the following features. *(Chap-10, Class-XI, Old NCERT) (IAS Pre 2019)*

1. Deification of the Buddha
2. Trading the path of Bodhisattvas
3. Image worship and rituals

Which of the above is/are the features of Mahayana Buddhism?

(a) Only 1 (b) 1 and 2 (c) 2 and 3 (d) 1, 2 and 3

Ans. (d)

Exp. All of the given features (1), (2) and (3) are of Mahayana Buddhism.

The two sect of Buddhism emerged after the fourth Buddhist Council convened by Kushan King, Kanishka in first century AD. Mahayana sect 1. Mahayana, 2. Hinayana characterised by worship of Buddha as God, image worship and conducting rituals. This sect also believed in the idea of the Bodhisattvas and followers were encouraged to follow the path of *Bodhisattva* in order to attain enlightenment.

39 Consider the following statements with reference to the religious history of India. *(Chap 10, Class-XI, Old NCERT) (IAS Pre 2016)*

1. The concept of Bodhisattva is central to Hinayana sect of Buddhism.
2. Bodhisattva is a compassionate one on his way to enlightenment.
3. Bodhisattva delays achieving his salvation to help all sentient beings on their path to it.

Which of the statements given above is/are correct?

(a) Only 1 (b) 2 and 3 (c) Only 2 (d) 1, 2 and 3

Ans. (b)

Exp. Statements (2) and (3) are correct with reference to the religious history of India. In Buddhism, *Bodhisattva* is considered as a compassionate one who is on his way to enlightenment. Once they attained enlightenment, they could live in complete isolation and meditate in peace.

However, instead of doing that, they remained in the world to teach and help other people. Thus, they delay achieving his own salvation to help all sentient beings on their path to it.

Statement (1) is incorrect because the concept of *Bodhisattva* is central to *Mahayana* sect of Buddhism.

40 In order to make his followers correctly understand the meaning of life, Buddha preached four noble truths. Arrange these noble truths in correct chronology from the codes given below. *(Chap 3, Class-IX, Old NCERT), (UPPSC Pre 2006)*

1. The cause of suffering is desire.
2. There is suffering in this world.
3. This suffering has a cause.
4. It is possible to put an end to suffering if desires are removed.

Codes

(a) 1, 2, 3, 4
(b) 2, 3, 4, 1
(c) 2, 3, 1, 4
(d) 3, 1, 2, 4

Ans. (c)

Exp. The correct chronology of noble truth taught by Buddha is as follows

There is suffering in the world, This suffering has a cause, The cause of suffering is desire, It is possible to put an end to suffering if desires are removed.

41 Which of the following was/were included in the Code of Conduct devised by the Gautama Buddha for his followers? *(Chap 9, Class-XI, Old NCERT)*

1. Do not covet the properties of the others.
2. Do not commit violence.
3. Do not speak a lie.
4. Do not take foreign voyages.

Codes

(a) 1 and 2 (b) 2, 3 and 4
(c) 1, 3 and 4 (d) 1, 2 and 3

Ans. (d)

Exp. Options (1), (2) and (3) are included in the Code of Conduct that Buddha laid down for his followers. The main items in this conduct are

Do not covet the properties of others, Do not commit violence, Do not use intoxicants, Do not speak a lie, Do not indulge in corrupt practices.

However, Code of Conduct didn't prohibit foreign voyages.

42 Which among the following Buddhist texts declared the cattle to be giver of food, beauty and happiness and pleaded for their protection? *(Chap 9, Class-XI, Old NCERT)*

(a) Sutta Nipata (b) Vinay Pitaka
(c) Abhidhamma Pitaka (d) Dipavamsa

Ans. (a)

Exp. The Buddhist text, *Sutta Nipata* declared the cattle to be giver of food, beauty and happiness and pleaded for its protection. *Sutta Nipata* is collection of more than 10000 teachings of Buddha of his close companions. It was originally written in Pali language.

With its emphasis on non-violence and sanctity of the animal life, Buddhism boosted the cattle wealth of the country.

43 Match the following lists correctly and choose the correct code. *(Chap 4, Class-XII, New NCERT)*

List I (Religious Symbolism in Buddhism)	List II (Meanings)
A. Empty seat	1. Enlightenment of Buddha
B. Wheel	2. Meditation of Buddha
C. Stupa	3. Mahaparinibbana
D. Bodhi trees	4. First sermon of Buddha

Codes
	A	B	C	D		A	B	C	D
(a)	1	2	3	4	(b)	2	4	3	1
(c)	2	1	4	3	(d)	3	1	4	2

Ans. (b)

Exp. The correct matching is A-2, B-4, C-3, D-1

Empty seat In Buddhism the empty seat is used to symbolise the meditation of the Buddha.

Wheel The symbol of wheel was used to indicate the first sermon of Buddha delivered at Sarnath.

Stupa In Buddhism, the symbol of Stupa is associated with Mahaparinibbana i.e. renunciation of the world by Buddha.

Bodhi tree Buddha attained enlightenment under the Bodhi tree in Bodh Gaya in Bihar. So, Bodhi tree is used to refer to the enlightenment of the Buddha.

44 Consider the following statements regarding causes of the decline of Buddhism in India. *(Chap 9, Class-XI, Old NCERT)*

1. From the first century AD onwards, they practised idol worship on large scale and received numerous offerings from devotees.
2. The enormous wealth of the monasteries with women living in them led to further degeneration of Buddhism in India.
3. It is characterised by establishment of seat of learning at Nalanda and Vikramshila .

Which of the statements given above are correct?

(a) 1 and 2 (b) 2 and 3 (c) 1 and 3 (d) 1, 2 and 3

Ans. (a)

Exp. Statements (1) and (2) are correct regarding the causes of the decline of Buddhism in India.

The decline of Buddhism started as the evils of Brahmanism seeped into it. Some monks started to treat Buddha as God and worship his idols and statues.

They started to take donations and offerings from devotees and turned into ease-loving people.

Monks started to see women as object of lust. Allowing of women in monasteries, which was done by mediation of disciple Ananda, led to further degeneration of Buddhism.

Statement (3) is incorrect because the development of schools of learning at Nalanda and Vikramshila was the characteristic of rise of Buddhsim as it to expansion of Buddhism.

Sect of Buddhism

45 With reference to the Spread of Buddhism, consider the following statements. *(Class XI, Old NCERT)*

1. Mahayana spread to Sri Lanka and Burma.
2. Hinayana spread to China and Japan.
3. Vikramshila University in Bihar was an important centre of Vajrayana Buddhism.

How many statements given above is/are correct with reference to the spread of Buddhism?

(a) Only one (b) Only two
(c) All three (d) None of these

Ans. (a)

Exp. Only one statement i.e., (3) is correct with reference to the spread of Buddhism.

The Vikramshila University in Bihar was an important centre of Vajrayana Buddhism. By the end of Gupta period, Vajrayana emerged. It was popular in Bengal and Bihar.

Statements (1) and (2) are incorrect because Mahayana or the Great vehicle became popular and influential in India. Mahayana spread to China and Japan.

Hinayana or the lesser vehicle became popular in Sri Lanka, Burma, Thailand and other South-East Asian countries.

46 Which one of the following is the most fundamental difference between Mahayana Buddhism and Hinayana Buddhism? *(Chap 9, Class-XI, Old NCERT) (IAS Pre 1994)*

(a) Emphasis on ahimsa
(b) Casteless society
(c) Worship of gods and goddesses
(d) Worship of stupa

Ans. (c)

Exp. The most fundamental difference between Mahayana and Hinayana Buddhism is the worship of gods and goddesses. Mahayana or 'great vehicle' believes in the heavenliness of Buddha and Idol worship of Buddhas and Bodhisattvas embodying Buddha nature. Hinayana are deficient vehicle, abandoned vehicle or defective vehicle. It believes in the original teaching of Buddha or Doctrine of elders. It does not believe in Idol worship and tries to attain individual salvation through self-discipline and meditation.

47 In the Mahayana Buddhism, the Bodhisattva Avalokitesvara was also known as *(Class XI, Old NCERT) (IAS Pre 1997)*

(a) Vajrapani (b) Manjusri
(c) Padmapani (d) Maitreya

Ans. (c)

Exp. In the mahayana Bddhism, the Bodisattva Avlaoites vara was alokanown as padmapni lotus bearer. Avalokitesvara (watchful lord) also called Padmapani (Lotus bearer), whose attribute is compassion, which reaches down to Avichi, the lowest Buddha Purgatory. His heaven is Akanishtha, and his Sakti is Tara. Avalokitesvara is given female form in China and Japan.

48 Consider the following statements regarding the contribution of Buddhism in India. *(Chap 9, Class-XI, Old NCERT)*

1. It boosted the animal wealth of the country by forbidding the killing of cattle.
2. They opposed the idol worship and laid emphasis on education of girl child.
3. It taught the people to not to take things for granted but to argue and judge them on the merit.

Which of the statements given above is/are incorrect?

(a) 1 and 2 (b) 2 and 3
(c) Only 2 (d) Only 3

Ans. (c)

Exp. Statement (2) is incorrect regarding the contribution of Buddhism in India because in its early form, Buddhism opposed idol worship but later, they started idol and image worship. It allowed women to be part of Sangha but there was no as such focus on education of girl child.

49 Match the following lists correctly and choose the correct code. *(Chap 9, Class-XI, Old NCERT)*

List I (Places related with Life of Buddha)	List II (Significances)
A. Sarnath	1. Birth
B. Lumbini	2. Enlightenment
C. Kushinagar	3. First Sermon
D. Bodh Gaya	4. Death

Codes

	A	B	C	D		A	B	C	D
(a)	1	2	3	4	(b)	2	1	4	3
(c)	4	2	3	1	(d)	3	1	4	2

Ans. (d)

Exp. The correct matching is A-3, B-1, C-4, D-2

Sarnath Gautama Buddha gave his first sermon in Sarnath near Varaṇasi. It is referred as *Dhammachakraparivartan* and is symbolised through Wheel.

Lumbini Gautama Buddha was born in 563 BC in Lumbini (presently in Nepal) in a Shakya Kshatriya clan.

Kushinagar Gautama Buddha died at the age of 80 in Kushinagar (presently in Uttar Pradesh) in 483 BC. It is referred as *Mahaparinibbana*.

Bodhgaya Gautama Buddha attained enlightenment at the age 35 in Bodh Gaya (presently in Bihar). It is symbolised through Bodhi tree.

50 Match the following lists correctly and choose the correct code. *(Chap 4, Class-XII, New NCERT)*

List I (Terms related with Buddhism)	List II (Meanings)
A. Sangha	1. Righteous path
B. Dhamma	2. Place where relics of Buddha and other monks were placed.
C. Stupas	3. Monastic order
D. Chaityas	4. Place where monks prayed

Codes

	A	B	C	D		A	B	C	D
(a)	1	2	3	4	(b)	2	1	4	3
(c)	4	2	3	1	(d)	3	1	2	4

Ans. (d)

Exp. The correct matching is A-3, B-1, C-2, D-4.

Sangha was a monastic order of monks who lived a life according to code of conduct at bare minimum necessities and with discipline.

Dhamma was teachings and path shown by Buddha. It included eight-fold path, which according to Buddha would lead to attainment of *Nirvana*.

Stupas were architecture of Buddhist period. Here, pictures, sculptures and idols of Buddha and *Bodhisattvas* were placed.

Chaityas were building for monks where they stayed for rest in times of rainy season and prayed.

51 The Buddhist text, which described that the Emperor Ashoka distributed portions of the Buddha's relics to every important town and ordered the construction of stupas over them was *(Chap 4, Class-XII, New NCERT)*

(a) Dipvamsa (b) Buddhaghosha
(c) Ashokavadana (d) Buddhacharita

Ans. (c)

Exp. The Buddhist text was Ashokavadana, which described that the Emperor Ashoka distributed portions of Buddha's relics to every important town and ordered the construction of Stupa over them. The tradition of erecting stupas may have been pre-Buddhist, but they came to be associated with Buddhism.

They contained relics regarded as sacred, the entire stupa came to be venerated as an emblem of both the Buddha and Buddhism.

52 In the Buddhist literature, Sutta and Vinaya Pitaka are considered as the most authentic text for understanding Buddhism. What was the main theme of both of these texts? *(Chap 4, Class-XII, New NCERT)*

(a) Sutta Pitaka consisted of Buddha's teachings and Vinaya Pitaka dealt with rules for maintaining the monastic orders.
(b) Vinaya Pitaka consisted of Buddha's teachings and Sutta Pitaka dealt with rules for maintaining the monastic orders.
(c) Sutta Pitaka comprises Buddha's sayings and Vinaya Pitaka dealt with Buddhist philosophy.
(d) Sutta Pitaka consisted of history of Buddhism in Ceylon (now Sri Lanka) and Vinaya Pitaka consisted of Buddha's teachings.

Ans. (a)

Exp. Statement (a) states the main theme of both of these texts.

Sutta Pitaka was composed of Buddha's teachings. *Vinaya Pitaka* included rules and regulations for those who joined monastic orders or *Sangha*.

Apart from these two *pitakas*, the third pitaka is *Abhidhamma Pitaka*, which dealt with philosophical matters.

53 Which among the following reason(s) helped in spread of Buddhism in Indian subcontinent and beyond? *(Chap 9, Class-XI, Old NCERT)*

1. More liberal and democratic outlook than Brahmanism.
2. The use of classical Indian language, Sanskrit.
3. Organised preaching under the auspices of Sangha.

Codes

(a) 1 and 2
(b) 2 and 3
(c) 1 and 3
(d) 1, 2 and 3

Ans. (c)

Exp. Statements (1) and (3) are correct reasons, which helped in spread of Buddhism in Indian subcontinent and beyond. Buddhism won the support of lower classes, it attacked the Varna system. People were admitted to Buddhist order without considering their castes.

Women were also allowed in *Sangha*. In comparison to Brahmanism, Buddhism was liberal and Gautama Buddha also organised Sangha or the religious order, whose doors were open to everybody. The only condition was that monks faithfully observe the rules and regulations of Sangha. As a result of organised preaching under Sangha, Buddhism made rapid strides.

Statement (2) is incorrect because Buddhism's early teachings were in Pali, which was language of common people.

54 Which among the following ancient rulers of India was/were antagonist to Buddhism and persecuted the followers of Buddhism? *(Chap 9, Class-XI, Old NCERT)*

(a) Pushyamitra Shunga (b) Mihirakula
(c) Shashanka (d) All of these

Ans. (d)

Exp. Pushyamitra Shunga, Mihirakula and Shashanka were ancient rulers, antagonist to Buddhism and persecuted the followers of Buddhism.

Pushyamitra Shunga who founded Shunga dynasty immediately after the fall of Mauryan empire, was supporter of Brahamanism. He persecuted the followers of Buddhism.

Similarly, they were also persecuted by the Huna king, Mihirakula.

The Shaivite Shashanka of Gauda (Bengal) cut-off Bodhi tree at Bodh Gaya, where Buddha had attained enlightenment.

55 Many of the Greeks, Kushans and Shakas embraced Buddhism rather than Hinduism because *(Chap 15, Class-XI, Old NCERT), (IAS Pre 1998)*

(a) Buddhism was in the ascendant at that time.
(b) They had renounced the policy of war and violence.
(c) Caste- ridden Hinduism did not attack them.
(d) Buddhism provided easier access to Indian society.

Ans. (d)

Exp. Statement (d) is correct with reference to the reason behind Kushans and Shakas embraced Buddhism rather than Hinduism. Many of the Greeks, Kushans and Shakas embraced Buddhism rather than Hinduism because Buddhism provided easier access to Indian society.

56 Which of the following can be regarded as the chief contribution of Buddhism to India? *(Class XI, Old NCERT) (IAS Pre 1985)*

(a) Art and literature
(b) Architecture
(c) Ahimsa and self purification
(d) Rituals

Ans. (c)

Exp. Statement (c) is Ahimsa and self-purification can be regarded as the chief contribution of Buddhism to India. Buddhism was emerged as reaction to Brahmanical rituals. Buddha discarded the Vedic religion in its totality.

He strongly opposed rituals, sacrifices and ceremonial worship Art and architecture mainly limited to Stupas in Buddhism and were not extraordinary. Buddha emphasised Ahimsa, by his love for human beings and all living creatures, he endeared himself to all. His religion was identical with morality and it emphasised purity of thought, word and deed. Buddha laid emphasis on self effort or self-sufficiency, i.e, one who looks unto himself.

Chapter 06

Mahajanapadas

Mahajanapadas

Emergence of Mahajanapadas

Sixteen Mahajanapadas

- Important city/states These were either kingdoms or republics. Emerged in 6th century AD. Total 16 in number

Mahajanapada	Capital	Present Day
Anga	Champa	Bhagalpur (Bihar)
Asmaka	Paithan	Telangana/ Maharashtra
Avanti	Mahismati and Ujjaini	Malwa (MP)
Chedi	Suktamati	Bundelkhand
Gandhara	Taxila	North-Wester frontier region (Pakistan)
Kashi	Kashi	Banaras (UP)
Kamboja	Rajapura	Afghanistan and Pakistan
Kosala	Shravasti	Eastern UP
Kuru	Indraprastha	Delhi and Meerut region
Magadha	Rajgriha and Patliputra	Bihar
Malla	Kushinagar and Pava	Eastern UP
Matsya	Viratnagar	Jaipur (Rajasthan)
Panchala	Ahichatra and Kampilya	UP
Surasena	Mathura	UP
Vajji	Vaishali	Bihar & (Nepal)
Vatsa	Kaushambi	UP

Foreign Invasion

Foreign Invasion

- **Iranian/Persian Invasion**
- In 516 BC, Achaemenian ruler Darius annexed parts of Punjab and Sindh
- Indian soldiers formed part of Achaemenid army who conquered Greece
- **Effects** Introduction of Aramaic form of writing, promotion of Indo-Iranian trade and fusion of Persian art
- **Greek Invasion**
- In 4th century BC, conquered North-Western part under Alexander
- **Effects** Opened trade route between Asia and Europe
- Fusion of Greek art, many Greek scholars came to India and disintegration of North-West India led to expansion of Mauryan empire

Battle of Hydaspes

- The Battle of Hydaspes was fought between Alexander the Great and King Porus in 326 BC. The Battle took place on the banks of the Jhelum river; which was known as Hydaspes to ancient Greeks
- In the battle, Porus surrendered and the Alexander emerged victorious
- After the battle, the Alexander was deeply impressed by the bravery and resistance by Porus and made Porus his satraps (Viceroy to the king)

Important Dynasties of Magadha

Haryanka Dynasty

- First to rule in the Magadha
- Founded by Bimbisara
- **Bimbisara** Contemporary of Gautama Buddha
- Defeated Anga and established matrimonial relation with Kosala, Lichchavi and Madra clan
- **Ajatashatru** Killed father Bimbisara
- Defeated Prasenjit (King of Kosala) and Lichchavi king. Convened First Buddhist Council
- **Udayin** Successor of Ajatashatru; Shifted capital from Rajgriha to Pataliputra

Shishunag Dynasty

- Established by Shishunaga who also conquered Avanti
- Magadha become the sole super Mahajanapada
- He was succeded by kalashoka
- Kalashoka shifted capital from Vaishali to Pataliputra and convened Second Buddhist Council

Nanda Dynasty

- Considered as first empire builders of India
- Defeated the Kalinga
- Prominent ruler Mahapadmananda
- Dhanananda was the last ruler of Nanda dynasty and was replaced by Chandragupta Maurya, who established Mauryan Dynasty

SOURCE *New NCERT Class VI (Kingdoms, Kings and Early Republics), Old NCERT Class VI (India from 600 BC to 400 BC), Old NCERT Class IX (Early Iron-Age Civilisation), New NCERT Class XI (State and Varna society in the Age of Buddha), New NCERT Class XI (Kings, Farmers and Towns), Old NCERT Class XI (Territorial States and First Magadhan Empire), New NCERT Class XII (Kinship, Caste, Class) Tamil Nadu Board Class XI (Rise of Territorial Kingdom), NIOS Module-1 (From Janpadas to Empire)*

The Sixteen Mahajanapadas

1 With respect to rise of territorial kingdom after Vedic age, consider the following statements.

(Unit 3, Class XI, Tamil Nadu Board)

1. Indo-Aryans began migrating Eastwards from about 1000 BC.
2. Wide spread use of iron provided impetus for urbanisation.
3. A spirit of scepticism developed that questioned orthodoxy in the belief system.

How many statements given above is/are correct?

(a) Only one (b) Only two
(c) All three (d) None of these

Ans. (c)

Exp. All three statements i.e., (1) (2) and (3) are correct with reference to the rise of the territorial kingdom after Vedic age.

Aryans began migrating Eastwards from about 1000 BC. As they moved Eastward, they encountered thick forests. Iron played a significant role in clearing the forests. The fertile soil of the Gangetic valley and the use of iron ploughshare improved agricultural productivity.This in turn, paved the way for urbanisation.

A spirit of scepticism began to pervade questioning every custom and orthodoxy in the belief system in the society leading to rise of new ideas and faiths.

2 With reference to formation of Mahajanapadas, consider the following statements.

(Class XI, Old NCERT)

1. Period between 1000-600 BC witnessed the transition from a tribal polity from lineage to a territorial state.
2. Mahajanapada had all elements of a state except sovereignty.
3. All Mahajanapada are classified as chiefdoms.

How many statements given above is/are correct?

(a) Only one (b) Only two
(c) All three (d) None of these

Ans. (b)

Exp. Only two statements i.e., (1) and (2) are correct with reference to formation of Mahajanapadas.

The later Vedic period (1000-600 BC) witnessed the transition from a tribal polity based on lineage to a territorial state. The Janas who migrated Eastwards began to settle down in various regions. The loyalty of people shifted from Jana(tribe or clan) to Janapada(territory). Some Mahajanapadas had all the elements of state i.e., territory, people, government except sovereignty. The Mahajanapadas represented the emergence of territorial kingdoms that ruled over people (Jana).

Statement (3) is incorrect because, not all Mahajanapadas were classified as chiefdoms. The Mahajanapadas are classified as Gana Sanghas and chiefdoms based on the nature of their polity. based on the nature of their polity.

3 Consider the following statements.

(Chap 10, Class-XI, Old NCERT)

1. Vatsa Mahajanapada was formed by the members of Kuru clan who had shifted from Hastinapur and settled down at Kaushambi near Allahabad.
2. The tribal republic of Kapilavastu was part of Kamboja Mahajanapada.
3. Kusinara was the capital of Malla Mahajanapada.

Which of the statements given above is/are incorrect?

(a) 1 and 2 (b) 2 and 3 (c) Only 2 (d) Only 3

Ans. (c)

Exp. Statement (2) is incorrect because tribal republic of Kapilavastu was part of Kosala Mahajanapada. The capital of Kapilavastu has been identified with Piprahwa in Basti district of Uttar Pradesh.

4 Identify the Mahajanapada with the help of statements given below. *(Chap 10, Class-XI, Old NCERT)*

1. It was divided into two parts; the Northern part with its capital at Ujjain and the Southern part with its capital at Mahishmati.
2. It specialised in the smelting and production of iron.
3. Chand Pradoyta was its most famous ruler.

Codes

(a) Magadha (b) Avanti
(c) Anga (d) Panchala

Ans. (b)

Exp. The Mahajanapada mentioned in the given statements is Avanti. In Central Malwa (Rajasthan and Madhya Pradesh border areas) lay the state of Avanti. It was divided into two parts.

The Northern part had its capital at Ujjain and the Southern part at Mahishmati (both Ujjain and Mahishmati in Madhya Pradesh). It had large scale working in iron and erected strong fortification. Magadha was most serious rival of Avanti.

Its king Chand Pradyota Mahasena fought Bimbisara, but they later became friends.

5 Match the following lists correctly and choose the correct code.

(Chap 10, Class-XI, Old NCERT) (UPPSC Pre 2020)

List I (Mahajanapadas)	List II (Capitals)
A. Matsya	1. Mathura
B. Kuru	2. Potali
C. Surasena	3. Viratnagar
D. Asmaka	4. Indraprastha

Codes

	A	B	C	D		A	B	C	D
(a)	1	2	3	4	(b)	2	3	4	1
(c)	4	2	3	1	(d)	3	4	1	2

Ans. (d)

Exp. The correct matching is A-3, B-4, C-1, D-2.

Matsya Mahajanapada was situated in the region adjoining modern-day Rajasthan. Viratnagar was its capital.

Kuru Mahanjanapada was situated in the region adjoining modern day Western Uttar Pradesh and Delhi. Its capital was Indraprastha.

Surasena Mahajanapada covered the modern day territories of Braj Region of Uttar Pradesh. Its capital was Mathura.

Asmak Mahajanapada was the Southernmost among all the sixteen Mahajanapadas. It was located on the bank of Godavari river with its capital at Potali or Paithan.

6 With reference to Mahajanapadas, consider the following statements. *(Class XI, Old NCERT)*

1. Polity of Vajji Mahajanapada could be classified as oligarchy.
2. Mahajanpada and the ruling clan have references in the epic Mahabharata.
3. Priestly class enjoyed a preeminent status equally both Mahajanapadas and Gana-sanghas.

How many statements given above is/are incorrect?

(a) Only one (b) Only two
(c) All three (d) None of these

Ans. (a)

Exp. Only one statement i.e., (3) is incorrect with reference to Mahajanapadas.

The priestly class enjoyed a pre eminent status in the Mahajanapadas unlike in the Gana-sanghas. The Brahman priests provided legitimacy to the king through various rituals.

7 With reference to Mahajanapadas, consider the following statements. *(Chap 2, Class-XII, New NCERT)*

1. In Ancient India, Dharmasutras laid down the norms for Kshatriya as well as for other social categories.
2. During the Mahajanapada period, Ujjain was known as Mahishmati.
3. Amatyas were ministers who helped the king in performance of their duties

How many statements given above is/are incorrect?

(a) Only one (b) Only two
(c) All three (d) None of these

Ans. (a)

Exp. Only one statement i.e., (2) is incorrect with reference to Mahajanapadas because during the period of Mahajanapada, Ujjain was known as Avantika. It was one of the capital of Avanti Mahajanapada.

8 With reference to socio-political structure of Mahajanapadas, consider the following statements. *(Class XI, Old NCERT)*

1. Kassakas were the richer landowner who employed labourers called dasas.
2. A new social category that emerged which was considered untouchables had their own language.
3. Bali was a voluntary contribution based on the amount of surplus produced.

How many statements given above is/are correct?

(a) Only one (b) Only two (c) All three (d) None of these

Ans. (a)

Exp. Only one statement i.e., (2) is correct with reference to the socio-political structure of Mahajanapadas.

A new social category that emerged during the period of Mahajanapadas was placed below the Shudras in the social hierarchy and considered untouchables. They were forced to live on the fringes of the settlements and subsisted on hunting and gathering their food.

Statements (1) and (3) are incorrect because the smaller landowners were known as Kassakas or Krishakas. The richest landowners were called grahapatis. Bali was not a voluntary tax rather it was a tax imposed based on the area of cultivable land.

9 Some of the Mahajanapadas were governed by oligarchy. It means *(Chap 2, Class-XII, New NCERT)*

(a) form of government, where people elected their rulers.
(b) form of government, where power is exercised by group of men.
(c) form of government, where priestly class ruled the state.
(d) form of government, where governance is carried out through popular assemblies.

Ans. (b)

Exp. Some of the Mahajanapadas were governed by oligarchy. It means a form of government, where power is exercised by group of men. Sakya of Kapilavastu and Vajji Sangha were some of the powerful oligarchies in the Mahajanapada era. The kings of each clan were known as *Raja* and they were jointly responsible for administration.

10 Which type of the pottery was the chief distinctive feature of the age of Mahajanapada? *(Chap 10, Class-XI, Old NCERT)*

(a) Northern Black Polished Ware (NBPW)
(b) Black and Red Ware (BRW)
(c) Painted Grey Ware (PGW)
(d) Ochre Coloured Pottery (OCP)

Ans. (a)

Exp. Northern Black Polished Ware (NBPW) was the chief distinctive feature of the age of Mahajanapada. It marked the second phase of urbanisation in India. They have been found in towns of Kaushambi, Shravasti, Ayodhya, Kapilavastu, Varanasi, Rajgir, Pataliputra and Champa. And in each case show signs of habitation and mud structures belonging to this phase.

11 In the Mahajanapadas, taxes on crops was most important. It was *(Chap 5, Class-VI, New NCERT)*

(a) 1/6th of the produce (b) 1/3rd of the produce
(c) 1/4th of the produce (d) 1/5th of the produce

Ans. (a)

Exp. In the Mahajanapadas, taxes on crops was most important and it was 1/6th of the produce. As the kings in Mahajanapadas started having armies and fortifying the cities, they started collecting taxes.

Taxes on crops were the most important as most people were farmers. Usually, the tax was fixed at 1/6th of what was produced and was known as *bhaga* or a share.

12 **The port of Bhrigukachchha played an important role in trading of goods from the Mahajanapadas. It is identical to modern day** *(Chap 6, Class-XI, Old NCERT)*

(a) Broach
(b) Kandla
(c) Mumbai
(d) Haldia

Ans. (a)

Exp. Bhrigukachchha port of Mahajanapada is identical to modern day as Broach (Bharuch) in Gujarat.

Trade in Mahajanapadas was not limited to a small area. Goods produced in the Ganga valley were sent across the Punjab to Taxila or across the Vindhya mountains to the port of Broach (Bhrigukachchha) from where it went to Western Asia or to South India.

13 **With reference to the socio-political structure of Mahajanapada, consider the following statements.** *(Chap 12, Class-XI, Old NCERT)*

1. Kammakaras in the Mahajanapada period were private spies of the kings.
2. Nishka and Satamana were the coins used during the Mahajanapada era.

Which of the statements given above is/are correct?

(a) Only 1
(b) Only 2
(c) Both 1 and 2
(d) Neither 1 nor 2

Ans.(b)

Exp. Only statement (2) is correct with reference to socio-political structure of the Mahajanapada.

The term 'Nishka' and Satamana referred in texts written during Mahajanapada era denoted coins.

Statement (1) is incorrect because Kammakaras in the Mahajanapada period were the landless agricultural labourers.

14 **Consider the following statements regarding the system of coinage in the Mahajanapada era.** *(Chap 12, Class-XI, Old NCERT)*

1. Gold coins were widely used for trade and commerce.
2. The earliest coins were largely made of silver and copper.

Which of the statements given above is/are correct?

(a) Only 1
(b) Only 2
(c) Both 1 and 2
(d) Neither 1 nor 2

Ans. (b)

Exp. Statement (2) is correct regarding the system of coinage in the Mahajanapada era. During the sixth century BC, the Central and Eastern India saw the period of second urbanisation characterised by the growth of trade and commerce. It led to the demand of introduction of coinage on the wide scale. For this Punch marked coins were introduced.

They were mostly made up of silver, though copper coins were also in circulation.

Statement (1) is incorrect because gold coins were first introduced in India in first century AD by the Kushan rulers.

15 **Consider the following statements regarding state of agriculture during the Mahajanapada era.** *(Chap 12, Class-XI, Old NCERT)*

1. Rice was the staple cereal produced in the Eastern Uttar Pradesh and Bihar.
2. All the village land was owned by the king who allotted to the families for producing crops.
3. Farmers also cultivated cotton, which was used for producing clothes.

Which of the statements given above is/are incorrect?

(a) 1 and 2
(b) 2 and 3
(c) Only 2
(d) Only 3

Ans. (c)

Exp. Statement (2) is incorrect regarding state of agriculture during the Mahajanapada era because the lands were owned by people but were divided into cultivable plots and allotted family-wise.

16 **Consider the following Assertion (A) and Reason (R) and choose the correct code.** *(Chap 12, Class-XI, Old NCERT)*

Assertion (A) The earliest coins made during the age of Mahajanapada were called Punchmarked coins.

Reason (R) The piece of the metals used in producing this type of coins were punched with the certain marks such as hills, trees, fish, bulls, etc.

Codes

(a) Both A and R are true and R is the correct explanation of A.
(b) Both A and R are true, but R is not the correct explanation of A.
(c) A is true, but R is false.
(d) A is false, but R is true.

Ans. (a)

Exp. Both Assertion (A) and Reason (R) are true and Reason (R) is the correct explanation of Assertion (A).

The earliest coins were called Punch marked because pieces of these metals were punched with certain marks such as bulls, elephant, tree, hills, crescent, etc.

They are usually found to be made of silver but few have also found of copper. They first start to appear around sixth century BC in age of Gautama Buddha.

17 **With reference to justice delivery in Mahajanapada, consider the following statements.**

(Chap 12, Class-XI, Old NCERT)

1. The civil and criminal laws during the age of Mahajanapada were based on the Varna division.
2. It was administered by the royal agents.
3. Punishment for the criminal offences were governed by the idea of rehabilitation.

How many statements given above is/are correct?

(a) Only one (b) Only two
(c) All three (d) None of these

Ans. (b)

Exp. Only two statements i.e., (1) and (2) are correct with reference to justice delivery in the Mahajanapadas.

The civil and criminal law during the age of Mahajanapada were based on the idea of division of Varna. Dharmasutras laid down duties of each Varna. The higher the Varna, the purer it was and higher was the order of moral conduct expected by civil and criminal law. In Mahajanapadas, justice and law was delivered and administered by royal agents, who inflected harsh punishment.

Statement (3) is incorrect as in Mahajanapada the punishment was based on the idea of revenge and not rehabilitation.

18 **Consider the following statements about the state of society during the Mahajanapada age.**

(Chap 12, Class-XI, Old NCERT)

1. Non-vedic tribal people were gradually absorbed into the Brahmanical social order.
2. Sudras were deprived of the religious and legal rights and relegated to the lowest position in the society.
3. Peasants were categorised as Shudras.

Which of the statements given above are correct?

(a) 1 and 2
(b) 2 and 3
(c) 1 and 3
(d) 1, 2 and 3

Ans. (a)

Exp. Statements (1) and (2) are correct about the state of society during the Mahajanapada age.

Although the Brahmanical law books took into account the social status of the different Varnas in framing law, they did not ignore the customs of the non-vedic tribal groups, which gradually absorbed into the Brahmanical social order, which went on expanding as a result of conquests.

Sudras who were accorded lowest position in Varna based social order were deprived of the religious and legal rights and relegated to the lowest position in the society

Statement (3) is incorrect bacause peasants were categorised as Vaishyas (not Shudras).

Magadha Empire

19 **The following maps shows four of the Sixteen Mahajanapadas that existed in ancient India. The place marked A,B,C and D respectively are**

(Unit 3, Class-XI, Tamil Nadu Board) (UPSC Pre 1997)

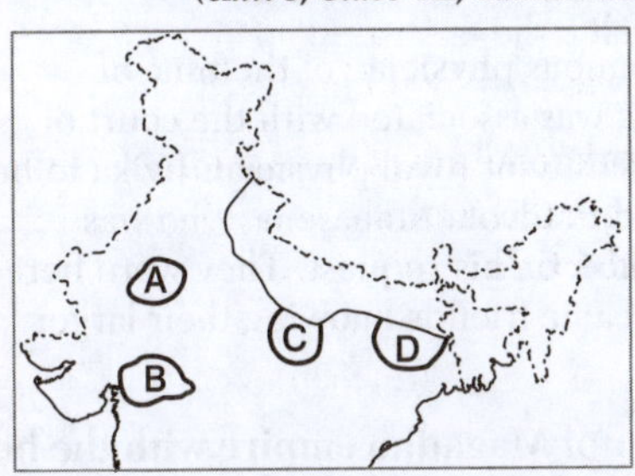

(a) Matsya, Chedi, Kosala, Anga
(b) Surasena, Avanti, Vatsa, Magadha
(c) Matsya, Avanti, Vatsa, Anga
(d) Surasena, Chedi, Kosala, Magadha

Ans. (c)

Exp. Option (c) is correct with reference to the Sixteen Mahajanapadas that existed in ancient India. Capital of Matsya Mahajanapada was Viratnagar, in present day Rajasthan. Capital of Avanti was Mahishmati and Ujjaini, in present day Malwa region of Madhiya Pradesh. Capital of Vatsa was Kaushambi in present day Uttar Pradesh and capital of Anga was Champa in present day Bhagalpur and Munger.

22 Mahajanapadas are mentioned in Ashtadhyayi of Panini. 16 Mahajanapadas are mentioned in Anguttara Nikaya of Sutta Pitaka.

20 **With reference to Magadha empire, consider the following statements.** *(Chap 5, Module-1, NIOS)*

1. Bimbisara was the contemporary of only Gautama Buddha and not Lord Mahavira.
2. Rich availability of Iron gave Magadha an advantage over other Janapada.
3. Capitals of the Magadha empire were vulnerable due to their geographical locations.

How many statements given above is/are incorrect?

(a) Only one (b) Only two
(c) All three (d) None of these

Ans. (b)

Exp. Only two statements i.e., (1) and (3) are incorrect with reference to the Magadha empire.

Bimbisara was the contemporary of both Mahavira and Buddha. Magadha came into prominence under his leadership, who belonged to the Haryanka dynasty.

Capitals, Rajgir and Pataliputra, of the Magadha empire were not vulnerable due to their geographical locations. Position of these capitals were invulnerable because of their geographical location. For instance, Pataliputara was surrounded by rivers on almost all sides.

21 Jivaka, the famous physician of the time of Mahatma Buddha, was associated with the court of *(Chap 10, Class-XI, Old NCERT) (UP UDA/LDA Pre 2006)*

(a) Bimbisara (b) Chand Pradyota
(c) Prasenjit (d) Udayin

Ans. (a)

Exp. Jivaka, the famous physician of the time of Mahatma Buddha, was associated with the court of Bimbisara. Bimbisara sent royal physician Jivika to help Avanti king Chand Pradyota Mahasena, who was attacked by jaundice, on his request. They were fierce rivals but later became friends knowing their larger interests.

22 Identify the ruler of Magadha empire with the help of statements given below. *(Chap 10, Class-XI, Old NCERT)*

1. He killed his father and seized the throne for himself.
2. Throughout his reign, he followed the aggressive policy of the expansion.
3. Under his reign, the Magadha capital Rajgir was fortified.

Codes

(a) Udayin (b) Mahapadma Nanda
(c) Ajatashatru (d) Bimbisara

Ans. (c)

Exp. The ruler of Magadha empire discussed in the given statements was Ajatashatru. He killed his father Bimbisara and took throne for himself and succeeded as King of Magadha.

He fought two wars and made preparation for third. Throughout his reign, he pursued an aggressive policy of expansion.

To avoid the danger of Avanti and face the invasion of Magadha by Avanti, he fortified the capital, Rajgir (Bihar). The walls of fortification can still be seen. The invasion did not happen in his lifetime.

23 Identify the ruler of Magadha empire with the help of statements given below. *(Chap 10, Class-XI, Old NCERT)*

1. He adopted the title of 'Ekrat', the sole monarch.
2. He acquired territories of Kalinga and Kosala.
3. He brought an image of 'Jina' from the Kalinga as victory trophy.

Codes

(a) Udayin (b) Mahapadma Nanda
(c) Ajatashatru (d) Bimbisara

Ans. (b)

Exp. The given statements refer to the Magadha King, Mahapadma Nanda. He was the founder of Nanda kingdom of the Magadha empire in fourth century BC and is considered as the most powerful rulers of the Magadha empire. He after defeating and uprooting many Kshatriya kings adopted the title of *Ekrat* i.e. the sole monarch.

During his reign, the territories of Kalinga and Kosala were annexed and made part of Magadha empire. After defeating the ruler of Kalinga, he brought an image of *Jina* from the Kalinga as victory trophy.

24 Match the following lists correctly and choose the correct code. *(Chap 10, Class-XI, Old NCERT)*

List I (Kings)	List II (Associated with)
A. Bimbisara	1. Married with Lichchhavi, Princess of Vaishali
B. Ajatashatru	2. Annexed the republic of Vaishali
C. Chand Pradyota Mahesena	3. King of Avanti
D. Mahapadma Nanda	4. Most powerful ruler of Magadha

Codes

	A	B	C	D		A	B	C	D
(a)	1	2	3	4	(b)	2	3	4	1
(c)	4	2	3	1	(d)	3	1	4	2

Ans. (a)

Exp. The correct matching is A-1, B-2, C-3, D-4.

Bimbisara had three wives. His second wife was Chellana who was a Lichchhavi who gave birth to Ajatashatru.

Ajatashatru had no respect for relations. Although, his mother was a Lichchhavi princess, he attacked Vaishali and annexed it.

Chand Pradyota Mahasena was king of Avanti, with its capital at Ujjain, in times of Bimbisara. They were rival.

Mahapadma Nand*a* was most powerful ruler of Magadha. He added Kalinga and Kosala to Magadha empire.

25 Consider the following Assertion (A) and Reason (R) and choose the correct code. *(Chap 10, Class-XI, Old NCERT)*

Assertion (A) The surplus agricultural production underlies the growth of Magadha empire.

Reason (R) The Magadha empire lay at the centre of the middle Gangetic plain.

Codes

(a) Both A and R are true and R is the correct explanation of A.
(b) Both A and R are true, but R is not the correct explanation A.
(c) A is true, but R is false.
(d) A is false, but R is true.

Ans. (a)

Exp. Both Assertion (A) and Reason (R) are true and Reason (R) is the correct explanation of Assertion (A). The area of Magadha was at centre of middle Gangetic plains, which made the area far more productive than the areas to the West of Allahabad. This led to more produce, which came to kings in form of taxes and it resulted in success of Magadha as an empire.

26 With reference to reign of Bimbisara, consider the following statements. *(Class XI, Old NCERT)*

1. In his reign, village headmen were permitted to directly speak with the king.
2. Conquest and defeat of Anga,Kashi, Avanti became the launching pad for expansion of Magadha.
3. Under the policy of Matrimonial alliance, he married the sister of King of Vajji.

How many statements given above is/are incorrect?

(a) Only one (b) Only two
(c) All three (d) None of these

Ans. (b)

Exp. Only two statements i.e., (2) and (3) are incorrect with reference to the reign of Bimbisara.

Bimbisara didn't acquire Kashi as a result of conquest; rather it was brought in dowry by the sister of King Kosala, with whom Bimbisara married, under his policy of Matrimonial alliance. The Shishunaga dynasty and not Bimbisara is credited with the conquest and defeat of Avanti (Malwa) making it a part of Magdha.

27 With reference to Magadha empire, consider the following statements. *(Class XI, Old NCERT)*

1. Hathigumpha inscription is indicative of the geographical extent of the Nanda empire.
2. A centralised state was established by Nandas which led to the development of cities.
3. The Nanda dynasty added Kalinga to his empire.

How many statements given above is/are correct?

(a) Only one (b) Only two
(c) All three (d) None of these

Ans. (c)

Exp. All statements i.e., (1), (2) and (3) are correct with reference to the Magadha empire.

An inscription known as the Hathigumpha from Udayagiri near Bhubaneshwar, Odisha is indicative of the geographical extent of the Nanda empire. It records the aqueduct built by King Nanda three hundred years earlier.

Nandas had established a centralised state. A centralised state required a new administrative framework to govern an extensive territory, the creation of a bureaucracy and such political formation led to the development of cities as administrative centers distinct from villages and rural areas.

The Nanda dynasty added Kalinga to the Magadha empire. Mahapadma Nanda defeated and killed the last of the series of the 32 Kshatriya kings and incorporated Kalinga to his extensive empire.

28 With reference to centre of learning during Magadha empire, consider the following statements. *(Chap 10, Class-XI, Old NCERT)*

1. Panini compiled his Ashtadhyayi here.
2. It was excavated in the 1940s by Sir John Marshall.
3. Between the fifth and fourth century, it was part of the Achaemenid empire of Persia.

Which of the following centers of learning is being suggested from the above statements?

(a) Taxila (b) Bodh Gaya
(c) Ujjain (d) Kosala

Ans. (a)

Exp. Takshashila or Taxila is the correct option with reference to the statements given to identify the centre of learning during the reign of Magadha empire.

Panini seems to have compiled his well-known work, Ashtadhyayi at Taxila. The city of Taxila was brought to light by the excavations carried out in the 1940s by Sir John Marshall. Between the fifth and fourth century, it was part of the Achaemenid empire of Persia.

29 With reference to the socio-political structure of India in 330-320 BC, consider the following statements. *(Chap 10, Class-XI, Old NCERT)*

Statement-I Alexandria near Kabul and Boukephala in Pakistan were some of the prominent Greek settlements.

Statement-II Alexander's invasion led to the establishment of Greek Satrapies in the North-Western region of the Indian subcontinent.

Which one of the following is correct in respect of the above statements?

(a) Both Statement-I and Statement-II are correct and Statement-II is the correct explanation for statement-I.
(b) Both Statement-I and Statement-II are correct and Statement-II is not the correct explanation for Statement-I
(c) Statement-I is correct but Statement-II is incorrect.
(d) Statement-I is incorrect but Statement-II is correct.

Ans. (a)

Exp. Both Statement-I and Statement-II are correct and Statement-II is the correct explanation for Statement-I. Alexander's invasion led to the establishment of Greek Satrapies in the North-Western region of the Indian subcontinent.

Trade routes opened up with the West. As trade confact increased, many Greek settlements were established in the North-West of India. Alexandria near Kabul, Boukephala near Peshwar (Pakistan) and Alexandria in Sindh were some of the prominent Greek settlements.

30 With references to Indo-Iranian contact in sixth century BC, consider the following statements. *(Class XI, Old NCERT)*

1. Iranian rulers annexed Punjab in the sixth century BC.
2. Kharosthi script introduced by Iranian is written from left to right.
3. Mauryan sculpture has perceptible Iranian influence.

How many of the statements given above is/are incorrect?

(a) Only one (b) Only two
(c) All three (d) None of these

Ans. (a)

Exp. Only one statement i.e., (2) is incorrect.

The Iranian scribes brought into India a form of writing which came to be known as Kharosthi script. It was written from right to left like the Arabic.

31 The Macedonian ruler Alexander invaded India in fourth century BC. He was tempted to invade India because *(Chap 11, Class-XI, Old NCERT)*

(a) Herodotus and other Greek writers had written about fabulous wealth of India.
(b) He possessed a strong passion for geographical enquiry and natural history.
(c) Absence of any strong state in the North-Western part of Indian subcontinent.
(d) All of the above

Ans. (d)

Exp. All the given statements highlight reasons due to which Alexander was tempted to invade India. From Iran, Alexander marched to India, obviously attracted by its great wealth.

'Herodotus' who is called the 'Father of History' and other Greek writers had painted India as a fabulous land, which tempted Alexander to invade it.

Alexander also possessed a strong passion for geographical inquiry and natural history. He had heard that the Caspian Sea continued on the Eastern side of India.

The political condition of North-West India suited his plans. The area was divided into many independent monarchies and tribal republics. There were no strong states.

32 Consider the following statements regarding Alexander invasion of India. *(Chap 11, Class-XI, Old NCERT)*

1. The ruler of Taxila, Ambhi put forth a strong resistance against Alexander.
2. The strongest resistance against Alexander in India came from Porus whose bravery and courage greatly impressed Alexander.
3. His army refused to enter India beyond the Beas river as they feared the strong army of Nanda Empire in Gangetic valley.

Which of the statements given above is/are incorrect?

(a) 1 and 2
(b) Only 1
(c) Only 2
(d) 1, 2 and 3

Ans. (b)

Exp. Statement (1) is incorrect regarding Alexander invasion of India because Ambhi, the ruler of Taxila, easily surrendered to the invader, augmented his army and replenished his treasure.

33 Consider the following statements regarding effect of Alexander invasion in India. *(Chap 11, Class-XI, Old NCERT)*

1. It opened up four distinct routes by land and sea between India and Greece.
2. The historians and geographers who accompanied Alexander left detailed account of India in the fourth century BC.
3. By destroying the power of petty states in North-West India, the Alexander invasion paved the way for expansion of Mauryan empire.

Which of the statements given above are correct?

(a) 1 and 2
(b) 2 and 3
(c) 1 and 3
(d) 1, 2 and 3

Ans. (d)

Exp. All the statements (1), (2) and (3) are correct regarding effect of Alexander invasion in India.

The important outcome of Alexander's was the establishment of direct contact between India and Greece. It opened up four distinct routes by land and sea. Alexander's historians have left valuable geographical accounts. They have left clearly dated records of Alexander's campaign, which enabled to build Indian chronology for subsequent events on a definite basis.

By destroying the power of petty states in North-West India, Alexander's invasion paved the way for the expansion of Mauryan empire in that area.

Chapter 07

Mauryan Empire

Mauryan Empire

Mauryan Empire

Sources of Mauryan Phase

- Kautilya's Arthashastra
- About economical, socio-political condition of Mauryan empire
- Mudrarakshasha by Vishakhadutta
- Rajatarangini of Kalhana,
- Kathasaritsagar of Somadeva and Indica by Megasthenes

Important Ruler

- **Chandragupta Maurya**
  - Overthrew Nanda ruler Dhanananda
  - Defeated Greek ruler Seleucus Nicator who sent ambassador Megasthenes to his court
- **Bindusara**
  - Referred as Amitrochatas in Greek literature; Ruler of Syria,
  - Antiochus I sent an ambassador Deimachus
- **Ashoka**
  - First Indian king, who gave Royal public orders through his edicts; Addressed his subjects as 'son' and called himself 'Davanampia and Piyadasi'
- **Successor Rulers**
  - After Ashoka, rule of his weak successors continued for next 50 years; Kunal was immediate successor and Brihadratha was last Mauryan ruler

Art and Architecture

- Stone and wood architecture began on massive scale
- 80 pillared grand hall at Pataliputra
- Rock-cut caves carved for Buddhist monks
- Started use of baked bricks in North-West India
- Northern Black Polished Ware (NBPW)—Pottery
- Fragments of stone pillars and their stubs have been found at Kumhrar
- Ringed wells first came into prevalence during the mauryan period
- Mahasthan script found in Bogra district
- Pottery, iron tools and punch-marked coins have also been found

Decline of Empire

- Weak and incapable rulers, foreign invasion, rise of new dynasty, decline of royal treasury and Brahmanical reaction

Society and Administration and Its Decline

Dhamma Policy

- Followed by Ashoka, Inspired by Buddhist ideology; Appointed Dhamma Mahamattas to propagate Dhamma; Sent missionaries to promote Buddhism in foreign countries promoted tolerance and non-violence

Provincial Administration

- Empire divided into several provinces which were further sub-divided into smaller units five provinces-Uttrapath, Avantika, Dakshinapatha, Magadha and Kalinga

Military Administration

- Six sub-committee governed military
  1. Infantry 2. Cavalry 3. Elephant 4. Chariot 5. Boat 6. Transport and provisions economy

Economy

- 27 Adhyakshas appointed to regulate economic functions; Facilities for irrigation provided; State had monopoly on sales of mines, alcohol and manufacturing of weapons
- Samaharta-supreme authority of tax assessment
- Punch- marked silver coins

Society

- Megasthenes divided society into seven categories (actual four categories/varnas); Joint family and Patriarchy was prevalent
- Women allowed to accumulate streedhan

Religion

- Witnessed rise and growth of Buddhism and Jainism
- Chandragupta Maurya followed Jainism
- Bindusara was followed of Sarmanas and Ajivikas
- Ashoka was great patron of Buddhism and convened third Buddhist Council

SOURCE *Old NCERT Class VI (The Mauryan Empire), New NCERT Class VI (Ashoka, the Emperor Who Gave up War), Old NCERT Class IX (Early Iron-Age Civilisation), Old NCERT Class XII (The Age of Mauryas), Old NCERT Class XI (Significance of the Mauryan Rule), New NCERT Class XII (Thinkers, Beliefs and Buildings), New NCERT Class XII (Kings, Farmers and Towns)*

Mauryan Empire

1 **With reference to Mauryan empire, consider the following statements.** *(Class-XI, Old NCERT)*

1. Junagadh rock inscriptions give information on the geographical extent of Chandragupta.
2. The usurping of the kingship of Chandragupta by Bindusara is the theme of Mudrarakshasa.
3. Chanakya is prolifically mentioned in Jain and Buddhist texts.

How many statements given above is/are incorrect?

(a) Only one (b) Only two
(c) All three (d) None of these

Ans. (a)

Exp. Only one statement i.e., (2) is incorrect with reference to the Mauryan empire. Theme of the play Mudrarakshasa is the intrigues and brilliant strategy of Chanakya to subvert the intended invasion of Magadha . He is credited with having devised the strategy for overthrowing the Nandas and helping Chandragupta to become the emperor of Magadha.

2 **With reference to Mauryan empire, consider the following statements.** *(Chap 13, Class-XI, Old NCERT)*

1. Justin was a Greek writer who wrote about the military conquests of Chandragupta.
2. Chandragupta liberated North-Western India from the rule of Seleucus.
3. The Mauryan empire ruled over the entire Indian subcontinent except North-Eastern India.

How many of the statements given above is/are correct?

(a) Only one (b) Only two (c) All three (d) None of these

Ans. (b)

Exp. Only two statements i.e., (1) and (2) are correct with reference to the Mauryan empire.

Justin was a Greek writer who wrote on the military conquest of Chandragupta Maurya. He wrote that Chandragupta overran the whole of India with an army of 600,000. Chandragupta liberated North-Western India from the thraldom of Seleucus who ruled over the area West of the Indus.

Statement (3) is incorrect because Chandragupta built up a vast empire which included not only Bihar and a good portion of Orissa and Bengal, but also Western and North-Western India and the Deccan. Leaving Kerala, Tamil Nadu and parts of North-Eastern India, the Mauryans ruled over the whole of the subcontinent.

3 **With reference to Mauryan empire, consider the following statements.** *(Chap 13, Class-XI, Old NCERT)*

1. Megasthenes wrote about the administration of the city of Pataliputra.
2. A specific committee was entrusted with the responsibility of weights and measures in the Pataliputra.
3. Mauryans maintained a huge standing army but no Navy.

How many of the statements given above is/are correct?

(a) Only one (b) Only two
(c) All three (d) None of these

Ans. (b)

Exp. Only two statements i.e., (1) and (2) are correct with reference to Mauryan empire. Megasthenes, a Greek ambassador sent by Seleucus to the court of Chandragupta Maurya, gave an elaborate account on the system of Mauryan administration. He lived in Mauryan capital of Pataliputra and wrote not only of the administration of the city of Pataliputra but also of the Mauryan empire as a whole. A specific committee was entrusted with the responsibility of weights and measures in the Pataliputra. The administration of Pataliputara, which was the capital of the Mauryans, was carried on by six committees, each committee consisting of five members. These committees were entrusted with sanitation, care of foreigners, registration of birth and deaths, regulations of weight and measures.

Statement (3) is not correct because according to Roman writer Pliny, Chandragupta maintained 600,000 foot soldiers, 30,000 cavalry and 9000 elephants. Another source tells us that the Chandragupta Maurya maintained a Navy.

3 **With reference to kingship in Mauryan empire, consider the following statements.** *(Class 13, Class-XI, Old NCERT)*

1. Kings should follow the laws laid down in Dharmashastras and not the customs.
2. Kautilya advised the kings to promulgate Dharma when the social order based on Varna and Ashrama deteriorates.
3. Dharmapravartaka is a term used to denote the monks who spread the message of Dharma.

How many of the statements given above is/are correct?

(a) Only one (b) Only two
(c) All three (d) None of these

Ans. (b)

Exp. Only two statements i.e., (1) and (2) are correct with reference to the kingship in the Mauryan empire.

The Brahmanical law books stressed that the king should be guided by the laws laid down in the Dharmashastra and by the customs prevalent in the country.

Kautilya advised the kings to promulgate Dharma when the social order based on the Varnas and Ashrama (stages of life) perishes. Ashoka promulgated Dharma and appointed officials to inculcate and enforce its essentials throughout the country.

Statement (3) is not correct because Kautilya calls the king as Dharmapravartaka or promulgator of the social order.

4 With reference to Mauryan emperor, consider the following statements. *(Class-XI, Old NCERT)*

1. During the last phase of his reign, Chandragupta Maurya converted to Jainism.
2. Chandragupta Maurya spent the last year of his life in Vallabhi as a Jain ascetic.
3. Bindusara conquered the ancient kingdom of South India and made them part of the Mauryan empire.

How many of the statements given above is/are correct?

(a) Only one (b) Only two
(c) All three (d) None of these

Ans. (b)

Exp. Only two statements i.e., (1) and (3) are correct with reference to the Mauryan emperor.

During the last phase of his reign, Chandragupta Maurya converted to Jainism. According to a late tradition, the spread of Jainism in Karnataka is attributed to Chandragupta Maurya (322-298 BC).

The ancient kingdom of South India, though accepted the suzerainty of Mauryan, was not part of the empire. During the reign of Bindusara the Mauryan empire extended as far South as Mysore.

Statement (2) is incorrect because Chandragupta spent his last year as an ascetic in Chandragiri, near Shravanabelagola, in Karnataka.

5 Assertion (A) The Mauryan kings did not bestow land grants on religious basis.

Reason (R) The peasants revolted against land grants. *(Unit 4, Class-XI, Tamil Nadu Board)*

Select the correct answer by using the codes given below.

(a) Both A and R are true and R is the correct explanation of A.
(b) Both A and R are true, but R is not the correct explanation of A.
(c) A is true, but R is false.
(d) A is false, but R is true.

Ans. (c)

Exp. Assertion (A) is true, but Reason (R) is false.

As the practice of giving land grants on the religious basis in India was started during the period of Satavahanas, it is attested by the epigraphic record from the Nashik, which highlights that the Satavahana rulers provided land grants to the Brahmanas and Buddhist monks. In the historical sources of Mauryan empire, most notably work the Arthashastra of Kautilya and Indica of Megasthenes, there is no mention about peasant revolt against land grants

6 With reference to the Mauryan emperor, consider the following statements. *(Class-XI, Old NCERT)*

1. Bindusara committed fratricide to capture the throne of the Mauryan empire.
2. Ashoka was chosen as the successor of Bindusara.
3. Last ruler of Mauryan empire Brihadratha was killed by his Commander-in-Chief Pushyamitra Shunga.

How many statements given above is/are incorrect?

(a) Only one (b) Only two
(c) All three (d) None of these

Ans. (b)

Exp. Only two statements i.e., (1) and (2) are incorrect with reference to the Mauryan emperor.

Chandragupta's son Bindusara succeeded him as emperor in 297 BC in a peaceful and natural transition.

Ashoka was not the chosen successor of Bindusara and the fact that he came to the throne only four years later in 268 BC would indicate that there was a struggle between the sons of Bindusara for the succession.

7 With reference to military structure of Mauryan empire, consider the following statements. *(Chap 13, Class-XI, Old NCERT)*

Statement-I The Mauryan empire maintained a larger military compared to the Nandas on the account of far more resources.

Statement-II The Mauryan empire brought new lands under cultivation which expanded the revenue base of the empire.

Which one of the following is correct in respect of the above statements?

(a) Both the Statement-I and Statement-II are correct and Statement-II is the correct explanation for Statement-I.
(b) Both the Statement-I and Statement-II are correct and Statement-II is incorrect explanation for Statement-I.
(c) Statement-I is correct, but statement-II is incorrect.
(d) Statement-I is incorrect, but statement-II is correct.

Ans. (a)

Exp. Both Statement-I and Statement-II are correct and Statement-II is the correct explanation for Statement-I.

The Mauryan military strength was almost three times that of the Nandas. This apparently happened to a large empire and far more resources.

The state brought new land under cultivation with the help of cultivators and Shudras labourers.

The virgin land which was opened to cultivation yielded handsome income to the state in the form of revenue collected from the newly settled peasants. This naturally brought money to the royal Exchequer.

8 With reference to Policy of Ashoka, consider the following statements. *(Chap 13, Class-XI, Old NCERT)*

1. Kalinga was made a sovereign territory after the Kalinga war.
2. Ashoka didn't make any ideological appeal to the tribal people to follow the principle of Dhamma.
3. Ashoka no longer treated foreign dominions as legitimate areas for military conquest post the Kalinga war.

How many of the statements given above is/are incorrect?

(a) Only one (b) Only two
(c) All three (d) None of these

Ans. (b)

Exp. Only two statements i.e., (1) and (2) are incorrect with reference polity of Ashoka. Kalinga was not made an independent sovereign territory after the war by Ashoka. The subjects of the independent states in Kalinga were asked to obey the kings as their father and to repose confidence in him.

Ashoka made an ideological appeal towards tribal people to follow principles of Dhamma. Ashoka maintained intimate contacts with the tribal people who were exhorted to observe Dharma. Ashoka launched a deliberate and systematic policy of acculturation.

9 With reference to Ashoka's Dhamma, consider the following statements. *(Chap 13, Class-XI, Old NCERT)*

Statement-I Ashoka disbanded the huge army maintained since the time of Chandragupta.

Statement-II The Kalinga war didn't make Ashoka an extreme pacifist.

Which one of the following is correct in respect of the above statements?

(a) Both Statement-I and Statement-II are correct and Statement-II is the correct explanation for Statement-I.
(b) Both Statement-I and Statement-II are correct and Statement-II is incorrect explanation for Statement-I.
(c) Statement-I is correct, but Statement-II is incorrect.
(d) Statement-I is incorrect, but Statement-II is correct.

Ans. (d)

Exp. Statement-I is incorrect, but Statement-II is correct with reference to the policy adopted by Emperor Ashoka. There is also nothing to show that he disbanded the huge army maintained from the time of Chandragupta Maurya. The policy of Ashoka to consolidate the empire through Dharma bore fruit.

It would be wrong to think that the Kalinga war made Ashoka an extreme pacifist. He didn't pursue a policy of peace for the sake of peace under all conditions. On the other hand, he adopted a practical policy of consolidating his Empires.

10 With reference to Policy of Ashoka, consider the following statements. *(Chap 13, Class-XI, Old NCERT)*

1. Rajukas could reward people for following dhamma but couldn't punish them.
2. Kandahar inscriptions gave details of hunters giving up killing of animals.

Which of the statements given above is/are incorrect?

(a) Only 1
(b) Only 2
(c) Both 1 and 2
(d) Neither 1 nor 2

Ans. (b)

Exp. Statement (1) is incorrect with reference to the policy adopted by Emperor Ashoka:

Ashoka appointed a class of officers known as the Rajukas, who were vested with the authority of not only rewarding people but also punishing them, wherever necessary.

11 After seeing the massacre and displacement of people in Kalinga war, Ashoka changed his policy of *bherighosha* with *dhammaghosha*. It meant *(Chap 14, Class-XI, Old NCERT)*

(a) he abandoned the policy of physical occupation in favour of policy of spiritual conquest.
(b) he initiated the policy of physical occupation in favour of policy of cultural conquest.
(c) he abandoned the policy of decentralisation in favour of policy of centralisation.
(d) he initiated the policy of secularism in favour of state patronage of Buddhism only.

Ans. (a)

Exp. Statement (a) means that Ashoka changed his policy of *bherighosha* with *dhammaghosha*. Ashoka was moved by the massacre in the Kalinga war. The war brought to the Brahmana priests and the Buddhist monks great suffering, which caused Ashoka much grief and remorse. He abandoned the policy of aggression and tried to conquer the hearts of people. In other words, Bherighosha was replaced with Dhammaghosha.

12 Who among the following rulers advised his subjects through the given inscription? *(Chap 7, Class-VI, New NCERT) (IAS Pre 2020)*

"Whosoever praises his religious sector blames other sects out of excessive devotion to his own sect, with the view of glorifying his own sect, he rather injures his own sect very severely".

(a) Ashoka (b) Samudragupta
(c) Chandragupta Maurya (d) Krishnadevaraya

Ans. (a)

Exp. Ashoka advised his subjects through the given inscription Ashoka got his messages inscribed on rocks and pillars, instructing his officials to read the messages to those who could not read it themselves.

People in the empire followed different religious and this sometimes led to conflict animals were sacrificed slaves and servants were ill-treated besides, there were quarrels in families and among neighbours.

13 Consider the following statements with reference to impact of Kalinga war on Ashoka. *(Chap 15, Class-XI, Old NCERT)*

1. He made an ideological appeal towards the tribal people and the frontier kingdom to follow the principles of Dhamma.
2. He disbanded the huge army maintained from the time of Chandragupta Maurya.
3. He allowed Kalinga to remain as an independent territory.

How many of the statements given above is/are incorrect?

(a) Only one (b) Only two
(c) All three (d) None of these

Ans. (b)

Exp. Only two statements i.e., (2) and (3) are incorrect with reference to impact of Kalinga war on Ashoka because he never neglected the army nor disbanded it. He also made Kalinga a part of his Empire rather than leaving it as independent territory.

14 With reference to conquest of Kalinga by Ashoka, consider the following statements. *(Unit 4, Class-XI, Tamil Nadu Board)*

Statement-I Ashoka annexed Kalinga to the Mauryan empire region.

Statement-II Kalinga controlled the land and sea routes to South India.

Which one of the following is correct in respect of the above statements?

(a) Both Statement-I and Statement-II are correct and Statement-II is the correct explanation for Statement-I.
(b) Both Statement-I and Statement-II are correct and Statement-II is incorrect explanation for Statement-I.
(c) Statement-I is correct, but Statement-II is incorrect.
(d) Statement-I is incorrect, but Statement-II is correct

Ans. (a)

Exp. Both Statement-I and Statement-II are correct and Statement-II is the correct explanation for Statement-I.

The main reason behind annexation of Kalinga by Ashoka in 261 BC was both political and economical.

The territories of Kalinga acted as bridge for cultural exchange between the North and South India.

Further, its strategic location and control of sea ports and trade routes encouraged Ashoka to annex it.

However, it was only war fought by Ashoka who after this war changed his policy towards cultural conquest.

15 With reference to the last phase of reign of Ashoka, which of the following statements is/are correct? *(Chap 14, Class XI, Old NCERT)*

1. The pacifist policies of Ashoka didn't made any lasting impression on the viceroys and vassals who declared themselves independent after the retirement of the king in 232 BC.
2. The outlying provinces under the control of Mauryan empire such as Taxila and Karnataka revolted against the imperial rule during the reign of Ashoka.

Codes

(a) Only 1 (b) Only 2
(c) Both 1 and 2 (d) None of these

Ans. (a)

Exp. Statement (1) is correct regarding the last phase of reign of Ashoka. Ashoka's policy did not make any lasting impression on his viceroys and vassals, who declared themselves independent in their respective areas after the retirement of the king in 232 BC.

Statement (2) is incorrect because Taxila and Karnataka didn't revolt during the reign of Ashoka.

16 With reference to Ashoka's Dhamma, consider the following statements. *(Class-XI, Old NCERT)*

1. It can't be regarded as a sectarian faith.
2. Its objective was to preserve the social order.
3. Ashoka held that if people followed Dhamma they would attain Nirvana.

How many of the statements given above is/are correct?

(a) Only one (b) Only two
(c) All three (d) None of these

Ans. (b)

Exp. Only two statements i.e., (1) and (2) are correct with reference to Ashoka's Dhamma was not a narrow dharma. It can't be regarded as a sectarian faith. His teaching were meant to strengthen the institutions of family and existing social classes.

Thus, his teaching was intended to maintain existing social order on the basis of tolerance. He doesn't seem to have preached any sectarian faith.

The broad objective of Ashoka's dhamma was to preserve the social order. He emphasised compassion towards animals and proper behaviour towards relative. Ashoka's teaching were thus intended to maintain existing social order on the basis of tolerance.

Statement (3) is incorrect because Nirvana was not the stated objective of Ashoka's understanding of Dhamma.

17 With reference to Ashoka's Policy of conquest, consider the following statements. *(Chap 13, Class-XI, Old NCERT)*

Statement-I Policy followed by Ashoka was in conjunction with the policy suggested by Kautilya for a king.

Statement-II Ashoka followed the policy of peace, non-aggression and cultural conquest.

Which one of the following is correct in respect of the above statements?

(a) Both Statement-I and Statement-II are correct and Statement-II is the correct explanation for Statement-I.
(b) Both Statement-I and Statement-II are correct and Statement-II is incorrect explanation for Statement-I.
(c) Statement-I is correct, but Statement-II is incorrect.
(d) Statement-I is incorrect, but Statement-II is correct.

Ans. (d)

Exp. Statement-I is incorrect, Statement-II is correct. Kautilya advised the king to always be intent on physical conquest. Ashoka followed just the reverse policy. Ashoka after the Kalinga war abandoned the policy of physical occupation in favour of a policy of cultural conquest. In other words, Bherighosa was replaced by Dhammaghosa. Ashoka followed the policy of peace, non-aggression and cultural conquest. He asked his successors to give up the policy of conquest and aggression, which had been followed by the Magadha prince till the Kalinga war. He consistently stuck to this policy.

18 With reference to policy of Ashoka, consider the following statements. *(Chap 13, Class-XI, Old NCERT)*

1. He took steps for the welfare of men and animals in foreign lands.
2. Ashoka followed the ideal of paternal Kingship.
3. Ashoka disapproved of all rituals except those observed by women.

How many of the statements given above is/are correct?

(a) Only one
(b) Only two
(c) All three
(d) None of these

Ans. (b)

Exp. Only two statements i.e., (1) and (2) are correct with reference to policy adopted by Ashoka.

Ashoka took steps for the welfare of men and animals in foreign lands, which was innovative. He sent ambassadors of peace to the Greeks kingdoms in Western Asia and Greece.

Ashoka was converted to Buddhism as a result of the Kalinga war. According to the tradition he became a monk, made huge gifts to the Buddhist and undertook pilgrimage to the Buddhist shrines. Ashoka set a very ideal for himself, and this was the ideal of paternal kingship.

Statement (3) is incorrect because Ashoka disapproved of rituals, especially those observed by women. He forbade killing of certain birds and animals and completely prohibited the slaughter of animals in the capital.

19 With reference to Ashoka's Policy, consider the following statements. *(Class-XI, Old NCERT)*

Statement-I Ashoka replaced the policy of Dhammaghosa with the Bherighosa after the Kalinga war.

Statement-II Ashoka's military conquest in Kalinga filled him with remorse.

Which one of the following is correct in respect of the above statements?

(a) Both Statement-I and Statement-II are correct and Statement-II is the correct explanation for Statement-I.
(b) Both Statement-I and Statement-II are correct and Statement-II is incorrect explanation for Statement-I.
(c) Statement-I is correct, but Statement-II is incorrect.
(d) Statement-I is incorrect, but Statement-II is correct.

Ans. (d)

Exp. Statement-I is incorrect, but statement-II is correct.

The ideology of Buddhism guided Ashoka's state policy at home and abroad. After his accession to the throne Ashoka fought only one major war called the Kalinga war. The war brought to the Brahmana priest and the Buddhist monks great suffering which caused Ashoka much grief and remorse.

He abandoned the policy of physical occupation in favor of a policy of cultural conquest. In other words, Bherighosa was replaced by Dhammaghosha.

Inscriptions

20 With reference to Mauryan inscriptions, consider the following statements.

(Class-XI, Old NCERT) (IAS Pre 2020, 1991)

1. In Shahbazgarhi relief sculpture inscriptions, 'Ranyo Ashoka' (King Ashoka) is mentioned along with the stone portrait of Ashoka.
2. The only inscription which mention the name of Ashoka is Minor rock inscription at Maski.

Which of the statements given above is/are incorrect?

(a) Only 1
(b) Only 2
(c) Both 1 and 2
(d) Neither 1 nor 2

Ans. (a)

Exp. Only statement (1) is incorrect with reference to Mauryan inscriptions as Kanganahalli inscription mentions Ranyo Ashoka along with a stone portrait of him.

21 With reference to Ashokan edicts, consider the following pairs. *(Class-XI, Old NCERT)*

Location of Edicts		Script of Inscriptions
1. Edicts in Central India	–	Brahmi Script
2. Edicts in North-Western	–	Aramaic Scripts
3. Edicts in Afganistan	–	Kharosthi Script

How many of the pairs given above is/are correctly matched?

(a) Only one
(b) Only two
(c) All three
(d) None

Ans. (a)

Exp. Only one pair i.e., (1) is correctly matched with reference to Ashokan edicts.

Ashoka was the first Indian king to speak directly to the people through his inscriptions. The inscriptions were composed in Prakrit languages and written in Brahmi script throughout central India.

Pairs (2) and (3) are not correctly matched because in North Western India the Ashokan inscriptions were composed in Kharosthi script.

In Kandahar (Afghanistan) Ashoka's inscription were composed in Aramaic, in Greek scripts and Greek languages.

22 Which among the following inscriptions speaks about the success of the Ashoka's Dhamma policy with hunters and fishermen, who gave up killing animals and possibly took to a settled agricultural life? *(Chap 14, Class-XI, Old NCERT)*

(a) Shoghura copper plate inscription
(b) Maski pillar inscription
(c) Kalinga inscription
(d) Kandahar inscription

Ans. (d)

Exp. The Kandahar inscription speaks about the success of Ashoka's Dhamma policy with the hunters and fishermen, who gave up killing animals and possibly took to a settled agricultural life.

23 The finely polished stone sculpture of the bull, which has now been placed in the Rashtrapati Bhavan had been taken from? *(Chap 7, Class-VI, Old NCERT)*

(a) Ashoka's pillar inscription at Rampurva
(b) Ashoka's pillar inscription at Sannati
(c) Ashoka's Major Rock Edict, Sarnath
(d) Ashoka's Minor Rock Edict, Kandahar

Ans. (a)

Exp. The finely polished stone sculpture of the bull which has now been placed in the Rashtrapati Bhavan (President house) had been taken from Ashoka's pillar inscription at Rampurva.

The bull capital of Rampurva was originally constructed in the West Champaran district of Bihar. It is one of the seven remaining animal capitals from the pillars of Ashoka. It has strong influence of Greek, Persian and Indian art.

24 With reference to Ashokan edicts/ inscriptions, consider the following pairs. *(Chap 14 & 15, Class-XI, Old NCERT)*

Inscriptions/Edicts		Information Inscribed
1. XIII Major Rock edicts	–	Account of Kalinga war
2. Kalsi pillar inscriptions	–	Reduction of land revenue rate of Lumbini
3. Rumindei pillar inscription	–	Directed Mahamatras not to torture

How many of the pairs given above is/are correctly matched?

(a) Only one
(b) Only two
(c) All three
(d) None of these

Ans. (a)

Exp. Only one pair i.e., (1) is correctly matched with reference to Mauryan edicts and inscriptions.

The account of Kalinga war is known to us by the Rock Edict-XIII. Ashokan XIII Major Rock Edict had expressed grief and disappointed over massacare of thousands due to the Kalinga war. This inscription is written in Kharosthi script and was discovered from Shahbaz Garhi in present day Pakistan. This inscription projects the grief and remorse felt by Ashoka.

Pairs (2) and (3) are not correctly matched because Rumindei inscriptions of Ashoka states that the land revenue rate of Lumbini (birth place of Gautama Buddha) was reduced to one-eighth.

Kalinga edict, found near Dhauligiri hill, Bhubaneswar, Odisha mentions that he had asked the Mahamatras not to torture townsmen without due cause.

25 Consider the following statements regarding inscriptions erected under the reign of Ashoka. *(Chap 15, Class-XI, Old NCERT)*

1. The name of Ashoka occurs only in copies of Minor Rock Edict I found at three places in Karnataka and at one in Madhya Pradesh.
2. All the other inscriptions referred Ashoka as Devanampriya Priyadarshi.
3. They throw light on the career of Ashoka, his external and domestic policies, and extent of his empire.

Which of the statements given above are correct?

(a) 1 and 2
(b) 2 and 3
(c) 1 and 3
(d) 1, 2 and 3

Ans. (d)

Exp. All of the given statements are correct regarding inscriptions erected under the reign of Ashoka.

The name of Ashoka occurs only in copies of Minor Rock Edict I found at three places in Karnataka and at one in Madhya Pradesh. All the other inscriptions mention only Devanampriya Priyadarshi, dear to Gods, and leave out the word Ashoka.

The history of Ashoka is reconstructed on the basis of his inscriptions, numbering 39. These inscriptions throw light on the career of Ashoka, his external and domestic policies and the extent of his empire.

26 Consider the following statements regarding Ashokan inscriptions. *(Chap 15, Class-XI, Old NCERT)*

1. The stone pillar were made in Vaishali near Pataliputra and from there it was transported to North and South India.
2. These inscriptions were erected on all the important highways.
3. These inscriptions conveyed Ashoka's messages to his subjects.

Which of the statements given above is/are incorrect?

(a) 1 and 2
(b) Only 1
(c) 1 and 3
(d) Only 3

Ans. (b)

Exp. Statement (1) is incorrect regarding Ashokan inscriptions because the stone pillars were made in Chunar, in Uttar Pradesh near Varanasi, from here they were transported to North and South India.

27. **Match the lists correctly and choose the correct codes.** *(Chap 12, Class-XII, New NCERT)*

List I (Inscriptions of Ashoka)	List II (Places)
A. Major Rock Edicts	1. Bairat
B. Minor Pillar Inscription	2. Kandahar
C. Pillar Inscription	3. Allahabad
D. Queen's Edict	4. Lauriya Nandangarh

Codes

	A	B	C	D
(a)	1	2	3	4
(b)	2	1	4	3
(c)	2	3	1	4
(d)	1	2	4	3

Ans. (b)

Exp. The correct matching is A-2, B-1, C-4, D-3.

Major Rock Edicts of Ashoka are found at Kandahar (Afghanistan), Girnar (Gujarat), Jaugada and Sisupalgarh in Orissa.

Minor Pillar Inscription found at Bairat, also known as Viratnagar in Rajasthan.

Pillar Inscription of Lauriya Nandangarh, is in West Champaran district in Bihar.

Queen's Edict was discovered from Kaushambi near Allahabad. It is dedicated to the wife of Ashoka, Tishyarakshita.

Mauryan Administration

28 **With reference to Mauryan administration, consider the following statements.** *(Chap 11, Class-XII, New NCERT)*

1. The Ashokan inscription mentions Tosali as an important provincial political center.
2. Taxila was the provincial center for important long-distance trade routes.
3. Ujjayini was an important center for tapping gold mines.

How many of the statements given above is/are correct?

(a) Only one (b) Only two
(c) All three (d) None of these

Ans. (b)

Exp. Only two statements i.e., (1) and (2) are correct with reference to Mauryan administration.

There were five major political centers in the empire – the capital Pataliputra and the provincial centers of Taxila, Ujjayini, Tosali and Suvarnagiri, all mentioned in Ashokan inscriptions.

Taxila and Ujjayini being situated on important long-distance trade routes.

Statement (3) is incorrect because Suvarnagiri (literally, the golden mountain) was an important provincial center for tapping the gold mines of Karnataka.

29 **With reference to Mauryan administration, consider the following statements.** *(Chap 11, Class-XII, New NCERT)*

1. Military activities were coordinated by a committee consisting of six sub-committees.
2. Propagation of the principle of Dhamma was also aimed at consolidation of the empire.
3. Dhamma Mahamatta was a special officer entrusted to spread the message of Dhamma.

How many of the statements given above is/are correct?

(a) Only one (b) Only two (c) All three (d) None of these

Ans(c)

Exp. All three statements are correct with reference to the Mauryan administration.

Megasthenes mentions a committee with six subcommittees for coordinating military activity. Of these, one looked after the navy, the second managed transport and provisions, the third was responsible for foot-soldiers, the fourth for horses, the fifth for chariots and the sixth for elephants. Ashoka tried to hold his empire together by propagating Dhamma, the principles of which were simple and virtually universally applicable. This, according to him, would ensure the well-being of people in this world. Special officers, known as the Dhamma Mahamatta, were appointed to spread the message of Dhamma.

30 **With reference to Mauryan empire, consider the following statements.** *(Chap 14, Class-XI, Old NCERT)*

1. Military conquest by Mauryan followed a policy of assertion of royal absolutism.
2. Mauryan empire maintained a large bureaucracy to control all the aspect of life of the state.
3. Administrative mechanism of Mauryan backed by an elaborate system of espionage.

How many of the statements given above is/are correct?

(a) Only one (b) Only two (c) All three (d) None of these

Ans. (b)

Exp. Only one statement i.e., (3) is incorrect.

The administrative mechanism of the Magadha was backed by an elaborate system of espionage. Various types of spies collected intelligence about foreign enemies and kept an eye on numerous officers. They also helped the collection of money from credulous people through deliberate resort to superstitious practices.

Statement (1) and (2) are incorrect because Mauryan never followed a policy of assertion of royal absolutism. Mauryan empire maintained a large bureaucracy to control various, not all the aspects of life of the state.

31 **With references to administrative structure of Mauryan, consider the following statements.** *(Chap 14, Class-XI, Old NCERT)*

1. Trithas referred to important functionaries of Mauryan empire.
2. Adhyakshas were responsible to regulate the economic activities of the state.

3. Important functionaries of the administration were paid in land grants.

How many of the statements given above is/are incorrect?

(a) Only one (b) Only two
(c) All three (d) None of these

Ans. (a)

Exp. Only one statement i.e., (3) is incorrect with reference to Mauryan administration. Important and highest functionaries of the state were paid in cash. They were paid generously as much as 48 thousands panas (pana being a silver coin equal to three fourth of a tola). In sharp contrast to them the lowest officers were given 60 panas in consolidated pay although some employees were given as little as 10 or 20 panas. Therefore, it would seem that there were enormous gaps between the highest and the lowest category of government servants.

32 The Emperor Ashoka appointed the official, Dhamma Mahamatras for *(Chap 2, Class-XII, New NCERT)*

(a) administering justice in the empire.
(b) converting people to the Buddhism.
(c) propagating dharma among various social groups.
(d) constructing pillars consisting of emperor's message to the general public.

Ans. (c)

Exp. The Emperor Ashoka appointed the official, Dhamma Mahamatras for propagating dharma among various social groups. Ashoka tried to hold his empire together by propagating Dhamma, the principles of which were simple and virtually universally applicable. According to him, this would ensure the well-being of people in this world and the next.

33 During the reign of which of the following Mauryan rulers, the citizen of Taxila complained against the misrule of bureaucrats? *(Chap 15, Class-XI, Old NCERT)*

(a) Ashoka (b) Brihadratha
(c) Bindusara (d) Chandragupta Maurya

Ans. (c)

Exp. During the reign of Bindusara, the citizens of Taxila bitterly complained against the misrule of wicked bureaucrats (*dushtamatyas*).

Their grievance was redressed by the appointment of Ashoka. But when Ashoka became emperor, a similar complaint was lodged by the same city.

34 Consider the following statements regarding administration of armed forces during the reign of Mauryan empire. *(Chap 14, Class-XI, Old NCERT)*

1. It was carried on by a board of 30 officers divided into six committees.
2. The six wings of the armed forces– the army, the cavalry, the elephants, the chariots, the navy and the transport were administered by a separate committee.

Which of the statements given above is/are correct?

(a) Only 1 (b) Only 2
(c) Both 1 and 2 (d) Neither 1 nor 2

Ans. (c)

Exp. Both the statements (1) and (2) are correct regarding administration of armed forces during the reign of Mauryan empire.

The administration of the armed forces, according to Megasthenes, was carried on by a board of 30 officers divided into six committees, each committee consisting of five members.

It seems that the six wings of the armed forces–the army, the cavalry, the elephants, the chariots, the navy and the transport were each assigned to the care of a separate committee.

35 Consider the following statements regarding administration during the reign of Ashoka. *(Chap 5, Class-VI, Old NCERT)*

1. He introduced the concept of paternal kinship in the administration.
2. The empire was divided into eight big provinces which were ruled by a viceroy reporting directly to the King.

Which of the statements given above is/are incorrect?

(a) Only 1 (b) Only 2
(c) Both 1 and 2 (d) Neither 1 nor 2

Ans. (b)

Exp. Statement (2) is incorrect regarding administration during the reign of Ashoka as in his time, empire was divided into four big provinces (not eight), and each was ruled by a viceroy who was under the king. Ashoka's edicts also carries information regarding state of administration during the Mauryan.

36 With reference to foreign policy of Ashoka, which of the following statements is/are correct? *(Chap 15, Class-XI, Old NCERT)*

1. Ashoka treated foreign dominions as legitimate areas for military conquests.
2. Ashoka had sent foreign mission to Syria, Egypt and Greece to spread ideas about the Dhammas.
3. Ashoka's son, Mahendra preached Buddhism in Sri Lanka.

Codes

(a) 1 and 2 (b) 2 and 3 (c) 1 and 3 (d) 1, 2 and 3

Ans. (b)

Exp. Statements (2) and (3) are correct regarding foreign policy of Ashoka. He sent ambassadors of peace to Greek Kingdoms in West Asia (Syria, Egypt) and Greece. It was done to propagate the message of Dhamma. He also sent missionaries for the propagation of Buddhism to Sri Lanka and Central Asia. He tried to enlarge his political influence through propaganda.

He had sent his son Mahendra to Sri Lanka to preach Buddhism.

Statement (1) is incorrect because Ashoka after witnessing the horrors of Kalinga war, didn't treat foreign dominion as legitimate areas for military conquests. Rather, he tried to conquer them ideologically.

37 The strategic location of Pataliputra helped Mauryan administration in which of the following ways? *(Chap 15, Class-XI, Old NCERT)*

1. It provided connectivity to all the four directions through waterways.
2. It was connected through North-Western India, Kalinga, Nepal and Central India through well developed road network.
3. It is located on the bank of Yamuna which served important function of inland navigation.

Codes

(a) 1 and 2 (b) 2 and 3 (c) 1 and 3 (d) 1, 2 and 3

Ans. (a)

Exp. Both the statements (1) and (2) highlights that the strategic position of Pataliputra helped Mauryan administration.

In the ancient times, the fort of Pataliputra was known as Jaldurga (water fort) as it was surrounded by the rivers from all its sides. It provided connectivity to all the four directions through waterways. Pataliputra also lays in centre of fertile valley which was strategically connected through North-Western India, Kalinga, Nepal and Central India through well-developed road network.

Statement (3) is incorrect about strategic position of Pataliputra because it is located on the bank of Ganga river.

38 Consider the following statements regarding the role of king in the administration under the Mauryan empire. *(Chap 15, Class-XI, Old NCERT)*

1. The kings were autocrat who concentrated all power in his hands.
2. The king was assisted by the Council whose members were noted for wisdom.
3. The advice rendered by the Council of the minister was binding on the king.

Which of the statements given above is/are correct?

(a) 1 and 2 (b) 2 and 3 (c) 1 and 3 (d) 1, 2 and 3

Ans. (a)

Exp. Statements (1) and (2) are correct regarding the role of king in the administration under the Mauryan empire. The Mauryan empire was monarchial one that means kings were autocrat who concentrated all power in hands. Another feature of Mauryan administration was high degree of Centralisation.

The king was assisted by the Council of Minister, who were assigned different portfolios based on their qualities. They were also noted for their wisdom.

Statement 3 is incorrect because king was free to accept or reject the advice tendered by the Council of Ministers.

39 Match the following lists correctly and choose the correct code. *(Chap 15, Class-XI, Old NCERT)*

List I (Officials in Mauryan Empire)	List II (Functions)
A. Rajukas	1. Reporter
B. Pativedaka	2. Chief custodian of the state treasury
C. Sannidhata	3. Administering justice
D. Samaharta	4. Highest officer in charge of assessment.

Codes

	A	B	C	D		A	B	C	D
(a)	1	2	3	4	(b)	2	1	4	3
(c)	4	2	3	1	(d)	3	1	2	4

Ans. (d)

Exp. The correct matching is A-3, B-1, C-2, D-4.

Rajukas were appointed by Ashoka for the administration of justice in his empire.

Pativedaka were reporters which according to a inscriptions were appointed by Ashoka. The Mauryas attached greater importance to assessment than to storage and depositing.

Sannidhata was the chief custodian of the state treasury and store-house. **Samaharta** was the highest officer in charge of assessment.

Economy

40 With reference to the revenue source of Mauryan empire, consider the following statements. *(Chap 13, Class-XI, Old NCERT)*

1. The Mauryan state didn't enjoy monopoly in the sales of liquor.
2. The Mauryan state enjoyed monopoly in the mining and manufacture of arms.
3. Tax collected from peasants varied from one-fourth to one-sixth of the produce.

How many of the statements given above is/are correct?

(a) Only one (b) Only two
(c) All three (d) None of these

Ans. (b)

Exp. Only two statements i.e., (2) and (3) are correct with reference to source of Mauryan revenue.

The Mauryan state enjoyed monopoly in the mining, sale of liquors and manufacture of arms etc. This naturally brought money to the royal Exchequer.

Tax collected from the peasants varied from one-fourth to one-sixth of the produce.

Statement (1) incorrect because as per Arthashastra state controlled all the economic activities of the state. State enjoyed a monopoly in the sale of liquor.

41 **Which among the following method(s) was/were utilised by the Mauryan emperors to increase the area under cultivation?** *(Chap 15, Class-XI, Old NCERT)*

(a) Remission in tax
(b) Provisions for cattle, seed and money
(c) Both a and b
(d) Irrigation facilities at the state expense

Ans. (c)

Exp. Remission in tax and provisions for cattle, seed and money were utilised by the Mauryan emperors to increase the area under cultivation. The Mauryan emperors in order to increase the area under cultivation, employed various strategies recommended in Arthashastra of Kautilya.

Some of the measures included-employing shudras for agricultural operation, providing remission in tax, ensuring provisions for cattle, seed and money to the new settlers. This policy led to the opening of large areas to cultivation and settlement.

Irrigation facilities at the state expense wasn't made for new cultivation areas.

42 **With reference to the state of economy under the Mauryan empire.** *(Chap 13, Class-XI, Old NCERT)*

1. The state brought new land under cultivation with the help of administrators and Shudra labourers.
2. The taxes collected from the peasants varied from one-eighth to one-tenth of the produce.
3. The Arthashastra, recommended comprehensive state control over agricultural production and marketing.

Which of the statements given above is/are correct?

(a) Only one (b) Only two
(c) All three (d) None of these

Ans. (b)

Exp. Statements (1) and (3) are correct regarding the state of economy under the Mauryan empire In the Mauryan empire, land revenue constituted chief source of revenue for the state. Thus, in order to increase production the state brought new land under cultivation with the help of administrators and Shudra labourers.

The Arthashastra, recommended comprehensive state control over agricultural production and marketing, with warehouse to store agricultural products and regulated markets, in order to maximise the revenues from this most important sector of the economy.

Statement (2) is incorrect because land revenue rate in the Mauryan Empire was one-sixth of the total produce.

43 **Consider the following statements regarding coinage prevalent in Mauryan age.** *(Chap 15, Class-XI, Old NCERT)*

1. The punch-marked silver coins which carried the symbols of peacock, hill and the crescent formed the imperial currency of the Mauryas.
2. All the taxes and salaries of officials were paid through these coins only.

Which of the statements given above is/are incorrect?

(a) Only 1 (b) Only 2
(c) Both 1 and 2 (d) None of these

Ans. (b)

Exp. Statement (2) is incorrect regarding the system of coinage prevalent in Mauryan empire because besides cash (coins), taxes and salaries of officials were also paid in kind i.e. grains or tax free land.

Art and Architecture

44 **Which one of the following ancient books highlights that "the happiness of the king lies in the happiness of his subjects"?** *(Chap 14, Class-XI, Old NCERT)*

(a) Arthashastra
(b) Indika
(c) Mudrarakshasha
(d) Raghuvansham

Ans. (a)

Exp. Ancient book Arthashastra highlights that in "the happiness of his subjects lay his happiness and in their troubles lay his troubles." It was written by Kautilya.

45 **With reference to Ashoka's Policy, consider the following statements.** *(Chap 15, Class-XI, Old NCERT)*

Statement-I In the Mauryan period, attempts were made to spread elements of the middle Gangetic basin culture in the distant areas.

Statement-II The Mauryan inscriptions, NBPW potsherds and punch marked coins were discovered from the parts of Bangladesh, Odisha and Karnataka.

Which one of the following is correct in respect of the above statements?

(a) Both Statement-I and Statement-II are correct and Statement-II is the correct explanation for Statement-I.
(b) Both Statement-I and Statement-II are correct and Statement-II is incorrect explanation for Statement-I.
(c) Statement-I is correct, but Statement-II is incorrect.
(d) Statement-I is incorrect, but Statement-II is correct.

Ans. (b)

Exp. Both Statement-I and Statement-II are correct and Statement-II is incorrect explanation for Statement-I. The Mauryan ruler through propagation of Dhamma, introduction of unified coinage, using a common language and erecting structures and monuments tried to spread elements of the middle Gangetic valley to the distant lands such as Kalinga (modern Odisha), Andhra, Karnataka, Bengal and Kamrup. This have been attested through discovery of Mauryan inscriptions, Northern Black Polished Ware (NBPW) potsherds, and punch marked coins from places lying in modern day Bangladesh, Odisha and Karnataka.

46 **The characteristic feature of the Mauryan pottery was** *(Chap 15, Class-XI, Old NCERT)*

(a) Painted Grey Ware
(b) Northern Black Polished Ware
(c) Ochre Coloured Pottery
(d) Black and Red Ware

Ans. (b)

Exp. Northern Black Polished Ware (NBPW) was the characteristic feature of Mauryan pottery. Megasthenes has mentioned in high praise the skill shown by artisans of Pataliputra palace.

They show high technical skills attained by them. The polishing of stone pillars, which are known as Northern Black Polished Ware are still found in sites of Mauryan empire. There are sculptures of peacock, bulls or lions made of them.

47 **Which of the following South kingdoms is not mentioned in the Ashokan inscriptions?** *(Chap 15, Class-XI, Old NCERT) (UPPSC Mains 2005)*

(a) Chola (b) Pandya (c) Satyaputras (d) Satavahana

Ans. (d)

Exp. The kingdom of Satavahana is not mentioned in the Ashokan inscriptions. This kingdom emerged in Peninsular India after the downfall of the Mauryan empire. The Rock Edict II and XIII mention that Chola, Chera, Pandya and Satyaputras lived on the borders of the Mauryan state.

48 **Which one of the following statements regarding Ashokan stone pillar is incorrect?** *(Chap 15, Class-XI, Old NCERT) (IAS Pre 1997)*

(a) These are highly polished. (b) These are monolithic.
(c) The shaft of pillars is tapering in shape.
(d) These are parts of architectural structures.

Ans. (d)

Exp. Statement (d) is incorrect regarding Ashokan stone pillar as the Mauryan stone pillars were usually not parts of architectural structures. They were erected stand-alone on all important highways and places. The chief characteristics of Ashokan stone pillar include

They were highly polished surface.
They were made from monolithic stone.
Their shaft of pillar is tapering in shape.
They used eloquent design including animals.
They used Chunar red sandstone.

49 **Which among the following monument(s) was/were constructed during the reign of Mauryan empire?** *(Chap 15, Class-XI, Old NCERT)*

1. Barabar Caves 2. Ajanta Caves
3. Sanchi Stupa 4. Kailasa Temple

Codes

(a) 1 and 2 (b) 2 and 3 (c) 1 and 4 (d) 1 and 3

Ans. (d)

Exp. Codes (1) and (3) are correct regarding the construction of monuments during Mauryan empire. Barabar Caves and Sanchi Stupa were constructed during the reign of Mauryan empire. The Mauryan artisans also started the practice of cutting out caves from rocks for monks to live in. Its examples are Barabar caves at the distance of 30 km from Gaya, Bihar.

Sanchi Stupa is in Madhya Pradesh. It was ordered to be constructed by Ashoka. It is also a rock cut structure.

Ajanta caves and Kailasa temples (Ellora) are in Maharashtra. They date back to different reigns (Satavahanas and Rashtrakutas) not to Mauryan empires.

50 **Which among the following statements regarding the Mauryan capital is correct?** *(Chap 15, Class-XI, Old NCERT)*

(a) It was located in Kumrahar on the outskirts of modern Prayagraj.
(b) The fragments of the stone pillars and stumps indicate existence of 80 pillared hall in the Mauryan capital.
(c) Chanakya in the Arthashastra states that the Mauryan palace was as beautiful as that of Iran.
(d) It was constructed by using unburnt bricks on the large scale.

Ans. (b)

Exp. Statement (b) is correct regarding the Mauryan capital. The Mauryas made a remarkable contribution to art and architecture. They introduced stone masonry on a wide scale. Megasthenes states that the Mauryan palace at Pataliputra was as splendid as that in the capital of Iran. Fragments of stone pillars and stumps, indicating the existence of a 80-pillared hall, have been discovered at Kumrahar on the outskirts of modern Patna.

51 **Consider the following regarding language and script used in the Mauryan Age.** *(Chap 2, Class-XII, New NCERT)*

1. In Indian part of the subcontinent, Aramaic language and Kharosthi script had been used.
2. In the North-Western part of India including territories in Afghanistan, Prakrit langauge and Brahmi script was used.

Which of the statements given above is/are incorrect?

(a) Only 1 (b) Only 2
(c) Both 1 and 2
(d) Neither 1 nor 2

Ans. (c)

Exp. Both the statements (1) and (2) are incorrect regarding language and script used in the Mauryan Age. Most Ashokan inscriptions were in the Prakrit language while those in the North-West of the subcontinent modern day (Afghanistan and Pakistan) were in Aramaic and Greek.

Prakrit inscriptions (used in present day Indian part of subcontinent) were written in the Brahmi script.

52 **Consider the following statements with reference to the contribution of Mauryan in the art and architecture.** *(Chap 15, Class-XI, Old NCERT)*

1. They introduced stone masonry on a wide scale.
2. The polished pillars were made up of a single piece of buff coloured sandstone.
3. They started the practice of hewing out caves from rocks for monks in India.
4. They started the use of burnt bricks for the first time in India.

Which of the statements given above are correct?

(a) 1 and 2
(b) 1, 2 and 3
(c) 2, 3 and 4
(d) 1 and 4

Ans. (b)

Exp. Statements (1), (2) and (3) are correct with reference contribution of Mauryan in the art and architecture.

Mauryans introduced stone masonry on a wide scale.

Mauryan artisans attained high technical skills in polishing the stone pillars, which are as shining as Northern Black Polished Ware (NBPW).

Each pillar is made of a single piece of buff coloured sandstone. Only their capitals, which are beautiful pieces of sculpture in the form of lions or bulls, are joined with the pillars on the top.

The Mauryan artisans also started the practice of hewing out caves from rocks for monks to live in.

The earliest examples are the Barabar caves at the distance of 30 km from Gaya, Bihar.

Statement (4) is incorrect because burnt brick was first used in Indus Valley Civilisation.

53 **With reference to Mauryan period, consider the following statements.** *(Class-XI, Old NCERT)*

1. Courtesans were accorded a special place in the social hierarchy.
2. Buddhist and Jain literature were primarily written in Prakrit.
3. Arthashastra is devoid of any mention of performing arts.

How many of the statements given above is/are correct?

(a) Only one
(b) Only two
(c) All three
(d) None of these

Ans. (a)

Exp. Only one statement i.e., (1) is correct with reference to the Mauryan period.

Courtesans were accorded a special place in social hierarchy and their contribution was highly valued.

Statements (2) and (3) are incorrect because Buddhist and Jain texts were primarily written in Pali. The Arthashastra notes the performing arts of the period, including music, instrumental music, bards, dance and theatre.

Society

54 **Which among the following statements regarding the state of society under the Mauryan Empire is incorrect?** *(Chap 15, Class-XI, Old NCERT)*

(a) Slaves were engaged in the agricultural operations.
(b) Ashoka tried to strengthen the institution of family and existing social classes.
(c) The Mauryan emperors prohibited the inter- mingling between the peasants and tribal societies.
(d) The Shudras were regarded as the collective property of the three higher varnas.

Ans. (c)

Exp. Statement (c) is incorrect regarding the state of society under the Mauryan Empire because Mauryan emperors supported the inter-mingling between the peasants and tribal societies.

This implies that tribal and other people would take to the habits of a settled, tax paying, peasant society and develop respect for paternal power, royal authority and for monks, priests and officers who helped enforce his authority.

55 **With reference to the welfare policy(s) undertaken by Ashoka, which of the following statements are correct?** *(Chap 15, Class-XI, Old NCERT)*

1. He taught people to live and let live and emphasised compassion towards animals.
2. He arranged for medical facilities for both human beings and animals.
3. He prohibited the practice of sati.

Codes

(a) 1 and 2 (b) 1, 2 and 3 (c) 2 and 3 (d) 1 and 3

Ans. (a)

Exp. Statements (1) and (2) are correct regarding welfare policies undertaken by Ashoka. Ashoka taught people to live and let live.

He emphasised compassion towards animals, birds and proper behaviour towards relatives. He built roads, dug wells and rest houses. He arranged for medical treatment for both human beings and animals.

Statement (3) is incorrect because there is no evidence of presence of sati during the reign of Ashoka, therefore the emperor didn't made any attempt to prohibit it.

56 **Consider the following statements with reference to Ashoka's perspective on religion.** *(Chap 7, Class-VI, New NCERT)*

1. He initiated Dhamma Yatras in which, he undertook pilgrimages to the Buddhist shrines.
2. He organised the first Buddhist Council and sent missionaries to South India and Sri Lanka.
3. He aspired to attain Nirvana, which was the goal of the Buddhist teaching.
4. He respected and made donations to religious sect other than the Buddhism.

Which of the statements given above are incorrect?

(a) 1 and 2
(b) 1, 2 and 3
(c) 2, 3 and 4
(d) 2 and 3

Ans. (d)

Exp. Statements (2) and (3) are incorrect with reference to Ashoka's perspective on religion because the Third Buddhist Council was conducted under the patronage of Emperor Ashoka. Further, instead of attaining Nirvana he sought a policy of development and empowerment of masses.

He never stated that his aim was to attain Nirvana.

Miscellaneous

57 Even before Ashoka, which among the following rulers had pursued pacifist policy of administration? *(Chap 14, Class-XI, Old NCERT)*

(a) Alexander of Macedonia
(b) Chandragupta Maurya of Magadha
(c) Akhenaton of Egypt
(d) Darius of Persia

Ans. (c)

Exp. The Akhenaton of Egypt had followed the pacifist policies even before Ashoka. However, Ashoka was probably unknown of his policies. He therefore, initiated his own policies based on the edifice of peace and compassion.

58 Which of the following best describes the term Maha-Sarthavaha, mentioned in the reference of Mauryan period. *(Class-XI, Old NCERT)*

(a) He was the officer in charge of the weight and measurements in Pataliputra.
(b) He was the head priest of the Buddhist Council.
(c) He was a caravan leader of long distance overland trade.
(d) He was the head of the espionage department of Pataliputra.

Ans. (c)

Exp. Option (c) is correct with related to Maha-Sarthavaha, mentioned in reference of the Mauryan period. In general, long distance overland trade was undertaken by merchant groups travelling together, as a caravan for security, led by a caravan leader known as the Maha-Sarthavaha.

59 Which among the following factor(s) was/were responsible for the downfall of the Mauryan empire? *(Chap 15, Class-XI, Old NCERT)*

1. Neglect of the North-West frontier
2. State patronage to the Buddhism
3. Oppressive rule in the Provinces
4. Highly centralised administration

Codes

(a) 1 and 2
(b) 1, 3 and 4
(c) 2, 3 and 4
(d) 1 and 4

Ans. (b)

Exp. Among the given factors (1), (3) and (4) were responsible for the downfall of Mauryan empire. The Mauryan empire fell shortly after Ashoka as the Brahamans were antagonised by state policies which were unfavourable to them.

The areas of North-West were left unchecked and Ashoka who was busy in his missionary activities didn't pay attention towards its safeguard measures.

The oppressive regime often leads to breaking up of an empire. Same happened with Mauryan Empire. Whose provincial governors were sometimes accused of Maladministration. Though Ashoka tried to do this away but couldn't succeed.

Factor mentioned in statement (2) is not responsible for the downfall as state patronage to Buddhism was not responsible for downfall of empire. It highly enriched the foreign relation of Mauryan empire.

60 With reference to Satavahana empire, consider the following statements. *(Chap14, Class-XI, Old NCERT)*

Statement-I Satavahana empire was a projection of the Mauryan empire in the Deccan.

Statement-II Satavahana rulers adopted the administrative units of the Mauryan empire.

Which one of the following is correct in respect of the above statements?

(a) Both Statement-I and Statement-II are correct and Statement-II is the correct explanation for Statement-I.
(b) Both Statement-I and Statement-II are correct and Statement-II is incorrect explanation for Statement-I.
(c) Statement-I is correct but, Statement-II is incorrect.
(d) Statement-I is incorrect but, Statement-II is correct.

Ans. (a)

Exp. Both Statement-I and Statement-II are correct and statement-II is the correct explanation for Statement-I. Magadha owed its expansion to certain basic material advantages.

Contacts established by administrators, traders, Jain and Buddhist monks led to the spread of the material culture of the Gangetic basin of the empire.

In some ways the Satavahana empire was a projection of the Mauryan empire in the Deccan.

The Satavahana rulers adopted some of the administrative units of Mauryan and in their times Buddhism flourished in the same manner as it did in the heart of the empire of Ashoka.

Chapter 08

Post-Mauryan Period

Post-Mauryan Period

Kingdoms of Post-Mauryan Period

Shunga Dynasty (185-75 BC)
- Founded by Pushyamitra Shunga who overthrew the last Mauryan king Brihadratha
- Followed Brahminism and made Vidisha as a capital
- Performed Ashvamedha, Rajasuya and Vajapeya sacrifice; Succeeded by Agnimitra, Sujyeshtha and Vasumitra

Kanva Dynasty (75-30 BC)
- Founded by Vasudeva; Followed Brahminism and made Vidisha as their capital
- Last ruler - Susarman

Satavahana Dynasty (230 BC-220 AD)
- Succeeded Mauryas in the Deccan region
- Referred as Andhras in Puranas
- Gautamiputra Satakarni was most important ruler who defeated Sakas, Pallavas and Yavanas (Nashik inscription)
- **Material Culture** Exploited rich minerals of Deccan such as iron-ores from Karimnagar and Warangal and gold from Kolar fields
- **Social Condition** Re-established social hierarchy mother enjoyed high status Ruling family was however patriarchal
- **Religious Lives** Promoted Brahminism; Cult of Bodhisattvas became popular and flourished Buddhism Important pilgrimage centre — Nagarjunakonda and Amravati
- **Administration** Ashokan administrative system retained, rural administration carried by Gaulmika. Granted tax- free villages to Brahmanas and Buddhist Monks
- **Art and Architecture** Built Chaityas and Viharas in Deccan prominent centres- Karle, Amravati and Nagarjunakonda
- **Economy** Development of 18 types of guilds; Agriculture was the main occupation
- **Ikshvaku Dynasty** Succeeded Satvahanas in Deccan region Matsya Purana mentioned Ikshvakus as Shriparvatiya Andhras

Indo-Greeks
- Started by Demetrius in 180 BC, who conquered Afghanistan and parts of Punjab;
- Most famous king Menander I
- They minted coins, which help to understand the history of their respective

Saka (Indo-Kingdoms)
- Central Asian nomadic tribe, first conquered Sindh and Saurashtra
- They were in constant confrontation with Satavahanas in South and Kushanas in North
- Most powerful ruler Rudradaman I who issued Junagarh inscription

Parthians
- Succeeded Saka rule in North-Western India;
- Migrated from Iran to India;
- Most renowned Parthian king- Gondophernes

Kushana
- Originally from the Chinese Turkestan; One of the five branches of the Yuezhi tribe
- Minted large number of coins
- Most famous ruler — Kanishka who convened Fourth Buddhist Council in Kashmir in 78 AD

Post-Mauryan Administration

Social Condition
- Foreigners incorporated into the caste structure
- Growth of trades, arts and crafts changed social status of Vaishyas and Shudras

Religious Condition
- Vedic ritualism, Bhagvatism, Buddhism and Jainism flourished
- Emergence of Mahayana and Hinayana sects in Buddhism

Trade
- Trade between India and Rome increased substantially
- Muslin, spices, pearls, jewellery and precious stones were exported-Large number of gold coins were exported to India

Coinage
- Indo-Greek rulers minted first gold coins
- Largest gold coin — Kushana period
- Dinar type gold coin issued by Kushana
- Coins made up of lead, potin and copper were used for day to day transactions

Art and Architecture
- Development of Gandhara, Mathura and Amravati school of art
- Important texts such as Milinda Panha, Buddhacharita, Mahavibhasha and Sushruta Samhita were compiled

Science and Technology
- Engineering skills in building of dams and irrigation tanks were developed
- In medicine, Charaka Samhita (by Charaka) and Sushruta Samhita (by Sushruta) were compiled

SOURCE **New NCERT Class VI** *(Traders, Kings and Pilgrimages)*, **Old NCERT Class VI** *(India from 200 BC to AD 300)*, **Old NCERT Class XI** *(Early Iron-Age Civilisation)*, **Old NCERT Class XI** *(Central Asian Contacts and Their Results)*, **New NCERT Class XII** *(The Age of Satvahanas)*, **New NCERT Class XII** *(King, Farmers and Towns)*, **New NCERT Class XII** *(Kinship, Caste and Class)*, **New NCERT Class XII** *(Thinkers, Beliefs and Buildings)*, **NIOS Module-1** *(Post Mauryan Developments)* **Tamil Nadu Board Class XI** *(Polity and Society in Post Mauryan Period)*

1 With reference to Post-Mauryan policy of ancient India, consider the following statements.

(Chap 15, Class-XI, Old NCERT)

1. Disintegration of the Mauryan empire was followed by the invasion from Central Asia and Western China.
2. Construction of Chinese wall created conditions for Bactrian Greeks to invade India.
3. Indo-Greek rulers instituted unified rule over India.

How many of the statements given above is/are correct?

(a) Only one (b) Only two
(c) All three (d) None of these

Ans. (b)

Exp. Only two statements i.e., (1) and (2) are correct with reference to post-Mauryan policy of ancient India.

Disintegration of the Mauryan empire was followed by the invasion by various groups of people based in Central Asia and Western China. These were Indo-Greeks, the Scythians or Shakas, the Parthians or the Pallavas and the Kushanas. It was through such a political process that India came in close contact with Central Asian politics and culture.

Construction of the Chinese wall created conditions for Bactrian Greeks to invade India. With the construction of the Chinese wall, the Scythians were now not in a position to push forward into China. So they turned their attention towards the neighbouring Greeks and Parthians. Pushed by the Scythian tribes, the Bactrian Greeks were forced to invade India.

Statement (3) is incorrect although Indo- Greek rulers occupied a large part of North-Western India, but the Indo-Greek rulers failed to establish united rule in India.

2 With reference to the historical period post 200 BC in India, consider the following statements.

(Chap 15, Class-XI, Old NCERT)

1. This period is marked by the coins which can be definitely attributed to the kings and dynasty unlike earlier punch-marked coins.
2. This period is marked by the introduction of Gandhara art which gave rise to Hellenistic art features.

How many of the statements given above is/are correct?

(a) Only 1 (b) Only 2
(c) Both 1 and 2 (d) Neither 1 nor 2

Ans. (a)

Exp. Only one statement i.e., (1) is correct with historical period post 200 BC in India. The Indo-Greeks were the first rulers in India to issue coins which can be definitely attributed to the kings. This is not possible in the case of the early punch- marked coins, which cannot be assigned with certainty to any dynasty.

Statement (2) is incorrect because the Greek rule is also memorable on account of the introduction of Hellenistic art features in the North-West frontier of India, giving rise to the Gandhara art.

Shunga Dynasty

3 With reference to post-Mauryan development, consider the following statements.

(Chap 6, Module, -1, NIOS)

1. Shungas dynasty was contemporary to Yavanas of Balkh.
2. Bhagabhadra was the ruler of the Kanvas dynasty, according to inscriptions found at Besnagar.

Which of the statements given above is/are correct?

(a) Only 1 (b) Only 2
(c) Both 1 and 2 (d) Neither 1 nor 2

Ans. (d)

Exp. Neither statements (1) nor (2) are correct with reference to post-Mauryan development.

While the Shungas were ruling in North India, the Indo-Greeks also known as Yavanas, emerged in Bactria (Balkh) as an independent power and soon started extending their rule in the North-Western and Northern parts of India.

Bhagabhadra was the ruler of the Shunga dynasty as per the inscriptions found at Besnagar.

4 With reference to the reign of Shunga dynasty, which of the following statements are correct?

(Chap 15, Class-XI, Old NCERT)

1. The rulers of this dynasty were ardent followers of Brahmanism and performed several Vedic sacrifices.
2. Contrary to the system of kingship suggested in the Dharamashastras, the rulers of this dynasty were Brahmana.
3. The great Sanskrit grammarian, Patanjali was contemporary of Pushyamitra Shunga.

Codes

(a) 1 and 2 (b) 2 and 3 (c) 1 and 3 (d) 1, 2 and 3

Ans. (d)

Exp. All the statements (1), (2) and (3) are correct with reference to the reign of Shunga dynasty.

The Mauryan empire was finally destroyed by Pushyamitra Shunga in 185 BC. Although Brahmana, was a General of the last Mauryan king Brihadratha, he is said to have killed Brihadratha, in public and forcibly usurped the throne of Pataliputra.

Shungas performed several Vedic sacrifices in order to mark the revival of the Brahmanical way of life. It is said that they persecuted the Buddhists. However, the Buddhist stupa at Bharhut was renovated during his reign. The great Sanskrit grammarian, Patanjali lived at the court of Pushyamitra Shunga. He compiled Mahabhashya, a commentary on Panini's Ashtadhyayi.

5 **Which one of the following epics of ancient India has the love story of the son of the founder of the Shunga dynasty?**

(Unit 7, Class-XI, Tamil Nadu Board) (IAS Pre 2016)

(a) Swapnavasavadatta (b) Malavikagnimitra
(c) Meghaduta (d) Ratnavali

Ans. (b)

Exp. Malavikagnimitra, narrates the love story of the son of the founder of the Shunga dynasty. It is the Sanskrit play written by Kalidasa in the 5th century AD.
It narrates the love story of King Agnimitra, the Shunga emperor at Vidisha. Agnimitra was the son of Pushyamitra Shunga, founder of the Shunga dynasty.

Kanva Dynasty

6 **With reference to the Kanva dynasty, which of the statements given below is/are correct?**

(Chap 15, Class-XI, Old NCERT)

1. It ruled Magadha after the downfall of Shunga dynasty.
2. They were greatest patron of Jainism in ancient India.

Codes

(a) Only 1 (b) Only 2
(c) Both 1 and 2 (d) Neither 1 nor 2

Ans. (a)

Exp. Only statement (1) is correct with reference to the Kanva dynasty. Shunga dynasty was followed by Kanva dynasty at Magadha. It was founded by Vasudeva, who killed the last Shunga king, Devabhuti. Its capital was at Pataliputra.
Statement (2) is incorrect because similar to Shungas, they were also followers of Brahmanism.

7. **Consider the following statements.**

(Chap 15, Class-XI, Old NCERT) (IAS Pre 2003)

1. The last Mauryan ruler, Brihadratha was assassinated by his commander in chief Pushyamitra Shunga.
2. The last Shunga king, Devabhuti was assassinated by his Brahmana minister Vasudeva Kanva who usurped the throne.
3. The last ruler of the Kanva dynasty was deposed by the Andhras.

Which of the statements given above is/are correct?

(a) 1 and 2 (b) Only 2 (c) Only 3 (d) 1, 2 and 3

Ans. (d)

Exp. All the statements are correct with reference to post Mauryan polity of ancient India. Emperor Brihadratha Maurya was the last Mauryan king of the Mauryan empire. He was killed by Pushyamitra Shunga, a Military General in the Mauryan army.
Devabhuti was the last Shunga ruler who was killed by his own minister Vasudeva Kanva in around 73 BC.
Vasudeva Kanva thus assassinated the last ruler of the Shunga dynasty and founded the Kanva dynasty.
According to the Vayu Purana the Kanva was a minor dynasty having only four rulers: Vasudeva, Bhumimitra, Narayana and Susaraman. The rulers of Kanva dynasty ruled for 45 years i.e., 73 to 28 BC Susaraman, the last ruler of Kanva dynasty was killed by the Andhra king Simuka.

Satavahana Dynasty

8 **Consider the following with reference to the Satavahana dynasty.** *(Chap 3, Class-XII, New NCERT)*

1. It succeeded the Mauryas in the Deccan and Central India after the gap of 100 years.
2. The rulers of this dynasty were identified through matronymics.
3. Similar to the Mauryas, the rulers of this dynasty established matrimonial alliances with Indo-Greeks.

Which of the statements given above is/are incorrect?

(a) 1 and 2 (b) 2 and 3
(c) Only 3 (d) Only 2

Ans. (c)

Exp. Statement (3) is incorrect with reference to the Satavahana dynasty because Satavahana practiced endogamy, marriage within the kin group, which was prevalent amongst several communities in South India. Such marriages amongst kinfolk (such as cousins) ensured a close-knit community. They didn't established matrimonial alliances with Indo-Greeks.

9 **With reference to Satavahana dynasty, consider the following statements.** *(Chap 16, Class-XI, Old NCERT)*

1. Early Satavahana kings appeared not in Maharashtra, but in Andhra, where most of their early inscriptions have been found.
2. Satavahanas defeated Sakas and their greatest competitors were Kanvas.
3. Nahapana was the important ruler of this dynasty who conquered Malwa and Kathiawar.

How many of the statements given above is/are incorrect?

(a) Only one (b) Only two
(c) All three (d) None of these

Ans. (c)

Exp. All three statements i.e., (1), (2) and (3) given above are incorrect with reference to Satavahana dynasty. The early Satavahana kings appeared not in Andhra, but in Maharashtra where most of their early inscriptions have been found.
They set up their power in the upper Godavari valley. Gradually, they extended their power over Karnataka and Andhra. Satavahana defeated the Kanvas in the first century BC and established their power in part of central India.

Sakas were the greatest competitors of Satavahana , who had established their power in the upper Deccan and Eastern India. Nahapana was an important ruler of the Western Kshatrapas, descendant of the Indo-Scythians, in North-Western India, who ruled during the 1st or 2nd century AD. Gautamiputra Satakarni (106-130 AD) defeated Nahapana and revived Satavahana dynasty.

10 With reference to Satavahana dynasty, consider the following statements. *(Chap 16 & 17 Class-XI, Old NCERT)*

1. They found mention in the Aitareya Brahmana and Matsya Purana.
2. Nashik inscriptions describes Hala (20-24 AD) as the destroyer of Sakas and Pallavas.
3. Hostilities between Sakas and Satavahana dynasty was contained by matrimonial alliances.

How many of the statements given above is/are incorrect?

(a) Only one (b) Only two
(c) All three (d) None of these

Ans. (a)

Exp. Only one statement i.e., (2) is incorrect with reference to Satavahana dynasty.

In a Nashik inscription of his mother Gautami Balashri, he is described as the destroyer of the Sakas, Pallavas and the Yavanas (Greeks).

11 For which of the following rulers, the term *Ekabrahmana* has been used?
(Chap 16, Class-XI, Old NCERT) (UP RO/ARO Pre 2016)

(a) Pushyamitra Shunga
(b) Kharavela
(c) Gautamiputra Shatakarni
(d) Susharman

Ans. (c)

Exp. For Gautamiputra Shatakarni, the term *Ekabrahmana* has been used. Gautamiputra Shatakarni (106-130 AD) was the greatest ruler of Satavahana dynasty and called himself the only Brahmana. He defeated the Shakas and destroyed many Kshatriya rulers including his adversary *Nahapana*. He also occupied Malwa and Kathiawar which lay under the control of Sakas.

12 With reference to Satavahana dynasty, consider the following statements.
(Chap 16 & 17 Class-XI, Old NCERT)

1. Terms Kataka and Skanadhavaras mentioned in Satavahana inscriptions meant coins in lead and gold respectively.
2. Satavahana kings mostly issued coins of lead and they used gold as bullion.

Which of the statements given above is/are correct?

(a) Only 1 (b) Only 2
(c) Both 1 and 2 (d) Neither 1 nor 2

Ans. (b)

Exp. Only statement (2) is correct with reference to Satavahana dynasty. The Satavahana mostly issued coins of lead, which is found in the Deccan. Satavahanas may have used gold as bullion for they did not issue gold coins as the Kushans did.

Statement (1) is incorrect because the terms Kataka and Skanadhavaras frequently mentioned in the Satavahana inscriptions meant military camps and settlements respectively. Skandhavaras were fortified and represented feudal character of kingdom. Both of these settlements served as administrative centre as long as king was there.

13 With reference to Satavahanas dynasty, consider the following statements. *(Chap 16, Class-XI, Old NCERT)*

1. Some elements of material culture appeared in North India centuries before they acquired importance in the Deccan.
2. Evidence of the use of perforated roof tiles and fire baked bricks have been found from the Peddabonkur site belonging to Satavahana dynasty.
3. Towns appeared simultaneously in Maharashtra and Eastern Deccan by the first century BC.

How many of the statements given above is/are correct?

(a) Only one (b) Only two
(c) All three (d) None of these

Ans. (b)

Exp. Only two statements i.e., (1) and (2) are correct with reference to Satavahanas dynasty. These elements of material life had become quite important in North India by 300 BC, but they acquired importance in the Deccan a couple of centuries later.

Peddabonkur (200 BC- 200 AD) in Karimnagar district, is a Satavahana site. Here we find regular use of fire-baked bricks and use of flat, perforated roof tiles.

Statement (3) is incorrect because Towns appeared in Maharashtra by the first century BC, when we find several crafts.

They emerged in the Eastern Deccan a century later.

14 With reference to the societal profile during the Satavahanas, consider the following statements.
(Chap 16, Class-XI, Old NCERT)

1. The absorption of the Sakas in Hindu society facilitated the intermarriage between the Sakas and the Satavahanas.
2. Gandhikas were the annual donations made by Satavahanas kings to Buddhist monks.
3. Satavahanas ruling family was patriarchal.
4. Satavahana show traces of a matrilineal social structure.

How many of the statements given above is/are incorrect?

(a) Only one (b) Only two (c) Only three (d) All of these

Ans. (a)

Exp. Only one statement i.e., (2) is incorrect with reference to societal profile during the Satavahanas. The term Gandhikas refers to denote all kinds of shopkeepers.

15 Consider the following statements with reference to the state of administration under the Satavahanas.

(Chap 17, Class-XI, Old NCERT)

1. Similar to the pattern of administration followed during the Mauryan age, the districts and officials were referred as Ahara and Amatyas respectively.
2. The Satavahana kingdom had three grades of feudatories headed by the Raja, Mahabhoja and Senapati.
3. The administration in the rural areas was placed in the hands of Gaulmika who was also the head of military regiments.

Which of the statements given above are correct?

(a) 1 and 2 (b) 2 and 3
(c) 1 and 3 (d) 1, 2 and 3

Ans. (d)

Exp. All the statements (1), (2) and (3) are correct regarding the state of administration under the Satavahana. The Satavahanas retained some of the administrative units found in Ashokan times. Their district was called *Ahara*, as it was known in the time of Ashoka.

Their officials were known as Amatyas and Mahamatras as they were known in Mauryan times.

The Satavahana kingdom had three grades of feudatories. The highest grade was formed by the king who was called *raja* and who had the right to strike coins. The second grade was formed by the *Mahabhoja*, and the third grade by the *Senapati*.

The administration in the rural areas was placed in the hands of *Gaulmika* who was the head of a military regiment consisting of 9 chariots, 9 elephants, 25 horses and 45 foot-soldiers.

16 With reference to Satavahanas Policy and administration, consider the following statements.

(Class-XI, Old NCERT)

1. Satavahanas kings were the first in Indian history to make tax free land grants to Buddhists Monks and Brahmanas.
2. Coercion played an important part in the Satavahana administration.
3. Administration of Satavahanas was devoid of any feudalistic elements for the first time in Indian history.

How many of the statements given above is/are correct?

(a) Only one (b) Only two
(c) All three (d) None of these

Ans. (b)

Exp. Only two statements i.e., (1) and (2) are correct with reference to the policy and administration of Satavahana. Satavahanas kings were the first in Indian history to make tax free land grants to Buddhists and Brahmanas.

This practice became more prominent in succeeding periods. Coercion played an important part in the Satavahana administration. Head of the army platoon was therefore posted in the countryside to maintain peace. The military character of the Satavahana rule is also evident from the common use of such terms as Kataka and Skandhavaras in their inscriptions.

Statement (3) is incorrect because there were certain feudalistic and military elements in the administration of Satavahanas. The Satavahanas kingdom had three grade feudatories i.e., raja, mahabhoja and Senapati.

17 Consider the following statements with reference to the religious policies followed by the Satavahanas.

(Chap 17, Class-XI, Old NCERT)

1. The Satavahana rulers called themselves Brahmanas and persecuted the followers of Buddhism and Jainism.
2. They started the practice of making land grants to the brahmanas.
3. The king was represented as the upholder of Dharma.

Which of the statements given above is/are incorrect?

(a) 1 and 2 (b) Only 1 (c) 1 and 3 (d) Only 3

Ans. (b)

Exp. Statement (1) is incorrect with reference to religious policies followed by the Satavahanas because although the Satavahanas were Brahmanas they didn't persecuted Buddhists and rather made land grants to them also. Mahayana sect of Buddhism had considerable followers in their times.

18 With reference to Amravati Stupa, which of the following statements are correct?

(Chap 4, Class-XII, New NCERT)

1. It was constructed during the reign of Satavahana rulers.
2. It is full of sculptures which depicts the various scenes from the life of the Buddha.
3. Similar to the Sanchi Stupa it was also preserved by the local authorities till the 19th century.

Codes

(a) 1 and 2 (b) 2 and 3
(c) 1 and 3 (d) 1, 2 and 3

Ans. (a)

Exp. Statements (1) and (2) are correct with reference to Amravati Stupa.

The construction of Amravati Stupa began in about 200 BC but was completely reconstructed in the second half of the second century AD. It was patronised by the Satavahana rulers.

It is full of sculptures which depicts the various scenes from the life of Buddha. The theme of this sculptures were drawn from *Jataka* and was narrative in outlook. Statement (3) is incorrect because Amravati Stupa is not well preserved and its stones and parts were taken to other places and used.

19 Consider the following statements with reference to the architecture in the reign of Satavahana. *(Chap 17, Class-XI, Old NCERT)*

1. Large number of Chaityas and Vihara were constructed in the regions of Maharashtra and Andhra Pradesh.
2. Influenced by the Mahayana tradition of Buddhism, the sculptures of Satavahana times depicted the image of Buddha and other Bodhisattva from the Jataka tales.
3. The construction of Buddhist monuments were commissioned by the rulers only.

Which of the statements given above is/are incorrect?

(a) 1 and 2 (b) Only 1
(c) Only 3 (d) 1, 2 and 3

Ans. (c)

Exp. Statement (3) is incorrect regarding the state of architecture in the reign of Satavahana as the construction of Stupa, Chaitya, Vihara etc were undertaken by the rulers as well as by merchant guilds.

20 With reference to the extraction of minerals during the age of Satavahana, which of the following statements are correct? *(Chap 17, Class-XI, Old NCERT)*

1. They exploited the iron-ores of Karimnagar and Warangal region of the Andhra Pradesh.
2. During the reign of Satavahana, iron was introduced in the Deccan and Central India for the first time.
3. Lead was used for the minting of coins on a very large scale.

Codes

(a) 1 and 2 (b) 2 and 3
(c) 1 and 3 (d) 1, 2 and 3

Ans. (c)

Exp. Statements (1) and (3) are correct regarding extraction of minerals during the age of Satavahana. The mines of Karimnagar and Warangal region of Andhra Pradesh was the chief source of iron-ore for the Satavahana. It greatly benefited their economy.

Under Satavahana, lead was the chief metal used for mining of coins. They also commissioned coins made up of potin (mixture of copper, tin and lead), copper and bronze.

Statement (2) is incorrect because iron had been used before the Satavahanas, the megalithic (stone builder) were familiar with iron.

21 Consider the following Assertion (A) and Reason (R) and choose the correct code. *(Chap 17, Class-XI, Old NCERT)*

Assertion (A) Coercion played a key role in the administration of Satavahana.

Reason (R) The tribal people in the Deccan were not thoroughly Brahmanised and reconciled to the new rule.

Codes

(a) Both A and R are true and R is the correct explanation of A.
(b) Both A and R are true, but R is not the correct explanation of A.
(c) A is true, but R is false.
(d) A is false, but R is true.

Ans. (a)

Exp. Both Assertion (A) and Reason (R) are true and Reason (R) is the correct explanation of Assertion (A). The military character of the Satavahana rule is also evident from the common use of such terms as *Kataka* and *Skandhavaras* in their inscriptions. Thus, coercion played a key role in the Satavahana administration.

The tribal people in the Deccan were not thoroughly Brahmanised and reconciled to the new rule, it was necessary to keep them under strong military control. The administration in the rural areas was placed in the hands of *gaulmika*.

22 With reference to the Satavahanas, consider the following statements. *(Class-XI, Old NCERT)*

Statement-I The Satavahana kingdom established in the Deccan had an administrative structure similar to the Mauryan.

Statement-II The Provincial governor of the Satavahanas had a considerable degree of autonomy.

Which one of the following is correct in respect of the above statements?

(a) Both Statement-I and Statement-II are correct and Statement-II is the correct explanation for Statement-I.
(b) Both statement-I and Statement-II are correct and Statement-II is not the correct explanation for Statement-I.
(c) Statement-I is correct, but Statement-II is incorrect.
(d) Statement-I is incorrect statement-II is correct.

Ans. (b)

Exp. Both Statement-I and Statement-II are correct and Statement-II is not the correct explanation for Statement-I. The Satavahanas kept some of the administrative units found in Ashokan times. Their officials were known as amatyas and mahamatras, as they were known in Mauryan times. However, Satavahana kingdom established in the Deccan area, comprising the modern states of Andhra Pradesh and Telangana, was not like the centralised empire of the Mauryas and the provincial governors of the Satavahanas had a considerable degree of autonomy.

Indo-Greek Invasions

23 With reference to the Indo- Greeks Invasions, consider the following statements. *(Class-XI, Old NCERT)*

1. They were the first to invade India after the downfall of the Mauryan empire.
2. They introduced a practice of military governorship in India.
3. Menander successfully attacked Pataliputra, but retreated without consolidating his conquest.

How many of the statements given above is/are incorrect?

(a) Only one (b) Only two
(c) All three (d) None of these

Ans. (d)

Exp. None of the statements given above are incorrect with reference to Indo-Greeks. They were the first to invade India after the downfall of the Mauryan empire. They introduced a practice of governorship in India. Menander (165/145-130 BC) was the best known of the Indo- Greeks Kings. He successfully attacked Pataliputra, but retreated without consolidating his conquest.

24 Consider the following statements about Indo-Greek King Menander. *(Chap 16, Class-XI, Old NCERT)*

1. From his base in Punjab, he invaded the Ganga-Yamuna doab.
2. He was converted to Buddhism by the monk Nagarjuna.

Which of the statements given above is/are correct?

(a) Only 1 (b) Only 2
(c) Both 1 and 2 (d) Neither 1 nor 2

Ans. (c)

Exp. Both the statements (1) and (2) are correct about Indo-Greek King Menander. The most famous Indo-Greek ruler Milinda also known as Menander (165-145 BC) had his capital at Sialkot, Punjab in Pakistan. He invaded the Ganga-Yamuna Doab from his base in Punjab. He was converted to Buddhism by Nagasena, who is also known as Nagarjuna. He had philosophical discourse with Nagarjuna and asked many questions about life.

These questions and answers are recorded in a form of book known as Milind Panho or Questions of Milinda.

25 With reference to the invasion of Indo-Greeks in India, which among the following statements are correct? *(Chap 16, Class-XI, Old NCERT)*

1. The weakness of Seleucid empire of Bactria and Parthia was one of the reasons behind Greek invasion in India.
2. Their territories were captured by Scythian tribes which compelled them to invade India.
3. They were successful in establishing united rule in India.

Codes

(a) 1 and 2 (b) 2 and 3 (c) 1 and 3 (d) 1, 2 and 3

Ans. (a)

Exp. Statements (1) and (2) are correct with reference to the invasion of Indo-Greeks in India.

The first to cross Hindukush were the Greeks, who ruled Bactria, lying in North Afghanistan. One important cause of invasion was the weakness of the Seleucid empire which had been established in Bactria and the adjoining areas of Iran called Parthia.

Due to the Scythian tribes the later Greeks were unable to hold their power in this area. So, they turned to invade India.

Statement (3) is incorrect because they were unable to establish United rule over India. Two different parallel dynasties ruled over North-West India.

The Shakas

26 Consider the following statements about the reign of Shakas in India. *(Chap 16, Class-XI, Old NCERT)*

1. They controlled much larger part of India than the Indo-Greeks.
2. There were five branches of the Shakas with their seats of power in different parts of India and Afghanistan.

Which of the statements given above is/are correct?

(a) Only 1 (b) Only 2
(c) Both 1 and 2 (d) Neither 1 nor 2

Ans. (c)

Exp. Both the statements (1) and (2) are correct about the reign of Shakas in India.

The Greeks were followed by the Shakas, who controlled a much larger part of India than the Greeks.

There were five branches of the Shakas with their seats of power in different parts of India and Afghanistan. One branch of the Shakas settled in Afghanistan. The second branch settled in Punjab with Taxila as its capital. The third branch settled in Mathura, where it ruled for about two centuries. The fourth branch established its hold over Western India, where the Shakas continued to rule until the fourth century AD. The fifth branch of the Shakas established its power in the upper Deccan.

27 With reference to Shaka rule in India, consider the following statements. *(Class-XI, Old NCERT)*

1. The first Shaka ruler in India was Maues (80 BC).
2. Shakas found it difficult to assimilate into Hindu society.

Which of the statements given above is/are correct?

(a) Only 1 (b) Only 2
(c) Both 1 and 2 (d) Neither 1 nor 2

Ans. (c)

Exp. Both statements (1) and (2) are correct with reference to Shaka rule in India. The first Shaka ruler in India was Maues or Moa/Moga (80 BC). He occupied Gandhara, driving a wedge into the Indo-Greek kingdoms, but it was his successor Azes who finally destroyed the last remnants of the Indo- Greek kingdoms and extended Shaka rule as far as Mathura.

In India, the Shakas became assimilated into Hindu society. They began to adopt Hindu names and religious beliefs, so much so that their coins had representations of Hindu gods on one side.

28 Consider the following statements with reference to the Sudarshana lake. *(Chap 2, Class-XII, New NCERT)*

1. It was an artificial reservoir constructed in the Girnar region of Gujarat.
2. It was built by the local governor during the reign of Mauryas.
3. A rock inscription of the Saka ruler, Rudradaman gives information about this lake.
4. It was destroyed by the Indo-Greek rulers in India.

Which of the statements given above is/are incorrect?

(a) 1 and 2 (b) Only 4 (c) Only 3 (d) 1 and 4

Ans. (b)

Exp. Statement (4) is incorrect because Sudarshana lake with reference to as terrible storm broke the embankments and water gushed out of the lake. It was not destroyed by the Indo-Greek rulers in India. Rudradaman, a Saka ruler, ruling in the area, claimed to have got the lake repaired using his own resources, without imposing any tax on his subjects.

The Parthians

29 Consider the following statements about the reign of the Parthians in India. *(Chap 6, Class-XI, Old NCERT)*

1. In comparison with the Greeks and the Shakas they occupied a large portion of North-Western India.
2. The most famous Parthian king was Gondophernes in whose reign St. Thomas visited India for the propagation of Christianity in India.

Which of the statements given above is/are incorrect?

(a) Only 1 (b) Only 2
(c) Both 1 and 2 (d) Neither 1 nor 2

Ans. (a)

Exp. Statement (1) is incorrect about the reign of the Parthians in India because in comparison with the Greeks and the Shakas they occupied only a small portion of North-Western India.

30 With reference to Rudradaman I, consider the following statements. *(Unit 5, Class-XI, Tamil Nadu Board)*

1. Junagarh inscriptions of Gujarat details the exploits of Shaka Kshatraps.
2. He commissioned the first ever long inscription in Chaste Sanskrit.
3. He ruled parts of Uttar Pradesh, Bihar and Bengal.

How many of the statements given above is/are incorrect?

(a) Only one (b) Only two
(c) All three (d) None of these

Ans. (b)

Exp. Only one statement i.e., (3) is incorrect with reference to Shaka kshatraps Rudradaman-I as ruled parts of Western India comprising modern territories of Sindh, Gujarat, Konkan, Malwa and Kathiawar.

The Kushans

31 With reference to Kushan dynasty, consider the following statements. *(Class-XI, Old NCERT)*

1. Kushans approached Shakas for war help against Parthians.
2. Kushans were one of the five clans into which the Yardung tribe was divided.

How many of the statements given above is/are correct?

(a) Only 1 (b) Only 2
(c) Both 1 and 2 (d) Neither 1 nor 2

Ans. (d)

Exp. None of the statements given above is correct with reference to the Kushans dynasty.

The Shakas approached the Kushans for war help against the Parthians. The Kushans belong to the Yuechis tribes of Central Asia. The Parthians were followed by the Kushans, who are also called Yuechis or Tocharians. The Kushans were one of the five clans into which the Yuechis tribe was divided.

32 Consider the following statements with reference to the Kushan dynasty. *(Chap 16, Class-XI, Old NCERT)*

1. The ruler of this dynasty controlled the silk route passing from China to the territories of the Roman empire.
2. It was the first dynasty to issue gold coins on the wide scale.

Which of the statements given above is/are correct?

(a) Only 1 (b) Only 2
(c) Both 1 and 2 (d) Neither 1 nor 2

Ans. (c)

Exp. Both the statements (1) and (2) are correct regarding Kushan dynasty.

The Kushans controlled the silk route, which started from China and passed through their empire in Central Asia and Afghanistan to Iran and Western Asia which formed part of the Roman empire.

Kushans were the first rulers in India to issue gold coins on a wide scale.

They levied heavy tolls on traders because of that they were able to manage prosperous empire.

33 Which one of the following pairs is correctly matched? *(Chap 16, Class-XI, Old NCERT) (CGPSC Pre 2008)*

(a) Harappan Civilisation – Painted Grey Ware
(b) Kushans – Gandhara School of Art
(c) Mughals – Ajanta Paintings
(d) Marathas – Pahari School of Painting

Ans. (b)

Exp. Pair (b) is correctly matched. The Gandhara School of Art flourished under the reign of Kushans. It was influenced by Graeco-Roman tradition and also incorporated some of the indigenous elements of sculpture. It used green-schist as the medium. Beautiful images of Buddha were created through this art form. While pairs (a), (c) and (d) are incorrectly matched because Painted Grey Ware was the characteristics of Vedic age (not Harappan Civilisation), Ajanta paintings was done during the reign of Gupta empire (not Mughal empire) and Pahari School of Painting flourished during the reign of Rajput kings of Basholi and Kangra (not Marathas).

34 The modern day territories of which of the following countries were part of the Kushan empire? *(Chap 16, Class-XI, Old NCERT)*

1. India
2. Iran
3. Afghanistan
4. Vietnam

Codes

(a) 1 and 2 (b) 2 and 3 (c) 1, 2 and 3 (d) All of these

Ans. (c)

Exp. With reference to the Kushan empire codes (1), (2) and (3) are correct. As per modern day territories of India, Iran and Afghanistan were the part of the Kushan empire. Kushan empire extended from the Oxus river to the Ganga, from Khorasan in Central Asia to Varanasi in Uttar Pradesh. A good part of Central Asia now included in the Commonwealth of Independent States (in former USSR), a portion of Iran, a portion of Afghanistan, almost the whole of Pakistan and almost the whole of Northern India were brought under one rule by the Kushans. Vietnam was not a part of the Kushan empire.

35 Consider the following statements about the Kushan dynasty. *(Chap 16, Class-XI, Old NCERT)*

1. Its kings adopted the pompous titles of king of kings and sons of God.
2. They introduced the satrap system of government.
3. Hereditary dual rule was also prevalent during the reign of the Kushan dynasty.

Which of the statements given above are correct?

(a) 1 and 2 (b) 2 and 3 (c) 1 and 3 (d) 1, 2 and 3

Ans. (d)

Exp. All the statements (1), (2) and (3) are correct about the Kushan dynasty.

Kushans solidified idea of their godly right of kingship. Kushan kings were called sons of God. It was used to legitimise the royal authority.

The Kushans also introduced the satrap system of government. In satrap system, the empire was divided into numerous satrapies and each satrapy was placed under the rule of a satrap.

The hereditary dual rule, two kings ruling in the same kingdom at same time, were also there.

36 Consider the following statements with reference to the geographical extent of the Kushan empire. *(Chap 16, Class-XI, Old NCERT)*

1. The inscriptions related with the Kushan rulers had been discovered at Mathura, Shravasti, Kaushambi and Varanasi.
2. Varanasi and Purushapura were the first and second capital of the Kushan empire in India.
3. It ruled vast area encompassing the present day modern territories of nine countries.

Which of the statements given above is/are incorrect?

(a) 1 and 3 (b) 1 and 2 (c) Only 2 (d) Only 3

Ans. (c)

Exp. Statement (2) is incorrect with reference to the geographical extent of the Kushan empire as coins, inscriptions, constructions pieces of sculpture found in Mathura show that it was their second capital in India, their first capital was Purushapura or Peshawar where Kanishka erected a monastery and a huge stupa. The empire of Kushans spread from Khorasan in Central Asia to Varanasi in Uttar Pradesh. This had given cultural and other processes to mingle between people of different countries of their empires which are now nine modern countries.

37 With reference to Kushan ruler, Kanishka, which of the following statements are correct? *(Chap 16, Class-XI, Old NCERT)*

1. He defeated the Chinese ruler from the Han dynasty in the first century AD.
2. To consolidate the teachings of Mahayana Buddhism, he convened a Buddhist Council in Kashmir.
3. He started the Saka Era in 78 AD.

Codes

(a) 1 and 2 (b) 2 and 3
(c) 1 and 3 (d) 1, 2 and 3

Ans. (b)

Exp. Statements (2) and (3) are correct with reference to Kushan ruler, Kanishka.

Kanishka (78-101 AD) was most famous Kushan ruler. Kanishka was a great patron of Mahayana Buddhism. He convened Buddhist Council in Kashmir, in which teachings of Mahayana Buddhism were finalised.

He started an era in 78 AD, which is now known as Saka era and used by Government of India.

Statement (1) is incorrect because he was defeated by the Han dynasty Chinese ruler in first century AD.

38 Which one of the following is the correct chronological order with reference to the invaders in ancient India?

(Chap 16, Class-XI, Old NCERT) (IAS Pre 2006)

(a) Greeks-Sakas-Kushans (b) Greeks-Kushans-Sakas
(c) Sakas-Greeks-Kushanas (d) Sakas-Kushans-Greeks

Ans. (a)

Exp. The correct chronological order with reference to the invaders in ancient India is Greeks-Sakas-Kushans.

The Indo-Greeks came to India first in second century BC.

The Shakas ruled over India from first century BC to fourth century AD.

The Shaka domination was followed by the Parthians. They ruled over India at the same time as Sakas but over lesser areas than them.

The Kushans ruled after Parthians, they were called Yuechis. They ruled from, Kadphises- 50 AD, to successors of Kanishka till 230 AD.

Impact of Central Asian Contacts on Indian Culture

39 Consider the following statements with reference to Indo-Greeks in India. *(Chap 16, Class-XI, Old NCERT)*

1. They issued coins which can be definitely attributed to the kings.
2. They were the first to issue gold coins in India.
3. They introduced features of Hellenistic art in the North-West frontier of India.
4. They introduced spoked wheel in India.

Which of the statements given above are correct?

(a) 1, 2 and 3 (b) 2, 3 and 4
(c) 1, 3 and 4 (d) All of these

Ans. (a)

Exp. Statements (1), (2) and (3) are correct with reference to Indo-Greeks in India.

The Indo-Greeks were the first rulers in India to issue coins which can be definitely attributed to the kings.

The Indo-Greeks were the first to issue gold coins in India, which increased in number under the Kushans.

The Greek rule introduced features of Hellenistic art in the North-West frontier of India. This art was not purely Greek. It was the result of Greek contact with non-Greeks.

Statement (4) is incorrect because spoked wheel were in use even in Mauryan rule.

40 With reference to impact of Central Asian contacts on Indian culture, consider the following statements. *(Chap 16, Class-XI, Old NCERT)*

1. Heliodorus set up a pillar in honour of Vasudeva in Mathura.
2. Image of Shiva and Buddha appeared on the coins of Kushans.
3. Period of Saka-Kushan phase in Indian history was characterised by Red ware potteries.

How many of the statements given above is/are incorrect?

(a) Only one (b) Only two
(c) All three (d) None of these

Ans. (a)

Exp. Only one statement i.e., (1) is incorrect with reference to impact of Central Asian contacts on Indian culture. The Greek ambassador Heliodorus set up a pillar in honour of Vasudeva near Vidisha (headquarters of Vidisha district) in Madhya Pradesh around the middle of the second century BC.

41 Which one of the following statements about the impact of the Shakas and Kushans on Indian culture is incorrect? *(Chap 16, Class-XI, Old NCERT)*

(a) They adopted the Indian names.
(b) They introduced their own language, script and religion in India.
(c) They became integral part of the Indian society.
(d) They introduced turban, tunic, trousers and heavy long coat.

Ans. (b)

Exp. Statement (b) is incorrect about the impact of the Shakas and Kushans on Indian culture because they belonged to the tribal culture of West and Central Asia and devoid of such elements in their culture.

Thus, they patronised and cultivated Sanskrit literature, converted to indigenous religious such as Buddhism and Vaishnavism and adopted Brahmi Script. They also adopted the Indian names and became integral part of the Indian Society. However, Kushan introduced turban, tunic, trousers and heavy long coat.

42 Consider the following statements with reference to the contribution of Shakas and Kushans in military technology. *(Chap 16, Class-XI, Old NCERT)*

1. They popularised the use of spears and lances for the horseman.
2. They introduced the use of caps, helmets and boots in warfare.
3. They also introduced the use of gun powder for storming the fortress of the adversaries.

Which of the statements given above are correct?

(a) 1 and 2 (b) 1 and 3
(c) 1 and 4 (d) 2, 3 and 4

Ans. (a)

Exp. Statements (1) and (2) are correct with reference to the contribution of Shakas and Kushans in military technology.

Shakas and Kushans brought better cavalry and the use of riding horse on a large scale. Some of their horsemen were heavily armoured and fought with spears and lances. They also brought caps, helmets and boots. They were used by warriors.

Statement (3) is incorrect because they didn't introduced gun powder. It was introduced later in medieval period.

43 With reference to the state of religion under the Kushan dynasty, which of the following statements is/are correct? *(Chap 16, Class-XI, Old NCERT)*

1. The Kushan ruler, Vasudeva was worshipped as an incarnation of God Krishna.
2. The Kushan ruler, Kanishka was the greatest patron of Buddhism after the Ashoka.

Codes

(a) Only 1
(b) Only 2
(c) Both 1 and 2
(d) Neither 1 nor 2

Ans. (b)

Exp. Only statement (2) is correct with reference to the state of religion under the Kushan dynasty. Kanishka became great patron of Mahayana Buddhism. He convened a Buddhist Council in Kashmir. The members of the council composed 3,00,000 words, which thoroughly explained the three pitakas or collections of Buddhist literature.

Kanishka got these commentaries engraved on sheets of red copper, enclosed them in a stone receptacle and raised a stupa over it. Kanishka set up many other stupas to perpetuate the memory of the Buddha.

Statement (1) is incorrect because Kushan ruler Vasudeva whose name is synonym for Krishna. He was worshipped as an incarnation of Lord Vishnu.

44 Consider the following statements with reference to Gandhara art. *(Chap 16, Class-XI, Old NCERT)*

1. It was synthesis of local, Greek, Romans and Central Asian elements under the influence of Buddhism.
2. In this art form, images of the Buddha were made in the Graeco-Roman style.
3. It was patronised by the rulers from Shaka dynasty.

Which of the statements given above are correct?

(a) 1 and 2
(b) 2 and 3
(c) 1 and 3
(d) 1, 2 and 3

Ans. (a)

Exp. Statements (1) and (2) are correct regarding Gandhara art. Kushan rulers brought artists and masons of Central Asian, Gandhara and Mathura together. Pieces of sculpture from Central Asia show synthesis of both local and Indian elements under the influence of Buddhism.

Indian craftsmen came into contact with the Central Asians, Greeks and Romans, especially in the North-Western frontier of India in Gandhara. This gave rise to a new kind of art in which images of the Buddha were made in the Graeco-Roman style. The hair of the Buddha was fashioned in the Graeco-Roman style.

Statement (3) is incorrect because Gandhara art was patronised by the rulers of Kushan dynasty.

45 Consider the following statements with reference to Mathura School of Art. *(Chap 16, Class-XI, Old NCERT)*

1. Similar to Gandhara School of Art, it also focused on Buddhism only.
2. It primarily used red sandstone for the construction of sculptures.
3. It was primarily a centre of indigenous art, promoted by the rulers of Kushan dynasty.

Which of the statements given above is/are incorrect?

(a) 1 and 2 (b) Only 1
(c) 1 and 3 (d) Only 3

Ans. (b)

Exp. Statement (1) is incorrect with reference to Mathura School of Art because this school of art not only depicts the image of Buddha, but also of Jain Tirthankaras and Hindu gods and goddesses. Mathura school was patronised by Kushana rulers.

46 Consider the following statements about Ashvaghosha. *(Chap 16, Class-XI, Old NCERT)*

1. He enjoyed the patronage of Kushans.
2. He wrote Buddhacharita, the biography of the Buddha.
3. He also composed the Saundarananda which is a fine example of Kavya in Prakrit language.

Which of the statements given above are correct?

(a) 1 and 2 (b) 2 and 3 (c) 1 and 3 (d) 1, 2 and 3

Ans. (a)

Exp. Statements (1) and (2) are correct regarding Ashvaghosha. Ashvaghosha was the greatest luminary at the court of Kanishka. He is credited with the composition of Buddhacharita, which is a biography of Buddha.

Statement (3) is incorrect because Saundarananda was also composed by Ashvaghosha in Sanskrit language (not Prakrit).

47 With reference to cultural contact between Indian and ancient Greek, which of the following statements are correct? *(Chap 16, Class-XI, Old NCERT)*

1. In Post-Mauryan times Indian astrology and astronomy profited from contact with the Greeks.
2. Greek rulers introduced Indian motifs on their coins.
3. The Greeks exported dogs, cattle, spices and ivory pieces from India.

Codes

(a) 1 and 2 (b) 2 and 3 (c) 1 and 3 (d) 1, 2 and 3

Ans. (d)

Exp. All the statements are correct with reference to cultural contact between Indian and ancient Greek. In Post-Mauryan times, Indian astrology and astronomy profited from contact with the Greeks. Many terms were taken about movement of planets from Greeks. Indian astrology was influenced by Greek ideas.

From Greek word, horoscope was derived horoshashtra, which is used for astrology in Sanskrit.

Greek rulers used the Brahmi script and represented some Indian motifs on their coins.

Dogs, cattle, spices and ivory pieces were exported by the Greeks from India.

48 Consider the following statements with reference to the development in the field of medicine in Post-Mauryan times. *(Chap 16, Class-XI, Old NCERT)*

1. The Indian benefitted immensely from the Greeks in the field of medicine.
2. The Charaka Samhita contains names of numerous plants and herbs from which drugs are to be prepared for the use of patients.
3. For the cure of ailments the ancient Indian physician relied chiefly on plants.

Which of the statements given above are correct?

(a) 1 and 2 (b) 2 and 3 (c) 1 and 3 (d) 1, 2 and 3

Ans. (b)

Exp. Statements (2) and (3) are correct with reference to the development in the field of medicine in Post-Mauryan times.

The ancient treatise on medicine, Charaka Samhita was written by Charak. It contains names of numerous plants and herbs from which drugs are to be prepared for the use of patients. For the cure of diseases, ancient Indian Physician relied mainly on plants, for which the Sanskrit word is *Oshadhi* and as a result medicine itself came to be known as Aushadhi.

Statement (1) is incorrect because Indians didn't benefit from Greeks in medicine, they relied on works of Charaka and Sushruta.

Miscellaneous

49 With reference to cultural history of Post-Mauryan India, consider the following statements. *(Chap 19, Class-XI, Old NCERT)*

1. Nagarjunakonda was a great center for the manufacturing of clothes called Shataka.
2. Largest number of terracotta and moulds of the Satavahanas period has been discovered from Yelleshwaram.
3. Ujjain was famous for its export of agate and carnelian stones.

How many of the statements given above is/are incorrect?

(a) Only one (b) Only two
(c) All three (d) None of these

Ans. (a)

Exp. Only one statement i.e., (1) is incorrect with reference to the cultural history of Post- Mauryan India. Mathura was one of the great centers for the manufacturing of the special type of clothes called Shataka.

50 The ancient cities of Khairadih and Mason, which prospered greatly during the Kushan phase is located in which of the following present-day state of India? *(Chap 19, Class-XI, Old NCERT)*

(a) Uttar Pradesh (b) Bihar
(c) Madhya Pradesh (d) Punjab

Ans. (a)

Exp. The ancient cities of Khairadih and Mason, which prospered greatly during the Kushan phase is located in present-day state of Uttar Pradesh.

During the reign of Kanishka, the territories of Kushan dynasty also covered parts of Uttar Pradesh and Eastern Bihar. Besides these two cities, Chirand, Sonpur and Buxar, in Bihar also witnessed prosperous Kushan phases.

51 Consider the following statements with reference to ports in ancient India. *(Chap 19, Class-XI, Old NCERT)*

1. Broach and Sopara were located on the Eastern coast of India.
2. Arikamedu and Tamralipti located on the Western coast provided connectivity to the Roman empire.

Which of the statements given above is/are correct?

(a) Only 1 (b) Only 2
(c) Both 1 and 2 (d) Neither 1 nor 2

Ans. (d)

Exp. Both the statements (1) and (2) are incorrect with reference to ports in ancient India. Broach in Gujarat and Sopara in Maharashtra were ancient port towns on the Western coast of India.

Arikamedu, in Puducherry and Tamralipti in West Bengal were situated on Eastern coast of India.

52 Consider the following statements about trade routes in ancient India. *(Chap 19, Class-XI, Old NCERT)*

1. The Shakas and the Kushans used two routes from the North-Western frontier to the Western coast of India.
2. Both of these routes converged at the Mathura and were connected with the silk route.
3. Uttarpatha was the most frequently used trade route.

Which of the statements given above is/are in correct?

(a) Only 1 (b) Only 2 (c) Only 3 (d) All of these

Ans. (b)

Exp. Statement (2) is incorrect because both these routes converged at Taxila and were connected with the silk route passing through Central Asia.

53 Which among the following cities lied on the ancient trade route called Uttarpatha? *(Chap 19, Class-XI, Old NCERT)*

1. Taxila 2. Mathura 3. Varanasi
4. Ujjain 5. Broach

Codes

(a) 1, 2, 3 and 4 (b) 2, 3, 4 and 5
(c) 1, 2, 4 and 5 (d) All of these

Ans. (c)

Exp. Taxila, Mathura, Ujjain and Broach lied on the ancient trade route called Uttarpatha. The Shakas and the Kushans used two routes from the North-Western frontier to the Western sea coast. Both these routes converged at Taxila and were connected with the silk route passing through Central Asia.

The second route called the *Uttarpatha* was in more frequent use. From Taxila, it passed through modern Punjab up to the Western coast of the Yamuna, Following the course of the Yamuna, it went southward to Mathura, Uttar Pradesh. From Mathura, it passed on to Ujjain in Malwa and again from Ujjain to Broach on the Western coast.

Varanasi was not on the Uttarpatha route.

54 Consider the following statements with reference to trade between India and Roman empire in the Post-Maurya age. *(Chap 19, Class-XI, Old NCERT)*

1. Articles of daily use of common people dominated the trade between Indian and Roman empire.
2. Roman mainly imported spices, muslins, pearls, jewels and precious stones from Central and South India.
3. India also served as the intermediary station for exporting goods from Central Asia and China to Roman empire.

Which of the statements given above is/are incorrect?

(a) 1 and 2 (b) Only 1
(c) Only 2 (d) 1, 2 and 3

Ans. (b)

Exp. Statement (1) is incorrect with reference to trade between India and Roman empire in the Post-Mauryan age as the volume of trade between India and Rome seems to have been large, but it was not carried on in articles of daily use for the common people. There was a trade in luxury goods, which are also called articles of aristocratic necessities.

55 Consider the following statements with reference to balance of trade between India and Roman empire in the Post-Maurya age. *(Chap 19, Class-XI, Old NCERT)*

1. Silk was the most traded commodity between India and Roman empire.
2. The maximum profit of trade with Roman empire in India was taken by the Satavahanas.
3. The Roman Emperors took steps to ban its trade with India in pepper and steel goods.

Codes

(a) 1 and 2 (b) 2 and 3
(c) 1 and 3 (d) 1, 2 and 3

Ans. (b)

Exp. Statements (2) and (3) are correct with reference to balance of trade between India and Roman empire in the Post-Maurya age.

Both Kushans and Satavahanas kingdom profited from trade with Romans, but the maximum profit went to Satavahanas.

Roman empire took measures to ban India made steel cutlery and pepper. Roman nobles used to pay high prices for these items which disturbed the balance of trade against the Romans. Hence, they ban its trade with India in pepper and steel goods.

Statement (1) is incorrect because the most traded item between India and Roman empire was Indian pepper as Westerners were fond of it. It was called Yavanapriya in Sanskrit.

56 With reference to the coinage in the Post-Mauryan age, which of the following statements are incorrect? *(Chap 19, Class-XI, Old NCERT)*

1. The Kushan issued the dinar type of gold coins in India.
2. For day to day transactions coins made up of lead and copper was used.
3. All the gold imported from the Roman Empire was used in mining of coins in India.

Codes

(a) 1 and 2 (b) Only 1
(c) 1 and 3 (d) Only 3

Ans. (d)

Exp. Statement (3) is incorrect with reference to coinage in the Post-Mauryan age as it is wrong to think that all Kushan gold coins were minted out of Roman gold. In fifth century BC, India had paid a tribute of 320 talents of gold to the Iranian empire. This gold may have been extracted from the gold mines in Sind.

The Kushans probably obtained gold from Central Asia. They may also have procured it either from Karnataka, or Dhalbhum in South Bihar.

57 Which among the following pairs is not correctly matched? *(Chap 19, Class-XI, Old NCERT)*

	Indigenous territories in Post-Maurya Age		Associated territories
(a)	Nagas	–	Eastern India
(b)	Mitras	–	Kaushambi and Mathura
(c)	Yaudheyas	–	Eastern Rajasthan
(d)	All of the above		

Ans. (a)

Exp. Pair (a) is not correctly matched because Nagas ruled over the Central India not Eastern India.

During the 3rd and the 4th centuries after the decline of the Kushan empire. Its capital was located at Padmavati.

58 **Consider the following statements with reference to the growth of urbanisation in Post-Mauryan phase.** *(Chap 19, Class-XI, Old NCERT)*

1. Most Indo-Greek towns in India lay exactly on the Uttarpatha route passing from Mathura to Taxila.
2. The rulers of Kushan dynasty ensured security on the important trade routes.
3. Ujjain was the most important city administered by the rulers of Saka dynasty.

Which of the statements given above are correct?

(a) 1 and 2 (b) 2 and 3
(c) 1 and 3 (d) 1, 2 and 3

Ans. (b)

Exp. Statements (2) and (3) are correct with reference to the growth of urbanisation in Post-Mauryan phase. The Kushan empire ensured security on the routes, which lay on Kushan towns. Its end in the third century AD dealt a great blow to these towns.

Ujjain was most important town of this period, as it lay on the nodal point of these two trade routes, one from Kaushambi and other from Mathura. It was also important because of its export of agate and carnelian stones.

Statement (1) is incorrect because most Kushan towns in India lay exactly on the North-Western or Uttarpatha route passing from Mathura to Taxila.

59 **Consider the following pairs.** *(Chap 16, Class-XI, Old NCERT)*

Towns in Post-Mauryan Phase		Present Indian States
1. Chirand	–	Bihar
2. Shringverpur	–	Uttar Pradesh
3. Ropar	–	Punjab
4. Dhanyakataka	–	Haryana

How many pairs given above is/are incorrectly matched.

(a) Only one (b) Only two
(c) Only three (d) All of these

Ans. (a)

Exp. Only one pair i.e., (4) is incorrectly matched Dhanyakataka was post-Mauryan town, presently located in Andhra Pradesh. It was a thriving town famous for its Stupa and trade and commerce during Satavahana period.

60 **Consider the following pairs.** *(Chap 16, Class-XI, Old NCERT)*

Terms associated with Post-Mauryan Phase		Meaning
1. Mleccha	–	Curtains
2. Gandhika	–	People outside Varna order
3. Yavanika	–	Pepper
4. Yavanapriya	–	Artisans specialising in manufacture of perfumes

How many of the pairs given above is/are incorrectly matched?

(a) Only one (b) Only two
(c) Only three (d) All of these

Ans. (d)

Exp. All of these pairs are incorrectly matched.

Mleccha were people who were kept outside the Varna order.

Gandhikas were artisans, who were perfumer. They manufactured perfumes and flourished during the age of Satavahanas.

Yavanika was a term used for curtains. Greeks contributed immensly to Indian theatre. Use of curtain in introduction was borrowed from Greeks.

Yavanapriya was Sanskrit word of Indian pepper. In Age of Satavahanas, Indian pepper was heavily traded with Romans.

61 **With reference to the institution of marriage in the Post-Mauryan phase, which of the following statements are incorrect?** *(Chap 3, Class-XII, New NCERT)*

1. Dharmashastras and Dharmasutras recognised eight forms of marriages.
2. After marriage, women retained their father's gotra.
3. The member of the same gotra could not marry.

Codes

(a) 1 and 2 (b) 2 and 3
(c) Only 2 (d) Only 3

Ans. (c)

Exp. Statement (2) is incorrect with reference to the institution of marriage in the Post-Mauryan phase because women were expected to give up their father's gotra and adopt that of their husband's.

Chapter 09

The Age of the Guptas

The Age of the Guptas

Sources and Rulers of Gupta Empire

Introduction

- Literary sources includes Puranas, Devichandraguptam and Mudrarakshasa (by Vishakhadatta) Works of Kalidas and Mrichchhakatika of Sudraka
- Prominent inscriptions-Allahabad pillar inscription of Samudragupta and Junagarh rock inscription of Skandagupta

Important Rulers

- **Chandragupta I (319-335 AD)** First most important king, first to assume title of Maharajadhiraja and ruled over Saket, Prayag and Magadha
- **Samudragupta (335-380 AD)** For military conquests known as Napolean of India, Harisena was his court poet; Meghavarman the ruler of Sri Lanka sent a missionary to ask for permission to build a Buddhist temple at Bodh Gaya
- **Chandragupta II (380-412 AD)** Extended the limits of empire of matrimonial alliances and conquests; Conquered Western Malwa and Gujarat from Saka; Adopted the title of Vikramaditya, Fa-Hien visited his court Chandragupta II appointed nine gems
- **Kumaragupta (415-455 AD)** Issued Ashvamedha type of coins. Laid the foundation of Nalanda University. Inscribed Bilsada edict
- **Skandagupta (455-467 AD)** Defeated Huna armies (Bhitari stone inscription), repaired Sudarshan lake

Society and Administration

Provincial and Local Administration

- Empire divided into divisions (Bhuktis) and placed under Uparika
- Districts — Were Known as Vishaya (placed under Vishayapati); In Eastern India, Vishayas divided into Vithis
- Promoted representative administration and guilds having administrative powers
- Religious functionaries granted tax free lands

Economy

- **Taxation** 1/4th to 1/6th of the agricultural produce
- Peasants required to provide for maintenance of royal armies; In Central and Western India prevalence of forced labour called Vishti

Judiciary

- Civil and criminal law clearly defined and demarcated
- Guilds of artisans, merchants and others were governed by their own laws

Bureaucracy

- First evidence of bureaucracy. Most important officials — Kumaramatyas
- Several offices were in the hands of the same person and posts became hereditary

Social Lives

- Division of castes into sub-castes
- Relatively positions of Shudras and women improved; Untouchable increased in number; Brahmanical supremacy reached new heights

Trade

- Traded with Eastern Roman empire, Western Asia and South-East Asia
- **Ports** Tamralipti (East), Broach, Sopara and Kalyan (West)

Other Aspects

Religion

- Hinduism became chief religion
- However Buddhism was also promoted
- Lord Vishnu emerged as God of devotion
- Gupta kings performed religious sacrifices
- Idol worship became prominent feature

Art and Architecture

- Patronised by Samudragupta and Chandragupta II
- Development of earliest Hindu temples in India
- Brick temples in Bhitargaon in Kanpur and Bhitari in Ghazipur
- Over 2m high bronze image of Buddha is found at Sultanganj

Literature

- 13 plays written by Bhasa (most famous—Urubhanga)
- Kalidasa wrote Abhijnanasakuntalam, Meghadutam and Raghuvansham
- Compilation of various Smritis and Amarakosha by Amarasimha

Science

- Development of Decimal system
- Work of Aryabhatta in astronomy and Brihat Samhita and Panchasiddhantika by Varahamihira in Mathematics
- Mathematician, Brahmagupta wrote Surya Siddhantika

Decline of Gupta Empire

- Foreign invasions, declaration of independence by feudatories, free land grant depleted royal treasury

SOURCE ***Old NCERT Class VI*** *(The Age of Guptas)*, ***Old NCERT Class XI*** *(The Rise and Growth of the Gupta Empire)*, ***Old NCERT Class XI*** *(Life in Gupta Age)*, ***NIOS Module-1*** *(The Guptas and their successors)*, ***Tamil Nadu Board Class XI*** *(The Guptas)*

Gupta Empire

1 With reference to the sources of Gupta empire, consider the following statements. *(Unit 7, Class-XI, Tamil Nadu Board)*

1. Kamandaka by Vishakadutta and Devichandraguptam by Nitisara are important literary sources of the Gupta empire.
2. Chinese traveller Fahien has provided an account of the Gupta empire and society.

Which of the statements given above is/are correct?

(a) Only 1
(b) Only 2
(c) Both 1 and 2
(d) Neither 1 not 2

Ans. (b)

Exp. Only statement (2) is correct with reference to the sources of the Gupta Empire.

Fahien was a Chinese traveller who provided an account of the Gupta Empire and society. Fahien describes the perils of the sea route between India and China. The goods traded from India were rare gems, pearls, fine textiles and aromatics. Indians imported silk and other articles from China.

Statement (1) is incorrect because Kamandaka by Nitisara and Devichandraguptam by Vishakadutta are important literary sources of the Gupta empire.

Kamandaka's Nitisara, a work on polity addressed to the king (400 AD) Devichandraguptam and Mudrarakshasam by Vishakadutta provide details about the rise of the Guptas.

2 With reference to Gupta empire, consider the following statements. *(Chap 7, Module-1, NIOS)*

1. The rulers of the Gupta empire were feudatories of Sakas.
2. Pallavas of Kanchi were contemporary of the Gupta dynasty.
3. The original kingdom of the Guptas comprised Uttar Pradesh and Bihar at the end of the third century AD.

How many statements given above is/are correct?

(a) Only one
(b) Only two
(c) All three
(d) None of these

Ans. (b)

Exp. Only two statements i.e., (2) and (3) are correct with reference to the Gupta Empire.

Pallavas of Kanchi were contemporary of the Gupta empire. After the decline of the Kushanas, North India witnessed the rise of the Gupta dynasty. The rulers of this dynasty were able to establish a Vast Empire that included almost the entire North India.

The original kingdom of the Guptas comprised Uttar Pradesh and Bihar at the end of the third century AD. They operated from Eastern Uttar Pradesh and Bihar which were very fertile.

Statement (1) is incorrect because rulers of Gupta Empire were feudatories of Kushanas. At many places in Uttar Pradesh and Bihar, the Kushana antiquities are immediately followed by the Gupta antiquities. After the decline of the Kushanas, North India witnessed the rise of the Gupta dynasty.

3 With reference to Gupta rule(335 AD-445 AD), consider the following statements. *(Chap 19, Class-XI, Old NCERT)*

1. Effective use of horses in warfare gave Gupta rulers an advantage over their rivals.
2. Iron-ores of South Bihar provided the Gupta ruler a material advantage.
3. Gupta rulers took advantage of the Silk trade of North India with the Byzantine empire.

How many of the statements given above is/are incorrect?

(a) Only one
(b) Only two
(c) All three
(d) None of these

Ans. (d)

Exp. None of the statements given above are incorrect with reference to the Gupta empire.

Effective use of horses in warfare gave Gupta rulers an advantage over their rivals.

Basic strength of Gupta Kings lay in the use of horses. All these gave them mobility and made them excellent horsemen.

Iron-ores of South Bihar provided the Gupta ruler a material advantage. The center of their operations lay in the fertile land of Madhyadesa covering Bihar, Uttar Pradesh.

Gupta rulers took advantage of their proximity to the areas in North India which carried on Silk Trade with the Eastern Roman Empire also known as the Byzantine empire.

4 Which of the following pairs is/are matched correctly? *(Chap 20, Class-XI, Old NCERT)*

	Territories under Gupta Empire		Modern name
(a)	Anuganga	–	Middle Gagetic Baser
(b)	Saketa	–	Allahabad
(c)	Prayag	–	Ayodhya

(d) None of the above

Ans. (a)

Exp. Pair (a) is matched correctly.

The ancient territory of **Anuganga** under the Gupta Empire is now identified with Middle Gangetic basin.

While pairs (b) and (c) are matched incorrectly.

The ancient territory of **Saketa** under the Gupta Empire is now identified with Ayodhya.

The ancient territory of **Prayag** under the Gupta Empire is now identified with Allahabad (Prayagraj).

Rulers of the Gupta Empire

5 With reference to Gupta rule(335 AD-445 AD), consider the following statements. *(Chap 19, Class-XI, Old NCERT)*

1. Gupta rulers assumed pompous titles similar to Mauryan rulers.
2. The Gupta Empire followed the practice of primogeniture in the inheritance of Kingship.
3. Coins of the Gupta Period bear no representation of Goddess or God.

How many of the statements given above is/are correct?

(a) Only one (b) Only two (c) All three (d) None of these

Ans. (d)

Exp. None of the statements given above are correct with reference to the Gupta Empire. In contrast to the Mauryan Empire, the Gupta Kings adopted pompous title such as Paramesvara, Maharajadhiraja and Parambhattaraka. This signifies they rule over lesser kings. Chandragupta I held the title of Maharajadhiraja. Kingship during the Gupta ruler was hereditary, but the royal power was limited by the absence of a firm practice of primogeniture. The throne didn't always go to the eldest son. This created uncertainties of which the chiefs and high officials could take advantage. The goddess Lakshmi is represented invariably on the other side of the coins as the wife of Vishnu.

6 With reference to Gupta Kings, consider the following statements. *(Class-XI, Old NCERT)*

Statement-I Historians call Chandragupta I the Napoleon of India.

Statement-II The Southern kings paid tribute, while the Northern kingdoms were annexed to the Gupta Empire under his reign.

Which one of the following is correct in respect of the above statements?

(a) Both Statement-I and Statement-II are correct and Statement-II is the correct explanation for Statement-I.
(b) Both Statement-I and Statement-II are correct and Statement-II is incorrect explanation for Statement-I.
(c) Statement-I is correct, but Statement-II is incorrect.
(d) Statement-I is incorrect, but Statement-II is correct.

Ans. (d)

Exp. Statement-I is incorrect, but Statement-II is correct with reference to the Gupta Kings. Historians call Samudragupta the Napoleon of India. This statement is undeniable. The Southern kings paid tribute, while the Northern kingdoms were annexed to the Gupta Empire under Samudragupta. His direct control was confined to the Ganges Valley, since the Sakas remained unconquered in Western India. Samudragupta's reign lasted for about 40 years, which must have given him ample time to plan and organise these campaigns. He performed the horse-sacrifice ritual to proclaim his military conquests.

7 Consider the following statements. *(Chap 20, Class-XI, Old NCERT)*

1. Raj Suryavarma, the ruler of Sri Lanka sent a missionary to Samudragupta seeking permission to built Buddhist temple at Bodhgaya.
2. The historian AL Bashm has referred Samudragupta as 'Napoleon of Ancient India'.

Which of the statements given above is/are incorrect?

(a) Only 1
(b) Only 2
(c) Both 1 and 2
(d) Neither 1 nor 2

Ans. (c)

Exp. Both the statements (1) and (2) are incorrect. During the reign of Samudragupta, the ruler of Sri Lanka, Meghavarman sent a missionary to Samudragupta seeking permission to built Buddhist temple at Bodhgaya.

Though majority of Gupta ruler were followers of Bhagvatism, they also supported and gave patronage to the other sect also.

The historian Vincent Arthur Smith has referred Samudragupta as 'Napoleon of Ancient India'.

8 During the reign of Samudragupta, the term 'Atavika Rajyas' was used for *(Chap 20, Class-XI, Old NCERT)*

(a) forest kingdoms situated in the Vindhya regions.
(b) republics situated in the Punjab region.
(c) kingdoms situated in the North-Eastern parts of the country.
(d) village assemblies headed by Gahapatis.

Ans. (a)

Exp. During the reign of Samudragupta, the term Atavika Rajyas was used for forest kingdoms situated in the Vindhya regions. These kingdoms were conquered by Samudragupta and were brought under the control of Gupta Empire.

9 Consider the following statements with reference to the reign of Samudragupta. *(Chap 7, Class-VI, Old NCERT)*

1. He defeated the four kings of Northern India and added the region of present day Delhi and Western Uttar Pradesh to his kingdom.
2. In one of his coins, he is shown playing a veena.
3. He incorporated the territories of nine tribal republics of Afghanistan.

Which of the statements given above is/are incorrect?

(a) 1 and 2 (b) 2 and 3 (c) Only 2 (d) Only 3

Ans. (d)

Exp. Only statement (3) is incorrect regarding reign of Samudragupta because he didn't incorporate areas of Afghanistan, but of Rajasthan. From the nine tribal areas of Rajasthan, he also collected taxes and received regular tributes.

10 With reference to Prayag Prashasti, which of the following statements is/are correct? *(Chap 2, Class-XII, New NCERT)*

1. It was composed by the court poet of Samudragupta, Harisena in Sanskrit.
2. It gives an elaborate account of the people and countries that were conquered by the Samudragupta.
3. According to this Prashasti, Samudragupta incorporated the territories of all the defeated kingdoms in the Gupta Empire.

Codes

(a) 1 and 2 (b) 2 and 3
(c) 1 and 4 (d) 1, 2 and 3

Ans. (a)

Exp. Statements (1) and (2) are correct regarding Prayag Prashasti. The Prayag Prashasti (also known as the Allahabad Pillar Inscription) was composed in Sanskrit by Harisena who was the court poet of Samudragupta. Poet Harisena wrote a glowing account of the military exploits of his patron. In a long inscription, the poet enumerates the people and countries that were conquered by Samudragupta.

Statement (3) is incorrect because territories of conquered areas were not included in Gupta kingdom.

11 With reference to the reign of Chandragupta Vikramaditya, which of the following statements is/are correct? *(Chap 20, Class-XI, Old NCERT)*

1. He extended the limits of the empire by marriage alliance and conquests.
2. He conquered Western Malwa and Gujarat from the rule of Vakataka.
3. During his reign, the Chinese pilgrim Fa-Hien (399-414 AD) visited India and wrote an elaborate account of the life of its people.

Codes

(a) 1 and 2 (b) 2 and 3
(c) 1 and 3 (d) All of these

Ans. (c)

Exp. Statements (1) and (3) are correct regarding the reign of Chandragupta Vikramaditya. He extended the limits of the Empire by marriage alliance and conquests. Chandragupta married his daughter Prabhavati with a Vakataka prince who belonged to the Brahmana caste and ruled in Central India.

It was in Chandragupta's time that the Chinese pilgrim Fa-Hien (399-414 AD) visited India and wrote an elaborate account of the life of its people.

Statement (2) is incorrect because Chandragupta II conquered Western Malwa and Gujarat, which had been under the rule of the Shaka Kshatrapas for about four centuries by that time conquests.

12 With reference to Gupta Kings, consider the following statements. *(Class-XI, Old NCERT)*

1. The name Simhavikrama mentioned in the Gupta coins refers to Chandragupta II.
2. Samundragupta was the first Gupta Ruler to issue silver coins.
3. Kumara Gupta is credited with the foundation of Nalanda University.

How many statements given above is/are incorrect?

(a) Only one (b) Only two
(c) All three (d) None of these

Ans. (a)

Exp. Only one statement i.e., (2) is incorrect with reference to the Gupta Kings. Chandragupta II was the first Gupta ruler to issue silver coins.

13 With reference to Samudragupta (AD 335-380), consider the following statements. *(Chap 19, Class-XI, Old NCERT)*

1. He followed the same policy of empire expansion as the one followed by Mauryan King Ashoka.
2. Harisena was the court poet of Samudragupta.
3. The Forest Kingdom of Vindhya regions remained outside his sphere of influence.
4. Pallavas dynasty of Kanchi recognised his suzerainty.

How many of the statements given above is/are correct?

(a) Only one (b) Only two
(c) Only three (d) All four

Ans. (b)

Exp. Only two statements i.e., (1) and (4) are correct with reference to Samudragupta.

The Gupta Kingdom was enlarged enormously by Chandrgupta I successor Samudragupta (335-380 AD). He was the opposite of Ashoka. Ashoka believed in a policy of peace and non- aggression, but Samundragupta didn't follow the same policy of cultural conquest, rather his policy of territorial expansion relied on military conquest.

Twelve rulers of Eastern Deccan and South India, who were conquered and liberated by Samudragupta. Samudragupta's arms reached as far as Kanchi in Tamil Nadu where the Pallavas were compelled to recognise his suzerainty.

Statements (2) and (3) are incorrect because Harisena was the court poet of Chandragupta II. The Gupta Rulers patronised art, literature and science. Kalidasa, Harisena, Amarsimha, Dhanvantri and Varahmihira adorned their court. The Allahabad pillar inscription was composed by Harisena. Forest Kingdoms situated in the Vindhya region and known as Atavika Rajyas, were brought under control of Samudragupta.

14 With reference to the conquests of Samudragupta, consider the following statements.

(Class-XI, Old NCERT)

Statement-I He adopted a different policy for different areas conquered by him.

Statement-II In Ganga-Yamuna doab he followed a policy of annexation while in South India he followed a policy of political conciliation.

Which one of the following is correct in respect of the above statements?

(a) Both Statement-I and Statement-II are correct and Statement-II is the correct explanation for Statement-I.
(b) Both Statement-I and Statement-II are correct and Statement-II is incorrect explanation for Statement-I.
(c) Statement-I is correct, but Statement-II is incorrect.
(d) Statement-I is incorrect, but Statement-II is correct.

Ans. (a)

Exp. Bath Statement-I and Statement-II are correct and Statement-II is the correct explanation for Statement-I.

According to Prayag Prashasti inscriptions, Samudragupta incorporated the territories of all the defeated kingdoms in the Gupta Empire as he adopted a different policy for different areas conquered by him. In Ganga-Yamuna doab, he followed a policy of annexation. However in South India, he followed a policy of political conciliation under which instead of annexing the kingdom of South India, he liberated and reinstated these kings on their thrones.

The policy of political conciliation for South India was adopted because he knew it was difficult to keep them under control and subservience once he returned to his capital in the North. So, it was enough for him that these states recognised his suzerainty and paid him tributes and presents.

Societies and Administration

15 Consider the following statements.

(Chap 21, Class-XI, Old NCERT) (CGPSC Pre 2008)

1. Gupta emperors claimed divine rights for themselves.
2. Their administration was highly centralised.
3. They extended the tradition of land grants.

Which of the statements given above are correct?

(a) 1, 2 and 3 (b) 1 and 2 (c) 1 and 3 (d) 2 and 3

Ans. (c)

Exp. Statements (1) and (3) are correct. Like their predecessors, Kushanas, the Gupta monarchs claimed divine rights for themselves. They assumed pompous titles. They also continued the system of land grants to learned persons including Brahmana started during the rule of Satavahana.

Statement (2) is incorrect because administration under Gupta was highly decentralised. They adopted feudal system of administration.

16 With reference to the provincial and local administration under the Gupta Empire, which of the following statements is/are correct?

(Chap 21, Class-XI, Old NCERT)

1. The empire was divided into divisions called bhuktis and were placed under the charge of Rajuka.
2. The bhuktis were divided into districts called Vishyas and were placed under the charge of Vishayapati.
3. In Eastern India, the Vishayas were divided into Vithis, which were further divided into villages.

Codes

(a) 1 and 2 (b) 2 and 3 (c) 1 and 3 (d) 1, 2 and 3

Ans. (b)

Exp. Statements (2) and (3) are correct regarding provincial and local administration under the Gupta empire. The Guptas organised a system of provincial and local administration. The Empire was divided into divisions which were called Bhuktis.

The bhuktis were divided into districts (Vishyas), which were placed under the charge of Vishayapati.

In Eastern India, the Vishyas were divided into Vithis, which again were divided into villages.

Statement (1) is incorrect because bhukti was placed under the charge of an Uparika.

17 Consider the following statements with reference to the urban administration under the Gupta Empire.

(Chap 21, Class-XI, Old NCERT)

1. The organised professional bodies such as guilds of artisans, merchants and scribes were included in the urban administrative bodies.
2. Their consent to land transactions was considered necessary.
3. Periodic elections were organised for the selection of the members of the urban administrative bodies.

Which of the statements given above is/are incorrect?

(a) 1 and 2 (b) Only 2
(c) Only 3 (d) 1, 2 and 3

Ans. (c)

Exp. Only statement (3) is incorrect regarding urban administration under the Gupta Empire. As there were no elections organised for the selection of members of the urban administrative bodies.

18 The vassals who lived on the fringes of the Gupta Empire were obliged to certain function(s), such as

(Chap 21, Class-XI, Old NCERT)

(a) homage to the sovereign by personal attendance at his court.
(b) regular tributes to the sovereign.
(c) to present their daughters in marriage.
(d) All of the above

Ans. (d)

Exp. The vassals who lived on the fringe of the Gupta Empire carried out three obligations i.e., they offered homage to the sovereign by personal attendance at his court; paid tribute to him and presented to him daughters in marriage. The major part of the Gupta Empire was held by feudatory chiefs, many of whom had been subjugated by Samudragupta.

19 **Consider the following statements regarding the pattern of administration during the reign of Gupta empire.** *(Chap 21, Class-XI, Old NCERT)*

1. Since much of the imperial administration was managed by feudatories and beneficiaries, the Gupta rulers did not require as many officials as the Mauryas did.
2. Religious functionaries were granted tax free land and were also authorised to collect taxes from the peasants.
3. Abundance of gold in the Gupta empire suggests that all the officials were paid in cash.

Which of the statements given above are correct?

(a) 1 and 2 (b) 2 and 3
(c) 1 and 3 (d) 1, 2 and 3

Ans. (a)

Exp. Statements (1) and (2) are correct regarding the pattern of administration during the reign of Gupta empire.

Most of the imperial administrations were managed by feudatories and beneficiaries, the Gupta rulers did not require as many officials as the Mauryas did. They did not require too many officers also because, unlike the Maurya state, the Gupta state did not regulate economic activities on any big scale.

In Gupta age, mainly in Madhya Pradesh, religious functionaries were granted land, free of tax and they were allowed to collect taxes from the peasants, all the taxes which could have gone to the king.

Statement (3) is incorrect because all officials of Gupta times were not paid in cash and only high officials were paid by land grants.

20 **Consider the following statements with reference to the difference between administrative mechanism of the Mauryas and Guptas.** *(Chap 21, Class-XI, Old NCERT)*

1. In the Mauryan empire, administration was highly centralised whereas in Gupta Empire, it was feudalistic in character.
2. The Mauryan empire regulated the major economic activities of the state whereas in Gupta Empire, guilds were authorised to carry out many important functions of regulation.
3. They retained the elaborate political machinery of the Mauryan times.

Which of the statements given above are correct?

(a) 1 and 2 (b) 2 and 3 (c) 1 and 3 (d) 1, 2 and 3

Ans. (a)

Exp. Statements (1) and (2) are correct regarding the difference between administrative mechanism of the Mauryas and Guptas. The Guptas neither needed nor possessed the centralised administrative machinery of Mauryan times and in some ways, their political system appears to be feudal.

Guptas did not require too many officers because, unlike the Mauryan state, the Gupta state did not regulate economic activities on any big scale. The participation of leading artisans, merchants, elders, etc., in rural and urban administration also reduced the need for maintaining a large numbers of officers.

Statement (3) is incorrect because they didn't keep the elaborate systems of Mauryas because they didn't need it.

21 **With reference to Kingship during Gupta Empire, consider the following statements.** *(Class-XI, Old NCERT)*

1. During the Gupta age, political hierarchies can be identified by the titles adapted.
2. Gupta Kings didn't claim divine status.

Which of the statements given above is/are correct?

(a) Only 1 (b) Only 2
(c) Both 1 and 2 (d) Neither 1 nor 2

Ans. (a)

Exp. Only statement (1) is correct with reference to kingship during Gupta empire as during the Gupta age, political hierarchies can be identified by the titles adopted. Kings assumed titles such as Maharajadhiraja, Parama-Bhattaraka and Parameshvara.

Statement (2) is incorrect because some historians have suggested that the Gupta Kings claimed divine status. For example, Samudragupta is compared to Purusha (Supreme Being) in the Allahabad inscription. These assertions can be seen as reflections of an attempt to claim divine status by the king.

22 **With reference to administration of Gupta Empire, consider the following statements.** *(Class-XI, Old NCERT)*

1. The post of high-ranking officials was not hereditary.
2. Artisans and merchants took active part in the town administration.
3. Important functionaries of the Gupta Empire were all recruited from the cadre of Kumaranatyas.

How many of the statements given above is/are incorrect?

(a) Only one (b) Only two
(c) All three (d) None of these

Ans. (a)

Exp. Only one statement i.e., (1) is incorrect with reference to the administration of the Gupta Empire. The post of high-ranking officials was hereditary.

One of the seals mentions a Mahadandanayaka named Agnigupta. The Allahabad Prashasti refers to three Mahadandanayakas. All these suggest that these posts were hereditary by nature.

23 With reference to forced labour (Vishti) in India during the Gupta period, which one of the following statements is correct? *(Class-XI, Old NCERT)*

(a) It was considered a source of income for the state, a sort of tax paid by the people.
(b) It was totally absent in the Madhya Pradesh and Kathiawar regions of the Gupta Empire.
(c) The forced labourer was entitled to weekly wages.
(d) The eldest son of the labourer was sent as the forced labourer.

Ans. (a)

Exp. Only statement (a) is correct with reference to forced labour (Vishti) in India during the Gupta period. It was considered a source of income for the State, a sort of tax paid by the people.

Statements (b), (c) and (d) are incorrect because Vishti was considered as a source of income for the state, a sort of tax by the people. Junagarh inscription mentions Vishti as one form of tax, which indicates that it was extracted from Gujarat and Malwa region.

The forced labourers were not entitled to any weekly wages. Anyone could be sent as a labourer for Vishti, not necessarily the eldest son of the labourer.

Society and Religion

24 With reference to societal structure during Gupta Put under society and Religion Empire, consider the following statements. *(Chap 7, Module-1 NIOS)*

1. Land was granted to Brahmanas with tax exemptions.
2. Shudras were allowed to listen to the Puranas.
3. Women were neither entitled to inherit property nor were given full right on her Stridhana.

How many of the statements given above is/are correct?

(a) Only one (b) Only two
(c) All three (d) None of these

Ans. (b)

Exp. Only two statements i.e., (1) and (2) are correct with reference to societal structure during the Gupta Period.

Brahmanas were getting large-scale land grants not only from the rulers but from other people also. The land was given along with administrative rights and tax exemptions. Thus, a new class of Brahmana landlords was created.

The position of Shudras improved somewhat during this period. They were allowed to listen to the epics and the Puranas They could also perform some domestic rituals that were earlier prohibited for them.

Statement (3) is incorrect because the status of women continued to decline in the Gupta period. The women were not entitled to inherit property. However, she had full right on her Stridhana. The free representation of females in art suggest that there was no purdah system.

25 Which one of the following statements is incorrect regarding the position of women in the Gupta period? *(Chap 21, Class-XI, Old NCERT)*

(a) The women were allowed to listen to the Ramayana and Mahabharata.
(b) The women of lower varna were free to earn their livelihood through agriculture.
(c) The women of upper varna enjoyed proprietary rights.
(d) The first example of immolation of widow after the death of her husband appears in Gupta era.

Ans. (c)

Exp. Only statement (c) is incorrect regarding the position of women in Gupta period because absence of proprietary right was the main reason for the subordination of women belonging to Gupta period.

The upper varna women were completely dependent on men for their livelihood. Whereas women's lower varna were free to earn their livelihood through agriculture.

26 Fa-Hien's mission to India was to *(Chap 21, Class-XI, Old NCERT)*

(a) learn about the administrative system of the Gupta kings.
(b) understand the social position of women during the Gupta period.
(c) visit the Buddhist institutions and to collect copies of Buddhist manuscripts.
(d) get full knowledge about the condition of peasants during the period of Gupta kings.

Ans. (c)

Exp. Fa-Hien's mission to India was to visit the Buddhist institutions and to collect copies of Buddhist manuscripts. Fa-Hien visited India during the reign of Chandragupta II.

He entered the Indian subcontinent through the North-West and stayed in India for 10 years. In order to collect copies of Buddhist manuscripts, he visited the renowned centres of education and Buddhist monasteries.

27 The society during the Gupta age was characterised by the emergence of numerous sub-caste. Which among the following reasons was/were responsible for the proliferation of castes into the sub-castes? *(Chap 21, Class-XI, Old NCERT)*

1. Assimilation of large number of foreigners into the Indian society.
2. Large number of tribal people were absorbed in the brahmanical social order.
3. Origin of Bhakti Movement in India.

Codes

(a) 1 and 2 (b) 2 and 3
(c) 1 and 3 (d) 1, 2 and 3

Ans. (a)

Exp. Reasons mentioned in statements (1) and (2) were responsible for proliferation of castes into the sub-castes during Gupta age. The castes proliferated into numerous sub-castes as a result of two factors. A large number of foreigners were assimilated into the Indian society and each group of foreigners was considered as a kind of caste.

The other reason for the increase in the number of castes was the absorption of many tribal people into brahmanical society through the process of land grants.

Reason mentioned in statement (3) is incorrect because Bhakti Movement first originated in South India in seventh and eighth centuries AD and it didn't play any role in proliferation of castes into the sub-castes.

28 With reference to the state of religion under the Gupta Empire, which of the following statements is/are correct? *(Chap 21, Class-XI, Old NCERT)*

1. Vaishnavism became the most prominent religion.
2. Idol worship in the temple became a common feature of Hinduism from the Gupta period onwards.
3. The Gupta kings, in order to promote Hinduism, persecuted the followers of Buddhism and Jainism.

Codes

(a) 1 and 2 (b) 2 and 3 (c) 1 and 3 (d) 1, 2 and 3

Ans. (a)

Exp. Statements (1) and (2) are correct regarding state of religion under the Gupta Empire.

Vaishnavism became the new prominent religion as took Vishnu, a Vedic God, Krishna, a legendary hero of *Vrishni* tribe and Narayana, a non-Vedic tribal God, and merged their worshippers into one.

Idol worship became a common feature of Hindu religion from Gupta period. And many festivals also started to be celebrated.

Statement (3) is incorrect because Gupta king didn't persecute different religious sects and follow tolerant religious policy.

Economy

29 Consider the following statements. *(Chap 21, Class-XI, Old NCERT)*

1. The largest number of gold coins in ancient India was issued by the Gupta Empire.
2. Kumargupta was the first Gupta ruler to issue silver coin.

Which of the statements given above is/are correct?

(a) Only 1 (b) Only 2
(c) Both 1 and 2 (d) Neither 1 nor 2

Ans. (a)

Exp. Statement (1) is correct as owing to thriving trade with Roman Empire, agricultural expansion and stable administration, the Gupta monarchs were able to issue largest number of gold coins in ancient India. It was referred as dinars and was characterised by regularity in size and weight.

Statement (2) is incorrect because the first Gupta ruler to issue silver coin was Chandragupta II.

30 Which one of the following ports was in use for the North India trade during the Gupta period? *(Chap 7, Class-VI, Old NCERT) (BPSC Pre 2019)*

(a) Tamralipti (b) Broach (c) Sopara (d) Kalyan

Ans. (a)

Exp. Among the given options, the ancient port of Tamralipti was used for North India trade during the Gupta period. Tamralipti in Ganga delta was situated on the East coast. It is in modern-day Midnapore district of West Bengal. It handled a large part of commerce with countries of South-East Asia, such as Burma, Java, Cambodia, etc.

31 With reference to the coins issued by the Gupta monarch, which of the following statements is/are correct? *(Chap 21, Class-XI, Old NCERT)*

1. The gold coins issued in the Gupta Empire were called as dinars.
2. After conquest of Bengal, Gupta monarchs issued large number of silver coins for local trade.
3. The lesser circulation of copper coins suggests that the use of money did not touch the common people so much as it did under the Kushans.

Codes

(a) 1 and 2 (b) 2 and 3 (c) 1 and 3 (d) 1, 2 and 3

Ans. (c)

Exp. Statements (1) and (3) are correct regarding coins issued by Gupta monarch. In ancient India, the Guptas issued the largest number of gold coins, which were called dinaras in their inscriptions.

In contrast to those of the Kushans, the Gupta copper coins are very few. This would suggest that the use of money did not touch the common people so much as it did under the Kushanas.

Statement (2) is incorrect because after the conquest of Gujarat (not Bengal), the Gupta monarch issued a good number of silver coins mainly for local exchange.

32 With reference to the economy of the Gupta period, consider the following statements. *(Chap 21, Class-XI, Old NCERT)*

Statement-I The middle of the sixth century AD witnessed the decline of trade between India and the Eastern Roman Empire.

Statement-II Around 550 AD, the people of the Eastern Roman Empire learnt the art of growing silk from the Chinese.

Which one of the following is correct in respect of the above statements?

(a) Both Statement-I and Statement-II are correct and Statement-II is the correct explanation for Statement-I.
(b) Both Statement-I and statement-II are correct and Statement-II is not the correct explanation for Statement-I.
(c) Statement-I is correct, but Statement-II is incorrect.
(d) Statement-I is incorrect, but Statement-II is correct.

Ans. (a)

Exp. Both Statement-I and Statement-II are correct and Statement-II is the correct explanation for Statement-I with reference to the economy of the Gupta period. In the middle of the sixth century, long-distance trade declined.

Till 550 AD, India carried on some trade with the Eastern Roman Empire to which it exported silk. Around 550 AD the people of the Eastern Roman Empire learnt from the Chinese the art of growing silk. It adversely affected Indian trade with Roman Empire.

33 With reference to agrarian structure during Gupta Empire, consider the following statements.

(Class-XI, Old NCERT)

1. Ustapala maintained records of all the land transactions in the district.
2. Jalanirgamah was constructed for the purpose of irrigation.
3. Position of peasantry was reduced to the position of serfs.

How many statements given above is/are correct?

(a) Only one
(b) Only two
(c) All three
(d) None of these

Ans. (b)

Exp. Only two statements i.e., (1) and (3) are correct with reference to agrarian structure. As per Paharpur plates, an officer called Ustapala maintained records of all the land transactions in the district and the village accountant preserved records of land in the village. The position of peasantry was undermined. They were reduced to the position of serfs due to granting of various privileges and land to others.

Statement (2) is incorrect because to prevent inundation, Jalanirgamah(drains) were constructed which is mentioned by Amarasimha.

34 With reference to the land grants, consider the following pairs. *(Class-XI, Old NCERT)*

1. Agrahara grants Features land grants for the repairs and worship of temples.
2. Secular grants Grant Made to fondatories of Guptas.
3. Devagrahara grants Perpetual hereditary and tax bree land.

How many of the pairs is/are correctly matched?

(a) Only one
(b) Only two
(c) All three
(d) None of these

Ans. (a)

Exp. Only one pair i.e., (2) is correctly matched as secular grants constituted grants made to feudatories of Guptas.

While pairs (1) and (3) are incorrectly matched.

Agrahara grants were given to Brahmins, it was perpetual, hereditary and tax free.

Devagrahara grants were land grants in favour of a Brahmin as well as gifts to merchants for the repair and worship of temples.

Trade

35 With reference to trade during Gupta Period, consider the following statements.

(Class-XI, Old NCERT)

1. Tamralipti in present day Karnataka was an important center of trade.
2. The Gupta Empire had trade relation with Persia and Byzantium.

Which of the statements given above is/are correct?

(a) Only 1
(b) Only 2
(c) Both 1 and 2
(d) Neither 1 nor 2

Ans. (b)

Exp. Only statement (2) is correct with reference to trade in the Gupta Empire. The Gupta Empire had trade relations with Persia and Byzantium. The ports and towns of the Gupta Empire were connected with those of Persia, Arabia and Byzantium on the one hand and Sri Lanka, China and Southeast Asia on the other. Fahien describes the perils of the sea route between India and China.

Statement (1) is incorrect because Fahien refers to Tamralipti in Bengal as an important center of trade on the Eastern coast.

36 With reference to the period of the Gupta dynasty in ancient India, the towns Ghantasala, Kadura and Chaul were well known as

(Class-XI, Old NCERT) (IAS Pre 2020)

(a) ports handling foreign trade.
(b) capitals of powerful kingdoms.
(c) places of exquisite stone art and architecture.
(d) important Buddhist pilgrimage centres.

Ans. (a)

Exp. With reference to the period of the Gupta dynasty in ancient India, the towns Ghantasala, Kadura and Chaul were well known as Ports handling foreign trade.

Ghantasala was a major port located on the East coast of India, near the Krishna Delta. Kadura was another important port located on the West coast of India, near present-day Mumbai.

Chaul was a bustling port located on the West coast of India, near present-day Raigad district in Maharashtra.

Art and Literature

37 With reference to prevalence of art in Gupta Dynasty, consider the following statements.
(Chap 21, Class-XII, Old NCERT)

1. In Sanskrit plays written during the Gupta period, women and Shudra spoke Prakrit language.
2. The two metre high bronze image of the Buddha sculpted during the Gupta times has been discovered from Sultanganj.
3. Allahabad pillar inscriptions compiled during the Gupta age suggests that the decimal system was known in India at the beginning of the fifth century AD.

How many of the statements given above is/are correct?

(a) Only one (b) Only two
(c) All three (d) None of these

Ans. (c)

Exp. All three statements i.e., (1), (2) and (3) are correct with reference to the prevalence of art in the Gupta Dynasty. In Sanskrit plays, such as Mrichchhakatika by Shudraka written during the Gupta period, women and Shudra spoke Prakrit language. The members of higher classes in these plays spoke Sanskrit. It reflected the social division prevalent in the age of Gupta, besides representing a clear social hierarchy.
The two meter high bronze image of Buddha sculpted during the Gupta times has been discovered from Sultanganj (near modern day Bhagalpur in Bihar). In this sculpture, Buddha is seen in the Abhay mudra or the pose of reassurance. Allahabad pillar inscription of 448 AD compiled during the Gupta age suggests that the decimal system was known in India at the beginning of the fifth century AD.

38 Consider the following statements.
(Chap 21, Class-XI, Old NCERT)

1. The ancient treatise 'Romanka Siddhanta' compiled during Gupta age deals with astronomy.
2. The craftsmen during the Gupta age had advanced knowledge of metal technology.

Which of the statements given above is/are correct?

(a) Only 1
(b) Only 2
(c) Both 1 and 2
(d) Neither 1 nor 2

Ans. (c)

Exp. Both the statements (1) and (2) are correct.
Romanka Siddhanta is an ancient treatise in the field of astronomy. It was influenced by Greek ideas and was written in Sanskrit during the Gupta age.
The workmanship quality of Gupta craftsmen in bronze and iron was quite high. Several bronze images of Buddha were produced by Gupta craftsmen.

39 The iron column, located in the courtyard of Delhi's Quwwat-ul-Islam mosque is retention of
(Chap 21, Class-XI, Old NCERT) (UPPSC Pre 2002)

(a) Ashoka (b) Chandra
(c) Harsha (d) Anangapal

Ans. (b)

Exp. The iron column, located in the courtyard of Delhi's Quwwat-ul-Islam mosque is retention of Chandra.
The king 'Chandra' mentioned in this pillar is identified with Chandragupta II. This pillar was erected by him in the honour of God Vishnu. It is greatest specimen of advancement of metallurgy achieved during the Gupta age, as this pillar has not been corroded yet.

Decline of the Gupta Empire

40 The control of the Gupta Empire over India was considerably weakened by the attack of Hunas. Which of the following statements is/are correct about the Hunas? *(Chap 7, Class-VI, Old NCERT)*

1. They were nomadic tribes from the Central Asia who excelled in horsemanship and used stirrups made of metal.
2. With repeated attacks, they became the rulers of the Punjab and Kashmir.
3. They settled permanently in India and became part of Indian culture.

Codes

(a) 1 and 2 (b) 2 and 3 (c) 1 and 3 (d) 1, 2 and 3

Ans. (d)

Exp. All the statements are correct regarding Hunas. Skandagupta, the last great Gupta ruler effectively handled the attacks of Hunas but later successors failed to counter them.
Hunas were nomadic tribes of Central Asia. They excelled in horsemanship and used stirrups made of metal. These helped them in moving quickly.
Their repeated attacks made Eastern Malwa and portion of Central India into their possession. Later regions of Punjab and Kashmir also were occupied by them. Hunas like other invaders became part of Indian culture and traditions.

Miscellaneous

41 With reference to the Gupta Empire, consider the following statements. *(Chap 22, Class-XI, Old NCERT)*

1. During the fourth century AD, the territories of Kosala and Mahakantara which were included in the regions conquered by the Samudragupta referred to the present day territories of North and West Odisha.
2. The ancient province of Pundravardhana bhukti comes under the modern territories of West and East Bengal.

Which of the statements given above is/are correct?

(a) Only 1
(b) Only 2
(c) Both 1 and 2
(d) Neither 1 nor 2.

Ans. (c)

Exp. Both statements (1) and (2) are correct with reference to the Gupta Empire.During the fourth century AD, the territories of Kosala and Mahakantara, which was included in the regions conquered by the Samudragupta, referred to the present day territories of North and West Odisha. During his South India campaign, Samudragupta defeated 12 kings. The king Mahendra of Kosala and Vyagraja of Mahakanara were also defeated but they were reinstated in their respective positions. They became his vassals and they accepted to pay tributes.

Ancient province of Pundravardhana bhukti comes under the modern territories of West and East Bengal during the Gupta age, this region was noted for its agricultural prosperity and important trading port of Tamralipti was also part of this province large number of copper plate containing records of land sale had been discovered from this province.

42 With reference to Gupta dynasty, consider the following statements. *(Class-XI, Old NCERT) (IAS Pre 2001)*

Statement-I The origin of feudal system in ancient India can be traced to military campaigns

Statement-II There was considerable expansion of the feudal system during the Gupta period.

Which one of the following is correct in respect of the above statements?

(a) Both Statement-I and Statement-II are correct and Statement-II is the correct explanation for Statement-I.
(b) Both Statement-I and Statement-II are correct and Statement-II is not the correct explanation for Statement-I.
(c) Statement-I is correct, but Statement-II is incorrect.
(d) Statement-I is incorrect, but Statement-II is correct

Ans. (d)

Exp. Statement-I is incorrect, but Statement-II is correct.

The sources of the Gupta period suggest that certain important changes were taking place in the agrarian society. Feudal development surfaced under the Guptas with the grant of fiscal and administrative concessions to priests and administrators. Started in the Deccan by the Satavahanas, the practice became a regular affair in Gupta times.

43 What was the capital of the Mukhari dynasty which rose to the power in Bihar and Uttar Pradesh in the sixth century AD? *(Chap 20, Class-XI, Old NCERT)*

(a) Pataliputra
(b) Prayagraj
(c) Kannauj
(d) Ayodhya

Ans. (c)

Exp. Kannauj in Uttar Pradesh was the capital of the Mukhari dynasty, which rose to the power in Bihar and Uttar Pradesh in the sixth century AD. Late Guptas of Magadha also established their power in Bihar alongside Mukharis.

44 Consider the following statements with reference to the Judicial system prevalent during the Gupta age. *(Chap 21, Class-XI, Old NCERT)*

1. For the first time, civil and criminal laws were clearly demarcated.
2. Theft and adultery came under the civil law whereas disputes regarding various types of property came under the criminal law.
3. The guilds of artisans, merchants and others were governed by their own laws.

Which of the statements given above is/are incorrect?

(a) 1 and 2
(b) 2 and 3
(c) Only 2
(d) Only 3

Ans. (c)

Exp. Only statement (2) is incorrect with reference to Judicial system prevalent during the Gupta age. As during the Gupta age, theft and adultery came under criminal law (not civil law) whereas disputes regarding various types of property came under civil law (not criminal law).

Chapter 10

Post-Gupta Era

Post-Gupta Era

Harshavardhana and Its Administration

Introduction

- Greatest ruler of Pushyabhuti dynasty was Harshavardhan (606-647 CE), who ruled from Thanesar to Kannauj and conquered many parts of Punjab, Eastern Rajasthan and Ganga valley

Administration

- Became more feudal and decentralised
- Based in patterns of Gupta administration;
- Rajasthaniya - foreign secretary; Mahasandhivigradhikrita - minister for war and peace; Mahabaladhikrita — officer in supreme command in the area

Revenue System

- Divided into four parts
  1. Dedicated for expenditure of kings
  2. Scholars 3. Endowment of officials
  4. Religious purposes

Law and Order

- According to Hiuen-Tsang, law and order was not well maintained
- Severe punishments for crime

Religious Policy

- Harsha followed a tolerant religious policy, used to organise assembly at Prayag every five years
- Nalanda became huge monastic establishment

Society

- Land grants to Brahmins - Agrahara/Brahmadeya
- Presence of artisans and traders in cities
- Shudras were poorest and were indulged in agriculture

Other Kingdom

Kamarupa Dynasty

- Ruled from 350 to 1140 AD
- Existed as an independent kingdom
- Covered the entire Brahmaputras Valley, parts of North Bengal, Bhutan

Pala Dynasty

- Founded by Gopala in 750 AD who built Odantapuri monastery
- His successor Dharamapala (770-810 AD) engaged in tripartite struggle for supremacy of Kannauj
- Also founded Vikramshila University. Greatest ruler - Devapala (810-850 AD)

Gurjara-Pratihara Dynasty

- Ruled part of North and North-Western India from 6th to 11th century AD
- Protected from Arab invasions for 11th century AD
- Nagabhata I was first important ruler who expelled Arabs in Battle of Rajasthan
- King Vatsaraja defeated Dharmapala King Nagabhata II rebuild Somnath temple in 815 AD
- Most important ruler—Mihira Bhoja who adopted title of Adivaraha

Rashtrakuta Dynasty

- Ruled Deccan from about 753 AD to 982 AD; Dantidurga founded the dynasty and he defeated Pratihara and Chalukyan kings.
- Krishna I was greatest ruler who defeated Gangas and the Eastern Chalukyas of Vengi;
- He also built rock-cut-monolithic Kailash temple at Ellora

Life in Post-Gupta Era

Language and Literature

- Apabhramsa the precursor of modern language like Hindi, Gujarati, Marathi and Bangla
- Number of Kavyas developed.
- Sanskrit remained language of learning

Society

- Distinct Jatis such as Kayasthas emerged; Women's right to inherit property was accepted and widow were entitled to succeed to the whole estate of her deceased husband

Economy

- Literary and inscriptional evidences show advanced state of agriculture, trade and economy; Large variety of cereals were cultivated and irrigation was done by Arahata (Persian wheel) and leather buckets

Religion and Philosophy

- Both Buddhism and Jainism developed theistic tendencies
- Jainism gained popularity among trading classes; Many Jain basadis (temples) and Mahastambhas (pillar) erected; Tantricism gained popularity in North-Eastern India

Education

- Imported through temples and monastic establishments
- Vikramshila, Odantapuri, Vallabhi and Nalanda emerged great centres of higher learning

Art and Architecture

- Temples of Odisha and Khajuraho developed in Deccan temples of Vatapi and Pattadakal

SOURCE ***Old NCERT Class VI*** *(The Age of Smaller Kingdoms)*, ***New NCERT Class VI*** *(New Empires and Kingdoms)*, ***New NCERT Class VI*** *(Traders, Kings and Pilgrimages)*, ***Old NCERT Class XI*** *(Formation of New States and Rural Expansion)*, ***Old NCERT Class XI*** *(Spread of Civilisation in Eastern India)*, ***Old NCERT Class XI*** *(Harsha and His Times)*, ***Tamil Nadu Board Class XI*** *(Harsha and Rise of Regional Kingdoms*, ***NIOS Module 1*** *(India between 750-1200 AD)*

Harshavardhana

1 With reference to rule of Harshavardhana, consider the following statements. *(Unit 8, Class-XI, Tamil Nadu Board)*

1. He accepted the throne on the advice of Avalokitesvara.
2. Thaneswar and Kannauj became united under Harsha's rule.
3. Hostilities between Harsha and Maithrakas ended in a matrimonial alliance.

How many of the statements given above is/are correct?

(a) Only one (b) Only two
(c) All three (d) None of these

Ans. (c)

Exp. All three statements i.e, (1), (2) and (3) are correct with reference to the rule of Harshavardhana. A reluctant Harsha accepted the throne on the advice of Avalokitesvara Bodhisattva with the title of Rajputra and Siladitya.

The two kingdoms of Thaneswar and Kannauj became united under Harsha's rule. Consequently, Harsha transferred his capital to Kannauj.

The hostilities between Harsha and the Maithrakas ended in the marriage of Dhruvabhatta with the daughter of Harsha. Soon, Valabhi became a subordinate ally of Harsha.

2 Consider the following statements. *(Chap 23, Class-XI, Old NCERT)*

Statement-I Harsha authored Priyadarshika ,the Ratnavali, Mricchakatika and the Nagananda .

Statement-II Harsha patronised literary and cultural activities. Bana, the author of Harshacharita and Kadambari, was a court poet of Harsha.

Which one of the following is correct in respect of the above statements?

(a) Both Statement-I and Statement-II are correct and Statement-II is the correct explanation for Statement-I.
(b) Both Statement - I and Statement-II are correct and Statement-II is not the correct explanation for Statement-I.
(c) Statement-I is correct, but Statement-II is incorrect.
(d) Statement-I is incorrect, but Statement-II is correct.

Ans. (d)

Exp. Statement-I is incorrect, but Statement-II is correct as Mricchakatika was not authored Harshavardhana the Sanskrit drama. Mricchakatika was written by Shudraka in third century AD.

Harsha is remembered for his patronage and learning and also for the authorship of Three Dramas the Priyadarshika, the Ratnawali and the Nagananda. Banabhatta, court poet of Harsha, attributes great poetical skills to him. Ban wrote Harshachitra and Kadambari.

3 Consider the following statements. *(Chap 8, Class-VI, Old NCERT)*

1. Pulakeshin II defeated Harshvardhana.
2. Pulakeshin II was the ruler of Chalukya dynasty of Badami.
3. Pulakeshin II was defeated by Narasimhavarman I of Pallava dynasty.

How many of the statements given above is/are correct?

(a) Only one (b) Only two
(c) All three (d) None of these

Ans. (c)

Exp. All three statements i.e., (1), (2) and (3) are correct as Pulakeshin II popularly known as Immadi Pulakeshi, was the greatest Chalukyan Emperor who reigned from Vatapi (present-day Badami in Karnataka, India). Krittivarman I was the father of Pulakeshin II. Pulakeshi II defeated Harshavardhana in the year 618 AD on the bank of river Narmada.With this defeat ,the ambition of Harshavardhana to form all Indian empire came to an end. Pulakeshin II was defeated by Narasimhavarman I of Pallava dynasty.

4 With reference to Pushyabhutis, consider the following statements. *(Class-XI, Old NCERT)*

1. The founder of the Vardhana dynasty was Harshavardhana.
2. Harshavardhana shifted his capital from Kannauj to Thanesar.

Which of the statements given above is/are correct?

(a) Only 1 (b) Only 2
(c) Both 1 and 2 (d) Neither 1 nor 2

Ans. (d)

Exp. Neither statements (1) nor (2) are correct with reference to the Vardhana dynasty. The founder of Vardhana dynasty was Pushyabhuti who ruled from Thaneswar. He served as a military general under imperial Guptas and rose to power after the fall of the Guptas.

Harsha shifted his capital from Thanesar to Kannauj because Thanesar was too close to the threat from the North-West.

5 Consider the following statements about Harshavardhana. *(Chap 10, Class-VI, New NCERT)*

1. He was born in Thanesar.
2. During the reign of his father, he served as the provincial Governor of Bihar and Bengal.
3. His brother-in-law was the ruler of Kannauj and was killed by the ruler of Bengal.
4. He conquered the territories of Magadha and Bengal.

How many of the statements given above is/are incorrect?

(a) Only one (b) Only two (c) Only three (d) All four

Ans. (b)

Exp. Only one statement i.e., (2) is incorrect about the early life of Harshavardhana. The territories of Bengal and Bihar was annexed before the reign of Harshavardhana. So, he was not the provincial Governor of Bengal and Bihar during the reign of his father.

6 **Which among the following sources helps in the historical reconstruction of the reign of Harshavardhana?** *(Chap 23, Class-XI, Old NCERT)*

1. Harshacharita
2. Account of Chinese pilgrim, Hiuen Tsang
3. Travelogues of Fa-Hien.

Codes

(a) 1 and 2 (b) 2 and 3 (c) 1 and 3 (d) All of these

Ans. (a)

Exp. Among the given options, Harshacharita and account of Chinese pilgrim, Hiuen Tsang help in the historical reconstruction of the reign of Harshavardhana. Harshacharita written by Banabhatta, the court poet of Harshavardhana gives biographical account of Harshavardhana. It also tells about important events and flora and fauna of the country. Hiuen Tsang stayed in India for about 15 years and was widely respected by Harsha. His account helps in understanding the rule of Harsha.

The Travelogues of Fa-Hien, who came to India during the reign of Gupta Empire, gives a detailed account of reign of Chandragupta Vikramaditya.

7 **With reference to the pattern of administration under the reign of Harshavardhana, which of the following statements is/are incorrect?** *(Chap 23, Class-XI, Old NCERT)*

1. The administration under Harshavardhana was feudalistic and decentralised.
2. He stopped the practice of making land grants to the priests started by the rulers of the Gupta Empire.
3. Every feudatory under the Harshavardhana contributed his quota of footmen and horses.

Codes

(a) 1 and 2 (b) 2 and 3 (c) Only 2 (d) Only 3

Ans. (c)

Exp. Statement (2) is incorrect with reference to the pattern of administration under region of Harshavardhana because the land grants continued to be made to the priests for special services rendered to the state in Harsha times. Harsha is also credited with the grant of land to the officers by charters.

8 **Consider the following statements.** *(Class-XI, Old NCERT)*

1. Bhaga, Hiranya and Bali were the three kinds of tax collected during Harsha's reign.
2. Bhaga was the land tax paid in kind.
3. One-sixth of the produce was collected as land revenue.
4. Hiranya was the tax paid by farmers and merchants in cash. The crown land was divided into four parts.

How many of the statements given above is/are correct?

(a) Only one (b) Only two
(c) Only three (d) All of four

Ans. (d)

Exp. All four statements i.e., (1), (2), (3) and (4) are correct. Bhaga, Hiranya and Bali were the three kinds of tax collected during Harsha's reign. Bhaga was the land tax paid in kind. One-sixth of the produce was collected as land revenue. Hiranya was the tax paid by farmers and merchants in cash. There is no reference to the tax Bali. The crown land was divided into four parts.

Part I - For carrying out the affairs of the state

Part II - For paying the ministers and officers of the crown

Part III- For rewarding men of letters

Part IV - For charity to religious institutions

9 **Consider the following statements.** *(Class-XI, Old NCERT)*

1. The Harsha empire was divided into the provinces then into districts (vishayas).
2. The principle officer of the province was Uparika and district was Vishayapati and village was Gramika.
3. The fiscal and administrative unit 'Dandabhukti' was formed in the seventh century AD.

How many of the statements given above is/are correct?

(a) Only one (b) Only two
(c) All three (d) None of these

Ans. (c)

Exp. All three statements i.e., (1), (2) and (3) are correct. King Harshavardhana set up his empire in North India and he ruled from 606 - 647 AD. The empire was divided into the provinces then into districts (vishayas). The last unit was the village. The principle officer of the province was Uparika and district was Vishayapati and village was Gramika, other officials referred in Harshacharita are Bhogapati, Ayuktaka, Pratipalaka and Purushas. Harsha used his feudatories for administration called as Mahasamanta or Samantamaharaja. High officials are not paid in cash, but assigned as jagirs.

The fiscal and administrative unit 'Dandabhukti' was formed in the border areas between Bengal and Odisha in the seventh century AD.

10 **Consider the following statements.** *(Chap 23, Class-XI, Old NCERT) (IAS Pre 2004)*

1. The Chinese pilgrim Fa-Hien attended the fourth Great Buddhist Council held by Kanishka.
2. The Chinese pilgrim Hiuen-Tsang met Harsha and found him to be antagonistic to Buddhism.

Which of the statements given above is/are incorrect?

(a) Only 1 (b) Only 2
(c) Both 1 and 2 (d) Neither 1 nor 2

Ans. (c)

Exp. Both statements (1) and (2) are incorrect because the Chinese pilgrim Fa-Hien came to India during the reign of the Gupta Emperor, Chandragupta-II. Another Chinese pilgrim Hiuen Tsang arrived India in 629 AD during the reign of Harshavardhana.

According to him, the king was kind, courteous and tolerant. He was a devout Buddhist and convened a grand assembly at Kannauj to widely publicise the doctrine of Mahayana.

11 Consider the following statements with reference to the Chinese traveller Hiuen Tsang. *(Chap 8, Class-VI, Old NCERT)*

1. He left China at the age of twenty-six and travelled through Central Asia to India.
2. He reckoned that Buddhism was not popular among masses.
3. He studied the Mahayana form of Buddhism in Vikramshila University.

Which of the statements given above are correct?

(a) 1 and 2 (b) 2 and 3 (c) 1 and 3 (d) 1, 2 and 3

Ans. (a)

Exp. Statements (1) and (2) are correct with reference to Chinese traveller Hiuen Tsang. One of sources for the history of Harsha period is the account left by the Buddhist visitor Hiuen Tsang.

He was a Chinese traveller and pilgrim who left China in 629 AD, at the age of twenty-six. He arrived India through Central-Asia and stayed approximate fifteen years to study Buddhism and to collect Buddhist literature. Hiuen Tsang noticed that Buddhism was not as popular in all parts of India as he had thought it would be but in Eastern India, it was still very popular.

Statement (3) is incorrect because Hiuen Tsang visited and studied Buddhism in Nalanda University.

12 With reference to the state of law and order during the reign of Harshvardhana, which of the following statements is/are incorrect? *(Chap 23, Class-XI, Old NCERT)*

1. Under the reign of Harsha, the state of law and order in the empire was not well maintained.
2. Robbery was considered to be a second treason for which the right hand of the robber was amputated.
3. Under the influence of Hiuen Tsang, the severity of punishment was mitigated and criminals were imprisoned for life.

Codes

(a) Only 3 (b) 2 and 3
(c) 1 and 3 (d) 1, 2 and 3

Ans. (a)

Exp. Statement (3) is incorrect with reference to the state of law and order during the reign of Harshavardhana because under the influence of Buddhism severity of punsihment was mitigated and criminals were imprisoned for life.

13 With reference to the account of Hiuen Tsang on state of society in India, consider the following statements. *(Chap 23, Class-XI, Old NCERT)*

1. The cities of Pataliputra and Vaishali were in state of decline.
2. Majority of Brahmanas and Kshatriyas were engaged in agriculture.
3. Contrary to the Gupta period, there was no untouchability prevalent in India.

How many of the statements given above is/are correct?

(a) Only one (b) Only two
(c) Only three (d) All of these

Ans. (b)

Exp. Only two statements i.e., (1) and (2) are correct with reference to the account of Hiuen Tsang on state of society in India. The Hiuen Tsang's account shows that prominent ancient cities such as Pataliputra and Vaishali were in state of decline. On the other hand, Prayag and Kannauj in the Doab had become important centres.

The Brahmanas and Kshatriyas were reported to have led a simple life. The majority in each one of them had taken to agriculture.

Statement (3) is incorrect because the Chinese pilgrim takes notice of untouchables in times of Gupta period.

14 Consider the following statements with reference to the state of Nalanda University during the reign of Harshavardhana. *(Chap 23, Class-XI, Old NCERT)*

1. Students and monks were taught Buddhist philosophy of Hinayana school.
2. The monastery at the Nalanda was supported from the revenue of the 100 villages.
3. Besides Hiuen Tsang, it was also visited by another Chinese traveller I-tsing in seventh century.

How many of the statements given above is/are correct?

(a) Only one (b) Only two
(c) All three (d) None of these

Ans. (b)

Exp. Only two statements i.e., (2) and (3) are correct with reference to the state of Nalanda University during the reign of Harshavardhana.

According to Hiuen Tsang, the monastery at Nalanda was supported by revenue of 100 villages. Another traveller I-tsing records it to be 200 villages.

I-tsing, another Chinese pilgrim visited Nalanda in 670 AD (7th century).

Statement (1) is incorrect because at Nalanda, Mahayana School of Buddhism was taught to students and monks.

15 **Consider the following statements with reference to the state of religion during the reign of Harshavardhana.** *(Chap 23, Class-XI, Old NCERT)*

1. The king Harshavardhana was follower of Vaishnavism before becoming a great patron of Buddhism.
2. An assembly at Kannauj was convened by the Harshavardhana to publicise the doctrine of Mahayana.
3. According to the Hiuen Tsang, Harshavardhana was kind, courteous and followed a tolerant religious policy.

Which of the statements given above is/are incorrect?

(a) 1 and 2 (b) Only 1 (c) 1 and 3 (d) Only 3

Ans. (b)

Exp. Statement (1) is incorrect with reference to the state of religion during the reign of Harshavardhana because Harshavardhana was follower of Shaivism in his early days. Gradually, he became a great patron of Buddhism.

16 **With reference to ancient city of Kannauj, which of the following statements is/are correct?** *(Chap 23, Class-XI, Old NCERT)*

1. It was well-fortified in the seventh century as it was situated on the elevated area of the Ganga-Yamuna doab.
2. Its strategic location allowed the movement of soldiers through both land and water routes.
3. It contained huge amount of iron-ore which was used for making arms.

How many of the statements given above is/are correct?

(a) Only one (b) Only two (c) All three (d) None of these

Ans. (b)

Exp. Only two statements i.e., (1) and (2) are correct. Kannauj was made capital by Harsha. Fortification of places in the plains was far more difficult, but Kannauj was situated on an elevated area which was easily fortifiable. As it was located in the middle of the doab, it was well-fortified in the seventh century. So, to exercise control over the Eastern and Western wings of the doab soldiers could be moved by both land and water routes.

Statement (3) is incorrect because there was not any source of iron-ore near the city of Kannauj.

17 **The Chinese traveller Yuan Chwang (Hiuen Tsang), who visited India recorded the general conditions and culture of India at that time. In this context, which of the following statements is/are correct?** *(Chap 23, Class-XI, Old NCERT), (IAS Pre 2013)*

1. The roads and river-routes were completely immune from robbery.
2. As regards punishment for offences ordeals by fire, water and poison were the instruments for determining the innocence or guilt of a person.
3. The tradesman had to pay duties at ferries and barrier stations.

How many of the statements given above is/are correct?

(a) Only one (b) Only two
(c) All three (d) None of these

Ans. (b)

Exp. Only two statements i.e., (2) and (3) are correct regarding account of Hiuen Tsang on general condition of India during the reign of Harshavardhana.

As regard punishment methods such as ordeals by fire, water and poison were employed for determining the innocence or guilt of a person. Severe punishments were inflicted for crime. According to Hiuen Tsang, in the empire of Harsha, law and order was not well maintained. The tradesman had to pay duties at ferries and barrier station.

Statement (1) is incorrect because despite the special care taken for Hiuen Tsang, he was robbed of his belonging.

18 **Match the following lists correctly and choose the correct codes.** *(Chap 10, Class-VI, New NCERT)*

List I (Officials)	List II (Functions)
A. Sandhi-Vigraha	1. Minister of War and Peace
B. Nagara Shreshthi	2. Leader of the merchant caravan
C. Sarthavaha	3. Chief banker of the city
D. Prathama-Kulika	4. Chief craftsmen

Codes

	A	B	C	D
(a)	1	3	2	4
(b)	2	1	4	3
(c)	4	2	3	1
(d)	3	1	2	4

Ans. (a)

Exp. The correct matching is A-1, B-3, C-2, D-4.

In times of Harsha, a person could hold two posts. **Sandhi-Vigrahika** meaning a Minister of War and Peace.

The **Nagara-Shreshthi** was chief banker or merchant of the city in times of Harsha.

The **Sarthavaha** was leader of the merchant caravans.

The **Prathama-Kulika** meant the chief craftsman.

19 **Consider the following statements.** *(Chap 23, Class-XI, Old NCERT)*

Statements-I As compared to the rulers of Gupta Empire, Harshavardhana didn't issue coins on the large scale.

Statement-II He started the feudal practice of rewarding and paying officers with grants of lands.

Codes

(a) Both Statement-I and Statement-II are correct and Statement-II is the correct explanation for Statement-I.
(b) Both Statement-I and Statement-II are correct and Statement-II is not the correct explanation for Statement-I.
(c) Statement-I is not correct, but Statements-II is correct.
(d) Statement-I is incorrect but Statement-II is correct.

Ans. (a)

Exp. Both Statement-I and Statement-II are correct and Statement-II is the correct explanation of Statement-I.

Harsha is credited with the grant of land to the officers by charters.

Hiuen Tsang also tells that ministers and high officers of the state were endowed with land. The feudal practice of rewarding and paying officers with grants of land seem to have begun under Harsha. This explains why too many coins are not found at times of Harsha.

Regional Kingdoms

20 Consider the following statements with reference to administration in Bengal in the Post-Gupta age. *(Unit 8, Class-XI, Tamil Nadu Board)*

1. Agharika was appointed for supervising the endowments of tax free land and villages to learned persons.
2. Harsha is credited with the grant of land to the officers by charters.
3. Visayapati was the district officer and Gramika was the village officer.

How many of the statements given above is/are correct?

(a) Only one (b) Only two
(c) All three (d) None of these

Ans (c)

Exp. All three statements are correct in times of after a special; officer called Agraharika was appointed to supervise these land grants.

Harsha is credited with the grant of land to the officers by charters.The high officials such as Mahasamantas and Maharajas were hereditary-local chiefs.

Provincial officers were Kumaramatyas, Uparikas, etc. Visayapati was the district officer and Gramika was the village officer.

21 Consider the following statements with reference to the King Shashanka. *(Chap 23, Class-XI, Old NCERT)*

1. He was ruler of Gauda (Bengal) in the late sixth and early seventh century AD.
2. He was the greatest patron of Mahayana school of Buddhism in Eastern India.

Which of the statements given above is/are incorrect?

(a) Only 1 (b) Only 2
(c) Both 1 and 2 (d) Neither 1 nor 2

Ans. (b)

Exp. Statement (2) is incorrect with reference to the King Shashanka because Shashanka cut off the Bodhi tree at Bodh Gaya. His death in 619 AD put an end to this hostility to Buddhism.

22 Consider the following statements with reference to the Kingdom of Matharas in the Odisha. *(Chap 22, Class-XI, Old NCERT)*

1. They began the practice of dividing the year into twelve months keeping the view of changing weather condition in mind.
2. They created the districts of Mahendrabhoga and Dantayavagubhoga in the Orissa.
3. They made endowments called agraharas for supporting religious and educational activities of Brahamana.

How many of the statements given above is/are correct?

(a) Only one (b) Only two (c) All three (d) None of these

Ans. (c)

Exp. All three statements i.e., (1), (2) and (3) are correct. Under the Matharas, in the middle of the fifth century, began the practice of dividing the year into twelve lunar months. This implied a detailed idea of weather conditions, which was useful for agricultural operations.

The Matharas created a district Mahendrabhoga in the area of the Mahendra mountains and also a district called Dantayavagubhoga, both being in Orissa.

The Matharas made endowments called agraharas, which consisted of land and income from villages and were meant for supporting religious and educational activities of the brahmanas.

23 With reference to the history of Bengal in the fourth and fifth century AD, which of the following statements is/are incorrect? *(Chap 22, Class-XI, Old NCERT)*

1. The deltaic portion of the river Brahmaputra and Ganga was referred as Samatata and it was surrounded by the state of Vanga in the West.
2. In the sixth century AD, it was ruled by the King Sama Hardeva who issued large number of gold coins.
3. The rulers of Samatata and Vanga were ardent supporter of Jainism.

How many of the statements given above is/are incorrect?

(a) Only one (b) Only two
(c) All three (d) None of these

Ans. (a)

Exp. Statement (3) is incorrect with reference to history of Bengal in fourth and fifth century AD because the rulers of Samatata were not ardent supporter of Jainism. They favoured different religious sects, Buddhism was one of them.

24 During the seventh century AD, the territories of South-East and Central Bengal were ruled by the state of Khadgas, Lokanatha, and Ratas. Which of the following statements regarding their administration is/are correct? *(Chap 22, Class-XI, Old NCERT)*

1. All of them were involved in expansion of cultivation and rural settlement.
2. They made endowments called agraharas for supporting religious and educational activities of the Brahamana.
3. Prakrit was the main language of these kingdoms.

Codes

(a) 1 and 2
(b) 2 and 3
(c) 1 and 3
(d) 1, 2 and 3

Ans. *(a)*

Exp. Statements (1) and (2) are correct regarding administration in the territories of South-East and Central Bengal. The state of Khadgas swordsmen in Dhaka region, Lokanatha (Brahmana feudatory), and Ratas, both in Comilla region. These states of South-East and Central Bengal issued land grants in the sixth and seventh centuries. Like the Orissa kings, they also created agraharas to maintain the supervision of land grants to monks and Brahamans.

They were also involved in expansion of cultivation and rural settlements.

Statement (3) is incorrect because their main language was Sanskrit not Prakrit.

25 Consider the following statements with reference to administration of land in the seventh century AD Bengal. *(Chap 22, Class-XI, Old NCERT)*

1. Land was under the possession of individual families.
2. The sale and purchase of the land was in control of the local communities dominated by leading artisans, merchants, landowners and scribes.
3. These communities were entitled to taxes and also possessed rights over waste and fallow land.

How many of the statements given above is/are correct?

(a) Only one (b) Only two
(c) All three (d) None of these

Ans. *(b)*

Exp. Only two statements i.e., (1) and (2) are correct in the seventh century AD, generally land was under the possession of individual family.

But it's sale and purchase was subject to local community. Local community was mainly dominated by leading artisans, merchants, land owners and scribes.

Statement (3) is incorrect because the king had right and tax over fallow and waste lands.

26 Consider the following statements with reference to Kamrupa kingdom. *(Chap 22, Class-XI, Old NCERT)*

1. The rulers of this kingdom adopted the title of Varman which symbolises a warrior.
2. Until the eight century AD, the use of Sanskrit and art of writing was not known to the people in Kamarupa kingdom.
3. The rulers of the Kamarupa kingdom strengthened their position through land grants to the Brahmanas.

Which of the statements given above is/are incorrect?

(a) 1 and 2 (b) 2 and 3 (c) Only 2 (d) Only 3

Ans. *(c)*

Exp. Statement (2) is incorrect with reference to Kamrupa kingdom because in the inscriptions of sixth century AD, the use of Sanskrit and art of writing have been found here.

27 Match the following lists correctly and choose the correct code. *(Chap 22, Class-XI, Old NCERT)*

List I (Regional Kingdoms in Odisha)	List II (Achievements)
A. Matharas	1. Devised calendar based on the seasons
B. Vashishthas	2. Ruled borders of Andhra in South Kalinga
C. Nalas	3. Issued gold coins in the Bastar tribal areas
D. Manas	4. Issued large number of copper coins

Codes

	A	B	C	D		A	B	C	D
(a)	1	2	3	4	(b)	2	1	4	3
(c)	3	2	4	1	(d)	4	3	2	1

Ans. *(a)*

Exp. The correct matching is A-1, B-2, C-3, D-4.

Matharas divided the year into three units, each of four months. This was on basis of seasons.

Vasishthas ruled over areas on the borders of Andhra in South Kalinga (Odisha). They were contemporary of Pitribhaktas who ruled the state of Matharas, between Mahanadi and Krishna river.

Nalas were contemporary of Matharas in ancient Odisha and Chhattisgarh. They issued gold coins in the Bastar tribal areas.

Manas ruled from the Coastal areas of Odisha and were famous for issuing large number of copper coins.

28 With reference to Indian history, which of the following is/are the essential element/elements of the feudal system? *(Chap 28, Class-XI, Old NCERT) (IAS Pre 2015)*

1. A very strong centralised political authority and a very weak provincial or local political authority.
2. Emergence of administrative structure based on control and possession of land.

3. Creation of lord-vassal relationship between the feudal lord and his overlord.

Codes

(a) 1 and 2
(b) 2 and 3
(c) Only 3
(d) All of the above

Ans. (b)

Exp. Statements (2) and (3) are correct regarding feudal system.

It is a type of administrative structure based on control and possession of land. It was one of the feature of agrarian society.

It was also marked by creation of lord-vasal relationship between the feudal lord and his overlord. In the lieu of grant of land titles, the vassal is obliged to provide services to the lord. Feudalism in ancient India gradually developed since the reign of Gupta Empire. Till the advent of Harshavardhana it became most prominent feature of administration.

Statement (1) is incorrect because feudalism is the characterstic feature of weak and decentralised authority.

Tripartite Struggle

29 With respect to Tripartite struggle, consider the following statements. ***(Class-XI, Old NCERT)***

1. Cholas were not involved in the Tripartite struggle from the eighth to the tenth century AD.
2. It is defined as a constant struggle among three pre-medieval dynasties of East, West and South India for the control and supremacy over Kannauj.
3. Due to constant struggle and military expeditions, these three kingdoms were not able to provide stable living conditions for the general population nor they patronised art and literature.

How many statements given above is/are correct?

(a) Only one (b) Only two
(c) All three (d) None of these

Ans. (b)

Exp. Only two statement i.e., (1) and (2) are correct with respect to Tripartite struggle. Cholas were not involved in the Tripartite struggle from the eighth to the tenth century AD. these Struggle for power in India from 750-1000 AD was between mainly three kingdoms of Pala, Pratiharas and Rashtrakutas, who dominated areas in East, West and Deccan regions of India, respectively. The struggle was also for the rich land of the upper Gangetic region of Kannauj which was rich in resources and trade. This constant struggle among these kingdoms is referred to as Tripartite struggle.

Statement (3) is incorrect because three empires, even if they fought among themselves, provided stable conditions of life over India and patronised arts and literature.

Pala Dynasty

30 Which Arab traveller calls the Pala kingdom as 'Ruhma'? ***(Chap 21, Class-XI, Old NCERT)***

(a) Al-Masudi (b) Al-Masher
(c) Sulaiman (d) Al-Beruni

Ans. (c)

Exp. The Arab traveller, Sulaiman visited the Bengal during the reign of Pala kingdom in ninth century AD. He in his memoir referred the Pala kingdom as 'Ruhma' and described about its military strength.

31 With reference to the archeological and literary sources of Pala dynasty, consider the follwing statements. ***(Chap 1, Class-XI, Old NCERT)***

1. Accounts of an Arab merchant Sulaiman
2. Tibetan chronicles
3. Manuscripts preserved at Nalanda University

How many of the above sources helps in the historical reconstrution of Pala dynasty?

(a) Only one (b) Only two
(c) All three (d) None of these

Ans. (b)

Exp. Only two statements i.e., (1) and (2) are correct regarding historical reconstruction of Pala dynasty. Arab trader Sulaiman travelled to India in middle of ninth century and has written about the Pala kingdom.

He calls it Ruhma, which means Dharma (short for Dharmapala). He tells that Palas were at wars with their neighbours.

Tibetan chronicles also give information about Pala rule. According to them, Pala rulers were patron of Buddhist learning and religion. Dharmapala founded the Vikramshila University in Bihar.

Statement (3) is incorrect because the manuscripts as well as Nalanda University itself was destroyed in 12th century AD by Turk invaders and some are in bad condition..

32 Consider the following statements with reference to the Pala dynasty. ***(Chap 3, Class-VI, Old NCERT)***

1. They organised their power partly by building a strong army and partly by making alliances with the neighbouring kingdoms.
2. They encouraged merchants to take part in the South-East Asian trade.
3. Under Dharmapala, they defeated the King of Tibet and made it as a part of Pala dynasty.

Which of the statements given above is/are incorrect?

(a) 1 and 2 (b) 2 and 3 (c) Only 2 (d) Only 3

Ans. (d)

Exp. Statement (3) is incorrect with reference to the Pala dynasty as Dharmapala didn't conquer Tibet but had close relations with it. There were exchange of Buddhist ideas between two regions.

33 **With reference to Pala empire, consider the following pairs.** *(Chap 1, Class-XI, Old NCERT)*

	Kings of Pala dynasty		Important events
1	Dharmapala	–	occupied Kannauj and held a grand darbar
2	Gopala	–	revived Nalanda University
3	Devapala	–	granted permission to a ruler of Sailendra dynasty to build a monastery at Nalanda

How many pairs given above is/are incorrectly matched?

(a) Only one (b) Only two
(c) All three (d) None of these

Ans. (a)

Exp. Only one pair i.e., (2) is incorrectly matched because Nalanda University of Magadha region was revived by Dharmapala, who was the son of Gopala, founder of Pala empire.

Dharmapala had also kept 200 villages apart only for upkeep and expenses of Nalanda University. Later, Dharmapala also founded the Vikramshila University.

34 **Consider the following statements with reference to administration under Pala dynasty.** *(Chap 1, Class-XI, Old NCERT)*

1. The empire consisted of areas administered directly and areas ruled over by the Vassal chiefs.
2. The directly administered territories under the Pala empires were divided into bhukti (province) and visaya (districts).
3. The Governor of the provinces was called samanta.

Which of the statements given above are correct?

(a) 1 and 2 (b) 2 and 3 (c) 1 and 3 (d) All of these

Ans. (a)

Exp. Statements (1) and (2) are correct with reference to administration under Pala dynasty. In the Pala dynasty, the empire consisted of areas administered directly and areas ruled by Vassal chiefs.

Areas under Vassal chiefs were mostly autonomous in character as far as internal matters were concerned and they had a general loyalty to kings. They paid fixed tributes and provided troops in need.

The areas ruled over by vassals were divided into provinces which were called bhukti and mandala or visaya, which were districts.

Statement (3) is incorrect because the Governor of the provinces or bhukti was called *uparika*.

35 **With reference to Pala dynasty, consider the following statements.** *(Class-XI, Old NCERT)*

1. The palas ruled eastern India from Pataliputra between the ninth and the early twelfth centuries.
2. Sanskrit, Prakriti and Pali were the languages in use in their Kingdom.
3. Dharmapala extended Pala control Eastward upto Assam.

How many statements given above is/are incorrect?

(a) Only one (b) Only two
(c) All three (d) None of these

Ans. (a)

Exp. Only one statement i.e., (3) is incorrect because Dharmapala's son Devapala extended Pala control Eastwards up to Kamarupa (Assam). He defeated Amoghavarsha, the Rashtrakuta ruler, by allying with all the states that regarded the Rashtrakutas as their common enemy. Devapala was also a great patron of Buddhism.

36 **With reference to literature of the Pala dynasty, consider the following statements.** *(Class-XI, Old NCERT)*

1. Philosophical text called Agama Shastra was composed by Sridhar Bhatta.
2. Nayaya Kundali was composed by Gaudapada.

Which of the statements given above is/are correct?

(a) Only 1
(b) Only 2
(c) Both 1 and 2
(d) Neither 1 nor 2

Ans. (d)

Exp. Neither statements (1) nor (2) are correct with reference to the literature during Pala dynasty. The notable Pala texts on philosophy include Agama Shastra composed by Gaudapada, and Nyaya Kundali composed by Sridhar Bhatta. Moreover, many texts on medicine were compiled by Chakrapani Datta, Sureshwar Gadadhara Vaidya and Jimutavahana.

37 **With reference to Pala dynasty, consider the following statements.** *(Class-XI, Old NCERT)*

1. Advance of the Cholas beyond the Ganges was checked by the Pala king Mahipala I.
2. Last ruler of the Pala dynasty was repelled by the Vijayasena of the Sena dynasty.

Which of the statements given above is/are correct?

(a) Only 1 (b) Only 2
(c) Both 1 and 2 (d) Neither 1 nor 2

Ans. (c)

Exp. Both statements (1) and (2) are correct with reference to the Pala dynasty. This was the most important event of the reign of Mahipala was the invasion of Northern India by Rajendra Chola between 1020 and 1025 AD. However, the advance of the Cholas beyond the Ganges was checked by Mahipala I.

Last ruler of the Pala dynasty, Madanapala was repelled by the Vijayasena of the Sena dynasty.

Vijayasena of the Sena dynasty who had become powerful by then in Northern Bengal expelled the last ruler Madanapala (1130-1150 AD) from Bengal and established his dynastic rule.

38 **With reference to the reign Pala dynasty , consider the following Buddhists scholar.** *(Chap 1, Class-XI, Old NCERT)*

1. Santarakshita
2. Nagarjuna
3. Dipankara
4. Dandapani

How many of the above Buddhist scholars were invited to Tibet during the reign of Pala dynasty?

(a) Only one (b) Only two
(c) Only three (d) All four

Ans. (b)

Exp. Only two Buddhist scholars i.e., (1) and (4) were invited to Tibet during the reign of Pala dynasty. Santarakshita and Dipankara, also known as Atisa. were invited to Tibet.

They introduced a new form of Buddhism there. Because of that, many people came to Universities of Nalanda and Vikramshila for studies.

39 **Consider the following statements.**

1. The Ikshvaku rulers of Southern India were antagonistic towards Buddhism.
2. The Pala rulers of Eastern India were patrons of Buddhism. *(Class-XI, Old NCERT) (IAS Pre 2006)*

Which of the statements given above is/are correct?

(a) Only 1 (b) Only 2
(c) Both 1 and 2 (d) Neither1 nor 2

Ans. (b)

Exp. Only statement (2) is correct as Pala dynasty, ruling dynasty in Bihar and Bengal, India, from 8th to the 12th century. The Palas were supporters of Buddhism, and it was through missionaries from their kingdom, that Buddhism was finally established in Tibet.

Statement (1) is incorrect because Andhra Ikshvakus were one of the earliest recorded ruling dynasties of the Guntur - Krishna - Nalgonda regions of Andhra Pradesh and Telangana.

Although the Ikshvakus rulers practiced the Vedic religion, they were also great patrons of Buddhism. Most of the kings and their household donated to the Buddhist cause.

Pratihara Dynasty

40 **With reference to Pratihara ruler Mihir Bhoja, which of the following statements are correct?** *(Chap 1, Class-XI, Old NCERT)*

1. During his reign, Pratihara became successful in capturing Kannauj in 836 AD.
2. He adopted the title of 'Adivaraha' which has been inscribed in some of his coins.
3. The Arab traveller, Al-Masudi visited the Empire of Pratihara during the reign of Mihir Bhoja.

Codes

(a) 1 and 2 (b) 2 and 3
(c) 1 and 3 (d) 1, 2 and 3

Ans. (a)

Exp. Statements (1) and (2) are correct with reference to Pratihara ruler Mihir Bhoja who re-established the Pratihara rule and won the capital city Kannauj in 836 AD. Kannauj remained capital of Pratiharas for next 100 years. He was a devotee of Vishnu and had adopted the title of 'Adivaraha', it has been found inscribed on coins of his period.

Statement (3) is incorrect because Al-Masudi travelled to Gujarat in 915 AD during the reign of Mahipala.

41 **With reference to Pratihara consider the following statements.** *(Class-XI, Old NCERT)*

1. The rise of the Pratiharas in Jalore under Mihira Bhoja brought about the decline of the Palas.
2. Sanskrit poet Rajashekhar lived at the court of Mahipala.

How many statements given above is/are correct?

(a) Only 1 (b) Only 2
(c) Both 1 and 2 (d) Neither 1 nor 2

Ans (c)

Exp. Both statements (1) and (2) are correct with reference to the rise of the Pratiharas in Jalore under Mihira Bhoja brought about the decline of the Palas. The Rashtrakutas and the Pratiharas took advantage of Narayanapala's disposition and defeated the Palas.

The great Sanskrit poet and dramatist Rajashekhar lived at the court of the Pratihara ruler Mahipala. He was grandson of the founder of Pratihara dynasty, Mihir Bhoja. Pratiharas patronised learning and literature. They also made many temples and buildings in the capital city of Kannauj.

Rashtrakuta Dynasty

42 **Consider the following statements with reference to Rashtrakuta ruler, Amoghavarsha.** *(Chap 1, Class-XI, Old NCERT)*

1. He is credited with writing the first Kannada book on poetics.
2. According to Al-Masudi, he was the greatest king of India and most of the rulers accepted his suzerainty.

Which of the statements given above is/are incorrect?

(a) Only 1 (b) Only 2
(c) Both 1 and 2 (d) Neither 1 nor 2

Ans. (b)

Exp. Only statement (2) is incorrect with reference to Rashtrakuta ruler, Amoghavarsha (814-878 AD) as Arab traveller, Al-Masudi had referred the Rashtrakuta king, Balhara or Vallabharaja, as the greatest king of India.

43 **Consider the following statements about Rashtrakutas.** *(Chap 1, Class-XI, Old NCERT)*

1. The great Apabhramsha poet Svayambhu lived at the Rashtrakuta court.
2. Chandrobalabbe, the daughter of Krishna III was entrusted with the responsibility of administering Raichur doab.

3. Amoghavarsha who ruled for 64 years was one of the greatest patron of Jainism.

How many statements given above is/are correct?

(a) Only one (b) Only two
(c) All three (d) None of these

Ans. (b)

Exp. Only two statements i.e., (1) and (3) are correct about Rashtrakutas. Rashtrakutas were patrons of arts and letters. They had Sanskrit scholars, poets and others who wrote in Prakrit at their courts. The great poet Svayambhu of Apabhramsha lived at a Rashtrakuta court.

Amoghavarsha (814-878 AD) ruled for 64 years and by nature was fond of art, poems and buildings. He was himself a Jain but respected all religions.

Statement (2) is incorrect because Chandrobalabbe was daughter of King Amoghavarsha 1. She was entrusted with the responsibility of administering Raichur doab.

44 With reference to Rashtrakuta dynasty, consider the following pairs. ***(Chap 1, Class-XI, Old NCERT)***

(1) Govinda III– annexed Malwa
(2) Amoghavarsha – defeated Mahipala of Pratihara dynasty
(3) Krishna III–erected a pillar of victory in Rameshwaram.

How many pairs given above is/are correctly matched?

(a) Only one (b) Only two
(c) All three (d) None of these

Ans. (b)

Exp. Only two pairs i.e., (1) and (3) are correctly matched.

Govinda III of the Rashtrakuta dynasty annexed Malwa from Nagabhata II. After the conquest of Malwa, Govinda III ensured the Paramara dynasty would rule as vassals of the Rashtrakutas in 800 AD.

Krishna III erected a pillar of victory in Rameshwaram. Krishna III defeated the Chola King Parantaka I (949 AD), annexed the Northern part of the Chola empire. He, then, pressed down to Rameshwaram and set up a pillar of victory there and built a temple.

Pair (2) is incorrectly matched because Indra III of the Rashtrakuta dynasty defeated Mahipala of the Pratihara Dynasty and took control of Kannauj.

45 Consider the following statements with reference to Rastrakuta dynasty. ***(Chap 1, Class-XI, Old NCERT)***

1. The kings of Rashtrakuta empire were great patron of Shaivism and Vaishnavism.
2. During the reign of Rashtrakutas, Kailasha temple at Ellora was built.
3. Its rulers didn't allow Muslim traders to settle and to preach Islam in their territory.

How many statements given above is/are correct?

(a) Only one (b) Only two
(c) All three (d) None of these

Ans. (b)

Exp. Only two statements i.e., (1) and (2) are correct with reference to the state of religion under Rashtrakuta. Rashtrakuta rulers were tolerant of all religions. They were great patrons of Shaivism and Vaishnavism. They also provided patronage to Jainism. The famous rock-cut temple of Shiva at Ellora was built by one of Rashtrakuta kings.

Statement (3) is incorrect because Rashtrakutas allowed Muslim traders to settle and permitted Islam to be preached in their territory.

46 Match the following lists correctly and choose the correct code. ***(Chap 1, Class-XI, Old NCERT)***

List I (Functionaries)	List II (Responsibilities)
A. Koshta-pala	1. Revenue officers
B. Nad-gavundas	2. Maintenance of law and orders in towns
C. Rashtrapati	3. Village elders to assist headmen
D. Grama-mahattara	4. Governor of provinces

Codes

	A	B	C	D		A	B	C	D
(a)	1	2	3	4	(b)	2	3	1	4
(c)	2	1	4	3	(d)	3	4	1	2

Ans. (c)

Exp. The correct matching is A-2, B-1, C-4, D-3.

Koshta-pala or Kotwal maintained law and orders in towns and areas in their immediate vicinity.

Nad-gavundas were revenue officers whose post was hereditary. They were also called desa-gramakutas.

Rashtrapati were Governors of provinces.

Grama-mahattara or grama- mahajana were village elders who helped headman in his duties.

47 Who among the following laid the foundation of Rashtrakuta Empire? ***(Class-XI, Old NCERT) (IAS Pre 2006)***

(a) Amoghavarsha I (b) Dantidurga
(c) Dhruva (d) Krishna I

Ans. (b)

Exp. The founder of the Rashtrakuta power was Dantivarman or Dantidurga was a contemporary of Chalukya King Pulakesin II. Rashtrakuta was a royal dynasty ruling large parts of the Indian subcontinent between the sixth and tenth centuries. Dantidurga occupied all territories between the Godavari and Bhima river.

48 With reference to Rashtrakuta dynasty, consider the following statements. ***(Class-XI, Old NCERT)***

1. They were feudatories of the Vakataka dynasty.
2. Kailasha temple of Ellora was constructed by Krishna I.

Which of the statements given above is/are incorrect?

(a) Only 1 (b) Only 2
(c) Both 1 and 2 (d) Neither 1 nor 2

Ans. (a)

Exp. Statement (1) is incorrect with reference to the Rashtrakuta dynasty. The Rashtrakutas were originally known to be the feudatories of the Western Chalukyas of Vatapi. Though Rashtrakutas were early rulers, the greatest ruler of the dynasty was Dandidurga.

Development of Indian Philosophy

49 Which of the following schools of philosophy has opinion that Vedas contain eternal truth? *(Chap 25, Class-XI, Old NCERT) (CGPSC Pre 2013)*

(a) Mimamsa (b) Nyaya
(c) Samkhya (d) Lokayata

Ans. (a)

Exp. The Mimamsa school of philosophy has opinion that Vedas contain eternal truth. In order to attain salvation, the Mimamsa strongly recommended the performance of Vedic sacrifices, which needed the services of the priests and legitimised the social distance between various varnas.

Through the propagation of the Mimamsa, the Brahmanas wanted to maintain their ritual authority and preserve the social hierarchy based on Brahmanism.

50 With reference to the development of Indian Philosophy, consider the following statements. *(Chap 25, Class-XI, Old NCERT)*

1. The 'Brahmasutra of Badarayana' compiled in the second century BC formed the basic tenant Vedanta schools of Indian Philosophy.
2. Vaishehika propounded the atom theory.
3. The Nyaya philosophical system was propagated by Kapila.

How many statements given above is/are incorrect?

(a) Only one (b) Only two
(c) All three (d) None of these

Ans. (a)

Exp. Only one statement i.e., (3) is incorrect with reference to the development of Indian philosophy. The Nyaya philosophical system was propagated by Gautama. It was developed as a system of logic. According to it, salvation can be attained through the acquisition of knowledge.

51 The ancient sages, Makkhali Gosala and Ajita Kesakambalin belonged to which of the following sects? *(Chap 4, Class-XII, New NCERT)*

(a) Lokayatas and Ajivika
(b) Ajivika and Lokayata
(c) Samkhya and Vedanta
(d) Vedanta and Samkhya

Ans. (b)

Exp. The ancient sages Makkhali Gosala and Ajita Kesakambalin belonged to the tradition of the Ajivikas and Lokayata respectively. They have often been described as fatalists; those who believe that everything is predetermined.

Ajita Kesakambalin belonged to the tradition of the Lokayatas, usually described as materialists.

Texts from these traditions have not survived, so knowledge about them comes from the works of other traditions.

52 With reference to cultural history of India, the term 'Panchayatana' refers to *(Chap 27, Class-XI, Old NCERT) (IAS Pre 2014)*

(a) an assembly of village elders.
(b) a religious sect.
(c) a style of temple construction.
(d) an administrative functionary.

Ans. (c)

Exp. With reference to cultural history of India, the term 'Panchayatana' refers to a style of temple construction. Panchayatana denotes type of temple building wherein chief God Shiva or any other was housed in the main building and was accompanied by four subsidiary shrines containing other four deities- Brahma, Ganapati, Vishnu and Shakti.

53 Match the following lists correctly and choose the correct code. *(Chap 25, Class-XI, Old NCERT)*

List I (Philosophies)	List II (Basic tenants)
A. Samkhya	1. Brahma is reality and everything else is unreal.
B. Nyaya	2. Salvation can be attained through meditation and physical application.
C. Vedanta	3. Knowledge can be acquired through perception, inference and hearing.
D. Yoga	4. Salvation can be attained through acquisition of knowledge.

Codes

	A	B	C	D
(a)	1	2	3	4
(b)	2	3	1	4
(c)	2	1	4	3
(d)	3	4	1	2

Ans. (d)

Exp. The correct matching is A-3, B-4, C-1, D-2.

Samkhya Philosophy laid emphasis on knowledge and it can be acquired through perception, inference and hearing. It had a typical methods of scientific inquiry to nature.

Nyaya meant school of analysis. It developed as a system of logic and salvation could be achieved through acquisition of knowledge.

According to **Vedanta** School of Philosophy, Brahma is the reality and everything else is unreal, maya. The soul (atma) is same as Brahma.

Yoga School of Philosophy emphasised on meditation and asanas. It also prescribed pranayama which is a breathing exercise. According to this philosophy, through the meditation and asanas salvation could be attained.

54 **Consider the following statements with reference to materialistic Philosophy Lokayata.** *(Chap 25, Class-XI, Old NCERT)*

1. Charvaka was the main expounder of this school of thought.
2. This school denied the existence of any divine or supernatural agency and underlined the importance of intimate contact with the world.
3. By the fifth century AD, it overshadowed the other idealist philosophies and became popular among the masses.

Which of the statements given above are correct?

(a) 1 and 2 (b) 2 and 3 (c) 1 and 3 (d) 1, 2 and 3

Ans. (a)

Exp. Statements (1) and (2) are correct with reference to materialistic Philosophy Lokayata. Charvaka was the main expounder of Lokayata Philosophy which was focused on materialistic nature of life. Lokayata means ideas from lives of common people.

Charvaka was against any quest for spiritual salvation and denied the existence of any divine or supernatural force of nature. He accepted only reality or existence which could be experienced by human beings.

Statement (3) is incorrect because it was overshadowed by other idealist philosophy and it went out of masses.

55 **With reference to Jainism, consider the following pairs.** *(Chap 4, Class-XI, Old NCERT)*

	Monuments related with Jainism		Associated dynasties
1.	Dilwara temple at Mount Abu	–	Chalukyas of Gujarat
2.	Statue of Bahubali at Sravana Belgola	–	Ganga dynasty of Karnataka
3.	Jaina temple at Naregal	–	Pallava dynasty of Karnataka

How many of the pairs given above is/are incorrectly matched?

(a) Only one (b) Only two
(c) All three (d) None of these

Ans. (a)

Exp. Only one pair i.e., (3) is incorrectly matched as Jaina temple of Naregal was built under the reign of Ganga rulers of Karnataka region. They were called basadis. Ganga rulers also constructed mahastambhas (pillars) at various places.

56 **Which among the following ancient texts composed by Bhakti saints from South India is also referred as the fifth Veda?** *(Chap 3, Class-XI, Old NCERT)*

(a) Tirumurai
(b) Nalayira Divya Prabandham
(c) Tiruthonda Thogai
(d) Thirrukural

Ans. (a)

Exp. Tirumurai is an ancient text composed by Bhakti saints from South India and it is also referred as the fifth Veda. It was compilation of teachings of Tamil devotees/saints of Vishnu and Shiva- Alvar and Nayanars. Compilation was done in eleven volumes in early part of 12th century.

57 **With reference to Bhakti movement in ancient India, consider the following statements.** *(Chap 4, Class-XI, Old NCERT)*

1. It was led by series of popular saints called Nayanars and Alvars.
2. All of them were from lower caste and they vehemently opposed the tradition of caste system.
3. They helped in development of regional languages.

How many statements given above is/are correct?

(a) Only one (b) Only two
(c) All three (d) None of these

Ans. (b)

Exp. Only two statements i.e., (1) and (3) are correct with reference to Bhakti movement in ancient India.

The Bhakti movement was led by a series of popular saints, called Nayanars and Alvars. These saints rejected austerities, they looked upon religion not as a matter of cold, formal worship but as a living bond based on love between the God and the worshipper.

They were devotees of God Shiva and Vishnu. They spoke and wrote in Tamil and Telugu, the languages which everyone could understand. In this way, they helped in the development of regional languages.

Statement (2) is incorrect as only some of them belonged to the lower classes and at least one of them was a Brahmana.

58 **Consider the following statements with reference to the religious changes in Post-Gupta times.** *(Chap 4, Class-XI, Old NCERT)*

1. The monastic organisations of the Jainas, Shaivites and Vaishnavites were divided into ranked hierarchy.
2. A new sect called Tantricism emerged in the sixth century AD and it admitted both women and shudras into its rank.
3. Tantricism was exclusively related to Buddhism and emphasised on the use of magical rituals for attaining salvation.

Which of the statements given above are correct?

(a) 1 and 2 (b) 2 and 3 (c) 1 and 3 (d) 1, 2 and 3

Ans. (a)

Exp. Statements (1) and (2) are correct with reference to the religious changes in Post-Gupta times as the monastic organisations of the Jainas, Shaivites, Vaishnavites, etc., came to be divided into about five ranks. The higher rank was occupied by the acharya, whose coronation took place in the same manner as the coronation of the prince. The Upadhyaya and Upasaka occupied lower positions. Spread of Tantricism happened in about the sixth century AD.

Tantricism admitted both women and shudras into its ranks and laid great stress on the use of magic rituals. It was popular in Eastern India.

Statement (3) is incorrect because tantricism permeated to Jainism, Brahminism, worshippers of Shiva and Vishnu and Buddhism.

Development of Science and Technology

59 With reference to the development of Science and Technology, consider the following statements. *(Chap 29, Class-XI, Old NCERT)*

1. Aryabhatta was the first to explain that the rotation of the Earth on its own axis accounts for daily rising and setting of the Sun.
2. In the context of the history of mathematics, the term hindsa' was used for the system of Indian algebra.

Which of the above statements given above is/are incorrect?

(a) Only 1 (b) Only 2
(c) Both 1 and 2 (d) Neither 1 nor 2

Ans. (b)

Exp. Only statement (2) is incorrect with reference to development of Science and Technology. In the context of the history of mathematics, the term 'hindsa' was used for the system of Indian numerals. The Indian numerals are called Arabic in English, but the Arabs themselves called their numerals 'hindsa' The use of these numbers could be found in inscriptions of Ashoka long before they were used in Western countries.

60 The chief export from India in ancient times, which later came to be known as 'wootz' was *(Chap 29, Class-XI, Old NCERT)*

(a) textile (b) steel (c) gold ornaments (d) tea

Ans. (b)

Exp. The Indian steel was chief export from India in ancient times and came to be called 'wootz' in later times. No other countries in the world could manufacture such steel swords as were made by Indian craftsmen. The Indians were great experts in the art of making steel. This craft was developed first in India.

61 With reference to the field of mathematics in ancient Indus, consider the following statements. *(Chap 29, Class-XI, Old NCERT)*

1. Notational system 2. Decimal system
3. Use of Zero 4. Trigonometry

How many of the above fields can be considered as destinactive contribution of Indians?

(a) Only one (b) Only two (c) Only three (d) All four

Ans. (c)

Exp. The codes 1, 2 and 3 are correct. In the field of Mathematics, the ancient Indians made three distinct contributions i.e., the notational system, the decimal system and the use of zero.

The earliest epigraphic evidence for the use of the decimal system is in the beginning of the fifth century AD. Zero was discovered by Indians in the second century BC.

Indians were also first to use the decimal system. Aryabhatta was also aware of this system. Indians, as early as 500 BC, had devised a system of different symbols for every number from one to nine. This notation system was adopted by the Arabs who called it the hind numerals.

In the field of Trigonometry, first significant work was done by Aryabhatta who devised method for obtaining an area of triangle.

62 Consider the following statements with reference to Aryabhatta. *(Chap 29, Class-XI, Old NCERT)*

1. He was one of the earliest exponents of the decimal system.
2. He formulated the rule for finding the area of a triangle.
3. He discovered the causes of solar and the lunar eclipses and correctly measured the circumference of the Earth.

Which of the statements given above are correct?

(a) 1 and 2 (b) 2 and 3 (c) 1 and 3 (d) 1, 2 and 3

Ans. (d)

Exp. All the statements (1), (2) and (3) are correct regarding Aryabhatta.

Aryabhatta (476-550 AD) was one of the greatest mathematicians of ancient world. He was one of the earliest exponents of the decimal system.

His major work, Aryabhatiya contains topics including arithmetic, algebra, plane and spherical trigonometry. He also formulated the rule for finding the area of a triangle.

In the fied of Astronomy, he discovered the causes of solar and the lunar eclipses and correctly measured the circumference of the Earth.

63 With reference to science of medicine practiced in ancient India, consider the following statements. *(Chap 29, Class-XI, Old NCERT)*

1. In Sushrutasamhita, Sushruta describes the method of operating cataract, stone disease and several other ailments.
2. Charakasamhita compiled by Charaka is considered as encyclopedia of Indian medicine.
3. Charaka is considered as the father of surgery.

How many statements given above is/are correct?

(a) Only one (b) Only two
(c) All three (d) None of these

Ans. (b)

Exp. Only two statements i.e., (1) and (2) are correct with reference to science of medicine practiced in ancient India.

In the second century AD, India produced two famous scholars of the Ayurveda, Sushruta and Charaka.

In the Sushrutasamhita, Sushruta explains the method of operating cataract, stone disease and many other diseases.

Charaka's Charakasamhita is said to be an encyclopedia of Indian medicine. It describes various types of fever, leprosy, hysteria (mirgi) and tuberculosis.

Statement (3) is incorrect because Sushruta (not Charaka) is considered to be the 'father of surgery'.

64 **Match the following lists correctly and choose the correct code.** *(Chap 29, Class-XI, Old NCERT)*

List I (Indian Scholars)	List II (Contributions)
A. Kanada	1. Calculation the position of planet based on the Babylonian method.
B. Aryabhatta	2. Described acute angle, obtuse angle and right angle.
C. Varahamihira	3. Developed the Atomic theory.
D. Apastamba	4. Moon rotated around the Earth and Earth rotated around the Sun.

Codes

	A	B	C	D		A	B	C	D
(a)	1	2	3	4	(b)	2	3	1	4
(c)	2	1	4	3	(d)	3	1	4	2

Ans. (d)

Exp. The correct matching is A-3, B-1, C-4, D-2.

Kanada (6th-4th century BC) was a philosopher of Vaisheshika School of Philosophy. He propounded the theory of atoms.

Aryabhatta (476-550 AD) was a fifth century mathematician from Pataliputra. He found out the positions of planets with the help of Babylonian methods. His book is known as Aryabhatiya.

Varahamihira (505-587 AD) was a contemporary scholar of Aryabhatta. He put forward that the Moon rotates around the Earth and the Earth rotates around the Sun. His work in the form of a book is known as Brihatsamhita.

Apastamba (600-540 BC). It introduced the concepts of practical geometry involving acute angles, obtuse angle and right angle worked on practical geography and helped in construction of altars or platforms for offering of sacrifices, which kings used.

India and the World : Cultural Contacts

65 **Consider the following statements with reference to temple of Angkor Wat in Cambodia.** *(Chap 26, Class-XI, Old NCERT)*

1. The stories of the Ramayana and Mahabharata are narrated in reliefs of the walls of the temple.
2. It was constructed in medieval times by the ruler of Champa who patronised Brahmanical religion.
3. It was constructed after demolishing the earlier Buddhist structure.

Which of the statements given above are correct?

(a) 1 and 2 (b) 2 and 3 (c) 1 and 3 (d) 1, 2 and 3

Ans. (a)

Exp. Statements (1) and (2) are correct with reference to temple of Angkor Wat in Cambodia.

In Indo-China, which is at present divided into Vietnam, Cambodia and Laos, the Indians set up two powerful kingdoms in Kamboja and Champa. The powerful kingdom of Kamboja, identical with modern Cambodia was founded in the sixth century AD. Its rulers were devotees of Shiva. It can be compared to the best artistic achievements of the Egyptians and Greeks.

Statement (3) is incorrect because it wasn't constructed after demolishing any earlier Buddhist structure.

66 **With reference to the impact of cultural contacts between India and the world, consider the following statements.** *(Chap 26, Class-XI, Old NCERT)*

1. Ancient Indian learnt the art of growing silk and betel leaves from China and Indonesia respectively.
2. The method of growing cotton spread from India to China and Central Asia.
3. As a result of Kushan rule, the use of Sanskrit written in Kharoshthi script spread to Central Asia.

How many statements given above is/are correct?

(a) Only one (b) Only two (c) All three (d) None of these

Ans. (b)

Exp. Only two statements i.e., (1) and (2) are correct with reference to the impact of cultural contacts between India and the world.

The Indians acquired the craft of minting gold coins from the Greeks and Romans. They learnt the art of growing silk from China, that of growing betel leaves from Indonesia and several other products from neighbouring countries. Similarly, the method of growing cotton spread from India to China and Central Asia.

Statement (3) is incorrect because Kharoshthi script was used to write Prakrit which spread in Central Asia.

67 **Consider the following pairs.** *(Chap 9, Class-VI, Old NCERT)*

Ancient name		Present name
1. Suvaranabhumi	–	Myanmar
2. Kambuja	–	Cambodia
3. Yavadvipa	–	Java
4. Jambudvipa	–	India

How many pairs given above is/are matched correctly?

(a) Only one (b) Only two
(c) All three (d) All of these

Ans. (d)

Exp. All of these pairs are correctly matched.

Suvaranabhumi was name given to Burma, present day Myanmar. It also encompassed region of Pegu.

Kamboja was ancient name of modern country Cambodia. It was founded in sixth century AD.

Yavadvipa was name of Java, presently part of Indonesia.

Jambudvipa was used for India in ancient times in many South-East countries. It comes from trees of Jambu.

Chapter 11

History of South India

History of South India

Sangam Age

Introduction

- Period between 3rd century BC to 3rd century AD in Southern India Present day- Tamil Nadu, Karnataka and Andhra Pradesh During the period of Cholas, Cheras and Pandyas
- Flourished under the patronage of the Pandya Kings of Madurai
- Three Sangams (Academy of Tamil poets) organised
- **Language** Sangam literature was regarded as the Age of Tamil literature; Tamil is the oldest among the spoken literary language of South India
- **Earliest Tamil Works** Tolkappiyam oldest extent Tamil grammar written by Tolkappiyar
- Pattupattu (collection of ten poems) and Ettutogai (collection of eight anthologies) and Pathinenkilkanakku (eighteen minor works)
- **Tamil Epics** Silappadikaram (The jewelled Anklet) by Ilango Adigal depicts tragic love story of a merchant named Kovalam of Puhar and Madhvi **Manimekalai** written by Satthanar depicts excellence of Buddhist religion through the painful life of Manimekalai
- **Megalith Culture** Graves encircled by big pieces of stone
- Practice of burying goods in the graves with the dead bodies
- Cultivated paddy and ragi

Three Early Kingdoms

Pandyan Kingdom

- Occupied Southernmost and South-Eastern portion of Indian Peninsula; Capital at Madurai; Profited from trade with Roman empire and Roman emperor Augustus sent embassy to them

Chola Kingdom

- Ruled over coromandel coast with its capital at Uraiyur; It was famous for cotton trade; Chola King Elora conquered Sri Lanka; Most famous King Karikala who founded city of Puhar and constructed 160 km of embankment on Kaveri river

Chera Kingdom

- Situated West and North of the land of the Pandyas; Romans setup two regiments at Muziris; Greatest king Sehguttuvan (The Red Chera)

Economy During Three Kingdoms

- Based on exploitation of natural resources and foreign trade
- Engaged in trade relations with Greek and Romans; Produced paddy, ragi and sugarcane

Social Lives During Three Kingdoms

- Brahmanas functioned as court poets and were rewarded by the kings; Kshatriyas and Vaishyas do not appear as regular Varna
- Ruling class Arasar; Peasantry-Vallalus low class artisans-Pulaiyans

Religious Lives

- Chief local deity worshipped - Murugan; People offered paddy to the dead; Brahmanical influence was confined to a small part of Tamil territory

New Kingdoms in Deccan

Vakatakas

- Contemporary of Guptas; Founded by Vindhyasakti
- Ruler Pravarasena assumed imperial titles such as Maharajadhiraja and Samrat
- Rudrasena II married Prabhavatigupta (daughter of Chandragupta II)

Chalukyas

- Ruled Deccan from 6th to 8th centuries AD
- Adopted paternalistic control over village administration;
- Patronised Sanskrit and Prakrit langauge
- Developed vesara style of temple construction
- Built temples at Aihole, Badami and Pattadakal; Most famous ruler Pulakeshin II

Pallavas

- Founded by Simha Vishnu in 5th century AD
- Most famous ruler - Narasimhavarman I who occupied Chalukyan capital Vatapi and killed Pulakeshin II
- Developed Ghatikas - centre of learning; Patronised scholars like - Bharavi, Dandin, Dignaga and Mayursarman

Kadambas

- Founded by Mayursharma in 345 AD and lasted till 540 AD; Ruled parts of Northern Karnataka

Imperial Cholas

- Founded by Vijayalaya in 9th century AD. Defeated both Pallavas and Pandyas

Other Aspects of Imperial Cholas

- Promoted local self-government
- Gave land grants such as — Vellanvagai (non-Brahmana), Brahmadeya (Brahmanas), Shalabhoga (maintenance of school); Build temples such as Brihadeeshwara at Tanjore

SOURCE **New NCERT Class VI** *(New Empires and Kingdoms)*, **New NCERT Class VI** *(What Books and Burials Tell Us)*, **New NCERT Class VI** *(Vital Villages, Thriving Towns, Buildings, Paintings and Books)*, **Old NCERT Class VI** *(The Age of Smaller Kingdoms)*, **Old NCERT Class XI** *(The Dawn of History in the Deep South)*, **Old NCERT Class XI** *(Formation of New States and Rural Expansion in the Peninsula)*, **New NCERT Class XII** *(Kings, Farmers and Towns)*, **Tamil Nadu Board Class XI** *(Evolution of Society in South India)*

Sangam Age

1 With reference to the Sangam age, consider the following statements. *(Unit 5, Class-XI, Tamil Nadu Board)*

1. The last three centuries before the common Era and the first three centuries of the common Era are widely accepted as the Sangam period.
2. The ancient Sangam poems frequently mention the term 'muvendar' which was used for songs praising the valour of soldiers.

Which of the statements given above is/are correct?

(a) Only 1 (b) Only 2
(c) Both 1 and 2 (d) Neither 1 nor 2

Ans. *(a)*

Exp. Only statement (1) is correct with reference to the Sangam age. The last three centuries before the common Era and the first three centuries of the common Era are widely accepted as the Sangam period. The details about this period are mainly derived from the Sangam literature. Based on the archaeological evidence apart from the literary sources we can assume that this Sangam Era was started at least two centuries earlier than what we widely believe. Generally this age can be taken as the beginning of historic age in Tamil Nadu.

Statement (2) is incorrect because the ancient Sangam poems frequently mention the term 'muvendar' which was used for three ruling families of Cholas, who became powerful in South India about 2300 years ago in Sangam period.

2 South India by the third century BC was divided into three kingdoms viz- Cholas, Cheras and Pandyas. *(Chap 18, Class-XI, Old NCERT)*

1. Spread of iron technology.
2. Distribution of the punch-marked coins.
3. Flourishing trade with the Roman empire.
4. Use of advanced navy.

How many of the factors given above played role in the formation of these three Kingdoms?

(a) Only one (b) Only two
(c) Only three (d) All four

Ans. *(c)*

Exp. Only three factors i.e., (1), (2) and (3) above in statements played a key role in the formation of Cholas, Cheras and Pandyas kingdoms. Cholas ruled over Coromandel coast area, Cheras in Kerala and Pandyas had political centre at Madurai, Tamil Nadu. These Southern kingdoms developed with the spread of iron technology which promoted forest clearing and plough cultivation.

The distribution of the punch-marked coins in areas ruled by Cholas, Cheras and Pandyas of the imperial Magadhan type show the development of North-South trade.

Flourishing trade with the Roman empire also contributed to the formation of the three states under the Cholas, Cheras and Pandyas.

However, use of advanced navy do not played a key role in the formation of these states as they developed their navies, years after consolidation of their powers in mainland India.

3 Which of the following statements best describes the Satyaputra mentioned in the Ashokan inscription? *(Class-XI, Old NCERT)*

(a) A philosopher in Chera kingdom.
(b) A military leader during the Sangam age.
(c) A prominent figure in Chola's court.
(d) A velir chief in Sangam literature.

Ans. *(d)*

Exp. Satyaputra (same as Athiyaman) mentioned in the Ashokan inscription is a velir chief in the Sangam poems.

Sangam Literature

4 Which one of the following explains the practice of 'Vattakirutal' as mentioned in Sangam poems? *(Unit 5, Class-XI, Tamil Nadu Board) (IAS Pre 2023)*

(a) Kings employing women bodyguards.
(b) Learned persons assembling in Royal courts to discuss religious and philosophical matters.
(c) Young girls keeping watch over agricultural fields and driving away birds and animals.
(d) a king defeated in a battle committing ritual suicide by starving himself to death.

Ans. *(d)*

Exp. The practice of 'Vattakirutal' as mentioned in Sangam poems can be understood in terms of a king defeated in a battle committing ritual suicide by starving himself to death accompanied by those who had been close to him during his lifetime. Sangam poems are pervaded with a warrior ethic. The goal of the hero of the puram poems was pukal (glory, fame) and a heroic death was greatly valued. It was believed that the spirit of a warrior who died in battle dwelt in paradise.

A poem in the Purananuru suggests that the bodies of warriors who did not die in battle were cut with swords before the funerary rites, to simulate death in battle.

5 With reference to the Sangam age, consider the following statements. *(Class-XI, Old NCERT)*

1. Tolkappiyam is the oldest extant Tamil grammar written by Tolkappiyar.
2. Pattupattu contains poetry of subjective experience.
3. Allananuru, part of Ettutogai, was compiled by Gudalur Kilar.

How many of the statements given above is/are correct?

(a) Only one
(b) Only two
(c) All three
(d) None of the above

Ans. *(b)*

Exp. Only two statements i.e., (1) and (2) are correct with reference to Sangam literature.

Tolkappiyam is the oldest extant Tamil grammar written by Tolkappiyar (one of the 12 disciples of sage Agastya). It is divided into three major parts, each consisting of nine iya's (sub-parts) and has a total of 1612 sutras.

Pattupattu contains poetry of subjective experience. The poetry in the Pattupattu (Ten poems) was divided into two main groups i.e., Aham (deals with matters strictly limited to one aspect of subjective experience viz love) and Puram (deals with matters capable of externalisation of objectification.

Statement (3) is incorrect because Ettutogai is a collection of eight anthologies. One of the eight anthologies was Aingurunuru, compiled by Gudalur Kilar, consisting of 500 erotic poems.

6 **With reference to Sangam literature, consider the following statements.** ***(Class-XI, Old NCERT)***

1. Brahmi script was used to write inscriptions in Tamil in ancient South India.
2. The narrative works are called Kilkanakku or Eighteen Minor Works.
3. The didactic works are called Melkanakku and comprises Eighteen Major Works consisting of eight anthologies and ten idylls.

How many of the statements given above is/are incorrect?

(a) Only one (b) Only two
(c) All three (d) None of these

Ans. (b)

Exp. Only two statements i.e., (2) and (3) are incorrect with reference to the Sangam literature. Sangam literature can roughly be divided into two groups-narrative and didactic. The narrative parts are called Melkanakku or Eighteen Major Works. They comprise eighteen major works consisting of eight anthologies and ten idylls. The didactic works are called Kilkanakku or Eighteen Minor Works.

7 **"In a space in which an elephant could lie, one can produce enough grains to feed seven". This was stated in Sangam poems for which of the following kingdom?** ***(Chap 18, Class-XI, Old NCERT)***

(a) Chola (b) Chera (c) Pandya (d) Rashtrakuta

Ans. (a)

Exp. The given statement from the Sangam poems highlights the agricultural productivity of Coromandel coast of Tamil Nadu in the Sangam age. It was drained by the Kaveri river and was famous for production of rice. It formed the territories of the Chola kingdom.

8 **With reference to the Art of writing in South India, consider the following statements.** ***(Chap 18, Class-XI, Old NCERT)***

1. It was introduced in the Southern India by the Brahmana priests in the second century AD.
2. More than 75 short inscriptions in the Brahmi script have been found in the caves near Madurai.

Which of the statements given above is/are correct?

(a) Only 1 (b) Only 2
(c) Both 1 and 2 (d) Neither 1 nor 2

Ans. (b)

Exp. Only statement (2) is correct with reference to the Art of writing in South India.

More than 75 short inscriptions in the Brahmi script have been found in natural caves, mainly in the Madurai region. It provide the specimens of the earliest form of Tamil mixed with Prakrit words. They belong to the second-first centuries BC when the Jaina and Buddhist missionaries appeared in this area.

Statement (1) is incorrect because the art of writing was known to the Tamils before the beginning of the Christian era, and Brahmanical influence.

9 **Consider the following statements about Tamil epics written during the Sangam age.** ***(Chap 18, Class-XI, Old NCERT)***

1. Silappadikaram written by a Buddhist monk deals with the love story of Kovalan and Madhavi.
2. Manimekalai written by the grain merchant of Madurai deals with the adventure of the daughter born of the union between Kovalan and Madhavi.
3. Both these epics throw light on the social and economic life of the Tamils upto the sixth century AD.

Which of the statements given above is/are incorrect?

(a) 1 and 2 (b) Only 1
(c) 1 and 3 (d) Only 3

Ans. (b)

Exp. Statement (1) is incorrect about Tamil epics written during the Sangam age because Silappadikaram was written by Ilango Adigal who was a Jaina monk. Also referred as 'story of anklet', it deals with love story of Kovalan and Madhavi.

10 **With reference to Megalithic culture in South India, consider the following statements.** ***(Chap 17, Class-XI, Old NCERT)***

Statement-I Megalithic people of South India did not practice an advanced type of agriculture.

Statement-II Tools that were meant for fighting and hunting were buried in the megaliths in larger number as compared to the agricultural tools.

Which one of the following is correct in respect of the above statements?

(a) Both Statement-I and Statement-II are correct and Statement-II is the correct explanation for Statement-I.
(b) Both Statement-I and Statement-II are correct and Statement-II is not the correct explanation for Statement-I.
(c) Statement I is correct, but Statement-II is incorrect.
(d) Statement I is incorrect, but Statement-II is correct.

Ans. (a)

Exp. Both Statement-I and Statement-II are correct and Statement-II is the correct explanation for Statement-I.

As compared to the number of agricultural tools that were buried in the graves, those meant for fighting and hunting are larger in number. This would show that the megalithic people did not practice an advanced type of agriculture.

These graves are called megaliths because they were encircled by big pieces of stone. They contain not only skeletons of people who were buried but also pottery and iron objects.

Pandyas

11 With reference to the Pandya kingdom, consider the following statements. *(Chap 18, Class-XI, Old NCERT)*

1. Its territory occupied the Southernmost and the South-Eastern portion of the Indian peninsula.
2. Madurai was the capital of the Pandya kingdom.
3. The Pandya kings profited from trade with the Roman empire and sent embassies to the Roman Emperor Augustus.
4. The rulers of Pandya kingdoms were ardent follower of Buddhism.

How many of the statements given above is/are correct?

(a) Only one (b) Only two (c) Only three (d) All four

Ans. (a)

Exp. Only one statement i.e., (4) is incorrect regarding the Pandya kingdom because the rulers of Pandya kingdom had Brahmanical influence from Northern kingdom and it enjoyed it's patronage. Pandya kings performed Vedic sacrifices in early centuries of Christian Era.

12 With reference to the history of South India in the third century BC, consider the following statements. *(Chap 17, Class-XI, Old NCERT)*

1. The rulers of Chola and Chera kingdom convened the three Sangam assemblies.
2. Hieun-Tsang first mentioned the kingdom of Pandyas and wrote that it was famous for pearls.

Which of the statements given above is/are incorrect?

(a) Only 1 (b) Only 2
(c) Both 1 and 2 (d) Neither 1 nor 2

Ans. (c)

Exp. Both statements (1) and (2) are incorrect with reference to the history of South India in the third century BC.

The rulers of Pandya kingdom convened the three Sangam assemblies.

Sangam was a college or assembly of Tamil poets held under chiefly or royal patronage.

The texts compiled in these assemblies is the main source of historical reconstruction of the reign of Cholas, Cheras and Pandyas.

Megasthenes was the Greek ambassador at the court of Mauryan Emperor, Chandragupta Maurya. Southern kingdom of Pandyas was known to Northern Magadha because it supplied pearls, gold and other precious metals to them. Megasthenes also mention that it was ruled by a woman which indicates matriarchal influence in Pandya society.

13 With reference to ancient South India, Korkai, Poompuhar and Muchiri were well-known as *(Class-XI, Old NCERT) (IAS Pre 2023))*

(a) capital cities
(b) ports
(c) centres of iron-and-steel making
(d) shrines of Jain Tirthankaras

Ans. (b)

Exp. With reference to ancient South India, Korkai, Poompuhar and Muchiri were well-known as ports. The premier Chola port was Puhar (also known as Kaveripumpattinam and Poompuhar), the major Pandya port was Korkai, while Tondi and Muchiri were the important ports in the Chera kingdom.

14 Consider the following statements with reference to the state of religion under the Pandya kingdom. *(Chap 18, Class-XI, Old NCERT)*

1. The kings of Pandya kingdom performed Vedic sacrifices and patronised the Brahmana.
2. Under the influence of Brahmana, Tamil language was replaced by the Sanskrit.

Which of the statements given above is/are incorrect?

(a) Only 1 (b) Only 2
(c) Both 1 and 2 (d) Neither 1 nor 2

Ans. (b)

Exp. Statement (2) is incorrect with reference to the state of religion under the Pandya kingdom.

The official language of the Pandyas were Tamil. The Pandyas founded a Tamil literary academy called the 'Sangam'.

The Sangam literature known as 'the poetry of the noble ones' connotes the ancient Tamil Literature. The Tamil tradition and legends link it to three Sangams held at Madurai and Kapatupuram. The Pandyas were the followers of Brahminism. They adopted the vedic religion of sacrifice and patronised Brahmin priests.

Cholas

15 During the reign of the Chola kingdom, what was the significance of the city of Uraiyur? *(Chap 18, Class-XI, Old NCERT)*

(a) It contained Roman settlements.
(b) Sangam assemblies held in the Uraiyur.
(c) It was famous for trade of cotton.
(d) It is considered as the birthplace of the classical dance, 'Bharatanatyam'.

Ans. (c)

Exp. During the reign of the Chola kingdom, the city Uraiyur was famous for trade of cotton. Uraiyur is a neighbouring region in Tiruchirappalli in Tamil Nadu. It was the capital of the early Cholas, who were one of the three fundamental realms of the old Tamil nation.

Uraiyur had a great expertise in the field of weaving and spinning of cotton clothes. There was a huge demand for cotton clothes of Uraiyur in the Western world.

The profound town of Uraiyur is also famous for the Azhagiya Manavala Perumal Temple, committed to Lord Vishnu.

16 Which among the following statement regarding Chola kingdom is incorrect?

(Chap 18, Class-XI, Old NCERT)

(a) It was situated to the North-East of the territories of Pandyas.

(b) It was mentioned in the inscription of Ashoka.

(c) Its rulers maintained an efficient navy and carried on trade with Roman empire.

(d) Ramnad was the most prominent city of the Chola Kingdom.

Ans. (d)

Exp. Statement (d) is incorrect regarding Chola kingdom because Ramnad was the most prominent city of Pandya kingdom. The Pandyas were occupied the region of modern districts of Tirunelveli, Ramnad and Madurai in Tamil Nadu. Madurai was their capital, which is situated on the bank of river Vagai.

Kallikudi inscription of Pandyan King Sriseevalla Devar states that Pandyas ruled over Ramnad Ramnathpuram which was the Southernmost district of Tamil Nadu.

17 Consider the following statements with reference to the ancient city of Puhar under the Chola kingdom.

(Chap 18, Class-XI, Old NCERT)

1. It was founded by the famous king karikala and served as the capital of the Chola Kingdom.
2. It was great centre of trade and commerce and had a large dock.
3. It is identical with the present day city of Chennai.

Which of the statements given above is/are incorrect?

(a) 1 and 2

(b) Only 2

(c) Only 3

(d) 1, 2 and 3

Ans. (c)

Exp. Statement (3) is incorrect with reference to the ancient city of Puhar under Chola kingdom. Puhar is identical with city of Kaveripattinam in Tamil Nadu and not with Chennai. Puhar was the capital of Cholas. Which was founded by Chola King Karikala. Excavations shows that it had a large dock and was a centre of trade and commerce.

The Port city of Puhar became an emporium of foreign trade in Sangam period as big ships entered this port with precious goods.

18 Consider the following statements.

(Chap 18, Class-XI, Old NCERT)

1. One of the main sources of the wealth of the Cholas was trade in cotton cloth.
2. The kingdom of ancient Cholas was destroyed by the repeated attacks of Pallavas.

Which of the statements given above is/are correct?

(a) Only 1 (b) Only 2

(c) Both 1 and 2 (d) Neither 1 nor 2

Ans. (c)

Exp. Both the statements (1) and (2) are correct. Chola dynasty was situated on the Coromandel coast and was famous for production of high quality cotton. The chief centre of political power of Chola empire lay at Uraiyur, a place famous for cotton trade. The trade in cotton cloth remained the main source of wealth for Chola dynasty. Under Karikala's successors, the Chola power rapidly declined, it was finally destroyed by the repeated attacks of Pallavas from the North in the fourth century AD.

19 With reference to the Chola kingdom, consider the following statements. *(Class-XI, Old NCERT)*

1. The Cholas controlled the Central and Northern part of Tamil Nadu.
2. The capital city of Chola was famous for its cotton trade.
3. Cholamandalam was located in the region of delta of Krishna river.

How many of the statements given above is/are incorrect?

(a) Only one (b) Only two (c) All three (d) None of these

Ans. (c)

Exp. All the statements given above are incorrect with reference to the Chola kingdom. The Cholas controlled the Central and Northern parts of Tamil Nadu. Their capital was Uraiyur which was famous for trade of cotton. Uraiyur is a neighbouring region in Tiruchirappalli in Tamil Nadu.

It was the capital of the early Cholas, who were one of the three fundamental realms of the old Tamil nation. The core area of rule of the Cholas was the Kaveri delta, later known as Cholamandalam.

Cheras

20 The Keralaputras mentioned in the inscription of Ashoka was identical with the Tamil kingdom of

(Chap 18, Class-XI, Old NCERT)

(a) Cholas (b) Cheras (c) Pandyas (d) Satyaputras

Ans. (c)

Exp. The Keralaputras mentioned in the inscription of Ashoka were identical with Cheras. The same inscription of Ashoka also mentions the Southern kingdom of Pandyas, Cholas and Satyaputras (not recognised yet). The ancient Chera kingdom covered modern day territories of Tamil Nadu and Kerala.

21 **With reference to Chera kingdom, consider the following statements.** *(Chap 18, Class-XI, Old NCERT)*

1. The first Chera king Udiyanjeral was called Imayavaramban.
2. Their great ruler was Sanuguttuvan or Red Chera.
3. They used modified version of Tamil.
4. They were in alliance with the Pandyas.

How many of the statements given above is/are correct?

(a) Only one (b) Only two (c) Only three (d) All four

Ans. (a)

Exp. Only one statement i.e., (1) is correct with reference to Chera kingdom because the first Chera king Udiyanjeral was not called Imayavarman, it was second king of Chera and son of Udiyanjeral (also spelled as - Uthiyan Cheralathan), Nedum Cheralathan was known as Imayavarman. Imayavarman Nedum Cheralathan (Nedunjeral Athan) was the second king of Chera dynasty of the Sangam era of South India.

22 **Consider the following statements regarding relations between the Cheras and the Roman empire.** *(Chap 18, Class-XI, Old NCERT)*

1. They carried lucrative trade with the Roman empire.
2. The Romans set up two regiments at Musiris in the Chera kingdom to protect their interests.

Which of the statements given above is/are incorrect?

(a) Only 1 (b) Only 2
(c) Both 1 and 2 (d) Neither 1 nor 2

Ans. (c)

Exp. Both the statements (1) and (2) are correct regarding the relations between the Cheras and the Roman empire. The Chera kingdom owing to its strategic location, carried lucrative trade with the Roman empire. The Romans set up two regiments at Musiris identical with Cranganore in the Chera kingdom to protect their interests. The temple of Roman Emperor, Augustus was also built by Romans in Musiris.

23 **With reference to Chera kingdom, consider the following statements.** *(Class-XI, Old NCERT)*

1. The Pooriya branch of the Chera family ruled from Karur.
2. Karikalan was a prominent Chera king who ensured the safety of the great port of Musiri.

Which of the statements given above is/are incorrect?

(a) Only 1 (b) Only 2
(c) Both 1 and 2 (d) Neither 1 nor 2

Ans. (b)

Exp. Only statement (2) is incorrect with reference to the Chera kingdom. Karikalan was the Chola king and his greatest military achievement was the defeat of the Cheras and the Pandyas, supported by as many as eleven velir chieftains at Venni. Chebguttuvan was a Chera Kingehi ensured the safety of the great port Musiri by putting down piracy.

Economy

24 **From the excavation of which ancient sites, information has been gathered regarding brisk trade relations between India and Rome, during the early centuries of Christian era?** *(Chap 6, Class-XI, Old NCERT) (UPPSC Pre 2003)*

(a) Madurai (b) Tamralipti
(c) Tondi (d) Arikamedu

Ans. (d)

Exp. From the excavation of Arikamedu, information has been gathered regarding brisk trade relations between India and Rome, during the early centuries of Christian era. Arikamedu was an important trading site as well as habitation site for the Romans in India.

It was located near Eastern coast and is identified with modern day Puducherry. Excavation at this site reveals large number of Roman artefacts. It was known to the author of "Periplus of the Erythrean Sea" as Paduoke.

25 **Consider the following statements.** *(Chap 18, Class-XI, Old NCERT)*

1. The words for rice, ginger, cinnamon and several other articles in Greek language were derived from Telugu language.
2. Pariyars were agricultural labourers specialising in animal skin.
3. Masattuvan were guilds of foreign exporters.

How many of the statements given above is/are correct?

(a) Only one (b) Only two
(c) Only three (d) None of these

Ans. (b)

Exp. Only two statements i.e., (1) and (3) are incorrect as in ancient times, the Tamils traded with the Greek or Hellenistic kingdom of Egypt and Arabia on the one side, and with the Malay archipelago and from there with China on the other. As a result of trade, the words for rice, ginger, cinnamon and several other articles in Greek language were derived from Tamil language.

Masattuvan were designated as successful merchants in Tamil and called set this and Sattavahas in praicsit. They were specialised in both Island as well as external trade.

26 **Consider the following steps undertaken by the rulers of three Tamil kingdoms.** *(Chap 18, Class-XI, Old NCERT)*

1. Appointment of custom officials
2. Regular collection of transit duties
3. Embassies to the foreign kingdoms

How many of the steps given above helped to promote and protect trade with foreign kingdom?

(a) Only one (b) Only two
(c) Only three (d) None of these

Ans. (d)

Exp. All the given steps i.e., (1), (2), (3) and (4) were undertaken by the rulers of three ancient Tamil kingdoms Cholas, Cheras and Pandyas.

Trade constituted the chief source of income for the rulers of Tamil kingdoms. Therefore, their rulers took several steps to protect and promote trade with foreign kingdoms. Some of them were

Appointment of custom officials to check entry and exit of goods.

Officials were appointed to collect transit duties on regular basis.

They also sent embassies to foreign kingdoms such as to Egypt and China.

27 Consider the following statements with reference to the sources of royal revenue in three ancient Tamil Kingdoms. *(Chap 18, Class-XI, Old NCERT)*

1. Both internal and external trade constituted the chief source of royal revenue.
2. Spoils of war also contributed to the income of royal treasury.
3. As land was not fertile, agricultural income was not taxed.

Which of the statements given above is/are incorrect?

(a) 1 and 2 (b) 2 and 3 (c) Only 2 (d) Only 3

Ans. (d)

Exp. Statement (3) is incorrect with reference to the sources of royal revenue in three ancient Tamil Kingdoms. As territories adjoining Cauvery river was very fertile and land revenue (agricultural income) constituted significant earning for three ancient Tamil Kingdoms.

28 With reference to the economy of the ancient South Indian Kingdom, consider the following statements. *(Chap 18, Class-XI, Old NCERT)*

Statement-I Many Roman gold silver coins belonging to the first and second centuries AD have been discovered in South India.

Statement-II Some parts of South India were under Roman occupation during this period.

Which one of the following is correct in respect of the above statements?

(a) Both Statement-I and Statement-II are correct and Statement-II is the correct explanation for Statement-I.
(b) Both Statement-I and Statement-II are correct and Statement-II is not the correct explanation for Statement-I.
(c) Statement-I is correct, but Statement-II is incorrect.
(d) Statement-I is incorrect, but Statement-II is correct.

Ans. (c)

Exp. Statement-I is correct, but Statement-II is incorrect.During the first and second centuries AD, trade and commerce flourished significantly between the three Kingdoms of Sangam age (i.e. Chola, Chera and Pandya) and the Roman empire.

The Balance of Trade was in favour of these three kingdoms, which led to the huge inflow of Roman gold and silver coins in India.

Excavation at ancient sites such as Arikamedu, Musiris etc had yielded a large number of Roman coins and artefacts.

However, there is no evidence suggesting that Romans occupied the territories of South India during the Sangam age. A Roman settlement, mostly occupied by traders, has been found in Arikamedu.

Society

29 With reference to Tamil society consider following statements. *(Chap 18, Class-XI, Old NCERT)*

1. Brahmanas enjoyed patronage of the kings and were generously rewarded with cash and land.
2. The ruling class had marriage relation with the families of rich peasants.
3. Social inequalities was not present in the Tamil society in the Sangam age.
4. The acute caste distinction as practised in the Northern India was absent in the ancient Tamil society.

How many of the statements given above is/are incorrect?

(a) Only one (b) Only two (c) Only three (d) All four

Ans. (a)

Exp. Only one statement i.e., (3) is incorrect in context of ancient Tamil society as there were sharp social inequalities in the Sangam age. Rich people lived in houses made of bricks and mortar and poor people in huts. In cities, rich merchants lived in the upper storey of their houses. But it is not clear whether rites and religion were used to maintain social inequalities. There was emergence of Brahmanas and the ruling caste, but acute caste distinctions which can be seen in later times are less in the beginning of Sangam age.

30 Consider the following statements. *(Chap 18, Class-XI, Old NCERT)*

1. The megalith practice of providing for the dead was discontinued.
2. Cremation was introduced.
3. Kings started performing vedic sacrifices.

With reference to the impact of Brahamanism. Which among the above was/were introduced in ancient Tamil society?

(a) 1 and 2 (b) 2 and 3 (c) 1 and 3 (d) 1, 2 and 3

Ans. (b)

Exp. Changes mentioned in statements (2) and (3) were introduced in the ancient Tamil society with reference to the impact of Brahmanism. Cremation was introduced in Tamil society with influence of Brahmanism. In Sangam age, Brahmanical influence was confined to a small part of the Tamil territory and mainly to the upper levels of society.

The kings started performing vedic sacrifices. The Brahmanas, who were the followers of the Vedas, carried on argumentative debates. The worship of Vishnu is also mentioned, although it seems to be adopted late in Sangam age.

Statement (1) do not include change introduced in the ancient Tamil society as megalithic practice of providing for the dead still continued. People offered paddy and other grains to the dead.

31 Consider the following pairs. *(Chap 18, Class-XI, Old NCERT)*

Social Classes in Tamil Literature		Descriptions
(a) Enadi	–	Captains of Navy
(b) Vellalas	–	Members of lowest class specialising in agricultural operations.
(c) Kadaisiyar	–	Rich peasants
(d) Arasar	–	Ruling class

Ans. (a)

Exp. Only pair (a) is incorrectly matched.

Enadi was a title offered to Captains of army. It was done at a special ceremony and was indicative of importance of warrior class in Sangam age.

32 Consider the following statements, with reference to the societal structure of ancient South India. *(Chap 18, Class-XI, Old NCERT)*

Statement-I The Kshatriyas and Vaishyas appear as regular varnas in the Sangam texts.

Statement-II Warrior class was an important element in the Tamil polity and society.

Which one of the following is correct in respect of the above statements?

(a) Both Statement-I and Statement-II are correct and Statement II is the correct explanation for Statement-I.
(b) Both Statement-I and Statement-II are correct and Statement-II is not the correct explanation for Statement-I.
(c) Statement-I is correct, but Statement-II is incorrect.
(d) Statement I is incorrect, but Statement-II is correct.

Ans. (b)

Exp. Both Statement-I and Statement-II are correct and Statement-II is incorrect explanation for Statement-I.
The Kshatriyas and Vaishyas were treated normally and not much importance was placed on them. It was because there was less influence of Brahmanism in early Sangam age in terms of varna division. Warrior class who fought wars were respected and given titles.

Vakataka Dynasty

33 With reference to the Vakataka kingdom, consider the following statements. *(Chap 24, Class-XI, Old NCERT)*

1. They succeeded Satavahanas in Southern Andhra Pradesh and Karnataka.
2. They were great patron of Brahmanical religion and performed numerous Vedic sacrifices.
3. They supported the Gupta rulers in conquering Gujarat and adjoining parts of Western India from the Shaka Kshatraps.

Which of the statements given above is/are correct.

(a) 1 and 2 (b) 2 and 3
(c) 1 and 3 (d) 1, 2 and 3

Ans. (b)

Exp. Statements (2) and (3) are correct with reference to the Vakataka kingdom. The Vakataka were Brahmans themselves.

They issued land charters to Brahmans, it had been found on large number of copper-plates. They were great patron of Brahmanical religion and performed numerous Vedic sacrifices.

The Vakataka had matrimonial relation with Gupta rulers. Chandragupta II married her daughter Prabhavati Gupta to Vakataka prince. And in consequence, Vakataka helped Gupta rulers in conquering Gujarat and nearby areas of Western India from Shaka Kshatraps.

Statement (1) is incorrect because Vakataka succeeded the Satavahanas in areas of Northern Maharashtra and Vidarbha.

34 With reference to Vakataka kingdom, consider the following statements. *(Chap 24, Class-XI, Old NCERT)*

1. It became a channel for transmitting Brahmanical ideas and social institutions to the South.
2. They had a matrimonial alliance with the Gupta dynasty.
3. Kalidasa wrote Meghadutam in the court of Pravarasena II.

How many of the statements given above is/are incorrect?

(a) Only one (b) Only two
(c) All three (d) None of these

Ans. (a)

Exp. Only one statement i.e., (3) is incorrect as Kalidasa wrote Meghadutam in the court of Chandra Gupta not (Pravarasena II). Pravarsena II built the temple of Ramachandra ar Pravarapura and composed the famous Prakrit poem Setubandha.

Ikshvakus

35 Immediately after the decline of power of Satavahana, which among the following dynasty arose in prominence in the Krishna-Guntur region? *(Chap 24, Class-XI, Old NCERT)*

(a) Pallava (b) Chalukya
(c) Ikshvaku (d) Vakataka

Ans. (c)

Exp. The Ikshvaku dynasty came in power immediately after the decline of the Satavahanas in Krishna-Guntur region.

Chamtamula is considered as founder of Ikshvakus dynasty who ruled parts of Andhra Pradesh from third to fourth century AD. Vijayapuri was the capital of this dynasty.

36 **Consider the following statements with reference to the Ikshvaku dynasty.** *(Chap 24, Class-XI, Old NCERT)*

1. They were descendants of the mythological Ikshvaku dynasty of Ayodhya.
2. They started the practice of land grants in the Krishna-Guntur region.
3. They constructed beautiful monuments at Nagarjunakonda and Dharanikota.

Which of the statements given above is/are incorrect?

(a) 1 and 2 (b) Only 1 (c) 1 and 3 (d) Only 3

Ans. (b)

Exp. Statement (1) is incorrect because the Ikshvaku dynasty (225-340 AD) was a feudatory tribe under the patronage of Satavahana Empire. That ruled the Krishna-Guntur region of Andhra Pradesh.

The Ikshvakus constructed many monuments at Nagarjunkoda and Dharanikota. Dharanikota (present-Amravati) was the capital of the Ikshvakus. They were the patronage of Amravati School of Art.

Chalukya Dynasty

37 **Consider the following statements with reference to the Aihole inscription.** *(Chap 24, Class-XI, Old NCERT)*

1. It was composed by Ravikirti, the court poet of Pulakeshin II.
2. It is an eulogy (Prashasti) appreciating the military victories and genoristy of Pulakeshin II.
3. It is an example of poetic excellence reached in Kannada language.

How many of the statements given above is/are incorrect?

(a) Only one (b) Only two
(c) All three (d) None of these

Ans. (a)

Exp. Only one statement i.e., (3) is incorrect with reference to the Aihole inscription because the Aihole inscription (Aihole Prashashti) is inscribed in Sanskrit language and old Kannada script. It is dated Saka 556 or 634 AD. The Aihole inscription was composed by Ravikriti, the court poet of Pulakeshin II.

The Aihole inscription is an eulogy about the victories of Chalukya king on Harshavardhana and Pallavas.

38 **With reference to the Chalukya ruler Pulakeshin II, which of the following statements is/are correct?** *(Chap 10, Class-VI, New NCERT)*

1. He led the victorious campaign against the Harshavardhana in the North and Mahendravarman of Pallava kingdom.
2. He started the practice of appointing feudal chief in the Southern India.
3. He sent an embassy to the Persian King, Khusrau II.

Codes

(a) 1 and 2 (b) 2 and 3
(c) 1 and 3 (d) 1, 2 and 3

Ans. (c)

Exp. Statements (1) and (3) are correct with reference to the Chalukya ruler Pulakeshin II.

He was the greatest ruler of Chalukya Kingdom of Badami. He defeated Harshavardhana at the bank of Narmada river in 618 AD. He also led successful military expedition against Mahendravarman of Pallava kingdom. To promote trade and ensure regular supply of good quality of horses, he also sent an embassy to Persian king Khusrau II.

Statement (2) is incorrect because practice of appointing Feudal Chief had already started by other kingdoms in the past.

39 **Which among the following places contains temples constructed under the reign of Chalukya rulers?** *(Chap 24, Class-XI, Old NCERT)*

1. Pattadakal 2. Aihole
3. Badami 4. Dharanikota

Codes

(a) 1, 2 and 3 (b) 2, 3 and 4
(c) 1, 2 and 4 (d) All of these

Ans. (a)

Exp. Among the given options, Pattadakal, Aihole and Badami i.e., 1, 2 and 3 contains temples constructed under the reign of Chalukya rulers.

Pattadakal has ten temples built by Chalukyas, in seventh and eighth century AD. Aihole contains almost 70 temples built by Chalukyas from 610 AD. Badami also had temples built by Chalukyas, it was a nearby town from Aihole, here Papanatha Temple in 680 AD was built.

40 **Consider the following statements.** *(Chap 24, Class-XI, Old NCERT)*

1. The Chalukya ruler sent an embassy of 72 merchants to China.
2. Rashtrakuta, the feudatory of Chalukyas annexed the Kingdom of Chalukyas in 757 AD.

Which of the statements given above is/are incorrect?

(a) Only 1
(b) Only 2
(c) Both 1 and 2
(d) Neither 1 nor 2

Ans. (c)

Exp. Both the statements (1) and (2) are incorrect because Chola Empire under the king Kulottunga I sent an embassy of 72 merchants to China.

Rashtrakuta the feudatory of Chalukyas annexed the kingdom of Chalukyas in 753 AD. Dantidurg, who was a feudutory of Chalukya defeated ruler Kritivarman II in 753 AD.

41 **With reference to the Chalukyas dynasty, consider the following statements.** *(Class-XI, Old NCERT)*

1. Capital city of Chalukyas was founded by Kritivarman.
2. Aihole inscriptions mention the victory of Pulikesin II.
3. Defeat of Pulikesin II by Harshavardhana's army led to the disintegration of the dynasty.

How many of the statements given above is/are incorrect?

(a) Only one (b) Only two
(c) All three (d) None of these

Ans. (a)

Exp. Only one statement i.e., (3) incorrect with reference to the Chalukyas dynasty. Pulikesin II was the defeat of Harshavardhana's army on the banks of the Narmada. The kings of Malwa, Kalinga and Eastern Devcan accepted his suzerainty.

42 **With reference to Chalukya administration, consider the following statements.** *(Class-XI, Old NCERT)*

1 Nala-Kavundas were the traditional revenue officials.
2. Purapatis were involved in the administration of the village.
3. Kamunda were involved in the administration of the town.

How many of the statements given above is/are correct?

(a) Only one (b) Only two
(c) All three (d) None of these

Ans. (a)

Exp. Only one statement i.e., (1) is correct with reference to the Chalukya administration. The traditional revenue officials of the villages were called the Nala-Kavundas.

Statements (2) and (3) are incorrect because Kamunda was a central figure in the village administration (not town). Nagarpatis or Purapatis were the officials of the towns.

43 **With reference to Chalukya Empire, consider the following statements.** *(Class-XI, Old NCERT)*

1. Saptavataram is a grammar work authored by Pulikesin II.
2. Chalukyas introduced the technique of building temples using soft sandstones as medium.
3. Chalukyas built temples dedicated only to Hindu God and Goddesses.

How many of the statements given above is/are correct?

(a) Only one (b) Only two
(c) All three (d) None of these

Ans. (a)

Exp. Only one statement i.e., (2) is correct with reference to the Chalukya Empire. Historically, in Deccan,Chalukyas introduced the technique of building temples using soft sandstones as medium. A temple dedicated to the goddess Durga was built on the model of Buddha Chaitya. Another temple, dedicated to the same goddess is called Huccimalligudi.

Statements (1) and (3) are incorrect because a chieftain of Pulikesin II authored a grammar work Saptavataram in Sanskrit. Chalukya used Sanskrit in pillar inscriptions such as in Aihole and Mahakudam.

Pallavas

44 **With reference to Pallavas, consider the following statements.** *(Chap 24, Class-XI, Old NCERT)*

1. The Pallavas were associated with the region of Tondaimandalam.
2. They were feudatories of Chalukya.
3. Kingship were considered to be of divine origin.

How many of the statements given above is/are correct?

(a) Only one (b) Only two
(c) All three (d) None of these

Ans. (b)

Exp. Only two statements i.e., (1) and (3) are correct with reference to Pallavas. Pallavas were associated with Tondaimandalam, the land between the North Pennar and North Vellar rivers. Under the Pallavas, kinship were held to be of divine origin and hereditary.

Statement (2) is incorrect because the Pallavas were the feudatorres of the Satavahanas Kingdom, and began their rule in the far South after the decline of the Satavahanas. They started as local rulers and gradually extended their rule Southwards to Kanchipuram, in Tamil Nadu.

45 **With reference to the administration of Pallavas, consider the following pairs.** *(Class-XI, Old NCERT)*

Officer	Role
1. Mainkkappand aram kappan	– Officer in Charge of Treasury
2. Kodukkappillai	– Officer of gifts
3. Rahasyadhikrita	– Members of the judicial courts

How many of the pairs given above is/are correctly matched?

(a) Only one (b) Only two (c) Only three (d) None of these

Ans. (b)

Exp. Only two pairs i.e., (1) and (2) are correctly matched with reference to the administration of the Pallavas.

Manikkappandaram Kappan was an officer in charge of the treasury. Kodukkappillai was the officer of gifts. They were central officers under the Pallava Kings. Rahasyadhikrita was a private secretary of the King (spy).

46 **Consider the following statements.**
(Chap 24, Class-XI, Old NCERT) (UPPSC Pre 2003)

1. Under the reign of Pallavas, Kanchipuram became a town of temples and Vedic learning.
2. Pallavas were contemporary with Kadamba Kingdom.

Which of the statements given above is/are correct?

(a) Only 1 (b) Only 2
(c) Both 1 and 2 (d) Neither 1 nor 2

Ans. (c)

Exp. Both the statements (1) and (2) are correct. Kanchipuram, served as the capital of Pallava dynasty. Under the reign of generous Pallava rulers, it become a town of temples and Vedic learning.

Pallavas were contemporary with Kadamba kingdom whose founder Mayursharman received education at Kanchipuram.

47 **The rulers of Pallavas and Chalukyas were engaged in bitter struggle over the supremacy of**
(Chap 24, Class-XI, Old NCERT)

(a) Kaveri delta.
(b) land lying between the Krishna and Tungabhadra.
(c) port of Arikamendu and Uraiyur in the Eastern coastal peninsula.
(d) the territories of Kalinga ruled by the Ganga dynasty.

Ans. (b)

Exp. The rulers of Pallavas and Chalukyas were engaged in bitter struggle over the supremacy of land lying between the Krishna and Tungabhadra river. The main interest in the political history of peninsular India from the sixth to the eighth century centres around the long struggle between the Pallavas of Kanchi and the Chalukyas of Badami for supremacy.

48 **With reference to Pallava Empire, consider the following pairs.** *(Chap 24, Class-XI, Old NCERT)*

Kings of Pallava dynasty	Important Events
1. Mahendravarman	– Poet and Musician
2. Narasimhavarman I	– Defeated Harshavardhana
3. Simhavarman	– Real founder of the Pallava power

How many of the pairs given above is/are incorrectly matched?

(a) Only one (b) Only two
(c) All three (d) None of these

Ans. (a)

Exp. Only one pair i.e., (2) is incorrectly matched Narasimhavarman I was a Pallava king, who ruled from 630-668 AD. He didn't defeat Harshavardhana. Chalukya ruler Pulakeshin II was defeated by Pallava ruler Narasimhavarman I in 642 AD at the battle of Uatapi. Before it, Pulakeshin II had defeated Harshavardhana on the banks of river Narmada in 618 AD.

49 **Consider the following statements with reference to the Pallava king Mahendravarman I.**
(Chap 8, Class-VI, Old NCERT)

1. He was the contemporary of Harshavardhana and Pulakeshin II.
2. He was converted to the Vaishanavism by the Tamil saint, Appar.

Which of the statements given above is/are incorrect?

(a) Only 1
(b) Only 2
(c) Both 1 and 2
(d) Neither 1 nor 2

Ans. (b)

Exp. Statement (2) is incorrect with reference to the Pallava King Mahendravarman I (600-630 AD) as he was a Jaina to begin with, but was later converted to Shaivism by Appar, one of the Tamil saints not vaishnavism.

50 **With reference to the Pallava King Narasimhavarman I, which of the following statements is/are correct?** *(Chap 8, Class-VI, Old NCERT)*

1. He assumed the title of Vatapikonda after defeating Pulakeshin II of the Chalukya dynasty.
2. He also founded the Port city of Mamallapuram.
3. The seven ratha temples at Kanchipuram was built under his reign.

Codes

(a) 1 and 2 (b) 2 and 3
(c) 1 and 3 (d) 1, 2 and 3

Ans. (d)

Exp. All the statements (1), (2) and (3) are correct with reference to the Pallava King Narasimhavarman. Narasimhavarman I (630-668 AD) assumed the title of Vatapikonda, which means the conqueror of Vatapi after defeating Pulakeshin II.

He also founded the port city of Mahabalipuram or Mamallapuram in Tamil Nadu. It is 65 km away from Chennai. It is famous for shore temples, which are part of UNESCO heritage.

He also ordered the construction of the seven ratha temple at Mahabalipuram in Seventh century AD.

51 **Consider the following statements with reference to the local assembly under the Pallava rulers.**
(Chap 10, Class-VI, New NCERT)

1. Sabha was the assembly of the Brahmin land owners.
2. Ur was a village assembly found in areas where the land owners were not Brahmins.

Which of the statements given above is/are correct?

(a) Both 1 and 2 (b) Only 1
(c) Only 2 (d) Neither 1 nor 2

Ans. (a)

Exp. Both the statements (1) and (2) are correct with reference to the local assembly under the Pallava rulers. The inscriptions of the Pallavas mention a number of local assemblies. These included the Sabha, which was an assembly of brahmin land owners. This assembly functioned through sub-committees, which looked after irrigation, agricultural operations, making roads, local temples, etc.

The Ur was a village assembly found in areas where the landowners were not brahmins. The organisation of merchants was called the 'Nagarams', these assemblies were controlled by rich merchants and landowners. These local assemblies survived for centuries in South India.

52 **With reference to the Kalabhras revolt in the sixth century AD, which of the following statements is/are incorrect?** *(Chap 24, Class-XI, Old NCERT)*

1. They put an end to the brahmadeya rights granted to the Brahmins in many villages of the Southern India.
2. It effected the Pallavas and their contemporaries and led to an era of anarchy in their territories.
3. It was put down under the leadership of Pallava ruler Mahendravarman and Chalukya ruler Pulakeshin II.

Codes

(a) 1 and 2 (b) 2 and 3
(c) Only 2 (d) Only 3

Ans. (d)

Exp. Statement (3) is incorrect with reference to the Kalabhras revolt in the sixth century AD. As the Kalabhras revolt could be put down with coordination of Pandyas, Pallavas and Chalukyas of Badami.

53 **Consider the following statements with reference to the state of religion under the Pallavas.** *(Chap 24, Class-XI, Old NCERT)*

1. The rulers of the kingdom lavishly patronised the Brahmanas and performed many vedic sacrifices.
2. The Tamil saints, Alvar popularised the worship of Shiva and Nayanar saints promoted the worship of Vishnu.
3. Under the influence of Brahmana, Sanskrit became the court language under the rulers of Pallava Kingdom.

Which of the statements given above is/are incorrect?

(a) 1 and 2 (b) 2 and 3
(c) Only 2 (d) Only 3

Ans. (c)

Exp. Statement (2) is incorrect with reference to the state of religion under the Pallavas because Alvars and Nayanars both preached the cult of Bhakti but Alvars preached Vaishnavism during the Pallava period and Nayanars had preached Shaivism and were known as Shaivaites.

After the establishment of the Pallava rule, the Brahmanism was revived. The Pallava rulers had patronised Brahmanism and performed many vedic sacrifices. They had built temples and made land grants to Brahmins.

Sanskrit was the court language under the Pallava rule. Dandin wrote Avanisundari Katha. Famous Pallava King Mahendravarman wrote Mattavilasprahasan in Sanskrit.

54 **Which among the following monuments was/were built under the auspice of Pallava rulers?** *(Chap 24, Class-XI, Old NCERT)*

1. Shore Temple at Mahabalipuram
2. Virupaksha Temple at Hampi
3. Kailashnath Temple at Kanchipuram

Codes

(a) 1 and 2 (b) 2 and 3 (c) 1 and 3 (d) 1, 2 and 3

Ans. (c)

Exp. Codes (1) and (3) are correct. The Shore Temple of Mahabalipuram or Mamallapuram and the Kailashnath Temple at Kanchipuram were built during the reign of the Pallava ruler Narasimhavarman II (Rajasimha) and it is the oldest structural temple of significance in South India.

These temples were constructed in 8th century AD. Virupaksha Temple at Hampi was constructed by Lakkan Dandesha, a chieftain under the ruler Deva Raya II of the Vijayanagara Empire.

Kadamba Dynasty

55 **Consider the following statements with reference to the ancient kingdom of Kadambas.** *(Chap 24, Class-XI, Old NCERT)*

1. They after defeating the rulers of Pallava dynasty established an independent kingdom with its capital at Vijayanti or Banvasi.
2. They initiated the grant of tax free lands to the Brahmanas for lieu of their services.

Which of the statements given above is/are incorrect?

(a) Only 1 (b) Only 2
(c) Both 1 and 2 (d) Neither 1 nor 2

Ans. (b)

Exp. Statement (2) is incorrect with reference to the ancient kingdom of Kadambas, as land grants were already being given by Pallavas who also patron Brahaminism.

56 **With reference to the Kadamba dynasty, consider the following statements.** *(Chap 24, Class-XI, Old NCERT)*

1. Satavahana Empire was followed by Kadambas in Northern Karnataka.
2. The capital of Kadamba Kings was Badami.

Which of the statements given above is/are incorrect?

(a) Only 1 (b) Only 2
(c) Both 1 and 2 (d) Neither 1 nor 2

Ans. (b)

Exp. Only statement (2) is incorrect with reference to the Kadamba dynasty. The capital of Kadamba Kings was Banvasi Kadamba kingdom was contemporary with Pallavas. It was founded by Mayurasharman who received education at Kanchi. He was successful in defeating the Pallava kings with the help of forest tribes. It was established in 345 AD.

Ganga Dynasty

57 With reference to the Western Ganga dynasty, which of the following statements is/are correct? *(Chap 18, Class-XI, Old NCERT)*

1. They were the feudatories of the Pallavas.
2. They made land grants mostly to the Jainas.

Codes

(a) Only 1 (b) Only 2
(c) Both 1 and 2 (d) Neither 1 nor 2

Ans. (c)

Exp. Both the statements (1) and (2) are correct with reference to the Western Ganga dynasty.

Western Ganga was an important ruling dynasty of ancient Karnataka, which ruled about 350 to 1000 AD. They were known as Western Ganges to distinguish them from the Eastern Ganges, who ruled over Kalinga region. The Western Ganges were subordinates of the Pallavas of Kanchi. Though, contrary evidences are present in the early inscription of King Madhavvarman I. The Western Ganges gave patronage to all the major religions, but scholars have argued that Gangas were ardent Jains.

Imperial Cholas

58 Consider the following statements. *(Chap 3, Class-XI, Old NCERT)*

1. Initially, the rulers of Chola empire were feudatories of Pallavas.
2. The founder of Chola empire was Vijayalaya.

Which of the statements given above is/are correct?

(a) Only 1 (b) Only 2
(c) Both 1 and 2 (d) Neither 1 nor 2

Ans. (c)

Exp. Both the statements (1) and (2) are correct.

The founder of the Chola empire was Vijayalaya, who was at first a feudatory of the Pallavas. He was successful in capturing Tanjore in 850 AD.

By the end of the ninth century AD, the Cholas had defeated both the Pallavas of Kanchi and weakened the Pandyas, bringing the Southern Tamil country (Tondamandala) under the control.

59 Consider the following statements with reference to the reign of Chola ruler, Rajaraja. *(Chap 3, Class-XI, Old NCERT)*

1. Before ascending the throne he had extensive experience of administration and warfare.
2. He led successful military expedition against the kingdom of Chera and Pandya and also annexed the Northern part of Sri Lanka.
3. He after the request of ruler of Sailendra dynasty endowed a village for upkeep of Buddhist monastery at Nagapatam.

Which of the statements given above is/are incorrect?

(a) 1 and 2 (b) 2 and 3
(c) Only 2 (d) Only 3

Ans. (d)

Exp. Statement (3) is incorrect with reference to the reign of Chola ruler, Rajaraja because Rajendra I had endowed a village for upkeep of Buddhist monastery at request of ruler Sailendra.

60 Consider the following statements with reference to the military campaign of Rajendra Chola in the North India. *(Chap 3, Class-XI, Old NCERT)*

1. He raided the North India in 1022 AD and took the same route, which the great conqueror Samudragupta had followed.
2. He defeated the Tomar Rajputs of Delhi and uprooted Pala king, Rampala.
3. To commemorate his victories, he assumed the title of 'Gangaikonda Chola' and built the new capital near the mouth of Kaveri and called it Gangaikonda Cholapuram.

Which of the statements given above are correct?

(a) 1 and 2 (b) 2 and 3
(c) 1 and 3 (d) 1, 2 and 3

Ans. (c)

Exp. Statements (1) and (3) are correct with reference to the military campaign of Rajendra Chola in North India.

Rajendra Chola led his army across Kalinga to Bengal in which the Chola armies crossed the Ganga. It took place in 1022 AD and followed the same route which the great conqueror Samudragupta had followed.

To commemorate his victories, Rajendra Chola assumed the title of 'Gangaikonda Chola' (or 'the Chola conqueror of Ganga'). He built the new capital near the mouth of the Kaveri and called it, Gangaikonda Cholapuram 'the city of the Chola conqueror of the Ganga rulers'.

Statement (2) is incorrect because Rajendra Chola didn't defeat Tomar Rajputs.

61 With reference to administration under the Chola Empire, the 'agraharas' were *(Chap 3, Class-XI, Old NCERT)*

(a) general assembly of villages inhabited by the peasants.
(b) assembly of adult men in the villages inhabited by Brahmana.
(c) irrigation tax collected by the head of village assemblies.
(d) system of land grant to learned people of the Empire.

Ans. (b)

Exp. Gathering or assembly of adult men in the villages inhabited by Brahmana in Chola Empire was called Agraharas. In these villages, Brahmanas, most of the land was rent-free. These villages enjoyed a large measure of autonomy.

62 With reference to the Imperial Cholas (850 – 1200 CE), consider the following statements.

(Class-XI, Old NCERT)

Statement-I We have much more information about Cholas than their predecessors.

Statement-II The Chola rulers adopted the practice of having inscriptions written on the walls of temples giving a historical narrative of their victories.

Which one of the following is correct in respect of the above statements?

(a) Both Statement-I and Statement-II are correct and Statement-II is the correct explanation for Statement-I.
(b) Both Statement-I and Statement-II are correct and Statement-II is incorrect explanation for Statement-I.
(c) Statement-I is correct, but Statement-II is incorrect.
(d) Statement I is incorrect, but Statement-II is correct.

Ans. (a)

Exp. Both Statement-I and Statement-II are correct and Statement-II is the correct explanation for Statement-I. Chola rulers Rajaraja and Rajendra I marked their victories by erecting a number of Shiva and Vishnu temples at various places. The most famous of these was the Rajarajeshwara temple at Tanjore which was completed in 1010 AD. The Chola rulers adopted the practice of having long inscriptions written on the walls of these temples, giving a historical narrative of their victories. That is why, we have more information about Cholas than their predecessors.

63 Consider the following statements with reference to village administration during the Chola Empire.

(Chap 3, Class-XI, Old NCERT)

1. During the reign of Chola Empire, the growth of feudalism led to more autonomy for village assemblies.
2. The affairs of the villages were managed by an executive committee to which educated persons owing property was elected either by drawing lots or by rotation.
3. Other committees were also constituted for assessment and collection of land revenue, maintaining law and order and delivering justice.

How many of the statements given above is/are correct?

(a) Only one (b) Only two (c) All three (d) None of these

Ans. (c)

Exp. All three statements i.e., (1), (2) and (3) are correct with reference to village administration during the Chola Empire.

The practice of land grants to officers and feudal lords led to more autonomous villages in Chola Kingdom.

In these villages, the affairs of the village were managed by an executive committee to which educated persons owning property were elected either by drawing lots or by rotation.

There were other committees for helping in the assessment and collection of land revenue for maintaining of law and order, justice, etc.

64 Consider the following statements with reference to temple architecture during the Chola Empire.

(Chap 3, Class-XI, Old NCERT)

1. During the reign of Chola Empire, Dravida style of temple architecture became prominent.
2. They started the practice of installing images of kings and queens in the temples.
3. The greatest specimen of Chola temple architecture is Kailashnath temple at Kanchipuram built under the reign of Rajaraja Chola.

Which of the statements given above is/are correct?

(a) 1 and 2 (b) 2 and 3
(c) Only 1 (d) Only 3

Ans. (d)

Exp. Only statement (3) is incorrect with reference to temple architecture during the Chola Empire, as an early example of the Dravida style of temple architecture is Kailashnath temple at Kanchipuram built by Pallava rulers.

65 Consider the following statements with reference to state of literature during the Chola Empire.

(Chap 3, Class-XI, Old NCERT)

1. One of the greatest Tamil poet Naniah enjoyed that patronage of the Chola rulers.
2. Kamban is credited with compilation of Ramayana in Tamil.
3. The age of Kamban who is placed in the second half of the 11th and early part of the 12th century is regarded as a golden age in Tamil Literature.

Which of the statements given above is/are correct?

(a) 1 and 2
(b) 2 and 3
(c) 1 and 3
(d) 1, 2 and 3

Ans. (b)

Exp. Statements (2) and (3) are correct with reference to state of literature during the Chola Empire.

Kamban's Ramayana is considered as classic in Tamil literature. Kamban is believed to have lived at the court of a Chola king.

The age of Kamban is placed in the second half of the 11th and the early part of the 12th century AD is regarded as a golden age in Tamil literature.

Statement (1) is incorrect because Naniah lived at court of a Chalukyan king and wrote Telugu version of Mahabharata.

66 **Which among the following cities had served as the capital of the Chola Empire?**

(Chap 3, Class-XI, Old NCERT)

1. Tanjore
2. Kanchipuram
3. Gangaikonda Cholapuram
4. Nagapattinam

Codes

(a) 1, 2 and 3 (b) 2, 3 and 4 (c) 1, 2 and 4 (d) All of these

Ans. (a)

Exp. Codes 1, 2 and 3 are correct. Tanjore, Kanchipuram and Gangaikonda Cholapuram served as the capitals of Chola Empire.

Founder of Chola Empire Vijayalaya had his kingdom at Tanjore which he captured in 850 AD. After defeating Pallavas, they also had city of Kanchipuram under their control and set their capital there.

Rajendra Chola I led his army North from Kalinga to Bengal and set up his capital near mouth of Kaveri river and named the city Gangaikonda Cholapuram, the city of Chola conqueror of Ganga ruler.

Nagapattinam was port city of Chola empire.

67 **Which of the following pairs is correctly matched?**

(Chap 3, Class-XI, Old NCERT)

Cities conquered by the Chola ruler		Associated Kingdoms
(a) Madurai	–	Chera
(b) Anuradhapur	–	Sri Lanka
(c) Trivandrum	–	Later Chalukyas
(d) Kalyani	–	Pandya

Ans. (b)

Exp. Only pair (b) is correctly matched .

Anuradhapur was ancient capital of rulers of Sri Lanka. It was destroyed by Chola rulers who treated their king and queens harshly.

While, pairs (a), (c) and (d) are incorrectly matched. Madurai was ruled by Pandyas of Sangam Age and was taken by Rajaraja of Chola kingdom.

Trivandrum was a Chera ruling area. It lies in Kerala. Rajaraja destroyed Chera Navy and captured this city from them.

Kalyani was capital of Later Chalukyas. Cholas plundered this city also.

68 **Match the following lists and choose the correct code.** *(Chap 3, Class-XI, Old NCERT)*

List I (Constituent structures in Dravida style)	List II (Characteristics)
A. Garbhagriha	1. Cheif deity room
B. Mandap	2. Pillared hall
C. Gopurams	3. Storied structure above the room of main shrine
D. Vimana	4. High walls surrounding the temple complex

Codes

	A	B	C	D		A	B	C	D
(a)	1	2	4	3	(b)	2	4	1	3
(c)	3	1	4	2	(d)	4	2	1	3

Ans. (a)

Exp. The correct matching is A-1, B-2, C-4, D-3.

Garbhagriha is the Chief deity room in Dravidian style temples.

Mandap was a pillared hall, which had well carved pillars.

Gopurams were high walls surrounding the temple to safeguard and defend.

Vimana is the structure over the garbhagriha or inner sanctum in temples in South India in North super structure over garbhagriha called 'Shikhara'.

69 **With reference to the imperial Chola (850-1200 CE), consider the following statements.**

(Class-XI, Old NCERT)

1. Chola kings dominated the Indian ocean but didn't venture into the Bay of Bengal.
2. The Cholas controlled both the Coromandel and the Malabar coast.

How many of the statements given above is/are correct?

(a) Only 1 (b) Only 2
(c) Both 1 and 2 (d) Neither 1 nor 2

Ans. (a)

Exp. Only one statement i.e., (1) is incorrect with reference to the Chola Empire.

Chola kings like Rajaraja I, not only dominated the Indian ocean but also ventured into the Bay of Bengal. The Chola ruler, Rajendra I (1014-1044 AD) converted the Bay of Bengal into a 'Chola lake'. He led a naval expedition against the ruler of Sri Vijaya Empire of Malay peninsula in the 11th century AD.

70 **With reference to Chola Empire (850-1200 CE), consider the following statements.**

(Class-XI, Old NCERT)

Statement-I The Chola administration represented a harmonious balance between the central authority and the local self-government.

Statement-II At the village level people looked after their administration with the help of self elected local bodies.

Which one of the following is correct in respect of the above statements?

(a) Both Statement-I and statement-II are correct and Statement-II is the correct explanation for Statement-I.
(b) Both Statement-I and Statement-II are correct and Statement-II is incorrect explanation for Statement-I.
(c) Statement-I is correct, but Statement-II is incorrect.
(d) Statement I is incorrect, but Statement II is correct.

Ans. (a)

Exp. Both Statement-I and Statement-II are correct and Statement-II is the correct explanation for Statement-I.

In the Chola Kingdom in South India, a great amount of autonomy was enjoyed by the local people. They looked after their administration with the help of self elected local bodies.

Two types of village assemblies are mentioned in the records. These were known as Sabha and Ur Sabha was the assembly in the villages which were inhabited predominantly by the Brahmanas. Whereas Ur was in the non brahmanical settlements. These assemblies looked after the local public works, tax collection, temple management, etc., with the help of the members elected through a procedure set by the villagers. It was a unique feature of the Chola administration as it represented a harmonious balance between the central authority and the local self-government.

71 With reference to Imperial Cholas (850 – 1200 AD), consider the following statements.

(Chap 3, Class-XI, Old NCERT)

Statement-I The Chola naval expedition conquered the territories of Kadaram and a number of other places in the Malay Peninsula from the ruler of Sailendra dynasty.

Statement-II Chola rulers wanted to remove obstacles to Indian traders and to expand Chola trade with China.

Which one of the following is correct in respect of the above Statements?

(a) Both Statement-I and Statement-II are correct and Statement-II is the correct explanation for Statement-I.
(b) Both Statement-I and Statement-II are correct and Statement-II is incorrect explanation for Statement-I.
(c) Statement-I is correct, but Statement-II is incorrect.
(d) Statement-I is incorrect, but Statement-II is correct.

Ans. (a)

Exp. Both Statement-I and Statement-II are correct and Statement-II is correct explanation for Statement-I.

Rajendra Chola led a navy expedition to Sri Lanka whose rule extended over the Malay Peninsula, Sumatra, Java and neighbouring islands. To remove the obstacle of doing trade with China led to hostile relations between Sri Lanka and rulers of Cholas. Ultimately a naval expedition from the Chola king, Rajendra I was successful in conquering the territories of Kadaram and a number of other places in Malay Peninsula from the ruler of Sailendra dynasty.

Miscellaneous

72 Consider the following statements with reference to the Samantas of Southern India.

(Chap 11, Class-XI, New NCERT) (UPPSC Pre 2003)

1. They were military leaders who supported the king with troops whenever he needed them.
2. They collected revenue from the land and used this to maintain soldiers.

Which of the statements given above is/are correct?

(a) Only 1 (b) Only 2
(c) Both 1 and 2 (d) Neither 1 nor 2

Ans. (c)

Exp. Both the statements (1) and (2) are correct with reference to the Samantas of Southern India. They were military leaders who supported the king with troops whenever he needed them.

They were not paid regular salaries, instead some of them received grants of land.

They collected revenue from the land and used this to maintain soldiers and horses, and provide equipment for warfare.

73 Which of the following pairs is not matched correctly?

(Chap 24, Class-XI, Old NCERT)

	Kingdoms		Modern Territories
(a)	Chalukya	–	Territories of Western Deccan
(b)	Ikshvaku	–	Krishna-Guntur region
(c)	Kadamba	–	Kerala
(d)	Vakataka	–	Northern Maharashtra

Ans. (c)

Exp. Pair (c) is matched incorrectly because Kadamba kingdom ruled over region of Northern Karnataka and Konkan.

74 With reference to the culture of ancient South India, consider the following statements.

(Class-XI, Old NCERT)

1. Pampa, Poona and Ranna were regarded as three gems of Kannada poetry.
2. Pallippadai was a memorial shrine built over the ruins of kings Chola period of South India.
3. Rajendra I composed the foundational text of the philosophical system called Saiva Siddhanta.
4. Koyilkanakku audited the accounts of the temple during the rule of the Chola empire (850-1200AD).

How many of the statements given above is/are incorrect?

(a) Only one (b) Only two
(c) Only three (d) All four

Ans. (a)

Exp. Only one statement i.e., (3) is incorrect with reference to cultural development in ancient South India.

Meikandar composed the foundational text of the philosophical system called Saiva Siddhanta. The foundational text of this philosophy was called Sivagnana Bodham.

A highly evolved philosophical system called Saiva Siddhanta was founded during this period. Fourteen texts, collectively called Saiva Siddhanta Sastram, form the core of this philosophy.

75 Match the following lists and choose the correct code. *(Chap 3, Class-XI, Old NCERT)*

List I (Temples)	List II (Associated dynasty)
A. Brihadisvara temple at Tanjore	1. Pallava
B. Kailashnatha temple at Kanchipuram	2. Hoysala
C. Papanatha temple at Pattadakal	3. Chola
D. Hoysalesvara temple at Halbeid	4. Chalukya

Codes

	A	B	C	D
(a)	1	2	4	3
(b)	2	4	1	3
(c)	3	1	4	2
(d)	4	2	1	3

Ans. (c)

Exp. The correct matching is A-3, B-1, C-4, D-2.

Brihadisvara temple at Tanjore was built under the patronage of Rajaraja I of the Chola dynasty.

Kailashnatha temple at Kanchipuram was built under the patronage of Rajasimha of Pallava dynasty. It is an example of early Dravida style of architecture in eighth century.

Papanatha temple at Pattadakal was built during the eighth century. It was built under the patronage of Chalukya rulers. This temple was built during the eighth century by the rulers of Early Chalukya dynasty.

Hoysalesvara temple at Halbeid was built under the patronage of king Vishnuvardhana of Hoysala dynasty.

76 Which among these was famous for Telugu translation of Mahabharata? *(Chap 3, Class-XI, Old NCERT) (UPPSC Pre 2012)*

1. Kamban 2. Kuttan 3. Nannaya 4. Tikkana

Codes

(a) 1 and 2 (b) 2 and 3 (c) 3 and 4 (d) 4 and 1

Ans. (c)

Exp. Among the given options, Nannaya and Tikkana were famous for Telugu translation of Mahabharata. Besides these two, Yerrapragada (Errana) was also involved in Telugu translation of Mahabharata. Together, they translated the Mahabharata from Sanskrit into Telugu over the period of the 11th to 14th century AD. They were patronised by Chalukyan kings.

77 Choose the correct chronological order. *(Class-XI, Old NCERT)*

(a) Rajadhiraja I , Parantaka I, Kulottunga I , Rajaraja I
(b) Kulottunga I , Parantaka I , Rajadhiraja I, Rajaditya I
(c) Parantaka I , Rajadhiraja I, Kulottunga I, Rajaraja I
(d) Parantaka I, Rajaraja I, Rajadhiraja I, Kulottunga I
(e) Answer not known

Ans. (d)

Exp. The correct chronological order is Parantaka I, Rajaraja I , Rajadhiraja I, Kulothunga I. Parantaka Chola ruled between 907 - 950 AD. He conquered Madurai and Sri Lanka. Rajaraja I ruled between 985-1014 AD. He built the Brihadeshwara temple in Thanjavur. Thirumurai, the important text had been texted during his rule. Rajadhiraja Chola ruled between 1044-1054 AD. He maintained the Chola authority over most of Lanka, Vengi and Kalinga region. Kulottunga Chola I ruled between 1070-1122 AD. He got the title Kulottunga, literally meaning the exalter of his race.

Arab and Turk Conquest in India

Arab and Turk Conquest in India

Arab Conquest

Arabs in India

- In 712 AD, the Arabs conquered Sindh under the leadership of Muhammad Bin Qasim
- In this part of India, Islam became an important religion for the first time
- Muhammad-Bin-Qasim was a military commander of Al-Hajjaj (Governor of Basra)
- They established several trading settlements on Western coast of India

Reasons for Failure

- New Khalifa put a break on military help
- Fight over Khilafat (Caliphate)
- Lack of communication and transport between Sindh and Baghdad
- Muhammad-bin-Qasim put to death by the caliph

Administration in Sindh

- Divided into a number of districts (iqtas)
- Iqtas made over of the Arab military officer on condition of military service
- Those who paid poll tax or Jizya were exempted from embracing Islam

Impact of Arab Rule

- Converted Sindh population of Islam
- The formal slavery system was introduced

Introduction

- An adventurer Alp-Tegin founded the principality of Ghazni in 962 AD.
- The period from 1000-1200 AD saw rapid changes, both in West and Central Asia. Which paved way to sudden attack of turks in Northern India

Mahmud of Ghazni

- Ascended the throne in 998 AD of Ghazni (Afghanistan)
- Led 17 expeditions in to India
- Encouraged Arabic language and literature
- AL-Biruni came of India with Ghazni wrote Kitab-ul-Hind in Arabic; Translated many Indian texts in to Arabic

Muhammad of Ghur

- Ascended the throne at Ghazni in 1173 AD
- Defeated by Prithviraj Chauhan-III in First Battle of Tarain in 1991 AD.
- Defeated Prithviraj Chauhan-II in Second Battle of Tarain in 1192 AD.
- Captured Hansi, Saraswati, Somara and Ajmer

Turkish Conquest

Turkish Conquest of Bihar and Bengal

- **Bakhtiyar Khilji** Raided Bihar and Bengal
- Destroyed Buddhist monastries of Nalanda and Vikramashila
- Defeated Sena ruler of Bengal and captured their capital, Lakhnauti; seuerely defeated by Magh ruler of Assam

Causes of Turkish Success

- Use of superior horses, presence of feudalism in India, division between Rajput rulers and advanced military skills

Effect of Turkish Invasion

- Development of central autocratic system, growth of urban economy, uniformity in revenue system, adoption of Islamic laws and development of Persian as an official language
- Introduction of Turkish architecture : arches, domes, lofty towers and minarets

SOURCE *Old NCERT Class VI (India and the World), Old NCERT Class XI (The Age of Conflict), New NCERT Class XII (Through the Eyes of Travellers), New NCERT Class XII (Bhakti and Sufi Tradition), Tamil Nadu Board Class XI (Advent of Arab and Turks), NIOS Chap 9, Module 2 (Establishment and Expansion of Delhi Sultanate)*

Arab Invasion

1 With reference to medieval history of Indian subcontinent, consider the following statements.

(Class-XI, Old NCERT)

1. Arabs were the first Muslim invaders of India.
2. Sindh was the first province to be conquered by first invaders .
3. The primary motive of the initial Arab military expedition was to strengthen their power in Central Asia.

How many of the statements given above is/are incorrect?

(a) Only one (b) Only two (c) All three (d) None of these

Ans. (d)

Exp. None of the statements given above are incorrect with reference to the medieval history of the Indian subcontinent.

The first Muslim invaders of India were Arabs.

They first invaded India in 712 AD in Sindh under the leadership of Muhammad Bin Qasim.

Arab military expeditions in 712 and subsequent Ghaznavid and the Ghori military raids, intended to loot and use the resources seized to strengthen their power in Central Asia, created a relationship of the conqueror and the conquered.

2 With reference to the advent of Arabs in the eighth centuries, consider the following statements.

(Unit 10, Class-XI, Tamil Nadu Board)

1. Pre-Islamic Arabs had maritime contacts with Eastern coasts of India.
2. Mappillais were the first Arab trader who settled in western India.

Which of the statements given above is/are correct?

(a) Only 1 (b) Only 2
(c) Both 1 and 2 (d) Neither 1 nor 2

Ans. (a)

Exp. Statement (1) is correct with reference to the advent of Arab in India in the 13th centuries. The geographical location of Arabia facilitated trade contact between India and Arabia. As sea-faring traders, the pre-Islamic Arabs had maritime contacts with the Western and Eastern coasts of India. Arabs too settled in Malabar and the Coromandel coast.

Statement (2) is incorrect. The Arabs who married Malabar women and settled down on the West Coast were called Mappillais (son-in-law).

3 With reference to the Arab Invasion, consider the following statements. *(Class-XI, Old NCERT)*

1. King Dahir's refusal to punish the pirates of Debol was one of the reasons behind the Sindh Invasion by Muhammad-Bin-Qasim.
2. In the early 8th century, the Invasion of India was part of the policy of Arab expansion.
3. Muhammad-Bin-Qasim was the general of the Umayyad caliphate.

How many of the statements given above is/are incorrect?

(a) Only one
(b) Only two
(c) All three
(d) None of the above

Ans. (d)

Exp. None of the above statements are incorrect with reference to the Arab Invasion.

King Dahir's refusal to punish the pirates of Debol was one of the reasons behind the Sindh Invasion by Muhammad-Bin-Qasim.

In the early 8th century, the Invasion of India was part of the policy of Arab expansion. By the 8th century AD, the Arabs had acquired a core position from Spain to India , connecting the trade of the Mediterranean and the Indian Ocean.

Muhammad-Bin-Qasim was the general of the Umayyad caliphate. Who led the Muslim conquest of Sindh from the last Hindu King, Raja Dahir in Battle of Aror.

4 With reference to regimes of Sultanate and Great Mughals, consider the following statements.

(Class-XI, Old NCERT)

Statement-I The regimes of the Sultanate were diminutive in their institutional advancement when compared to Great Mughals.

Statement-II In terms of class relations, the medieval state served as the agent of the ruling class.

Which one of the following is correct in respect of the above statements?

(a) Both Statement-I and Statement-II are correct and Statement-II is the correct explanation for Statement-I.
(b) Both Statement-I and Statement-II are correct and Statement-II is not the correct explanation for Statement-I.
(c) Statement-I is correct, but Statement-II is incorrect.
(d) Statement-I is incorrect, but Statement-II is correct.

Ans. (a)

Exp. Both Statement-I and Statement-II are correct and Statement-II is the correct explanation for Statement-I.

Historians focusing on the history of class relations, have argued that the medieval state served as the agent of the ruling class and hence, the regimes of the Sultanate were diminutive in their institutional advancement when compared with the Great Mughals.

Thus, there is no consensus yet amongst scholars in determining the true nature of the Sultanate.

Ghaznavi

5 With reference to Samanid empire, consider the following territory. *(Chap 5, Class-XI, Old NCERT)*

1. Transoxiana 2. Khorasan 3. Parts of Iran

How many of the above territories were ruled by Samanid Empire towards the end of ninth century?

(a) Only one (b) Only two
(c) All three (d) None of these

Ans. (c)

Exp. Towards the end of ninth century, Samanid empire ruled over the Transoxiana, Khorason and in some parts of Iran. This empire was founded by four brothers Nuh, Ahmed, Yahya and Ilyas towards the end of the ninth century AD.

These brothers ruled territory under Abbasid suzerainty before the establishment of independent empire.

6 Consider the following statements. *(Chap 5, Class-XI, Old NCERT)*

1. Mahmud was closely associated with the renaissance of the Iranian spirit.
2. Firdausi was the poet laureate at the court of Mahmud.
3. Mahmud proclaimed descent from the Iranian legendary King Afrasiyab.

Which of the statements given above is/are correct?

(a) Only 1 (b) 1 and 2 (c) 2 and 3 (d) 1, 2 and 3

Ans. (d)

Exp. All the given statements are correct. Mahmud was closely associated with the renaissance of the Iranian spirit Firdausi, the poet laureate at the court of Mahmud, was the author of Shahnama. Mahmud proclaimed descent from the Iranian legendry King Afrasiyab. Mahmud Ghazni was the third ruler of the Ghaznavid Empire. He ascended to throne in 998 AD at the age of 27. He was the first Turk ruler to be known as Sultan.

7 Consider the following statements. *(Chap 5, Class-XI, Old NCERT)*

1. Jayapala in his fight against the Mahmud of Ghazni was supported by the Muslim ruler of Multan.
2. After being defeated by Mahmud of Ghazni, Jayapala was imprisoned and killed by him.
3. Waihind was the capital of rulers of Hindushahi dynasty.

Which of the statements given above is/are incorrect?

(a) Only 1 (b) 1 and 2 (c) 2 and 3 (d) Only 2

Ans. (d)

Exp. Statement (2) is incorrect because Jaypala was defeated badly by the Mahmud of Ghazni. He was imprisoned by him and later he was released. Jayapala was humiliated over his defeat, therefore, he decided to kill himself by entering a funeral pyre.

8 With reference to invasion of Sindh, consider the following statements. *(Unit 10, Class-XI, Tamil Nadu Board)*

Statement-I The Arab conquest of Sindh has been described as a triumph without results.

Statement-II After the expedition of Muhammad-Bin-Qasim Sindh had a respite from invasion for about three centuries.

Which one of the following is correct in respect of the above statements?

(a) Both Statement I and Statement-II are correct and Statement-II is the correct explanation for Statement-I.
(b) Both Statement-I and Statement-II are correct and Statement-II is not the correct explanation for Statement-I.
(c) Statement-I is correct, but Statement-II is incorrect.
(d) Statement-I is incorrect, but Statement-II is correct.

Ans. (a)

Exp. Both Statement-I and Statement-II are correct and Statement-II is the correct explanation for Statement-I. The Arab conquest of Sindh has been described as a "triumph without results" because it touched but a fringe of the country, which, after Qasim's expedition had a respite from invasions for about three centuries.

9 Consider the following statements with reference to the Ghaznavid dynasty. *(Class-XI, Old NCERT)*

1. Ghazni was the capital of Samanid Kingdom established by Sabuktigin.
2. They relied on a permanent, professional army.
3. The later rulers of Ghaznavid dynasty could exercise their authority only in Lahore regions.

How many of the statements given above is/are incorrect?

(a) Only one (b) Only two
(c) All three (d) None of the above

Ans. (a)

Exp. Only one statement i.e., (1) is incorrect with reference to the Ghaznavid dynasty.

Alaptigin laid down the foundation of the Ghaznavid Kingdom. He was the governor under the Samanid dynasty of Iran. Ghazni was the capital of his new kingdom. He was succeeded by his slave and son-in-law, Sabuktigin.

10 With reference to the military raid of India by Ghaznavid dynasty, consider the following statements. *(Class-XI, Old NCERT)*

Statement-I Plundering raids and looting of the temples were more of political and economic character than of religious chauvinism.

Statement-II Desecration of temples and vandalisation of deities were all part of asserting one's authority in medieval India.

Which one of the following is correct in respect of the above statements?

(a) Both Statement-I and Statement-II are correct and Statement-II is the correct explanation for Statement-I.

(b) Both Statement-I and Statement-II are correct and Statement-II is not the correct explanation for Statement-I.

(c) Statement-I is correct Statement-II is incorrect.

(d) Statement-I is incorrect Statement-II is correct.

Ans. (a)

Exp. Both Statement-I and Statement-II are correct and Statement-II is the correct explanation for Statement-I.

Many scholars argue that these plundering raids were more of political and economic character than of religious chauvinism. Politically, Desecration of temples, vandalising the images of deities were all part of asserting one's authority in medieval India.

Economically, the plundering raids of invaders like Mahmud were meant to replenish the treasury to maintain his huge army.

Though the motive was to loot, there was also a military advantage in demolishing temples and smashing idols. The Ghaznavid soldiers viewed it also as a demonstration of the invincible power of their God.

11 With reference to Al-Biruni, consider the following statements. *(Class-XI, Old NCERT)*

Statement-I He was the inter-civilisational connect between India and the rest of the world.

Statement-II He translated the Greek work of Euclid into Sanskrit and transmitted the Aryanhata's Aryattiyam to the West.

Which one of the following is correct in respect of the above statements?

(a) Both Statement-I and Statement-II are correct and Statement-II is the correct explanation for Statement-I.

(b) Both Statement-I and Statement-II are correct and Statement-II is not the correct explanation for Statement-I.

(c) Statement-I is correct Statement-II is incorrect.

(d) Statement-I is incorrect Statement-II is correct.

Ans. (a)

Exp. Both Statement-I and Statement-II are correct and Statement-II is the correct explanation for Statement-I.

Al-Biruni was inter-civilisational connection between India and the rest of the world. Al-Biruni, mathematician, philosopher, astronomer, and historian, came to India along with Mahmud of Ghazni. He learned Sanskrit, studied religious and philosophical texts before composing his work Kitab-Ul-Hind. He also translated the Greek work of Euclid into Sanskrit. He transmitted Aryabhata's magnum opus Aryabattiyam (the thesis that Earth's rotation around its axis creates day and night) to the West.

12 With reference to expedition of Mahmud Ghaznavi, consider the following pairs. *(Chap 5, Class-XI, Old NCERT)*

Expedition of Mahmud Ghaznavi		Year
1. Waihind	–	1008-09 AD
2. Kannauj	–	1025 AD
3. Somnath	–	1026 AD

How many of the pairs given above is/are incorrectly matched?

(a) Only one
(b) Only two
(c) All three
(d) None of these

Ans. (b)

Exp. Only two pairs i.e., (2) and (3) are incorrectly matched with reference to expedition of Mahmud Ghaznavi. Kannauj (in present day Uttar Pradesh) was attacked by Mahmud Ghaznavi in the year 1018-19 AD. During this raid, he also attacked Mathura.

Kannauj and Mathura were part of the territory ruled by Pratihar Rajyapal. In 1025 AD, Mahmud Ghazni raided Gujarat looting the Somnath temple and breaking its Jyotirlinga. He took 2 million dinars in body.

13 Consider the following statements. *(Chap 5, Class-XI, Old NCERT)*

1. A decisive battle between Mahmud and Anandpala was fought in 1001-1004 AD at Waihind.
2. Many princes of North-Western India, including the rulers of Kannauj and Rajasthan, took part in the battle.

Which of the statements given above is/are incorrect?

(a) Only 1
(b) Only 2
(c) Both 1 and 2
(d) Neither 1 nor 2

Ans. (a)

Exp. Statement (1) is incorrect because a decisive battle between Mahmud and Anandpala was fought in 1009 AD, near Hazro. This battle was known as Battle of Chach or Battle of Chaach.

14 Consider the following statements in context of Al-Biruni. *(Chap 5, Class-XII, New NCERT)*

1. He came into service of Mahmud when Mahmud Ghaznavi invaded Khwarizm.
2. His literary work was influenced by Indian scholar of that time.
3. He was well-versed in Sanskrit.
4. He was against the study of Indian literature.

How many of the statements given above is/are correct?

(a) Only one
(b) Only two
(c) Only three
(d) All of these

Ans. (c)

Exp. Only three statements i.e., (1), (2) and (3) are correct in context of Al Biruni.

Al-Biruni was born in 973 AD, in Khwarizm in present day, Uzbekistan. In 1017 AD, when Sultan Mahmud invaded Khwarizm, he took several scholars and poets back to his capital, Ghazni was one of them.

He was an impartial writer on the customs and creeds of different nations. He was well-versed in several languages such as Syrian, Arabic, Persian, Hebrew, Sanskrit, etc.

Statement (4) is incorrect because he was not against the study of Indian literature. He was considered as the founder of Indology.

15 Consider the following statements with reference to the Kitab-ul-Hind. *(Chap 5, Class-XI, New NCERT)*

1. It was written by Al-Biruni in Arabic language.
2. It covered only religion and philosophy.
3. He adopted a distinctive structure in each chapter, beginning with a question, following this up with a description based on Sanskrit traditions.

Which of the statements given above is/are incorrect?

(a) Only 1 (b) 1 and 2
(c) Only 2 (d) 1, 2 and 3

Ans. (c)

Exp. Statement (2) is incorrect with reference to the Kitab-ul-Hind because Kitab-ul-Hind is divided into 80 chapters on subjects such as religion and philosophy, festivals, astronomy, alchemy, manners and customs, social life, weights and measures, iconography, laws and metrology.

He is considered as the 'first anthropologist' for his keen observation on Indian society and the cultural ethos of the time. He was also the 'first indologist'.

16 The first Muslim who studied *Puranas* was
(Chap 5, Class-XII, New NCERT) (UPPSC Pre 2002)

(a) Abul Fazal (b) Abdul Qadir Badayuni
(c) Al-Biruni (d) Dara Shikoh

Ans. (c)

Exp. The first Muslim who studied *Puranas* was Al-Biruni. He was not only historian but also took keen interest in the wide level of subjects.

Besides Puranas, he also studied Vedas, the Bhagwad Gita, Patanjali, the Manusmriti, etc. He also translated Patanjali's Yoga sutra into Arabic.

Ghurids

17 Battle that laid the foundation of Muslim domination in India was
(Chap 5, Class-XI, Old NCERT) (UPPSC Pre 1995)

(a) First Battle of Tarain (b) Second Battle of Tarain
(c) First Battle of Panipat (d) Second Battle of Panipat

Ans. (b)

Exp. Battle that laid the foundation of Muslim domination in India was Second Battle of Tarain (1192 AD).

This battle was fought between Muhammad Ghori and Prithviraj Chauhan, near Tarain. In this battle, Prithviraj Chauhan was defeated by Muhammad Ghori. This was the turning point in the Indian history as it laid the foundation of Muslim rule in India.

18 Which of the following is/are correct in the context of the Turkish conquest in India?
(Chap 5, Class-XI, Old NCERT)

(a) In the year 1194, Jayachandra was defeated in battle of Chandawar.
(b) In this battle, Turkish forces were led by Qutb-ud-Din Aibak.
(c) Both a and b
(d) Neither a nor b

Ans. (a)

Exp. After establishing his rule over Delhi, Muhammad Ghori returned to Ghazni. In the year 1194 AD, he launched military expedition against Jayachandra who was the ruler of the Gahadavala dynasty.

Battle was fought at Chandawar between Muhammad Ghori and Jayachandra. In this battle, Turkish forces were led by Muhammad Ghori (not Qutb-ud-Din Aibak) and he emerged victorious. The reason behind this expedition was to get control over the fertile land of the Ganga Valley.

19 Which of the following rulers had defeated Muhammad Ghori and Prithviraj in different battles, however, Qutb-ud-Din Aibak was successful in defeating him? *(Chap 5, Class-XI, Old NCERT)*

(a) Anandpala (b) Jayachandra
(c) Bhima II (d) Jayapala

Ans. (c)

Exp. Bhima II defeated Muhammad Ghori and Prithviraj Chauhan in different battles. He was the ruler of the Chalukya (also known as Solanki) dynasty. In 1178 AD, the Ghurid king Muhammad Ghori invaded the Chalukya kingdom, but was defeated in the Battle of Kayadara. However, Qutb-ud-Din Aibak was successful in defeating him in the year 1197 AD.

20 Consider the following statements with reference to the Bakhtiyar Khalji. *(Chap 5, Class-XI, Old NCERT)*

1. He attacked and destroyed famous monasteries like Nalanda and Vikramshila.
2. He established Lakhnauti as his capital in North Bihar.

Which of the statements given above is/are correct?

(a) Only 1 (b) Only 2
(c) Both 1 and 2 (d) Neither 1 nor 2

Ans. (a)

Exp. Statement (1) is correct with reference to the Bakhtiyar Khalji.

He attacked and destroyed famous monasteries like Nalanda and Vikramshila because of his radical Islamic ideology. He was one of the generals of Muhammad Ghori. He was appointed as Governor of Bihar and Bengal by Muhammad Ghori.

Statement (2) is incorrect because he established Lakhnauti as his capital in North Bengal.

21 **With reference to Ghurids dynasty, consider the following statements.** *(Class-XI, Old NCERT)*

Statement-I The motive of invasions by the Ghurids dynasty was narrower than the Ghaznavid dynasty.

Statement-II Ghurids enlarged their scope to establish garrison towns to ensure the regular flow of plunder.

Which one of the following is correct in respect of the above statements?

(a) Both Statement-I and Statement-II are correct and Statement-II is the correct explanation for Statement-I.
(b) Both Statement-I and Statement-II are correct and Statement-II is not the correct explanation for Statement-I.
(c) Statement-I is correct, but Statement-II is incorrect.
(d) Statement-I is incorrect, but Statement-II is correct.

Ans. (d)

Exp. Statement I is incorrect, but Statement II is correct with reference to the Ghurids dynasty. The motive of invasions by the Ghurids dynasty was broader than the Ghaznavid dynasty.

If Ghaznavid invasions were intended for loot, the Ghurids enlarged their scope to establish garrison towns to ensure the regular flow of plunder and tribute. The Muizzuddin Muhammad of the Ghori dynasty, generally known as Muhammad Ghori, invested in territories he seized. Through the 1180s and 1190s, Ghori established garrisons in the modern provinces of Punjab, Sind and Haryana.

22 **With reference to the period of invasions by Ghurids dynasty, consider the following statements.** *(Class-XI, Old NCERT)*

1. In 1175 Muhammad Ghori seized Multan and captured the fort of Uch.
2. Chalukyas of Gujarat inflicted a crushing defeat on Muhammad Ghori at Mt. Abu.
3. Tabarhinda was a strategic point for the Chalukyas of Gujarat.

How many of the statements given above is/are incorrect?

(a) Only one
(b) Only two
(c) All three
(d) None of these

Ans. (a)

Exp. Only one statement i.e., (3) is incorrect in reference to the period of invasions by Ghurids dynasty. Tabarhinda was a strategic point for the Chauhans of Ajmer. Ghori attacked the fortress of Tabarhinda (Bhatinda), a strategic point for the Prithviraj Chauhan.

The ruler Prithviraj Chauhan marched to Tabarhinda and faced the invader in the First Battle of Tarain (1191). He was an Indian King from the Chahmana (Chauhan) dynasty.

23 **Consider the following statements, with reference to the Battle of Tarain.** *(Class-XI, Old NCERT)*

1. The First Battle of Tarain was fought between Muhammad Ghori and Prithviraj Chauhan.
2. Prithviraj Chauhan consolidated his position after emerging victorious in the First Battle of Tarain.
3. Muhammad Ghori restored Prithviraj Chauhan to his throne after the Second Battle of Panipat.

How many of the statements given above is/are incorrect?

(a) Only one
(b) Only two
(c) All three
(d) None of these

Ans. (a)

Exp. Only one statement i.e., (2) is incorrect with reference to Battle of Tarain. Prithviraj scored a brilliant victory in the First Battle of Panipat in 1191 AD, however he failed to consolidate his position believing this battle to be a frontier fight, and did not expect the Ghurids to make regular attacks.

24 **With reference to Muhammad Ghori, consider the following statements.** *(Class-XI, Old NCERT)*

1. The Battle of Tarain and Chandwar laid the foundations of Turkish rule in northern India.
2. He defeated Jai Chand at the Battle of Anhilwara.

Which of the statements given above is/are correct?

(a) Only 1
(b) Only 2
(c) Both 1 and 2
(d) Neither 1 nor 2

Ans. (b)

Exp. Statement (2) is incorrect with reference to Muhammad Ghori. He gave a crushing defeat to Jai Chand at Chandwar near Kannauj. Thus the battle of Tarain and Chandwar laid the foundations of Turkish rule in northern India.

At the Battle of Anhilwara, Chalukya ruler of Gujarat, Bhima II defeated Muhammad Ghori at battle.

Chapter 13

Delhi Sultanate

Delhi Sultanate

Mamluk and Khilji Dynasty

Mamluk Dynasty (1206-1290 AD)

- **Qutb-ud-din Aibak** Established Turkish rule in India. Made Lahore as capital; Also known as Lakh Baksh (and the foundations of Qutub Minar and Adhai din Ka jhonpra)
- **Iltutmish** Shifted capital from Lahore to Delhi; Saved Sultanate from destruction by Mongols; Issued two basic coins— Tanka and Jital; Densed Iqta system and established Turkan-i-Chahalgani
- **Raziya Sultan** First woman ruler of Delhi Sultanate; Rule of Raziya Sultan marked the beginning of a struggle for power between the monarchy and the *Turkan-i-Chahalgani*
- **Balban** Ruled in autocratic manner and declared himself descendent of Iranian King Afrasiab; Broke the power of Turkan-i-Chahalgani; Assumed title of *Zil-i-Ilahi*

Khilji Dynasty (1290-1320 AD)

- **Jalaluddin Khilji** First ruler to put forward the view that the state should be based on the willing support of the people
- **Alauddin Khilji** Earlier served as Iqtedar of Awadh and Kara; Led first Turkish expedition to Southern India Curbed the power of nobles and interference by Ulema; Started practice of assessing land revenue based on measurement of area under cultivation

Tughlaq and Sayyid Dynasty

Tughlaq Dynasty (1320-1414 AD)

- **Ghiyasuddin Tughlaq** Earlier served as an important official in reign of Alauddin Khilji founded Tughlaq dynasty
- **Muhammad bin Tughlaq** Consolidated the Delhi Sultanate by annexing navar territories; Defeated Rai Rudra Dev of Warangal and Bhanudeva II of Jajnagas; Promoted religious tolerance; Appointed Ibn Battuta as Qazi of Delhi. Failed experiments —
  - Transfer of capital from Delhi to Daultabad
  - Expeditions of Khurasan and Qarachil
  - Introduction of Token currency
  - Taxation in Doab
- **Firoz Shah Tughlaq** By using policy of appeasement prevented imminent breakup of Delhi Sultanate, Established department for public work and founded city of Jaunpur. Jizya became a separate tax : Repaired and dug number of canals

Sayyid Dynasty (1414-1415 AD)

- **Khizr Khan** Taimur appointed Khizr Khan as the ruler of Multan; Founded this dynasty after invasion of Delhi in 1398 AD; Claimed to be descendants of Prophet Muhammad
- **Mubarak Shah** After Khizr Khan's death Mubarak Shah and Muhammad Shah ascended the throne one after another

Lodi Dynasty and Mongol Invasion

Lodi Dynasty (1451-1526 AD)

- **Bahlol Lodi** Had Afghan ancestry successfully suppressed the revolts in Mewat and Doab; In 1476 AD, defeated the Sultan of Jaunpur
- **Sikander Lodi** Re-imposed Jizya on non-Muslims; Harsh treatment to nobles and Amirs; Founded the city of Agra in 1510 AD and made it second capital; Introduced Gaz-i-Sikandari, a system of land measurement
- **Ibrahim Lodi** Defeated by Babur in 1526 AD in First Battle of Panipat; First Sultan of Delhi who was killed in battle field

Mongol Invasion in Delhi Sultanate

- **During Rule of Iltutmish** Saved Delhi Sultanate from wrath of Genghis Khan by not giving assylum to Prince of Khwarizm
- **During Rule of Balban** Mongols under leadership of Tair Bahadur captured Lahore; In 1245 AD, Mongol attacked the Sultanate but defeated by Balban
- **During Rule of Khilji** In 1292, Mongol commander Abdullah attacked Delhi but defeated by Jalaluddin Khilji; During the reign of Alauddin many battles were fought between Mongols and his army, but Alauddin crushed the Mongols decisively

SOURCE *Old NCERT Class VII* (*Sultan of Delhi*), *New NCERT Class VII* (*The Delhi Sultans*), *Old NCERT Class XI* (*Delhi Sultanate I*), *Old NCERT Class XI* (*Delhi Sultanate II*), *Old NCERT Class XI* (*Government, Economic and Social Life Under the Delhi Sultanate*) *NIOS Class XI* (*Establishment and Expansion of Delhi Sultanate*)

Slave/Mamluk Dynasty

1 The position or authority of Qutb-ud-din Aibak was challenged by whom among the following? *(Chap 6, Class-XI, Old NCERT)*

1. Muizz-ud-Din 2. Illtutmish
3. Yalduz 4. Sher Khan

Codes

(a) 1 and 2 (b) 2 and 3
(c) Only 3 (d) 1 and 3

Ans. (c)

Exp. The position or authority of Qutb-ud-din Aibak was challenged by Yalduz. Qutb-ud-din Aibak and Yalduz were the slaves of Muiz-ud-Din or Muhammad Ghori. Qutb-ud-din Aibak succeeded in Delhi as Sultan. On the other hand, the another slave of Muhammad Ghori, Yalduz succeeded at Ghazni.

As the ruler of Ghazni, Yalduz claimed to rule over Delhi as well. It was unacceptable for Aibak, who discontinued its links with Ghazni.

It also enabled the Delhi Sultanate to develop on its own independent lines, without depending on countries outside India.

2 With reference to Iltutmish, consider the following statements. *(Chap 6, Class-XI, Old NCERT)*

1. Iltutmish was the son-in-law of Qutb-ud-din Aibak.
2. At the time of his accession, Qubacha, declared himself an independent ruler of Multan.
3. His accession was not accepted by some of the nobles in Delhi.

Which of the statements given above is/are correct?

(a) 1 and 2 (b) 2 and 3
(c) 1 and 3 (d) 1, 2 and 3

Ans. (d)

Exp. All the given statements are correct.

Iltutmish was the son-in-law of Qutb-ud-din Aibak.

But, before he could be succeeded to the throne, he had to fight and defeat the son of Aibak. Thus, the principle of heredity i.e., son succeeding his father was also checked after this accession.

At the time of his accession, Qubacha, a fellow slave of Aibak, had declared himself an independent ruler of Multan. He also seized Lahore and parts of Punjab.

His accession was not accepted by some of the nobles in Delhi. They were reluctant to accept his authority.

3 Consider the following statements with reference to Iltutmish. *(Chap 6, Class-XI, Old NCERT)*

1. He established Delhi as the capital of the Slave dynasty.
2. He was successful in defeating Chalukya ruler of Gujarat.

Which of the statements given above is/are correct?

(a) Only 1 (b) Only 2
(c) Both 1 and 2 (d) Neither 1 nor 2

Ans. (a)

Exp. Only statement (1) is correct with regard to Iltutmish. He succeeded to throne in 1210 AD. He was an Ilbari Turk, who was associated with the Shamsi dynasty.

After becoming Sultan, he established Delhi as the capital of the Slave dynasty because nobles in Lahore were against his accession. He received the title of Sultan by Caliph of Baghdad in 1229 AD and was also known as 'slave of a slave'.

Statement (2) is incorrect because he was not successful in defeating Chalukya ruler of Gujarat. His expedition against Chalukya ruler was a failure.

4 Consider the following statements regarding Raziya Sultan. *(Chap 6, Class-XI, Old NCERT)*

1. She received support from the nobles.
2. Under her reign, Gujarat was subdued under Delhi Sultanate.
3. She was captured by the Altunia on the orders of rebellion of her brother.
4. She was killed in battle against her brother Muiz-ud-Din Bahram, who crowned himself as a king.

Which of the statements given above is/are incorrect?

(a) 1 and 3 (b) 1, 2 and 4
(c) 2 and 4 (d) Only 4

Ans. (b)

Exp. Statements (1), (2) and (4) are incorrect regarding Raziya Sultan.

Raziya Sultan was nominated as the ruler by Iltutmish as his sons were not worthy. Turkish nobles wanted her to be puppet in their hands but she discarded them. She even gave up the female apparel and started holding court with her face unveiled. This led them to accuse her of violating feminine modesty and hence, did not support her.

She was killed by bandits when she was on her way to recapture Delhi. Under her reign, Gujarat was not subdued under Delhi Sultanate.

5 Consider the following statements with reference to Raziya Sultan. *(Chap 6, Class-XI, Old NCERT)*

1. Nizam-ul-Mulk Junaidi revolted against her.
2. Her friendship with Abyssinian Noble, Yakut Khan was one of the reasons for hatred to nobles towards her.

Which of the statements given above is/are incorrect?

(a) Only 1 (b) Only 2
(c) Both 1 and 2 (d) Neither 1 nor 2

Ans. (d)

Exp. Neither statements (1) nor (2) are incorrect with reference to Raziya Sultan. Nizam-ul-Mulk Junaidi was the wazir of Raziya Sultan. He had opposed her elevation to the throne. Thus, he backed and supported a rebellion of nobles against her. But, he was defeated and forced to flee. Nobles also hated her because she gave importance and preference to Abyssinian Noble, Yakut Khan.

She appointed him to an office of the Amir-i-Akhur (master of the horse). Yakut was later killed by rebellion.

6 **With reference to Balban, consider the following statements.** *(Chap 6, Class-XI, Old NCERT)*

1. The real name of Balban was the Ulugh Khan.
2. He held the position of Naib or deputy to Nasiruddin Mahmud, a younger son of Iltutmish.
3. Balban undertook a campaign to destroy the Mewatis.

How many of the statements given above is/are correct?

(a) Only one (b) Only two
(c) All three (d) None of these

Ans. (c)

Exp. All three statements i.e., (1), (2) and (3) are correct with reference to Balban.

The real name of Balban was Ulugh Khan. He was Turkish chief, known in history by his later title of Balban. He gradually arrogated all power to himself, and finally ascended the throne in 1265 AD.

During the earlier period, Balban held the position of Naib or deputy to Nasiruddin Mahmud, a younger son of Iltutmish. He had helped him in securing the throne in 1246 AD. Balban undertook a campaign to destroy the Mewatis.

7 **With reference to Balban, consider the following statements.** *(Chap 6, Class-XI, Old NCERT)*

1. Balban appointed spies in every department to keep himself well-informed.
2. He emphasised on the centralisation of administration.
3. He declared himself as a descendant of Iranian King Afrasiyab.

Which of the statements given above is/are correct?

(a) Only 1 (b) 1 and 2 (c) 2 and 3 (d) 1, 2 and 3

Ans. (d)

Exp. All the given statements are correct. Balban founded the second Ilbari dynasty in the year 1265 AD. He also declared himself as a descendant of Iranian King Afrasiyab so that his accession will be not challenged by other nobles and people.

After accession, he emphasised on the centralisation of administration. This step was taken to increase the power and authority of Sultan. He also appointed spies in every department to keep himself well-informed about activities and intention of nobles.

8 **With reference to the Balban, consider the following statements.** *(Chap 6, Class-XI, Old NCERT)*

Statement-I Balban made his government firm, stable and centralised all authority in his hands.

Statement-II He wanted to protect the North-West frontier against Mongol invasion.

Which one of the following is correct in respect of the above statements?

(a) Both Statement-I and Statement-II are correct and Statement-II is the correct explanation for Statement-I.
(b) Both Statement-I and Statement-II are correct and Statement-II is not the correct explanation for Statement-I.
(c) Statement-I is correct, but Statement-II is incorrect.
(d) Statement-I is incorrect, but Statement-II is correct.

Ans. (b)

Exp. Both Statement-I and Statement-II are correct and Statement-II is not the correct explanation for Statement-I.

Balban made his government firm, stable and centralised all authority in his hands. It is because he was mindful of the intrigues of nobles, who wanted to continue their power and influence in the court, even at the expense of the king.

It was an age in which authority and power was supposed to be the privilege of those born in noble houses and this was also one of the reasons for concentrating powers in his hands.

He wanted to protect the North-West frontier against Mongol invasions as they were posing a threat through the North-West frontier. Although he fought against the Mongols stoutly, the frontiers of Delhi gradually receded from the river Jhelum to the Beas.

9 **Balban succeeded in finally breaking and destroying the power of *Turkan-i-Chahalgani*. What was the main issue he had faced by *Turkan-i-Chahalgani*?** *(Chap 6, Class-XI, Old NCERT)*

(a) Inviting Mongols to invade Sultanate
(b) Interference in the administration
(c) They followed un-Islamic practices
(d) None of the above

Ans. (b)

Exp. The main issue Balban faced by *Turkan-i-Chahalgani* was interference in the administration. *Turkan-i-Chahalgani* was a group of 40 nobles constituted by the Sultan Iltutmish to consolidate the power of nobility under one group. After his death, nobles of this group intrigued in court politics and administration.

This was visible after the death of Iltutmish. Balban also faced these problems as a result he decided to break and destroy the power of *Turkan-i-Chahalgani* and finally, he was successful.

10 Consider the following statements about Balban. *(Chap 6, Class-XI, Old NCERT)*

1. He adopted policy of 'Blood and Iron' against the Hindu in order to realise the dream of Dar-ul-Islam.
2. He created *Diwan-i-Arz* or department of military affairs.
3. He restored peace in the Doab.
4. His son was killed in battle against Mongol.

Which of the statements given above are correct?

(a) 1, 2 and 3
(b) 1, 3 and 4
(c) 2, 3 and 4
(d) All of the above

Ans. (c)

Exp. Statements (2), (3) and (4) are correct about Balban. He created *Diwan-i-Arz* or department of military affairs to bring efficiency in warfare.

He was successful in restoring peace in the Doab, which was the main source of revenue for Sultanate.

One of its main objectives was check Mongol invasions. His son was killed in battle against Mongol.

Statement (1) is incorrect because Balban adopted the policy of Blood and Iron to control the rebellious elements in the court.

11 With reference to Balban, consider the following statements. *(Chap 6, Class-XI, Old NCERT)*

1. He introduced the practice of *Sijada* and *Paibos*.
2. He started celebration of Persian festival Nauroz.
3. He campaigned against Mongols.
4. He allowed women's recruitment in army.

How many of the above policies/initiatives were taken by Balban?

(a) Only one
(b) Only two
(c) Only three
(d) All four

Ans. (c)

Exp. Only three statements i.e., (1), (2) and (3) are correct with reference to the policies/initiatives undertaken by Balban.

During his reign from 1275 to 1286 AD, Balban had taken many initiatives. He introduced the practice of *Sijada* and *Paibos*, which were a form of salutation to the king.

He also started celebration of Persian festival Nauroz in the court for the first time. He launched many campaign against Mongols as they wanted to bring Delhi under their control.

Statement (4) is not correct because Balban did not allow women's recruitment in army.

Khilji Dynasty

12 Consider the following statements with reference to the Jalaluddin Khilji. *(Chap 7, Class-XI, Old NCERT)*

1. He was the first ruler of the Delhi Sultanate to clearly put forward the view that the state should be based on the willing support of the governed.
2. He also tried to gain the goodwill of the nobility by following policy of tolerance.
3. Jalaluddin Khilji faced opposition on the ground that he was a Afghan and not a Turk.

How many of the statements given above is/are correct?

(a) Only one (b) Only two
(c) All three (d) None of these

Ans. (c)

Exp. All three statements i.e, (1), (2) and (3) are correct with reference to Jalaluddin Khilji.

He was the first ruler of the Delhi Sultanate to clearly put forward the view that the state should be based on the willing support of the governed. He ascended the throne in 1290 AD and reigned till 1296 AD.

He also tried to gain the goodwill of the nobility by following policy of tolerance and avoiding harsh punishments. He was assassinated by his nephew and son-in-law Alauddin Khilji near Kara in Uttar Pradesh.

Jalaluddin Khilji faced opposition on the ground that he was a Afghan and not a Turk.

13 With reference to history of India between 1290 to 1296, consider the following statements. *(Chap 7, Class-XI, Old NCERT)*

1. Prataprudra Deva was the ruler of Devagiri at the time of Alauddin Khilji.
2. Alauddin Khilji constructed a new garrison town named Siri for his soldiers.

Which of the statements given above is/are incorrect?

(a) Only 1 (b) Only 2
(c) Both 1 and 2 (d) Neither 1 nor 2

Ans. (a)

Exp. Only statement (1) is incorrect with reference to Alauddin Khilji because Ramchandra Deva was the ruler of Devagiri at the time of Alauddin Khilji's invasion. During the invasion, Ramchandra Deva, the ruler of Devagiri, promised to pay an yearly tribute to Delhi, but he failed to pay.

14 With reference to Alauddin Khilji , consider the following statements. *(Chap 9, Module-2, NIOS)*

1. He decided to revive Balban's policies of ruthless governance.
2. He ordered nobles not to have social gatherings without his permission.
3. He established a permanent standing army.

How many of the statements given above is/are incorrect?

(a) Only one (b) Only two
(c) All three (d) None of these

Ans. *(d)*

Exp. None of these statements are incorrect with reference to Alauddin Khilji.

Alauddin Khilji decided to revive Balban's policies of ruthless governance. He decided to curb the powers of the nobles and interference of Ulema in the matters of the state.

In order to prevent the reoccurrence of rebellion, he formulated certain regulations and implemented them, for instance he ordered nobles not to have social gatherings or inter-marriage without his permission.

He established a huge permanent, standing army to satisfy his ambition of conquest and to protect the country from Mongol invasion.

15 Consider the following statements with reference to the expansion of Delhi Sultanate.
(Chap 7, Class-XI, Old NCERT)

1. Ratan Singh was the ruler of Ranthambore.
2. He defeated Alauddin Khilji's army which was led by Malik Kafur.
3. It is believed that Alauddin Khilji marched against Chittor for Padmini, wife of Ratan Singh.

Which of the statements given above is/are incorrect?

(a) Only 1
(b) 1 and 2
(c) Only 3
(d) 1, 2 and 3

Ans. *(b)*

Exp. Statements (1) and (2) are incorrect with reference to the expansion of Delhi Sultanate because Ratan Singh was the rulers of Mewar Kingdom. His capital was Chittor.

In the battle against Alauddin Khilji in 1303 AD, he was defeated and killed.

16 Which of the following statements is correct with regard to the campaigns of Malik Kafur?
(Chap 7, Class-XI, Old NCERT)

(a) Malik Kafur led campaign against Warangal in year 1309.
(b) In the same year, he also defeated ruler of Dwar Samudra.
(c) After his successful campaign in South India, he was appointed as Wazir.
(d) All of the above

Ans. *(a)*

Exp. Statements (a) is correct with regard to the campaigns of Malik Kafur. Malik Kafur led military campaign against Warangal in the 1309 AD on the order of Alauddin Khilji. Warangal was ruled by Kakatiya kingdom who was defeated very badly by Malik Kafur.

Statements (b) and (c) are incorrect because Malik Kafur launched military campaign against ruler of Dwar Samudra in the year 1311. Dwar Samudra was under the control of Hoysala dynasty. This campaign marked the end of Hoysala dynasty.

When Alauddin fell seriously ill in 1315 AD, Kafur was recalled to Delhi, where he exercised power as Na'ib (Viceroy) not wazir.

Tughlaq Dynasty

17 With reference to the Muhammad bin Tughlaq, consider the following statements.
(Chap 7, Class-XI, Old NCERT)

1. He transferred his capital to Deogir to keep Deccan under control.
2. He lived at bank of river Ganges near Kannauj in camp for 2 years when Delhi was reeling under famine.

Which of the statements given above is/are correct?

(a) Only 1 (b) Only 2
(c) Both 1 and 2 (d) Neither 1 nor 2

Ans. *(c)*

Exp. Both the statements (1) and (2) are correct regarding Muhammad bin Tughlaq.

He transferred his capital to Deogir to keep Deccan under control. He renamed Deogir as Daulatabad. However, this initiative was not successful and he again transferred capital to Delhi.

He lived at bank of river Ganges near Kannauj in camp for 2 years when Delhi was suffering from famine.

Tughlaq dynasty was established by the Ghiyas-ud-din Tughlaq (real name was Ghazi Malik) in the year 1320 AD. His son Muhammad bin Tughlaq ascended the throne in 1325 AD.

18 Arrange the following programmes of Muhammad bin Tughlaq in their chronological orders.
(Chap 6, Class-XI, Old NCERT)

1. Transfer of capital
2. Increase in taxation in Doab
3. Promulgation of token currency
4. Khurasan expedition

Codes

(a) 1, 2, 3, 4 (b) 2, 3, 1, 4 (c) 2, 1, 3, 4 (d) 3, 2, 1, 4

Ans. *(c)*

Exp. The correct chronology of Muhammad bin Tughlaq's initiatives is 2, 1, 3, 4 that is Increase in Taxation in Doab, Transfer of capital, Promulgation of token currency, Khurasan Expedition.

After ascending the throne in 1325 AD, his first major initiative was to increase the taxation in Doab region of North India in (1326 AD). His next main initiative was to transfer capital from Delhi to Deogir in 1327 AD.

He then promulgated token currency in 1329 AD. He launched Khurasan expedition in 1329 AD to occupy Khurasan and Iraq.

19 Which of the following statements is correct in the context of territorial expansion under Tughlaq dynasty? *(Chap 7, Class-XI, Old NCERT)*

(a) Bengal was subdued under Delhi Sultanate.
(b) Kampili was annexed in the year 1328.
(c) Territorial expansion on large scale caused administrative and financial problems.
(d) All of the above

Ans. (d)

Exp. All of the above given statements are correct regarding territorial expansion under Tughlaq dynasty. Territorial expansion of Delhi Sultanate reached at zenith during the reign of Muhammad bin Tughlaq. Bengal was subdued under Delhi Sultanate by Muhammad bin Tughlaq. He also annexed Kampili in the year 1328 AD. Territorial expansion on large scale caused administrative and financial problems.

Tughlaq dynasty was the third dynasty of Delhi Sultanate followed by Slave and Khilji dynasty.

20 Qarachil expedition was launched by the Muhammad bin Tughlaq in which of the following region? *(Chap 7, Class-XI, Old NCERT)*

(a) Central Asia
(b) Kumaon region of the Himalayas
(c) Bihar and Bengal
(d) Deccan

Ans. (b)

Exp. Qarachil expedition was launched by the Muhammad bin Tughlaq in 1330 AD in the Kumaon hills in the Himalayas. This expedition was carried out to counter the Chinese incursion.

21 With reference to Muhammad bin Tughlaq, consider the following statements. *(Unit 10, Class-XI, Tamil Nadu Board)*

1. He held religious and philosophical discussions with the Jinaprabha Suri.
2. Bronze coins introduced by him were withdrawn due to devaluation.
3. He died without naming his successors.

How many of the statements given above is/are correct?

(a) Only one (b) Only two
(c) All three (d) None of these

Ans. (c)

Exp. All three statements i.e, (1), (2) and (3) are correct with reference to the Muhammad Bin Tughlaq. He held discussions with the Jain saint Jinaprabha Suri to discuss various issues related with the religious affairs and philosphy.

Bronze coins was introduced by him, these coins replaced with silver coins due to devaluation.

He died without naming his successor. The claim by Muhammad's sister to his son was not supported by the nobles.

22 Assertion (A) Muhammad bin Tughlaq issued a new gold coin which was called Dinar by Ibn Battuta.
Reason (R) Muhammad bin Tughlaq wanted to issue token currency in gold coins to promote trade with West Asian and North African countries. *(Chap 7, Class-XI, Old NCERT) (IAS Pre 2006)*

(a) Both A are R are true and R is the correct explanation of A.
(b) Both A and R are true, but R is not the correct explanation of A.
(c) A is true, but R is false.
(d) A is false, but R is true.

Ans. (c)

Exp. Assertion (A) is true, but Reason (R) is false with reference to Muhammad bin Tughlaq. He issued bronze coins as the token currency which was a great Fiasco.

When Muhammad issued bronze coins, fake coins were minted which could not be prevented by the government. The new coins were devalued to such an extent that the government had to withdraw the bronze coins and replace them with silver coins, which told heavily on the resources of the empire.

23 Consider the following statements with reference to the Firoz Shah Tughlaq. *(Chap 7, Class-XI, Old NCERT)*

1. He adopted policy to appease the nobles.
2. He made no attempt to re-assert his authority over South India and the Deccan.
3. He allowed entry of hereditary system into army and revenue administration.

Which of the statements given above is/are correct?

(a) Only 1 (b) 1 and 2
(c) 2 and 3 (d) 1, 2 and 3

Ans. (d)

Exp. All the given statements are correct with reference of Firoz Shah Tughlaq.

Firoz Shah Tughlaq ascended the throne in the year 1351 AD and reigned till 1388 AD. In order to consolidate the power, he adopted the policy of appeasement towards nobles.

He made no attempt to re-assert his authority over South India and the Deccan.

This was done by him to keep them satisfy and prevent rebellion. He also allowed entry of hereditary system into army and revenue administration.

24 Firoz Shah Tughlaq was one of the most renowned rulers of the Delhi Sultanate. Which of the following works was/were done by him? *(Chap 7, Class-XI, Old NCERT)*

1. He set up a special department for spies.
2. He repaired and dug large number of canals.
3. Hissar in Haryana was established by him.

Codes

(a) Only 1 (b) Only 2
(c) 2 and 3 (d) All of these

Ans. (c)

Exp. Statements (2) and (3) are correct with reference to works done by Firoz Shah Tughlaq. He is known for his large number of initiatives which were launched for the welfare of common people. In agriculture sphere, he repaired and dug large number of canals to increase the irrigation facility. His major canals include Sirsa to Hansi, Sutlej to Hansi and Yamuna to Hisar. He also established many cities throughout the Sultanate; Hisar in Haryana was one among them.

Statement (1) is incorrect because he did not set up any special department for spies.

25 Consider the following statements with reference to the Timur Lang. *(Chap 7, Class-XI, Old NCERT)*

1. He invaded India during the reign of Nasiruddin Tughlaq.
2. After defeating Delhi Sultan, he established Timurid dynasty which ruled for short period of time.

Which of the statements given above is/are incorrect?

(a) Only 1 (b) Only 2
(c) Both 1 and 2 (d) Neither 1 nor 2

***Ans.* (b)**

Exp. Statement (2) is incorrect with reference to Timur Lang because he did not established Timurid dynasty in India. He was from Turk-Mongol ethnicity. He was the ruler and founder of the Timurid empire. His Empire was spread in the region of Central and West Asia.

Sayyid and Lodi Dynasty

26 With reference to the Sayyid dynasty, which of the following statements is/are correct? *(Chap 3, Class-VII, Old NCERT)*

1. It was established as a consequence of Timur's attack.
2. Mubarak Shah was an important ruler of this dynasty.
3. It ruled for shortest period of time among all dynasties.
4. Khizr Khan was the last ruler of this dynasty.

Codes

(a) 1 and 2 (b) 1, 2 and 3 (c) 2, 3 and 4 (d) All of these

***Ans.* (a)**

Exp. Statements (1) and (2) are correct with reference to the Sayyid dynasty. It was the fourth dynasty of Delhi Sultanate. It ruled from 1414 to 1451 AD.

Khizr Khan was the Governor of Multan under the Tughlaq ruler. Later, after the attack of Timur, he was appointed at Delhi by Timur. Then, he laid the foundation of this dynasty.

Mubarak Shah was an important ruler of this dynasty. He was son of Khizr Khan. He ruled from 1434 to 1443 AD. Alauddin Alam Shah was the last ruler of this dynasty, who reigned from 1445 to 1451 AD.

Statements (3) and (4) are incorrect because the Khilji dynasty ruled for the shortest period among all dynasties of Delhi Sultanate. While, Khizr Khan was the first ruler of Sayyid dynasty.

27 Consider the following statements with reference to the Lodi dynasty. *(Chap 4, Class-VII, Old NCERT)*

1. Kingdom of Jaunpur was subdued under the rule of Lodi dynasty.
2. Sikandar Lodi reigned from 1489 to 1520.

Which of the statements given above is/are correct?

(a) Only 1
(b) Only 2
(c) Both 1 and 2
(d) Neither 1 nor 2

***Ans.* (a)**

Exp. Only statement (1) is correct regarding the Lodi dynasty as Bahlol Lodies annexed Sharqi dynasty of Jaunpur and appointed his son Barbak Khan as the Governor of Jaunpur.

Statement (2) is incorrect because Sikandar Lodi was the successor of the Bahlul Lodi. He reigned from 1489 to 1517 AD. He shifted his capital from Delhi to Agra in 1504 AD.

It was the last dynasty of Delhi Sultanate. It came into existence in 1451 AD and ruled till 1526 AD.

Its foundation was laid by Bahlul Lodi. He was invited by the Wazir of last Sayyid ruler to ascend on throne.

28 Consider the following statements with reference to the Lodi dynasty. *(Chap 4, Class-VII, Old NCERT)*

1. Lodi rulers were of Turkish origin.
2. Sikandar Lodi was defeated by the Babur.
3. Nobles discontent towards the last ruler of the Lodi dynasty led to decline of Delhi Sultanate.

How many of the statements given above is/are incorrect?

(a) Only one (b) Only two
(c) All three (d) None of these

***Ans.* (b)**

Exp. Only statements i.e., (1) and (2) are incorrect with reference to the Lodi dynasty because the Lodi rulers were of Afghan origin not Turkish. It was founded by Bahlul Lodi. He declared himself as one of the Afghan peers not the king. He also adopted the title 'Bahlul Shah Ghazi'. Sikandar Lodi was son of Bahlul Lodi. Sikander Lodi was defeated by Raja Man Singh to take control of the Gwalior Fort.

Chapter 14

Delhi Sultanate: Administration, Economy, Society and Arts

Delhi Sultanate: Administration, Economy, Society and Arts

Administration

Central Administration

- Sultan assisted by several ministers who were chosen by him and remained in office at his pleasure
- Wazir was key officer dealing with the revenue affairs

Major Department

- Diwan-i-Risalat (religious affairs)
- Diwan-i-Arz (military)
- Diwan-i-Insha (correspondence)
- Wakil-i-Dar (Roya Household)
- Diwan-i-Amir-Kohi (agriculture)

Army

- Alauddin introduced the branding system (Dagh) of the horses
- Also had largest standing army
- He was also first sultan to pay soldiers in cash
- Ariz-i-Mumalik served as the head of Diwan-i-Arz department

Local Administration

- Divided administration into several Iqtas headed by Muqtis and Walis
- They were responsible to maintain law, order and collect land revenue
- Iqtas later became provinces known as Subas
- It was further divided into shiqs and pargana headed by Shiqdar and Amil respectively
- Villages were administered by Khut (landowners) and Muqaddam (headmen)

Economy

Taxation

- Based on Sharia four kinds of taxes sanctioned
- Zakat - to be paid by Wealthy Muslims for poors welfare
- Jizyah levied on the non-Muslims
- Kharaj-land tax Khams - of the booty captured during war

Types of Land

- **Khalisa** Land directly administered by Central Government
- **Waqf** Land given to Muslim saints and scholar
- **Iqta** Part of land granted by the Sultan to its military chiefs for the maintenance of a given number of troopers

Trade of Industry

- Growth of major cities - Delhi, Lahore, Multan, Kara, Lakhnauti, Anhilwara and Cambay
- Indian textiles were in high demand in West and China
- India imports from West : High grade textiles, items made of silk, gold and silverware
- Gujarat and Bengal important centres for textile trade

Social Life

- Development of feudalism, growing powers of Samanta, Ranak and Rautta (Rajput)
- Existence of poverty, Practice of Sati

Social and Art

Literary Work

- Persian became official language and Urdu was camp language
- Amir Khusrau innovated Khayal, invented tabla, sitar and modified veena. Also wrote — Khazain-ul-Futuh, Nuh-i-Sipihar and Tughlaqnama
- Ibn-Battuta came to India from Morocco during the reign of Muhammad bin Tughlaq. In his work Rihla, he talks about the contemporary social, economic, cultural and religious practices

Architecture

- Emergence of Indo-Islamic architecture
- Use of arch and dome. Tomb of Balban-first true arch and Alai Darwaza - first true dome. Used the combined principle of Slab and Beam method

Caste System

- The caste system continued to be the basis of the society. But there were important changes within the caste system
- Thus, there was considerable strengthening of the position of the Brahmans

Condition of Women

- The practice of sati was made obligatory by some writers, but condemned by others
- According to an Arab writer, Sulaiman wives of kings sometimes burnt themselves on the funeral pyre of their husbands

SOURCE ***Old NCERT Class VII*** *(Kingdom of the North),* ***Old NCERT Class XI*** *(Delhi Sultanate- II),* ***Old NCERT Class XI*** *(Control and Agrarian Policy of Allauddin),* ***Tamil Nadu Board, Class XI*** *(Advent of Arab and Turks),* ***NIOS Module 2*** *(Establishment and Expansion of Delhi Sultanate)*

Central Administration

1 With reference to the central administration during Delhi Sultanate, consider the following statements.
(Chap 4, Class-VII, Old NCERT) (Chap 7, Class-XI, Old NCERT)

1. The Iqta system was the military system under the administration of the Delhi Sultanate.
2. Sahana was the officer who used to collect revenue from the farmers.

How many of the statements given above is/are incorrect?

(a) Only 1 (b) Only 2
(c) Both 1 and 2 (d) Neither 1 nor 2

Ans. (c)

Exp. Both statements (1) and (2) are incorrect with reference to the central administration during the Delhi Sultanate.

The Iqta system was the grant of revenue from a territory. It was an important administrative system of the Delhi Sultanate. This system was mainly developed by the Iltutmish.

During the period of the Delhi Sultanate Sahana was the officer who used to regulate markets.

2 Consider the following pairs.
(Chap 8, Class-XI, Old NCERT)

Department	Responsibility
1. Diwan-i-Arz	– Dealt with military affairs
2. Diwan-i-Insha	– Dealt with state's correspondence
3. Diwan-i-Wizarat	– Dealt with religious affairs

How many of the pairs given above is/are correctly matched?

(a) Only one (b) Only two
(c) All three (d) None of these

Ans. (b)

Exp. Only two pairs i.e., (1) and (2) is/are correctly matched.

Diwan-i-Arz was a military department. It was established by Sultan Balban. It was headed by Ariz-i-Mamalik.

Diwan-i-Insha was department of state correspondence. This department was responsible for sending and receiving correspondence within Sultanate and also outside.

Pair (3) is incorrectly matched because Diwan-i-Wizarat was associated with finance department. It was most important department. It was headed by Wazir (considered as a Prime Minister).

3 What was/were the main reasons behind the introduction of market and other reforms by the Alauddin Khilji? *(Chap 7, Class-XI, Old NCERT)*

1. To collect revenue for raising large army in order to check Mongol invasion.
2. To implement the principle of Sharia law over the non-Muslim population.
3. To ensure supply of cheap food grain to armed forces and common people.

Codes

(a) 1 and 3 (b) 2 and 3
(c) Only 3 (d) All of these

Ans. (a)

Exp. Only reasons mentioned in statements (1) and (3) were responsible for the introduction of market and other reforms by Alauddin Khilji. One among them was market reform. The main objectives behind the market reform were to collect revenue to raise large army in order to check Mongol invasion and ensure supply of cheap food grain to armed forces and common people.He reigned from 1296 to 1316 AD. He introduced many reforms during his reign.

Statement (2) is incorrect because reforms did not aim at implementing the principle of Sharia law over the non-Muslim population.

4 Consider the following statements.
(Chap 8, Class-XI, Old NCERT) (IAS Pre 2019)

1. In the revenue administration of Delhi Sultanate, the in-charge of revenue collection was known as Amil.
2. The Iqta system of Sultans of Delhi was an ancient indigenous institution.
3. The office of Mir Bakshi came into existence during the reign of Khilji Sultans of Delhi.

Which of the statements given above is/are incorrect?

(a) Only 1 (b) 2 and 3
(c) Only 3 (d) 1, 2 and 3

Ans. (b)

Exp. Statements (2) and (3) are incorrect because the Iqta system was mainly introduced by Turkis conqueror. The holders of these offices were called Walis or Muqtis. It was developed by Iltutmish. Thus, it was not an ancient indigenous institution. The office of Mir Bakshi came into existence during the reign of Mughals. It used to head the military department.

5 Match the following lists correctly and choose the correct code. *(Chap 4, Class-VII, Old NCERT)*

List I (Officer)	List II (Assign Duty)
A. Qazi	1. Supervised the accounts
B. Wazir	2. Pay-master
C. Mushrif	3. Chief judge
D. Bakshi	4. Supervised the work of all other officers

Codes

	A	B	C	D
(a)	2	4	1	3
(b)	3	4	1	2
(c)	1	3	2	4
(d)	4	1	2	3

Ans. (b)

Exp. The correct matching is A-3, B-4, C-1 and D-2.
Qazi was chief judge in the administration. He used to listen cases and solved them on the basis of religious texts.
Wazir was responsible for supervising the work of all other officers. It was the highest position in the court.
Mushrif were responsible for supervising the accounts.
Bakshi was associated with military system. He was the pay-master.

6 **Consider the following statements.**
(Chap 8, Class-XI, Old NCERT)

Statement-I Alauddin Khilji was able to contain the Mongol invasions while conquering the Deccan at the same time.
Statement-II Due to reforms, his military system was quite efficient.
Which one of the following is correct in respect of the above statements?
(a) Both Statement-I and Statement-II are correct and Statement-II is the correct explanation for Statement-I.
(b) Both Statement-I and Statement- II are correct and Statement-II is not the correct explanation for Statement-I.
(c) Statement-I is correct and Statement-II is incorrect.
(d) Statement I is incorrect and Statement-II is correct.
Ans. (a)

Exp. Both Statement-I and Statement-II are correct and Statement-II is the correct explanation for Statement-I.
Alauddin Khilji was able to contain the Mongol invasions while conquering the Deccan at the same time. This became possible due to military reforms introduced by Alauddin Khilji, which made his army efficient and disciplined.

Military Department

7 **Consider the following statements.**
(Chap 8, Class-XI, Old NCERT)

1. Ariz-i-Mamalik was Commander-in-Chief of Army.
2. The head of military department was known as Ariz-i-Mamalik.
3. Ariz-i-Mamalik's responsibility included recruitment, equip and pay the army.

How many of the statements given above is/are correct?
(a) Only one (b) Only two
(c) All three (d) None of these
Ans. (b)

Exp. Only two statements i.e., (2) and (3) are correct. The head of military department was known as Ariz-i-Mamalik. His responsibility included recruitment and ensuring provisions of equipment and salary to the army.
Statement (1) is incorrect because Sultan used to be Commander-in-Chief of Army. All other officers were under him.

8 **With reference to the administration of Delhi Sultanate, consider the following statements.**
(Chap 3, Class-VII, New NCERT)

1. Bandagan were special slaves purchased for military service.
2. Muqtis were the landowners of Iqta given by the Sultan.
3. The duty of the Muqtis was to lead military campaigns.

How many of the statements given above is/are incorrect?
(a) Only one (b) Only two
(c) All three (d) None of these
Ans. (d)

Exp. None of the statements given above are incorrect with reference to the administration of Delhi.
During the period of the Delhi Sultanate, the term Bandagan was used in the administration. It refers to special slaves purchased for military service.
Muqtis were the landholders of Iqta (land) given by the Sultan. They were responsible for maintaining law and order in their iqtas.
The duty of the Muqtis was to lead military campaigns whenever summoned by the Sultan for it.

9 **Consider the following statements.**
(Chap 8, Class-XI, Old NCERT)

1. Of all the Delhi rulers, Alauddin Khilji had the largest standing army.
2. Muhammad bin Tughlaq paid great attention to revenue department.

Which of the statements given above is/are correct?
(a) Only 1
(b) Only 2
(c) Both 1 and 2
(d) Neither 1 nor 2
Ans. (c)

Exp. Both the statements (1) and (2) are correct.
Of all the Delhi rulers, Alauddin Khalji had the largest standing army. The strength of his army is placed at 300000 by Barani which appears to be an exaggeration. He was also the first Sultan to pay his soldiers fully in cash.
Muhammad bin Tughlaq paid close attention to revenue department. Hence, he used to give more attention to Wazir (the head of revenue department). His Wazir Khwaja Jahan, was widely respected, and was left in charge of capital when Muhammad bin Tughlaq went out to deal with the rebellions.

10 **Consider the following reforms.**
(Chap 8, Class-XI, Old NCERT)

1. Regular muster of the armed forces
2. Branding (dagh) of the horses
3. Descriptive role of each soldier was maintained
4. Paid salaries in cash

How many of the above reference were introduced by Alauddin Khilji?

(a) Only one (b) Only two
(c) Only three (d) All four

Ans. (d)

Exp. All the reforms given in the question were introduced by Alauddin Khilji. Alauddin Khilji introduced many reforms in military administration to cherish his dream of becoming Sikandar-i-Sani (Second Alexander the Great). For this, he implemented regular muster of the armed forces, branding (dagh) of the horses, descriptive role of each soldier was maintained and they were paid salaries in cash. These steps enhanced efficiency of the army.

11 Consider the following statements in the context of spies system in Delhi. *(Chap 8, Class-XI, Old NCERT)*

1. The rulers posted intelligence agents were called Barids.
2. Wazir also served as the head of intelligence department.

Which of the statements given above is/are correct?

(a) Only 1 (b) Only 2
(c) Both 1 and 2 (d) Neither 1 nor 2

Ans. (a)

Exp. Statement (1) is correct in the context of spies system in the Delhi Sultanate. The rulers posted intelligence agents were called Barids in different parts of the empire to keep themselves informed.

Statement (2) is incorrect because Barid-i-Mumalik was the head of Intelligence department. Only a nobleman who enjoyed the fullest confidence of Sultan was appointed as Chief Braid.

Revenue System and Local Administration

12 Consider the following statements with reference to the administration under the Delhi Sultanate. *(Chap 4, Class-VII, Old NCERT)*

1. Generally the amount of land revenue was fixed at one-third of the total produce.
2. Muqaddam was the hereditary headman of the villages.
3. Gaj-e-Sikandari was introduced by Alauddin Khilji as a measurement of land.

How many of the statements given above is/are correct?

(a) Only one (b) Only two
(c) All three (d) None of these

Ans. (b)

Exp. Only two statements i.e., (1) and (2) are correct regarding the administration under Delhi Sultanate. Land revenue was the main source of revenue for the kingdoms of the medieval period. Generally, the amount of land revenue was fixed at one-third of the total produce. However, it kept on changing under different rulers.

Muqaddam was the hereditary headman of the villages. They were responsible for collecting tax. They were like zamindars. During the reign of Alauddin Khilji, their power was curbed.

Statement (3) is incorrect because Sikandar Lodi introduced Gaj-e-Sikandari as a measurement of land, in his kingdom.

13 Consider the following statements. *(Unit 10 & 12, Class-XI, Tamil Nadu Board) (IAS Pre 2021)*

1. It was during the reign of Iltutmish that Genghis Khan reached the Indus in pursuit of the fugitive Khwarizm prince.
2. It was during the reign of Muhammad bin Tughluq that Taimur occupied Multan and crossed the Indus.
3. It was during the reign of Deva Raya II of Vijayanagara Empire that Vasco da Gama reached the coast of Kerala.

Which of the statements given above is/are correct?

(a) Only 1 (b) 1 and 2
(c) Only 3 (d) 2 and 3

Ans. (a)

Exp. Statement (1) is correct. It was during the reign of Iltutmish that Genghis Khan reached the Indus in pursuit of the fugitive Khwarizm prince. Genghis Khan attacked the Khwarizm Prince Jalaluddin Magbrani, who sought refuge in the court of Iltutmish but Iltutmish decided not the give refuge to Jalalauddin, and hence he avoided the invasion of Genghis Khan to India.

Statements (2) and (3) are incorrect because Taimur invaded India in 1398. During this period, Nasiruddin Muhammad Tughlaq was the ruler and not Muhammad bin Tughlaq (1325-1350).

Vasco da Gama came to India in 1498. He was welcomed by the ruler of Calicut-Manna Vikrama also called as Zamorin. Krishnadeva Raya, the Vijayanagara ruler came to power in 1509 onwards.

14 With reference to Delhi Sultanate, consider the following statements. *(Chap 8, Class-XI, Old NCERT)*

1. The term Rahat was associated with irrigation.
2. Zawabits were secular decrees issued by the kings.

Which of the statements given above is/are correct?

(a) Only 1
(b) Only 2
(c) Both 1 and 2
(d) Neither 1 nor 2

Ans. (c)

Exp. Both the statements (1) and (2) are correct with reference to Delhi Sultanate.

During the period of Delhi Sultanate, the term Rahat was associated with irrigation. It was an improved version of Persian wheel which helped in lifting the water from deeper levels.

During the period of the Delhi Sultanate, Zawabits were concerned with state laws. These are also known as secular decrees issued by the King. It was non-shariat state laws which was made according to the needs of the state.

15 **With reference to the economy of Delhi Sultanate, consider the following pairs.**

(Chap 8, Class-XI, Old NCERT)

Taxes		Description
1. Zakat	–	Paid by well to do Muslims.
2. Kharaj	–	Land tax paid by Hindus
3. Sharab	–	An irrigation tax
4. Khums	–	Part of the booty captured during war.

How many of the pairs given above is/are correctly matched?

(a) Only one (b) Only two
(c) Only three (d) All four

Ans. (d)

Exp. All four pairs i.e., (1), (2), (3) and (4) are correctly matched with reference to the economy of the Delhi Sultanate.

Zakat To be paid by wealthy Muslims for helping the needy peoples.

Kharaj Land tax paid mainly by Hindus which was equal to 1/10th of the produce of land.

Khums It was 1/6th of the booty captured during the war. Abwabs Excess taxes like house tax, grazing tax, etc.

Sharab is an irrigation tax.

16 **With reference to the economy of the Delhi Sultanate, consider the following statements.**

(Unit 10, Class-XI, Tamil Nadu Board)

Statement-I India's external trade, both overland and oceanic, declined significantly during this period.

Statement-II Mongol raids and conquest of the western Borderlands posed a critical threat to the sultanate.

Which one of the following is correct in respect of the above statements?

(a) Both Statement-II and Statement-II are correct and Statement-II is the correct explanation for Statement-I.
(b) Both Statement-I and Statement-II are correct and Statement-II is not the correct explanation for Statement-I.
(c) Statement-I is correct, but Statement-II is incorrect.
(d) Statement-I is incorrect, but Statement-II is correct.

Ans. (d)

Exp. Statement-I is incorrect, but Statement-II is correct. Despite the Mongol conquests of the Western borderlands, in the view of Historian Irfan Habib, India's external trade, both overland and oceanic, grew considerably during the period of Delhi Sultanate.

This can be attested by the fact that The Delhi Sultans began their gold and silver mintage alongside copper from early in the 13th century and that indicated brisk commerce.

Also in the 14th century, Delhi and Daulatabad (Devagiri) emerged as great cities of the world. There were other large towns such as Multan, Kara, Awadh, Gaur, Cambay (Khambayat) and Gulbarga.

17 **With reference to the economy of the Delhi Sultanate, consider the following statements.**

(Class-XI, Old NCERT)

1. Payment of land tax to the level of rent in cash was one of the changes introduced during this period.
2. This period was marked by the existence of a great number of trade guilds.
3. Yarn production increased greatly by discovery of spinning wheels in Bengal in the 14th century.

How many of the statements given above is/are incorrect?

(a) Only one (b) Only two
(c) All three (d) None of these

Ans. (b)

Exp. Only two statements i.e., (2) and (3) are incorrect with reference to the economy of Delhi Sultanate.

There is no evidence of the existence of trade guilds, which had played a crucial role in the economy in the classical age.

The spinning wheel invented by the Chinese came to India through Iran in the 14th century and enabled the spinner to increase her output some six-fold and enlarged yarn production greatly.

Economic/Social/Religious Status

18 **With reference to the economy of Delhi Sultanate, consider the following statements.**

(Class-XI, Old NCERT)

1. Tanka and Jital were the main currencies during the Sultanate period.
2. Dirham used during the Sultanate period was made of gold.
3. Jaunpur was the largest city during the Sultanate period.

How many of the statements given above is/are incorrect?

(a) Only one (b) Only two
(c) All three (d) None of these

Ans. (b)

Exp. Only two statements i.e., (2) and (3) are incorrect with reference to the Economy of Delhi Sultanate.

Dirham was made up of silver not gold, it was promoted by Muhammad bin Tughlaq.

Delhi was the largest city during the Sultanate period.

19 Consider the following statements.
(Chap 8, Class-XI, Old NCERT)

1. Road from Peshawar to Sonargaon was built by Muhammad bin Tughlaq.
2. Canbay and Anhilware were the centre of Mercantile activities of Khurasanis and Iranians.
3. Relay system was used for posts.

Which of the statements given above is/are correct?

(a) Only 1 (b) 1 and 2 (c) 2 and 3 (d) 1, 2 and 3

Ans. (d)

Exp. All the statements are correct.

Road from Peshawar to Sonargaon was built by Muhammad bin Tughlaq. Canbay and Anhilwara along with Delhi, Lahore, Multan, Kara Lakhnauti and Daultabad were important cities that thrived on Mercantile activities of Jain Marwari, Hindu Multains and Muslim Bohras, Khurasanis, Afghans and Iranians Relay system was used for ports. During the period of Delhi Sultanate, attention was also paid towards the improvement of the means of transportation and communication.

20 Consider the following statements with reference to the society of Sultanate period.
(Chap 8, Class-XI, Old NCERT)

1. Muslim law Sharia was also imposed on Hindus.
2. Hindu masses received the status of zimmis.

Which of the statements given above is/are correct?

(a) Only 1 (b) Only 2
(c) Both 1 and 2 (d) Neither 1 nor 2

Ans. (b)

Exp. Statement (2) is correct with reference to society of Sultanate period. During the Sultanate period, Hindu masses received the status of zimmis. It was a term used for non-Muslims living in an Islamic state with legal protection.

Statement (1) is incorrect because Muslim law Sharia was not imposed on Hindus. It was only imposed on Muslims.

21 The historian Barani refused to consider the state in India under Delhi Sultans as truly Islamic because
(Chap 8, Class-XI, Old NCERT)

(a) majority of the population did not follow Islam.
(b) the Muslim theologist were often disregarded.
(c) the Sultan supplemented the Muslim Law by framing his regulations.
(d) the religious freedom was accorded to non-Muslims.

Ans. (a)

Exp. The historian Barani refused to consider the state in India under Delhi Sultans as truly Islamic because majority of the population did not follow Islam. He further stated that during Sultanate period, the Islamic or Shariat laws were not being only followed but it was based on worldly or secular considerations also. He was the author of Tarikh-i-Firoz Shahi (also called Tarikh-i-Firuz Shahi). He was contemporary to Muhammad bin Tughlaq and Firuz Shah.

22 With reference to the account provided by the Ibn Battuta, which of the following statements is/are correct?
(Chap 8, Class-XI, Old NCERT)

1. He said only one crop was produced in a year
2. He gave account of roads.
3. He also shed light on the life of people.

Codes

(a) Only 1 (b) 1 and 2 (c) 2 and 3 (d) 1, 2 and 3

Ans. (c)

Exp. Statements (2) and (3) are correct with reference to the account provided by the Ibn Battuta.

Ibn Battuta was Moroccan traveller who visited India during the reign of Muhammad bin Tughlaq. In his travelogue, Rihla, he had mentioned various socio-economic information of India. He gave account of roads. He also shed light on the life of people.

Statement (1) is incorrect because he said that crops were grown twice in a year.

23 Consider the following statements.
(Chap 4, Class-VII, Old NCERT)

1. In Delhi Sultanate, Indian Muslims were not appointed as the officer.
2. Noble influenced the state policy.
3. Most of the nobles were of Turkish or Afghan in origin.

Which of the statements given above is/are correct?

(a) Only 1 (b) 1 and 2 (c) 2 and 3 (d) 1, 2 and 3

Ans. (c)

Exp. Statements (2) and (3) are correct. Nobles were most important official in the State after Sultan in the Delhi Sultanate. They played a key role in the administration and influenced the state policy. Most of the nobles were of Turkish or Afghan in origin.

Statement (1) is incorrect because Indian Muslims were also appointed as the officer in Delhi Sultanate.

24 With reference to the Mongol attack, which of the following statements is/are correct?
(Chap 3, Class-VII, New NCERT)

1. The Mongols under Genghis Khan invaded Transoxiana in North-East Iran in 1219 AD.
2. Mongol attacks on the Delhi Sultanate increased during the reign of Alauddin Khilji.

Codes

(a) Only 1 (b) Only 2
(c) Both 1 and 2 (d) Neither 1 nor 2

Ans. (c)

Exp. Both the statements (1) and (2) are correct with reference to the Mongol attack.

The Mongols under Genghis Khan invaded Transoxiana in North-East Iran in 1219 AD. Genghis Khan was most powerful Mongol ruler. He came to power by uniting many of the nomadic tribes of North-East Asia.

Mongol attacks on the Delhi Sultanate increased during the reign of Alauddin Khilji. In 1305 Mangols were defeated in Battle of Amroha and in 1306 near river Ravi by the forces of Alauddin Khilji.

25 **Consider the following statements with reference to the Khwarizmi Empire.** *(Chap 6, Class-XI, Old NCERT)*

1. The boundaries of Khwarizmi Empire reached the river Indus.
2. Many battles were fought between Khwarizmi Empire and Delhi Sultanate over territorial expansion.
3. Genghis Khan destroyed the Khwarizmi Empire in 1320 AD.

Which of the statements given above is/are incorrect?

(a) Only 1 (b) 1 and 2
(c) Only 2 (d) 1, 2 and 3

Ans. (c)

Exp. Statement (2) is incorrect with reference to Khwarizmi Empire because battles were not fought between Khwarizmi Empire and Delhi Sultanate over territorial expansion.

26 **Consider the following statements regarding Alauddin Khilji.** *(Chap 6, Class-XI, Old NCERT)*

1. He set up three distinct markets one for food grains, one for cloth and the third for horses.
2. A Shahna was posted in the market.
3. The Peasants had to pay land revenue in kind.
4. Slaves were transacted in market during his time.

Which of the following are correct?

(a) 1, 2 and 3 (b) 2, 3 and 4
(c) 1, 2 and 4 (d) 1 and 4

Ans. (c)

Exp. Statements (1), (2) and (4) are correct. Alauddin's measures to control the markets were one of the most important policy initiatives.

Since, Alauddin wanted to maintain a large army, he, therefore, lowered and fixed the price of the commodities of daily use. To control the prices, he set up three different markets for different commodities in Delhi. Each market was under the control of a higher officer called Shahna who maintained a register of merchants and strictly controlled the shopkeepers and the prices. Slaves were transacted in market during his time. Peasant has to pay taxes in cash.

27 **Assertion (A)** The scheme of the token currency of Muhammad bin Tughlaq proved unsuccessful.

Reason (R) Muhammad bin Tughlaq did not have the proper control over currency issue.

(Chap 6, Class-XI, Old NCERT)

Codes

(a) Both A and R are true and R is the correct explanation of A.
(b) Both A and R are true, but R is not the correct explanation of A.
(c) A is true, but R is false.
(d) A is false, but R is true.

Ans. (a)

Exp. Both Assertion (A) and Reason (R) are true and Reason (R) is the correct explanation of Assertion (A).

In 1330 AD, after his failed expedition to Deogiri, Muhammad bin Tughlaq issued token currency, that is coins of brass and copper were minted, whose value was equal to that of gold and silver coins.

Barani had also written that the Sultan's treasury had been exhausted by his action of giving rewards and gifts in gold. In the rural areas, officials like the Muqaddams paid the revenue in brass and copper coins and also used the same coins to purchase arms and horses. As a result, the value of coins decreased and the coins became 'as worthless as stones'. This also disrupted trade and commerce. The token currency had inscriptions in Persian and Arabic marking the use of new coins instead of the royal seal and so, the citizens could not distinguish between the official and the forged coins. Finally Muhammad -bin Tughlaq decided to withdraw the token currency.

Chapter 15

Vijayanagara and Bahmani Empire

Vijayanagara and Bahmani Empire

Vijayanagara Empire

Sangama Dynasty (1336-1485 AD)
- First dynasty of Vijayanagara Empire founded by Harihara I and Bukka I in 1336 AD
- Harihara I founded city of Vijayanagara and annexed Hoysala state
- Harihara II assumed titles such as Raja Parmeshwara and annexed Belgaum and Goa from Bahmani kingdom
- Deva Raya I was defeated by Bahmani Sultan Firoz Shah

Saluva Dynasty (1485-1505 AD)
- Founded by Saluva Narasimha
- He conquered the Western part of Kannada, Honnavar, Bakanur and Bhatkal

Tuluva Dynasty (1505-1570 AD)
- Founded by Vira Narasimha
- Krishnadeva Raya defeated rulers of Orissa and Bijapur
- He wrote Usha Parinayam and Jambavati Kalyanam in Sanskrit and Amuktamalyada in Telugu
- Adopted the title of Yavanaraja Sthapanacharya and Abhinava Bhoja Krishnaswamy, Hazara Ramaswamy and Vittalaswami were some of famous temples built by Sri Krishnadevaraya

Aravidu Dynasty (1570-1652 AD)
- Founded by Tirumala II who also shifted his capital from Hampi to Penugonda

Bahmani Empire

Introduction
- First independent Islamic kingdom in South India
- Founded by Alauddin Hasan Bahman Shah in 1347 AD with its capital at Gulbarga
- Later, on this kingdom split into five independent kingdoms – Bijapur, Ahmednagar, Berar, Bidar and Golconda

Prominent Bahmani Kings
- **Muhammad Shah** (1358-1375 AD) Established a Council of eight ministers known as 'Ashta-Pradhan'
- **Ahmad Shah I** (1422-1435 AD) Associated with Sufi Saint Gesu Daraz invaded Warangal and shifted the capital from Gulbarga to Bidar in 1429 AD
- **Alauddin Humayun** (1458-1461 AD) Appointed Mahmud Gawan as Prime Minister who introduced gunpowder in India and also built Mahmud Gawan Madrasa in Bidar
- **Muhammad Shah III** (1463-1482 AD) Last ruler of Bahmani kingdom
- **Decline of Bahmani Empire** After the death of Mahmud Gawan, the nobles were divided into the native and long established Dakhanis and the new-comers Afaqis

Other Features of Vijayanagara Empire

Central Administration
- Kings assisted by Council of Ministers enjoyed absolute authority in executive, judicial and legislative matters

Provincial/Local Administration
- Kingdom was divided into Mandalam (provinces)-Nadu (district) - Sthala (sub-district) and Grama (village)
- Nayakara were a category of officers appointed by the king with rights overland and assigned a piece of land called Amaram

Revenue Administration
- Crown land-most important source of revenue
- Taxes were collected on basis of assessment fixed after thorough survey

Society
- Considerable growth of towns and urbanisation
- High position of Brahmins and position of women was fairly high

Economic Condition
- Agricultural prosperity, development of textiles, mining and metallurgy industries
- Promotion of guilds, cloth, rice, iron, saltpetre, sugar and spices were exported

Art and Architecture
- Addition of pillared halls, Pavilions, Raya Gopuram and sculptures in temples
- Mahanavami Dibba a rectangular shaped structure was built during the reign of Krishnadevaraya

SOURCE *Old NCERT Class XI* (The Age of Vijayanagara and the Bahmani's and the Coming of the Portuguese), *Old NCERT Class XI* (Struggle for Empire in North India), *New NCERT Class XII* (The Imperial Capital Vijayanagara), *Tamil Nadu Board, Class XII* (Bahmani and Vijayanagara Kingdom), *NIOS Module 2* (Emergency of Regional States in India)

Vijayanagara Empire

1 Which of the following statements is/are incorrect in the context of Harihara and Bukka? *(Chap 9, Class-XI, Old NCERT)*

(a) Harihara and Bukka were enslaved by Firuz Shah Tughlaq.
(b) They established Vijayanagara Empire in the year 1436.
(c) They belonged to Sangama dynasty.
(d) Both a and b

Ans. (d)

Exp. Both the statements (a) and (b) are incorrect in the context of Harihara and Bukka because Harihara and Bukka were enslaved by Muhammad bin Tughlaq. It was happened when Kampili (Kingdom in Deccan) was attacked by Tughlaq for giving refuge to Muslim rebel.

They established Vijayanagara Empire in the year 1336 AD and its capital at Hampi, located on Tungabhadra river.

2 With reference to Harihara and Bukka, which of the following statements is/are incorrect? *(Chap 9, Class-XI, Old NCERT)*

1. They had been feudatories of the Yadavas of Devagiri.
2. They also served as the ministers in the Kingdom of Kampili.

Codes

(a) Only 1 (b) Only 2
(c) Both 1 and 2 (d) Neither 1 nor 2

Ans. (a)

Exp. Statement (1) is incorrect with reference to Harihara and Bukka because Harihara and Bukka had been feudatories (person who holds land under the conditions of the feudal system) of the Kakatiyas of Warangal.

3 Consider the following statements with reference to Harihara and Bukka. *(Chap 9, Class-XI, Old NCERT)*

1. They were imprisoned by Muhammad bin Tughlaq and later converted to Islam by him.
2. Saint Vidyasagar inspired them to lay the foundation of Vijayanagara Empire.

Which of the statements given above is/are correct?

(a) Only 1
(b) Only 2
(c) Both 1 and 2
(d) Neither 1 nor 2

Ans. (a)

Exp. Statement (1) is correct with reference to Harihara and Bukka. They were the Ministers in the Kingdom of Kampili (modern Karnataka).

The Kampili Kingdom was attacked by Muhammad bin Tughlaq for giving refuge to a Muslim rebel. In this course of action, they were imprisoned and converted to Islam by him.

Statement (2) incorrect because after a short time, Harihara and Bukka forsook their new master and their new faith. At the instance of their Guru Vidyaranya, they were re-admitted to Hinduism and laid the foundation of Vijayanagara Kingdom.

4 Consider the following statements. *(Chap 9, Class-XI, Old NCERT)*

1. Harihara and Bukka merged Hoysala Kingdom with their empire.
2. Bukka succeeded Harihara in the year 1356 AD.
3. Under Harihara and Bukka, Vijayanagara empire was kind of cooperative society.

Which of the statements given above is/are correct?

(a) Only 1 (b) 1 and 2 (c) 2 and 3 (d) 1, 2 and 3

Ans. (d)

Exp. All the given statements (1), (2) and (3) are correct. Harihara and Bukka merged Hoysala Kingdom with their empire. This merger was held when Hoysala ruler was badly defeated by the Sultan of Madurai.

Harihara was the first ruler of the Vijayanagara Empire. He was succeeded by Bukka in the year 1356 AD who ruled till 1377 AD.

Under Harihara and Bukka, Vijayanagara Empire was kind of cooperative society. It means that the central authority was weak and ruler coordinated with other feudal chief in order to run the administration.

5 Consider the following statements with reference to the Harihara II. *(Chap 9, Class-XI, Old NCERT)*

1. He reigned from 1377 to 1418 AD.
2. He embarked on policy of extension towards Eastern coast.
3. He also sent an expedition to Northern Sri Lanka.

Which of the statements given above is/are incorrect?

(a) Only 1 (b) 1 and 2 (c) 2 and 3 (d) 1, 2 and 3

Ans. (a)

Exp. Statement (1) is incorrect with reference to the Harihara II because he reigned from 1377 to 1404 AD. He was the successor of Bukka I. He was the first ruler of Vijayanagara Empire to assume the title of Raja Parmeshwara and Maharajadhiraja.

6 With reference to Deva Raya I, consider the following statements. *(Chap 9, Class-XI, Old NCERT)*

1. He constructed dam on Tungabhadra river.
2. The famous Hazara temple was built during the reign of Deva Raya I.
3. He inducted Muslims archers in the army.

How many of the statements given above is/are correct?

(a) Only one (b) Only two
(c) All three (d) None of these

Ans. (b)

Exp. Only two statements i.e., (1) and (2) are correct with reference to Deva Raya I. He launched different initiative for the welfare of his subjects such as construction of dam on Tungabhadra river for the purpose of irrigation and also, large numbers of canals were constructed. He also built a dam on the river Haridra.

Hazara Rama Temple was also built during his reign. Statement (3) is incorrect because Deva Raya II inducted Muslims archers in the army not Deva Raya I. Deva Raya I emphasised on the modernisation of the army.

7 Consider the following statements.

(Chap 9, Class-XI, Old NCERT)

1. Vijayanagara ruler Deva Raya II received tribute from king of Sri Lanka.
2. Deva Raya II is popularly known as 'Gajabetekara'.

Which of the statements given above is/are correct?

(a) Only 1 (b) Only 2

(c) Both 1 and 2 (d) Neither 1 nor 2

***Ans.* (c)**

Exp. Both the statements (1) and (2) are correct regarding Deva Raya II. Vijayanagara ruler Deva Raya II received tribute from king of Sri Lanka. Nuniz, a Portuguese writer of 16th century tells that the Kings of Quilon, Sri Lanka, Pulicat, Pegu and Tenasserim (Burma and Malaya) also paid tribute to Deva Raya II.

Deva Raya II (1425 to 1446 AD) was a great elephant hunter. Hence, he is popularly known as 'Gajabetekara'.

8 Which one of the following statements is incorrect about King Krishnadeva Raya is?

(Chap 9, Class-XI, Old NCERT)

(a) He was a great scholar of Telugu and Sanskrit.

(b) Foreign travellers Paes and Nuniz visited his court.

(c) Barbosa praised him for the great justice and equity prevailing in his empire.

(d) He belonged to Saluva dynasty.

***Ans.* (d)**

Exp. Statement (d) is incorrect about the King Krishnadeva Raya because he belonged to Tuluva dynasty of Vijayanagara Empire. He reigned from 1509 to 1530 AD. He was successor of Viranarasimha. He was a great scholar of Telugu and Sanskrit. He wrote Ushaparinayam and Jambavati Kalayana in Sanskrit and Amuktamalyada in Telugu. Foreign travellers Paes and Nuniz visited his court. Barbosa praised him for the great justice and equity prevailing in his empire.

9 Consider the following statements with reference to the King Krishnadeva Raya.

(Chap 9, Class-XI, Old NCERT)

1. He compelled ruler of Orissa to subdue.
2. In order to fight with Portuguese, he raised a strong navy.

Which of the statements given above is/are correct?

(a) Only 1 (b) Only 2

(c) Both 1 and 2 (d) Neither 1 nor 2

***Ans.* (a)**

Exp. Statement (1) is correct with reference to the King Krishnadeva Raya because King Krishnadeva Raya was successful in compelling the Gajapati ruler Prataparudra of Orissa in 1513 AD to subdue.

He also launched military expedition against the Bijapur frontier in 1512 AD and took possession of Raichur. Statement (2) is incorrect because in order to fight with Portuguese, he did not raise a strong navy instead he maintained friendly relations with the Portuguese and granted them some concessions.

He gave permission to British to build a fort at Bhatkal, which was granted after the Portuguese had captured Goa from the Muslims.

10 Read the given description.

(Chap 7, Class-XII, New NCERT)

A king should improve the harbours of his country and so encourage its commerce that horses, elephants, precious gems, sandalwood, pearls and other articles are freely imported..... .

This statement was made by which of the following Vijayanagara rulers in his book?

(a) Krishnadeva Raya (b) Narasimha

(c) Deva Raya II (d) Tirumala

***Ans.* (a)**

Exp. The given statement was made by Vijayanagara ruler Krishnadeva Raya. He was a great patron of art and literature. In his court, he gave patronage to Ashtadiggajas (8 famous scholars of Telugu).

11 With reference to the India of the fourteenth century, consider the following statements.

(Unit 12, Class-XI, Tamil Nadu Board)

1. Expeditions of Malik Kafur brought defeat to Kakatiyas of Warangal and Hoysalas of Dvarasamudra.
2. Shifting of capital back to Delhi was followed by the declaration of Independence by the Subordinate of Muhammad Tughlaq in the South.

Which of the statements given above is/are incorrect?

(a) Only 1 (b) Only 2

(c) Both 1 and 2 (d) Neither 1 nor 2

***Ans.* (c)**

Exp. Both the statements (1) and (2) are correct with reference to India of the fourteenth century. During the two expeditions of the general Malik Kafur, first in 1304 and then in 1310, the Yadavas of Devagiri (Western Deccan or present Maharashtra), the Hoysalas of Dvarasamudra (Karnataka), the Kakatiyas of Warangal (Eastern part of present Telengana) and the Pandyas of Madurai (Southern Tamil Nadu) faced defeat one after another and lost most of their accumulated wealth to the plundering raids of the Sultanate army.

When Muhammad Tughlaq (1325-51) shifted the capital back to Delhi, his subordinates in the South declared independence. Thus Madurai became an independent Sultanate in 1333.

12 With reference to the Bahmani Sultanate and Vijayanagara kingdom consider the following statements. *(Chap 9, Class-XI, Old NCERT)*

1. Konkan became a point of contention between them as strategic ports of Goa were located here.
2. Both wanted to control the fertile Krishna-Tungabhadra Doab.

Which of the statements given above is/are correct?

(a) Only 1 (b) Only 2
(c) Both 1 and 2 (d) Neither 1 nor 2

Ans. (c)

Exp. Both the statements (1) and (2) are correct with reference to Bahmani Sultanate and Vijayanagara kingdom. Both the Bahmani Sultanate and Vijayanagara kingdom fought for the control over the Konkan region because of its fertile land and location of Goa (strategic port) in this region.

The bone of contention between the Bahmani Sultanate and Vijayanagara Kingdom was Krishna-Tungabhadra Doab because of its fertile land.

13 With reference to the Vijayanagara Kingdom consider the following statements. *(Unit 12, Class-XI, Tamil Nadu Board)*

1. Its ruler adopted the emblem of the Chalukyas.
2. Pandya country was not annexed to the Vijayanagara kingdom.
3. Krishna river was the dividing line between the Vijayanagara kingdom and Bahmani kingdom.

How many of the statements given above is/are incorrect?

(a) Only one (b) Only two
(c) All three (d) None of these

Ans. (a)

Exp. Only one statement i.e., (2) is incorrect with reference to Vijayanagara Kingdom. The Pandya country including Madurai was not annexed to the Vijayanagara Kingdom in the beginning however.

It became a part of the Kingdom only around 1500. Until then only the Northern and central parts of the Tamil country up to the Kaveri Delta were under the direct administration of the Sangama and Saluva dynasties.

14 With reference to Vijayanagara Kingdom, consider the following statements. *(Chap 7, Class-XI, New NCERT)*

1. Nicolo Conti was a Portuguese traveller who visited the Vijayanagara empire.
2. Remains of the Vijayanagara empire are found in Hampi.

Which of the statements given above is/are incorrect?

(a) Only 1 (b) Only 2
(c) Both 1 and 2 (d) Neither 1 nor 2

Ans. (a)

Exp. Statement (1) is incorrect with reference to the Vijayanagara Empire. Nicolo Conti was an Italian traveller who visited Vijayanagara empire during the reign of Deva Raya II. In his travelogue, he said that Vijayanagara is covered with lofty and massive stone walls everywhere across the valleys and mounted over the hillsides.

15 Consider the following statements with reference to Krishnadeva Raya. *(Chap 7, Class-XII, New NCERT)*

1. During his reign, the land between the Tungabhadra and Krishna rivers (the Raichur doab) was acquired.
2. He composed a work on statecraft in Telugu known as the Amuktamalyada.
3. He also founded a suburban township near Vijayanagara called Nagalapuram after his father.

Which of the statements given above is/are incorrect?

(a) Only 1 (b) 1 and 2
(c) 2 and 3 (d) 1, 2 and 3

Ans. (c)

Exp. Statements (2) and (3) are incorrect regarding Krishnadeva Raya because his literary work 'Amuktamalyada' was based on the story of Andal rather than on statecraft. He also founded a suburban township near Vijayanagara called Nagalapuram after his mother. During his reign, famous Vittalaswamy and Tirupati temples were built.

16 Consider the following statements. *(Chap 7, Class-XII, New NCERT)*

1. He adopted the adventurous policy to play off various Muslim powers against one another.
2. This policy led the Sultans to combine together and decisively defeat him.

Which of the following personality is mentioned in the above statements?

(a) Krishnadeva Raya
(b) Bukka III
(c) Sadasiva Raya
(d) Rama Raya

Ans. (d)

Exp. The given statements are associated with the Vijayanagara de facto ruler Rama Raya. He was regent of King Sadasiva Raya (1543-1567 AD). He adopted the adventurous policy to play off one Sultan against another when Sultans understood his policy, they joined hand together and defeated him. He was killed in the Battle of Talikota. He was son-in-law of Emperor Krishnadeva Raya and the progenitor (procreator) of the Aravidu dynasty of Vijayanagara Empire.

17 **Consider the following statements.**

(Chap 7, Class-XII, New NCERT)

1. The Vijayanagara kings claimed to rule on behalf of God Virupaksha.
2. Vijayanagara kings also used the little 'Hindu Suratrana'.

Which of the statements given above is/are correct?

(a) Only 1 (b) Only 2
(c) Both 1 and 2 (d) Neither 1 nor 2

Ans. (c)

Exp. Both the statements (1) and (2) are correct. The Vijayanagara Kings claimed to rule on behalf of God Virupaksha. Virupaksha was recognised as the form of Lord Shiva. A famous Virupaksha temple was also built by Lakkana Dandesha, a nayaka (Chieftain) under the ruler Deva Raya II.

Vijayanagara rulers also indicated their close links with the gods by using the title 'Hindu Suratrana'. This was a sanskritisation of the Arabic term sultan, meaning king, so it literally meant 'Hindu Sultan.'

18 **With reference to the Vijayanagara Empire consider the following pairs.**

(Chap 9, Class-XI, Old NCERT)

Traveller		King
1. Abdur Razzaq	–	Deva Raya II
2. Nuniz	–	Achyuta Raya
3. Barbosa	–	Deva Raya I

How many of the pairs given above is/are correctly matched?

(a) Only one
(b) Only two
(c) All three
(d) None of the above

Ans. (b)

Exp. Only two pairs i.e., (1) and (2) are correctly matched with reference to Vijayanagara Empire. Abdur Razzaq visited Vijayanagara Empire during the reign of Deva Raya II.

Nuniz visited Vijayanagara during the reign of Achyuta Raya. He was a portuguese traveller.

Pair (3) is incorrectly matched because Barbosa visited Vijayanagara during the reign of Krishnadeva Raya.

He was Portuguese writer and explorer. He had given a vivid account of governance of Vijayanagara under Krishnadeva Raya in his book.

19 **Arrange the following in the correct chronology (From earliest to latest).** *(Chap 7, Class-XII, New NCERT)*

1. Tuluva 2. Sangama
3. Saluva

Codes

(a) 1, 2, 3 (b) 2, 3, 1
(c) 3, 2, 1 (d) 2, 1, 3

Ans. (b)

Exp. The correct chronology of dynasties of Vijayanagara Empire from earliest to latest is 2, 3, 1 i.e., Sangama (1336-1485), Saluva (1485-1505) and Tuluva (1491-1570). Sangama dynasty was established by the Harihara and Bukka year in 1336 AD. Saluva dynasty was established by the Narasimha in 1485 AD and came to end in 1505 AD. Then, Tuluva dynasty came into existence, which remained in power since 1570.

20 **Consider the following statements.**

(Chap 9, Class-XI, Old NCERT)

1. Deva Raya II was the ruler of Sangama dynasty
2. Krishna Dev Raya was the ruler of Saluva dynasty
3. Sadasiva Raya was the ruler of Tuluva dynasty

Which of the statements given above is/are correct?

(a) 1 and 2 (b) 2 and 3 (c) 1 and 3 (d) 1, 2 and 3

Ans. (c)

Exp. Statements (1) and (3) are correct. Deva Raya II was the ruler of Sangama Dynasty. He ruled from 1424 to 1446 AD.

Sadasiva Raya was the ruler of Tuluva Dynasty. He ruled from 1542 to 1570 AD.

Statement (2) is incorrect because Krishna Dev Raya was the ruler of Tuluva dynasty. He ruled from 1509 to 1529 AD.

Administration

21 **With reference to the Administration of the Vijayanagara Empire, consider the following statements.** *(C1ass-XI, Old NCERT)*

1. Assignment of revenue yielding territory in return for military service was a common feature of Delhi Sultanate, Kakatiya Kingdom and Vijayanagara Empire.
2. The practice of Nayaktanam became established during the reign of Krishnadeva Raya and Achyuta Devaraya.
3. Practice of Nayaktanam is supported by the evidence of Nunis and Peas.

How many of the statements given above is/are correct?

(a) Only one (b) Only two
(c) All three (d) None of these

Ans. (c)

Exp. All three statements i.e., (1), (2) and (3) are correct with reference to the administration of Vijayanagara Empire. Assignment of revenue yielding territory in return for military service was a common feature of Delhi Sultanate, Kakatiya Kingdom and Vijayanagara Empire. Assignment of the revenue of a particular locality to the Nayak for their military service is found in the Kakatiya kingdom during the thirteenth century.

The practice became established during the reign of Krishnadeva Raya and Achyuta Devaraya.

This is supported by the evidence of inscriptions and by the accounts of Nuniz and Paes.

22 **Consider the following statements.**
(Chap 7, Class-XII, New NCERT)

1. The Amara-nayaka system was a major political innovation of the Vijayanagara Empire.
2. The Amara-nayakas were military commanders who were given territories to govern by the Raya.
3. They were not given power to collect tax.

Which of the statements given above is/are correct?

(a) Only 1 (b) 1 and 2 (c) 2 and 3 (d) 1, 2 and 3

Ans. (b)

Exp. Statements (1) and (2) are correct. The 'Amar-nayaka' system was a major political innovation of the Vijayanagara Empire. Many features of this system were derived from Iqta System of the Delhi Sultanate.

The Amar-nayakas were military commanders who were given territories to govern by the Raya. The Amar-nayakas sent tribute to the king annually and personally appeared in the royal court with gifts to express their loyalty.

Statement (3) is incorrect as Amar-nayakas collected taxes and other dues from peasants, crafts persons and traders in the area. They retained parts of the revenue for personal use and for maintaining a stipulated contingent of horses and elephants.

23 **With reference to nayakas of the Vijayanagara Empire, consider the following statements.**
(Chap 7, Class-XII, New NCERT)

1. They controlled forts and had armed supporters.
2. They often rebelled and had to be subdued by military action.

Which of the statements given above is/are incorrect?

(a) Only 1 (b) Only 2
(c) Both 1 and 2 (d) Neither 1 nor 2

Ans. (d)

Exp. Neither statements (1) nor (2) are incorrect with reference to Vijayanagara Empire. The nayakas controlled forts and had armed supporters. Whenever any nayaka rebelled and tried to carve out their own kingdom then such nayakas were subdued by military action.

24 **Arrange the following in the correct sequence (lowest to highest in hierarchy).**
(Chap 9, Class-XI, Old NCERT)

1. Mandalam 2. Nadu 3. Sthala

Codes

(a) 3, 2, 1 (b) 2, 1, 3 (c) 1, 2, 3 (d) 1, 3, 2

Ans. (a)

Exp. The correct sequence of administrative unit of Vijayanagara Empire from lowest to highest hierarchy is as follows

Sthala (sub-district), Nadu (district) and Mandalam (Province).

The lowest unit of governance was Grama. The chief officer of a Mandalam was known as Pradhani.

Society

25 **With reference to societal structure during Vijayanagara Empire, consider the following statements.**
(C1ass-XI, Old NCERT)

1. All the Nayak of the Vijayanagara administration belonged to the social background of Brahmana.
2. Revolt took place in 1430 AD in the Central parts of Tamil Nadu against harsh tax collection.
3. Continuous warfare, migration of people and widening gap between ruling class ruled was an enduring feature of Vijayanagara.

How many of the statements given above is/are correct?

(a) Only one (b) Only two
(c) All three (d) None of these

Ans. (b)

Exp. Only two statements i.e., (2) and (3) are correct with reference to Vijayanagara Empire. Revolt took place in 1430 AD in the Central parts of Tamil Nadu against harsh tax collection. This was the revolt in which all the basic producers joined, forgetting their caste differences. Continuous warfare, migration of people and widening gap between ruling class ruled was an enduring feature of Vijayanagara.

Statement (1) is incorrect because most of these Nayak were the Kannadiga and Telugu warriors besides some local chiefs. They belonged to different castes, Brahmana as well as non-Brahmana.

Economy

26 **With reference to the economy of the Vijayanagara Empire, consider the following statements.**
(C1ass-XI, Old NCERT)

1. Taxing the people was the chief source of revenue for the state.
2. Vijayanagara period witnessed striking development in the field of non-agrarian crafts.
3. Non-agrarian groups were generally called the Pattadai.

How many of the statements given above is/are correct?

(a) Only one (b) Only two
(c) All three (d) None of these

Ans. (c)

Exp. All three statements i.e., (1), (2) and (3) are correct with reference to Vijayanagara Empire. The state had to derive their revenue only by taxing the people. It is found that during the Sangama dynasty when the Vijayanagara rule was extended to new areas, their officers were harsh in tax collection, which provoked the toiling people to rise in revolt.

The Vijayanagara period witnessed striking development in the field of non-agrarian crafts. Until the thirteenth century the economy was mainly agrarian. Artisans like weavers, smiths, and masons became more prominent in the society. These non-agrarian groups were generally called the Pattadai (workshop people) or kasaya-vargam that is the group that pays taxes in cash.

Miscellaneous

27 According to Portuguese writer Nuniz, the women in the Vijayanagara empire were experts in which of the following areas? *(C1ass-XI, Old NCERT) (IAS Pre 2022)*

1. Wrestling
2. Astrology
3. Accounting
4. Soothsaying

Select the correct answer using the codes given below.

(a) 1, 2 and 3 (b) 1, 3 and 4
(c) 2 and 4 (d) 1, 2, 3 and 4

Ans. (d)

Exp. All the above given options are correct with reference to Vijayanagara empire. As per Portuguese writer Nuniz, the women in the Vijayanagara empire were experts in Wrestling, Astrology, Accounting Soothsaying.

Nuniz writes "he (the king of Vijayanagara) has also women who wrestle and others who are astrologers and soothsayers; and he has woman who write all the accounts of expenses that are incurred inside the gates and others whose duty it is to write all the affairs of the kingdom and compare their books with those of the writers outside he has women also for music, who play instruments and sing".

28 Who among the following rulers of Vijayanagara empire constructed a large dam across Tungabhadra river and a canal-cum-aqueduct several kilometres long from the river to the capital city? *(Chap 11, Module-2, NIOS) (IAS Pre 2023)*

(a) Deva Raya I (b) Vira Vijaya
(c) Mallikarjuna (d) Virupaksha

Ans. (a)

Exp. Deva Raya I constructed a large dam across Tungabhadra river and a canal-cum-aqueduct several kilometres long from the river to the capital city. He was the third ruler of the Vijayanagara empire, and he reigned from 1406 to 1422.

29 Regarding the taxation system of Krishna Deva, the ruler of Vijayanagara, consider the following statements. *(Chap 1, Class-XII, New NCERT) (IAS Pre 2016)*

1. The tax rate on land was fixed depending on the quality of the land.
2. Private owners of workshops paid an industry tax.

Which of the statements given above is/are correct?

(a) Only 1 (b) Only 2
(c) Both 1 and 2 (d) Neither 1 nor 2

Ans. (c)

Exp. Both the statements (1) and (2) are correct with reference to the Taxation system of Vijayanagara empire. The tax rate on land was fixed depending on the quality of the land as evident from the travelogue written by Persianenvoy Abdur Razzaq in the court of Vijayanagara. Private owners of workshops paid an industry tax. The government also levied other taxes like the grasing tax, the customs duty, tax on gardening and industries taxes on manufacture of various articles.

30 With reference to Vijayanagara Empire, consider the following statements. *(Chap 1, Class-XII, New NCERT)*

1. Parados used in the administration of Vijayanagara Empire referred to the currency.
2. The term Amaram was used for grants given to scholar and poets.
3. Mahanavami Dibba referred to a stone platform that supported a wooden structure.

How many of the statements given above is/are correct?

(a) Only one (b) Only two (c) All three (d) None of these

Ans. (b)

Exp. Only two statements i.e., (1) and (3) are correct with reference to the Vijayanagara Empire. The term Parados was widely used in the administration of Vijayanagara Empire which refers to currency.

Mahanavami Dibba is a beautiful stone platform located within the Royal Enclosure of Hampi.lt was built during the Vijayanagara period by King Krishnadeva Raya to commemorate his victory over Udaygiri.

Statement (2) is incorrect because the term Amaram in the Vijayanagara Empire was used for Military grants. It was land with a fixed revenue given to Nayakas. The most of the Nayakas were the Kannadiga and Telugu warriors have maintained a fixed number of soldiers, horses and elephants. They were also known as Palaiyagar and Palegar.

31 Consider the following statements. *(Chap 7, Class-XII, New NCERT)*

1. The ruins at Hampi were brought to light by Colin Mackenzie in 1800 AD.
2. He was the second Surveyor General of India.

Which of the statements given above is/are correct?

(a) Only 1 (b) Only 2
(c) Both 1 and 2 (d) Neither 1 nor 2

Ans. (a)

Exp. Statement (1) is correct as the ruins at Hampi were brought to light by Colin Mackenzie in 1800 AD. He was engineer, surveyor and Cartographer. By studying Vijayanagara, Mackenzie believed that East India Company would gain much useful information on many of these institutions.

Statement (2) is not correct because in 1815 AD, he was appointed as the first surveyor General of India, a post he held till his death in 1821 AD.

32 The term kudiraichettis was widely used in Deccan during 15th-16th century. It denotes

(Chap 7, Class-XII, New NCERT)

(a) local communities of merchants
(b) landlords
(c) government officials
(d) low caste farmers

Ans. (a)

Exp. The term kudiraichettis was widely used in Deccan during 15th-16th century AD. It denotes local communities of merchants. They were generally horse traders. They use to live in cities, trade centres, ports, towns and villages.

33 Consider the following statements about the Lotus Mahal. *(Chap 7, Class-XII, New NCERT)*

1. The most beautiful buildings in the royal centre is the Lotus Mahal.
2. It had nine towers – a high central one and eight along the sides.
3. One suggestion, found in a map drawn by Mackenzie, is that Lotus Mahal may have been a council chamber, a place where the king met his advisors.

Which of the statements given above is/are correct?

(a) Only 1 (b) 1 and 2
(c) 1 and 3 (d) All of these

Ans. (d)

Exp. All the given statements (1), (2) and (3) are correct about the Lotus Mahal. The most beautiful buildings in the royal centre is the Lotus Mahal.

It had nine towers, a high central one, and eight along the sides. There is no exact information about the Lotus Mahal.

According to Mackenzie, is that it may have been a Council chamber, a place where the king met his advisors. The royal centre was located in the South-Western part of the Vijayanagara, which had over 60 temples.

34 A building Kalyaana Mandapas was a notable feature in the temple construction in the kingdom of

(Chap 7, Class-XII, New NCERT) (IAS Pre 2019)

(a) Chalukya
(b) Chandela
(c) Rashtrakuta
(d) Vijayanagara

Ans. (d)

Exp. Kalyaana Mandapas was a notable feature in the temple construction in the kingdom of Vijayanagara. Kalyaana Mandapas meant to celebrate divine weddings.

Mandapas or pavilions are long, pillared corridors that often ran around the shrines within the temple complex. Gopuram is also one of the important feature in the temple construction in the kingdom of Vijayanagara.

35 Where is the famous Vijaya Vitthal Temple, having its 56 carved pillars emitting musical notes located?

(Chap 7, Class-XII, New NCERT) (IAS Pre 2007)

(a) Belur (b) Bhadrachalam
(c) Hampi (d) Srirangam

Ans. (c)

Exp. The famous Vijaya Vitthal temple, having its 56 carved pillars emitting musical notes is located in Hampi. The principal deity in this temple is of Vitthala, a form of Vishnu generally worshipped in Maharashtra. This temple has several halls and a unique shrine designed as a chariot. It is extended from the temple Gopurams in a straight line. It was built by the king of Tuluva dynasty, Krishnadeva Raya.

Bahmani Kingdom

36 Consider the following statements with reference to the Bahmani Kingdom. *(Chap 9, Class-XI, Old NCERT)*

1. Its first capital was Daulatabad.
2. It was established by the Alauddin Hasan.

Which of the statement(s) given above is/are incorrect?

(a) Only 1 (b) Only 2
(c) Both 1 and 2 (d) Neither 1 nor 2

Ans. (a)

Exp. Statement (1) is incorrect with reference to the Bahmani Kingdom because first capital of Bahmani Kingdom was Gulbarga not Daulatabad.

37 With reference to Bahmani Kingdom, consider the following statements. *(Chap 9, Class-XI, Old NCERT)*

1. Alauddin Hasan who laid the foundation of the new Muslim Empire belonged to Turkish ethnicity.
2. Ahmad Shah I transferred his capital from Gulbarga to Bidar.

Which of the statements given above is/are incorrect?

(a) Only 1 (b) Only 2
(c) Both 1 and 2 (d) Neither 1 nor 2

Ans. (a)

Exp. Statement (1) is incorrect with reference to Bahmani Kingdom. Alauddin Hasan laid the foundation of the new Muslim Empire in South India. He belonged to Afghan ethnicity. He reigned from 1347 to 1358 AD. Towards the end of his reign, the kingdom stretched from the Wainganga river to Krishna and East to West from Bhongir to Daulatabad.

38 Which of the following statement is incorrect in the context of Alauddin Hasan and Bahmani Kingdom?

(Chap 9, Class-XI, Old NCERT)

(a) He was also known as Hasan Gangu.
(b) He traced his origin from mythological hero of Iran Bahman Shah.
(c) The name of Bahmani Kingdom derived its name from Bahman Shah.
(d) Alauddin Hasan was defeated by Deva Raya II.

Ans. (d)

Exp. Statement (d) is incorrect in the context of Alauddin Hasan and Bahmani Kingdom because he was not defeated by Deva Raya II. Both of them were not contemporary to each other.

39 With reference to the Firuz Shah Bahmani, which of the following statements is/are correct? *(Chap 9, Class-XI, Old NCERT)*

1. He appointed Hindus on a large scale in administration.
2. He built an observatory near Daulatabad.

Codes

(a) Only 1 (b) Only 2
(c) Both 1 and 2 (d) Neither 1 nor 2

Ans. (c)

Exp. Both the statements (1) and (2) are correct. Firuz Shah Bahmani reigned from 1397 to 1422 AD.

He adopted the title of Taj-ud-din Firuz Shah.

He appointed Hindus on a large scale in administration. He built an observatory near Daulatabad. He defeated rulers of Vijayanagara in 1389 AD and in 1408 AD. Later, he was defeated by Deva Raya I in 1419 AD.

40 With reference to Bahmani Kingdom, consider the following statements. *(C1ass-XI, Old NCERT)*

1. Bhaman Shah divided the Kingdom into five territorial divisions called Tarafs.
2. Mohammed I assumed the title of Second Alexander on his coins.
3. The reign of the Bahmani Kingdom was marked by rivalry between Deccani Muslim and Pardesi Muslims.

How many of the statements given above is/are incorrect?

(a) Only one (b) Only two
(c) All three (d) None of these

Ans. (b)

Exp. Only two statements i.e., (1) and (2) are incorrect with reference to the Bahmani Kingdom. In order to facilitate smooth administration, as followed in the Delhi Sultanate, he divided the kingdom into four territorial divisions called tarafs, each under a governor.

Bahman Shah assumed the title Second Alexander on his coins. For the greater part of his reign of eleven years Bahman was engaged in subduing the unruly in his kingdom and in establishing order. Bahman Shah emerged victorious in all these expeditions and assumed the title Second Alexander on his coins.

41 Consider the following statements with reference to the Ahmad Shah I. *(Chap 9, Class-XI, Old NCERT)*

1. During his period Bahmani Kingdom was defeated by Warangal.
2. He was popularly known as Wali by the common people.
3. He was associated with the Sufi Saint Gesu Daraz.

Which of the statements given above is/are incorrect?

(a) Only 1 (b) 1 and 2 (c) 2 and 3 (d) 1, 2 and 3

Ans. (a)

Exp. Statement (1) is incorrect because Ahmad Shah I in 1424-1425 AD invaded Warangal and killed its ruler. He was popularly known as Wali by the common people because he was associated with the Sufi Saint Gesu Daraz.

42 Which one among the following was not a reform measure carried out by Mahmud Gawan of Bahmani Kingdom? *(Chap 9, Class-XI, Old NCERT)*

(a) The Kingdom was divided into eight provinces or Tarafs.
(b) Nobles were paid salaries and were asked to maintain contingents of horses.
(c) A tract of land, Khalisa was set apart for the expenses of the Tarafdar.
(d) Lands were measured and land taxes were fixed on that basis.

Ans. (c)

Exp. Statement (c) was not a reform measure carried out by Mahmud Gawan of Bahmani Kingdom because Khalisa land was set apart for the expenses of the Sultan (not Tarafdar).

43 Consider the following statements with reference to the Mahmud Gawan. *(Chap 9, Class-XI, Old NCERT)*

1. He was granted title Malik-ul-Tujjar.
2. He died in battle against the Vijayanagara Empire.

Which of the statements given above is/are incorrect?

(a) Only 1 (b) Only 2
(c) Both 1 and 2 (d) Neither 1 nor 2

Ans. (b)

Exp. Statement (2) is incorrect because he did not die in battle against the Vijayanagara Empire. He was executed on the orders of Bahmani Sultan in 1482 AD.

44 Which of the following was not one of the states formed after the disintegration of Bahmani Kingdom? *(Chap 9, Class-XI, Old NCERT)*

1. Ahmednagar 2. Bijapur 3. Berar
4. Warangal 5. Golconda

Codes

(a) Only 1 (b) Only 2 (c) Only 3 (d) Only 4

Ans. (d)

Exp. Warangal was not among the states which were formed after the disintegration of Bahmani Kingdom. After the death of Mahmud Gawan, Bahmani Kingdom started declining and ultimately it was disintegrated into following five kingdoms :

Kingdom	Dynasty
Ahmednagar	Nizam Shahi dynasty
Bijapur	Adil Shahi dynasty
Golconda	Qutb Shahi dynasty
Bidar	Barid Shahi dynasty
Berar	Imad Shahi dynasty

45 With reference to the administration of Bahmani Kingdom, consider the following pairs. *(Class-XI, Old NCERT)*

Council of Ministers	Function
1. Vakil-us-sultana	Immediate Subordinate of Sovereign
2. Amir-i-jua	Minister of Finance
3. Sadr-i-jahana	Minister of Foreign Affairs

How many of the pairs given above is/are incorrectly matched?

(a) Only one (b) Only two (c) All three (d) None of these

Ans. (a)

Exp. Only one pair i.e., (3) is incorrectly matched, as Sadr-i-jahana were the Chief Justice and Minister of religious affairs and endowments. They were appointed by Mohammed I, who appointed a council of eight ministers of state. Mohammed-I established a good system of government that was followed by all the successor Sultanate as well as by the Marathas later.

46 With reference to Vijayanagara Kingdom, consider the following statements. *(Class-XI, Old NCERT)*

Statement-I Vijayanagara Kingdom and Bahmani Sultanate had a matrimonial alliance.

Statement-II Virupaksha Raya I married his daughter to the Bhamani Sultan Firuz Shah.

Which one of the following is correct in respect of the above statements?

(a) Both Statement-I and Statement-II are correct and Statement-II is the correct explanation for Statement-I.

(b) Both Statement-I and Statement-II are correct and Statement-II is not the correct explanation for Statement-I.

(c) Statement-I is correct, but Statement-II is incorrect.

(d) Statement I is incorrect, but Statement-II is correct.

Ans. (c)

Exp. Statement-I is correct, but Statement-II is incorrect. Deva Raya I married his daughter to the Bhamani Sultan Firuz Shah. In 1406, Firuz Bahmani, the ruler of the Bahmani Sultanate, invaded Vijayanagara. Deva Raya I, the ruler of Vijayanagara, led his army to fight against the Bahmani Sultanate.

However, the Vijayanagara army was decisively defeated by Firuz Bahmani. Consequences of the war as a result of the war, Deva Raya I was forced to pay a huge war indemnity to Firuz Bahmani.

He also had to offer his daughter in marriage to Firuz Bahmani as a sign of surrender.

This marriage alliance between the two kingdoms was meant to establish peace and stability in the Deccan region.

47 Choose the incorrect pair regarding the foreign chronicles of the Vijayanagara period. *(Class-XI, Old NCERT)*

(a)	Abdur Razzaq	–	Described the conditions during the reign of Devaraya II
(b)	Domingo Paes	–	Described the rule of Krishna devaraya
(c)	Caesar Frederick	–	Wrote about the conditions of Vijayanagara after the Battle of Rakshasi Tangadi
(d)	Nikitin	–	Visited during the reign of Achyuta Deva Raya

Ans. (d)

Exp. Pair (d) is incorrectly matched because Afanasy Nikitin visited India during the Bahmani ruler, Muhammad Shah III.

He was a Russian traveller. He described his journey in 'Journey Beyond Three Sea'.

He described the condition of the Bahmani kingdom nder Muhammad in his voyage to India.

Chapter 16

Rise of Provincial Kingdoms

Rise of Provincial Kingdom

Western India

Gujarat

- Ahmad Shah I was real founder who shifted the capital from Patan to new city of Ahmedabad in 1413 AD
- Most famous ruler - Mahmud Begada who ruled over Gujarat for more than 50 years; He formed a naval alliance with the Sultans of Turkey and Egypt and defeated the Portuguese in Battle of Chaul
- Bahadur Shah was last able ruler who recaptured Gujarat from Humayun, but was killed by the Portuguese

Malwa

- Earliest ruler Hoshang Shah, adopted a broad policy of religious toleration
- Lalitpur temple was built during Hoshang Shah period

Mewar

- First ruled by Guhila dynasty with its capital Nagada. Rana Kumbha of Sisodiya dynasty carried out continuous warfare against Gujarat and Malwa
- He built Vijay Stambha at Chittor in 1448. Rana Sanga was defeated by Babur in the Battle of Khanwa in 1527 AD

Eastern India

Bengal

- Made part of Delhi Sultanate by Bakhtiyar Khilji in 1204 AD.
- In 1345 AD Haji Ilyas became ruler of Bengal
- King Ghiyasuddin Azam Shah sent an ambassador in China
- Alauddin Hussain Shah established Hussain Shahi dynasty in 1494 AD
- He promote Bengali language and culture
- Chaitanya preached Vaishnavism during the reign of Nasiruddin-Nusrat Shah
- During his rule, Mahabharata was translated in Bengali

Assam

- Two kingdoms — Kamata (Kamrup) in West and Ahom in East ruled Assam
- An attack by Alauddin Hussain Shah of Bengal led to the destruction of the city of Kamtapur
- Suhungmung, the greatest Ahom ruler repulsed Muslim attack. Shankaradeva belonged to his reign

Orissa

- Ruled by the Ganga dynasty during the Delhi Sultanate period. Firoz Shah Tughlaq attacked Orissa in 1340 AD
- Gajapati rulers were mainly instrumental in building the famous Jagannath temple and the Sun temple (Konark)

North-West and North India

Jaunpur

- First ruler Malik Sarwar
- During the reign of Ibrahim Shah Sharqi a distinctive architecture, Sharqi style developed
- Jaunpur was called the 'Sheraz of India'

Kashmir

- Independent Muslim kingdom in Kashmir was formed by Shah Mirza Sultan Zain-ul-Abidin (1420-1470 AD) the greatest ruler who followed liberal and benevolent policies
- He abolished Jizya, withdrew Sati and abolished Cow slaughter
- In 1540 AD, Mirza Haider conquered Kashmir and later, Akbar annexed Kashmir into the Mughal empire in 1588 AD

Other Regional Kingdoms

- **Marwar** Rao Chunda, ruled Marwar from 1404-1421 AD; He was succeeded by Jodha
- **Amber** Dulha Rai was the founder of Kachhawaha dynasty which ruled Amber; Most famous ruler - Hammir Deva

SOURCE *Tamil Nadu Board Class XI* (*Bahmani and Vijayanagara Kingdom*), *Old NCERT Class XI* (*The Age of the Vijayanagara and Bahmanis and the coming of the Portuguese*), *NIOS Module-2* (*Emergence of Regional States*)

Regional Kingdoms (1400-1525 AD)

1 Consider the following statements with reference to the Bengal Province. *(Chap 10, Class-XI, Old NCERT)*

1. Under the rule of Ilyas Khan, Bengal emerged as a regional power.
2. He was succeeded by his son Sikandar.

Which of the statements given above is/are correct?

(a) Only 1 (b) Only 2
(c) Both 1 and 2 (d) Neither 1 nor 2

Ans. (c)

Exp. Both the statements (1) and (2) are correct with reference to Bengal Province. Under the rule of Ilyas Khan, Bengal emerged as a regional power.

In 1342 AD, he United Bengal and became its ruler under the title of Shamsuddin Ilyas Khan. He founded the Ilyas Shah dynasty. He extended his dominion in West from Tirhut to Banaras.

In 1358 AD, he was succeeded by his son Sikandar Shah.

2 Which of the places was/were adorned as the capital by Bengal rulers? *(Chap 10, Class-XI, Old NCERT)*

1. Gaur 2. Murshidabad
3. Pandua

Codes

(a) Only 1 (b) Only 2
(c) Only 3 (d) 1 and 3

Ans. (d)

Exp. Gaur and Pandua were adorned as the capital by Bengal rulers. Gaur (also known as Gauda and Lakhnauti) was the earliest capital of Bengal Kingdom.

Pandua was established as the capital by the Ilyas Khan when he laid the foundation of Ilyas Shah dynasty. In 1450 AD, Sultan Mahmud Shah of Bengal announced the transfer of Bengal's capital from Pandua to Gaur. The transfer was completed by 1453 AD.

3 Consider the following statements. *(Chap 9, Class-XI, Old NCERT)*

1. Alauddin Husain Shah was the contemporary of Vaishnava Saint 'Chaitanya'.
2. He became the ruler of Bengal after assassinating Shamsuddin Muzaffar Shah.

Which of the statements given above is/are correct?

(a) Only 1 (b) Only 2
(c) Both 1 and 2 (d) Neither 1 nor 2

Ans. (c)

Exp. Both the statements (1) and (2) are correct. Alauddin Husain Shah was the contemporary of Vaishnava Saint 'Chaitanya' (1486-1534 AD).

He became the ruler of Bengal after assassinating the Abyssian Sultan, Shamsuddin Muzaffar Shah, whom he had served under as 'Wazir'. He laid the foundation of Hussain Shahi dynasty. He reigned from 1494 to 1519 AD.

4 With reference to the Bengal Province, consider the following statements. *(Class-XI, Old NCERT)*

1. In the 12th century AD Muhammad Bin Bakhtiyar annexed Bengal to the conquered territories of Muhammad Ghori.
2. Iltutmish invaded Bengal to counter the influence of Haji Iliyas.
3. Treaty signed between Firuz Shah Tughlaq and Haji Iliyas made river Kosi the boundary line between the two kingdom.

How many of the statements given above is/are incorrect?

(a) Only one (b) Only two
(c) All three (d) None of these

Ans. (a)

Exp. Only one statement i.e., (2) is incorrect with reference to the Bengal Province. To counter increasing influence of Haji lliyas Firuz Shah Tughlaq invaded Bengal but did not meet with success. He had to sign a treaty with lliyas. According to the treaty, river Kosi was accepted as the boundary line between two kingdoms. Haji lliyas died in AD 1357 and his son Sikandar succeeded the throne.

5 With reference to the Bengal province, consider the following statements. *(Class-XI, Old NCERT)*

1. Balban partitioned Bengal into three independent administrative divisions.
2. Ghiyasuddin Azam maintained friendly relations with the King of China.
3. In AD 1538 Sher Shah Suri defeated Ghiyasuddin Mahmud Shah and made Bengal a part of his empire.

How many of the statements given above is/are incorrect?

(a) Only one (b) Only two
(c) All three (d) None of these

Ans. (a)

Exp. Only one statement i.e., (1) is incorrect with reference to Bengal Province. Ghiyasuddin Tughlaq tried to solve the problem of keeping Bengal under the sovereignty of Delhi Sultanate, by partitioning Bengal into three independent administrative divisions namely Lakhnauti, Satgaon and Sonargaon. Still, the problems remained and eventually, Bengal surfaced as an independent indigenous state in the 14th century.

6 The two important warring Kingdoms in North Bengal and Assam included *(Chap 10, Class-XI, Old NCERT)*

1. Kamata 2. Ahom 3. Sharqi 4. Malwa

Codes

(a) 1 and 2 (b) 2 and 3
(c) Only 3 (d) All of these

Ans. (a)

Exp. Options (1) and (2) are correct. The two important warring Kingdoms in North Bengal and Assam included Kamata and Ahom, respectively.

Kamata Kingdom came into existence in the year 1257 AD. The last rulers of Kamata Kingdom were displaced in 1498 AD by Alauddin Husain Shah of Bengal. The Ahom Kingdom was established in 1228 AD by Sukaphaa.

7 Consider the following statements. *(Chap 7, Class-XII, New NCERT)*

1. During the period of Vijayanagara Empire Gajapati dynasty ruled over Orissa.
2. The capital of Gajapati Dynasty was Puri.
3. Kapilendra Deva was the founder of Gajapati Dynasty.

Which of the statements given above is/are correct?

(a) 1 and 2 (b) 2 and 3 (c) 1 and 3 (d) 1, 2 and 3

Ans. (c)

Exp. Statements (1) and (3) are correct. During the period of Vijayanagara Empire Gajapati dynasty ruled over Orissa. It ruled from 1434-1541 AD. The reign of Vijayanagara Empire was 1336-1646 AD. Thus, it was the contemporary of Vijayanagara Empire.

Kapilendra Deva was the founder of Gajapati Dynasty. He founded this dynasty in 1434 AD.

Statement (2) is incorrect because Cuttack was the capital of Gajapati kingdom of Orissa.

8 With reference to the Gujarat ruler Ahmad Shah I, which of the following statements is/are incorrect? *(Class 10, Class-XI, Old NCERT)*

1. Ahmad Shah I is known as real founder of Kingdom of Gujarat.
2. He attacked Sidhpur, the famous Hindu temple.

Codes

(a) Only 1 (b) Only 2
(c) Both 1 and 2 (d) Neither 1 nor 2

Ans. (d)

Exp. Neither statements (1) nor (2) are incorrect with reference to the Gujarat ruler Ahmad Shah I. He is known as real founder of Kingdom of Gujarat. He was the grandson of Zafar Khan (founder of Gujarat Kingdom). He attacked Sidhpur, the famous Hindu temple in the Saurashtra region of Gujarat.

9 With reference to the Provincial Kingdom of Western India, consider the following statements. *(Class-XI, Old NCERT)*

1. Sultan Alauddin Khalji was the first sultan who annexed Gujarat to the Delhi Sultanate.
2. In 1572 Akbar conquered Gujarat and annexed it to the Mughal Empire.

Which of the statements given above is/are incorrect?

(a) Only 1 (b) Only 2
(c) Both 1 and 2 (d) Neither 1 nor 2

Ans. (d)

Exp. Neither statements (1) nor (2) are incorrect with reference to the Provincial Kingdom of Western India. Sultan Alauddin Khalji was the first sultan who annexed Gujarat to the Delhi Sultanate.

In 1572 Akbar conquered Gujarat and annexed it to the Mughal Empire. Gujarat has always attracted the invaders due to its geographical location, prosperity and fertility.

10 Consider the following statements. *(Chap 10, Class-XI, Old NCERT)*

1. He shifted the capital from Patan to new city of Ahmedabad.
2. He also imposed a Jizyah on Hindus in Gujarat for the first time.

Identify the king of Gujarat on the basis of given description.

(a) Zafar Khan (b) Muzaffar Khan
(c) Ahmad Shah I (d) None of these

Ans. (c)

Exp. Ahmad Shah I of Gujarat shifted the capital from Patan to new city of Ahmedabad. The city of Ahmedabad was founded by him in the year 1413 AD. He also imposed a Jizyah on Hindus in Gujarat for the first time. He also appointed Malik Chand and Moti Chand as ministers.

11 Consider the following statements with reference to the Hoshang Shah. *(Chap 10, Class-XI, Old NCERT)*

1. He adopted policy of religious intolerance towards Hindus.
2. He was defeated and imprisoned by Zafar Khan.

Which of the statements given above is/are incorrect?

(a) Only 1 (b) Only 2
(c) Both 1 and 2 (d) Neither 1 nor 2

Ans. (a)

Exp. Statement (1) is incorrect with reference to the Hoshang Shah because he was ruler of Malwa who adopted policy of religious tolerance towards Hindus and people of other religion. This is mentioned in the inscription of the Lalitpur temple. Hoshang Shah reigned from 1406 to 1435 AD.

12 Consider the following statements with reference to the Rana Kumbha. *(Chap 10, Class-XI, Old NCERT)*

1. Rana Kumbha belonged to Mewar.
2. He is known for constructing Vijay Stambha.
3. He was murdered by his son Uda.

Which of the statements given above is/are correct?

(a) Only 1 (b) 1 and 2 (c) 2 and 3 (d) 1, 2 and 3

Ans. (d)

Exp. All the given statements are correct with reference to Rana Kumbha. He belonged to Mewar. He is known for constructing Vijay Stambha at Chittor after defeating Mahmud Khilji.

He was murdered by his son Uda in the greed of throne. Uda was removed by Maharana Raimal (another son of Rana Kumbha).

13 Rana Sanga defeated Sultan Ibrahim Lodi in, which of the following battles? *(Chap 10, Class-XI, Old NCERT)*

(a) Battle of Khatoli
(b) Battle of Saragaon
(c) Battle of Khanwa
(d) Battle of Chittor

Ans. (a)

Exp. Among the given battles, Rana Sanga of Mewar defeated Sultan Ibrahim Lodi in the Battle of Khatoli. It took place in the year 1518 AD. Sultan Ibrahim Lodi waged a war against Rana Sanga when latter encroached into territory of Delhi Sultanate.

Sultan was defeated very easily and in a very short span. In this battle, Rana Sanga lost an arm by a sword cut and an arrow also hit him in the leg which made him lame for rest of the life.

14 Match the following lists correctly and choose the correct code. *(Chap 10, Class-XI, Old NCERT)*

List I (Rulers)	List II (Kingdoms)
A. Ghiyasuddin Azam Shah	1. Bengal
B. Muzaffar Shah	2. Mewar
C. Hoshang Shah	3. Malwa
D. Rana Kumbha	4. Gujarat

Codes

	A	B	C	D		A	B	C	D
(a)	2	1	3	4	(b)	1	4	3	2
(c)	1	2	3	4	(d)	2	4	1	3

Ans. (b)

Exp. The correct matching is A-1, B-4, C-3, D-2.

Ghiyasuddin Azam Shah was the ruler of the Bengal.

Muzaffar Shah was the ruler of the Gujarat. He was also known as Zafar. He proclaimed himself an independent ruler after Timur's invasion and assumed the title 'Muzaffar Shah'.

Hoshang Shah was the ruler of the Malwa. He was also known as Alp Khan. He founded the city Hoshangabad in Madhya Pradesh.

Rana Kumbha was the ruler of the Mewar. He reigned from 1508 to 1528 AD. He was grandson of Kumbha.

15 Consider the following statements. *(Chap 9, Module-2, NIOS)*

1. Malik Sarwar laid the foundation of the Sharqi dynasty.
2. Varanasi was known as 'Shiraz of East' during the regime of Sharqi rulers.
3. There is distinctive style of architecture associated with Sharqi dynasty.

Which of the statements given above is/are incorrect?

(a) Only one
(b) Only two
(c) All three
(d) None of these

Ans. (a)

Exp. Only one statement i.e., (2) is incorrect with reference to the Sharqi dynasty. Jaunpur was known as the 'Shiraz of East' during the regime of Sharqi rulers. Jaunpur was established by Firuz Shah Tughlaq and named in the memory of his cousin Muhammad bin Tughlaq whose name was Jauna Khan.

16 With reference to Sharqi Sultans consider the following statements. *(Chap 10, Class-XI, Old NCERT)*

1. They were patrons of art and culture.
2. Well-known work Padmavat was written during this period.
3. During the period of Lodi dynasty, Sharqi rule declined and ended.

How many of the statements given above is/are incorrect?

(a) Only one
(b) Only two
(c) All three
(d) None of these

Ans. (d)

Exp. None of the above statements are incorrect.

The Sharqi Sultans patronised art and culture. Atala Masjid and Lal Darwaza Masjid are some of the specimen of architecture of Sharqi Sultans.

The well-known work Padmavat was written during this period by Malik Muhammad Jaisi.

During the period of Lodi dynasty, Sharqi rule declined and ended. In 1484 AD, Bahlul Lodi occupied Jaunpur and annexed the Sharqi Kingdoms.

17 With reference to the regional kingdom of Kashmir, consider the following statements. *(Chap 10, Class-XI, Old NCERT)*

1. It was centre of Vaishnavism.
2. It was attacked by Mongol invader Dalucha.
3. Sikandar Shah followed the policy of intolerance in Kashmir.

How many of the statements given above is/are incorrect?

(a) Only one
(b) Only two
(c) All three
(d) None of these

Ans. (a)

Exp. Only one statement i.e., (1) is incorrect with reference to the regional kingdom of Kashmir because the Regional Kingdom of Kashmir was centre of Shaivism (not Vaishnavism).

18 Consider the following statements with reference to the Zain-ul-Abidin. *(Chap 10, Class-XI, Old NCERT)*

1. He followed liberal policies towards Hindus.
2. The Raja of Gwalior sent him two rare Sanskrit works on music.
3. He prohibited cow slaughter.

Which of the statements given above is/are correct?

(a) Only 1
(b) 1 and 3
(c) 2 and 3
(d) 1, 2 and 3

Ans. (d)

Exp. All the given statements are correct with reference to the Zain-ul-Abidin (1420-1470 AD). He followed liberal policies towards Hindus and called back those Hindus who had left the state due to intolerant policies of Sikandar Shah. He prohibited cow slaughter.

The Raja of Gwalior sent him two rare Sanskrit works on music as Zain-ul-Abidin was fond of music. He also patronised art and culture.

19 Which among the following Ruler abolished Jizya first time?

(Chap 10, Class-XI, Old NCERT) (UK UDA Mains 2006)

(a) Zain-ul-Abidin (b) Muhammad bin Tughlaq
(c) Hussain Shah Sarqi (d) Akbar

Ans. (a)

Exp. Zain-ul-Abidin, a Kashmiri ruler abolished Jizyah first time. He was a learned and tolerant ruler. He is still called Badshah (the Great Sultan) by the Kashmiris. He also unified the Kashmiri Kingdom. He was also a great builder and fostered many crafts in Kashmir, such as stone cutting, bottle making, gold bearing, etc.

20 Choose the right matches. *(Chap 9, Module-2, NIOS)*

1. Khizr Khan – Orissa
2. Durgavati – Gondwana
3. Rana Udai Singh – Mewar
4. Kunwar Man Singh – Ajmer

Codes

(a) 1 and 2 are correct. (b) 2 and 3 are correct.
(c) 1 and 4 are correct. (d) 3 and 4 are correct.

Ans. (b)

Exp. Only two pairs (2) and (3) are correctly matched. Durgavati was the ruler in Gondwana region in Madhya Pradesh. In 1542, she married Dalpat Shah, the eldest son of king Sangram Shah of the Gondwana kingdom.

Rana Udai Singh was the Maharana of Mewar and the founder of the city of Udaipur in Rajasthan.

Pairs (1) and (4) are not correctly matched. Kunwar Man Singh was the prince of Amber from 1589-1614. He served in the imperial Mughal army under Emperor Akbar.

Khizr Khan was belong to Punjab region. He was a founder of Sayyid dynasty.

21 Which of the following pairs is correctly matched?

(Class-XI, Old NCERT)

Medieval Indian States		Current Sectors
1. Champaka	–	Central India
2. Durgara	–	Jammu
3. Kuluta	–	Malabar

Codes

(a) 1 and 2 (b) Only 2
(c) 1 and 3 (d) Only 3

Ans. (b)

Exp. Pair (2) is correctly matched as Durgara is the old name of Jammu.

Pairs (1) and (3) are incorrectly matched because Champaka currently known as Chamba is located in Himachal Pradesh. Kuluta currently known as Kullu is located in Himachal Pradesh.

Chapter 17

Bhakti and Sufi Movements

Bhakti and Sufi Movements

Bhakti Movement

Nayanars
- Tamil Shavite Bhakti saints called Nayanars. Total 63 in numbers
- Famous saints- Appar, Tirugyansambandar and Sundarmurti
- Tirumarai is compilation of hymns of Nayanars

Alvars
- Tamil Vaishnavite Bhakti saints emerged during the reign of Pallava's
- Total -12 saints; Famous saints- Nammalvar, Thirumangai and Andal

Virashaiva Tradition in Karnataka
- Established in 12th century AD by Basavanna
- Followers worship Shiva as a linga and are known as Lingayats
- Source of Virashaiva tradition compiled as Vachanas

Bhakti Movement in Maharashtra
- From the 13th to 17th centuries saints such as Dnyaneshwar, Namdev, Eknath and Tukaram preached the message of Bhakti
- Helped in development of Marathi language

Schools of Bhakti
- Emerged in North India; Divided into 2 schools
- **Nirguna** Believed in invisible formless God and God without attributes; Major saints- Dadu Dayal, Kabir, Guru Nanak
- **Shaguna Saints** Belived in God with forms and attributes; Major saints- Ramananda, Tulsidas, Chaitanya Mahaprabhu

Prominent Bhakti Saints

Shankaracharya (788-920 AD)
- Advocated Advaita (doctrine of oneness);
- Established four mathas at Dwarka, Puri, Sringeri and Badrinath

Ramanujacharya (1017-1137 AD)
- Advocated Vishishtadvaita or qualified oneness; Best means of attaining salvation was through intense devotion to Vishnu

Vallabhacharya (1475-1531 AD)
- Founded the Krishna-centered Pushti-marg sect of Vaishnavism; Proposed Shuddha Advaita (pure non-dualism)

Dadu Dayal (1544-1603 AD)
- Founded the Brahma Sampradaya in Gujarat; Teaching compiled in book- Bani

Kabir (1440- 1510 AD)
- Disciple of Ramananda
- Teaching compiled in book- Bijak

Guru Nanak (1469- 1539 AD)
- Advocated middle path of spiritual growth
- Laid emphasis on purity of character and conduct

Ramananda (1299- 1411 AD)
- Founded Ramanandi Sampradaya
- Preached Bhakti in Hindi

Tulsidas (1544-1623 AD)
- Belonged to Ram Bhakti sect
- Contemporary of Akbar

Chaitanya Mahaprabhu (1483- 1538 AD)
- Founded Gaudiya Vaishnavism
- Preached in Bengal

Mirabai (1498- 1546 AD)
- Rathore princess who devoted her life to Krishna

Shankardeva (1449-1568 AD)
- Leading proponent of Vaishnavism in Assam

Sufi Movement

Emergence
- Emerged after the fall of Abbasid Caliphate in 12th century AD
- Opposed orthodoxy in Islam Preached the message of love and peace

Sufi Silsilahs
- Sufi order led by a prominent mystic who lived in Khanqah along with his disciples
- **Chishti Silsilah** Introduced by Khwaja Moinuddin in 1161 AD in Ajmer
- Other saints- Bakhtiyar Kaki, Fariduddin Ganj-i-Shakar and Nizamuddin Auliya
- **Qadiri Silsilah** Founded by Abdul-Qadir Gilani in 1166 AD; Popular among Muslims of South India; Dara Shikoh was a follower of Qadiri order
- **Naqshbandi Silsilah** Founded by Baha-ud-din Naqshband Bukhari; Sheikh Ahmed Sirhindi opposed liberal policies of Akbar
- **Firdausi Silsilah** Popularised by Sheikh Sharfuddin Yahya in Bihar
- Practiced ascetic practices and believed in philosophy of Wahadat-ul- Wajood

SOURCE ***New NCERT Class VII*** *(Devotional Paths to the Divine),* ***Old NCERT Class VII*** *(Life of the People),* ***Old NCERT Class XI*** *(Cultural Development in India From the Thirteenth to the Fifteenth Century),* ***New NCERT Class XII*** *(Bhakti Sufi Traditions Changes in Religious Beliefs and Devotional Texts)* ***NIOS Module 2*** *(Cultural Development in Medieval India)*

Bhakti Movement

1 Consider the following statements with reference to the Bhakti movement. *(Chap 11, Class-XI, Old NCERT)*

1. It emerged in the seventh century AD in the South India after taking inspiration from Sufi saints who were settled in Malabar region.
2. Nayanar saints were devoted to Lord Vishnu.

Which of the statements given above is/are incorrect?

(a) Only 1 (b) Only 2
(c) Both 1 and 2 (d) Neither 1 nor 2

Ans. (c)

Exp. Both the statements (1) and (2) are incorrect regarding Bhakti movement.

The Bhakti Movement emerged in the seventh century AD in the South India. It was basically started by the Alvar and Nayanar saints to revive the Hinduism and reduce the dominance of Brahmanical element. It was not inspired by the Sufi saints because Sufi Movement gained prominence in medieval period. Nayanar saints were devoted to Lord Shiva.

2 Consider the following statements regarding Alvar and Nayanar Saints. *(Chap 11, Class-XI, Old NCERT)*

1. They were sharply critical of the Buddhists and Jainas.
2. They drew upon the ideals of love and heroism as found in the Ramayana and Mahabharata.
3. They came from all castes including those considered 'untouchables.'

How many of the statements given above is/are correct?

(a) Only one (b) Only two
(c) All three (d) None of these

Ans. (b)

Exp. Only two statements i.e., (1) and (3) are correct regarding Alvar and Nayanar Saints.

They were sharply critical of the Buddhists and Jainas. They came from all castes including those considered 'untouchables.' Bhakti saints criticised discrimination on the basis of class and caste.

Statement (2) is incorrect because they drew upon the ideals of love and heroism as found in the Sangam literature. The Bhakti Movement was started by the Alvar and Nayanar saints in the backdrop of rise of Jainism and Buddhism in South India.

3 Consider the following statements. *(Chap 6, Class-XII, New NCERT)*

1. Saguna saint worshipped an abstract form of God.
2. Ramananda was a Saguna saint, who was popular in North India.
3. Mirabai was a Nirguna saint.

Which of the statements given above is/are incorrect?

(a) Only 1 (b) 1 and 3 (c) Only 3 (d) 2 and 3

Ans. (b)

Exp. Statements (1) and (3) are incorrect because Saguna Bhakti saints believe in worship and devotion to a manifested deity who takes the form of an idol, an image or an incarnation. The famous Saguna saints are Mirabai, Tulsidas, Surdas, etc.

Nirguna Bhakti is the devotion towards a formless, all-encompassing God. The word 'nirgun' means 'devoid of realities', referring to the lack of physical attributes of God.

4 The Saivaite Nayanars and Vashanavaite Alwars preached the Bhakti Cult under, which of the following rulers? *(Chap 8, Class-VII, New NCERT)*

(a) Pallavas, Pandyas and Cholas
(b) Pallavas, Cheras and Rashtrakutas
(c) Pallavas, Vijayanagara and Bahmani Kingdoms
(d) Cheras and Pandavas

Ans. (a)

Exp. The Saivaite Nayanars and Vashanavaite Alwars preached the Bhakti Cult under Pallavas, Pandyas and Cholas. Many of these saints received patronage from the rulers of these dynasties. All these dynasties actively promoted Hinduism in their territories and areas under influence.

5 Consider the following statements regarding important Bhakti saints Shankara from Kerala and Ramanuja from Tamil Nadu. *(Chap 11, Class-XI, Old NCERT)*

1. Both Shankara and Ramanuja are contemporaries and they believed in non-dualism, that is, the God and the world is one.
2. Shankara argued that the way forward to salvation was strengthened by knowledge.
3. Ramanuja argued that the grace of God is more important than the knowledge about him in order to attain salvation.
4. Shankara upheld the Vedas as the fountain-head of true knowledge and Ramanuja believed the path of Bhakti was open to all, irrespective of caste.

Which of the statements given above are correct?

(a) 1, 2 and 3 (b) 2, 3 and 4
(c) 1, 3 and 4 (d) 1 and 2

Ans. (b)

Exp. Statements (2), (3) and (4) are correct with respect to Shankaracharya and Ramanuja.

Shankaracharya synthesised the Advaita Vedanta teaching and argued that the way forward to salvation was strengthened by knowledge.

He was the most important exponent of the Sri Vaishnavism tradition within Hinduism. According to Ramanuja, the grace of God is important to attain salvation. He believed the path of Bhakti was open to all, irrespective of caste. The shankaracharya was the Vedic scholar. He considered Veda is the fountain head of true knowledge.

Statement (1) is incorrect because Shankaracharya was scholar of eighth century and Ramanuja was 11th century scholar. They were not contemporary.

6 Which of the following saints belong to Nayanars? *(Chap 8, Class-VII, New NCERT)*

1. Sambandar
2. Appar
3. Sundarar
4. Nammalvar

Codes

(a) 1, 2 and 3 (b) 2 and 4 (c) 2, 3 and 4 (d) All of these

Ans. (a)

Exp. Sambandar, Appar and Sundarar belonged to Nayanars Bhakti saints. These saints were followers of the Lord Shiva. The total number of Nayanars was 63. Most of them belonged to Tamil Nadu.

7 Consider the following statements. *(Chap 14, Module-2, NIOS)*

1. Saint Nimbarka was contemporary of Akbar.
2. Saint Kabir was greatly influenced by Sheikh Ahmad Sirhindi.

Which of the statements given above is/are correct?

(a) Only 1 (b) Only 2
(c) Both 1 and 2 (d) Neither 1 nor 2

Ans. (d)

Exp. Neither (1) nor (2) statement is correct. Nimbarka was not a contemporary of Akbar because Nimbarka lived during 11th-12th centuries AD. Akbar ruled during 15th-16th centuries.

Saint Kabir (1398-1518) was born much before the Sheikh Ahmad Sirhindi (1564-1624). Thus, he was not influenced by Sheikh Ahmad Sirhindi. Nimbarka was a philosopher, who followed Vaishnava doctrine of Bhedabheda Dvaita-Advaita (dualities in unity).

8 According to the historians, what was the main reason behind the hostility between Nayanars and Buddhist and Jain saints on one side? *(Chap 6, Class-XII, New NCERT)*

(a) Due to competition between members of these religious traditions for royal patronage.
(b) Due to difference in their ideology.
(c) Rising influence of Buddhism and Jainism posed danger to Hinduism.
(d) All of the above

Ans. (a)

Exp. According to the historians, the hostility between Nayanars and Buddhist and Jain saints on one side was due to competition between members of these religious traditions for royal patronage. During that period, royal patronage was important as it played significant role in the spread of religions.

9 The image of, which of the following saints was/were consecrated by the Chola ruler Parantaka? *(Chap 6, Class-XII, New NCERT)*

1. Appar
2. Sambandar
3. Sundarar

Codes

(a) 1 and 3 (b) 1 and 2
(c) 2 and 3 (d) 1, 2 and 3

Ans. (d)

Exp. The Chola ruler Parantaka had consecrated metal images of Appar, Sambandar and Sundarar in a Shiva temple inscriptional evidence from around 945 AD. These kings also introduced the singing of Tamil Shaiva hymns in the temples under royal patronage. Appar, Sambandar and Sundarar belonged to Shaiva sect and they were from Tamil Nadu.

10 Consider the following statements with respect to Shankaracharya. *(Chap 8, Class-VII, New NCERT)*

1. He was not an advocate of Advaita philosophy.
2. He taught that Brahman, the only or ultimate reality, was formless and without any attributes.
3. He was born in Kerala in the eighth century.

How many of the statements given above is/are correct?

(a) Only one (b) Only two
(c) All three (d) None of these

Ans. (b)

Exp. Only two statements i.e., (2) and (3) are correct about Shankaracharya.

Shankaracharya was the most important Bhakti saint. He taught that Brahman, one only or ultimate reality, was formless and without any attributes. He considered the world around us to be an illusion or maya. His time period was from (788 – 820 AD).

Statement (1) is incorrect because he was an advocate of Advaita philosophy, which means the reality of the world is denied and Brahman is considered the only reality.

11 Consider the following statements with reference to Ramanujacharya. *(Chap 8, Class-VII, New NCERT)*

1. He was deeply influenced by the Nayanars.
2. According to him, the best means of attaining salvation was through intense devotion to Shiva.

Which of the statements given above is/are incorrect?

(a) Only 1 (b) Only 2
(c) Both 1 and 2 (d) Neither 1 nor 2

Ans. (c)

Exp. Both the statements (1) and (2) are incorrect with reference to Ramanujacharya.

Ramanujacharya was deeply influenced by the Alvars. According to him, the best means of attaining salvation was through intense devotion to Vaishnavism.

Ramanujacharya was one of the earliest Bhakti saints. His time period was from (1017-1137 AD).

He advocated prabattimarga or the path of self-surrender to God. He invited downtrodden people to Vaishnavism and advocated salvation by Bhakti. He promoted the concept of Vishista Advaitavada (qualified monism).

12 Which of the following statements is/are incorrect about Virashaivism? *(Chap 8, Class-VII, New NCERT)*

(a) Andhra Pradesh was main centre of Virashaivism.
(b) The Virashaivas were against the Brahmanical ideas about caste and the treatment of women.
(c) They were also against all forms of ritual and idol worship.
(d) This movement began in the mid-twelfth century.

***Ans.* (a)**

Exp. Statement (a) is incorrect about Virashaivism, because Virashaiva movement was initiated by Basavanna and his companions like Allama Prabhu and Akkamahadevi. This movement began in Karnataka in the mid-twelfth century AD.

13 Consider the following statements. *(Chap 8, Class-VII, New NCERT)*

1. Virashaiva worship Lord Shiva in his manifestation as a Linga.
2. They believe that on death, the devotee will unite with Shiva and will not return to this world.

Which of the statements given above is/are correct?

(a) Only 1 (b) Only 2
(c) Both 1 and 2 (d) Neither 1 nor 2

***Ans.* (c)**

Exp. Both the statements (1) and (2) are correct. Virashaiva worship Lord Shiva in his manifestation as a Linga. Men usually wear a small Linga in a silver case on a loop strung over the left shoulder. They are also known as Lingayats or wearers of Linga.

Virashaiva believe that on death, the devote will be united with Shiva and will not return to the world. Therefore, they do not practice funerary rites, such as cremation, prescribed in the Dharmashastra.

14 Match List I with List II and select the correct answer from the codes given below the lists. *(Chap 14, Module-2 NIOS)*

List I (Philosopher)	List II (Philosophy)
A. Ramanuja	1. Shuddhadvaita
B. Madhavacharya	2. Dvaita-Advaita
C. Nimbarka	3. Dvaita
D. Vallabhacharya	4. Vishishtadvaita

Codes

	A	B	C	D		A	B	C	D
(a)	3	1	4	2	(b)	4	3	2	1
(c)	2	4	1	3	(d)	1	2	3	4

***Ans.* (b)**

Exp. The correct matching is A-4, B-3, C-2, D-1.

Vishishtadvaita was a philosophical school, also known as qualified non-dualism, was propounded by Ramanuja. He was a prominent philosopher and theologian who lived in the 11th and 12th centuries.

Dvaita or dualism, was propounded by Madhavacharya, also known as Anandatirtha. He was a philosopher and theologian who lived in the 13th and 14th centuries.

Dvaita-Advaita, or dualistic non-dualism, was propounded by Nimbarka. He was a philosopher and theologian who lived around the 12th century.

Shuddhadvaita or pure non-dualism, was propounded by Vallabhacharya, also known as Vallabha. He was a philosopher, scholar and devotional poet who lived in the 15th century.

15 A common feature to all Bhakti saints was that they *(Chap 11, Class-XI, Old NCERT) (BPSC Pre 2005)*

(a) composed of their verses in the languages understood by their followers.
(b) rejected the authority of the priestly class.
(c) encouraged women to go to the temples.
(d) encouraged idol worship.

***Ans.* (a)**

Exp. A common feature to all the Bhakti saints was that they composed of their verses in the languages (generally vernacular language) understood by their followers. Bhakti saints belonged from different region and their time period was also different.

They also encouraged universal brotherhood and denied caste system. They also emphasised on the concept of the self-surrender to God without being dependent over the mediatory.

16 Which of the following statements is/are correct regarding the Bhakti saint Chaitanya? *(Chap 8, Class-VII, New NCERT)*

1. He popularised the Krishna cult in Bengal.
2. He believes that through love and devotion, song and dance, a devotee can feel the presence of God.

Codes

(a) Only 1 (b) Only 2
(c) Both 1 and 2 (d) Neither 1 nor 2

***Ans.* (c)**

Exp. Both the statements (1) and (2) are correct regarding the Bhakti saint Chaitanya.

Bhakti saint Chaitanya popularised the Krishna cult in Bengal. He believes that through love and devotion, song and dance, a devotee can feel the presence of God.

The system of songs and dance by several people in a group is known as sankirtan/kirtan system. He accepted disciples from all classes and castes.

One of the most important things about him was that he did not rejected the scriptures and idol worship.

17 **Which one of the following sequences indicates the correct chronological order of Bhakti saints?** *(Chap 8, Class-VII, New NCERT) (JPSC Pre 2011)*

(a) Shankaracharya, Ramanuja, Chaitanya
(b) Ramanuja, Shankaracharya, Chaitanya
(c) Ramanuja, Chaitanya, Shankaracharya
(d) Shankaracharya, Chaitanya, Ramanuja

Ans. (a)

Exp. The correct chronological order of given Bhakti saints is Shankaracharya, Ramanuja, and Chaitanya. Shankaracharya (788-820 AD) was a Bhakti Saint and the Propounder of Advaita Philosophy. He played an important role in reviving Hinduism when Buddhism was gaining popularity.

Ramanuja (1017-1137 AD) was one of the earliest Bhakti Saint. He was Alvar Saint and he advocated Vaishnavism as the best means of attaining salvation. Chaitanya (1486-1534 AD) was a Bhakti Saint from Bengal. He popularised the Krishna cult in Bengal and is considered to be the combined avatar of Radha and Krishna.

18 **Consider the following statements with reference to Kabir.** *(Chap 8, Class-VII, New NCERT)*

1. His collection of verses is called sakhis and pads.
2. His verses are preserved in the Guru Granth Sahib.
3. He belonged to community of fishermen.
4. Kabir believed in a formless Supreme God.

How many of the statements given above is/are correct?

(a) Only one (b) Only two (c) Only three (d) All of these

Ans. (c)

Exp. Only three statements i.e., (1), (2) and (4) are correct regarding Kabir. He was one of the most famous disciples of Ramananda. His collection of verses is called sakhis and pads. His verses are preserved in the Guru Granth Sahib. He was a popular Nirguna saint (believed in a formless Supreme God).

Statement (3) is incorrect because Kabir was brought up in a family of Muslim Julahas or weavers settled in or near the city of Varanasi (Banaras).

19 **Which one of the following statements about the teachings of Kabir is incorrect?** *(Chap 11, Class-XI, Old NCERT)*

(a) He was not against pilgrimage and idol worship.
(b) He believed in universal love.
(c) He emphasised on one God and the spread of devotionalism.
(d) He did not consider it necessary to abandon the normal life of a householder.

Ans. (a)

Exp. Statement (a) is incorrect regarding the teachings of Kabir. Kabir was a renowned Nirguna saint therefore, he was against the pilgrimage and idol worship. He declared that God is one and he is the same for both Hindus and Muslim.

20 **Which of the following statements is/are correct with reference to the Tulsidas?** *(Chap 8, Class-VII, New NCERT)*

1. He conceived of God in the form of Krishna.
2. His composition the Ramcharitmanas was written in Braj language.

Codes

(a) Only 1 (b) Only 2
(c) Both 1 and 2 (d) Neither 1 nor 2

Ans. (d)

Exp. Neither statement (1) nor (2) is correct regarding Tulsidas. Tulsidas was born in 1511 in a Brahmana family in Uttar Pradesh. He was a Saguna saint.

He conceived of God in the form of Rama. His composition the Ramcharitmanas was written in Awadhi language. The other important literary of his includes Gitawali, Vinaya Patrika, etc.

21 **Surdas was one of the important Bhakti saints. His composition included** *(Chap 6, Class-XII, New NCERT)*

1. Bijak
2. Surasaravali
3. Sahitya Lahiri

Codes

(a) 1 and 2 (b) 2 and 3
(c) Only 3 (d) All of these

Ans. (b)

Exp. Options (2) and (3) are correct with reference to Bhakti saints Surdas. He was one of the important Bhakti saints.

His composition included Surasaravali, Sur Sagar and Sahitya Lahiri. He was born in 1478 AD in Agra, Uttar Pradesh. He was disciple of Vallabhacharya. He was a blind. He was contemporary to the Mughal emperor Akbar.

22 **Consider the following statements regarding Shankaradeva.** *(Chap 8, Class-VII, New NCERT)*

1. He was responsible for the introduction of Bhakti Movement in Assam.
2. He composed poems and plays in Bengali.
3. He began the practice of setting up *namghars*.

Which of the statements given above are correct?

(a) 1 and 2 (b) 2 and 3
(c) 1 and 3 (d) All of these

Ans. (c)

Exp. Statements (1) and (3) are correct regarding Shankaradeva. Shankaradeva was responsible for the introduction of Bhakti Movement in Assam.

He was the follower of Vaishnavism. He was the leading proponent of spreading the ideas of Bhagavad Gita. He began the practice of setting up namghars or satra, type of monasteries. Ekasarana Dharma was founded by him.

Statement (2) is incorrect because he composed poems and plays in Assamese language.

23 **Consider the following statements in the context of Mirabai.** *(Chap 6, Class-XII, New NCERT)*

1. She was a Rajput princess married into the royal family of Mewar.
2. She was a disciple of Saint Dadu.
3. She was a devotee of Lord Krishna.

Which of the statements given above is/are incorrect?

(a) 1 and 2 (b) Only 2 (c) 1 and 3 (d) None of these

Ans. (b)

Exp. Statement (2) is incorrect in the context of Mirabai because she was a disciple of Saint Raidas who was a leather worker. Mirabai (15th-16th centuries AD) was a renowned Saguna saint from Rajasthan. She was born in a princely Rajput family.

24 **Consider the following statements with reference to the Jnaneshvara.** *(Chap 8, Class-VII, New NCERT)*

1. He preached bhakti in Maharashtra.
2. He wrote a commentary on Bhagavad Gita in Marathi.

Which of the statements given above is/are correct?

(a) Only 1 (b) Only 2
(c) Both 1 and 2 (d) Neither 1 nor 2

Ans. (c)

Exp. Both the statements (1) and (2) are correct with reference to Jnaneshvara. He was a Bhakti saint from Maharashtra. His time period was from 1275 to 1296 AD. He wrote a commentary of Bhagavad Gita called Jnaneswari. His other important work includes Changdev Prasasti and Amrit Anubhava. He was associated with the Krishnamargi sect.

25 **Which of the following statements is correct in the context of Ramananda?** *(Chap 11, Class-XI, Old NCERT)*

(a) He was a follower of Tulsidas.
(b) He was born at Prayag.
(c) He substituted worship of Vishnu on the place of Rama.
(d) Kabir is not considered among his closest disciples.

Ans. (b)

Exp. Statement (b) is correct as Ramananda was born at Prayag in 15th century AD.

Statements (a), (c) and (d) are incorrect because Ramananda was a follower of Ramanuja.

He substituted worship of Rama on the place of Vishnu. He preached in local languages to popularise his teachings. He taught the doctrine of Bhakti to all Varnas. He enrolled disciples from all castes including lower castes.

Kabir was one of his closest disciples along with Raidas, Sena and Dhanna.

26 **Consider the following statements.** *(Chap 11, Class-XI, Old NCERT)*

1. Bhakti saint Vallabha was a renowned follower of Vedantist philosophy.
2. He was a Tailang Brahmana.
3. He was not contemporary of the saint Jnaneshvara.

How many of the statements given above is/are correct?

(a) Only one (b) Only two
(c) All three (d) None of these

Ans. (b)

Exp. Only two statements i.e., (1) and (2) are correct. Vallabhacharya was an important Bhakti saint who followed Vedantist philosophy.

He was born in Banaras in a Telugu Tailang Brahmana family. His time period was from (1479-1531 AD). He propounded the philosophy of Shuddhadvaita. He founded Pustimarga and Rudra Sampradaya.

Statement (3) is incorrect because he was contemporary of the saint Jnaneshvara.

27 **Consider the following Bhakti saints with the modern state to, which he belonged?** *(Chap 11, Class-XI, Old NCERT)*

(1) Shankaradeva – Assam (2) Kabir – Uttar Pradesh
(3) Narsi Mehta – Gujarat (4) Tukaram – Bengal

How many of the pairs given above is/are incorrect?

(a) Only one (b) Only two
(c) Only three (d) None of these

Ans. (a)

Exp. Only one pair i.e., (4) is not correctly matched as Tukaram was Bhakti saint from Maharashtra. He was born in 1608 at Pune. He was a Nirguna saint. He was a devotee of Vithoba or Vitthala, incarnation of Lord Vishnu. He laid emphasis on community-based worship with spiritual songs called Kirtans. He wrote abhangas in Marathi language.

28 **Match the following lists and choose the correct code.** *(Chap 11, Class-XI, Old NCERT), (IAS Pre 2001)*

	List I (Bhakti Saints)		List II (Profession)
A.	Namdev	1.	Barber
B.	Kabir	2.	Weaver
C.	Ravidas/Raidas	3.	Tailor
D.	Sena	4.	Cobbler

Codes

	A	B	C	D		A	B	C	D
(a)	2	3	1	4	(b)	3	2	4	1
(c)	3	2	1	4	(d)	2	3	4	1

Ans. (b)

Exp. The correct matching is A-3, B-2, C-4, D-1.

Namdev was a tailor by profession. *Namdev* (1270-1350 AD) was a Bhakti saint from Maharashtra. He was devotee of Lord Vitthal of Pandher Pura.

Kabir was a weaver by profession. Kabir (1398-1518 AD) was a renowned Nirguna saint. He was against pilgrimage and idol worship.

Ravidas or Raidas was a cobbler by profession. He was born in 1450 at Varanasi (Uttar Pradesh).

Sena was a barber by profession. He worshipped Vithoba or Vitthala, incarnation of Lord Vishnu.

29 **Consider the following statements.** *(Chap 8, Class-VII, New NCERT)*

1. Nathpanthis, Siddhacharas and *Yogis* advocated the renunciation of the world.
2. They strongly advocated the rituals and other aspects of conventional religion.
3. These groups became particularly popular among 'Low castes'.

Which of the statements given above are correct?

(a) 1 and 2 (b) 2 and 3 (c) 1 and 3 (d) 1, 2 and 3

Ans. (c)

Exp. Statements (1) and (3) are correct. Nathpanthis, Siddhacharas and Yogis advocated the renunciation of the world. To them, the path to salvation lay in meditation on the formless ultimate reality and the realisation of oneness with it.

These groups became particularly popular among 'Low castes'. Their criticism of conventional religion created the ground for devotional religion to become a popular force in Northern India.

Statement (2) is incorrect because Nathpanthis, Siddhacharas and *Yogis* criticised the rituals and other aspects of the conventional religion.

Sikhism

30 **Consider the following statements with reference to the Guru Nanak.** *(Chap 8, Class-VII, New NCERT)*

1. He was born at Talwandi, which is located in Punjab province of Pakistan.
2. The sacred space created by Baba Guru Nanak for community kitchen is known as Dharmsala.
3. Guru Angad compiled the teaching of Baba Guru Nanak.

How many of the statements given above is/are correct?

(a) Only one (b) Only two
(c) All three (d) None of these

Ans. (b)

Exp. Only two statements i.e., (1) and (3) are correct with reference to Guru Nanak. He was born in 1469 AD at Talwandi, which is now located in Punjab province of Pakistan. He was a Nirguna saint.

Guru Angad (Second Sikh Guru) compiled the teaching of Baba Guru Nanak.

Statement (2) is incorrect because the sacred space created by Baba Guru Nanak for community kitchen is known as Langar. Guru Nanak was the founder of Sikh religion.

31 **Consider the following statements with reference to the teachings and principles of Guru Nanak .** *(Chap 11, Class-XI, Old NCERT)*

1. He wanted to establish a new religion by denouncing Hinduism.
2. He advocated a middle path in which spiritual life could be combined with the duties of the householder.

Which of the statements given above is/are correct?

(a) Only 1 (b) Only 2
(c) Both 1 and 2 (d) Neither 1 nor 2

Ans. (b)

Exp. Statement (2) is correct with reference to the teachings and principles of Guru Nanak. He advocated a middle path in which spiritual life could be combined with the duties of the householder.

He preached about the unity of God. He criticised idol-worship, pilgrimages and other tradition and rituals. He was the first Guru of Sikh.

Statement (1) is incorrect because he did not want to establish a new religion by denouncing Hinduism.

32 **Consider the following statements.** *(Chap 8, Class-VII, New NCERT)*

1. The city of Amritsar was established by Guru Ramdas.
2. Guru Ramdas was the fifth Guru of Sikhism.

Which of the statements given above is/are correct?

(a) Only 1
(b) Only 2
(c) Both 1 and 2
(d) Neither 1 nor 2

Ans. (a)

Exp. Statement (1) is correct as the city of Amritsar was established by Guru Ramdas. He also composed the four 'Laavn' of 'Anand Karaj' (Marriage code for Sikhs). He also received grants for the construction of Harmandir Sahib.

Statement (2) is incorrect because Guru Ramdas was the fourth of the ten Gurus of Sikhism.

33 **In the sacred text of the Sikh, Guru Granth Sahib the verses of, which among the following saints was/were included?** *(Chap 8, Class-XI, Old NCERT)*

1. Shaikh Farid 2. Saint Kabir
3. Namdev 4. Guru Teg Bahadur

Codes

(a) 1 and 2 (b) 2 and 3
(c) 1, 2 and 3 (d) All of these

Ans. (d)

Exp. In the sacred text of the sikh, Guru Granth Sahib the verses of Shaikh Farid, Saint Kabir, Namdev and Guru Teg Bahadur. The Adi Granth, its first rendition, was compiled by the fifth guru, Guru Arjan (1564–1606 AD). The Guru Granth Sahib is written in the Gurumukhi script.

Besides the teaching of these saints and Gurus, the teachings of Ramananda and five more Sikh Gurus namely, Guru Nanak, Guru Angad, Guru Aman Das, Guru Ram Das, Guru Arjan have also been included.

Sufi Movement

34 **Consider the following statements with reference to the Sufism.** *(Chap 6, Class-XII, New NCERT)*

1. Most Sufi silsilas were named after a founding figure.
2. The Qadiri order was named after Shaikh Nasriuddin Wahab Jilani.

Which of the statements given above is/are correct?

(a) Only 1 (b) Only 2
(c) Both 1 and 2 (d) Neither 1 nor 2

Ans. (a)

Exp. Statement (1) is correct with reference to the Sufism. Most Sufi silsilas were named after a founding figure. However, some like the chishti order, were named after their place of origin. It was the liberal movement in the Islam. It rejected rituals, orthodoxy and unscientific traditions.

Statement (2) is incorrect because the Qadri order was named after Shaikh Abdul Qadir Jilani.

35 **Consider the following statement with reference to the Abu'l Hasan al Hujwiri.** *(Chap 6, Class-XII, New NCERT)*

1. He settled in Lahore and wrote a book in Persian called the Kashful-Mahjub.
2. He was forced to cross the Indus as a captive of the invading Arab army.
3. He is revered as Data Ganj Bakhsh or 'Giver who bestows treasures'.

How many of the statements given above is/are incorrect?

(a) Only one (b) Only two
(c) All three (d) None of these

Ans. (a)

Exp. Only one statement i.e., (2) is incorrect regarding Abu'l Hasan al Hujwiri because in 1039 AD, he was forced to cross the Indus as a captive of the invading Turkish army.

36 **Consider the following statements about Sufism.** *(Chap 11, Class-XI, Old NCERT)*

1. The most influential group of sufis in India was the Suhrawardi.
2. Sufis were organised in 15 silsilas.

Which of the statements given above is/are incorrect?

(a) Only 1 (b) Only 2
(c) Both 1 and 2 (d) Neither 1 nor 2

Ans. (c)

Exp. Both the statements (1) and (2) are incorrect regarding sufism.

The most influential group of sufis in India was the Chisti not Suhrawardi. Over the course of period, sufism was organised into 12 silsilas. Silsilas were organised on the basis of spiritual genealogy of Sufi teachers. They followed a distinct method of instruction and way of devotion to God.

The Sufi movement in India emerged in the 11th century AD. Abu'l Hasan al Hujwiri laid the foundation of Sufism in India.

37 **Consider the following statements with regards to Khwaja Moinuddin Chishti.** *(Chap 11, Class-XI, Old NCERT)*

1. Khwaja Moinuddin is popularly known as 'Gharib Nawaz' (comforter of the poor).
2. Firoz Shah Tughlaq was the first Sultan to visit his shrine.

Which of the statements given above is/are incorrect?

(a) Only 1 (b) Only 2
(c) Both 1 and 2 (d) Neither 1 nor 2

Ans. (b)

Exp. Statement (2) is incorrect regarding Khwaja Moinuddin Chishti.

The Sultan of Delhi Sultanate (Muhammad bin Tughlaq) and Mughal Empire (Akbar) paid visit to Dargah of Khwaja Moinuddin Chishti.

38 **Arrange the following Sufi saints in their chronological order.** *(Chap 5, Class-VII, Old NCERT)*

1. Nasiruddin Chiragh-i-Delhi
2. Farid-ud-din Ganj-i-Shakar
3. Bakhtiyar Kaki
4. Khwaja Moinuddin Chishti

Codes

(a) 2, 1, 3, 4 (b) 4, 3, 2, 1 (c) 1, 4, 2, 3 (d) 4, 1, 3, 2

Ans. (b)

Exp. The correct chronological order of Sufi saints is 4, 3, 2, 1 i.e., Khwaja Moinuddin Chishti, Bakhtiyar Kaki, Farid-ud-din Ganj-i-Shakar, Nasiruddin Chiragh-i-Delhi.

Khwaja Moinuddin Chishti introduced the *Chishti Silsila* in India around 1192 AD.

Bakhtiyar Kaki was disciple and spiritual successor of Moinuddin Chishti. His base was in Delhi.

Farid-ud-din Ganj-i-Shakar was the disciple of Bakhtiyar Kaki. He was popularly known as Baba Farid or Shaikh Farid by people of all religions.

Nasiruddin Chiragh-i-Delhi was disciple and spiritual successor of Sufi saint Nizamuddin Auliya (1274-1337 AD).

39 **Consider the following statements about a Sufi saint.** *(Chap 6, Class-XII, New NCERT)*

1. His dargah is located in Delhi.
2. He was associated with the Chisti Silsila and died in the year 1235 AD.

The above statements are about which of the following saint?

(a) Shaikh Moinuddin Chishti
(b) Khwaja Qutubuddin Bakhtiyar Kaki
(c) Shaikh Fariduddin Ganj-i Shakar
(d) Shaikh Nizamuddin Auliya

Ans. (b)

Exp. The above given statements are about Sufi saint Khwaja Qutubuddin Bakhtiyar Kaki. His Dargah is located in Mehravli, Delhi (adjacent to Zafar Mahal). He was associated with the *Chisti Silsila* and died in the year 1235 AD.

Delhi Sultanate ruler, Iltutmish built a stepwell, Gandhak ki Baoli for him and Sher Shah Suri built a grand gateway at his dargah.

40 Consider the following statements. *(Chap 11, Class-XI, Old NCERT)*

1. Shaikh Nizamuddin's hospice was on the bank of the river Yamuna in Ghiyaspur (Delhi).
2. He adopted the yogic breathing exercise and because of which he gained the name *Sidh*.
3. He belonged to Sufi silsila, which believed in an austere and a simple life.

Which of the statements given above is/are correct?

(a) Only 1 (b) 1 and 2
(c) 2 and 3 (d) 1, 2 and 3

Ans. (d)

Exp. All the given statements are correct. Nizamuddin Auliya was one of the important Sufi saints of India. His hospice was on the banks of the river Yamuna in Ghiyaspur (Delhi). He was born in 1238 AD and died in 1325 AD.

He adopted the yogic breathing exercise and because of which he gained the name Sidh. He belonged to sufi silsila which believed in an austere and a simple life. He was also popularly known as Mahbub-e-Ilahi (Beloved of God).

41 Consider the following statements. *(Chap 6, Class-XII, New NCERT)*

1. Amir Khusrau was disciple of Shaikh Nizamuddin Auliya.
2. Amir Khusrau gave a unique form to the Chishti sama by introducing the *ziyarat* and *qaul*.
3. Shaikh Nizamuddin Auliya was contemporary to Mughal Emperor Akbar

Which of the statements given above is/are correct?

(a) Only 1 (b) 1 and 2
(c) 1 and 3 (d) 1, 2 and 3

Ans. (b)

Exp. Statements (1) and (2) are correct. Shaikh Nizamuddin Auliya was Sufi saint of Chishti order based in Delhi. The great poet and musician Amir Khusrau was his disciple.

Amir Khusrau gave a unique form to the Chishti sama by introducing the ziyarat and qaul. Later, Shaikh Nizamuddin Auliya always started his recital with the qaul.

Statement (3) is incorrect because Shaikh Nizamuddin Auliya was contemporary to Alauddin Khilji.

42 Consider the following pairs. *(Chap 11, Class-XI, Old NCERT)*

Sufi Saints	Dargahs
1. Shaikh Moinuddin Chishti	Ajmer
2. Shaikh Fariduddin Ganj-i Shakar	Ajodhan (Pakistan)
3. Shaikh Nizamuddin Auliya	Lahore
4. Khwaja Qutubuddin Bakhtiyar Kaki	Delhi

How many of the above given pairs is/are incorrectly matched?

(a) Only one (b) Only two
(c) Only three (d) None of these

Ans. (c)

Exp. Only one pair i.e., (c) is incorrectly matched because the Dargah of Shaikh Nizamuddin Auliya is located in Delhi not Lahore. Hazrat Nizamuddin Dargah is the Dargah of the sufi saint Khwaja Nizamuddin Aulia. He was sufi saint of the Chishti order. He was the disciple of Qutubuddin Bhaktiyar Kaki.

43 In the early year Delhi was the most important centre of Chishti Silsila. Which one of the following is the reason for decline of influence of Chishti Silsila in Delhi? *(Chap 11, Class-XI, Old NCERT)*

(a) After the death of Nasiruddin Chiragh-i-Delhi, the *Chishti* did not have commanding figure.
(b) Delhi Sultan denied patronage to Sufi's of *Chishti Silsila*.
(c) Due to instability in Delhi, they moved their centre to Southern India.
(d) None of the above

Ans. (a)

Exp. In the early year, Delhi was the most important centre of Chishti Silsila. Over the course of period, the influence of this Silsila declined in Delhi. This was mainly due to unavailability of any commanding figure after the death of Nasiruddin Chiragh-i-Delhi.

He is considered as the last pillar of Chishti Silsila in Delhi. His followers called him 'Roshan Chirag-e-Delhi', which in Persian, means 'Illuminated Lamp of Delhi'.

44 Consider the following statements with reference to the Shaikh Salim Chishti. *(Chap 6, Class-XII, New NCERT)*

1. The dargah of Shaikh Salim Chishti is located in Ajmer.
2. He was a direct descendant of Baba Farid.

Which of the statements given above is/are incorrect?

(a) Only 1 (b) Only 2
(c) Both 1 and 2 (d) Neither 1 nor 2

Ans. (a)

Exp. Statement (1) is incorrect with reference to Shaikh Salim Chishti because his dargah is located in Fatehpur Sikri, Agra, Uttar Pradesh not in Ajmer. He was highly revered by Mughal emperor Akbar. He named his first son Salim (later Emperor Jahangir) in honour of Chishti.

45 **Consider the following statements.**

(Chap 6, Class-XII, New NCERT)

1. Suhrawardi Silsila was popular in the Central India.
2. Sufis of this Silsila accepted the service of the state.
3. Shaikh Shihabuddin Suhrawardi was associated with this Silsila.

Which of the statements given above is/are incorrect?

(a) Only 1 (b) 1 and 2 (c) 2 and 3 (d) 1, 2 and 3

Ans. (a)

Exp. Statement (1) is incorrect because the activities of Suhrawardi Silsila were confined largely to the Punjab and Multan not in the Central India. This silsila was founded by Shihabuddin Suhrawardi in Baghdad and was established in India by Bahauddin Zakaria.

46 **With reference to the religious history of medieval India, the Sufi mystics were known to pursue, which of the following practices?**

(Chap 11, Class-XI, Old NCERT) (IAS Pre 2012)

1. Meditation and control of breath.
2. Severe ascetic exercise in lonely place.
3. Recitation of holy songs to arouse a state of ecstasy in their audience.

Codes

(a) 1 and 2 (b) 2 and 3 (c) Only 3 (d) 1, 2 and 3

Ans. (d)

Exp. All the given practices were pursued by Sufi mystics. These sufi saints practiced meditation and control of breath, which are traced to the Buddhist and Yogi influence. Sufis had risen in Islam at a very early state. These Sufi Saints helped to spread peace and harmony in Medieval India.

These Sufis turned to asceticism and mysticism in protest against growing materialism of the caliphate as a religious and political institution.

They laid emphasis on seeking salvation through intense devotion and love for God.

They also recited the holy songs to arouse a state of ecstasy in their audience.

47 **Consider the following Assertion (A) and Reason (R) and choose the correct code.**

(Chap 11, Class-XI, Old NCERT)

Assertion (A) Many Sanskrit works on music were translated into Persian during the medieval period.

Reason (R) The early Chisti Sufis were fond of musical assemblies called sama.

Codes

(a) Both A and R are true and R is the correct explanation of A.
(b) Both A and R are true, but R is not the correct explanation of A.
(c) A is true, but R is false.
(d) A is false, but R is true.

Ans. (b)

Exp. Both Assertion (A) and Reason (R) are true, but (R) is not the correct explanation of Assertion (A).

Many Sanskrit works on music were translated into Persian during the medieval period. Rulers of Delhi sultanate and Mughal Emperor promoted the translation work. Sufism did not only influence religious and social sphere but was also influenced cultural sphere.

The early *Chisti Sufis* were fond of musical assemblies called *sama*. It is considered as a form of worship in Sufism. It often includes singing, playing instruments, dancing, recitation of poetry and prayers, wearing symbolic attire and other rituals.

48 **Who, of the following saints were Sufi?**

(Chap 6, Class-XII, New NCERT)
(UPPSC Pre 1998, UP Lower 1998)

1. Rahim
2. Nizamuddin Auliya
3. Moinuddin Chishti
4. Rashkhan

Codes

(a) 1 and 3 (b) 1, 2 and 3
(c) 2 and 3 (d) 2 and 4

Ans. (c)

Exp. Moinuddin Chishti and Nizamuddin Auliya were the Sufi saints. Moinuddin Chishti promulgated the famous Chishti order of Sunni mysticism.

This particular tariqa (order) became the dominant Muslim spiritual group in medieval India and many of the most beloved and venerated Indian Sunni saints were Chishti in their affiliation, including Nizamuddin Auliya and Amir Khusrau.

49 **Qalandars, Madaris, Malangs and Haidaris mystics were considered different from other Sufi saints because of, which of the following reason?**

(Chap 6, Class-XII, New NCERT)

(a) They followed rituals and observed extreme forms of asceticism.
(b) They ignored rituals and observed extreme forms of asceticism.
(c) They enjoyed luxurious life.
(d) They followed principles of other religion.

Ans. (b)

Exp. Qalandars, Madaris, Malangs and Haidaris mystics also emerged along with Sufism. However, they were different from other Sufi saints because they ignored rituals and observed extreme forms of asceticism.

Sufi saints were against some orthodox rituals but they never promoted or observed extreme forms of asceticism.

50 **Consider the following pairs.**

(Chap 11, Class-XI, Old NCERT)

Sufi Terminology		Meaning
1. Pir	–	Successor of the Sufi saint
2. Murid	–	Sufi teacher
3. Wali	–	Place where Sufi saints live
4. Khanquah	–	Disciple

How many of the above pairs is/ are correctly matched?

(a) Only one (b) Only two
(c) Only three (d) None of these

Ans. (d)

Exp. None of the above pairs are correctly matched.

Pir refers to Sufi teacher. In Sufism, the tradition of Pir and Murid has played a very significant role. They provided guidance to their disciples.

Murid refers to disciple. Amir Khusrau was the famous murid of Shaikh Nizamuddin Auliya.

Wali refers to successor of the Sufi saint. When a Sufi saint died then he was succeeded by Wali.

Khanquah refers to Sufi hermitage. It was the place where Sufi saints use to live. It was considered as main centre.

51 With reference to Sufism in Indian history, consider the following statements. *(Chap-6, Class-XII, New NCERT)* *(IAS Pre 2002)*

1. Sheikh Ahmad Sirhindi was a contemporary of Ibrahim Lodi.
2. Sheikh Nasiruddin Chirag-i-Dehlavi was a disciple of Sheikh Nizamuddin Auliya.
3. Aurangzeb was a contemporary of Sheikh Salim Chishti.
4. The Qadiri order of Sufis was first introduced in India by Sheikh Niamatullah and Makhdum Muhammad Jilani.

Which of the statements given above are correct?

(a) 1 and 2 (b) 1 and 3
(c) 2 and 3 (d) 2 and 4

Ans. (d)

Exp. Statements (2) and (4) are correct with reference to Sufism in Indian history. Nasiruddin Mahmud Chirag-i-Dehlavi (1274 - 1337) was a 14th century mystic poet and a Sufi saint of the Chishti order.

He was a disciple of Sufi saint Sheikh Nizamuddin Auliya. He was the last important Sufi of the Chishti order from Delhi.

The Qadiri order of Sufis was first introduced in India by Sheikh Niamatullah and Makhdum Muhammad Jilani.

It was introduced in India during Babur period. A great follower of Qadri order was Dara Shikoh, who was the eldest son of the Mughal Emperor Shah Jahan.

52 Consider the following pairs. *(Chap 6, Class-XII, Old NCERT)*

Term		Meaning
1. Malfuzat	–	Conversations of sufi saint
2. Tazkiras	–	Treatises or manuals
3. Maktubat	–	Collections of letters

Which of the above pairs is/are correctly matched?

(a) 1 and 2 (b) 1 and 3 (c) 2 and 3 (d) Only 2

Ans. (b)

Exp. Pairs (1) and (3) are correctly matched.

Malfuzat refers to records of teaching of the Sufi saints, Pirs and Shaikhs. Some of the famous Malfuzat are Khair-al-Majalis, Fawa'id-al-Faud, etc.

Maktubat refers to collection of letters, which were generally addressed to their murids.

Pair (2) is incorrectly matched because Tazkiras refers to biographical accounts of the Sufi saints. Siyar-ui-Auliya is considered as a first Tazkiras.

53 Which of the principle are common for Bhakti and Sufi movement? *(Chap 11, Class-XI, Old NCERT)* *(Andhra Pradesh PCS Pre 2023)*

1. Monotheism
2. Asceticism
3. Religious tolerance
4. Accepted the idol worship to some extent

(a) 1, 2 and 3 (b) 2, 3 and 4
(c) 1, 3 and 4 (d) 1, 2 and 4

Ans. (a)

Exp. Among the following options (1), (2) and (3) are correct i.e., monotheism, asceticism and religious tolerance are common for Bhakti and Sufi movement. Both movement focuses on devotion to God. They believed that this was the best way to connect with God. Asceticism was the basic principle for one to have devotion. Religious tolerance was the significant role for both movement in promotion of harmony in medieval India.

Chapter 18

The Mughal Empire and Its Decline

The Mughal Empire and Its Decline

Origin
- The name 'Mughal' derives from Mongol
- Descendants of two great lineages of Genghis Khan and Timur
- Founded by Babur

Babur (1526-1530 AD)
- Defeated Ibrahim Lodi in first Battle of Panipat; Laid the foundation of Mughal empire in India; Wrote his autobiography Tuzuk-i- Baburi in Turkhish language
- **Major War Won by Babur** Battle of Khanwa against Rana Sanga; Battle of Chanderi against Medini Rai; and Battle of Ghagra against Eastern Afghanistan confederation
- **Significance** Kabul and Qandahar became integral parts of India
- Strengthened foreign trade with India; Introduced new modes of warfare; Laid number of gardens

Humayun (1530-1540 AD and 1555-1556 AD)
- Divided his empire among brothers- Hindal, Askari and Kamran
- Annexed Kalinjar fort
- Defeated Mahmood Lodhi in Battle of Dauhariya

Sur Empire (1540- 1555 AD)
- Afghan in origin; founded by Sher Shah Suri after defeating Humayun

Contribution of Sher Shah Suri
- Continued the strong central machinery of administration
- **Army** Direct recruitment of soldiers; set up cantonment in different parts of the empire with strong garrison
- **Land Revenue System** Crop rate was developed and share of state was 1/3 of the produce
- **Trade and Commerce** Restored the old imperial road called the Grand Trunk road
- Introduced Rupaya (a silver coin) and Dam (a copper coin)
- **Art and Architecture** Built his tomb at Sasaram
- Constructed old- fort in Delhi

Akbar (1556- 1605 AD)
- Won Second Battle of Panipat against Hemchandra with the assistance of his regent Bairam Khan
- Appointed 9 gems (navratnas)- Miyan Tansen, Raja Birbal, Faizi, Abdul Rahim Khan-i-Khana, Raja Todarmal, etc
- **Territorial Consolidation** Conquered parts of Malwa, Gujarat, Bihar, Khandesh and Ahmednagar
- **Social and Religious Reforms** Abolished Jizyah and practice of forcibly converting prisoners of war to Islam
- Initiated policy of Sulh-i-Kul
- Set up a new religion- Din-i-Ilahi

Jahangir (1605-1627 AD)
- Stabilised India's relation with Iran, Uzbeks and Ottoman Turks; Settled outstanding dispute with Mewar
- Ordered execution of 5th Sikh Guru Arjan Dev
- Married Nur Jahan

Shah Jahan (1628-1658 AD)
- Golden era of Art and Architecture in Medieval India
- Conquest of Deccan
- Continuous struggle with Safavid empire for the Territory of Qandhar

Aurangzeb (1658- 1707 AD)
- Defeated brothers- Shuja and Dara Sikoh in three successive wars of succession at Dharmat, Samugarh and Deorai
- Empire reached its territorial climax
- **Religious Policies** Reversed Akbar's policy of religious toleration
- Re-introduced Jizyah; Ordered destruction of many temples
- Discontinued the festival of Nauroz, Jharokha darshan

Decline of Mughal Empire
- Highly centralised administration
- Aurangzeb Deccan policy
- Rise of Marathas
- Jagirdari crisis
- Religious fanaticism

SOURCE *New NCERT Class VII (The Mughal Empire), Old NCERT Class VII (The Coming of the Mughals and the Europeans), NCERT Class VII (Akbar Old), Old NCERT Class VII (The Age of Magnificence), Old NCERT, Class XI (Struggle for Empire in North India–II (Mughals and Afghans 1525–1555), Old NCERT Class XI (Consolidation of the Mughal Empire (Age of Akbar), Old NCERT Class XI (The Deccan and South India), Old NCERT, Class XI (India in the First Half of the Seventeenth Century), Old NCERT, Class XI (Climax and Disintegration of the Mughal Empire–I), Old NCERT, Class XI (Economic and Social Life under Mughals)*

Babur

1 Consider the following statements in the context of Babur. *(Chap 4, Class-VII, New NCERT)*

1. He succeeded the throne of Ferghana, when he was only 11 years old.
2. In 1526, he defeated the Sultan of Delhi, Sikandar Lodi at Panipat and captured Delhi and Jaipur.
3. He was forced to leave Ferghana due to the invasion of Arab group, the Uzbeks.
4. He ruled over India for 10 years and consolidated his Empire in India.

How many of the statements given above is/are correct?

(a) Only one (b) Only two
(c) Only three (d) All of the above

Ans. (a)

Exp. Only one statement i.e., (1) is correct in context of Babur. Umar Shaikh Mirza was the ruler of Ferghana and father of Babur. Due to sudden death of his father, Babur succeeded the throne at the age of 11.

Statements (2), (3) and (4) are incorrect because he defeated Sultan Ibrahim Lodi of Delhi at Panipat in 1526 AD and founded Mughal Empire in India. He did not capture Jaipur in 1526 AD.

He was forced to leave Ferghana due to frequent invasion of Turk group. The Uzbeks under the leadership of the Shaibani Khan captured Ferghana. He ruled in India for about four years (1526 AD - 1530 AD).

2 Consider the following statements. *(Chap 12, Class-XI, Old NCERT)*

1. Babur was invited to invade India by Daulat Khan Lodi and Rana Sanga.
2. Ustad Ali and Mustafa played key role in utilisation of gunpowder.
3. Rana Sanga supplied troops and other help to Babur in the Battle of Panipat.

Which of the statements given above is/are correct?

(a) Only 1
(b) 1 and 2
(c) 2 and 3
(d) 1, 2 and 3

Ans. (b)

Exp. Statements (1) and (2) are correct as Babur marched towards Delhi on the invitation of Daulat Khan Lodi and Rana Sanga. Daulat Khan Lodi was the Governor of Lahore and he was not happy with the policies of Ibrahim Lodi. Rana Sanga was the ruler of Mewar, who wanted to remove Ibrahim Lodi from Delhi.

In the First Battle of Panipat, Ustad Ali and Mustafa played key role in the utilisation of the gunpowder for the armies of Babur.

Statement (3) is incorrect because Rana Sanga did not supply troops and other help to Babur in the Battle of Panipat.

3 Who among the following defeated Babur in the Battle of Sar-e-pul? *(Chap 12, Class-XI, Old NCERT) (UP Lower Pre 2015)*

(a) Abdullah Khan Uzbek (b) Shaibani Khan
(c) Ubaydullah Khan (d) Jani Begh

Ans. (b)

Exp. Shaibani Khan defeated Babur in the Battle of Sar-e-pul. Shaibani Khan also known as Shahi Beg Khan, was an Uzbek leader. He was the descendant of Shaiban, the fifth son of Jochi (Genghis Khan's eldest son).

4 The main reason of Babur's victory in the Battle of Panipat was *(Chap 6, Class-VII, Old NCERT)*

(a) his horse riding force
(b) his skilled warfare
(c) support of local people
(d) internal disputes among Afghans

Ans. (b)

Exp. The main reason of Babur's victory in the Battle of Panipat was his skilled warfare.

Babur used gunpowder, firearms and field artillery in such a way that Ibrahim's army in the Battle of Panipat was not able to stabilise itself. The tactics used by Babur in this battle is popularly known as *Tulghuma*.

5 Consider the following pairs regarding the military campaigns of Babur. *(Chap 6, Class-VII, Old NCERT)*

	Year		Campaigns
1.	1524 AD	–	Captured Lahore
2.	1527 AD	–	Defeated the Rajputs at Chanderi
3.	1528 AD	–	Defeated Rana Sanga, Rajput rulers and allies at Khanwa.

Which of the pairs given above is/are incorrectly matched?

(a) Only 1 (b) 2 and 3 (c) Only 3 (d) Only 2

Ans. (b)

Exp. Pairs (2) and (3) are incorrectly matched because Babur defeated the Rajput forces led by Rana Sanga at Khanwa in 1527 AD (not 1528 AD). In the next year (1528 AD), the Battle of Chanderi was fought between the Rajput ruler Medini Rai and the Babur. In this battle, Babur emerged victorious.

6 Consider the following statements. *(Chap 4, Class-VII, New NCERT) (Chap 9, Module-2) (IAS Pre 2015)*

The arrival of Babur in India led to the

1. introduction of gunpowder in the subcontinent.
2. introduction of the arch and dome in the region architecture.
3. establishment of Timurid dynasty in the region.

Select the correct answer by using the codes given below.

(a) 1 and 2 (b) Only 3 (c) 1 and 3 (d) All of these

Ans. (b)

Exp. Only statement (3) is correct as the arrival of Babur in India led to the establishment of Timurid dynasty in India.

Statements (1) and (2) are incorrect because gunpowder was introduced much earlier in the Indian subcontinent, probably in the 13th century by Mongols. Arch and domes were introduced in India by the Turkish rulers.

7 The Empire of Babur included the areas of

(Chap 6, Class-VI, NCERT) (UKPSC Pre 2003)

1. Kabul
2. Punjab
3. modern Uttar Pradesh
4. modern Rajasthan

Which of the options given above is/are correct?

(a) 1 and 2 (b) 2 and 3
(c) 1, 2 and 3 (d) 2, 3 and 4

Ans. (c)

Exp. Kabul, Punjab and Modern Uttar Pradesh were included in the empire of Babur. The Mughal Empire during the reign of Babur included modern day territories of Kabul, Punjab and Delhi and Gangetic plain of Uttar Pradesh. Except Kabul, these territories were annexed by Babur after defeating Ibrahim Lodi in the Third Battle of Panipat (1526 AD). In the subsequent battles (at Khanwa and Chanderi), he was able to consolidate his control over parts of Eastern Rajasthan and Madhya Pradesh.

While territories encompassing modern Rajasthan came under full control of the Mughals during the reign of Jahangir in 1615 AD.

8 Consider the following statements.

(Chap 6, Class-VII, Old NCERT)

1. Babur was a poet and writer and his mother tongue was Persian.
2. He was always keen to make gardens in all the places where he lived.
3. He made polo game popular amongst Indian nobles.

Which of the statements given above is/are correct?

(a) Only 1 (b) 1 and 2 (c) 2 and 3 (d) 1, 2 and 3

Ans. (c)

Exp. Statements (2) and (3) are correct.

Apart from military conquest, Babur is also known for his other talent and interests. He was always keen to make gardens in all the places, where he lived such as in Kabul where he created many gardens. He was also interested in Polo game, due to him it became popular amongst Indian nobles.

Statement (1) is incorrect because Babur was an excellent poet and writer and his mother tongue was Turkish. His memoir *Tujuk-e-Babri* was written by him in Turkish language.

9 Which one of the following pairs is not correctly matched? *(Chap 12, Class-XI, Old NCERT) (UPPSC Pre 2015)*

(a) First Battle of Panipat – 1526
(b) Battle of Khanwa – 1527
(c) Battle of Ghaghra – 1529
(d) Battle of Chanderi – 1530

Ans. (d)

Exp. Pair (d) is not correctly matched because Battle of Chanderi was fought in 1528 (not in 1530) between Babur and Medini Rai.

It took place in the aftermath of the Battle of Khanwa in which the Mughal emperor Babur had defeated a confederacy of Rajputs and Afghans which was headed by Rana Sanga of Mewar.

Humayun

10 From the following names, identify the one who was not the brother of Humayun?

(Chap 12, Class-XI, Old NCERT)

1. Kamran 2. Usman
3. Askari 4. Hindal

Codes

(a) 1 and 2 (b) 2 and 3
(c) Only 2 (d) None of these

Ans. (c)

Exp. Usman was not the brother of Humayun. Babur had four sons namely Humayun, Kamran, Askari and Hindal. Humayun was eldest among them. He succeeded the throne after his death till 1530 AD.

He reigned from 1530 to 1540 AD and again from 1555 to 1556 AD. Kabul and Qandhar were under the charge of Humayun's younger brother, Kamran.

11 Consider the following statements with reference to Humayun. *(Chap 6, Class-VII, Old NCERT)*

1. He divided his inheritance according to the will of his father.
2. Sher Khan, a Turk noble defeated Humayun at Chausa and Kannauj and forced him to flee to Iran.

Which of the statements given above is/are incorrect?

(a) Only 1 (b) Only 2
(c) Both 1 and 2 (d) Neither 1 nor 2

Ans. (b)

Exp. Statement (2) is incorrect with reference to Humayun. Due to sudden death of Babur, the responsibility of consolidating newly formed Empire came on his shoulders. In the Eastern India, Sher Khan an Afghan posed challenge to Mughal Empire.

Humayun marched against him but he was defeated by Sher Khan in the Battle of Chausa (1539 AD) and Kannauj (1540 AD) and he lost his empire. Ultimately, ruler of Iran gave him refuge.

12 Humayun during his short reign carried out many military expeditions. In this context, which of the following was/were captured by him? ***(Chap 6, Class-VII, Old NCERT)***

1. Gujarat 2. Golconda 3. Malwa

Codes

(a) 1 and 3 (b) 2 and 3
(c) Only 2 (d) All of these

Ans. (a)

Exp. Gujarat and Malwa were caputured by Humayun. He launched many military expeditions to expand the territory of his Empire. He marched against the Gujarat, which was ruled by Bahadur Shah and defeated him. He was also able to defeat ruler of Malwa.

13 Consider the following statements. ***(Chap 6, Class-VII, Old NCERT)***

1. In Iran, Humayun received help from the Safavid Shah.
2. The ambitions of his brother Mirza Kamran weakened Humayun's cause against Afghan competitors.
3. He died in the year 1556 AD in a battle against the Afghan nobles.

Which of the statements given above is/are correct?

(a) Only 1 (b) 1 and 2 (c) 2 and 3 (d) 1, 2 and 3

Ans. (b)

Exp. Statements (1) and (2) are correct.

Sher Shah Suri forced Humayun to leave Delhi. After, which, he wandered in North-West India but he did not receive any help.

Even his brothers didn't help him. It was the ambition of his brother Mirza Kamran, which weakened Humayun's cause against Afghan competitors.

Safavid ruler of Iran, helped him to recapture his lost territories by providing monetary and military support.

Statement (3) is incorrect because Humayun died in 1556 AD due to his fall from the staircase of his library.

14 Arrange properly as per dates of four important battles fought by Humayun, the names of battlefields are given below. ***(Chap 12, Class-XI, Old NCERT) (Chap 9, Module-2, NIOS) (41st BPSC Pre 1996)***

(a) Chausa, Devara, Kannauj, Sirhind
(b) Devara, Kannauj, Chausa, Sirhind
(c) Sirhind, Devara, Chausa, Kannauj
(d) Devara, Chausa, Kannauj, Sirhind

Ans. (d)

Exp. The correct chronological order of battles fought by Humayun is Devara, Chausa, Kannauj and Sirhind.

In the Battle of Devara or Dauharia (1532) Humayun defeated Mahmud Lodi, a relative of Ibrahim Lodi.

Battle of Chausa (26th June, 1539) was fought between Humayun and Sher Shah Suri. Humayun was defeated by Sher Shah.

Battle of Kannauj (May, 1540) Mughal forces once again clashed with Sher Shah. This time Humayun was decisively defeated and he left India and went into exile for 15 years.

Battle of Sirhind (22nd June, 1555) was fought between Humayun and Sikandar Shah Suri. Mughal victory led to be re-establishment of the Mughal empire.

15 What was/were the main reasons behind the establishment of a new city, of Delhi by Humayun, which he named Dinpanah? ***(Chap 12, Class-XI, Old NCERT)***

1. It can serve as a second capital.
2. Agra was under constant threat due to rising power of the Bahadur Shah.

Codes

(a) Only 1 (b) Only 2
(c) Both 1 and 2 (d) Neither 1 nor 2

Ans. (c)

Exp. Both the statements (1) and (2) were reasons behind establishing Delhi. Humayun is credited for the establishment of a new city of Delhi, named Dinpanah. The reason for its establishment is to create another seat of capital, as Agra was under constant threat due to rising power of the Bahadur Shah and Delhi will also serve as second capital.

Sher Shah

16 Consider the following statements with reference to Sher Shah. ***(Chap 6, Class-VII, Old NCERT)***

1. His real name was Farid.
2. He was the son of nobleman, who had a small estate under the rulers of Jaunpur.

Which of the statements given above is/are correct?

(a) Only 1 (b) Only 2
(c) Both 1 and 2 (d) Neither 1 nor 2

Ans. (a)

Exp. Only statement (1) is correct with reference to Sher Shah. In 1540 AD, Suri dynasty was established by the Sher Shah. His real name was Farid.

Statement (2) is incorrect because he was the son of Hasan Khan, who was the small Jagirdar at Sasaram (Bihar). He received the title Sher Khan by Bahar Khan Lahori (Governor of Bihar).

17 Which of the following statements is/are incorrect regarding the founder of the Suri dynasty?
(Chap 6, Class-VII, Old NCERT)

1. He built the Grand Trunk road from Peshawar to Allahabad (now Prayagraj) on line of highway built by Guptas.
2. He issued the coin named rupiah.

Codes

(a) Only 1 (b) Only 2
(c) Both 1 and 2 (d) Neither 1 nor 2

Ans. (a)

Exp. Only statement (1) is incorrect regarding to the founder of Suri dynasty because apart being a great soldier and general, Sher Shah was also a great administrator.

He had taken many initiatives for the welfare of people. He built the Grand Trunk road from Peshawar to Allahabad (now Prayagraj) on the line of highway built by Mauryas not Guptas.

18 Consider the following statements regarding administration during Sher Shah Suri.
(Chap 12, Class-XI, Old NCERT)

1. He divided his empire into *Sarkars*, which in turn was divided into *Parganas*.
2. He administered *Sarkar* and *Pargana* directly without using any other officials.

Which of the statements given above is/are correct?

(a) Only 1 (b) Only 2
(c) 1 and 2 (d) Neither 1 nor 2

Ans. (a)

Exp. Only statement (1) is correct regarding administration during Sher Shah Suri. To bring efficiency in the administration Sher Shah Suri divided his empire into *Sarkars*.

A *Sarkar* consists of various *Parganas*.

Statement (2) is incorrect because *Pargana* was under the charge of officials such as *Shiqdar, Amin, Fotedar* and *Karkuns*.

19 Consider the following statements regarding Sher Shah.
(Chap 12, Class-XI, Old NCERT)

1. During Sher Shah's reign, the village panchayats and zamindars were not allowed to deal with civil and criminal cases at the local level.
2. Sher Shah set up army cantonment in different parts of the Empire and a strong garrison was posted in each of them.

Which of the statements given above is/are correct?

(a) Only 1
(b) Only 2
(c) Both 1 and 2
(d) Neither 1 nor 2

Ans. (b)

Exp. Only statement (2) is correct regarding Sher Shah. Sher Shah had set up army cantonment in different parts of the empire and a strong garrison was posted in each of them. This was done with an objective of ensuring fast mobilisation of forces.

Statement (1) is incorrect because during his reign, the village panchayats and zamindars were allowed to deal with civil and criminal cases at the local level.

20 Sher Shah reign saw development of many new innovations in the administration. One such innovation was Patta system. What do you mean by Patta? *(Chap 12, Class-XI, Old NCERT)*

(a) Revenue system based on the system initiated by Alauddin Khilji
(b) It was a currency system developed by the Sher Shah
(c) Document contained details about the crop, area sown and amount paid by farmer
(d) It was related with the spies system of the state

Ans. (c)

Exp. Patta was a document that contained details about the crop, area sown and amount paid by farmer. Sher Shah innovated the Patta system for the welfare of farmers. It was also done to increase the efficiency of land revenue system.

21 Consider the following statements regarding the Sarai built by Sher Shah for convenience of travellers. *(Chap 12, Class-XI, Old NCERT)*

1. A Sarai was a fortified lodging or inn where travellers could spend the night and also keep their goods in safe custody.
2. Separate lodgings for Hindus and Muslims were provided in *Sarais*.
3. Brahmanas were appointed for providing bed and food to the Hindu travellers and grains for their horses.

Which of the statements given above is/are correct?

(a) Only 1
(b) 1 and 2
(c) 2 and 3
(d) All of the above

Ans. (d)

Exp. All the statements (1), (2) and (3) are correct regarding the *Sarai* built by Sher Shah for the convenience of travellers.

During Sher Shah's reign, large number of *Sarais* (resting houses) were built. A *Sarai* was a fortified lodging or inn where travellers could spend the night and also keep their goods in safe custody.

Separate lodgings for Hindus and Muslims were provided in *Sarais*.

Moreover, Brahmanas were appointed for providing bed and food to Hindu travellers and grains for their horses.

Akbar

22 **Consider the following statements regarding the early life of Akbar.** *(Chap 7, Class-VII, Old NCERT)*

1. He was of only 13 years in 1556 AD when his father died and he was proclaimed as the King.
2. Bairam Khan became his regent as he was too young to manage throne.
3. His first conflict held with his uncle Hindal just after coronation.

Which of the statements given above is/are correct?

(a) Only 1 (b) 1 and 2
(c) 2 and 3 (d) 1, 2 and 3

Ans. (b)

Exp. Statements (1) and (2) are correct regarding early life of Akbar. Humayun was succeeded by Akbar in 1556 AD. He was crowned at the age of 13. Bairam Khan was an important military General of Humayun. He became his regent as Akbar was too young to manage throne.

Statement (3) is incorrect as his uncle Hindal Mirza died in 1551 AD and Akbar was coronated in 1556 AD.

23 **Consider the following statements with reference to the Second Battle of Panipat.** *(Chap 7, Class-VII, Old NCERT)*

1. It was fought between Akbar and Mirza Hakim.
2. It was won by Akbar's generals Khan Zoman-1 and Bairam Khan.

Which of the statements given above is/are incorrect?

(a) Only 1
(b) Only 2
(c) Both 1 and 2
(d) Neither 1 nor 2

Ans. (c)

Exp. Both the statements (1) and (2) are incorrect regarding the second Battle of Panipat.

The Second Battle of Panipat was fought in the year 1556 AD. It was fought between Akbar and Hemu (General of Afghan ruler of Bengal).

Akbar's Army was led by Bairam Khan (Patron of Akbar). In this battle, Mughals were on the verge of defeat meanwhile an arrow pierced into eye of Hemu. In this battle, Hemu's army was defeated by Mughals.

24 **Consider the following statements with reference to the Royal court of Akbar.** *(Chap 7, Class-VII, Old NCERT)*

1. *Diwan-i-Aam* was the large hall where he would meet the special guest.
2. *Diwan-i-Khas* was the large hall where he would meet the large audience (common people).

Which of the statements given above is/are incorrect?

(a) Only 1 (b) Only 2
(c) Both 1 and 2 (d) Neither 1 nor 2

Ans. (c)

Exp. Both the statements (1) and (2) are incorrect. During the reign of Akbar two special assemblies were convened for an efficient administration i.e., *Diwan-i-Aam* and *Diwan-i-Khas*.

Diwan-i-Aam was the large hall where Mughal Emperor had meeting with common people. In this assembly, people listed out their grievances against inefficient rules of the nobles and *mansabdar*.

Diwan-i-Khas was the large hall where Mughal Emperor met with special dignitaries including his officials. It was a hall of private audience.

25 **Match the following list correctly and choose the correct code.** *(Chap 7, Class-VII, Old NCERT)*

List I (Year)	List II (Military Campaign of Akbar)
A. 1568 AD	1. Ahmednagar
B. 1595 AD	2. Malwa
C. 1581 AD	3. Chittor
D. 1561 AD	4. Kabul

Codes

	A	B	C	D		A	B	C	D
(a)	1	2	3	4	(b)	2	3	4	1
(c)	4	2	3	1	(d)	3	1	4	2

Ans. (d)

Exp. The correct matching is A-3, B-1, C-4, D-2.

In **1568 AD**, Chittor was annexed from Rana Udai Singh. In the siege of Chittor, Jaimal and Patta showed exceptional valour to save it from Mughals.

In **1595 AD**, Akbar annexed the territories of Ahmednagar ruled by Chand Bibi.

In **1581 AD**, Akbar defeated Mirza Hakim (ruler of Kabul) and gave its charge to his sister Bakhtunnisa Begum.

In **1561 AD**, he sent expedition to Malwa. It was again occupied and came under the control of Mughals.

26 **Consider the following statements with reference to the revolt in Akbar's reign.** *(Chap 13, Class-XI, Old NCERT)*

1. Mirza Hakim, ruler of Kabul abetted rebellion in the area ruled by Akbar.
2. The period between 1580-81 AD was marked by major rebellion.
3. During the revolts, Mirza Hakim received the support of the Raja Man Singh.

Which of the statements given above is/are correct?

(a) Only 1 (b) 1 and 2 (c) 2 and 3 (d) 1, 2 and 3

Ans. (b)

Exp. Statements (1) and (2) are correct as Mirza Hakim, ruler of Kabul played key role in revolts against the Akbar. The period between 1580-81 AD was marked by major rebellion against the Akbar. The rebellions were mainly happened in Bengal, Bihar, Gujarat and North-West areas.

Statement (3) is incorrect because during the revolts, Mirza Hakim did not receive the support of Raja Man Singh.

27 **Consider the following statements with regard to the Battle of Haldighati.** *(Chap 13, Class-XI, Old NCERT)*

1. Akbar's army was led by the Raja Man Singh.
2. War was happened when Rana Pratap denied accepting Mughal suzerainty.
3. In this battle, Raja Man Singh was defeated very badly.

How many of the statements given above is/are incorrect?

(a) Only one (b) Only two
(c) All three (d) None of these

Ans. (a)

Exp. Only one statement i.e., (3) is incorrect with regard to the Battle of Haldighati. The Battle of Haldighati is one of the most important battles of Mughal period. It was fought in 1576 AD between Maharana Pratap of Mewar and Akbar.

It happened when Rana Pratap denied to accept Mughal suzerainty. In this battle, Mughal forces were led by the Raja Man Singh of Amber, who defeated Maharana Pratap of Mewar.

28 **Consider the following statements.** *(Chap 14, Class-XI, Old NCERT)*

1. Chand Bibi ruled over the Ahmednagar as a regent.
2. She accepted Mughal suzerainty in the year 1596 AD.
3. She ceded Berar to Mughals in return of their recognition of the claim of Bahadur as a ruler of Ahmednagar.

Which of the statements given above is/are correct?

(a) Only 1 (b) 1 and 2
(c) 2 and 3 (d) 1, 2 and 3

Ans. (d)

Exp. All the given statements (1), (2) and (3) are correct. Chand Bibi ruled over the Ahmednagar as a regent. In the year 1595 AD, Mughal forces invaded Ahmednagar and defeated her.

She accepted the Mughal suzerainty in the year 1596 AD. She also ceded Berar to Mughals in return of their recognition of the claim of Bahadur as a ruler of Ahmednagar. She also acted as a regent of Bijapur.

29 **Consider the following statements with reference to Mughals territorial expansion in Deccan.** *(Chap 14, Class-XI, Old NCERT)*

1. Abdur Rahim Khan-i-Khanan was Mughal Commander in Deccan.
2. He was defeated by Malik Ambar in 1601 AD at a place called Nander.

Which of the statements given above is/are correct?

(a) Only 1 (b) Only 2
(c) Both 1 and 2 (d) Neither 1 nor 2

Ans. (a)

Exp. Only statement (1) is correct with reference to Mughals territorial expansion in Deccan.

Abdur Rahim Khan-i-Khanan was the Mughal Commander in Deccan.

When differences grew between Prince Murad and Abdur Rahim Khan-i-Khanan, latter was called back. He inflicted a crushing defeat on Malik Ambar in 1601 AD at a place called Nander.

However, he decided to make friendship with Ambar since, he considered it beneficial that there should be stability in the remaining Nizam Shahi Kingdom.

30 **Ibadat Khana at Fatehpur Sikri was** *(Chap 13, Class-XI, Old NCERT) (IAS Pre 2014)*

(a) the mosque for use of royal family.
(b) Akbar's private chamber prayer.
(c) the hall in which Akbar held discussion with scholars at various religions.
(d) the room in which the nobles belonging to different religions gathered to discuss religious affairs.

Ans. (c)

Exp. Ibadat Khana at Fatehpur Sikri was the hall in which Akbar held discussion with scholars at various religions.

Earlier it was opened for only Muslim scholars but later he opened to people of all religions i.e. Christians, Zoroastrians, Hindus, Jains, even Atheists. This broadened the discussions and debates began even on issues on, which all Muslims were agreed.

31 **Arrange the following events of Akbar's regime in their chronological order.** *(Chap 7, Class-VIII, Old NCERT) (UPPSC Mains 2004) (UPUDA/LDA 2010)*

1. Abolition of Jizya
2. Construction of Ibadat Khana
3. Singing of Mahzar
4. Foundation of Din-i-Ilahi

Codes

(a) 1, 2, 3, 4 (b) 2, 3, 4, 1
(c) 1, 3, 2, 4 (d) 3, 4, 1, 2

Ans. (a)

Exp. The correct chronological order is 1, 2, 3, 4. In 1564, Akbar abolished the Jizya tax as part of his efforts to foster harmony among people of different religious backgrounds.

The Ibadat Khana was built around 1575 - 1576 and served as a meeting place for the religious scholars and thinkers. The discussions held in the Ibadat Khana were known as 'Ibadat Khana debates' or 'Diwan-i- Khas.'

In 1579, he issued Mahzarnama, which was decree of infallible nature, in which he declared himself the supreme in all religious matters.

The foundation of Din- i- Ilahi is attributed to the year 1582. The Din- i- Ilahi, also known as the 'Divine Faith' was a syncretic religious and philosophical belief system introduced by emperor Akbar.

32 About whom the following statements are related? *(Chap 7, Class-VIII, Old NCERT)(MPSC Pre 2023)*

1. Religion was separated from politics.
2. Adopted a policy of seclusion towards brave women who followed Sati.
3. To stop child marriage and widow remarriage was encouraged.
4. Claimed that the final decision regarding the social law will be his.

Codes

(a) Babur (b) Humayun (c) Akbar (d) Aurangzeb

Ans. (c)

Exp. The given statements are related to King Akbar. During Akbar's rule, religion was separated from politics.

Akbar pursued a policy of religious tolerance and inclusivity, promoting a syncretic form of governance that sought to united people from different faiths under a single imperial framework. This policy, known as 'Sulh-i- Kul' or 'Din- i- Ilahi,' emphasised religious harmony and coexistence.

He also adopted a policy of seclusion towards brave women who followed Sati. One way Akbar discouraged Sati was by implementing regulations that required the consent of the widow before Sati could take place.

Akbar encouraged widow remarriage and discouraged child marriages and also claimed that the final decision regarding the social law will be his.

33 Which of the following social reforms were not initiated by the Akbar? *(Chap 13, Class-XI, Old NCERT)*

1. He abolished female infanticide.
2. He imposed pilgrimage tax on all the subjects irrespective of religion.
3. He banned forceful Sati.
4. Widow remarriage was legalised.

Codes

(a) 1 and 2 (b) 3 and 4 (c) 1, 2 and 3 (d) 1, 2 and 4

Ans. (a)

Exp. Social reforms mentioned in statements (1) and (2) were not initiated by Akbar.

Akbar had initiated a number of social and education reforms. He stopped Sati, the burning of a widow, unless she herself, of her own free will, persistently desired it. Widow remarriage was also legalised. He was against anyone having more than one wife unless the first wife was barren. The age of marriage was raised to 14 for girls and 16 for boys. The sale of wines and spirits were also prohibited.

34 Which of the following statements is/are incorrect? *(Chap 13, Class-XI, Old NCERT)*

1. Akbar tried to fix the age of marriage for boys and girls.
2. Akbar gave freedom to girls to marry at their own will and not under parental pressure.

Codes

(a) Only 1
(b) Only 2
(c) Both 1 and 2
(d) Neither 1 nor 2

Ans. (b)

Exp. Statement (2) is incorrect because there is no literary evidence available, which provide information that Akbar gave freedom to girls to marry at their own will and not under parental pressure.

Jahangir

35 Consider the following statements with reference to the rebellion during the period of Jahangir. *(Chap 15, Class-XI, Old NCERT)*

1. Both Khusrau and Khurram revolted against Jahangir.
2. Both of them were killed by the Mahabat Khan, General of Jahangir.

Which of the statements given above is/are incorrect?

(a) Only 1 (b) Only 2
(c) Both 1 and 2 (d) Neither 1 nor 2

Ans. (b)

Exp. Statement (2) is incorrect with reference to the rebellion during the period of Jahangir because Mahabat Khan do not killed them. Khusrau was murdered by his half brother Khurram.

Jahangir faced many rebellions. Khusrau, his eldest son revolted against him in 1606 AD. He was defeated by Jahangir in Battle near Lahore.

Khurram (later known as Shah Jahan) revolted against him in 1622 AD. His rebellion distracted the empire for 4 years resulting in loss of Kandahar. He revolted because of the influence of Nur Jahan had increased drastically on Jahangir.

36 Consider the following statements with reference to Chain of Justice. *(Chap 8, Class-VII, Old NCERT)*

1. It was an initiative of Nur Jahan in the reign of Jahangir.
2. Chain of Justice was installed to ensure that common people can register their complaints and grievances about the officers of the empire.

Which of the statements given above is/are incorrect?

(a) Only 1
(b) Only 2
(c) Both 1 and 2
(d) Neither 1 nor 2

Ans. (a)

Exp. Statement (1) is incorrect with reference to Chain of Justice as this initiative was started by Jahangir not Nur Jahan.

It was installed to ensure that common people can register their complaints and grievances about the officers of the empire. It was installed at the gate of Agra Fort.

37 **In the medieval India, many women were able to influence the policies of the court. Nur Jahan was one of those women. Consider the following about her.** *(Chap 15, Class-XI, Old NCERT)*

1. Her real name was Mehrunnisa.
2. Jahangir issued silver coins bearing his own titles on one side and the name of Nur Jahan on other side.

Which of the statements given above is/are correct?

(a) Only 1 (b) Only 2
(c) Both 1 and 2 (d) Neither 1 nor 2

Ans. (c)

Exp. Both the statements (1) and (2) are correct about Nur Jahan. The real name of Nur Jahan was Mehrunnisa. She married Jahangir after the death of her husband. With time, her influence increased in the Mughal Court. Jahangir issued silver coins bearing his own title on one side and her name on the other side.

38 **Consider the following pairs.** *(Chap 15, Class-XI, Old NCERT)*

Emperor		Noble
1. Akbar	–	Man Singh
2. Humayun	–	Bairam Khan
3. Jahangir	–	Sawai Jai Singh
4. Aurangzeb	–	Jaswant Singh

How many of the pairs given above is/are incorrectly matched?

(a) Only one (b) Only two (c) Only three (d) All four

Ans. (d)

Exp. Only one pairs i.e., (3) is incorrectly matched because Sawai Jai Singh was the ruler of Kingdom of Amber (Rajasthan). He served as a vassal of the Mughal Emperor Aurangzeb (not Jahangir). He also founded Jaipur. He played a key role in signing the treaty of Purandar in 1665 AD.

39 **Consider the following Assertion (A) and Reason (R) and choose the correct code.** *(Chap 14, Class-XI, Old NCERT)*

Assertion (A) Jahangir did not try to enlarge the conquest made by Akbar in the Deccan.

Reason (R) It was due to military weakness on the part of Jahangir.

Codes

(a) Both A and R are true and R is the correct explanation of A.
(b) Both A and R are true, but R is not the correct explanation of A.
(c) A is true, but R is false.
(d) A is false, but R is true.

Ans. (c)

Exp. Assertion (A) is true, but Reason (R) is false. Jahangir did not try to enlarge the conquest made by Akbar in the Deccan.

This was not due to any military weakness on the part of Jahangir, as he has been sometimes imagined, but due to deliberate policy. Apparently, Jahangir did not want to extend Mughal commitments in the Deccan, or become too deeply embroiled in its affairs.

Moreover, he was still hopeful that his moderation would enable the Deccan states to settle down, and live in peace with the Mughals.

40 **During the Mughal period, the geo-politics of the Central and Arab land was quite complex. In this context, which of the following refused to become part of tripartite struggle against the Persians?** *(Chap 15, Class-XI, Old NCERT)*

1. Mughals
2. Ottoman
3. Uzbek

Codes

(a) Only 1 (b) Only 2
(c) 1 and 2 (d) All of these

Ans. (a)

Exp. During the Mughal period, the geo-politics of the Central Asia was quite complex. The Mughals refused to be drawn into tripartite as it would have upset the Asian balance of power and left them alone against the mighty Uzbeks.

Shah Jahan

41 **The mother of which of the following Mughal emperors belonged to Rajput community?** *(Chap 8, Class-VII, Old NCERT)*

1. Jahangir 2. Akbar
3. Shah Jahan 4. Aurangzeb

Codes

(a) 1 and 3 (b) 1 and 2
(c) 2 and 3 (d) 1, 3 and 4

Ans. (a)

Exp. Among the given Mughal Emperors, mother of Jahangir and Shah Jahan belonged to Rajput Community. Jahangir was son of Jodha Bai and Akbar. Shah Jahan was a son of Jagat Gosain (Princess of Marwar) and Jahangir. Akbar and Aurangzeb were son of Muslim mothers.

42 **Who among the following was appointed as the Viceroy of Deccan by Mughal Emperor Shah Jahan to handle the rising revolt in the Deccan?** *(Chap 8, Class-VII, Old NCERT)*

(a) Shahryar Mirza (b) Dawar Bakhsh
(c) Aurangzeb (d) Prince Murad

Ans. (c)

Exp. Aurangzeb was appointed as the Viceroy of the Deccan by the Mughal Emperor Shah Jahan to handle the rising revolt. During the reign of Shah Jahan, his sons were appointed as Viceroy of the key provinces.
Shuja in Bengal, Murad in Gujarat and Aurangzeb in Deccan. Prince Dara was nominated by Shah Jahan as his successor, however he was ultimately defeated by Aurangzeb in Battle of Deorai near Ajmer in 1659 AD.

43 **Consider the following statements with reference to the Military campaign of Shah Jahan.**
(Chap 8, Class-VII, Old NCERT)

1. Kandahar was claimed by Safavids of Iran.
2. He made multiple attempts to capture Kandahar and in the end he gave up the attempt.

Which of the statements given above is/are incorrect?
(a) Only 1 (b) Only 2
(c) Both 1 and 2 (d) Neither 1 nor 2
Ans. (c)

Exp. Both the statements (1) and (2) are incorrect regarding military campaign of Shah Jahan.
Shah Jahan was the successor of the Jahangir. He succeeded throne in 1628 AD and reigned till 1658 AD. Kandahar was located in Afghanistan. It was claimed by Safavids of Iran.
He conquered Kandahar in 1639 AD and after some time it was again captured by Persians. He launched many efforts to recapture but realising the futility of his ambition, he stopped fighting.

44 **Consider the following statements.**
(Chap 8, Class-VII, Old NCERT)

1. Shah Jahan nominated Aurangzeb as his successor.
2. In the last days, he was kept as prisoner at the fort of Agra.
3. He was buried alongside of his father Jahangir.

Which of the statements given above is/are not correct?
(a) Only 1 (b) Only 2 (c) 1 and 3 (d) 1, 2 and 3
Ans. (c)

Exp. Statements (1) and (3) are not correct because when Shah Jahan died in 1666 AD, he was buried alongside his wife in the Taj Mahal. Also Shan Jahan had nominated Dara Shikoh as his successor (not Aurangzeb).

45 **Consider the following statements.**
(Chap 15, Class-XI, Old NCERT)

1. Balkh campaigned was launched under Prince Dara.
2. Nazr Muhammad ruler of Balkh asked for help from Shah Jahan.
3. Nazr Muhammad was reinstated as the ruler of Balkh.
4. The Mughal routed the Uzbeks outside the gates of Balkh.

Which of the statements given above is/are incorrect?
(a) Only 1 (b) 1 and 2 (c) 2 and 3 (d) 1 and 3
Ans. (d)

Exp. Statements (1) and (3) are incorrect as Balkh campaign was launched under the leadership of Prince Murad. Nazr Muhammad was not reinstated as the ruler of Balkh rather he declined the Mughal offer to make an apology and humble submission to Prince Aurangzeb. The Mughal army while on their way to retreat from Balkh in 1647 AD suffered grievous losses from the attacks of Uzbeks.

46 **Consider the following statements with reference to motive behind Shah Jahan's Balkh campaign.**
(Chap 15, Class-XI, Old NCERT)

1. Secure a friendly ruler in Balkh and Badakhan which bordered Kabul.
2. Conquer Samarkand and Ferghana, the Mughal homelands.
3. Fix the Mughal frontier on the 'Scientific line' near Amu Daria.
4. Expand the Mughal Empire beyond the subcontinent.

How many of the statements given above is/are correct?
(a) Only one (b) Only two
(c) Only (d) All of these
Ans. (a)

Exp. Only one statement i.e., (1) is correct as the motive behind Shah Jahan's Balkh campaign was to secure a friendly ruler at Balkh and Badakhan, which bordered Kabul. He wanted to seek help and support from Mughals.
However, his plan failed due to his son Murad who captured the fort of Balkh and compelled its ruler to flee.

47 **Consider the following statements with regard to Dara Shikoh.** ***(Chap 18, Class-XI, Old NCERT)***

1. He was nominated as his successor by the Shah Jahan.
2. He was an orthodox person who wanted to make India a land of Dar-ul-Islam.
3. He was defeated by Aurangzeb in the Battle of Samugarh.

How many of the statements given above is/are incorrect?
(a) Only one (b) Only two
(c) All three (d) None of these
Ans. (a)

Exp. Only one statement i.e., (2) is incorrect with regard to Dara Shikoh because he was liaberal person and denied the ideology of radical Islam.
Shan Jahan was designated with the title *Padshahzada-i-Buzug Martaba.*

Aurangzeb

48 **Consider the following statements.**

(Chap 18, Class-XI, Old NCERT)

1. In the war of succession, Aurangzeb had defeated Shuja at Khajwah near Allahabad (now Prayagraj).
2. The Battle of Deorai near Ajmer was the last major battle that Dara fought against Aurangzeb.

Which of the statements given above is/are correct?

(a) Only 1
(b) Only 2
(c) Both 1and 2
(d) Neither 1 nor 2

Ans. (c)

Exp. Both the statements (1) and (2) are correct.
Aurangzeb had defeated Shuja at Khajwah near Allahabad (now Prayagraj) in the war of succession, in December 1658 AD. Shuja was hounded out of India into Arakan (April 1660 AD).
Soon, he and his family was executed by Arakanese on a charge of fomenting rebellion.
The Battle of Deorai near Ajmer (March, 1659 AD) was the last major battle that Dara fought against Aurangzeb. In this battle, Dara Shikoh was defeated.

49 **Which of the following Mughal Emperors spent a greater part of his reign to overthrow the Deccan kingdoms?** *(Class-XI, Old NCERT)*

(UPPSC Mains 2006, 2009) (JPSC Pre 2012)

(a) Akbar (b) Jahangir
(c) Shah Jahan (d) Aurangzeb

Ans. (d)

Exp. Mughal Emperor Aurangzeb spent a greater part of his reign to overthrow the Deccan kingdoms. After Aurangzeb's accession in 1658, he wanted to overthrow the Deccan kingdoms. The three powers in the Deccan were the Marathas and the two Shah States of Bijapur and Golconda. His wars against Bijapur and Golconda alienated the Shia Muslim sentiment.

50 **Consider the following statements with regards to region of Aurangzeb.** *(Chap 8, Class-VII, Old NCERT)*

1. The territorial expansion of Mughal Empire reached at zenith during his reign.
2. He had to face large number of revolts, which occurred in different parts of empire.

Which of the statements given above is/are correct?

(a) Only 1 (b) Only 2
(c) Both 1 and 2 (d) Neither 1 nor 2

Ans. (c)

Exp. Both the statements (1) and (2) are correct with regards to region of Aurangzeb.
Aurangzeb was enthroned in the year 1658 AD after defeating his brother. He reigned till 1707 AD. The territorial expansion of Mughal Empire reached at zenith during his reign. He was an able General and bring most of Deccan under his reign. He had to face large number of revolts from different region of empire such as Jats, Sikhs, Marathas, etc. The main reason behind revolts were his religious policy, taxation and territorial expansion.

51 **Consider the following statements with regard to the context of the Aurangzeb.** *(Chap 8, Class-VII, Old NCERT)*

1. He followed liberal policies against people of other religion.
2. Jats of Mathura and the Sikhs revolted against him.
3. He was defeated by British forces when he led an expedition to drive out English from Chittagong.

How many of the statements given above is/are correct?

(a) Only one (b) Only two
(c) All three (d) None of these

Ans. (a)

Exp. Only one statement i.e., (2) is correct in the context of reign of Aurangzeb. The Jats of Mathura and the Sikhs revolted against him because of his exploitative policies.
Statements (1) and (3) are incorrect because Aurangzeb was alike from his descendants. He was an orthodox Muslim and strictly followed the Principles of Islam. Therefore, he did not follow liberal policies against people of other religion. He was not defeated by British forces when he led an expedition to drive out English from Chittagong. The Mughal armies not only captured Chittagong but also annexed the Eastern part of Bengal.

52 **During the reign of Mughal Emperor Aurangzeb, the interest of Mughals and Sikhs conflicted with each other. Which Sikh Guru was killed on the order of Aurangzeb in the year 1675 AD?**

(Chap 8, Class-VII, Old NCERT)

(a) Guru Har Krishan (b) Guru Teg Bahadur
(c) Guru Govind Singh (d) Guru Har Rai

Ans. (b)

Exp. Among the given options, the ninth Sikh Guru, Guru Tegh Bahadur was killed on the order of Aurangzeb in 1675 AD. The main reason behind the execution of the Guru was his growing popularity among both Hindus and Sikhs, subjects and support to Kashmiri Brahmins who approached Guru to save themselves from the prosecution. Under the reign of Guru Tegh Bahadur, Sikhs were gradually organising themselves as a military unit.
Earlier the fifth Sikh Guru, Guru Arjan Dev was killed on the order of Jahangir.

53 **Consider the following Assertion (A) and Reason (R) and choose the correct code.**

(Chap 18, Class-XI, Old NCERT)

Assertion (A) A battle in 1672 AD between Mughal forces and peasants was fought at Narnaul.

Reason (R) It was led by a religious body called Satnamis.

Codes

(a) Both A and R are true and R is the correct explanation of A.
(b) Both A and R are true, but R is not the correct explanation of A.
(c) A is true, but R is false.
(d) A is false, but R is true.

Ans. (b)

Exp. Both Assertion (A) and Reason (R) are true, but Reason (R) is not the correct explanation of Assertion (A).

In 1672 AD, an armed conflict between the peasants and the Mughals was held at Narnaul (near Mathura). The conflict was led by a religious body called Satnamis. The Satnamis were mostly peasants, artisans and low caste people. The battle began after the killing of a Satnami leader by the Mughal Soldier.

54 Arrange the following battles in the chronological order by choosing the correct answer from the codes given below. *(Chap 18, Class-XI, Old NCERT)*

1. Battle of Samugarh
2. Battle of Bilgram
3. Battle of Dharmat
4. Battle of Deorai

Codes

(a) 2, 3, 1, 4 (b) 2, 3, 4, 1
(c) 3, 2, 1, 4 (d) 3, 1, 2, 4

Ans. (a)

Exp. The correct chronology of given battles is 2, 3, 1, 4 i.e., Battle of Bilgram (1540 AD), Dharmat (April, 1658 AD), Samugarh (May, 1658 AD) and Deorai (March, 1659 AD).

Battle of Bilgram was fought between Humayun and Sher Shah Suri in 1540 AD.

Battle of Dharmat was fought between Aurangzeb and Dara Shikoh in April, 1658 AD for throne. In this battle, Aurangzeb had defeated forces of Dara Shikoh.

Battle of Samugarh was fought between Dara Shikoh and Aurangzeb in May, 1658 AD. After this battle, Aurangzeb coronated himself at Agra.

Battle of Deorai was the last battle of war of succession. It was fought in 1659 AD between Mughal Emperor Aurangzeb and Dara Shikoh.

55 Consider the following statements regarding the Aurangzeb. *(Chap 18, Class-XI, Old NCERT)*

1. He allowed the nobles to celebrate the Navroz festival.
2. He was proficient in playing tabla.
3. The grandeur of *jarokha darshan* was increased by him.

How many of the statements given above is/are incorrect?

(a) Only one (b) Only two
(c) All three (d) None of these

Ans. (c)

Exp. All three statements i.e., (1), (2) and (3) are incorrect regarding Aurangzeb. He abolished the celebration of Navroz festival in the court.

He was proficient in playing veena not tabla.

He also stopped the practice of *jarokha darshan*, which was started by former Mughal ruler Akbar.

56 With the departure of Kandahar, the Mughal Empire reached a setback *(Class-XI, Old NCERT) (IAS Pre 1998)*

(a) from the point of view of natural resources.
(b) from the point of view of intermediate territory.
(c) from the point of view of communication system.
(d) from the point of view of the centre of strategic importance.

Ans. (d)

Exp. With the departure of Kandahar, the Mughal Empire reached a setback from the point of view of the centre of strategic importance.

When the Mughal occupied India, it became necessary for them to make a strong hold on Kandahar because of its strategic location that connected Persia with India.

Shah Jahan recovered Kandahar in 1638 from the Iranians but lost it again in 1649.

57 Which of the following reason is the most prominent for the decline of Mughal Empire after the death of Aurangzeb? *(Chap 19, Class-XI, Old NCERT)*

(a) Successors of Aurangzeb were incapable
(b) War of succession
(c) Revolt of Shah Shuja
(d) Revolt of Dara Sikoh

Ans. (a)

Exp. The decline of Mughal Empire started after the death of Aurangzeb. The main reason behind the decline of Mughal Empire was that the successors of Aurangzeb were inefficient and incapable. They were unable to keep a check on the *mansabdars* and the *subedars*. There were many other factors which also contributed in the decline of Mughal Empire such as emergence of regional powers, problem of *jagirs*, foreign invasions, etc.

58 Consider the following statements with reference to the decline of Mughal Empire. *(Chap 19, Class-XI, Old NCERT)*

1. Internal conflict among the nobles were responsible for the decline in the power of central authority.
2. *Subedars* of the *subas* started to behave in the independent way.
3. Marathas started to attack the North-Western boundaries of empire.

How many of the statements given above is/are correct?

(a) Only one (b) Only two
(c) All three (d) None of these

Ans. (b)

Exp. Only two statements i.e., (1) and (2) are correct regarding the decline of Mughal Empire.

The decline of Mughal Empire started after the death of Aurangzeb in 1707 AD. Internal conflict among the nobles were responsible for the decline in power of central authority. Nobles were divided on the basis ethnicity and interest. They played role of kingmaker. *Subedars* of the *subas* started behaving in the independent way because the power of Mughal authority weakened.

Statement (3) is incorrect because Marathas started to attack the Southern boundaries of empire where Mugals were getting weak.

59 Who was the Mughal Emperor during the Nadir Shah's invasion of India ? *(Class-XI, Old NCERT)* *(UPPSC Pre 2004) (WBCS Pre 2012)*

(a) Farrukh Siyar (b) Bahadur Shah
(c) Muhammad Shah (d) Shah Alam

Ans. (c)

Exp. Muhammad Shah was the Mughal Emperor when Nadir Shah invaded India. In 1739 AD, Nadir Shah invaded the Mughal Empire and defeated Muhammad Shah in the Battle of Karnal (Haryana). Nadir Shah took away Takht - i - Taus (the peacock throne) and Kohinoor diamond from Muhammad Shah.

After the invasion, the Mughals rapidly disintegrated.

60 Which of the following social factors contributed in the decline of the Mughal of rule in India? *(Chap 19, Class-XI, Old NCERT)*

1. Agricultural community and Zamindars arose in rebellion against Mughal ruler.
2. Untouchable people were made landless.
3. Untouchable people started living a settled life.

Codes

(a) Only 1 (b) 1 and 2
(c) 2 and 3 (d) 1, 2 and 3

Ans. (b)

Exp. Statements (1) and (2) are correct regarding social factors contributed in the decline of the Mughal of rule in India. Agricultural community and Zamindars played a significant role in the decline of Mughal rule in India. Agricultural community and Zamindars were responsible for rising rebellion against the Mughal ruler.

Untouchable people were made landless by Zamindars which increased inequality in the society. This gave birth to dissatisfaction among the people.

Statement (3) is incorrect because life of untouchable people didn't improved during the reign of later Mughal rulers. They didn't started living a well settled life.

61 Which of the following who had rebelled against the Mughal Emperor Jahangir? *(Class-XI, Old NCERT) (UPPSC Pre 2013)*

1. Asaf Khan 2. Khurram
3. Mahabat Khan 4. Khusrau

Codes

(a) 1 and 2 (b) 2 and 3
(c) 2 and 4 (d) 2, 3 and 4

Ans. (d)

Exp. Khurram, Mahabat Khan and Khusrau rebelled against the Mughal Emperor Jahangir.

Khurram rebelled against Jahangir in 1623-24, when he tried to get independent sovereignty in Bihar and Bengal. But he was defeated by the Mughal General Mahabat Khan and was brought into submission.

Mahabat Khan was a famous Mughal General and statesman, best known for his coup against the Mughal Emperor Jahangir in 1626. He abducted Jahangir, but later was defeated by Nur Jahan's forces and thus Jahangir was freed.

Khusrau Mirza, the eldest son of Jahangir rebelled against Jahangir in 1606. He was defeated later by the Mughal forces.

Asaf Khan was the brother of Nur Jahan. He never rebelled against Jahangir. He supported Shah Jahan accession to throne.

62 Mansabdari system was backbone of Mughal administration but later it also became one of the important reasons for its decline. Under the rule of which of the following ruler number of Mansabdar was highest? *(Chap 19, Class-XI, Old NCERT)*

(a) Jahangir (b) Shah Jahan
(c) Aurangzeb (d) Muhammad Shah Rangila

Ans. (c)

Exp. Mansabdari system was backbone of Mughal administration but later it also became one of the important reasons for its decline. Under the rule of Aurangzeb, the number of Mansabdar was highest. The number of Mansabdars rose from 2069 at the time of Jahangir's accession to 11,456 during the later half of Aurangzeb's reign.

Though the number of nobles increased, but the revenue resources did not increase in that proportion. This caused tension among the nobles and rulers, which resulted in the decline of Mughal Empire.

63 Consider the following statements in the context of relationship between Mughals and Landlords. *(Chap 19, Class-XI, Old NCERT)*

1. The policy of Mughals towards Landlords was contradictory.
2. They were considered as threat for the stability of the Empire.
3. Mughals tried to associate them with the provincial administration.

How many of the statements given above is/are correct?

(a) Only one (b) Only two
(c) All three (d) None of these

Ans. (c)

Exp. All three statements i.e., (1), (2) and (3) are correct in context of relationship between Mughals and Landlords. Landlords or Zamindars belonged to dominant sections of the Indian society during Medieval period. The policy of Mughals towards Landlords was contradictory.

They were considered as threat for the stability of the Empire. On the other hand, they tried to associate them with the provincial administration.

64 Consider the following facts about the policies of Aurangzeb with reference to the decline of Mughal Empire. *(Chap 19, Class-XI, Old NCERT)*

1. He reserved Bijapur and Golconda as a *Khalisa* land.
2. He wanted to use *Khalisa* revenue in battles.

Which of the statements given above is/are correct?

(a) Only 1 (b) Only 2
(c) Both 1 and 2 (d) Neither 1 nor 2

***Ans.* (c)**

Exp. Both the statements (1) and (2) are correct with reference to the decline of Mughal Empire.

Under the reign of Aurangzeb, territorial expansion of the empire was on zenith. Most of the Deccan was brought under the direct rule of central authority. Bijapur and Golconda were also captured and reserved as a *Khalisa* land (land under emperor). He did so because he wanted to use *Khalisa* land revenue in the battles.

65 Which of the following historian had considered that problem of *Jagir* is one of the most prominent reasons for the decline of Mughal Empire? *(Chap 19, Class-XI, Old NCERT)*

(a) Bhim Sen (b) Khafi Khan
(c) Satish Chandra (d) Abbas Khan Sarbani

***Ans.* (b)**

Exp. Khafi Khan had considered that problem of Jagir is one of the most prominent reasons for the decline of Mughal Empire. His real name was Muhammad Hashim. He was given the title Khafi Khan (or Khwafi Khan) by emperor Muhammad Shah.

66 Consider the following facts regarding the *Jagir* during the declining phase of Mughal Empire. *(Chap 19, Class-XI, Old NCERT)*

1. During the period of Aurangzeb, problem of Jagir escalated.
2. His victory over the Deccan Kingdom solved the problem.

Which of the statements given above is/are correct?

(a) Only 1 (b) Only 2
(c) Both 1 and 2 (d) Neither 1 nor 2

***Ans.* (c)**

Exp. Both the facts in statements (1) and (2) are correct regarding, the Jagir during declining phase of Mughal Empire.

When Mughal Empire was in its last phase, shortage of Jagirs was one of the biggest crises in the administration. During the period of Aurangzeb, problem of Jagir escalated.

His victory over the Deccan Kingdom solved the problem, but it was not permanent solution.

67 In the context of roles of nobles in the decline of Mughal Empire, which of the following statements is incorrect? *(Chap 19, Class-XI, Old NCERT)*

(a) Nobles contributed in the decline of Mughal rule.
(b) They were divided on the basis of ethnicity.
(c) Development of nationalist attitude among the nobles.
(d) None of the above

***Ans.* (c)**

Exp. Statement (c) is incorrect in the context of roles of nobles in the decline of Mughal Empire as nationalist attitude never developed among the Mughal nobles. They were always interested in consolidating their own power. In the Mughal administration, the nobles were placed at the second in hierarchy after the King. They played key role in the policy formulation and running of the administration.

68 Consider the following statements about the role of administration in the decline of Mughal Empire. *(Chap 19, Class-XI, Old NCERT)*

1. Mughal administration was centralised in nature.
2. Under incapable ruler, central administration got weakened.
3. *Wazirs* were able to control the centralised administration.

Which of the statements given above is/are correct?

(a) Only 1 (b) 1 and 2
(c) 2 and 3 (d) 1, 2 and 3

***Ans.* (b)**

Exp. Statements (1) and (2) are correct about the role of administration in the decline of Mughal empire. Mughal administration was also responsible for the decline of empire upto a large extent. The administration was centralised in nature.

But after the death of Aurangzeb, incapable rulers were not able to control it and it got weakened.

Mughal administration was highly centralised and needed a competent monarch to run it.

Statement (3) is incorrect because In the absence of such monarchs, *Wazirs* tried to fill the gap, but they failed.

69 Consider the following statements. *(Chap 19, Class-XI, Old NCERT)*

1. Aurangzeb was unsuccessful in solving the problems of Maratha.
2. He gave *mansab* to many Maratha *Sardars*.
3. He was successful in creating an alliance with Deccan Kingdoms against the Marathas.

How many of the statements given above is/are correct?

(a) Only one (b) Only two
(c) All three (d) None of these

Ans. (b)

Exp. Only two statements i.e., (1) and (2) are correct as Aurangzeb was quite successful in defeating and capturing Deccan Kingdoms but he was not able to completely ruin the Maratha power. During the period of Aurangzeb, Marathas signed treaties with him. As a result of which, he gave *mansab* to many Maratha *Sardars*.

Statement (3) is incorrect because Aurangzeb failed to unite with the Deccan kingdoms against the Marathas.

70 What does the given map specifies? *(Chap 7, Class-VII, Old NCERT)* *(IAS Pre 2000)*

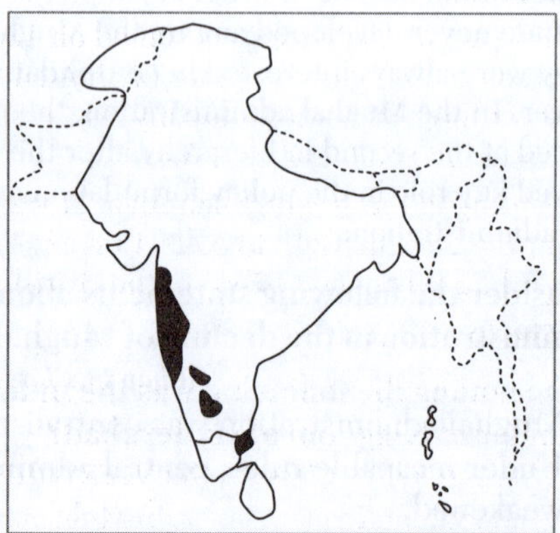

(a) Akbar's kingdom at the time of his conquest of Khandesh in 1601.
(b) Akbar's kingdom at the time of his death in 1605.
(c) Aurangzeb's kingdom at the time of Hyderabad conquest.
(d) Aurangzeb's kingdom at the time of his death in 1707.

Ans. (d)

Exp. The given map specifies the Aurangzeb's kingdom at the time of his dealth in 1707. He spent most of his time in the campaigns of Rajasthan and the Deccan. By 1687, the Deccan states of Bijapur and Golconda were annexed to the Mughal empire.

The major success of Aurangzeb in the North-East was annexation of Assam. This was followed by the capture of Chittagong in 1664.

71 Consider the following statements in the context of role of Rajput rulers in the decline of Mughal Empire. *(Chap 19, Class-XI, Old NCERT)*

1. Differences grew between Marwar rulers and Mughal kings.
2. Aurangzeb had destroyed Mewar.
3. In the Deccan war, Rathore Rajput of Marwar supported Aurangzeb.

How many of the statements given above is/are incorrect?

(a) Only one (b) Only two
(c) All three (d) None of these

Ans. (a)

Exp. Only one statement i.e., (3) is incorrect in the context of role of Rajput rulers in the decline of Mughal Empire because in the Deccan war, Rathore Rajput of Marwar did not supported Aurangzeb.

From the period of Akbar, Rajput had played key role in the consolidation and expansion of Mughal Empire.

72 Consider the following statements with reference to the role of Aurangzeb in the decline of Mughal Empire. *(Chap 19, Class-XI, Old NCERT)*

1. Aurangzeb was bounded by the complex situations.
2. The situations were created by him only.

Which of the statements given above is/are correct?

(a) Only 1
(b) Only 2
(c) Both 1 and 2
(d) Neither 1 nor 2

Ans. (c)

Exp. Both the statements (1) and (2) are correct with reference to the role of Aurangzeb in the decline of Mughal Empire.

Reign of Aurangzeb is quite contradictory. During his period, Mughal Empire reached at zenith and seeds of decline were also showed during his period. He was bounded by the complex situations, which were created by him only.

73 Consider the following statements with reference to religious policy/policies of Aurangzeb. *(Chap 19, Class-XI, Old NCERT)*

1. He tried to remain within the framework of the Islamic law.
2. His failure to respect the susceptibilities of his non-Muslims subjects.
3. Re-imposition of *Jizyah*.

How many of the statements given above is/are correct?

(a) Only one (b) Only two
(c) All three (d) None of these

Ans. (c)

Exp. All three statements i.e., (1), (2) and (3) are correct with reference to religious policies of Aurangzeb.

Aurangzeb was an orthodox in his outlook. He tried to remain within the framework of the Islamic law.

He failed to respect the susceptibilities of his non-Muslim subjects on many occasions.

He was the religious bigot who ordered destruction of temples and re-imposed *Jizyah* on her Hindu subjects.

These policies of Aurangzeb alienated segments of the Hindus and strengthened the hands of those section which were opposed to the Mughal empire. This ultimately resulted in the disintegration of Mughal empire.

74 Consider the following statements.
(Class-XI, Old NCERT)

1. In 1703, Aurangzeb opened negotiations with the Marathas.
2. Aurangzeb tried to capture Maratha states till his last breath.

Which of the statements given above is/are correct?

(a) Only 1 (b) Only 2
(c) Both 1 and 2 (d) Neither 1 nor 2

Ans. (c)

Exp. Both the statements (1) and (2) are correct. In 1703, Aurangzeb opened negotiations with the Marathas. He released Sahu, the son of Sambhaji. He was given the title of Raja and the Mansab of 7000.

Aurangzeb till his last breath in 1706 AD tried to capture and annex Maratha states. However, he was not successful and died in Aurangabad.

75 Consider the following statements with reference to Mughal nobles and Governors emerged as independent rulers. *(Chap 10, Class-VII, New NCERT)*

1. They were not transferred frequently.
2. They were transferred frequently.
3. Their policies were liked by people.

How many of the statements given above is/are correct?

(a) Only one (b) Only two
(c) All three (d) None of these

Ans. (a)

Exp. Only one statement i.e., (1) is correct. In the 18th century, many of the Mughal nobles and Governors emerged as independent ruler because they were not transferred frequently.

This was done in order to check their power. But later, they were not transferred frequently. This helped them in consolidating their power.

With the decline in central authority, they declared themselves as independent rulers. Their policies were not liked by people.

76 Emperor Shah Alam II gave the Diwani of Bengal, Bihar and Orissa to East India Company on
(Chap 13, Class-XI, Old NCERT)
(48th-52nd BPSC Pre 2008)

(a) 12th August, 1765 (b) 18th August, 1765
(c) 19th August, 1765 (d) 21st August, 1965

Ans. (a)

Exp. Emperor Shah Alam II gave the Diwani of Bengal, Bihar and Orissa (now Odisha) to East India Company on 12th August, 1765.

The Treaty of Allahabad was signed on 12th August, 1765 between the Mughal Emperor Shah Alam II and Robert Clive of the East India Company, as a result of the Battle of Buxar of 22nd October, 1764.

According to this treaty, Shah Alam II was forced to grant the Diwani (right to collect revenue) of Bengal (including Bihar and Orissa) to the British East India Company.

77 Who among the following was the independent founder of Kingdom of Hyderabad?
(Chap 13, Class-XI, Old NCERT) (UPPSC Mains 2002)

(a) Qamaruddin Khan (b) Muhammad Amin Khan
(c) Asad Khan (d) Chin Qilich Khan

Ans. (d)

Exp. Chin Quilich Khan or Asaf Jha was the founder of independent Kingdom of Hyderabad. In 1724 AD, he established autonomous rule over the Deccan region and founded the Asaf Jahi dynasty.

After eliminating Sayyid brothers in 1720 and 1722 with the support of Emperor Muhammad Shah, he served as a Mughal Grand Vizier (1722- 1724 AD).

Chapter 19

Mughal Administration, Society, Economy and Arts

Mughal Administration, Society, Economy and Arts

Administration

Central Administration
- Highly centralised in nature; Employed a system of checks and balances
- Emperor considered as of divine origin

Provincial Administration
- Empire divided into 15 Subas (province)
- Governor of Suba, Subedar directly appointed by Emperor
- They were responsible for welfare of the people and army

Local Administration
- **Sarkar (District)**
  - Faujdar was executive head; Amalguzar was revenue collector
- **Pargana**
  - Administrative unit below Sarkar; Headed by Shiqdar; Amil- revenue collector; Qanungos- record keeper
- **Mauza (Villages)**
  - Administered by Patwari and Muqaddam (village headmen)

Judicial System
- Followed Islamic justice system; Separate personal laws for civil matters and Islamic laws for criminal matter

Monetary System
- Akbar introduced gold coins named Asharafi; He also introduced practice of inscribing Persian poetry praising the ruler on coins (Silver coin)
- Nisar was started by Jahangir

Revenue Administration
- Land revenue was the main source of income; Zakat tax on Muslims
- Jaziya tax on Hindus and Khums (booty of war) were source of

Society and Economy

Society During Mughal Period
- Society during Mughal phase was feudal and majority of its population is dependent on agriculture
- Farmers, workers, servants, slaves, beggars etc. came under lower class and middle class
- In North India, people use wheat, dal and vegetables
- In Southern and East India rice and fish was consumed more
- Banjaras were important trader class of medieval era

Economy during Mughal Period
- India had a large class of rich traders and merchants, spread out all over the country, well organised and highly professional
- Some traders specialised in long distance, inter-regional trade and were called Seth, Bohra, Modi and Beoparis or Banik
- There was a special class of traders, the Banjaras, who specialised in carrying bulk goods, such as textiles, silks, etc
- Boat traffic on waterways and coastal trade along the seashore was highly developed during this period

Art and Architecture

Paintings
- Development of miniature painting and portraits introduced new themes depicting the court, battle scenes and animals
- European painting was introduced in Mughal court by Portuguese priests
- Two famous painters of Akbar- Daswant and Baswan
- Under Jahangir special progress made in portrait paintings and paintings of animals

Literature
- Development of Persian language
- Baburnama- biography of Babur
- Humayunama written by Gulbadan Begum
- Akbarnama written by Abul Fazl
- Tuzuk-i-Jahangiri – Autobiography of Jahangir
- Padshahnama gives detailed account of Jahangir's rule

Music
- Tansen was among Maharatnas of Akbar court; Invented many ragas

Art and Architecture
- Introduction of bulbous domes
- Slender minarets, Large halls, massive vaulted gateways and delicate ornamentation was the main characteristics
- Humayun's tomb, Agra fort, Fatehpur Sikri, Buland Darwaza and Panch Mahal were built during the reign of Akbar
- Shah Jahan ordered the construction of Red Fort, Jama Masjid and Taj Mahal

SOURCE *New NCERT Class VII* (The Mughals), *Old NCERT Class XI* (Mughal Empire), *NIOS Module 2* (Cultural Development in Medieval India)

Mughal Administration

1 Consider the following statements regarding the divisions of ranks under the Mansabdari system. *(Chap 4, Class-VII, New NCERT)*

1. The ranks were divided into two; *zat* and *sawar*.
2. The word *zat* means personal which fixed the personal status of a person.
3. The *sawar* indicated the number of cavalrymen (sawars), a person was required to maintain.

Which of the statements given above is/are correct?

(a) Only 1 (b) Only 2 (c) 1 and 2 (d) All of these

Ans. (d)

Exp. All the given statements (1), (2) and (3) are correct regarding divisions of ranks under the Mansabdari system.

The ranks were divided into two categories namely *zat* and *sawar*.

Zat means personal status of a person and *sawar* indicated the number of cavalrymen (*sawars*), a person was required to maintain.

Mansabdari system was the most important pillar of the Mughal administration. It was developed during the reign of Akbar. Under this, Mansabdar was assigned a *mansab* (rank).

2 Consider the following statements regarding the Mansabdari system. *(Chap 4, Class-VII, New NCERT)*

1. Mansabdars received their salaries as revenue assignments called *jagirs*, which was somewhat like *iqtas*.
2. The numbers of Mansabdars were lowest during the reign of Aurangzeb.
3. They only had rights to the revenue of their assignments, which was collected for them by their servants.
4. In Akbar's reign, these *jagirs* were carefully assessed, which was not followed by the successive rulers.

Which of the statements given above is/are incorrect?

(a) Only 1 (b) Only 2
(c) All of these (d) None of these

Ans. (b)

Exp. Only statement (2) is incorrect regarding Mansabdari system. The number of Mansabdars were highest during the reign of Aurangzeb.

3 Read the statements (A) and (B) below and choose the correct answer from the codes given below *(Chap 15, Class-XI, Old NCERT) (RAS/RTS Pre 2013)*

Statement (A) Not all the Mansabadars were military officers.

Statement (B) Those who held high civil posts under the Mughals were also Mansabdars and were graded accordingly.

Codes

(a) Both A and B are false.
(b) Both A and B are true.
(c) A is true, while B is false
(d) A is false, while B is true

Ans. (b)

Exp. Both the statements are true. The Mansabdari system was the administrative system of the Mughal Empire. It was first introduced by Akbar. The Mansabdari System was not confined to the military officers. The system was common to both the military and civil department.

The officials holding high civil posts under the Mughals were called Mansabdars and the Mansabs were granted to them accordingly.

4 Consider the following statements in regards with the modification in the Mansabdari system. *(Chap 15, Class-XI, Old NCERT)*

1. Jahangir introduced *du-aspah sih-aspah* system.
2. In Shah Jahan reign, number of *sawars* were increased drastically.

Which of the statements given above is/are correct?

(a) Only 1
(b) Only 2
(c) Both 1 and 2
(d) Neither 1 nor 2

Ans. (a)

Exp. Only statement (1) is correct regarding modification in the Mansabdari system.

Mansabdari system evolved under different rulers. Jahangir introduced *du-aspah sih-aspah* system (literally trooper with 2 or 3 horses).

Statement (2) is incorrect because the number of *sawars* increased during the reign of Aurangzeb.

5 Consider the following statements about Raja Todar Mal and his revenue system. *(Chap 4, Class-VII, New NCERT)*

1. Todar Mal was brilliant Revenue Minister of Akbar.
2. He carried out a careful survey of crop yields, prices and areas cultivated for a 15-year period.
3. His revenue system was also implemented in far-flung provinces such as Gujarat and Bengal.

Which of the statements given above is/are incorrect?

(a) Only 1 (b) 1 and 2
(c) Only 3 (d) 2 and 3

Ans. (d)

Exp. Statements (2) and (3) are incorrect regarding Raja Todar Mal and his revenue system because he carried out a 10 years careful survey of crop yields, prices and areas cultivated for a period.

His revenue system was implemented from Malwa to Gujarat and Lahore to Allahabad (but not in Bengal).

6 **During the period of Mughal empire many rulers were assigned *Watan Jagir*.**

(Chap 4, Class-VII, New NCERT)

1. Jagir assigned to sons of the rulers.
2. Jagir assigned to rulers in their homeland.
3. Jagir exempted from taxation.

Which of the following denotes the meaning of the *Watan Jagir*?

(a) Only 1 (b) Only 2
(c) 2 and 3 (d) None of the above

Ans. (b)

Exp. During the period of Mughal Empire, many rulers were assigned *Watan Jagir*. It denotes the *Jagirs*, which were assigned to rulers in their homeland. It was hereditary and non-transferable.

7 **Assertion (A)** Mansabdari system existed during the Mughal period.

Reason (R) Mansabdars were selected on the basis of merit. ***(Chap 14, Class-VII, New NCERT)(CGPSC Pre 2008)***

Codes

(a) Both A and R are true and R is the correct explanation of A.
(b) Both A and R are true, but R is not the correct explanation of A.
(c) A is true, but R is false.
(d) A is false, but R is true.

Ans. (b)

Exp. Both Assertion (A) and Reason (R) are true, but Reason (R) is not the correct explanation of Assertion (A).

Mansabdari system was the administrative system introduced by Akbar in Mughal empire during 1571 AD. It was a system of ranking the Government officials and determined their civil and military duties, along with their renumerations.

Mansabdars were selected on the basis of qualifications and given ranks as per their land holdings.

8 **During the reign of Akbar, the role of an official called *Amalguzar* was** ***(Chap 13, Class-XI, Old NCERT)***

1. to be in-charge of law and order.
2. to make an assessment and collection of land revenue.
3. to be in-charge of imperial household.
4. to maintain the royal treasury.

Which of the statements given above is/are correct?

(a) Only 1 (b) 1 and 3 (c) 2 and 4 (d) Only 2

Ans. (d)

Exp. Statement (2) is correct. During the reign of a Akbar, the role of an official called *Amalguzar* was to make an assessment and collection of land revenue.

Amalguzar was the provincial officer in Sarkar. He was responsible for assessing and collecting land revenue. He was also known as Amil. He also used to send daily reports of expenditure and receipts to provincial Diwan.

9 **Which one of the following pairs of term and meaning is not correctly matched?**

(Chap 13, Class-XI, Old NCERT)

(a) Khalisa - Villages whose income went directly to the state treasury
(b) Mauza -Rebellious territory
(c) Inam-Land allotted to learned and religious man
(d) Jagir-Territorial land allocated to farmers

Ans. (d)

Exp. Pair (d) is not correctly matched because under Jagirdari system, *Jagirs* were assigned to nobles and they were allowed to collect revenue from it. Jagirs were of different types, namely, *Tankhwa*, *Mashrut*, *Watan* and *Altamgha Jagir*.

10 **Consider the following statements with reference to the revenue system under Mughals.**

(Chap 13, Class-XI, Old NCERT)

1. In 1580 AD, Akbar instituted new system of revenue called *Dahsala*.
2. In *Dahsala*, state share was one-fourth.
3. Under this system, revenue was collected in cash.

Which of the statements given above is/are incorrect?

(a) Only 1 (b) Only 2
(c) 1 and 3 (d) 1, 2 and 3

Ans. (b)

Exp. Statement (2) is incorrect with reference to the revenue system under Mughals because in *Dahsala* one-third of the average produces was the state share.

Akbar had instituted a new system of revenue called *Dahsala* in 1580 AD. Under this system, the average produce of different crops as well as the average prices prevailing over the last ten (*dah*) years were calculated.

11 **Consider the following pairs.**

(Chap 13, Class-XI, Old NCERT)

	Soil Type		Description
1.	Polaj	—	Uncultivated land
2.	Chachar	—	Fallow for 3-4 years
3.	Banjar	—	Fallow for longer period of time

Which of the pairs given above is/are correctly matched?

(a) 1 and 2 (b) 2 and 3
(c) Only 3 (d) Only 2

Ans. (b)

Exp. Pairs (2) and (3) are correctly matched. Under the reign of Mughal Emperor Akbar, land was divided into different categories on the basis of their productivity. The division is as follows

Polaj – It was land cultivated every year.
Parati – It was land cultivated once in 2 year
Chachar – It was land allowed to be fallow for 3-4 years.
Banjar – It was worst kind of land and was left fallow for longer period of time.

12 **Match List I with List II and select the correct answer by using the codes given below the lists.**
(Chap 13, Class-XI, Old NCERT) (Haryana PCS Pre 2023)

List I (Characteristics)		List II (Foreign Travellers)	
A.	Description of Indian Trade and Society	1.	Manucci
B.	Visited India six times	2.	Bernier
C.	Came to India and never went back to Europe	3.	Barbosa
D.	Scientist of Mughal Empire Danishmand Khan	4.	Tavernier

Codes

	A	B	C	D
(a)	2	3	4	1
(b)	3	4	1	2
(c)	1	2	3	4
(d)	4	3	2	1

Ans. (b)

Exp. The correct matching is A-3, B-4, C-1, D-2.

Duarte Barbosa's book called 'Livro de Duarte Barbosa,' which translates to 'Book of Duarte Barbosa' provides valuable insights into the society, economy and culture of South India during the 16th century.

Jean Baptist **Tavernier** (from France) a traveller and merchant, visited India for six times between 1630- 1688. He is best known for the discovery of the 116- carat diamond.

Niccolo Manucci, a versatile traveller from Venice, Italy, settled in India till his last in Chennai, 1720.

Francois Bernier was associated with the Mughal court as a personal physician of Dara Shikoh (eldest son of Emperor Shah Jahan) and later as a scientist with Danishmand Khan (Nole at Mughal court).

13 **Consider the following statements regarding Zabti system.** *(Chap 13, Class-XI, Old NCERT)*

1. It was system of measurement and assessment.
2. It was introduced in the area from Lahore to Allahabad and in Malwa and Gujarat.

Which of the statements given above is/are correct?

(a) Only 1 (b) Only 2
(c) Both 1 and 2 (d) None of these

Ans. (c)

Exp. Both the statements (1) and (2) are correct regarding Zabti system of Akbar. Zabti system is the other name of Bandobast system. It was introduced during the reign of Akbar. It was developed by his revenue minister Todar Mal.

It was system of measurement and assessment of land. It was introduced in the areas from Lahore to Allahabad and Malwa to Gujarat.

14 **Consider the following statements with reference to the Mughal administration.**
(Chap 13, Class-XI, Old NCERT)

1. The department of intelligence was headed by Mir Bakshi.
2. The news reporters were known as *waqia-navis*.

Which of the statements given above is/are correct?

(a) Only 1 (b) Only 2
(c) Both 1 and 2 (d) Neither 1 nor 2

Ans. (c)

Exp. Both the statements (1) and (2) are correct with reference to Mughal administration.

In Mughal administration, the department of intelligence was headed by Mir Bakshi. The personnel who gathered information were known as barids.

The news reporters were known as *waqia-navis* and they were controlled by Mir Bakshi.

15 **Akbar played key role in consolidating administration. In regards with it, consider the following statements and identify the reforms introduced by him.** *(Chap 13, Class-XI, Old NCERT)*

1. The authority of the post *Wakil* was reduced.
2. Akbar popularised the title of *Diwan-i-Ala* on the place of *Wazir*.
3. The number of *subas* were reduced to 12 under his reign.
4. He prohibited the tradition *Jharokha*.

Codes

(a) 1 and 2 (b) Only 2 (c) 1 and 3 (d) 1, 3 and 4

Ans. (c)

Exp. Statements (1) and (3) are correct regarding administrative reforms introduced by Akbar. Akbar introduced many reforms and initiative for the consolidation of administration and his authority. He reduced or curbed the power utilised by the *Wakils*. Also, number of subas were reduced to 12 for the better governance.

Statements (2) and (4) are incorrect because Akbar did not popularised the title of *Diwan-i-Ala* on the place of *Wazir*. He started the tradition of *Jharokha*.

16 **Which of the following pairs is correctly matched?**
(Chap 4, Class-VII, New NCERT)

(a) Bakshi – Military commanders
(b) Sadr – Military paymaster
(c) Kotwal – Town police commander
(d) Faujdars – Main gatekeeper of fort

Ans. (c)

Exp. Pair (c) is correctly matched as in Mughal administration, *Kotwal* was a town police commander. He was responsible for maintaining law and order situation in the urban areas.

Pairs (a), (b) and (d) are incorrectly matched because *Bakshi* was the military paymaster in Mughal period. *Sadr* was the chief religious officers in Mughal Period. Faujdar was the administrative head of *Sarkar* (District) in Mughal Period.

17 Consider the following statements with reference to the administration under Mughals.

(Chap 7, Class-VII, Old NCERT)

1. The *wazir* looked after the revenue administration.
2. *Khan-i-saman* attended to the royal households.
3. The Bakshi was the chief commander of the army.
4. *Wazir* acted as the Emperor in absence of the Mughal Emperor due to health issue or military expedition.

Which of the statements given above is/are incorrect?

(a) 1 and 2 (b) 3 and 4 (c) 1, 2 and 3 (d) 1, 2 and 4

Ans. (b)

Exp. Statements (3) and (4) are incorrect with reference to the administration under Mughals because king was the chief commander of the army.

Wazir did not act as the Emperor in the absence of the Mughal Emperor due to health issue or military expedition.

18 Consider the following statements regarding the approach of Mughal Emperors towards nobles.

(Chap 16, Class-XI, Old NCERT)

1. Babur was a Turk but he never followed a narrow, socialist policy and tried to win the leading Afghan nobles to his side.
2. During Akbar's period, Rajput nobles were given prominent position.
3. From the time of Jahangir, Afghans also began to be recruited in the nobility and the Indian Muslims who were called *Shaikhzadas* or *Hindustanis* were also recruited in service.

Which of the statements given above is/are correct?

(a) Only 1 (b) 1 and 2 (c) 2 and 3 (d) All of these

Ans. (d)

Exp. All the given statements (1), (2) and (3) are correct regarding the approach of Mughal Emperors towards nobles. Babur was Turk by ethnicity but he never followed a narrow, socialist policy toward Afghan nobles. When Mughal dynasty was in early immature phase he tried to lead Afghan nobles to his side but they did not proved to be trustworthy.

During Akbar reigns, a new policy was launched towards the nobility. He gave prominence to Rajput nobles.

From the time of Jahangir, Afghans also began to be recruited in the nobility and the Indian Muslims who were called *Shaikhzadas* or *Hindustanis* were also recruited.

19 Consider the following statements with reference to state of nobility during the reign of Aurangzeb.

(Chap 18, Class-XI, Old NCERT)

1. Hindu contributed very less percentage in the total nobles of Aurangzeb.
2. Mir Jumla was one of his most important noble.

Which of the statements given above is/are incorrect?

(a) Only 1

(b) Only 2

(c) Both 1 and 2

(d) Neither 1 nor 2

Ans. (a)

Exp. Statement (1) is incorrect with reference to state of nobility during the reign of Aurangzeb because in comparison to other Mughal rulers, Hindu contributed very high percentage in the total nobles of Aurangzeb. there is contrast between religious ideology and Constitution of nobility by Aurangzeb.

20 *Ahadis* were those troopers who

(Chap 15, Class-XI, Old NCERT)

1. were directly under the control of Mughal ruler.
2. were highly trusted corps.
3. mustered upto five hörses.
4. attached themselves to Mirzas.

Which of the statements given above is/are correct?

(a) 1, 3 and 4 (b) 1, 2 and 3

(c) 2 and 3 (d) 1 and 4

Ans. (b)

Exp. Statements (1), (2) and (3) are correct regarding *Ahadis*. *Ahadis* were part of the Mughal army. They were given special place in the army. They were under the direct control of Mughal rulers.

They were highly trusted corps. An *Ahadi* had to muster up to five horses. However, sometimes two of them shared a horse.

Statement (4) is incorrect as they did not attached themselves to *Mirzas* (Nobles).

21 In the context of the Mughal army, the term *Walashasis* refers to ***(Chap 15, Class-XI, Old NCERT)***

1. officer responsible for the household of Emperor.
2. officer responsible for checking the fitness of the soldiers.
3. royal body guard of Emperor.

Codes

(a) Only 1 (b) Only 2

(c) Only 3 (d) None of these

Ans. (c)

Exp. In the context of the Mughal army, *Walashahis* were royal body guard of the Emperor. Mughal king was the powerful and central authority of the administration. Thus, his protection was quite important.

Economic and Social Life

22 Read the statements (A) and (B) below and choose the correct answer by using the codes given below.

(Chap 4, Class-VII, New NCERT) (RAS/RTS Pre 2013)

Statement (A) Not all the Mansabdars were military official.

Statement (B) Those who held high civil posts under the Mughals were also Mansabdars and were graded accordingly.

Codes

(a) Both A and B are false. (b) Both A and B are true.
(c) A is true, but B is false. (d) A is false, but B is true.

Ans. (b)

Exp. Both the statements (A) and (B) are true.

Not all the Mansabdars were military officials, they were appointed to all civil and military posts.

Mansabdars were nobles, high civil or military officials, provincial Governors who had the right to hold Jagir.

This system was also used as a grading system by the Mughals to fix ranks, salary and military responsibilities.

23 Consider the following statements with reference to the social and economic life under Mughals.

(Chap 16, Class-XI, Old NCERT)

1. There was no middle class in the Mughal society.
2. Qazis and theologians were included in the middle class strata.

Which of the statements given above is/are incorrect?

(a) Only 1 (b) Only 2
(c) Both 1 and 2 (d) Neither 1 nor 2

Ans. (a)

Exp. Statement (1) is incorrect with reference to social and economic life under Mughals. In Mughal period, society was divided into different classes. There was also a middle class.

24 Consider the following statements.

(Chap 16, Class-XI, Old NCERT)

1. The Hundi was letter of credit payable after a period of time at a discount.
2. The sarrafs were specialised in dealing with the Hundis.
3. Hundis were issued by the Mughal officer who was in charge of market.

Which of the statements given above is/are correct?

(a) Only 1 (b) 1 and 2 (c) 2 and 3 (d) All of these

Ans. (b)

Exp. Statements (1) and (2) are correct.

Hundi was part of the trading system of medieval period. It was letter of credit payable after a period of time at a discount. The sarrafs were specialised in dealing with Hundis.

Statement (3) is incorrect because Hundis were not issued by the Mughal officer who was in-charge of market.

25 Consider the following statements with reference to the cultural history of India.

(Chap 14, Module-2 NIOS) (IAS Pre 2018)

1. In the construction of Buland Darwaza and Kharah at Fatehpur white marble was used.
2. In the construction of Bara Imambara and Rumi Darwaza in Lucknow red sandstone and marble were used.

Which of the statements given above is/are correct?

(a) Only 1
(b) Only 2
(c) Both 1 and 2
(d) Neither 1 nor 2

Ans. (d)

Exp. Neither statements (1) nor (2) are correct the Buland Darwaza is made up of red and buff sandstone, decorated with white and black marble and it is higher than the courtyard of the mosque.

The Buland Darwaza is symmetrical and topped by large free standing kiosks, which are the Chhatris.

The architectural style of the Rumi Darwaza is completely in sync with the Nawabi architecture of Lucknow and it is significantly different from the Mughals.

The material used for the Darwaza is bricks and then it is coated with lime, while the Mughals often used the red sandstone. This is why the detailing on the Darwaza is more intricate, which would be impossible to achieve in stone.

26 During the period of Aurangzeb, Muhtasib were appointed in every province. What was/were main responsibilities of Muhtasib?

(Chap 18, Class-XI, Old NCERT)

1. They checked that people live their life in accordance with sharia.
2. They were also responsible for checking weight and measures.

Select the correct answer using the codes given below.

(a) Only 1
(b) Only 2
(c) Both 1 and 2
(d) Neither 1 nor 2

Ans. (c)

Exp. Both the statements (1) and (2) are correct regarding responsibility of Muhtasib who were appointed in every province during the reign of Aurangzeb.

The officials Muhtasib were responsible for maintaing and upholding the sharia law in the provinces. They checked that wine and intoxicants, such as 'Bhang' were not consumed in public places. They were also responsible for regulating the houses of ill-repute, gambling dons etc and for checking weights and measures.

27 In the reign of Aurangzeb, Muslim subjects were given relaxation for not paying abwabs. It denotes

1. a kind of cess *(Chap 18, Class-XI, Old NCERT)*
2. irrigation tax paid by people
3. household tax paid by Muslim nobles
4. tax paid by Muslims on employing Hindu salves

Which of the options given above is/are correct?

(a) Only 1 (b) Only 2 (c) Only 3 (d) Only 4

Ans. (a)

Exp. In the reign of Aurangzeb, Muslim subjects were given relaxation for not paying abwabs. It was kind of cess paid by Muslims. Aurangzeb was orthodox Muslim, therefore, he decided to give relaxation to Muslims for not paying abwabs.

28 Assertion (A) Akbar like Sher Shah, tried to regulate the circulation of state coins.

Reason (R) Similar to the currency system of Sher Shah, the major copper coin of Akbar's time was the Dam. *(Class-XI, Old NCERT) (UPPSC Pre 2019)*

Codes

(a) Both A and R are true and R is the correct explanation of A.

(b) Both A and R are true, but R is not the correct explanation of A.

(c) A is true, but R is false.

(d) A is false, but R is true.

Ans. (a)

Exp. Both Assertion (A) and Reason (R) are true and Reason (R) is the correct explanation of Assertion (A). The monetary system of Akbar was inspired largely by the innovations of Sher Shah Suri. Emperor Akbar issued coins in all three principal metals used for coinage. His copper coins in the denomination of one-half were known as Nisfi, one-half as Dam and one-eight part as Dam or Damdi.

Copper Dam was also associated with Akbar's system of weights.

The Akbar Dam weighed 20.9 grams and was exchanged at 40 per rupee. The Akbari unit of weight is 'The Ser' and it was fixed at 30 Dams to the one Ser.

29 According to Abul Fazal, Akbar started one thousand karkhanas for producing woollen clothes. At which among the following places did he established them? *(Chap 14, Module-2 NIOS) (Telangana PCS Pre 2023)*

(a) Surat (b) Dacca

(c) Lahore (d) Amritsar

Ans. (c)

Exp. Akbar started one thousands karkhanas for producing wollen clothes at Lahore. Karkhana were the manufacturing houses and workshops for raftmen, established by the Mughals in their empire.

These were the small manufacturing units for various arts and crafts as well as for the emperor's household and military needs.

Emergence of Maratha Empire

Emergence of Maratha Empire

Origin

Origin
- Unique geographical location helped chieftains developed a sense of autonomy; Bhakti movement provided impetus to creating Maratha identity

Maratha Rulers
- **Shahji Bhonsle** Father of Shivaji; Acquired practical experience of war and tactics under his father Maloji and Malik Amber of Ahmednagar
- **Shivaji** Raised under the guardianship of Dadaji Konddev; At Raigarh fort in 1674 crowned as King
- Adopted the title of Haindava Dharmodharak

Military Expedition of Shivaji

Defeated Adilshahi General Afzal Khan in Battle of Pratapgarh
- Defeated Mughal in Battle of Pawan Khind ;In Battle of Sinhagarh, recaptured Sinhagarh fort

Successors of Shivaji
- **Shambhaji** Continued struggle with Mughals; Was captured and executed by Aurangzeb in 1689 AD
- **Rajaram I** Reign 1689-1700 AD marked constant struggle against Mughals
- **Shahu** Son of Shambhaji who was earlier taken prisoner along with his mother in 1689 by Mughals

Local Administration

Central Administration

Established Ashta Pradhana, a council of ministers to assist king
- Astha Pradhan were
  - Peshwa (Prime Minister), Mazumdar (Auditor), Wakins, Dabir, Surnis (Superintendent), Pandit Rao, Senapati, Nyayadhish

Provincial Administration
- Empire was divided into Mauzas, Tarafs and Prants

Prants (province) were under the rule of Subedar

Military Administration

Largely based on fort system; Havaldar, Sabnis and Sarnobat were in-charge of forts; Navy fleet was equipped with Ghurabs and Gallivats

Revenue Administration
- Introduced Ryotwari system; Mirasdars had hereditary rights in land; Revenue system was patterned on the Kathi system of Malik Amber

Judicial Administration
- King was the supreme and last authority in Judicial matters; Nyayadhish and Pandit Rao appointed by Kings; Patel was village officials who had administrative revenue and Judicial responsibilities

Rise of Peshwa

Introduction
- Under Ashta- Pradhana system, Peshwa were head of both civil and military affairs

Balaji Vishwanath (1713- 1720 AD)
- Better known as Peshwa Balaji Vishwanath was the first of a series of hereditary Peshwa gained effective control of the Maratha Empire

Baji Rao I (1720-1740 AD)

He was a General of the Maratha Empire before serving as the Peshwa; Baji Rao I is credited with expanding the Maratha Empire in India

Balaji Baji Rao (1740-1761 AD)
- Also known as Nana Saheb; He was appointed as Peshwa in 1740 AD; Balaji Baji Rao was not a great military leader as like his father

Madhav Rao (1761-1772 AD)
- After the death of Balaji Bajirao, his son Madhav Rao succeeded him as Peshwa

Narayan Rao (1772-1773 AD)

Narayan Rao was the fifth Peshwa of the Maratha empire from November, 1772 till his death by murder in August, 1773

Peshwa Baji Rao II (1796-1818 AD)
- After the death of Madhav Narayan Rao (1795 AD), The son of Raghunath Rao, Baji Rao II became the Peshwa

SOURCE *Old NCERT Class XI (Climax and Disintegration of the Mughal Empire–II)*

1 With reference to the rise of Marathas, which of the following statements is/are correct? *(Chap 19, Class-XI, Old NCERT)*

1. Shahaji Bhosale acted as a kingmaker in Ahmednagar and joined the services of Bijapur.
2. He tried to set up a semi-independent principality at Hyderabad.

Codes

(a) Only 1 (b) Only 2
(c) Both 1 and 2 (d) Neither 1 nor 2

Ans. (a)

Exp. Only statement (1) is correct with reference to the rise of Marathas. Shahaji Bhosale (Father of Shivaji) served under Malik Ambar who was minister under Ahmed Shah of Ahmednagar. After his death, he played a significant role in the politics of Ahmednagar. After the treaty of 1636 AD, he joined the services of Sultan of Bijapur.

Statement (2) is incorrect because he tried to set up a semi-independent principality at Bangalore. However, he was not able to accomplish this task.

2 Consider the following statements. *(Chap 19, Class-XI, Old NCERT)*

1. Shivaji received Jagir of Kolhapur from his father Shahji.
2. Dadaji Kondadev acted as Shivaji's guardian.
3. He conquered Kondana fort from the Maratha chief Chandrarao More.

Which of the statements given above is/are incorrect?

(a) Only 1 (b) Only 2
(c) 1 and 3 (d) 1, 2 and 3

Ans. (c)

Exp. Statements (1) and (3) are incorrect because Shivaji received Jagir of Poona from his father Shahaji. He conquered Javli Kingdom from the Maratha chief Chandrarao More in 1656 AD. The conquest of Javli Kingdom had made him undisputed leader of the Konkan region.

3 Consider the reign of following Peshwas and arrange them in chronological order. *(Chap 19, Class-XI, Old NCERT)*

1. Balaji Vishwanath 2. Baji Rao I
3. Narayan Rao 4. Madhav Rao I

Select the correct answer by using the codes given below.

(a) 1, 2, 4, 3 (b) 2, 1, 4, 3
(c) 1, 2, 3, 4 (d) 1, 3, 2, 4

Ans. (a)

Exp. The correct chronological order is 1, 2, 4, 3.

Balaji Vishwanath (also known as Balaji Vishwanath Bhatt). He served as the first Peshwa of the Maratha empire from 1713-1720.

Baji Rao I (also known as Baji Rao Ballal). He was the second Peshwa and served from 1720-1740.

Madhav Rao I (also known as Madhav Rao Peshwa). He was the son of Nanasaheb and played a crucial role in consolidating Maratha power after the third Battle of Panipat.

Narayan Rao (also known as Narayan Rao Baji Rao). He was the fifth Peshwa and served from 1722-1773.

4 Consider the following statements in the context of Shivaji and Shaista Khan. *(Chap 19, Class-XI, Old NCERT)*

1. Shaista Khan occupied Poona in 1660 AD.
2. Shaista Khan was sent by ruler of Golconda.
3. Shaista Khan plundered the Maratha territory and forced Shivaji to take shelter at Khandesh.

How many of the statements given above is/are correct?

(a) Only one (b) Only two
(c) Only three (d) None of these

Ans. (a)

Exp. Only one statement i.e., (1) is correct. He occupied Poona in 1660 AD from Shivaji.

Statements (2) and (3) are incorrect because Shaista Khan was appointed by Mughal Emperor Aurangzeb with a special objective of crushing Shivaji. When Shivaji started re-occupying his territories of Deccan, Shaista Khan was transferred from Bengal to Deccan. When Shaista Khan plundered the Maratha territory, then Shivaji had not taken shelter at Khandesh. When Shaista Khan occupied Poona, Shivaji was in Konkan region.

5 Consider the following statements with reference to the Treaty of Purandar. *(Chap 19, Class-XI, Old NCERT)*

1. It was signed between Jai Singh and Shivaji in 1665 AD.
2. As per the treaty, Shivaji gave 23 forts out of 35 to Mughals.
3. A mansab of 5000 was granted to his son Sambhaji.

Which of the statements given above is/are correct?

(a) Only 1
(b) 1 and 2
(c) 2 and 3
(d) 1, 2 and 3

Ans. (d)

Exp. All the given statements (1), (2) and (3) are correct with reference to the Treaty of Purandar. After the plundering of Surat by Shivaji in 1664 AD, Jai Singh of Amber was sent by Mughal Emperor Aurangzeb to defeat Shivaji.

Jai Singh sieged the Purandar Fort, which led to sign of Treaty of Purandar between Jai Singh and Shivaji in the year 1665 AD. As per the Treaty, Shivaji gave 23 forts out of 35 to Mughals. His son Sambhaji was granted a mansab of 5000.

6 **Consider the following statements.**
(Chap 19, Class-XI, Old NCERT)

1. On the assurance of Jai Singh, he visited Agra.
2. With an intent to attain 'Hindavi Swarajya' Shivaji met Mughal Emperor Aurangzeb.
3. He did not pay much attention on the development of trade.

How many of the statements given above is/are incorrect about Shivaji?

(a) Only one (b) Only two
(c) All three (d) None of these

Ans. (a)

Exp. Only one statement i.e., (2) is incorrect about Shivaji because Shivaji did not meet Mughal Emperor Aurangzeb with intent to attain 'Hindavi Swarajya'. He visited Agra to meet the Emperor but due to disrespect, he walked away from imperial court. On this attitude, he was imprisoned by the Emperor. However, he was successful in escaping.

7 **Arrange the following in the correct chronological order.** *(Chap 19, Class-XI, Old NCERT)*

1. Chhatrapati Shahuji 2. Rajaram I
3. Sambhaji 4. Shivaji II

Select the correct answer from the codes given below.

(a) 3, 2, 1, 4 (b) 3, 2, 4, 1
(c) 2, 3, 1, 4 (d) 1, 2, 3, 4

Ans. (b)

Exp. The correct chronological order is 3, 2, 4, 1.

Sambhaji Bhonsle was the second Chhatrapati of the Maratha empire, ruling from 1681-1689 AD. He was the eldest son of Shivaji, the founder of the Maratha empire.

After Sambhaji's death, his brother Rajaram I succeeded him as the next Chhatrapati. Rajaram Bhonsle I (1670-1700 AD) was the third Chhatrapati of Maratha empire, who ruled from 1689 to his death in 1700 AD.

Shivaji II (1696-1726 AD), later Shivaji I of Kolhapur was the son of the Maratha Chhatrapati, Rajaram I. He served as Raja of Kolhapur from 1710-1714 AD.

Sahu Bonsle I (1682-1749 AD) was the fifth Chhatrapati of the Maratha empire. He was the son of Sambhaji. After his death, his Ministers and Generals such as the Peshwas, Bhonsle of Nagpur, Gaekwad, Shinde and Holkar carved out their own fiefdoms and turned the empire into a confederacy.

8 **Given below are two statements, one labelled as Assertion (A) and the other labelled as Reason (R).**
(Chap 19, Class-XI, Old NCERT) (MPSC Pre 2023)

Assertion (A) The Marathas emerged as the strongest regional power in India after the decline of the Mughal empire.

Reason (R) The Marathas were the first to have a clear concept of a United Indian Nation.

Codes

(a) Both A and R are true and R is the correct explanation of A.
(b) Both A and R are true, but R is not the correct explanation of A.
(c) A is true, but R is false.
(d) A is false, but R is true.

Ans. (c)

Exp. Assertion (A) is true, but Reason (R) is false. The Maratha empire emerged as one of the strongest regional powers in India after the decline of the Mughal empire. The decline of the Mughal empire in the 18th century created a power vacuum, leading to the rise of regional powers, including the Marathas. Under the leadership of capable military leaders and administrators, such as Shivaji and later the Peshwas, the Marathas expanded their territories and established a formidable empire.

Ashoka was the first Indian ruler to clear the concept of United Indian Nation.

9 **Consider the following statements.**
(Chap 19, Class-XI, Old NCERT)

1. Sambhaji was executed by the Mughal Emperor Aurangzeb on being rebel and infidel.
2. Execution of Sambhaji helped in curbing the rebellion among Marathas.
3. After execution of Sambhaji, Mughals attacked Raja Ram.

Which of the statements given above is/are correct?

(a) Only 1 (b) 1 and 3
(c) 2 and 3 (d) 1, 2 and 3

Ans. (b)

Exp. Statements (1) and (3) are correct as Sambhaji was the successor of Shivaji. He gave shelter to rebel son of Mughal Emperor Aurangzeb, Prince Akbar. After the battle of Sangameshwar, which was fought between Sambhaji and Mughal forces, Sambhaji was defeated. Then, he was executed by the Aurangzeb on being rebel and infidel in 1689 AD. After execution of Sambhaji, Mughals attacked Raja Ram, successor of Sambhaji.

Statement (2) is incorrect because execution of Sambhaji aroused the rebellion among Marathas.

10 **Assertion** (A) By 1750, the Maratha kingdom had become a confederacy presided by the Peshwa.

Reason (R) The successor of Sahu depended on the Peshwa. *(Chap19, Class-XI, Old NCERT)*

Codes

(a) Both A and R are true and R is the correct explanation of A.
(b) Both A and R are true, but R is not the correct explanation of A.
(c) A is true, but R is false.
(d) A is false, but R is true.

Ans. (a)

Exp. Both Assertion (A) and Reason (R) are true and Reason (R) is the correct explanation of Assertion (A). In 1750, Rajaram Bhonsle II (reign 1749-1777 AD) signed the famous Sangola agreement, whereby he invested the Peshwa with more authority and reduced himself to a titular king. In this condition, the power of the Maratha empire passed into the hands of Peshwa.

11 **Arrange the following Maratha rulers in the correct chronological order.** *(Chap 19, Class-XI, Old NCERT)*

1. Shahu 2. Rajaram 3. Sambhaji

Select the correct answer using the codes given below.

(a) 3, 1, 2 (b) 3, 2, 1 (c) 2, 3, 1 (d) 1, 2, 3

Ans. (b)

Exp. The correct chronological order of Maratha rulers is : 3, 2, 1 i.e., Sambhaji (1681-89 AD), Raja Ram (1689-1707 AD) and Shahu (1707-1749 AD).

Rajaram was the successor of Sambhaji. He reigned from 1689 to 1707 AD. He ruled on the behalf of Shahu. His headquarters was Jinji. He was frequently attacked by Mughal forces, as a result of which he ran from one place to another. He died in 1707 AD, which led to war of succession between Tarabai (regent of her son Shivaji II), widow of Rajaram and Shahu. Ultimately, Shahu emerged as victorious.

12 **Consider the following statements regarding Ashtapradhan.** *(Chap 19, Class-XI, Old NCERT)*

1. It was a council of eight ministers created by Shivaji for general administration and consultation.
2. Shivaji was bound to accept the recommendations of this council.
3. Every minister was chief of his own department.
4. All the ministers held military commands besides their civil duties.

Which of the statements given above are incorrect?

(a) 1 and 3 (b) 1, 2 and 3
(c) 2 and 4 (d) All of these

Ans. (c)

Exp. Statements (2) and (4) are incorrect regarding Ashtapradhan of Shivaji because Shivaji was not bound to accept the recommendations of this council. It was not mandatory for ministers to hold military commands besides their civil duties.

13 **Consider the following statements about Shivaji's military expertise.** *(Chap 19, Class-XI, Old NCERT)*

1. He was a master in guerrilla tactics and swift cavalry warfare.
2. He had built a series of fortified strongholds on the table mountains of the Western Deccan.

Which of the statements given above is/are correct?

(a) Only 1 (b) Only 2
(c) Both 1 and 2 (d) Neither 1 nor 2

Ans. (c)

Exp. Both the statements (1) and (2) are correct about Shivaji's military expertise. He was a master in guerrilla tactics and swift cavalry warfare. The rough terrain of Konkan region helped in execution of guerrilla tactics. Due to guerrilla tactics rival forces were not able to defeat Maratha forces easily.

He had built a series of fortified strongholds on the table mountains of the Western Deccan. These forts were located at strategic location and winning over them was literally impossible for enemy.

14 **Which of the following statements is incorrect?** *(Chap 19, Class-XI, Old NCERT)*

1. Chauth – Tax realised by the Marathas from the areas outside their domain equal to one-fourth of the revenue paid to the Mughal empire.
2. Sardeshmukhi – Tax realised by the Marathas equal to one-tenth of the land revenue.
3. Misl – Political unit among the Rajputs, each loyal to its own particular leader.

Select the correct answer using the codes given below.

(a) Only 1 (b) 2 and 3
(c) Only 3 (d) None of these

Ans. (c)

Exp. Statement (3) is incorrect because the Misls were the 12 sovereign states of the Sikh confederacy, which rose during the 18th century in the Punjab region in the Northern part of the Indian subcontinent.

The Misls formed a commonwealth that was described by Swiss adventurer Antoine Polier as a natural 'aristocratic republic'.

15 **The following were the officers in the Ashtapradhan of Shivaji.** *(Chap 19, Class-XI, Old NCERT) (CGPSC Pre 2007)*

1. Mazumdar 2. Dabir 3. Waknis 4. Surnis

Select the correct answer using the codes given below.

(a) 1, 2, 3 (b) 2, 3, 4 (c) 1, 2, 4 (d) 1, 2, 3, 4

Ans. (d)

Exp. All of the given officers were in Ashtapradhan of Shivaji.

Mazumdar was the accountant.

Dabir was master of ceremonies and also helped the king in his dealing with foreign powers.

Waknis or Waqia-Navis was responsible for intelligence, posts and household affairs.

Surnis or Surnavis or Chitnis helped the king with his correspondence.

16 **Arrange the following rulers in the chronological order of their rule.** *(Chap 2, Class-XII, Old NCERT) (UPPSC Mains 2004)*

1. Bajirao 2. Balaji Bajirao
3. Balaji Vishwanath 4. Madhavrao

Select the correct answer using the codes given below.

(a) 4, 3, 1, 2 (b) 1, 2, 3, 4 (c) 3, 1, 2, 4 (d) 2, 1, 4, 3

Ans. (c)

Exp. The correct chronological order of rulers is 3, 1, 2, 4 i.e., Balaji Vishwanath reigned from 1713-1720 AD.

In 1713 AD, Sahu made him his Peshwa or the Mukh Pradhan (Chief Minister). The system of Peshwa in Maratha government evolved under his leadership only.

Bajirao, the eldest son of Balaji Vishwanath, was made Peshwa in 1720 AD and he remained at this post till 1740 AD. During his tenure, the peshwa because the functional head of the Maratha empire.

Balaji Bajirao (widely known as Nana Saheb) was the Peshwa from (1740-1761 AD).

Madhav Rao became Peshwa in 1761 AD at the age of 17 and he remained in position till 1772 AD.

17 Arrange the following events related to Chhatrapati Shivaji in chronological order and select the correct answer from the codes given below.

(Chap 19, Class-XI, Old NCERT)

1. The victory of the Fort of Chakan.
2. The episode of Afzal Khan.
3. Start of clash with the Mughals.
4. Attack and sack of Surat.

Select the correct answer using the codes given below.

(a) 1, 3, 2, 4 (b) 1, 2, 3, 4
(c) 2, 4, 3, 1 (d) 2, 3, 1, 4

Ans. (a)

Exp. The correct chronological order of events related to Chhatrapati Shivaji is 1, 3, 2, 4.

In 1646 AD, Shivaji took several important forts near Pune, including Purandar, Kondhana and Chakan. Shivaji's confrontations with the Mughals began in 1657 AD, when two of Shivaji's officers raided the Mughal territory near Ahmednagar.

In the ensuing Battle of Pratapgarh fought between Maratha forces led by Shivaji and Afzal Khan, a veteran General of Bijapur Sultanate in 1659 AD, Shivaji's forces decisively defeated the Bijapur Sultanate's forces. Battle of Surat, also known as the 'Sack of Surat' was a land battle that took place in 1664 AD, near the city of Surat, Gujarat between Maratha Chhatrapati Shivaji and Inayat Khan, a Mughal captain. Shivaji sacked the port city of Surat, a wealthy Mughal trading centre.

18 Assertion (A) In matters of state, Shivaji was adviced by a Council of Ministers.

Reason (R) Each Minister held independent charge of his department. *(Chap 19, Class-XI, Old NCERT)*

Codes

(a) Both A and R are true and R is the correct explanation of A.
(b) Both A and R are true, but R is not the correct explanation of A.
(c) A is true, but R is false.
(d) A is false, but R is true.

Ans. (c)

Exp. Assertion (A) is true, but Reason (R) is false.

The Council of eight ministers or Ashtapradhan was an administrative and advisory Council set-up by Shivaji. It consisted of eight ministers who regularly advised Shivaji on political and administrative matters.

The Ashtapradhan was designed to encompass all the primary administrative functions of the state, with each minister being given charge of one role in the administration, but they were directly answerable to the Maratha king.

The Ashtapradhan is somewhat similar to the court arrangements of other famous emperors such as the Navaratnas of the courts of both Vikramaditya and Akbar, as also of the Astadiggajas of Krishnadevaraya's court.

19 Consider the following statements with reference to the administration of Marathas.

(Chap 19, Class-XI, Old NCERT)

1. Havaldars were supervised by the Sihahars.
2. Saranjam was not associated with the military administration of Marathas.

Which of the statements given above is/are incorrect?

(a) Only 1 (b) Only 2
(c) Both 1 and 2 (d) Neither 1 nor 2

Ans. (c)

Exp. Both the statements (1) and (2) are incorrect with reference to the administration of Marathas because Sihahars were supervised by the Havaldars. They were part of the auxiliary force of Maratha King.

Saranjam was associated with the military administration of Marathas. Many Military chief were given Saranjam (revenue grants). It was also known as Saranjami system.

20 Consider the following statements in the context of Revenue administration of Maratha.

(Chap 19, Class-XI, Old NCERT)

1. Total tax levied by Shivaji.
2. Irrigation tax levied by Rajaram.
3. A levy on the neighbouring territories by Shivaji which was one-fourth of land revenue in lieu of protection against Maratha invasion.

How many of the statements given above is/are correct?

(a) Only one (b) Only two
(c) All three (d) None of these

Ans. (a)

Exp. Only one statement i.e., (3) is correct in the context of the revenue administration of Maratha. Chauth was a levy on the neighbouring territories by Shivaji, which was one-fourth of land revenue in lieu of protection against Maratha invasion. Sardeshmukhi was an additional levy of 10% demanded from the areas outside from the Kingdom. Both of these taxes were main source of income for Maratha Kingdom.

Chapter 21

Later Mughals (18th Century)

Later Mughals (18th Century)

Later Mughal Rulers

- The death of Aurangzeb in 1707 resulted into rapid decline
- Mughal court became site of fighting among the nobles
- Provincial governors began to act in an independent manner
- In 1803 Delhi was occupied by British Army

Bahadur Shah I (1707-1712 AD)

- Tried to restore the goodwill of the Mughal Empire by conciliating the Maratha and Rajput rulers
- Reversed narrow- minded policies of Aurangzeb
- Led expedition against Sikhs
- Granted the Sardeshmukhi of Deccan to the Marathas but rejected their demands of Chauth
- Made peace with Chhatrasal (Bundela Chief) and Churaman (Jat Chief)

Jahandar Shah I (1712-1713AD)

- Till his reign, nobles became owner of power and used princes as mere puppets to capture the seat of authority
- Was supported by the noble Zulfiqar Khan who indirectly ruled the Empire
- Was incapable ruler
- Abolished Jizyah
- Introduced the Ijarah system of contract revenue farming

Farrukhsiyar (1713-1719 AD)

- Supported by Sayyid brothers-Abdullah Khan and Hussain Ali Khan who were awarded with the offices of Wazir and Mir Bakshi respectively
- Maratha Peshwa helped Sayyid brothers in overthrowing Farrukhsiyar

Downfall of Sayyid Brothers

Abdullah Khan and Hussain Ali were known as King-makers in Indian history

- Their attempt to save the empire from administrative disintegration failed because of constant political rivalry in nobility

Muḥammad Shah (1719-1748 AD)

- Selected by Sayyid brothers
- Considered as weak-minded ruler
- Wazir Nizam-ul-Mulk left the empire and founded the State of Hyderabad
- In many parts Zamindars, Rajas and Nawabs raised the banner of rebellion and independence
- Defeated and imprisoned by Nadir Shah in Battle of Karnal
- Delhi was plundered and looted in 1739
- Nadir Shah carried away the famous Koh-i-Noor diamond and jewel studded peacock throne of Shah Jahan

Ahmed Shah (1748-1754 AD)

- Reign is marked by series of plundering raids by Afghan ruler Ahmed Shah Abdali
- Marathas successfully annexed the Mughal territories of Malwa and Bundelkhand

Shah Alam II (1759-1806AD)

- Third Battle of Panipat was fought in 1761
- Joined Mir Qasim of Bengal and Shuja-ud-Daula of Awadh to fought British in Battle of Buxar
- After defeat in this battle, lived several years at Allahabad as a pensioner of the East India Company
- British secured the Diwani or the right to collect revenue of Bihar, Bengal and Orissa

Akbar II (1837-1837 AD)

- Gave the title of Raja to Rammohan Roy

Bahadur Shah II (1837-1858 AD)

- Last Mughal ruler
- Wrote Urdu poems under the pen name of Zafar
- During the Revolt of 1857, he was recognised as the Emperor of India by the rebel soldiers and Zamindars
- Tried and exiled to Rangoon

Reason for Decline

- Aurangzeb's intolerant attitude
- Weak successor
- Invasion of Nadir Shah and Ahmed Shah Abdali
- Division among nobility
- Revolts by Rajputs, Sikhs, Jats and Marathas

SOURCE ***New NCERT, Class VIII*** *(How, When and Where),* ***Old NCERT, Class VIII*** *(India in the 18th Century),* ***Old NCERT, Class VIII*** *(India and the Modern World),* ***Old NCERT, Class-XII*** *(India in the 18th Century),* ***Old NCERT, Class XII*** *(Indian States and Society in 18th Century)*

Later Mughals

1 Consider the following statements.

(Chap 1, Class-XII, Old NCERT)

1. Mirza Muhammad Muazzam also known as Bahadur Shah I, was the eighth Mughal emperor from 1707 to 1712.
2. He was the second son of Mughal emperor Aurangzeb, who he conspired to overthrow in his youth.
3. He was also Governor of Agra, Kabul and Lahore and had to face revolts of Rajputs and Sikhs.

How many of the statements given above is/are correct?

(a) Only one (b) Only two
(c) All three (d) None of these

Ans. (c)

Exp. All three statements i.e., (1), (2) and (3) are correct as Mirza Muhammad Muazzam also known as Bahadur Shah I was the eighth Mughal emperor from 1707 to 1712.

He emerged as victorious in the conflict of succession after the death of Mughal emperor Aurangzeb in 1707 AD. He was the Governor of Agra, Kabul and Lahore and the last Mughal ruler who enjoyed all the authority in real term. His reign was disturbed by several rebellions, the Sikhs under the leadership of Banda Singh Bahadur, Rajputs under Durgadas Rathore and fellow Mughal Kam Bakhsh.

2 Which of the following statements is incorrect in the context of Mughal Emperor Jahandar Shah?

(Chap 1, Class-XII, Old NCERT)

(a) In the civil war following the Bahadur Shah's death, one of his less able sons, Jahandar Shah emerged as victorious.
(b) Jahandar Shah was supported by Zulfiqar Khan, the most powerful noble of the time.
(c) Jahandar Shah re-imposed Jizyah practice.
(d) During Jahandar Shah's reign, Jai Singh of Amber was given title of Mirza Raja Sawai and appointed as Governor of Malwa.

Ans. (c)

Exp. Statement (c) is incorrect because in the context of Mughal Emperor Jahandar Shah because the Jizyah practice was formally abolished by him in 1712 AD, on the advice of Turani noble Asad Khan.

Jizyah was a tax paid by non-Muslim population to their Muslim rulers.

3 In the context of Bahadur Shah I, which statements is/are correct? *(Chap 1, Class-XII, Old NCERT)*

(a) He adopted more tolerant attitude towards the Hindu chiefs and rajas.
(b) There was no destruction of temples in his reign.
(c) He granted Chauth of the Deccan to Maratha chiefs.
(d) Both a and b

Ans. (d)

Exp. Statements (a) and (b) are correct in the context of Bahadur Shah I.

He adopted a more tolerant attitude towards the Hindu chiefs and rajas. There was no destruction of temples in Bahadur Shah's reign.

Statement (c) is incorrect because Bahadur Shah I granted the right to collect Sardesh Mukhi of Deccan but not Chauth to the Marathas.

4 Consider the following statements.

(Chap 1, Class-XII, Old NCERT)

1. Jahandar Shah 'The Owner of the World', was the ninth Mughal emperor from 1712 to 1713.
2. He was the son of emperor Bahadur Shah I and the grandson of emperor Aurangzeb.
3. Jahandar Shah was Mughal India's first puppet king. Zulfiqar Khan (Wazir) backed him up.

How many of the statements given above is/are correct?

(a) Only one (b) Only two
(c) All three (d) None of the above

Ans. (c)

Exp. All three statements i.e., (1), (2) and (3) are correct as Jahandar Shah was the ninth Mughal emperor from 1712 to 1713. He was the son of emperor Bahadur Shah I and the grandson of emperor Aurangzeb.

Jahandar Shah was the first puppet ruler of the Mughal dynasty, placed on the throne by powerful noble Zulfiqar Khan. His reign was short and turbulent, lasting less than a year. He was deposed by the Sayyid brothers and succeeded by his nephew Farrukh Siyar. His reign came to an early end in 1713 AD when he was defeated at Agra by his nephew Farrukh Siyar.

5 Consider the following statements.

(Chap 1, Class-XII, Old NCERT)

1. The term Ijarah was used in Mughal administration for Revenue farming.
2. It was opposite to the fixed land revenue as designed by Todar Mal.
3. The Ijarah system is known as a system in which a fixed amount is paid by the farmers to the state.

How many of the statements given above is/are correct?

(a) Only one (b) Only two
(c) All three (d) None of these

Ans. (c)

Exp. All three statements i.e., (1), (2) and (3) are correct as Ijarah system/revenue farming was introduced during the reign of the Mughal emperor Jahandar Shah. It was introduced by his powerful noble Zulfiqar Khan.

It was opposite to the fixed land revenue as designed by Todar Mal. Under Ijarah system, the Government began to contract with the revenue farmers and middlemen to pay the government a fixed amount of money while they were free to collect whatever they could from the peasants. This led to increased oppression of the peasants.

6 **Consider the following statements.**

(Chap 1, Class-XII, Old NCERT)

Statement-I Mughal Emperor Farrukh Siyar issued Royal Farman (charter).

Statement-II Under this Farman, the Noble was authorised to issue Dastaks (passes) for the transportation of Goods.

Which one of the following is correct in respect of the above statements?

(a) Both Statement-I and Statement-II are correct and Statement-II is the correct explanation for Statement-I.

(b) Both Statement-I and Statement-II are correct and Statement-II is not the correct explanation for Statement-I.

(c) Statement-I is correct, but Statement-II is incorrect.

(d) Statement-I is correct, but Statement-II is correct.

Ans. (c)

Exp. Statement-I is correct, but Statement-II is incorrect. The Mughal Emperor, Farrukh Siyar granted duty-free trading facilities to the English in Bengal, in 1717 AD. Under this Farman, the Company was authorised to issue Dastaks (passes) for the transportation of Goods. It included permission to export and import British goods in Bengal without paying taxes.

7 **Consider the following statements.**

(Chap 2, Class-VIII, Old NCERT)

1. The Sayyid brothers refers to Syed Hassan Ali Khan Barha and Syed Hussain Ali Khan.
2. They were Indian Muslims belonging to the Sadaat-e-Bara clan of the Barha dynasty.
3. The Sayyid brothers became highly influential in the Mughal Court after Aurangzeb's death in 1707.

How many of the statements given above is/are correct?

(a) Only one (b) Only two
(c) All three (d) None of these

Ans. (c)

Exp. All three statements i.e., (1), (2) and (3) are correct as they were Indian Muslims belonging to the Sadaat-e-Bara clan of the Barha dynasty, who claimed to be Sayyids or the descendants of the Islamic prophet Muhammad. The two Sayyid brothers were Abdullah Khan and Hussain Ali Khan. They became highly influential in the Mughal Court after Aurangzeb's death in 1707 and become king makers.

8 **Which one of the following is the correct chronology of later Mughal rulers?** *(Chap 2, Class-VIII, Old NCERT)*

(a) Jahandar Shah–Farrukh Siyar– Muhammad Shah–Bahadur Shah

(b) Muhammad Shah–Jahandar Shah– Bahadur Shah–Farrukh Siyar

(c) Farrukh Siyar–Bahadur Shah–Jahandar Shah–Muhammad Shah

(d) Bahadur Shah–Jahandar Shah– Farrukh Siyar–Muhammad Shah

Ans. (d)

Exp. The correct chronology of later Mughal rulers is Bahadur Shah I (1707-1712 AD), Jahandar Shah (1712-1713 AD), Farrukh Siyar (1713-1719 AD) Muhammad Shah (1719-1748 AD). The later Mughals refers to the period of the Mughal empire after the death of Aurangzeb in 1707 AD. The era of the great Mughals is generally considered to have ended at this point.

9 **Consider the following statements.**

(Chap 2, Class-VIII, Old NCERT)

1. The last Mughal ruler Muhammad Shah ruled for the longest period.
2. He was given the title of Rangeela.
3. On 21st February, 1722, Muhammad Shah appointed the Asaf Jah I as Grand Wazir.

How many of the statements given above is/are correct?

(a) Only one (b) Only two
(c) All three (d) None of these

Ans. (c)

Exp. All three statements i.e., (1) (2) and (3) are correct as the last Mughal ruler Muhammad Shah ruled for the longest period. He was the Mughal Emperor of India from 1719 to 1748 AD. He was fond of a luxurious life like music, dance, alcohol, women and animal fights for these reasons.

He was given the title of Rangeela.

On 21st February, 1722, Muhammad Shah appointed the Asaf Jah I as Grand Wazir. He advised Muhammad Shah to be "as cautious as Akbar and as brave as Aurangzeb".

10 **Consider the following statements.**

(Chap 2, Class-VIII, Old NCERT)

1. Mirza Nasir-ud-Din Muhammad Shah was the thirteenth Mughal emperor from 1719 to 1748.
2. Muhammad Shah's reign was marked by Nadir Shah's invasion of India.
3. Muhammad Shah was the last Mughal emperor to sit on Mayur Singhasan.

How many of the statements given above is/are correct?

(a) Only one (b) Only two
(c) All three (d) None of these

Ans. (c)

Exp. All three statements i.e., (1) (2) and (3) are correct as Mirza Nasir-ud-Din Muhammad Shah was the thirteenth Mughal emperor from 1719 to 1748. He was son of Khujista Akhtar, the fourth son of Bahadur Shah I. Muhammad Shah's reign was marked by rapid and irreversible decline of the Mughal empire that was exacerbated by Nadir Shah's invasion of India and the sacking of Delhi in 1739.

In February, 1739 Nadir Shah captured Delhi and took away the Mayur Singhasan with him as the trophy of victory.

Muhammad Shah was the last Mughal emperor to sit on Mayur Singhasan.

11 **Arrange the following into chronological order and select the correct answer by using the codes given below.** *(Chap 1, Class-XII, Old NCERT)* *(MPPSC Pre 2017) (UPPSC Pre 2018)*

1. Muhammad Shah
2. Jahandar Shah
3. Alamgir II
4. Ahmad Shah

Codes

(a) 1, 3, 4, 2 (b) 2, 1, 4, 3
(c) 3, 1, 2, 4 (d) 4, 2, 3, 1

Ans. (b)

Exp. The correct chronological order is 2, 1, 4, 3.

Jahandar Shah was the ninth Mughal emperor, who ruled for 1712–1713 AD. He was succeeded by his nephew Farrukhsiyar in 1713 AD.

Muhammad Shah was the 13th Mughal emperor, who reigned from 1719-1748 AD.

Ahmad Shah was the 14th Mughal emperor. He succeeded his father, Muhammad Shah to the throne in 1748 AD.

Alamgir II was the 15th Mughal emperor of India, who reigned from 1754-1759 AD. He was the son of Jahandar Shah.

12 **With reference to Indian history, which of the following statements is/are correct?** *(Chap 2, Class-VIII, Old NCERT) (IAS Pre 2021)*

1. The Nizamat of Arcot emerged out of Hyderabad state.
2. The Mysore kingdom emerged out of Vijayanagara empire.
3. Rohilkhand kingdom was formed out of the territories occupied by Ahmad Shah Durrani.

Select the correct answer by using the codes given below.

(a) 1 and 2
(b) Only 2
(c) 2 and 3
(d) Only 3

Ans. (a)

Exp. Statements (1) and (2) are correct with reference to Indian history. The Mysore kingdom emerged out of Vijayanagara empire, while Nizamat of Arcot emerged out of Hyderabad state.

After the decline of Vijayanagara empire, Mysore became independent under the Wodeyar dynasty in 1565 AD. In 1761, Hyder Ali overthrew the Wodeyars and established his own control in Mysore.

Statement (3) is not correct as the Rohilkhand state arose in the modern districts of Rampur, Bareilly, etc. Under the declining of Mughal empire in 1721 AD. Ahmad Shah Durrani started invading India in 1748 AD.

13 **Which one among the following was not a possible reason for the success of Nadir Shah's military campaign in Delhi?** *(Chap 2, Class-VIII, Old NCERT)*

(a) Weak Mughal emperor.
(b) Use of superior military technology by the invading army.
(c) Lack of strong defence in the North-West Frontier.
(d) Late preparation for the defence of Delhi.

Ans. (b)

Use of superior military technology by the invading army was not a possible reason for the success of Nadir Shah's military campaign in Delhi. Emperor Nadir Shah, the Shah of Persia (1736–1747) and the founder of the Iranian Afsharid dynasty of Persia invaded Northern India, eventually attacking Delhi in 1739 AD.

Chapter 22

Arrival of European Powers in India

Arrival of European Powers in India

Portuguese

- In 1498, Vasco da Gama of Portugal discovered a new all-sea route from Europe to India
- Since the 16th century, Portuguese enjoyed a virtual monopoly of highly profitable Eastern India
- Successful in maintaining their possession in India for a century due to naval superiority

Franciso de Almeida (1505-1509 AD)

- Defeated the combined naval fleet of Sultan of Egypt and ruler of Gujarat in 1509
- Pursued blue water policy and believed ' that holding India is only possible if they are powerful at sea'.

Alfonso De Albuquerque (1509-1515 AD)

- Real founder of Portuguese power in India
- Captured Goa from Bijapur in 1510

Nino da Cunha (1529-1538 AD)

- Transferred his capital from Calicut to Goa in 1530
- Annexed Diu and Bassein in 1534 from the ruler of Gujarat

Contribution of Portuguese

- Introduced first printing press at Goa in 1556
- Started cultivation of tomatoes, potatoes, tobacco and chilies in India
- Credited with first scientific work on

Decline

- Intense competition among European powers
- In Battle of Swally lost Surat to British; Emergence of powerful Marathas in Maharashtra

Dutch

English

- The East India Company (EIC) was a joint stock company founded in 1600 and dissolved in 1874

Expansion in West Coast

- William Hawkins arrived at the Jahangir's court in 1609 AD
- In 1613 AD, a farman issued by Jahangir allowed them to open a factory at Surat
- Royal ambassador Thomas Roe succeeded in getting two farmans in 1618 to trade and erect factories in different parts of Empire

Expansion in East Coast

- Permitted to trade in Masaulipatnam in 1611 AD
- Secured golden farman from sultan of Golconda in 1632 AD; in 1639 AD, Francis Day obtained the site of Madras from Raja of Chandragiri

Bengal

- In 1633 AD, Mughal Governor of Orissa gave English the permission to open factories at Hariharapur Balasore and Pipli
- Permitted by Governor of Bengal, Azimuth Shah to purchase the Zamindari of three villages of Sutanati, Kalikata and Govindpur
- Dutch East India Company was formed in 1602; Their main interest was in Indonesian islands for trading spices
- Established themselves at Masulipatnam
- Constructed trading depots at Surat, Cambay, Cochin, Nagpur, Patna
- After defeat against British in Battle of Bedara, decided to focus on spices trade from Indonesia

French

- French East India Company was founded in 1664
- Firmly established at Chandernagore and Pondicherry
- Heavily dependent on French government for finances
- Under Governor-General Joseph Francois Dupleix, French started interfering in internal affairs of native rulers

Carnatic Wars

- Fought between French and English for supremacy of India

First Carnatic War (1746-1748 AD)

- Caused due to Austrian war of succession in Europe
- French emerged victorious
- Peace was negotiated through Treaty of Aix-La- Chapelle

Second Carnatic War (1749-1754 AD)

- Fought because both rival companies supported different claimants to the post of Nizam of Hyderabad and the Nawab of Carnatic
- Resulted in defeat of French

Third Carnatic War (1756-1763 AD)

- English General Eyre Coote defeated the French Governor-General Count de Lally in Battle of Wandiwash in 1760 AD
- Treaty of Paris in 1763 was signed

Danes (Danish)

- Came from Denmark in 1616 AD
- Operated from headquarters in Serampore in Bengal
- At Serampore they established a printing press in 1800 AD and a college in 1818 AD

SOURCE **New NCERT, Class VIII** (How, When and Where), **Old NCERT, Class VIII** (India in the 18th Century), **Old NCERT, Class VIII** (India and the Modern World), **Old NCERT, Class-XII** (India in the 18th Century), **Old NCERT, Class XII** (Indian States and Society in 18th Century) **Tamil Nadu Board XI** (Effects of British Rule) **NIOS Module 3** (Establishment of British Rule in India Till 1857)

Advent of European Power

1 **Consider the following statements about Portuguese in India.** *(Chap 2, Class-XII, Old NCERT)*

1. The Portuguese built their first fortress (Fort Emmanuel) at Cochin in 1503.
2. Fort Emmanuel was built by the Portuguese Viceroy Francisco De Almeida.
3. Alfonso de Albuquerque was the real founder of Portuguese power in India.

How many of the statements given above is/are correct?

(a) Only one (b) Only two (c) All three (d) None of these

Ans. (b)

Exp. Only two statements i.e., (1) and (3) are correct regarding Portuguese in India.

The Portuguese did establish Fort Emmanuel in Cochin during their early presence in India. The fortress, named Fort Emmanuel after King Manuel I of Portugal, was constructed with the permission of the ruler of the Kingdom of Kochi.

Alfonso de Albuquerque was considered as a real founder of the Portuguese power in India. In the year 1510 AD, captured Goa from the Sultan of Bijapur and established Portuguese authority over Ormuz in the Persian Gulf.

Statement (2) is incorrect because Fort Emmanuel was constructed by the Portuguese Viceroy Alfonso de Albuquerque.

2 **Consider the following statements with reference to the Portuguese.** *(Chap 2, Class-VIII, New NCERT)*

1. Vasco da Gama had discovered the sea route to India in 1498 AD.
2. The urge to secure markets led to fierce battles between the trading companies.

Which of the statements given above is/are correct?

(a) Only 1 (b) Only 2
(c) Both 1 and 2 (d) Neither 1 nor 2

Ans. (c)

Exp. Both the statements (1) and (2) are correct with reference to Portuguese.

Vasco da Gama was a Portuguese explorer, who reached India by Sea on 17th May,1498 AD. His fleet reached Kappakadavu near Calicut in the modern state of Kerala.

The primary factor that led to fierce battles between trading companies in India was trading rivalry. Each company wanted to establish a trading monopoly in India to extract maximum profit.

3 **Consider the following statements in the context of Portuguese.** *(Chap 2, Class-XII, Old NCERT)*

1. In India, Portuguese had established their trading settlements at Cochin, Goa, Diu and Daman.
2. They seized Indian territories in the hinterland.
3. Portuguese had to face the might of Mughal Empire in the South.

How many of the statements given above is/are correct?

(a) Only one (b) Only two
(c) All three (d) None of these

Ans. (a)

Exp. Only one statement i.e., (1) is correct in the context of Portuguese. Portugal had a monopoly of the highly profitable Eastern trade for nearly a century. In India, they established her trading settlements at Cochin, Goa, Diu and Daman. From the beginning, the Portuguese combined the use of force with trade.

Statements (2) and (3) are incorrect because Portuguese seized Indian territories on the coast and waged constant war to expand their trade. However, they were not able to seize Indian territories upto the hinterland.

Apart from this, they clashed with the Mughal power in Bengal in 1631 AD and were driven out of their settlement at Hugli.

4 **Consider the following statements.** *(Chap 2, Class-VIII, New NCERT)*

1. In 1600 AD, the East India Company acquired a charter from the ruler of England, Queen Elizabeth I.
2. Charter granted East India Company the sole right to trade with the East.
3. The Portuguese had established their presence in the Eastern coast of India.

Which of the statements given above is/are correct?

(a) Only 1 (b) 1 and 2
(c) 2 and 3 (d) 1, 2 and 3

Ans. (b)

Exp. Statements (1) and (2) are correct.

The East India Company acquired a royal charter by Queen Elizabeth I on 31st December, 1600 AD.

This charter granted the Company, the exclusive privilege to trade in the East. The first voyage of the English East India Company was made in 1601 AD, when its ships sailed to the Spice Islands of Indonesia.

Statement (3) is incorrect because the Portuguese have established their presence in the Western coast of India Cochin, Goa, Daman and Diu and Bombay were some of the important settlements of Portuguese on Western coast of India.

5 **With the reference to the entry of European powers into India, consider the following statements.** *(Chap 3, Class-XII, Old NCERT) (IAS Pre 2003)*

1. The Portuguese captured Goa in 1499 AD.
2. The English opened their first factory in South India at Masulipatnam.
3. In Eastern India, the English Company opened its first factory in Orissa in 1633 AD.
4. Under the leadership of Dupleix, the French occupied Madras in 1746 AD.

How many of the statements given above is/are not correct?

(a) Only one (b) Only two
(c) Only three (d) All four

Ans. (a)

Exp. Only one statement i.e., (1) is not correct with reference to the entry of European powers into India because the Portuguese Governor Alfanso de' Albuquerque, captured Goa from rulers of Bijapur in 1510 AD.

Thus, the Portuguese established their domination over the entire Asian coast from Hormuz in the Persian Gulf to Malacca in Malaya and the spice islands in Indonesia.

6 **With reference to Indian history, consider the following statements.** *(Chap 2, Class-XII, Old NCERT) (IAS Pre 2004)*

1. The Dutch established their factories/warehouses on the East coast on lands granted to them by Gajapati rulers.
2. Alfonso de' Albuquerque captured Goa from the Bijapur Sultanate.
3. The English East India Company established a factory at Madras on a plot of land leased from a representative of the Vijayanagara empire.

Which of the statements given above are correct?

(a) 1 and 2 (b) 2 and 3 (c) 1 and 3 (d) 1, 2 and 3

Ans. (b)

Exp. Statements (2) and (3) are correct with reference to Indian history.

In 1510 AD, Alfonso de Albuquerque captured Goa from the Sultan of Bijapur, Ismail Adil Shah. He is considered to be the real founder of the Portuguese power in India. English East India Company established a factory in Madras in 1639 on land leased from representatives of Vijayanagara Empire called the Nayakas.

Statement (1) is incorrect because Dutch East India Company was established in 1602 AD and it established factories in India at Masulipatnan in 10605 AD. However Gajpati rulers ruled over Kalinga, Andhra Pradesh and West Bengal from 1435 to 1541 CE.

Establishment of British Rule

7 **Consider the following statements.** *(Chap 3, Class-XII, Old NCERT)*

1. Captain Hawkins was given a mansab of 400 by emperor Jahangir.
2. Later, he was expelled from Jahangir's court as a result of Dutch intrigue.

Which of the statements given above is/are correct?

(a) Only 1 (b) Only 2
(c) Both 1 and 2 (d) Neither 1 nor 2

Ans. (a)

Exp. Statement (1) is correct. When East India Company decided to open its factory in Surat then it sent captain Hawkins to Jahangir's court to obtain royal favours. He was given a mansab of 400 and Jagir by Jahangir.

Statement (2) is incorrect because, he was expelled from Jahangir's court from Agra as a result of Portuguese intrigue. This convinced the British of the need to overcome Portuguese influence at the Mughal court, if they were to obtain any concessions from the imperial government.

8 **Match List I with List II.** *(Class-XI, Old NCERT) (CGPSC Pre 2023)*

	List I		List II
A.	Alfonso de' Albuquerque	1.	Change of Portuguese headquarter from Cochin to Goa
B.	Nuno da Cunha	2.	Arrival in India in September 1500 AD
C.	Pedro Alvares Cabral	3.	Blue Water Policy
D.	Francisco de Almeida	4.	Acquiring Goa in 1510

Codes

	A	B	C	D		A	B	C	D
(a)	3	4	1	3	(b)	2	4	3	1
(c)	4	1	2	3	(d)	3	1	2	4

Ans. (c)

Exp. The correct matching is A-4, B-1, C-2, D-3.

Alfonso de' Albuquerque was the Portuguese viceroy (1509-1515) who acquired Goa in 1510. Governor **Nuno da Cunha** moved the capital from Cochin to Goa in 1530. **Pedro Alvares Cabral** arrived in India in September 1500 AD. **Francisco de Almeida** was the first Governor appointed by the Portuguese to India. He implemented the 'Blue Water Policy'.

9 **After Madras, British made Bengal as their important centre. In the context of establishing their control over the Bengal, consider the following statements.** *(Chap 2, Class-VIII, New NCERT)*

1. In 1645, East India Company was given permission to trade at Hugli in Bengal.
2. Company received zamindari rights over three villages. One of these was Kalikata, which later grew into the city of Calcutta.
3. Through the early 18th century, the conflict between the Company and the nawabs of Bengal intensified.

How many of the statements given above is/are not correct?

(a) Only one (b) Only two
(c) All three (d) None of these

Ans. (a)

Exp. Only one statement i.e., (1) is not correct because the English succeeded to establish their factory at Hugli in 1651 AD followed by those at Patna, Dacca and Kasim Bazar. In 1667 AD, Aurangzeb gave the English a farmen for trade in Bengal.

10 Consider the following description.
(Chap 3, Class-VIII, Old NCERT)

The Battle was fought between British and Nawab of Bengal in the year 1757 AD. This Battle changed the destiny of East India Company. This was their first ever important success in Indian sub continent. They won the battle without much effort and shedding blood.

Which of the following battles can be identified from above description?

(a) Battle of Plassey (b) Battle of Buxar
(c) Battle of Karnal (d) Battle of Calcutta

Ans. (a)

Exp. The given description is related to the Battle of Plassey. It was fought on 23rd June, 1757 AD between the British East India company led by Robert Clive and the Nawab of Bengal, Siraj-ud-Daulah.

The Battle is regarded as a historic turning point for British in India as it established political and military supremacy of the British in Bengal.

11 Consider the following statements.
(Chap 3, Class-VIII, Old NCERT)

1. Battle of Plassey was fought between Mir Jafar and the East India Company.
2. In Battle of Plassey, the troops led by Mir Jafar and others, who had already entered into a conspiracy with the English did not join the battle.
3. After the Battle of Plassey, the English Company became the real power in Bengal, with Nawab as its puppet.

Which of the statements given above is/are correct?

(a) Only 1 (b) 1 and 2 (c) 2 and 3 (d) 1, 2 and 3

Ans. (c)

Exp. Statements (2) and (3) are correct.

In Battle of Plassey, the leading men of Nawab's court, such as Mir Jafar, the Mir Bakshi, Manik Chand, Amichand, Jagat Seth intrigued with British army and did not join the battle. It contributed in Nawab's defeat.

After the Battle of Plassey, Robert Clive proclaimed Mir Jafar as the Nawab of Bengal thus making him a mere puppet in the hands of British.

Statement (1) is incorrect because Battle of Plassey was fought between Nawab of Bengal Siraj-ud-Daulah and the East India Company.

12 With reference to Battle of Plassey in India, consider the following statements. *(Chap 2, Class-VIII, New NCERT)*

1. After the defeat at Plassey, Mir Jafar was assassinated and Siraj-ud-Daulah became Nawab.
2. Siraj-ud-Daulah seized the English factory at Kashimbazar and occupied the Fort William on 19th July, 1757.
3. In 1760, Robert Clive led the Company's army against Siraj-ud-Daulah at Plassey.
4. The Battle of Plassey became famous because it was the first major victory of the East India Company in India.

How many of the statements given above is/are correct?

(a) Only one (b) Only two (c) Only three (d) All four

Ans. (a)

Exp. Only one statement i.e., (4) is correct with reference to Battle of Plassey in India as the Battle of Plassey established political and military supremacy of the Britishers. It was the first major victory of the East India Company in India.

Statements (1), (2) and (3) are incorrect because after the defeat at Plassey, Siraj-ud-Daulah was assassinated and Mir Jafar became Nawab of Bengal.

The British East India Company challenged the Nawab's sovereignty directly by demanding absolute right to trade freely in Bengal. This angered Siraj-ud-Daulah, which seized the English factory at Kasimbazar and occupied fort William on 20th June, 1756 AD.

In 1757 AD, Robert Clive led the Company's army against Siraj-ud-Daulah at Plassey.

13 Consider the following statements about the Battle of Plassey. *(Chap 16, Class-XI, Tamil Nadu Board)*

1. Nawab of Bengal Siraj-ud-Daulah's act of seizing Fort of Calcutta and imprisoning many East Indian Officials was reason behind the battle.
2. Lord Dalhousie was commanding-in-Chief from the side of East India Company.
3. The Battle of Plassey paved the way for British dominance over Bengal and eventually all of India.

How many of the statements given above is/are correct?

(a) Only one (b) Only two
(c) All three (d) None of these

Ans. (b)

Exp. Only two statements i.e., (1) and (3) are correct regarding Battle of Plassey.

The conflict between Siraj-ud-Daulah and the British escalated due to the incident at Fort William in Calcutta, where several British officials were imprisoned by the Nawab. The Battle of Plassey was fought on the banks of Bhagirathi river near Calcutta on 23rd June, 1757 between the Nawab of Bengal and his French allies and the British East India Company. The Battle of Plassey was of immense historical importance.

It paved way for British Mastery of Bengal and eventually the whole of India.

The British Company successfully established their monopoly over Bengal trade, marginalising the French and Dutch companies.

Statement (2) is incorrect as Robert was commanding in-chief from the side to East India Company.

14 **Consider the following statements in regards with the expansion of English power in India.** *(Chap 2, Class-VIII, New NCERT)*

1. In early years Company's main objective was the expansion of trade.
2. In 1765 AD, the Mughal emperor granted the *Diwani* of the Province of Bengal to Company.
3. Company never interfered in the internal matters of provinces.

Which of the statements given above are correct?
(a) 1 and 2 (b) 2 and 3 (c) 1 and 3 (d) 1, 2 and 3

Ans. (a)

Exp. Statements (1) and (2) are correct regarding the expansion of English power in India because in early years, Company's main objective was the expansion of trade. It was unwilling to take responsibility of administration. In 1765 AD, the Mughal emperor appointed the Company as the *Diwani* of the Province of Bengal.

Statement (3) is incorrect because after gradual conquest of India, the Company started appointing residents in Indian states. With this, the Company officials began interfering in the internal affairs of Indian states.

15 **Consider the following statements with reference to the treaty signed in 1765 AD.** *(Chap 3, Class-VIII, Old NCERT)*

1. The *Nawab* of Awadh ceded Allahabad and Kara to the Mughal Emperor as per Treaty of Allahabad.
2. English secured the *Diwani* of Bengal, Bihar and Central India.

Which of the statements given above is/are correct?
(a) Only 1 (b) Only 2
(c) Both 1 and 2 (d) Neither 1 nor 2

Ans. (a)

Exp. Statement (1) is correct with reference to the treaty signed in 1765 AD, as the *Nawab* of Awadh Shuja-ud-Daulah surrendered Allahabad and Kara to Mughal Emperor Shah Alam II as per Second Treaty of Allahabad. After victory over Nawab of Awadh and Mughal Emperor in Battle of Buxar, the Company signed two separate treaties with them at Allahabad.

Statement (2) is incorrect because the Mughal Emperor issued a *farman* granting the *Diwani* of Bengal, Bihar and Orissa to the East India Company in lieu of an annual payment of ₹ 26 Lakh.

16 **Consider the following statements about the Battle of Wandiwash.** *(Chap 16, Class-XI, Tamil Nadu Board)*

1. The Battle of Wandiwash took place between Eyre Coote and Lally at Vandavasee in January 1760.
2. The war concluded with the signing of the Treaty of Paris in 1763.
3. According to the Treaty of Paris in 1763, Pondicherry and Chandernagore were ceded to the French.

How many of the statements given above is/are correct?
(a) Only one (b) Only two
(c) All three (d) None of these

Ans. (c)

Exp. All three statements i.e., (1), (2) and (3) are correct regarding the Battle of Wandiwash. The Battle of Wandiwash, also known as the Third Carnatic War, occurred in January 1760 between the British forces led by General Eyre Coote and the French forces under Arthur de Lally.

The decisive battle of the Third Carnatic War was won by the English. The war ended with the signing of the Treaty of Paris in 1763, marking the end of the Seven Years' War. According to the treaty, Pondicherry and Chandernagore were returned to the French.

17 **Consider the following statements about Hyder Ali.** *(Chap 1, Class-XII, Old NCERT)*

1. He defeated British Forces in the First Anglo-Mysore War.
2. He established a modern arsenal at Dindigul in 1755 with the help of British expert.
3. He died in 1782 AD in the course of the Third Anglo-Mysore War.

How many of the statements given above is/are not correct?
(a) Only one (b) Only two
(c) All three (d) None of these

Ans. (b)

Exp. Only two statements i.e., (2) and (3) are not correct. Statements about Haider Ali.

He established a modern arsenal at Dindigul in 1755 AD with the help of French experts. He died in 1782 AD in the course of the Second Anglo-Mysore War.

18 **Consider the following statements with respect to First Anglo-Mysore War.** *(Chap 2, Class-XII, Old NCERT)*

1. In this war the Nizam of Hyderabad, the Marathas and the English allied together against Hyder Ali.
2. The war was concluded with Treaty of Madras which provided for the exchange of prisoners and the conquered areas.
3. Hyder Ali along with the Nizam attacked the Nawab of Arcot.

How many of the statements given above is/are correct?
(a) Only one (b) Only two
(c) All three (d) None of these

Ans. (c)

Exp. All three statements i.e., (1), (2) and (3) are correct with respect to first Anglo-Mysore war. The British, after their success in the Battle of Buxar with the Nawab of

Bengal, signed a treaty with the Nizam of Hyderabad persuading him to give them the Northern Circars for protecting the Nizam from Hyder Ali who already had disputes with the Marathas. The Nizam of Hyderabad, the Marathas and the English allied together against Hyder Ali.

The Treaty of Madras, signed in 1769, ended the First Anglo-Mysore War. It restored the conquered territories to their original owners and facilitated the exchange of prisoners.

Hyder Ali, along with the Nizam, attacked the Nawab of Arcot. Hyder displayed diplomatic skills. He paid the Marathas to maintain neutrality and persuaded the Nizam to become his ally by promising to share the conquered territories.

19 Consider the following statements with reference to the Tipu Sultan. *(Chap 1, Class-XII, Old NCERT)*

1. Tipu Sultan was defeated in Fourth Anglo-Mysore War.
2. French occupied Mysore after defeating and killing Tipu in 1899 AD.

Which of the statements given above is/are incorrect?

(a) Only 1
(b) Only 2
(c) Both 1 and 2
(d) Neither 1 nor 2

Ans. (b)

Exp. Statement (2) is incorrect with reference to Tipu Sultan because the Britishers occupied Mysore after defeating and killing Tipu Sultan in 1799 AD.

20 Which of the following pairs is correctly matched? *(Chap 3, Class-XII, Old NCERT) (UPPSC Mains 2014)*

(a) First Anglo-Mysore War - Hyder Ali was defeated.
(b) Second Anglo-Mysore War - Hyder Ali defeated the British.
(c) Third Anglo-Mysore War - Tipu Sultan won the battle and did not cede his territory to the British.
(d) Fourth Anglo Mysore War - Tipu was defeated and was killed in the Battle.

Ans. (d)

Exp. Pair (d) is correctly matched. Fourth Anglo-Mysore War was fought in 1799 AD between the Britishers led by Lord Wellesley and Tipu Sultan. In this battle, Tipu Sultan was killed and British annexed his Srirangapatanam Fort.

Pairs (a), (b) and (c) are incorrectly matched because the First Anglo-Mysore War was held in 1767-69, which ended with the Treaty of Madras. In this battle, Hyder Ali defeated the British forces.

Second Anglo-Mysore War was fought in 1780-84 AD in which Hyder Ali was defeated and this war ended with Treaty of Manglore.

Third Anglo-Mysore War was held in 1790-92 AD and ended with the treaty of Srirangapatanam in, which Tipu Sultan ceded his territory to the British.

21 With reference to the Kitoor and Rani Chennamma, which of the following statements is/are correct? *(Chap 3, Class-VIII, Old NCERT)*

1. When the British tried to annex the small state of Kitoor (in Karnataka today), Rani Chennamma led armed rebellion against British East India Company.
2. She was arrested in 1824 AD and died in prison in 1829 AD.

Select the correct answer using the codes given below.

(a) Only 1
(b) Only 2
(c) Both 1 and 2
(d) Neither 1 nor 2

Ans. (c)

Exp. Both the statements (1) and (2) are correct with reference to Kitoor and Rani Chennamma. She was the Indian queen of Kitoor, a princely state in present-day Karnataka.

She led an armed rebellion against British East India Company in 1824 AD in defiance of Doctrine of Lapse in an attempt to maintain Indian control over the region. However, she was defeated and arrested by East India Company in the war. She died in the British prison in 1829 AD.

22 Consider the following pairs. *(Class-XI, Old NCERT)*

1.	Warren Hastings	–	Abolished Dual system
2.	Lord Cornwallis	–	Permanent Settlement in Bengal
3.	Sir John Shore	–	Policy of Non-Interference
4.	Lord Wellesley	–	Subsidiary Alliance system

How many of the pairs given above is/are correctly matched?

(a) Only one
(b) Only two
(c) Only three
(d) All four

Ans. (d)

Exp. All four pairs are correctly matched. Warren Hastings abolished the Dual system which was established by Robert Clive. In this Dual System of Government in Bengal, the Company had Diwani rights that is the rights to collect revenue and the Nizam or Indian chiefs had the power on administrative authority.

Permanent Settlement was introduced by the second Governor-General of Bengal, Cornwallis, in 1793. It was a settlement system that was first enacted in Odisha, Bihar and Bengal.

The Policy of Non- Interference is associated with Sir John Shore. He was the first President of British and Foreign Bible Society.

Lord Wellesley introduced the Policy of Subsidiary Alliance; it came into effect in the year 1798. It was a Military Protection Agreement between the East India Company and the Indian States.

23 Which of the following statements is/are incorrect regarding Policy of Non-Intervention?

(Chap 3, Class-VIII, Old NCERT)

(a) After the defeat of Britain in the War of American Independence this policy was followed.
(b) Under this policy, British Government decided not to interfere in neighbouring states of India.
(c) The British adhered to the policy of Non-Intervention when it suited their interest.
(d) This period was utilised mainly to consolidate the power and to prepare themselves for the next phase of expansion.

Ans. (b)

Exp. Statement (b) is incorrect regarding Policy of Non-Intervention. According to the Non-Intervention Policy, every ruler in India had to accept to pay a subsidy to the British for the maintenance of the British army.

In return, the British would protect them from their enemies. This gave the Company enormous control over the Indian states.

24 Consider the following statements with reference to the Subsidiary Alliance. *(Chap 3, Class-VIII, Old NCERT)*

1. The first ruler to accept the Subsidiary Alliance was the Nizam of Hyderabad.
2. Under this policy, Indian rulers were forced to have a British official called the resident at his court.
3. Under this policy, Indian rulers made to keep a large British force within their territory and pay for its maintenance.

Which of the statements given above is/are correct?

(a) Only 1 (b) 1 and 2
(c) 2 and 3 (d) 1, 2 and 3

Ans. (d)

Exp. All the given statements are correct with reference to the Subsidiary Alliance.

Lord Wellesley in the year 1798 introduced, the Subsidiary Alliance, which was a new intervention policy to expand the British territory in India. The first ruler in India who accepted the Subsidiary Alliance was the Nizam of Hyderabad, Asaf Jah II.

Under the Subsidiary Alliance, Indian princely states were forced to keep British resident at their court. The Indian ruler would not employ any other European at their court.

An Indian ruler entering into a Subsidiary Alliance with the British, had to accept British forces in his territory and also agreed to pay for their maintenance.

In return, the East India Company, undertook to protect the state from external dangers and internal disorders. Nizam of Hyderabad was the first to accept the Subsidiary Alliance.

25 What were the main negative consequences of the Subsidiary Alliance Policy of the British?

(Chap 2, Class-XII, Old NCERT)

1. Indian rulers lost all vestiges of sovereignty in case of external matters.
2. British Resident interfered in day-to-day administration of the state.
3. British provided training to the soldiers of the state, which signed a Subsidiary Alliance.

Select the correct answer using the codes given below.

(a) 1 and 2 (b) 1 and 3 (c) 2 and 3 (d) All of these

Ans. (a)

Exp. Statements (1) and (2) were the negative consequences of the Subsidiary Alliance Policy of the British. Indian rulers had give up their Independence and had to accept the suzerainty of the English East India Company.

Besides this, the British Residents who were stationed at the court of Indian states, under the Subsidiary Alliance, interfered in day to day administration of the state.

Statement (3) is incorrect because British provided military protection to those, who signed the Subsidiary Alliance.

26 Consider the following statements in the context of the Governor-General Lord Wellesley.

(Chap 2, Class-XII, Old NCERT)

1. During his reign, British army attacked and defeated Tipu Sultan in 1799 AD.
2. In 1801 AD, Lord Wellesley forced a new treaty upon the puppet Nawab of Carnatic compelling him to cede his kingdom to the Company in return for a pension.
3. Arthur Wellesley defeated the combined armies of Sindhia and Bhonsle in 1803 AD.
4. In 1808 AD, Wellesley was recalled from India.

Which of the statements given above are correct?

(a) 1 and 2 (b) 1, 2 and 3
(c) 2, 3, and 4 (d) All of these

Ans. (b)

Exp. Statements (1), (2) and (3) are correct in the context of the Governor-General Lord Wellesley.

Lord Wellesley was the Governor-General of Bengal from 1798 to 1805 AD. During his tenure, the fourth and last Anglo-Mysore War was fought in 1799 AD. In this battle, Tipu Sultan was killed.

He also forced a new treaty upon, *Nawab* of Carnatic compelling him to cede his kingdom to the Company in return for a pension.

The Second Anglo-Maratha war was also fought during his tenure in which Bhonsle, Sindhia and Holkar were defeated.

Statement (4) is incorrect because Wellesley was recalled from India in 1805 and once again Lord Cornwallis was sent to India.

27 **Consider the following Princely states of the British rule in India.** *(Chap 2, Class-VIII, New NCERT) (IAS Pre 2004)*

1. Jhansi 2. Sambhalpur 3. Satara

The correct chronological order in which they were annexed by the British is

(a) 1, 2, 3 (b) 1, 3, 2 (c) 3, 2, 1 (d) 3, 1, 2

Ans. (c)

Exp. The correct chronology in which Princely states were annexed by the British was 3, 2, 1 i.e., Satara – Sambhalpur – Jhansi

Doctrine of Lapse was propounded by Lord Dalhousie. Under this doctrine, any state in India, which was not having any male heir would be handed over to the East India Company.

Satara was annexed by Lord Dalhousie in 1848 AD.
Sambhalpur was annexed by Lord Dalhousie in 1849 AD.
Jhansi was annexed by Lord Dalhousie in 1853 AD.

28 **With reference to the Hindu Nawab Wazirs of Awadh Sultanate, which of the following statements is/are correct?**
(Chap 2, Class-XII, Old NCERT) (UP RO/ARO Mains 2016)

1. Raja Tikait Rai was 'Artha Mantri' of Nawab Asaf-ud-Daula.
2. Usually there were certain Hindu castes who were placed at the high positions in the state of Nawabs of Awadh.

Select the correct answer using the codes given below.

(a) Only 1 (b) Only 2
(c) Both 1 and 2 (d) Neither 1 nor 2

Ans. (c)

Exp. Both the statements (1) and (2) are correct with reference to the Hindu Nawab Wazirs of Awadh Sultanate. Raja Tikait Rai Bahadur (1760 -1808) was the Diwan (Finance Minister) of Awadh from 1791 to 1796 AD. In the regime of Asaf - ud-Daula, usually there were certain Hindu castes who were placed at high positions in the state of Nawabs of Awadh. Nawab Asaf-ud-Daula became Nawab of Awadh at the age of 26, in 1775. He was known for his liberal policies and secular governance.

29 **Consider the following description.**
(Chap 2, Class-VIII, New NCERT)

The policy was mainly utilised by the Lord Dalhousie. Under this policy, British denied to recognise adopted son of the Indian ruler who did not have natural heir. They acquired the territory of rulers who did not have legal heirs.

Which of the following British policy is best described by above descriptions?

(a) Policy of Subsidiary Alliance
(b) Doctrine of Lapse
(c) Policy of Non-Intervention
(d) Policy of Ring-Fence

Ans. (b)

Exp. The given description is related to Doctrine of Lapse policy by Lord Dalhousie. Under this policy, British denied to recognise adopted son of the Indian ruler, who did not have natural heir. The princely state of Satara, Sambhalpur and Jhansi under the pretext of his policy.

30 **Consider the following statements about the Doctrine of Lapse.** *(Class-XI, Old NCERT)*

1. Under this policy any princely state where the ruler did not have a legal male heir would be annexed by the Company.
2. Satara was the first state to be annexed under the policy of the Doctrine of Lapse.
3. Dalhousie annexed Awadh in 1856 by giving reason for misgovernance.

How many of the statements given above is/are correct?

(a) Only one (b) Only two
(c) All three (d) None of these

Ans. (c)

Exp. All three statements i.e., (1), (2) and (3) are correct regarding the Doctrine of Lapse. The Doctrine of Lapse policy was introduced by Lord Dalhousie, in 1856. According to this policy, any princely state (also known as a native Indian state) under the suzerainty of the British East India Company would be annexed by the Company if the ruler died without a legitimate male heir.

Satara was one of the first princely states to be annexed under the Doctrine of Lapse. It happened in 1848 after the death of the ruler, Pratap Singh. Awadh, a significant princely state in Northern India, was annexed by Lord Dalhousie in 1856.

The pretext for annexation was the alleged misgovernance by Nawab Wajid Ali Shah, the ruler of Awadh. The British accused him of mismanagement, inefficiency and maladministration.

31 **Consider the following statements.**
(Chap 4, Class-XII, Old NCERT)

1. The conquest of Sindh occurred as a result of growing Anglo-Russian rivalry in Europe and Asia.
2. Sindh was annexed by British in 1837 AD.

Which of the statements given above is/are correct?

(a) Only 1 (b) Only 2
(c) Both 1 and 2 (d) Neither 1 nor 2

Ans. (a)

Exp. Statement (1) is correct as the conquest of Sindh occurred as a result of growing Anglo-Russian rivalry in Europe and Asia. There was constant fear by the British that Russia might attack India through Afghanistan or Persia.

To counter Russia, the British Government decided to increase its control over Afghanistan and Persia. Therefore, they decided to conquer Sindh.

Statement (2) is incorrect because Sindh was annexed by British in 1843 AD.

32 **Consider the following statements.**

(Chap 3, Class-VIII, Old NCERT)

1. The British denied helping Nawab of Awadh against the Rohillas.
2. The British relations with Awadh were strengthened and this helped in making the British rule in Bengal safe and secure.

Which of the statements given above is/are correct?

(a) Only 1 (b) Only 2
(c) Both 1 and 2 (d) Neither 1 nor 2

Ans. (b)

Exp. Statement (2) is correct as the strong relation between Awadh and Britishers strengthened the British rule in Bengal.

Awadh was envisioned as the buffer state against armies of Marathas. However, with the subsequent defeat of Marathas and consolidation of its territories in rest of India, Britishers, ultimately annexed the Awadh kingdom in 1856 AD.

Statement (1) is incorrect because the Nawab of Awadh was supported by the British East India Company in war under the Governor-General of Bengal, Warren Hastings. In this war, the Rohillas were defeated.

33 **Consider the following statements.**

(Chap 3, Class-VIII, Old NCERT)

1. The Treaty of Bassein was signed in 1802 AD.
2. The Treaty of Bassein was signed between English and Sikhs.
3. This Treaty was a decisive step in breaking up of the Sikh states.

Which of the statements given above is/are correct?

(a) Only 1 (b) 1 and 2 (c) 2 and 3 (d) 1, 2 and 3

Ans. (a)

Exp. Statement (1) is correct as the Treaty of Bassein was signed on 31st December, 1802 AD.

Statements (2) and (3) are incorrect because the Treaty of Bassein was signed between the British East India Company and Baji Rao II, the Maratha Peshwa of Poona, after the Battle of Poona.

Hence, this treaty was a decisive step in breaking up of the Maratha Confederacy. This pact ultimately led to the East India Company's annexation of the Peshwa's territories in Western India in 1818 AD.

34 **Consider the following statements.**

(Chap 3, Class-VIII, Old NCERT)

1. The Pindaris were military plunderers.
2. The Pindaris were suppressed by Lord Hastings in Pindari war.

Which of the statements given above is/are correct?

(a) Only 1 (b) Only 2
(c) Both 1 and 2 (c) Neither 1 nor 2

Ans. (c)

Exp. Both the statements (1) and (2) are correct.

The Pindaris were an irregular army not paid by the state but allowed to plunder during the war. Initially, they were attached by the Mughal army, later the Maratha army and finally after disintegration of both these Empires, they started raiding their neighbouring territories on their own.

The Pindaris were suppressed by Lord Hastings in Pindari war (in 1817-19 AD).

35 **Consider the following statements.**

(Chap 2, Class-XII, Old NCERT)

1. The Peshwa attacked the British Residency at Poona in November, 1817 AD.
2. Governor-General Lord Mayo compelled Sindhia to accept British suzerainty.
3. The small kingdom of Satara was founded out of the Peshwa's land and given to descendant of Chhatrapati Shivaji.

How many of the statements given above is/are not correct?

(a) Only one (b) Only two
(c) All three (d) None of these

Ans. (a)

Exp. Only one statement i.e., (2) is not incorrect because Governor- General Lord Wellesley compelled Sindhia to accept British suzerainty.

The Sindhias signed the Treaty of Surji-Anjanagaon in 1803 AD through which, the British got the territories of Rohtak, Ganga-Yamuna doab, Gurgaon, Delhi-Agra region, Broach, some districts in Gujarat, parts of Bundelkhand and Ahmednagar fort.

36 **Consider the following pairs.**

(Chap 2, Class-VIII, New NCERT)

	Anglo-Maratha War		Years
1.	First Anglo-Maratha War	–	1775-1785 AD
2.	Second Anglo-Maratha War	–	1803-1805 AD
3.	Third Anglo-Maratha War	–	1817-1819 AD

How many of the pairs given above is/are not correctly matched?

(a) Only one (b) Only two
(c) Only three (d) None of these

Ans. (a)

Exp. Only one pair i.e., (1) is not correctly matched because the First Anglo- Maratha war (1775-1782 AD) was fought between the British East India Company and Maratha Empire in India. The war began with the treaty of Surat and ended with the Treaty of Saibai.

37 **Which of the following statements is/are incorrect?**

(Chap 3, Class-VIII, Old NCERT)

1. The only area, which the British attacked but failed to conquer was Afghanistan.
2. In 1843 AD, Sind was annexed to the British Empire.

Codes

(a) Only 1 (b) Only 2
(c) Both 1 and 2 (d) Neither 1 nor 2

Ans. (d)

Exp. Neither statements (1) nor (2) are incorrect.

The only area, which the British attacked but failed to conquer was Afghanistan. The territories of Sind were annexed by the Bombay Presidency of British India in 1843 AD, following a British Indian conquest led by the then Major-General Charles Napier, in order to quell the insurrection of Sindhi rulers who had remained hostile to the British Empire following the First Anglo-Afghan war.

38 Consider the following statements.

(Chap 2, Class-XII, Old NCERT)

1. The chief of Sindh signed a Subsidiary Treaty in 1839 AD with British.
2. Lord Ripon had played a key role in the annexation of Sindh.

Which of the statements given above is/are correct?

(a) Only 1
(b) Only 2
(c) Both 1 and 2
(d) Neither 1 nor 2

Ans. (a)

Exp. Statement (1) is correct as the chief of Sindh, known as *amirs*, were made to sign a Subsidiary Treaty in 1839 AD with British. Finally, Sindh was annexed by British in spite of previous assurances that its territorial integrity would be respected.

Statement (2) is incorrect because Sindh was annexed in 1843 AD after a brief campaign by Sir Charles Napier. He received seven lakhs of rupees as Prize money for accomplishing this task.

39 Consider the following statements about the Maharaja Ranjit Singh. *(Class-XI, Old NCERT)*

1. Maharaja Ranjit Singh was the leader of the Sikh empire, which ruled the North-West Indian Subcontinent.
2. The capital of the Kingdom of Maharaja Ranjit Singh was Karachi.
3. Ranjit Singh got famous Kohinoor diamond from Shah Shuja who was the king of Afghanistan.

How many of the statements given above is/are correct?

(a) Only one (b) Only two
(c) All three (d) None of these

Ans (b)

Exp. Only two statements i.e., (1) and (3) are correct regarding Maharaja Ranjit Singh.

Maharaja Ranjit Singh popularly known as Sher-e-Punjab, was the leader of the Sikh empire, which ruled the North-West Indian Subcontinent in the early half of the 19th century.

Ranjit Singh got famous Kohinoor diamond from Shah Shuja who was the king of Afghanistan. In 1813, he presented Kohinoor to Ranjit Singh for saving his life. Statement (2) is incorrect because the capital of Kingdom of Maharaja Ranjit Singh was Lahore. It is located in the present day of Pakistan and became the political and culturay centre of the Sikh empire during Maharaja Ranjit Singh's rule.

40 With reference to the Anglo-Sikh conflict, which of the following statements is/are correct?

(Chap 3, Class-VIII, Old NCERT)

1. Punjab was annexed when Dalhousie became the Governor-General.
2. Second Anglo-Sikh War was fought in 1848 AD.

Select correct answer using the codes given below.

(a) Only 1 (b) Only 2
(c) Both 1 and 2 (d) Neither 1 nor 2

Ans. (c)

Exp. Both the statements (1) and (2) are correct with reference to the Anglo-Sikh Conflict.

During the reign of Dalhousie, East India Company annexed Punjab in 1849 AD. In 1858 AD, the Punjab along with the rest of British India, came under the direct rule of the British crown.

The Second Anglo-Sikh War was fought in between 1848-1849 AD.

It resulted in the fall of the Sikh empire and the annexation of the Punjab, which subsequently become the North-West Frontier Province, of the East India Company.

41 Match the following lists and choose the correct codes. *(Chap 3, Class-VIII, Old NCERT)*

List I (State Annexed)	List II (Years)
A. Awadh	1. 1843 AD
B. Punjab	2. 1856 AD
C. Sindh	3. 1818 AD
D. Maratha's Territory	4. 1849 AD

Codes

	A	B	C	D		A	B	C	D
(a)	3	1	4	2	(b)	1	3	2	4
(c)	2	4	1	3	(d)	4	3	2	1

Ans. (c)

Exp. The correct matching is A-2, B-4, C-1, D-3.

Awadh was annexed in 1856 AD by the British under the pretext of misgovernance.

Punjab was annexed by British in 1849 AD. It was annexed by British after Second Anglo-Sikh war that took place in 1848 to 1849 AD.

Sindh was annexed by British in 1843 AD.

Maratha's Territories were annexed by British in 1818 AD.

42 Consider the following statements.
(Chap 2, Class-XII, Old NCERT)

1. The Anglo-Nepalese War ended with the Treaty of Sagauli.
2. The First Burma War ended with the Treaty of Yandabo.
3. The Second-Anglo Afghan War ended with the Treaty of Gandamak.

How many of the statements given above is/are correct?

(a) Only one (b) Only two
(c) All three (d) None of these

Ans (c)

Exp. All three statements i.e., (1), (2) and (3) are correct.

The Anglo-Nepalese War took place between 1814 and 1816. It was fought between the British East India Company and the Kingdom of Nepal (ruled by the Gurkha dynasty). The Treaty of Sagauli was signed on 4th March, 1816 and it officially ended the war.

The Treaty of Yandabo was signed on 24th February, 1826, and it formally ended the war. The First Burma War took place between 1824 and 1826. It was fought between the British East India Company and the Burmese empire (ruled by the Konbaung dynasty).

The Treaty of Gandamak officially ended the first phase of the Second Anglo-Afghan War. Mohammad Yaqub Khan ceded various frontier areas as well as Afghanistan's control of its foreign affairs to Britain.

43 With reference to British India relations with neighbouring countries, consider the following statements. *(Chap 2 Class-XII, Old NCERT)*

1. Nepal didn't lose any territories as per Treaty of Sagauli (1816).
2. Need to check French ambitions in Burma and the rest of South-East Asia resulted in three Anglo-Burmese Wars.
3. As per Treaty of Lhasa (1904), Tibet agreed that the British Indian Government would occupy the Chumbi valley.

How many of the statements given above is/are incorrect?

(a) Only one
(b) Only two
(c) All three
(d) None of the above

Ans (a)

Exp. Only one statement i.e., (1) is incorrect with reference to British India relations with neighbouring countries becauses as per Treaty of Sagauli (1816) Nepal Suffered loss of territories.

Nepal ceded the districts of Garhwal and Kumaon and abandoned claims to Terai. Nepal also accepted a British resident. Nepal also withdrew from Sikkim.

44 With reference to Pondicherry (now Puducherry), consider the following statements.
(Chap 2, Class-XII, Old NCERT) (UPPSC Mains 2006)

1. The first European power to occupy Pondicherry were the Portuguese.
2. The second European power to occupy Pondicherry were the French.
3. The English never occupied Pondicherry.

Which of the statement(s) given above is/are correct?

(a) Only 1 (b) 2 and 3
(c) Only 3 (d) 1, 2 and 3

Ans. (a)

Statement (1) is correct with reference to Pondicherry as Portuguese were the first European power to set up a factory and occupy the Pondicherry region during the 16th century.

After Independence, incorporation of Pondicherry into the Union of India was done in 1962.

Statements (2) and (3) are incorrect because after the Portuguese, the second European power to capture Pondicherry was the Dutch.

In the year 1761, the British captured Pondicherry from the French, but later had to returned it back to the French under the Treaty of Paris in 1763.

Chapter 23

Rise of New and Autonomous States

Rise of New and Autonomous States

Successor State

Hyderabad

- Founded by Nizam-ul-Mulk Asaf Jah in 1724
- Never openly declared his independence but acted in independent manner
- Constantly engaged in a struggle against the Marathas

Carnatic

- Mughal suba which came under the Nizam of Hyderabad's authority
- Nawab Saadutullah Khan of Carnatic had made his hepen Dost Ali Khan his successor

Awadh

- Founded by Saadat Khan Burhan-Ul- Mulk in 1722
- Extended from Kannauj in West to river Karmnasa in East

Bengal

- **Murshid Quli Khan (1717-1727 AD)**
    - Became Governor of Bengal in 1717 freed himself from central control
    - Established peace by freeing Bengal of internal and external danger
- **Alivardi Khan**
    - Ruled for 15 years between 1740-1756 AD
    - Had constant struggle against Marathas

Siraj-Ud-Daula (1756-1757 AD)

- Faced internal rivals such as Shaukat Jang, Ghasiti Begum and others- Jagat Seth, Omichand, Rai Ballabh and Rai Durlabh

Independent State

Mysore

- Emerged as important power under the rule of Haidar Ali
- He established a modern arsenal in Dindigul with French assistance
- Engaged in war with Marathas
- **Anglo-Mysore War**
    - First (1767-1769 AD) concluded by Treaty of Madras
    - Second (1779-1784 AD) concluded by Treaty of Mangalore
    - Third (1790- 1792 AD) concluded by Treaty of Seringapatnam
- **Rajput Raja Sawai**
    - Jai Singh of Amber (1681- 1743 AD) founded the city of Jaipur based upon strictly scientific principles and regular plan
    - Erected observatories at Delhi, Jaipur, Ujjain, Varanasi and Mathura

Punjab

- Kingdom founded by Maharaja Ranjit Singh who captured Lahore in 1799 and Amritsar in 1802
- Built up a powerful, disciplined and well-equipped army along European lines

Kerala

- Kingdom of Travancore rose into prominence after 1729 under king Martanda Varma
- He conquered Quilon and Elay Adam and defeated the Dutch
- Established a modern arsenal Jats Revolted against the oppressive policies of Aurangzeb

Rohilkhand

- Afghan adventurer Muhammad Khan Bangash founded this rule over the territory and Farrukhabad

Socio-Economic Condition

Agriculture

- Technically backward and stagnant
- The state, zamindars and jagirdars and revenue produce from him
- It was common across all the autonomous states

Trade and Industry

- Self -sufficient in handicrafts and agriculture products
- Exports were more than imports
- Trade was balanced by imports of silver and gold and India was known as sink of precious metal
- Item of export- cotton textiles, raw silk, indigo, saltpeter, opium

Society

- Characterised by traditional outlook and stagnation
- People were divided by case, religion, region, tribe and language

Position of Women in Society

- In the patriarchal family system in India, women possessed little individuality of their own
- While upper class women remained at home, lower class women worked in fields and outside their homes supplementing the family income
- Traditions such as the purdah, sati, child marriage, polygamy did exist in 18th century

Art and Architecture

- Migration of artists in courts like Hyderabad, Lucknow, Murshidabad
- Construction of Bada Imambara in Lucknow and Padmanabhapuram palace in Kerala

SOURCE *New NCERT Class VIII (From Trade to Territory), Old NCERT Class XII (Decline of Mughal Empire) Tamil Nadu Board, Class XI (The Marathas), (The Coming of the Europeans)*

Rise of Provincial States

1 **Consider the following statements.**
(Chap 1, Class-XII, Old NCERT)
1. The State of Hyderabad was founded by Nizam-ul-Mulk Asaf Jah in 1724.
2. He was intermittently Viceroy of the Deccan under the Rajput Emperors.

Which of the statements given above is/are correct?
(a) Only 1 (b) Only 2
(c) Both 1 and 2 (d) Neither 1 nor 2

Ans. *(a)*

Exp. Statement 1 is correct as the state of Hyderabad was founded by Nizam-ul-Mulk Asaf Jah in 1724 AD, during the reign of Muhammad Shah Rangila, the 12th Mughal Emperor (1719 AD-1748 AD). But after the death of Nizam-ul-Mulk Asaf Jah in 1748, Hyderabad fell prey to the disruptive forces.
Statement (2) is incorrect because he was intermittently Viceroy of the Deccan under the Mughal Emperors from 1713 to 1721.

2 **Consider the following statements.**
(Chap 1, Class-XII, Old NCERT)
(Unit 16, Class-XI, Tamil Nadu Board)
1. Nizam-ul-Mulk Asaf Jah followed the intolerant policy towards Hindus.
2. The Carnatic was one of the *subahs* of the Mughal Deccan and it came under the Nizam of Hyderabad.
3. The repeated struggles for its Nawabship of Carnatic provided an opportunity to the European companies to directly interfere in Indian politics.

Which of the statements given above is/are correct?
(a) Only 1 (b) 1 and 2
(c) 2 and 3 (d) 1, 2 and 3

Ans. *(c)*

Exp. Statements (2) and (3) are correct.
Under the Mughal empire, Carnatic was one of the subah under the Governor of Deccan and came under the Nizami of Hyderabad.
But later, the Nawab of Carnatic Saadat-Ullah-Khan established an independent state of Carnatic by making his office hereditary.
After 1740 AD, the affairs of the Carnatic deteriorated because of the repeated struggle for its Nawabship.
This provided for the opportunity to the European trading companies to directly interfere in Indian Politics.
Statement (1) is incorrect because Nizam-ul-Mulk followed the tolerant policy towards the Hindus. For example, Puran Chand, a Hindu was a Diwan in his court.

3 **Which one of the following is the correct chronology of Bengal rulers?** *(Chap 1, Class-XII, Old NCERT)*
(a) Murshid Quli Khan–Shuja-ud-din- Sarfaraz Khan–Alivardi Khan
(b) Shuja-ud-din–Sarfaraz Khan–Alivardi Khan–Murshid Quli Khan
(c) Sarfaraz Khan–Alivardi Khan– Shuja-ud-din- Murshid Quli Khan
(d) Murshid Quli Khan–Sarfaraz Khan– Alivardi Khan–Shuja-ud-din

Ans. *(a)*

Exp. The correct chronology of Bengal rulers is Murshid Quli Khan - Shuja-ud-din-Sarfaraz Khan - Alivardi Khan.
Murshid Quli Khan–(1717-1727 AD) was the founder of independent regional kingdom of Bengal.
Shuja-ud-din–(1727-1739 AD) was the Nawab of Bengal and son-in-law of Murshid Quli Khan.
Sarfaraz Khan–(1739-1740 AD) He was successor of Shuja-ud-din. He ascended the *masnad* of Murshidabad in 1739 with the title of 'Alauddin Haider Jang'.
Alivardi Khan–(1740-1756 AD) He succeeded Sarfaraz Khan. He is known for his victory during the Battle of Burdwan against the Maratha empire.

4 **Consider the following statements.**
(Chap 1, Class-XII, Old NCERT)
1. The Subah of Bengal gradually became independent of Mughal control after Siraj-ud-Daula became the Governor in 1715.
2. Murshid Quli Khan transferred the capital from Dacca to Murshidabad.
3. Siraj-ud-Daula signed the Treaty of Alinagar with the British in 1757.

How many of the statements given above is/are correct?
(a) Only one (b) Only two (c) All three (d) None of these

Ans. *(b)*

Exp. Only two statements i.e., (2) and (3) are correct as Murshid Quli Khan, shifted the capital from Decca to Murshidabad. He died in 1727 and his son -in law Shuja -ud-din ruled Bengal till 1739. Siraj-ud-Daula signed the treaty of Alinagar with the British in 1757 and he seized the English factory at Kasim Bazar and Calcutta.
Statement (1) is incorrect because after Murshid Quli Khan became Governor in 1717, the Subah of Bengal gradually became independent of Mughal control.

5 **With reference to Saadat Khan, consider the following statements.** *(Chap 1, Class-XII, Old NCERT)*
1. He was the first Nawab of Awadh.
2. He tried to increase Mughal influence in the Awadh region by reducing the number of jagirdars appointed by Mughals.
3. He started Ijarah system in his province.

How many of the statements given above is/are correct?

(a) Only one (b) Only two
(c) All three (d) None of these

Ans. (b)

Exp. Only two statements i.e., (1) and (3) are correct as the first Nawab of Awadh was Saadat Khan also known as Saadat Khan Burhan-ul-Mulk (1722-1739AD). He was the founder and first Nawab of Awadh, an autonomous state in 1722 AD. The state depended on local bankers and Mahajans for loans .He started Ijarah system in his province. Ijarah system or revenue farming was a feature of the revenue system in Mughal India.

Statement (2) is incorrect because he tried to reduce the Mughal influence in the Awadh region by decreasing the number of jagirdars appointed by the Mughals.

6 **Consider the following statements.** *(Chap 1, Class-XII, Old NCERT)*

1. Saadat Khan carried out fresh revenue settlement in 1723 AD.
2. Saadat Khan was succeeded by his nephew Safdar Jung.
3. Lucknow became an important city under the patronage of Saadat Khan.

Which of the statements given above is/are correct?

(a) Only 1 (b) 1 and 2 (c) 2 and 3 (d) 1, 2 and 3

Ans. (b)

Exp. Statements (1) and (2) are correct.

Saadat Khan Burhan-ul-Mulk carried out a fresh revenue settlement in 1723 AD, as he was asked to improve the peasants' condition by protecting them from oppression by the big zamindars. Saadat Khan was succeeded by his nephew Safdar Jung.

Statement (3) is incorrect because it was under the rule of Asaf-ud-Daula, the city of Lucknow became utterly magnificent and acquired great splendour.

7 **Which of the following statements is incorrect with reference to province of Awadh?** *(Chap 1, Class-XII, Old NCERT)*

(a) Safdar Jung organised an equitable system of justice.
(b) Lucknow developed as an important centre of handicraft.
(c) During the invasion of Ahmad Shah Abdali, Shuja-ud-Daula supported Peshwa.
(d) None of the above

Ans. (c)

Exp. Statement (c) is incorrect with reference to province of Awadh because according to an agreement, Peshwa was to help the Mughal Empire against Ahmad Shah Abdali and to protect it from such internal rebels as the Indian Pathans and the Rajput rajas.

However, in the third Battle of Panipat (1761 AD), the Afghan forces under Ahmed Shah Abdali was supported by Nawab of Awadh, Shuja-ud-Daula. In this battle, Marathas were badly defeated.

8 **Consider the following statements regarding the poligar rebellion.** *(Chap 1 , Class-XII, Old NCERT)*

1. Poligars were local militia in Southern India who were given land in exchange for military service when called upon.
2. After crushing the revolt, the British replaced the Poligar system with the Zamindari system.

Which of the statements given above is/are correct?

(a) Only 1 (b) Only 2
(c) Both 1 and 2 (d) Neither 1 nor 2

Ans. (c)

Exp. Both statements (1) and (2) are correct as Poligar was used for warrior chieftains and zamindars of South India. Poligar was the feudal title for a class of territorial administrative and military Governors appointed by the Nayaka rulers of South India during the 16th and 18th centuries AD. The Poligar system, which had flourished for two and half centuries came to a violent end and the company introduced the Zamindari settlement in its place.

9 **Consider the following statements.** *(Chap 1, Class-XII, Old NCERT)*

1. Hyder Ali was succeeded by his son Tipu Sultan.
2. Tipu Sultan planted a 'Tree of Liberty' at Srirangapatnam and he became member of a Jacobin club.
3. Tipu Sultan's infantry was armed with muskets and bayonets in the European's fashion.

Which of the statements given above is/are correct?

(a) Only 1 (b) 1 and 2 (c) 2 and 3 (d) 1, 2 and 3

Ans. (d)

Exp. All the statements (1), (2) and (3) are correct. The regional kingdom of Mysore was founded by Hyder Ali in 1761 AD. He had established a modern arsenal in Dindigul with the French assistance.

He was succeeded by his son, Tipu Sultan in 1782 AD. He was modern and innovative ruler, who introduced new scales of weights and measures. He had keen interest about the important developments in the world, he planted a 'Tree of Liberty' at Srirangapatnam and became a member of Jacobin Club. He was inspired by the French revolution of 1789 AD. Tipu Sultan also started modernisation of Mysore army. His infantry was armed with muskets and bayonets in the European's fashion.

10 **Given below description is related to which of the following rulers?** *(Chap 1, Class-XII, Old NCERT)*

He made an effort to build modern navy after 1796 AD. He used to say "better to live a day as a lion than a lifetime as a sheep". He sent emissaries to France, Turkey, Iran and Pegu (Myanmar) to develop foreign trade.

(a) Hyder Ali (b) Safdar Jung
(c) Murshid Quli Khan (d) Tipu Sultan

Ans. (d)

Exp. The given description is related to Tipu Sultan. Tipu Sultan was Hyder Ali's son and a great warrior. He was also known as the Tiger of Mysore. He was a well-educated man fluent in Arabic, Persian, Kanarese and Urdu.

He introduced a number of administrative innovations during his rule. In order to boost foreign trade and develop bilateral relation with foreign countries, he sent emissaries to France, Turkey, Iran and Pegu (Myanmar).

11 Consider the following statements. *(Chap 1 ,Class-XII, Old NCERT)*

1. Indian ruler Tipu Sultan established embassies in foreign countries on modern lines.
2. He succeeded his father in 1782 and concluded peace with British in 1784.
3. During Second Mysore War, he defeated Col. John Brathwaite.

How many of the statements given above is/are correct?

(a) Only one (b) Only two
(c) All three (d) None of these

Ans. (c)

Exp. All three statements i.e., (1), (2) and (3) are correct as the ruler of Mysore kingdom, Tipu Sultan established embassies in foreign countries. He succeeded his father and ruled Mysore from 1782 to 1799 AD.

During his tenure he sent embassies to France, Turkey, Iran and Pegu (Myanmar), and was one of the first Indian rulers to understand the threat posed by foreign trading companies. During the Second Mysore War, he defeated Col. John Brathwaite on the banks of the Kollidam river.

12 Which one of the following pairs is not correctly matched? *(Chap 1, Class-XII, Old NCERT) UPPSC (Pre) 2021*

Rulers		States
(a) Rana Hamir	–	Mewar
(b) Rana Chunda	–	Marwar
(c) Malik Raja Faruqi	–	Khandesh
(d) Malik Sarwar Khwaja	–	Malwa

Ans. (d)

Exp. Pair (d) is not correctly matched as Malik Sarwar Khwaja Jahan was the founder of Sharqi dynasty of Jaunpur.

He was in service of the Delhi Sultan Firuz Shah Tughlaq, but declared his independence in 1394 AD.

13 Consider the following statements in the context of the Marthanda Varma. *(Chap 1, Class-XII, Old NCERT)*

1. He was one of the leading statesmen of 18th century.
2. He organised a strong army on the Western model with the help of European officers.

Which of the statements given above is/are correct?

(a) Only 1 (b) Only 2
(c) Both 1 and 2 (d) Neither 1 nor 2

Ans. (c)

Exp. Both the statements (1) and (2) are correct regarding Marthanda Varma.

Marthanda Varma was the king of Travancore during 18th century (1729-1758 AD). He combined rare foresight and strong determination with courage and daring.

He organised a strong army on the Western model with the help of European officers and armed it with modern weapons.

14 Consider the following statements in the context of the Rajput ruler Sawai Jai Singh of Amber. *(Chap 1, Class-XII, Old NCERT)*

1. He was distinguished law maker, statesmen and reformer.
2. He founded the city of Jaipur.
3. He was well-known painter and musician.
4. He ruled nearly for 44 years from 1699 to 1743 AD.

Which of the statements given above is/are incorrect?

(a) 1 and 2 (b) 2 and 3 (c) Only 3 (d) Only 4

Ans. (c)

Exp. Statement (3) is incorrect regarding Rajput ruler Sawai Jai Singh of Amber because he was a man of science in an age when Indians were oblivious to scientific progress. However, he was not associated with painting and music.

15 At which of the following places observatories were built by Sawai Jai Singh II of Amber? *(Chap 1, Class-XII, Old NCERT) (UPPSC Mains 2007)*

1. Ujjain 2. Varanasi 3. Delhi
4. Mathura 5. Lucknow

Codes

(a) 1, 2 and 3 (b) 2, 3, 4 and 5
(c) 1, 2 and 4 (d) 1, 2, 3 and 4

Ans. (d)

Exp. Sawai Jai Singh II, Maharaja of Amber and Jaipur, constructed five observatories in the second quarter of the 18th century in the North Indian cities of Delhi, Jaipur, Ujjain, Mathura and Varanasi.

16 Consider the following statements. *(Chap 1, Class-XII , Old NCERT)*

1. The book Zij Muhammad Shahi was written by Swai Jai Singh Jaipur.
2. Mirza Jai Singh II was the Hindu Rajput ruler of the Kingdom Amber.
3. He was given the title Mirza by Aurangzeb in 1699.

How many of the statements given above is/are correct?

(a) Only one (b) Only two
(c) All three (d) None of these

Ans. (c)

Exp. All three statements i.e., (1), (2) and (3) are correct as Mirza Sawai Jai Singh II wrote the, Zij Muhammad Shahi' book an accurate table of a constellation of stars in 1733. He was the Hindu Rajput ruler of the kingdom Amber. He founded the fortified city Jaipur and made it capital from Amber. He was given the title Mirza by Aurangzeb in 1699. He has great interest in Mathematics, Astronomy and Architecture.

17 Consider the following statements.

(Chap 1, Class-XII, Old NCERT)

1. Sikh religion was founded by Guru Nanak at the end of 15th century AD.
2. The transformation of Sikhs into a militant and fighting community was begun by Guru Hargobind.
3. Guru Gobind Singh was the last Guru of Sikhs.

How many of the statements given above is/are correct?

(a) Only one (b) Only two
(c) All three (d) None of these

Ans. (c)

Exp. All three statements i.e., (1), (2) and (3) are correct regarding Sikhism. Guru Nanak, the first Sikh guru is considered as the founder of Sikh religion at the end of 15th century AD. It was adopted by lower caste and the Jat peasantry for its simplicity and austerity.

Guru Hargobind was the sixth guru of Sikhism, he transformed the Sikhs into a militant and fighting community. Guru Gobind Singh was the last Sikh Guru; he founded the Khalsa Panth.

18 Consider the following statements.

(Chap 1, Class-XII, Old NCERT)

1. The Sikhs were organised into 20 *misls* or confederacies.
2. The invasion of Nadir Shah and Ahmad Shah Abdali and consequent dislocation of Punjab administration gave the Sikhs an opportunity to rise again.
3. The Sikh power reached at zenith under Ranjit Singh.

Which of the statements given above is/are correct?

(a) Only 1 (b) 1 and 2 (c) 2 and 3 (d) 1, 2 and 3

Ans. (c)

Exp. Statements (2) and (3) are correct as the invasion of Nadir Shah in 1738-1739 AD and Ahmad Shah Abdali in 1761 AD led to the condition of chaos in territories covering modern Punjab. It gave the opportunity to the Sikhs to rise again and lay a foundation for the strong kingdom.

Maharaja Ranjit Singh (1801-1839 AD) was the greatest Sikh ruler. Under him, Sikh power reached at zenith.

Statement (1) is incorrect because Sikhs were organised into 12 *misls* or confederacies, which operated in different part of the province.

19 Consider the following statements.

(Chap 2, Class-VIII, Old NCERT)
(Chap 15, Class-XI, Tamil Nadu Board)

1. Maharaja Ranjit Singh came from Karorasinghia Mai Misl.
2. Jean-Francois Allard and Jean Baptiste Ventura were the two Napoleonic generals in service of Maharaja Ranjit Singh.

Which of the statements given above is/are correct?

(a) Only 1 (b) Only 2
(c) Both 1 and 2 (d) Neither 1 nor 2

Ans. (b)

Exp. Statement (2) is correct as the Napoleonic generals in Ranjit Singh's employ were Jean- Francois Allard and Jean-Baptiste Ventura.

Statement (1) is incorrect because Ranjit Singh belonged to Sukerchakia Misl. He was the first Maharaja of the Sikh empire. He was the grandson of Charat Singh ,who was the founder of the Sukerchakia Misl.

20 Consider the following statements with reference to the Raja Ranjit Singh. *(Chap 1, Class-XII, Old NCERT)*

1. He did not make any changes in the system of land revenue promulgated earlier by the Mughals.
2. He also recruited Gurkhas, Oriyas, Pathans, Dogras and Punjabi Muslims in his army.

Which of the statements given above is/are correct?

(a) Only 1
(b) Only 2
(c) Both 1 and 2
(d) Neither 1 nor 2

Ans. (c)

Exp. Both the statements (1) and (2) are correct with reference to the Raja Ranjit Singh.

Raja Ranjit Singh did not make any changes in the system of land revenue promulgated earlier by the Mughals. The amount of land revenue was calculated on the basis of 50% of the gross produce. His new army was not confined to the Sikhs. He also recruited Gurkhas, Oriyas, Pathans, Dogras and Punjabi Muslims.

21 Consider the following statements.

(Chap 1, Class-XII, Old NCERT)

1. After the death of Aurangzeb in 1707 AD, a war of succession broke out.
2. Civil war broke between the Maratha rulers.
3. Maratha rule in Thanjavur which started from 1674 continued until the death of Serfoji II in 1832.

How many of the statements given above is/are correct?

(a) Only one (b) Only two
(c) All three (d) None of these

Ans (c)

Exp. All three statements i.e., (1), (2) and (3) are correct as after the death of Aurangzeb in 1707 AD, a war of succession broke out among his three sons-Muazzam (the Governor of Kabul), Muhammad Kam Baksh (the Governor of Deccan) and Muhammad Azam Shah (the Governor of Gujarat). Muazzam emerged victorious and ascended the throne with the title of Bahadur Shah I. A civil war broke out between Shahu at Satara and his aunt Tarabai at Kolhapur for gaining control over Maratha empire. Maratha rule in Thanjavur which started from 1674 continued until the death of Serfoji II in 1832. Nayak rule ended in 1674 at Thanjavur region.

22 Which of the following statements are correct with reference to evolution and consolidation of Peshwaship? *(Chap 1, Class-XII, Old NCERT)*

1. The period of Peshwa domination started from the time of Shahu.
2. Baji Rao I made the Peshwa the functional head of the Maratha empire.
3. Under Peshwa rule, Maratha empire was extended to North India.
4. Balaji Baji Rao was also known as Nana Saheb.

Codes

(a) 1 and 2 (b) 1 and 4
(c) 2 and 3 (d) All of these

Ans. (d)

Exp. All the given statements are correct regarding evolution and consolidation of Peshwaship. Peshwas were the hereditary ruler who acted as a Prime Minister to the king of the Maratha empire. During the reign of Shahu, Peshwa Balaji Vishwanath became most powerful. It started the period of Peshwa domination. His son, Baji Rao I made the Peshwa the functional head of the Maratha empire. During the reign of Baji Rao I and his successor Balaji Baji Rao (also known as Nana Saheb), the Maratha empire extended to North India.

23 Which of the following statements is incorrect regarding Third Battle of Panipat? *(Chap 1, Class-XII, Old NCERT)*

(a) The Third Battle of Panipat was fought in 1671 AD.
(b) The Maratha army was completely routed in third Battle of Panipat.
(c) Ahmad Khan Abdali was supported by Najib-ud-Daulah of Rohilkhand and Shuja-ud-Daulah of Awadh.
(d) Ahmad Khan Abdali was an Afghan ruler who defeated Maratha.

Ans. (a)

Exp. Statement (a) is incorrect because the Third Battle of Panipat was fought in 1761 AD (not 1671 AD). It was fought between the Maratha empire and a coalition of the king of Afghanistan, Ahmad Shah Durrani with Rohila Afghans of the Doab and Shuja-ud-Daula, the Nawab of Awadh. The Marathas were defeated in the battle.

24 Match the following lists correctly and choose the correct code. *(Chap 1, Class-XII, Old NCERT)*

List I (Kingdoms)	List II (Territories)
A. Sindhia	1. Gwalior
B. Gaekwad	2. Indore
C. Holkar	3. Baroda
D. Bhonsle	4. Nagpur

Codes

	A	B	C	D		A	B	C	D
(a)	3	1	4	2	(b)	1	3	2	4
(c)	2	4	1	3	(d)	4	3	2	1

Ans. (b)

Exp. The correct matching is A-1, B-3, C-2, D-4.

Sindhia This dynasty ruled the erstwhile state of Gwalior. The Gwalior state was a princely state under the British Raj during the 19th and 20th centuries AD.

Gaekwad The Gaekwads of Baroda ruled the princely state of Baroda in Western India from the early 18th century until 1947 AD.

Holkar The Holkars were generals under Peshwa Baji Rao I and later, became Maharajas of Indore in Central India as an independent member of Maratha empire.

Bhonsle The kingdom of Nagpur came under the rule of the Marathas of the Bhonsle dynasty in the mid-18th century AD. The city of Nagpur was the capital of the state.

25 Consider the following statements. *(Chap 1, Class-XII, Old NCERT)*

1. Tarabai was the queen of Rajaram I and daughter -in-law of the Shivaji I.
2. Tarabai came from Mohite clan.
3. She personally led the war and continued the fight against the Mughals.

How many of the statements given above is/are correct?

(a) Only one (b) Only two
(c) All three (d) None of these

Ans. (c)

Exp. All three statements i.e., (1), (2) and (3) are correct as Tarabai Bhonsle was the regent of the Maratha empire from 1700 until 1708. She was the queen of Rajaram I and daughter-in-law of the empire's founder Shivaji I. She is acclaimed for her role in keeping alive the resistance against Mughal occupation of Maratha territories after the death of her husband and acting as the regent during the minority of her son, Shivaji II. She came from Mohite clan and she personally led the war and continued the fight against the Mughals.

26 **Consider the following pairs.**

(Chap 1, Class-XII, Old NCERT)

Battle of Panipat		Between
1. First	–	Babar and Ibrahim Lodi
2. Second	–	Hemu and Humayun's Army
3. Third	–	Ahmad Shah Abdali and Maratha's

Which of the pairs given above is/are incorrectly matched?

(a) 1 and 2 (b) 2 and 3 (c) 1 and 3 (d) Only 2

Ans. (d)

Exp. Pair (2) is incorrectly matched because the second Battle of Panipat took place on 5th November, 1556 AD between the Emperor of North India, Hemu and the forces of the Mughal Emperor Akbar. The battle ended with a decisive Mughal victory.

27 **Which one of the following statements is incorrect regarding trade and commerce in 18th century?**

(Chap 1, Class-XII, Old NCERT)

(a) Indian agriculture during the 18th century was technically forward and dynamic.

(b) Extensive trade within the country and between India and other countries of Asia and Europe was carried under the Mughals.

(c) Tin was imported from Singapore.

(d) None of the above

Ans. (a)

Exp. Statement (a) is incorrect regarding trade and commerce in 18th century because the Indian agriculture during the 18th century was technically backward and stagnant. The techniques of production had remained stationary for centuries. The peasants' condition was very miserable.

The State, the zamindars, the jagirdars and the revenue farmers tried to extract the maximum from peasants.

28 **Consider the following statements with reference to the education in 18th century.**

(Chap 1, Class-XII, Old NCERT)

1. Education was given highest priority in 18th century.
2. Persian education being based on the official language of the time was equally popular among the Hindus and the Muslims.

Which of the statements given above is/are incorrect?

(a) Only 1 (b) Only 2

(c) Both 1 and 2 (d) Neither 1 nor 2

Ans. (a)

Exp. Statement (1) is incorrect regarding state of education in the 18th century AD because education was not given highest priority in the 18th century. It was neglected to some extent. It was traditional and out of touch with the rapid developments in the West. It did not focus on the study of physical and natural sciences, technology and geography.

29 **Which of the following statements is incorrect?**

(Chap 1, Class-XII, Old NCERT)

(a) The Jat power reached its highest glory under Suraj Mal.

(b) After the death of Suraj Mal, Jat power continued to rise.

(c) The Jat rulers took active part in the court intrigues at Delhi.

(d) Suraj Mal is referred as Plato of Jat tribe.

Ans. (b)

Exp. Statement (b) is incorrect because the death of Suraj Mal resulted in decline of unity among Jats. The territories controlled under the Jats were split up among petty zamindars.

30 **Consider the following statements.**

(Chap 1, Class-XII ,Old NCERT)

1. Ahilyabai Holkar was the Rani of Indore, within the Maratha Confederacy.
2. She established Maheshwar as the seat of the Holkar dynasty.

Which of the statements given above is/are correct?

(a) Only 1 (b) Only 2

(c) Both 1 and 2 (d) Neither 1 nor 2

Ans. (c)

Exp. Both the statements are correct as Ahilyabai administered the territory of Indore within the Maratha Confederacy. She established Maheshwar (Madhya Pradesh) as the seat of the Holkar dynasty. She is acclaimed for her role in keeping alive the resistance against Mughal occupation of Maratha territories after the death of her husband and acting as the regent during the minority of her son, Shivaji II.

31 **Which one of the following statements is incorrect regarding development of art in 18th century?**

(Chap 1, Class-XII, Old NCERT)

(a) Many of the painters of Mughal School migrated to provincial courts and flourished at Hyderabad, Lucknow, Patna and Kashmir.

(b) Significant progress was made in the music field in the reign of Bahadur Shah.

(c) The paintings of the Kangra and Rajputana Schools revealed vitality and taste.

(d) Urdu gradually became the medium of social intercourse among the upper classes of Northern India.

Ans. (b)

Exp. Statement (b) is incorrect regarding development of art in 18th century because significant progress was made in the music field during the reign of Muhammad Shah (not Bahadur Shah I).

He was a great patron of the arts, including musical, cultural and administrative developments. During his reign, *Qawwali* was re-introduced in the Mughal imperial court.

Chapter 24

Administrative & Economic Policies Under British Rule

Administrative & Economic Policies Under British Rule

Regulating Act, 1773
- Governor of Bengal was nominated as Governor-General for all three presidencies of Bengal, Madras and Bombay
- Establishment of Supreme Court, 1774

Charter Act, 1793
- Trade monopoly of company extended for another 20 years; Board of control and their staff paid out of Indian revenue

Charter Act, 1813
- Abolished trade monopoly of East India Company
- Provided for spread of Western education and Christian missionaries in India

Charter Act, 1833
- Made Governor-General of Bengal as Governor-General of India with all civil and military powers

Charter Act, 1853
- Established Indian Central Legislative Council
- Macaulay Committee was appointed on Indian Civil Services in 1854

Government of India Act, 1858
- Also known as Act of Good Governance of India; System of dual government abolished
- Office of Secretary of State for India was formed
- Designation of Governor-General of India was changed to Viceroy of India

Indian Council Act, 1892
- Function of Legislative Council was increased and was conferred power to discuss budget and to ask questions

Indian Councils Act,1909
- Also known as Morley Minto reforms Increased size of both Central and Provincial Legislative Council

Government of India Act, 1919
- Also known as Montagu-Chelmsford reform; Dyarchy system introduced in province in which subjects were divided into two parts- transferred and reserved
- This act introduced bicameral legislature on central level.

Government of India Act, 1935
- Established All India Federation
- Divided the power between center and States into- federal, provincial and concurrent list
- Abolished dyarchy in states

India Independence Act, 1947
- British rule in India came to an end and India was partitioned

Judicial Policies
- Warren Hastings established Diwani Adalats in every district to solve civil disputes
- Fauzdari courts were set up to try criminal disputes; Indian High Court Act, 1861; establishment of High Court at Calcutta, Bombay and Madras

Police System
- Lord Cornwallis denied the zamindars of their policing powers and divided the district into thana

Provincial and Local Administration
- Lord Mayo separated Central and Provinces finances
- Lytton transferred important subjects such as land, revenue, excise, law and Justice to province

Land Revenue System
- Permanent Settlement introduced in Bengal, Bihar and Orissa
- Banaras and Northern districts of Madras by Lord Cornwallis

Ryotwari System
- Introduced by Thomas Munroe and Captain Reed in 1820; Ryots were recognised as owners of land

Mahalwari System
- Introduced in 1822 by Holt Mackenzie
- Implemented in North-West Provinces, Central India, Punjab and Ganga valley; Revenue was fixed on the basis of assessment of production of complete villages

Development of Banking System
- First modern bank set up in India was Bank of Hindustan in 1770
- Bank of Calcutta (1806), Bombay (1840) and Madras (1843) were merged in 1921 and rechristened as Imperial Bank of India

Evolution of Civil Services
- Cornwallis code was enacted in 1793
- He is referred as Father of Civil Services in India; Concept of a merit based modern civil services introduced in 1854

SOURCE ***New NCERT Class VIII*** *(From Trade to Territory, Ruling the Country Side, Civilising the 'Native', Educating the Nation),* ***Old NCERT Class VIII*** *(Administrative Structure, Policies and Impact of British Rule),* ***Old NCERT Class X*** *(Indian Awakening),* ***Old NCERT Class XII*** *(The Structure of Government and Economic Policies of the British Empire of India, 1757-1857, European Penetration and British Conquest of India, Economic Impact of Rule)*

Administrative Structure

1 **Which of the following statements is incorrect in the context of the Dual Government in Bengal?** *(Chap 3, Class-XII, Old NCERT)*

(a) It was established after the Battle of Plassey.
(b) It was abolished in 1772.
(c) In this system, Indian officials were allowed to function as before but under the control of British Governor.
(d) It was formulated with the motive to carry on their profitable trade and to collect taxes for remission to England.

Ans. (a)

Exp. Statement (a) is incorrect in the context of the Dual Government in Bengal because the system of Dual Government was introduced in Bengal by Robert Clive in 1765 after the Battle of Buxar.

Under this system, the administration of Bengal was divided into *Diwani* and *Nizamat*. Through *Diwani* the Company was granted the right to raise revenue and through *Nizamat*, Nawab was given administrative powers.

The Dual System of Government was finally abolished by Warren Hastings in 1772.

2 **Which of the following is incorrect with reference to the early British administration?** *(Chap 2, Class-VIII, New NCERT)*

(a) British territories were broadly divided into administrative units called Presidencies.
(b) In 1775, a new system of Judiciary was established. Each district was to have two courts – a Criminal Court (*Faujdari adalat*) and a Civil Court (*Diwani adalat*).
(c) Under the Regulating Act of 1773, a new Supreme Court was established.
(d) None of the above

Ans. (b)

Exp. Statement (b) is incorrect regarding as early British administration because in 1772 (not 1775), a new system of Judiciary was established. Under this system, each district was provided two courts-a Criminal Court (*Faujdari adalat*) and a Civil Court (*Diwani adalat*). *Maulvis* and Hindu *Pandits* interpreted Indian laws for the European district collectors who presided over civil courts. The criminal courts were still under a *quazi* and *mufti*, but under the overall supervision of the collectors.

3 **Consider the following statements with reference to the Dual Government.** *(Chap 2, Class-XII, Old NCERT)*

1. As the *Diwan*, the Company directly controlled the police and judicial power.
2. Under the power of *Nizamat*, Company directly collected the revenues.

Which of the statements given above is/are incorrect?

(a) Only 1
(b) Only 2
(c) Both 1 and 2
(d) Neither 1 nor 2

Ans. (c)

Exp. Both the statements (1) and (2) are incorrect regarding Dual Government. Under the Dual System of Government, the Company was authorised to collect revenues of the province as the Diwan, while through the right to nominate, the Deputy Subahdar, was in a position to control the *Nizamat* or the police and judicial powers.

The Company got *Diwani* from the Mughal Emperor and *Nizamat* from the Nawab of Bengal.

4 **With reference to the administrative structure during British, which of the following statements is/are correct?** *(Chap 4, Class-VIII, Old NCERT)*

1. In early years, the British territories were divided into three presidencies i.e., Bengal, Madras and Surat.
2. In 1836, North-West province was formed by the British administration.

Codes

(a) Only 1
(b) Only 2
(c) Both 1 and 2
(d) Neither 1 nor 2

Ans. (b)

Exp. Statement (2) is correct regarding administrative structure during British as the North-West provinces were established in 1836, through merging the administrative divisions of the ceded and conquered provinces.

Statement (1) is incorrect because British territories were broadly divided into administrative units called Presidencies. There were three such presidencies – Bengal, Madras and Bombay. Each Presidency was under the charge of the Governor.

5 **With reference to Nabbos, consider the following statements.** *(Chap 4, Class-VIII, Old NCERT)*

1. Many British officials were called Nabbos.
2. Nabbos played a key role in defeating Nawab .
3. They were appointed as residents in the Court of Nawabs .
4. They followed the style of life of the Indian Democracy.

How many of the statements given above is/are correct?

(a) Only one
(b) Only two
(c) Only three
(d) All four

Ans. (b)

Exp. Only two statements i.e., (1) and (4) are correct as those British official, who through corruption earned great fortunes and adopted the lifestyle of Indian aristocracy were mockingly called as Nabbos. The term is an anglicised version of the Indian word Nawab. These were servants of the East private trade practices and other corrupt.

They followed the style of life of the Indian Democracy.

6 **Consider the following statements.**
(Chap 17, Class-XI, Tamil Nadu Board)

Statement-I The British Government introduced different land revenue system in different parts of India.

Statement-II It led to creation of different classes in Indian peasantry.

Which one of the following is correct in respect of the above statements?

(a) Both Statement-I and Statement-II are correct and Statement-II is the correct explanation for Statement-I.
(b) Both Statement-I and Statement-II are correct and Statement-II is not correct explanation for Statement-I.
(c) Statement-I is correct, but Statement-II is incorrect.
(d) Statement-I is incorrect, but Statement-II is correct.

Ans. (a)

Exp. Both Statement-I and Statement-II are correct and Statement-II is the correct explanation for Statement-I. The different land revenue systems in different parts of India introduced by the British were Permanent Settlement (Bengal and Bihar), Ryotwari System (Madras) and Mahalwari System (Uttar Pradesh and Madhya Pradesh). It led to creation of different classes in Indian peasantry.

7 **Consider the following statements.**
(Chap 4, Class-VIII, Old NCERT)

1. The cities were placed in the charge of *kotwals*.
2. The districts were divided into *thanas*, each of which was put under the charge of *daroga*.
3. The hereditary village policemen became *chowkidar*.

Which of the statements given above is/are correct?

(a) Only 1 (b) 1 and 2
(c) 2 and 3 (d) 1, 2 and 3

Ans. (d)

Exp. All the statements are correct as to ensure good administration, Lord Cornwallis created a permanent police force in India.

The cities were placed under the *kotwals*. Each district were divided into number of *thanas*, each of which was headed by a *daroga*. The hereditary village policemen became *chowkidar*.

8 **Consider the following statements with reference to the Charter Act.** *(Chap 3, Class-XII, Old NCERT)*

1. By the Charter Act, 1813, the trade monopoly of the Company was ended in India.
2. The Charter Act, 1833 restored the trade monopoly of the Company.

Which of the statements given above is/are incorrect?

(a) Only 1 (b) Only 2
(c) Both 1 and 2 (d) Neither 1 nor 2

Ans. (b)

Exp. Statement (2) is incorrect with reference to the Charter Act of 1833 because it ended the remaining monopoly of East India Company in tea trade and trade in China. Hence, all restrictions on European immigration into India were abolished.

9 **Consider the following pairs.**
(Chap 3, Class-XII, Old NCERT)

	Acts		Provisions
1.	Regulating Act of 1773	–	Supreme Court
2.	Charter Act, 1813	–	Trade monopoly of the Company was ended.
3.	Charter Act, 1833	–	India came under the direct rule of Britain.

Which of the pairs given above is/are correctly matched?

(a) 1 and 2 (b) 2 and 3
(c) Only 3 (d) Only 2

Ans. (a)

Exp. Pairs (1) and (2) are correctly matched as the Regulating Act of 1773 provided for the establishment of a Supreme Court at Calcutta (1774) having one Chief Justice and three other judges.

The Charter Act, 1813 ended the Company's trading monopoly except for the tea trade and the trade with China.

Pair (3) is incorrectly matched because with the Government of India Act, 1858, the rule of British East India Company was abolished and the Government of India was directly taken over by the crown with Queen Victoria as the Supreme monarch.

Economic Policies of British Period

10 **With reference to Ryotwari Settlement, consider the following statements.** *(Chap 3, Class-VIII, New NCERT)*

1. The rent was paid directly by the peasants to the government.
2. The government gave pattas to the ryots.
3. The lands were surveyed and assessed before being taxed.

How many of the statements given above is/are correct?

(a) Only one (b) Only two
(c) All three (d) None of these

Ans. (c)

Exp. All three statements i.e., (1), (2) and (3) are correct with reference to Ryotwari Settlement. The rent in the Ryotwari System was paid directly by the peasants to the government.

Under this system, government gave pattas to the ryots. The land under Ryotwari System were surveyed before being taxed. The rates were 50% in dry land and 60% in the wetland.

11 What was the consequence of Permanent Settlement on rural society in Bengal?

(Chap 3, Class-VIII, New NCERT)

(a) The zamindars invested capital and enterprise to improve agriculture along lines of British Yeoman farmers.

(b) A group of rich peasants known as *jotedars*, who succeeded in consolidating their position in the villages.

(c) The *ryots* prospered as a result of fixed revenue levy imposed on them.

(d) The system of collectorate introduced by the Company for exercising supervisory control on Zamindars failed to take off.

Ans. (b)

Exp. The main consequence of Permanent Settlement on rural society in Bengal was rise of group of peasants known as *jotedars*, who succeeded in consolidating their position in the villages. *Jotedars* were rich peasants in Bengal. They controlled trade and commerce including money lending business at the local level. They owned big areas of land under cultivation. Many a time they would buy estates of zamindar. It would be auctioned due to failure to pay up land revenue.

12 Consider of the following features of the Permanent Settlement of 1793. *(Chap 3, Class-VIII, New NCERT)*

1. The Permanent Settlement vested land ownership rights in the peasants.
2. The Permanent Settlement vested land ownership rights in the zamindars.
3. The zamindars had to pay a fixed amount of rent by a particular date.
4. The zamindars benefitted hugely from the Permanent Settlement while the peasants suffered.

How many of the statements given above is/are correct?

(a) Only one (b) Onle two (c) Only three (d) All four

Ans. (b)

Exp. Only two statements i.e., (2) and (3) are correct regarding features of Permanent Settlement of 1793 because zamindars were given hereditary rights of succession of the lands under them. The amount to be paid by the landlords was fixed and they were made liable to pay rent by a particular date.

Statements (1) and (4) are incorrect because the revenue rates were so high that many zamindars became defaulters. Thus, zamindars did not get benefit from the system.

The Permanent Settlement of 1793 enacted by Lord Cornwallis recognised landlords or zamindars as the owners of the land.

13 Consider the following Assertion (A) and Reason (R) and choose the correct code.

(Chap 3, Class-VIII, Old NCERT) (UPPSC Pre 2020)

Assertion (A) The British Government introduced different land revenue system in different parts of India.

Reason (R) The major aim of the British East India Company was to increase their land revenue collection.

Codes

(a) Both A and R are true and R is the correct explanation of A.

(b) Both A and R are true, but R is not the correct explanation of A.

(c) A is true, but R is false.

(d) A is false, but R is true.

Ans. (a)

Exp. Both Assertion (A) and Reason (R) are true, but Reason (R) is the correct explanation of Assertion (A). The British introduced different land revenue systems in different parts of the country. Under colonial rule three system of land revenue settlement prevailed i.e., Permanent settlement, Ryotwari system and the Mahalwari system. The major aim of British East India Company was to increase their land revenue collection. They aimed at getting maximum income from land without caring about its consequences on cultivators and peasants. It led to the creation of different classes in Indian peasantry such as zamindars, jotedars, tenant farmers and landless farmers.

14 Consider the following statements.

(Chap 3, Class-VIII, New NCERT)

1. The Mahalwari Settlement aimed to address the exploitative nature of the Zamindari System by directly engaging with individual cultivators.
2. It empowered village headmen, leading to potential abuse of power and exploitation of weaker cultivators.
3. It was devised by Holt Mackenzie.

How many of the statements given above is/are correct?

(a) Only one (b) Only two

(c) All three (d) None of these

Ans. (c)

Exp. All three statements i.e., (1), (2) and (3) are correct as the Mahalwari Settlement aimed to address the exploitative nature of the Zamindari System by directly engaging with individual cultivators.

In this system, the land revenue was collected by the village headmen and it was not fixed. The peasants were the owner of the land and every peasant had to give his share of the revenue.

The Mahalwari Settlement was devised by Holt Mackenzie in 1822 and it was reviewed under Lord William Bentick in 1833.

15 Who was associated with the introduction of Ryotwari Settlement in India?

(Chap 3, Class-VIII, New NCERT)

1. Alexander Reed 2. Holt Mackenzie
3. Thomas Munro 4. Charles Cornwallis

Codes
(a) 1 and 2
(b) 1 and 3
(c) 2 and 3
(d) 3 and 4

***Ans.* (b)**

Exp. Alexander Reed and Thomas Munro were associated with the introduction of Ryotwari settlement India during the British rule.

It was first introduced in Madras Presidency. Under this, British Government collected taxes directly from the peasants.

16 Which of the following statements about Mahalwari system is/are not correct? *(Chap 3, Class-VIII, New NCERT)*

(a) The charge of collecting the revenue and paying it to the Company was given to the village headman.
(b) The estimated revenue of each plot within a village was added up to calculate the revenue.
(c) The demand of revenue was permanently fixed.
(d) All of the above

***Ans.* (c)**

Exp. Statement (c) is not correct about Mahalwari system because in the Mahalwari system, the revenue was to be revised periodically.

The Mahalwari system is one of the three major land revenue systems introduced by the British in India.

In this system, the land was divided into *Mahals*. Each *Mahal* comprised one or more villages.

Ownership rights were vested with the peasants and the Villages Committee was responsible for collection of the taxes.

17 Which of the following statements about Ryotwari Settlement is/are correct? *(Chap 3, Class-VIII, New NCERT)*

1. It recognised the cultivators as the owner of land.
2. Revenue official fixed revenue rate too high.
3. It was introduced later than the Permanent Settlement.

Codes
(a) 1 and 2 (b) 1, 2 and 3
(c) Only 1 (d) 2 and 3

***Ans.* (b)**

Exp. Statements (1), (2) and (3) are correct regarding Ryotwari Settlement. The individual cultivator called Ryot had full rights regarding sale, transfer and leasing of the land.

The ryots could not be evicted from their land as long as they paid the rent. The revenue rates of the Ryotwari were 50% where lands were dry and 60% in irrigated areas.

It was introduced in 1820s in Madras Presidency by Alexander Reed and Thomas Munro.

Under the Ryotwari system the land revenue was paid by the farmers directly to the state.

18 Consider the following pairs.
(Chap 3, Class-VIII, New NCERT)

	Features		Land Revenue System
1.	Land allotted to big feudal landlords	–	Zamindari System
2.	Land allotted to revenue farmers or rent collectors	–	Jagirdari System
3.	Land allotted to each peasant with the right to sublet, mortgage, gift or sell	–	Ryotwari System
4.	Land was divided into *Mahals*, each *Mahal* comprises one or more villages	–	Mahalwari System

How many of the pairs given above is/are correctly matched?

(a) Only one (b) Only two (c) Only three (d) Only two

***Ans.* (b)**

Exp. Only two pairs i.e., (3) and (4) are correctly matched. The land allotted to each peasant with the right to sublet, mortgage or transfer was called Ryotwari system.

Pair (1) and (2) are incorrectly matched.

The settlement made at village level was called Mahalwari system. In this land was divided into Mahals, each Mahal comprises one or more villages.

The system in which land allotted to a big landlords was called Jagirdari system.

The system in which land allotted to revenue farmers or rent collectors was known as Zamindari system.

19 Which of the following statements is/are correct about evolution of Civil Services in India?
(Chap 4, Class-VIII, Old NCERT)

1. The steel frame of the British administration was its Civil Services.
2. Lord Cornwallis was the real founder of the British Civil Services in India.
3. Indians were given equal opportunities in the Civil Services.

How many of the statements given above is/are correct?

(a) Only one (b) Only two
(c) All three (d) None of these

***Ans.* (b)**

Exp. Only two statements i.e., (1) and (2) are correct regarding evolution of Civil Services in India. The Civil Services were the steel frame of the British administration. Lord Cornwallis was the real founder of Civil Services in India and hence he is called the 'Father of Indian Civil Services.'

Statement (3) is not correct because Indians were not given equal opportunities in the civil services. The exam was conducted only in London and age limit was set between 18 years and 23 years. The syllabus was moulded in favour of British residents which made it difficult for Indians to succeed.

20 **Consider the following statements with reference to the organisation of Civil Services.**

(Chap 4, Class-VIII, Old NCERT)

1. Lord Cornwallis separated the commercial and revenue branches of the administration.
2. In 1857, a system of open competition through examination was introduced.

Which of the statements given above is/are incorrect?

(a) Only 1
(b) Only 2
(c) Both 1 and 2
(d) Neither 1 nor 2

Ans. (b)

Exp. Statement (2) is incorrect with reference to the organisation of Civil Services because the Charter Act of 1853 provided for an open competitive examination for the recruitment of civil servants and had deprived the Court of Directors of the power of appointments based on patronage.

21 **Consider the following statements.**

(Chap 4, Class-VIII, Old NCERT)

1. The College of Fort William was started in Calcutta in 1801.
2. The East India College was set up at Haileybury in England.
3. Both of these colleges were established to provide training to Civil Servants in India.

How many of the statements given above is/are correct?

(a) Only one (b) Only two
(c) All three (d) None of these

Ans. (b)

Exp. Only two statements i.e., (2) and (3) are correct. In year 1809, East India College was established at Haileybury in England. Both of these were established to provide training to the Civil Servants.
Statement (1) is not correct because Fort William College was founded by Lord Wellesley on 10th July, 1800 at Calcutta (now Kolkata).

22 **Consider the following statements regarding effective contribution made by Dadabhai Naoroji.**

(Chap 17, Class-XI, Tamil Nadu Board)

1. He exposed the economic exploitation of India by the British.
2. He interpreted the Ancient Indian texts and restored the self-confidence of Indians.
3. He stressed the need for eradication of all the social evils before anything else.

Which of the statements given above is/are correct?

(a) Only 1 (b) 2 and 3
(c) 1 and 3 (d) 1, 2 and 3

Ans. (a)

Exp. Statement (1) is correct as the most significant and effective contributions made by Dadabhai Naoroji was his relentless efforts to expose and bring attention to the economic exploitation of India by the British colonial administration.
His analysis of the economic drain from India and his advocacy for economic justice laid the groundwork for understanding the adverse effects of British colonial policies on the Indian economy.

23 **Which of the following statements is/are incorrect regarding the administration of justice during British Period?** *(Chap 4, Class-VIII, Old NCERT)*

(a) An Act of 1781 provided that Indian Law will also be applicable to Englishmen.
(b) Courts to administer justice were set up in every district.
(c) In 1833, Law Commission was appointed.
(d) All of the above

Ans. (a)

Exp. Statement (a) is incorrect about administration of justice during British Period.
The Amending Act of 1781 was passed by British Parliament on 5th July, 1781 to remove the defects of Regulating Act, 1773.
The key provision of this Act was to demarcate the relations between the Supreme Court and Governor-General in Council.

24 **In 1833, Law Commission was appointed by the British Government. It was entrusted with the responsibilities of** *(Chap 4, Class-VIII, Old NCERT)*

1. to codify the Indian system of law.
2. to present a draft for curbing Indian nationalism.
3. to codify court procedure.

Codes

(a) Only 1 (b) 2 and 3
(c) 1 and 3 (d) All of these

Ans. (c)

Exp. Law Commission was entrusted with the responsibilities to codify the Indian System of law and court procedure. The Law Commission was established in 1834 under the Charter Act of 1833 under the Chairmanship of Lord Macaulay.

25 **Consider the following statements.**

(Chap 4, Class-VIII, Old NCERT)

1. Rule of Law implies that everybody is equal in the eye of law.
2. In British India, Rule of Law was implemented successfully.
3. There were same courts for the Britishers living in India.

Which of the statements given above is/are correct?

(a) Only 1 (b) 1 and 2 (c) 2 and 3 (d) 1, 2 and 3

Ans. (a)

Exp. Statement (1) is correct as the Rule of Law means that all laws apply equally to all citizens of the country and no one can be above the law.

Statements (2) and (3) are incorrect because in British India, Rule of Law was not implemented as there was discrimination between the Indians and Britishers. Separate courts were there for cases related to Indians and Britishers.

26 In the context of development of modern education in India, which of the following statements is correct? *(Chap 4, Class-VIII, Old NCERT)*

(a) The Calcutta Madrasa was established in 1781.
(b) Banaras Sanskrit College was established in 1881.
(c) The Fort William College was started in Bombay.
(d) The Charter Act of 1833 sanctioned one lakh rupees for the purpose of education in India.

Ans. (a)

Exp. Statement (a) is correct regarding development of modern education in India as in 1781, Warren Hastings founded the Madrasa Aliya or Calcutta Madrasa.

Statements (b), (c) and (d) are incorrect because in 1791-92, Jonathan Duncan founded the Sanskrit College at Banaras to provide study of Hindu Law and Philosophy. Fort William College was founded in 1800 by Lord Wellesley in Calcutta.

By the Charter Act of 1813, the Company granted an expenditure of one lakh rupees each year for the education in India.

27 Consider the following pairs. *(Class-XI, Old NCERT) (IAS Pre 2020)*

1. Aurang - In-charge of treasury of the state
2. Banian - Indian agent of the East India Company
3. Mirasidar - Designated revenue payer to the state

How many of the pairs given above is/are correctly matched?

(a) Only one (b) Only two
(c) Only three (d) None of these

Ans. (b)

Exp. Only two pairs i.e., (2) and (3) are correctly matched. The term Banian means Merchant. Banian was engaged by an individual Western merchant or a firm to work for them as a broker, interpreter and an agent. Under the Ryotwari Settlement System, the government recognised Mirasidars as the sole proprietors of land. They acted as the designated for revenue payer to the state.

Pair (1) is incorrectly matched because Aurang was a Persian term means a warehouse. It is a place where goods are collected before being sold.

28 What was the main motive of British to promote modern education in India? *(Chap 4, Class-VIII, Old NCERT)*

1. For the welfare of Indians.
2. To train Indians so that they could help the Company's British officials in administration.

Codes

(a) Only 1 (b) Only 2
(c) Both 1 and 2 (d) Neither 1 nor 2

Ans. (b)

Exp. The main motive of British to promote modern education in India was to train Indians for holding subordinate posts in administration and British business concerns.

29 Consider the following statements with reference to the orientalist. *(Chap 7, Class-VIII, New NCERT)*

1. Those with a scholarly knowledge of the language and culture of Asia were called orientalists.
2. William Jones and Henry Thomas Colebrooke were orientalist.
3. Asiatic Society of Bengal opposed orientalists.

Which of the statements given above is/are correct?

(a) Only 1 (b) 1 and 2 (c) 2 and 3 (d) 1, 2 and 3

Ans. (b)

Exp. Statements (1) and (2) are correct with reference to the orientalist because those who were in favour of continuation of the existing institutions of oriental learning and promotion of Indian classical tradition were called orientalists. William Jones and Henry Thomas Colebrooke were orientalists.

Statement (3) is incorrect because Asiatic Society of Bengal was founded by William Jones to encourage oriental studies.

30 Who is known for making this statement 'a single shelf of a good European library was worth the whole native literature of India and Arabia'? *(Chap 7, Class-VIII, New NCERT)*

(a) Thomas Babington Macaulay
(b) William Jones
(c) James Mill
(d) Henry Thomas Colebrooke

Ans. (a)

Exp. Thomas Babington Macaulay is known for making the statement given in the question. This statement was his part of speech to attack the orientalists. He was famous British historian and politician of 19th century. He saw India as an uncivilised country that need to be civilised. No branch of Eastern knowledge, according to him, could be compared to what England had produced.

31 With reference to the Fort William College Calcutta, which of the statements is/are correct? *(Chap 4, Class-VIII, Old NCERT)*

1. It was founded on 10th June, 1800 AD within the Fort William Complex in Calcutta.
2. The main purpose of establishing this college, was to teach Indian languages to British officers.

Codes

(a) Only 1 (b) Only 2
(c) Both 1 and 2 (d) Neither 1 nor 2

Ans. (a)

Exp. Statement (2) is correct with reference to the Fort William College, Calcutta. The main purpose of establishing Fort William College was to provide education in Indian languages to British officers and civil servants. It aimed to train British administrators and officials in the languages and customs of the Indian subcontinent to facilitate better governance and communication between the British rulers and the Indian subjects.

Statement (1) is incorrect because Fort William College in Calcutta (now Kolkata) was founded on 10th November, 1800 AD. It was established by Lord Wellesley, who was the Governor-General of India at the time.

32 Consider the following pairs. *(Chap 7, Class-VIII, New NCERT)*

	Educational institutions		Establishers
1.	Calcutta Madrasa	–	Lord Wellesley
2.	Sanskrit College	–	Raja Ram Mohan Roy
3.	Vedanta College	–	Jonathan Duncan
4.	Hindu College	–	David Hare

How many of the pairs given above is/are correctly matched?

(a) Only one (b) Only two (c) Only three (d) All four

Ans. (a)

Exp. Only one pair i.e., (4) is correctly matched as Hindu Vedanta college was founded by David Hare. He was an Scottish watchmakers and philanthropist in Bengal, India. He founded educational institution in Calcutta.

Pairs (1), (2) and (3) are incorrectly matched because Calcutta Madarsa was founded by Warren Hasting in 1781.

Sanskrit College was established at Varansi in 1791 by Jonathan Duncan,

Vedanta School was founded by Raja Ram Mohan Roy in 1825, he introduced machanics and voltaire's philosophy.

33 Which of the following led to the introduction of English Education in India? *(Chap 7, Class-VIII, New NCERT)*

1. Charter Act of 1813
2. General Committee of Public Instruction, 1823
3. Orientalist and Anglicist Controversy

Codes

(a) 1 and 2 (b) Only 2 (c) 1 and 3 (d) All of these

Ans. (d)

Exp. All the given statements led to the introduction of English Education in India. The Charter Act of 1813 provided a grant of 1 lakh per annum for the promotion of education in India.

In 1823, the Governor-General Council appointed a General Committee of Public Instruction, which had the responsibility to grant the 1 lakh for education. The committee was headed by Lord Macaulay consisting of 10 European members.

The Charter Act of 1813 created a controversy between the Anglicists and Orienta lists on the medium of instruction.

34 Consider the following statements regarding Wood's Despatch of 1854. *(Chap 7, Class-VIII, New NCERT)*

1. It recommended English as the medium of instruction for higher studies.
2. It laid stress on female education and vocational training.

Which of the statements given above is/are correct?

(a) Only 1 (b) Only 2
(c) Both 1 and 2 (d) Neither 1 nor 2

Ans. (c)

Exp. Both the statements (1) and (2) are correct with respect to Wood's Despatch of 1854. It recommended English as the medium of instruction for higher studies and vernacular language at primary or elementary education. It laid stress on female education and vocational training in order to create a wider range of products, as well as to create a healthy market for the purchase of such product.

35 Consider the following statements with reference to the report of William Adam. *(Chap 7, Class-VIII, New NCERT)*

1. Lord William Bentinck, the Governor-General of India appointed Adam in 1835 to survey the state of education in Madras and Bombay and suggest reform.
2. He suggested the need to incorporate flexible system of education.

Which of the statements given above is/are correct?

(a) Only 1 (b) Only 2
(c) Both 1 and 2 (d) Neither 1 nor 2

Ans. (a)

Exp. Statement (1) is incorrect with reference to the report of William Adam because William Adam was appointed by the Governor-General, William Bentinck in 1835, to survey the state of education in Bengal and Bihar and suggest reforms.

36 In the context of development of National Education, the goal of it according to Sri Aurobindo Ghose was to *(Chap 7, Class-VIII, New NCERT)*

(a) create employment opportunities.
(b) awaken the spirit of nationality among the students.
(c) create moral character among the students.
(d) None of the above

Ans. (a)

Exp. In the context of development of National Education, the goal of it according to Sri Aurobindo Ghose was to awaken the spirit of nationality among the students. According to Sri Aurobindo, the education must emphasis on the whole aspects of human life such as physical, psychic, mental, knowledge and love.

37 Consider the following Assertion (A) and Reason (R) and choose the correct code.

(Chap 4, Class-VIII, Old NCERT)

Assertion (A) British made English as a medium of instruction.

Reason (R) Three universities were set up at Calcutta, Bombay and Madras.

Codes

(a) Both A and R are true and R is the correct explanation of A.
(b) Both A and R are true, but R is not the correct explanation of A.
(c) A is true, but R is false.
(d) A is false, but R is true.

Ans. (b)

Exp. Both Assertion (A) and Reason (R) are true, but Reason (R) is not the correct explanation of Assertion (A). British made English as a medium of instruction with the passage of English Education Act, 1835. The aim was that British wanted to establish their cultural domination with spread of English language.

Three universities in three Presidency towns of Calcutta, Bombay and Madras were set up on the recommendations of the Despatch in 1856. However, Wood's Despatch also recommended that teaching and learning at primary level must have to be in vernacular language.

38 How villages were influenced by the economic policies of the British Government?

(Chap 4, Class-VIII, Old NCERT)

1. The villages lost their self-sufficiency.
2. The Village Panchayats lost their authority.

Codes

(a) Only 1 (b) Only 2
(c) Both 1 and 2 (d) Neither 1 nor 2

Ans. (c)

Exp. Both (1) and (2) are correct regarding economic policies of the British Government.

High tarrifs on export of Indian goods and relatively free imports of machine made British goods crippled the Indian handicraft sector.

Added to it, the high land revenue demand increased poverty in India. Due to this reason the Indian villages lost their self-sufficiency.

The Village Panchayats lost their authority as now it came directly under the British rule.

39 Economically, one of the result of the British rule in India in the 19th century was the

(Chap 4, Class-VIII, Old NCERT) (IAS Pre 2018)

(a) increase in the exports of Indian handicrafts.
(b) growth in the number of Indian owned factories.
(c) commercialisation of Indian agriculture.
(d) rapid increase in urban population.

Ans. (c)

Exp. Economically, one of the results of British rule in India in the 19th century was the commercialisation of Indian agriculture by introducing cash crops such as tea, coffee, indigo, opium, cotton, jute, sugarcane and oilseeds were introduced with different intentions.

40 British promoted indigo cultivation in India. What was/were the main reasons that raised the demand of the Indian Indigo? *(Chap 3, Class-VIII, New NCERT)*

1. Indigo produced a rich blue colour.
2. Expansion of cotton industries in England.

Codes

(a) Only 1 (b) Only 2
(c) Both 1 and 2 (d) Neither 1 nor 2

Ans. (c)

Exp. Both the statements (1) and (2) are correct regarding, promotion of Indigo cultivation in India by British. The 17th and 18th century saw large scale industrialisation in England. It enabled opening of large number of textile mills in England driven by machine. Gradually, it became one of the biggest manufacturer of cotton textile. These industries in England were dependent on Indian Indigo as dye, as it was of better quality and produced a rich blue colour, whereas dye from wood (grown in Europe) was pale and dull.

41 Which factor contributed in the decline of Indian cottage and handicraft sector?

(Chap 3, Class-VIII, Old NCERT)

1. Gradual disintegration of the princely states in the British territories.
2. British officials did not patronise craftsmen.
3. Britain prohibited the entry of many types of Indian products.
4. Indian products were not able to compete with cheap products of the English.

How many of the statements given above is/are correct?

(a) Only one (b) Only two (c) Only three (d) All four

Ans. (d)

Exp. All four statements i.e., (1), (2), (3) and (4) are correct regarding causes for the decline of Indian cottage and handicraft sector.

Through discriminatory tariff policy, the British Government successfully destroyed the demand of handicraft goods. They prohibited the entry of many types of Indian products in European markets.

With the British rule, Nawab who were main patrons of Indian handicraft product disappeared. There was no one to protect these handicrafts. Similarly, the disintegration of Princely states who were the main customers of Indian handicrafts products resulted in decline of Indian cottage and handicraft industry.

Indian handicraft products could not compete with machine-made products which were cheap and durable.

A new class of Indian society was affected by the culture of Britain. It adopted Western style of living.

42 **What were the main characteristics of commercial policy of British in India?** *(Chap 3, Class-XII, Old NCERT)*

1. It acquired monopolistic control over Indian trade.
2. It utilised the revenue to finance its export of Indian goods.
3. Labours were forced to work in company at low wages.
4. Handicrafts products were promoted in England.

How many of the statements given above is/are correct?

(a) Only one (b) Only two (c) Only three (d) All four

Ans. (c)

Exp. Only three statements i.e., (1), (2) and (3) depicts about the characteristics of commercial policy of British in India. The main focus of the economic policies pursued by the colonial government was to make India a mere supplier of Britain's own flourishing industrial base. Britishers acquired monopolistic control over Indian trade and utilised its revenue to finance its export of Indian goods.

The interest of the Indian economy were completely ignored. The Indian exports became costlier and its demand in the international market fell drastically that led to the collapse of Indian industries. In order to appropriate maximum profits labours were forced to work in company at low wages.

Statement (4) is incorrect because, Britishers discouraged the use of Indian handicraft products in England.

43 **Consider the following statements.** *(Chap 4, Class-VIII, Old NCERT)*

Which of the following was/were the main reason for decline in the handicrafts sector during the British rule in India?

1. New patterns of the demand for handicrafts.
2. The tariff policy followed by the British.
3. The competition in the sector due to man-made machines

How many of the statementsv given above is/are correct?

(a) Only one (b) Only two
(c) All three (d) None of these

Ans. (c)

Exp. All three statements i.e., (1), (2) and (3) are correct as the decline of the handicraft industry in India during the British rule can be attributed to several factors. The main reason behind this decline was the economic policies of the British that favoured the British textile industry over Indian handicrafts. The demand for traditional handicrafts declined and artisans found it difficult to sustain their livelihoods. The decay of handicrafts in India was caused by a combination of factors, including the British tariff policy, competition from man-made machines and changing demand patterns.

44 **The cause of decline of textile industries in 18th century in Bengal was** *(Chap 3, Class-XII, Old NCERT)*

(a) decline in quality of production.
(b) non-availability of raw material.
(c) high tariff rates on exports to Britain.
(d) non-availability of craftsmen.

Ans. (c)

Exp. The cause of decline of textile industries in 18th century in Bengal was high tariff rates on exports to Britain. Before the consolidation of British power in India, the Indian cotton products were in high demand in European markets. However, Britishers after conquest of India increased the tarrif rates on export to Britian, it made Indian textile products costlier in Britian, thus discouraging its consumption. At the same time, imports of machine- made cheap British textile products flooded the Indian market. Thus, Indian textile industry lost its domestic market resulting into its decline.

45 **The ship-building industry in the 17th and 18th centuries had earned fame. The main yards of ship-building were at** *(Chap 4, Class-VIII, Old NCERT)*

1. Goa 2. Surat 3. Lucknow 4. Hyderabad

Codes

(a) 1 and 2 (b) 2 and 3 (c) 2 and 4 (d) 3 and 4

Ans. (a)

Exp. During 17th and 18th centuries, the main yards of ship-building were at Goa and Surat. Located on the Western coast of India, they were helpful in promotional international trade in India.

46 **During British period, Muslin was one of the most important trading commodities. Which one of the following was the most important centre of Muslin in India?** *(Chap 4, Class-VIII, Old NCERT)*

(a) Dhaka (b) Delhi (c) Calcutta (d) Chennai

Ans. (a)

Exp. Dhaka was the most important centre of Muslin in India.

The word 'Muslin' was used to refer to all finely woven textiles. It was one of the most important trading commodities during British period. Armenian merchants traded Muslin from Bengal to Syria. As Muslin business expanded many European companies established their factories in Dhaka. The Dutch made their factory in 1663, British in 1699 and French in 1682. Establishment of factories also helped Dhaka is becoming most important textile centre at that time.

47 **There was no independent development of industries in India during British rule because of** *(Chap 8, Class-XII, Old NCERT)*

(a) absence of heavy industries.
(b) scarcity of foreign capital.
(c) scarcity of natural resources.
(d) preference of the rich to invest in land.

Ans. (a)

Exp. There was no independent development of industries in India during British rule because there was absence of heavy industries.

The establishment of a few manufacturing units here and there was no substitute to the near wholesale displacement of the country's traditional handicraft industries.

48 The staple commodities of export by the English East India Company from Bengal in the middle of the 18th century were

(Chap 5, Class-XII, Old NCERT) (IAS Pre 2018)

(a) raw cotton, oil-seeds and opium
(b) sugar, salt, zinc and lead
(c) copper, silver, gold, spices and tea
(d) cotton, silk, salt petre and opium

Ans. (d)

Exp. The staple commodities of export by the English East India Company from Bengal in the middle of the 18th century were; cotton, silk, salt petre and opium. After the Victory in Battle of Plassey and Buxar, the Company consolidated its rule in Bengal.

Gradually, it became biggest exporter of agricultural raw material which were used in production of finished goods in England. These goods were also sold by the Company in European and Chinese markets.

49 Consider the following statements in the context of de-industrialisation. ***(Chap 8, Class-XII, Old NCERT)***

1. It was started in 1813.
2. Ending of trade monopoly of East India Company have speed up this process.

Which of the statements given above is/are correct?

(a) Only 1 (b) Only 2
(c) Both 1 and 2 (d) Neither 1 nor 2

Ans. (c)

Exp. Both statements (1) and (2) are correct about the de-industrialisation. The de-industrialisation in India was started in 1813. The reason behind it was the ending of trade monopoly of East India Company which speeded up its process. After that Indian market was flooded with machine-made British goods, as large number of British companies started to trade with India. The trade policies under the colonial rule favoured the imports of goods from Britain.

50 Consider the following statements regarding the impact of Industrial Revolution on India during the first half of the 19th century.

(Chap 8, Class-XII, Old NCERT)

1. Indian handicrafts were ruined.
2. Machines were introduced in the Indian textile industry in large numbers.
3. Railway lines were laid in many parts of the country.
4. Heavy duties were imposed on the imports of British manufacturers.

How many of the statements given above is/are correct?

(a) Only one (b) Only two
(c) Only three (d) All four

Ans. (a)

Exp. Only one statement i.e., (1) is correct regarding the impact of Industrial Revolution on India during the first half of the 19th century. Indian textiles had to face stiff competition from English textiles in the European and American markets.

Heavy duties were imposed on imported Indian textiles in Britain. Britain started producing machine made goods and textiles that were much cheaper than Indian goods. It led to the ruination of Indian handicraft industries.

51 Consider the following statements in the context of industrialisation during British rule.

(Chap 8, Class-XII, Old NCERT)

1. The first cotton mill was started in 1853.
2. In 1905, the famous Tata Iron and Steel industry was established.
3. Industrialisation was promoted in all the regions of the country.

How many of the statements given above is/are correct?

(a) Only one (b) Only two
(c) All three (d) None of these

Ans. (d)

Exp. None of the given above statements are correct in the context of industrialisation during British rule.

In 1854, the first cotton mill was set up in Bombay and it grew as an important port for the export of raw cotton from India to England and China.

Tata Iron and Steel Company (TISCO) is the oldest steel plant in the country. It was established in 1907.

Industrialisation was promoted in the few regions of the country.

52 What was/were the main factor, which led to impoverishment of the rural economy in British India? ***(Chap 7, Class-VIII, Old NCERT)***

1. High revenue demand
2. De-industrialisation
3. Establishment of banking institution

Codes

(a) Only 1 (b) Only 2
(c) 1 and 2 (d) All of these

Ans. (c)

Exp. The main factor that led to impoverishment of the rural economy are high revenue demand and de-industrialisation.

Besides this, the colonial authorities neglected rural education and investment in agricultural sector which also contributed to impoverishment of rural economy.

53 With reference to the famines in India, which of the following statements is/are incorrect?

(Chap 8, Class-XII, Old NCERT)

1. A famine code was framed by British Government.
2. Many famine commissions were formed during British period.

Codes

(a) Only 1 (b) Only 2
(c) Both 1 and 2 (d) Neither 1 nor 2

Ans. (d)

Exp. Neither statements (1) nor (2) are incorrect. The repressive economic policies, de-industrialisation and impoverishment of agricultural sector, resulted in frequence occurence of famine in British India. In order to mitigate these crises, British Government initiated few reforms some of which are given below

Famine code was formulated in 1883 under Viceroyship of Lord Ripon.

First Famine Commission in 1878 under the Chairmanship of Sir Richard Strachey.

Second Famine Commission in 1897 under the Chairmanship of Sir James Lyall.

Third Famine Commission in 1900 under the Chairmanship of Sir Anthony MCD Panel.

54 The most important centre of Jamdani textile during British time were at

(Chap 6, Class-VIII, New NCERT)

1. Dacca in Bengal
2. Lucknow in the United Provinces
3. Lahore in North-Western Province
4. Surat in Bombay Province

Codes

(a) 1 and 2 (b) 2 and 3
(c) 1 and 3 (d) 2 and 4

Ans. (a)

Exp. Dacca in Bengal and Lucknow in the United Provinces were the most important centres of Jamdani textile during British time. Jamdani is a fine muslin cloth on which decorative motifs are woven on the loom. Dacca is now known as Dhaka (capital of Bangladesh).

55 With reference to 'De-industrialisation', which of the following statements is/are correct ?

(Chap 11, Class-XII, Old NCERT)

1. This process started in 1813.
2. Abolition of monopoly trade rights of East India Company aggravated the process.

Codes

(a) Only 1 (b) Only 2
(c) Both 1 and 2 (d) Neither 1 nor 2

Ans. (c)

Exp. Both the statements (1) and (2) are correct with reference to 'De-industrialisation'. After the Charter Act of 1813, which allowed one way free trade for British citizens, cheap and machine- made imports flooded the Indian market. The newly established rail network aided European products in reaching the most remote parts of the country. The Charter Act ended the commercial trade monopoly of the East India Company except for trade in tea and trade with China. This aggravated the process of De-industrialisation.

56 Consider the following statements.

(Chap 3, Class-XII, Old NCERT)

1. Through 'investments' Bengal's revenue was sent to England.
2. The drain of wealth decreased after 1858.
3. Salaries and other income of English officials were main component of the drain of wealth.

Which of the statements given above is/are correct?

(a) Only 1
(b) Only 2
(c) 1 and 3
(d) 1, 2 and 3

Ans. (c)

Exp. Statements (1) and (3) are correct because before 1865, the company had purchased goods in India by importing gold and silver from Britain. But, after 1865 revenue collected in Bengal could finance the purchase of goods for export.

Salaries and other income of English officials were major components that drained the Indian wealth, because large amount of revenue was paid in the form of salaries and other expenses to the English officials.

Statement (2) is incorrect, because the drain of Indian wealth has increased in the British reign.

57 Consider the following Assertion (A) and Reason (R) and choose the correct code.

(Chap 3, Class-XII, Old NCERT) (UPPSC Pre 2017)

Assertion (A) Generally, India had a favourable balance of trade during the British rule.

Reason (R) The drain of wealth took the form of unrequited exports.

Codes

(a) Both A and R are true and R is the correct explanation of A.
(b) Both A and R are true, but R is not the correct explanation of A.
(c) A is true, but R is false.
(d) Both A and R are false.

Ans. (d)

Exp. Both Assertion (A) and Reason (R) are false.

Even though Britishers maintained monopoly in foreign trade, India never had favourable Balance of Trade during British rule. This is because imports were higher than exports.

India used to import finished products which were manufactured in Britain at commercial level. This led to drain of wealth however it was not taking the form of unrequited exports.

Chapter 25

Civil Uprisings, Peasant, Tribal and Labour Movements

Civil Uprisings, Peasant, Tribal and Labour Movements

Civil and Peasant Uprisings

Sanyasi Revolt (1763-1800 AD)
- Provoked by disastrous famine of 1770 in Bengal and restriction on people from visiting holy places
- Important leaders- Chirag Ali, Musa Shah, Bhawani Pathak and Debi Chaudhurani

Poligar Revolt (1795-1805 AD)
- Led by Kattobomman Nayakan in North Arcot, Madurai, Sivagiri, Ramanathapuram and Tirunelveli

Velu Thampi Revolt (1808-1809 AD)
- Dean of Travancore, Velu Thampi rose up in rebellion against the British attempt to remove him from the Diwanship

Paika Rebellion (1817 AD)
- Traditional landlord militia who enjoyed rent free land tenures
- Rose up in rebellion against oppressive land revenue

Revolt of Mysore (1830-31 AD)
- **Main causes** increased revenue demand, corruption and extortion of local officials

Moplah Rebellion (1835-1921 AD)
- In Malabar region of Kerala; By Muslim peasants
- Directed against British and Hindu trader

Gadkari Revolt (1844 AD)
- Occurred around Kolhapur region by Gadkari who were hereditary servants attached to Maratha forts; Led by Daji Krishna Pandit

Indigo Revolt (1859- 1860 AD)
- Occurred in Nadia and Pabna district of Bengal who refused to grow indigo
- Led by Biswas brothers of Nadia, Rafiq Mondal and Kader Molla of Pabna

Pabna Rebellion (1873-1875 AD)
- Occurred in East Bengal against forceful collection of rents and land taxes by landlords
- Agrarian league was formed in Yusuf Shahi Pargana of Pabna district
- Organisation of rent strikes and use of litigation by farmers

Deccan Riots (1874-1875 AD)
- Occurred in Ryotwari areas of Pune and Ahmednagar
- High land revenue and its imposition even in bad seasons were main cause

Eka Movement (1926 AD)
- Occurred in Hardoi, Bahraich and Sitapur in United Province
- Main cause- excessive rents, oppression by thekedars

Tribal and Labour Movements

Khasi Uprising (1793-1833 AD)
- Occurred in hilly regions between Garo and Jaintia hills
- Protested against mobilisation of workers for road construction
- Led by Tirut Singh

Bhil Uprising (1819 AD)
- Occurred in Khandesh region because of incursion of outsiders
- Britishers used both military forces and conciliatory measures to suppress the rebels

Pagal Panthi Revolt (1825-1835 AD)
- Semi- religious sect founded by Karam Shah I
- Participated by Hajong and Garo tribe
- Occurred because of zamindari oppression in North Bengal

Ahom Revolt (1828-1833 AD)
- Occurred against British intrusion to Ahom territories; Led by Gomdhar Kohwar; Finally, company ceded part of territories to Maharaja Purandar Singh

Kol Uprising (1831-1832 AD)
- Kols of Singhbhum revolted against transfer of tribal lands

Khond Uprising (1831-1832 AD)
- Led by Chakra Bisoi against the British forces

Santhal Rebellion (1855-1856 AD)
- Occurred in Raj Mahal region against oppression of police

SOURCE *Old NCERT Class VIII (Revolts against British Rule), New NCERT Class VIII (Tribals, Dikus and the Vision of a Golden Age), Old NCERT Class VIII (Rise of Nationalism), New NCERT Class VIII (The Making of the National Movement : 1870s-1947), Old NCERT Class XII (Struggle for Swaraj II [1927-1947]), New NCERT Class XII (The Nationalist Movement : Civil Disobedience and Beyond)*

Tribal Movement

1 With reference to the tribal revolts, consider the following statements. *(Chap 4, Class-VIII, New NCERT)*

1. The 1917 Paika Rebellion in Odisha's Khurda is referred to as the 'original' first war of Indian Independence.
2. The Kols, tribal people from the Chota Nagpur area, rose in revolt against the British in 1831.

Which of the statements given above is/are correct?

(a) Only 1 (b) Only 2
(c) Both 1 and 2 (c) Neither 1 nor 2

Ans. (c)

Exp. Both the statements (1) and (2) are correct with reference to tribal revolts. The Paika Rebellion is sometimes referred to as the 'original' first war of Indian Independence because it pre-dates the 1857 War of Independence.

The Paika Rebellion was an armed rebellion against British colonial rule in India in 1817. The rebellion occurred in the region of Odisha, which was then under British control. The

Kol Rebellion was a major uprising in the Chota Nagpur region of India between 1831 and 1832. The Kols were upset over exploitation by agents of the East India Company (EIC). The transfer of tribal lands and the coming of moneylenders, merchants and British laws created a lot of tension among them.

2 Consider the following statements about Bhil Rebellion. *(Chap 5, Class-VIII, Old NCERT)*

1. The name of the Bhil tribe owes its origin to the word 'Bhillu' which means bow.
2. The rebellion was against the British feudalism and imperialism in Rajputana.
3. The states had given the contract to extract liquor to traders, which angered the natives of the tribe.

How many of the statements given above is/are correct?

(a) Only one (b) Only two
(c) All three (d) None of these

Ans. (c)

Exp. All three statements i.e., (1), (2) and (3) are correct regarding Bhil Rebellion.The name of Bhil tribe comes from the word "Bhillu" which means bow. The natives of the tribe had expertise in archery with practical experience in the art of bow-making and hunting was their main occupation.

The Bhil Rebellion of 1818 was one of the first resistance movements against the British empire and feudalism in Rajputana. The rebellion was led by Bhil leaders like Kazi Singh and Sewaram.

The natives of the tribe were prohibited to distil liquor openly in their homes. The states gave the contract of distilling liquor to the traders and earned income out of it.

3 Consider the following statements with reference to the Bhil Tribal Movement. *(Chap 5, Class-VIII, Old NCERT)*

1. It occurred in the North-Eastern part of India.
2. It started in 1820 and continued till 1841 AD.

Which of the statements given above is/are incorrect?

(a) Only 1 (b) Only 2
(c) Both 1 and 2 (d) Neither 1 nor 2

Ans. (c)

Exp. Both the statements (1) and (2) are incorrect with reference to the Bhil Tribal Movement. The Bhils were primitive tribes living in the Western Ghats with their strongholds in Khandesh.

British occupancy of this region in 1818 AD brought in the outsiders accompanying dislocations in their community life. A general Bhil insurrection in 1817-1819 AD was crushed by British Military forces. Some conciliatory measures were taken to pacify them. They again revolted under the leadership of Seva Ram in 1825 AD. Minor revolts again took place in 1836 AD and 1846 AD as well.

4 Consider the following events. *(Chap 1, Class-XII, New NCERT) (39th BPSC Pre 2019)*

1. Neel Rebellion 2. Santhal Rebellion
3. Deccan Rebellion 4. Sipahi Rebellion

Based on the given events, what is the correct chronological order of these rebellions?

(a) 4, 2, 1 and 3 (b) 4, 2, 3 and 1
(c) 2, 4, 3 and 1 (d) 2, 4,1 and 3

Ans. (d)

Exp. The correct chronological order is 2,4,1 and 3.

The Santhal Rebellion also known as Santhal Hool, which was led by two brothers Siddhu and Kanhu in the year 1855-1856 was mainly centered between Bhagalpur and Rajmahal (Bihar).

The Sipahi Rebellion of 1857 was a major uprising in India in 1857-1858 against the rule of the British East India Company, which functioned as a sovereign power on behalf of the British Crown.

Neel Revolt also known as Indigo Revolt. It was a Peasant Movement and subsequent uprising of indigo farmers against the indigo planters that arose in Bengal in 1859 and continued for over a year.

The Deccan Riots took place in 1875, which targeted conditions of debt peonage (Kamiuti) to moneylenders. The peasants began a systematic attack on the moneylenders' houses and shops.

5 After the Santhal uprising subsided, what was/ were the measures taken by Colonial Government? *(Chap 4, Class-VIII, New NCERT) (IAS Pre 2018)*

1. The territories called 'Santhal Parganas' were created.
2. It became illegal for a Santhal to transfer land to a non-Santhal.

Codes

(a) Only 1 (b) Only 2
(c) Both 1 and 2 (d) Neither 1 nor 2

Ans. (c)

Exp. Both the statements (1) and (2) are correct regarding measures taken by Colonial Government after Santhal uprising. The Santhal rebellion occurred in Chota Nagpur region of Bihar (modern Jharkhand) in 1855-1856. After the suppression of the revolt, the British Government accepted the demand of a separate Santhal Pargana. Besides creating a separate district, a Santhal Pargana Tenancy Act was also passed by the British Government. Under this Act, it became illegal for a Santhal to transfer land to a non-Santhal.

6 **Consider the following statements with reference to the 'Ulgulan'.** *(Chap 4, Class-VIII, New NCERT)*

1. It occurred in the Chota Nagpur region.
2. Chand and Bhairav were the main leaders of the movement.
3. The Chota Nagpur Tenancy Act was passed as a result of the Ulgulan revolt.

How many of the statements given above is/are correct?

(a) Only one (b) Only two (c) All three (d) None of these

Ans. (b)

Exp. Only two statements i.e. (1) and (3) are correct regarding Ulgulan.

The Ulgulan (Munda) movement took place primarily in the Chota Nagpur plateau region, which is part of present-day Jharkhand. The Munda Ulgulan (rebellion) is one of the most prominent tribal revolts in the history of Indian Independence. The British colonial administration enacted the Chota Nagpur Tenancy Act (1908) in response to the Ulgulan movement. This act restricted the transfer of tribal land to non-tribal individuals and recognised tribal rights, including the prohibition of certain practices.

Statement (2) is incorrect because the main leader of the Ulgulan movement was Birsa Munda, a prominent tribal freedom fighter. Chand and Bhairav were one of the main leaders of the Santhal Movement.

7 **Consider the following pairs with reference to the tribal uprising and their Leaders.** *(Chap-1, Class-XII, New NCERT)*

	Tribal Uprising		Organisation Leader
1.	Kondh	–	Bhola Nath Sahay
2.	Pahariya	–	Raja Jagganath
3.	Ramosi	–	Tirot Singh
4.	Chuar	–	Durjan Singh

How many of the pairs given above is/are correctly matched?

(a) Only one (b) Only two
(c) Only three (d) All of these

Ans. (b)

Exp. Only two pairs i.e., (2) and (4) are correctly matched as Pahariya rebellion was started in 1778 by King Jagannath against the British expansion of agriculture established in the hilly areas. The Pahariya tribe, facing similar challenges as other tribal communities, rose against oppressive policies. The Chuar rebellion occurred among the Chuar tribe in the Bundelkhand region (now part of Uttar Pradesh and Madhya Pradesh). Durjan Singh, a Chuar leader, spearheaded this movement in the late 19th century.

Pairs (1) and (3) are incorrectly matched because the Kondh rebellion took place in Orissa between 1837 and 1856. Its main leader was Chakra Bisoi. In 1822, Chittoor Singh of Satara led the Ramosi rebellion. The Ramosis, a tribal community in the Western ghats (Karnataka, Maharashtra and Madhya Pradesh), once served in the lower ranks of the Maratha army.

8 **Consider the following statements with reference to the Birsa Munda and Munda Movement.** *(Chap 4, Class-VIII, New NCERT)*

1. In 1895, he urged his followers to recover their glorious past.
2. He wanted to drive out missionaries, moneylenders and Hindu landlords.
3. With his death in 1900, the movement faded out.

Which of the statements given above is/are correct?

(a) Only 1 (b) 1 and 2 (c) 2 and 3 (d) 1, 2 and 3

Ans. (d)

Exp. All the statements (1), (2) and (3) are correct with reference to the Birsa Munda and Munda Movement.

In 1895, Birsa urged his followers to recover their glorious past. He talked of a golden age in the past. The Birsa Movement wanted to drive out missionaries, moneylenders, Hindu landlords and the government set up a Munda Raj. Birsa Munda died in jail on 9th June, 1900. After his death the movement became weak and eventually ended.

9 **Consider the following statements about the Santhal Hool of 1855-1856.** *(Chap 4, Class-VIII, New NCERT) (MPSC Pre 2010)*

1. The Santhals were in a desperate situation as tribal lands were leased out.
2. The Santhal rebels were treated very leniently by the British officials.
3. Santhal inhabited areas were eventually constituted into separate administrative units called 'Santhal Parganas'.
4. The Santhal Rebellion was the only major rebellion in mid-19th century India.

How many of the statements given above is/are correct?

(a) Only one (b) Only two
(c) Only three (d) All of these

Ans. (b)

Exp. Only two statements i.e (1) and (3) are correct about Santhal Hool of 1855-1856. The Santhals were in a desperate situation as tribal lands were leased out. The rebellion was led by the four Murmu brothers i.e., Siddhu, Kanhu, Chand and Bhairav. Santhal inhabited areas eventually constituted into separate administrative units called 'Santhal Parganas'.

Statements (2) and (4) are incorrect because Santhals were treated harshly by the British officials and the rebellion was crushed by the end of 1856. This was not the only major rebellion of mid-19th century. The Revolt of 1857 and other rebellions took place during this period.

10 Consider the following statements about the Santhal revolt. *(Chap 4, Class-VIII, New NCERT)*

1. Phulo and Jhano, two prominent women leaders of the Santhal rebellion, actively participated in the rebellion.
2. Santhals used advanced weapons and artillery against the British.
3. The Santhal Parganas Tenancy Act was enacted which provided the tribes some protection against the oppressive British rule.

Which of the statements given above are correct?

(a) 1 and 2 (b) 2 and 3 (c) 1 and 3 (d) All of these

Ans. (c)

Exp. Statements (1) and (3) are correct regarding the Santhal revolt.

Phulo and Jhano Murmu were two prominent women leaders of the Santhal rebellion, which took place from 1855-1856. The sisters joined their brothers, Siddhu, Kanhu, Chand and Bhairav Murmu, in the fight against the Zamindari system and the British East India Company. After the end of the war, the Santhal Parganas Tenancy Act was enacted which provided the tribes some protection against the oppressive British Rule. This was successful in inculcating nationalist feelings among the people.

Statement (2) is incorrect because traditional weapons like bow and arrow were used by the Santhals while modern weapons and artillery were used by the British. However, guerrilla tactics, which was a new phenomenon for Bihar in fighting against the British, gave the advantage to the Santhals.

11 Consider the following statements with reference to the Tribal Movement in India. *(Chap 4, Class-VIII, New NCERT)*

1. New revenue system and exploitation by traders were the main reasons behind tribal movement.
2. The Warli revolt took place in Maharashtra.

Which of the statements given above is/are correct?

(a) Only 1 (b) Only 2
(c) Both 1 and 2 (d) Neither 1 nor 2

Ans. (c)

Exp. Both the statements (1) and (2) are correct with reference to the Tribal Movement in India.

The colonial rule in India witnessed large number of tribal revolts. The introduction of new revenue system, which made land a perishable commodity, promulgation of forest laws, which restricted the movement of tribals in the forest and exploitation of traders and moneylenders were the main reasons behind the tribal movement.

The Warli Adivasi revolt began in Zari village, Talasari Taluka (Maharashtra) in 1945. In this revolt, tribals who were affected from the exploitation of the landlords and moneylenders, gathered and refused to work on fields of landlords until they received 12 annas a day in wages.

12 Consider the following pairs. *(Chap 4, Class-VIII, New NCERT)*

	Tribal Movement		Year
1.	Kol	–	1910
2.	Bastar	–	1831-1832
3.	Warli	–	1945
4.	Santhal	–	1855

How many of the above pairs is/are correctly matched?

(a) Only one (b) Only two
(c) Only three (d) All of the these

Ans. (b)

Exp. Only two pair i.e., (3) and (4) are correctly matched.

Warli revolt took place in 1945 in Zari village, Talasari Taluka of Maharashtra.

Santhal rebellion took place in 1855, by the two leaders Siddhu and Kanhu Murmu against the East India Company.

Pairs (1) and (2) are incorrectly matched because Kol rebellion was a revolt of the Adivasi Kol people of Chota Nagpur during 1831-1832.

Bastar rebellion also known as the Bhumkal was an Adivasi rebellion in 1910 against British Raj in the Princely State of Bastar.

13 Which amongst the following provided a common factor for tribal insurrection in India in the 19th century? *(Chap 4, Class-VIII, New NCERT) (IAS Pre 2011)*

(a) Introduction of a new system of land revenue and taxation of tribal products.
(b) Influence of foreign religious missionaries in tribal areas.
(c) Rise of a large number of moneylenders, traders and revenue farmers as middleman in tribal areas.
(d) The complete disruption of the old agrarian order of the tribal communities.

Ans. (d)

Exp. The main reason behind tribal insurrection in India in the 19th century was complete disruption of the old agrarian order of the tribal communities. The tribals living in Central India such as Bhils, Gonds, Santhals and Mundas were deprived of forest rights of collecting fuel and fodder from the forest under the laws enacted by the British colonial authorities. It completely disrupted their old agrarian order.

Peasant Movement

14 Consider the following statements with reference to the indigo cultivation. *(Chap 3, Class-VIII, New NCERT)*

1. British pressurised the village headman to sign a contract on the behalf of the ryots.
2. Ryots received very less price for their indigo.

Which of the statements given above is/are correct?

(a) Only 1 (b) Only 2
(c) Both 1 and 2 (d) Neither 1 nor 2

Ans. (c)

Exp. Both the statements (1) and (2) are correct with reference to the indigo cultivation. Sometimes, they pressurised the village headmen to sign the contract on behalf of the *ryots*.

However, peasants received very less price for their produce. It resulted into their economic exploitation. Under the Ryotwari system, indigo cultivation was done by the ryots. The planters made the ryots to sign a contract or an agreement.

15 With reference to Indigo rebellion, consider the following statements. *(Chap 3, Class-VIII, New NCERT)*

1. It took place in Gujarat.
2. Village headman and Zamindars supported rebellion.
3. As a result of rebellion, the Indigo Commission was appointed.
4. The Commission held the planters guilty.

How many of the statements given above is/are not correct?

(a) Only one (b) Only two
(c) Only three (d) None of these

Ans. (a)

Exp. Only one statement i.e. (1) is not correct in the context of the Indigo rebellion because it was a peasant movement and subsequent uprising of indigo farmers against the indigo planters. It arose in Changacha village of Nadia in Bengal in 1859.

16 Arrange the following events in chronological order. *(Chap 1, Class-XII, New NCERT)*

1. Pabna Movement 2. Deccan Riots
3. Indigo Rebellion 4. Pagal Panthis

Codes

(a) 1-2-3-4 (b) 1-3-2-4
(c) 2-4-1-3 (d) 4-3-2-1

Ans. (d)

Exp. The correct chronological order is 4-3-2-1.

Pagal Panthi is a peasant movement which was started by religious monks named Pagal Panthi in the year 1825-1833. Its main leaders were Karam Shah and Tipu Shah.They were known for their ecstatic and unconventional behaviour often dancing, singing and wandering from place to place.

The Indigo Rebellion took place in Bengal during 1859-1860. It was a significant agrarian movement led by peasants (ryots) against the oppressive practices of indigo planters and the British colonial administration.

The Deccan riots were a series of peasant uprisings that occurred in the Deccan region of India during the late 19th century. This movement took place in 1875 in Poona, Satara and Ahmednagar areas.

The Pabna Movement (also called the Pabna Peasant Uprising) occurred between 1873 and 1876 in the Yusufshahi Pargana (now part of Sirajganj District, Bangladesh). Led by Ishan Chandra Roy, who was known as the 'Rebel King'.

17 Consider the following statements. *(Chap 13, Class-XII, Old NCERT)*

1. Bardoli Satyagraha occurred in the year 1928.
2. It was headed by the Sardar Vallabhbhai Patel.
3. He also organised a No Tax Campaign by the peasants.

Which of the statements given above is/are correct?

(a) Only 1 (b) 1 and 2 (c) 2 and 3 (d) 1, 2 and 3

Ans. (d)

Exp. All the statements (1), (2) and (3) are correct.

Bardoli Satyagraha was a Peasant movement launched in 1928 by Sardar Vallabhbhai Patel. In this Satyagraha, farmers of Bardoli in Gujarat opposed unjust increase in land revenue by 22%. A No Tax Campaign based on Gandhian principle was launched by farmers of Bardoli under the leadership of Sardar Patel. Because of the exemplary leadership of Sardar Patel and Commitment of farmers, the British colonial authorities were compelled to reduce land revenue rates.

18 Consider the following pairs. *(Chap 1, Class-XII, New NCERT)*

Revolt/ Movement		Led by
1. Pabna Movement	–	Karam Shah
2. Pagal Panthis	–	Bishnucaharan Biswas
3. Indigo Revolt	–	Ishan Chandra Roy
4. Eka Movement	–	Madari Pasi

How many of the above pairs is/are correctly matched?

(a) Only one (b) Only two
(c) Only three (d) All of the these

Ans. (a)

Exp. Only one pair i.e., (4) is correctly matched.

The Eka Movement took place in 1921 in Awadh, Uttar Pradesh. Madari Pasi was a prominent leader of this movement. The main reasons for this revolt were the Spanish flu, six years of drought, price rise and a shortage of food grains and fuel.

While, pairs (1), (2) and (3) are incorrectly matched.

The Pabna movement took place in the year 1873-1885. Its main leaders were Ishan Chandra Roy, Shambhu Nath Pal, Khodi Mulla.

The Pagal Panthi rebellion started in the year 1825-1833. It was a peasant movement led by religious mendicants called Pagal Panthi. Its main leaders were Karam Shah and Tipu Shah.

Indigo Revolt (Indigo Rebellion) was started in 1959, Biswas brothers (specifically, Bishnucaharan Biswas and Digambar Biswas) of Nadia, Rafique Mondal of Malda, and Kader Molla of Pabna were prominent leaders of this revolt.

19 **Consider the following Assertion (A) and Reason (R) and choose the correct code.** *(Chap 13, Class-XII, Old NCERT)*

Assertion (A) The two nationalist mass movements of 1920-1922 and 1930-1934 had politicised the peasants and workers on a large scale.

Reason (R) The exploitation of peasants and workers led them to raise their voice against the British.

Codes

(a) Both A and R are true and R is the correct explanation of A.

(b) Both A and R are true, but R is not the correct explanation of A.

(c) A is true, but R is false.

(d) A is false, but R is true.

Ans. (a)

Exp. Both Assertion (A) and Reason (R) are true and Reason (R) is the correct explanation of Assertion (A).

The Non-Cooperation Movement of 1920-1922 and Civil Disobedience Movement of 1930-1934 had politicised the peasants and workers on large scale.

The peasants and workers suffered from high rents, illegal levies, arbitrary evictions and unpaid labour in Zamindari areas. The Government levied heavy land revenue which led them to raise their voice against British.

Civil Rebellion

20 **Which one of the following was the primary cause of majority of civil rebellions against the British rule, before 1857?** *(Chap 5, Class-VIII, Old NCERT)*

(a) Exploitation of the village artisans and farmers by moneylenders along with Britishers.

(b) The rapid changes that the British introduced in the economy, administration and land revenue system.

(c) The Colonial Policy of intensifying demands for land revenue and extracting as large amount as possible.

(d) Not even a part of the enhanced revenue was spent on the development of agriculture or the welfare of the cultivator.

Ans. (b)

Exp. The primary cause of majority of civil rebellions against the British rule, before 1857 was rapid changes that the British introduced in the economy, administration and land revenue system.

These laws and reforms completely altered the way of life of people. They were deprived of traditional forest and civil rights enjoyed hitherto in previous regimes under princely rule. Further, the high demand of land revenue also led to the misery of the peasants.

21 **Consider the following statements about the Sanyasi Revolt.** *(Chap 4, Class-VIII, New NCERT)*

1. The Sanyasi revolt started against the British in the Murshidabad and Baikunthpur forests of Bengal.
2. Apart from Sanyasis, the rebellion saw the participation of Zamindars, peasants and artisans.
3. The main leaders of the revolt were Shambhu Nath Pal and Khodi Mulla.

How many of the statements given above is/are correct?

(a) Only one (b) Only two
(c) All three (d) None of these

Ans. (b)

Exp. Only two statements i.e., (1) and (2) are correct about the Sanyasi Revolt. Sanyasi Revolt was a rebellion that occurred in late 18th century Bengal, India, specifically in the Murshidabad and Baikunthpur forests of Jalpaiguri. The Sanyasi rebellion was a significant uprising against the British East India Company and the oppressive Zamindari system in the late 18th century. The Sanyasi rebellion (1763-1800) involved a group of Sanyasis, who were originally peasants, apart from Sanyasis and Fakirs, the revolt saw active participation of displaced Zamindars, peasants, artisans and disbanded armies of Nawabs.

Statement (3) is incorrect because the revolt took place under the leadership of Pandit Bhabani Charan Pathak and other significant figures included Majnum Shah, Chirag Ali, Musa Shah, and Debi Chaudhurani against the administration and revenue policy of the British Government.

22 **Consider the following statements.** *(Chap 4, Class-VIII, New NCERT)*

1. The Sanyasis Uprisings took place in Bengal after the great famine of 1770.
2. The Bankim Chandra Chatterjee's novel Anandamath talks of the Sanyasi Rebellion in Bengal.
3. Pandit Bhawani Sharan Pathak was the prominent leader of the 'Sanyasi Rebellion' against British control and exploitation in Bengal in the 18th century.
4. It is suppressed by Warren Hastings first Governor of Bengal.

How many of the statements given above is/are correct?

(a) Only one (b) Only two (c) Only three (d) All four

Ans. (d)

Exp. All four statements i.e., (1), (2), (3) and (4) are correct regarding Sanyasi Revolt.

The Sanyasi Rebellion took place in Bengal from 1770-1777. The rebellion was a result of the 1770 Bengal famine, which caused widespread chaos and misery. Bankim Chandra Chatterjee's novel Anandamath is set against the backdrop of the Sanyasi Rebellion of 1763-1800. The novel's plot is inspired by the Indians' fight for independence from the British. Pandit Bhawani Charan Pathak emerged as the prominent leader during the Sanyasi Rebellion. He played a crucial role in leading the Sannyasis and Sadhus in their revolt against British rule and exploitation in Bengal.

In 1771, around 150 saints were put to death, which further fueled distress and violence, especially in Natore. Warren Hastings, Governor-General of Bengal, ordered the execution of 150 unarmed Sannyasis in 1771. Despite the superior training and forces of the British East India Company, sporadic clashes with migrating ascetics continued until 1802.

23 Which of the following statements is/are correct in the context of the Paika revolt?

1. It took place in 1790. *(Chap 4, Class-VIII, New NCERT)*
2. It was led by Bakshi Jagabandhu.
3. Paikas attacked the police station and other Government establishments.
4. The Zamindars and Ryots joined the Paikas.

Codes

(a) 1, 2 and 3 (b) 2, 3 and 4
(c) 1, 2 and 4 (d) 1, 2, 3 and 4

Ans. (b)

Exp. Statements (2), (3) and (4) are correct in the context of Paika revolt.

The Paika rebellion also known as the Paika Vidroh was an armed rebellion against Company rule in Odisha. The Paikas rose in rebellion under their leader Bakshi Jagabandhu.

Bakshi Jagabandhu was the hereditary chief of the militia army of the Gajapati King of Khurda. The Paikas attacked British symbols of power, setting ablaze police stations, administrative offices and the treasury during their march towards Khurda.

The Paikas were supported by the rajas, zamindars, village heads and ordinary peasants.

Statement (1) is incorrect because Paika revolt was started in 1817.

24 Match List I with List II.

(Chap 1, Class-XII, New NCERT) (UPPSC Mains 2006)

List-I (Events)		List-II (Years)	
A.	Barrackpore Mutiny	1.	1806
B.	Behrampore Revolt	2.	1824
C.	Santhal Revolt	3.	1855-1856
D.	Vellore Mutiny	4.	1857

Select the correct answer using the codes given below.

	A	B	C	D		A	B	C	D
(a)	3	1	2	4	(b)	2	4	3	1
(c)	2	1	4	3	(d)	3	1	4	2

Ans. (b)

Exp. The correct matching is A-2, B-4, C-3, D-1.

The **Barrackpore Mutiny** was a rising of native Indian sepoys against their British officers in Barrackpore in November, 1824. During first Anglo-Burmese War (1824-1826), troops refused to participate in a mission.

Behrampur Revolt was started in February, 1857. The 19th Regiment of Bengal Native Infantry refused to receive percussion caps due to fears about new greased cartridges until confronted by cavalry and artillery.

The **Santhal Rebellion** also known as Santhal Hool, which was led by two brothers Siddhu and Kanhu in the year 1855-1856 was mainly centered between Bhagalpur and Rajmahal (Bihar).

The **Vellore Mutiny** occurred on 10th July, 1806 and it was the first instance of a large scale and violent mutiny by the Indian sepoys against the British East India Company.

25 Which of the following is/are correct in the context of the Phadke armed revolt?

(Chap 9, Class-VIII, Old NCERT)

(a) It took place in the year 1879.
(b) It was headed by the Vasudev Balwant Phadke.
(c) It was launched against the British rule.
(d) All of the above

Ans. (d)

Exp. All of the given statements are correct in the context of the Phadke armed revolt. The Phadke armed revolt or the Hamaso revolt was led by Vasudev Balwant Phadke in 1877-1879 in the Vashi and Panvel area of Maharashtra. Phadke is known as the father of the armed struggle for India's independence. It was launched against the British rule.

26 Consider the following statements with reference to the Kuka movement. *(Chap 9, Class-VIII, Old NCERT)*

1. Kuka movement was led by the Guru Ram Singh.
2. They revolted against the corrupt Mahants supported by the British.

Which of the statements given above is/are correct?

(a) Only 1 (b) Only 2
(c) Both 1 and 2 (d) Neither 1 nor 2

Ans. (a)

Exp. Statement (1) is correct with reference to the Kuka movement because the Kuka movement was the first major movement of the people in the Punjab to the new political order initiated by the British after 1849. This movement was led by Guru Ram Singh.

Statement (2) is incorrect because Kuka Movement was started with the aim to overthrow the British rule.

Miscellaneous

27 **Consider the following statements with reference to the Wahabis.** *(Chap 5, Class-VIII, Old NCERT)*

1. It was founded by Sayyid Ahmad Barelvi.
2. Bengal and Bihar were the main base of this sect.
3. They urged people to join in a holy war to overthrow the British rule.

Which of the statements given above is/are correct?

(a) Only 1 (b) 1 and 2
(c) 2 and 3 (d) 1, 2 and 3

Ans. (d)

Exp. All the given statements (1), (2) and (3) are correct regarding Wahabis.

Wahabi movement in India was a vigorous movement for socio-religious reforms in Indo-Islamic society in the 19th century. It was founded by Sayyid Ahmad of Rai Bareilly. Bengal and Bihar were the main base of this sect. Wahabis urged people to join in a holy war to overthrow the British rule.

28 **At which of the following places popular Sepoy Mutinies were held before the Revolt of 1857?** *(Chap 5, Class-VIII, Old NCERT)*

1. Vellore 2. Lucknow
3. Barrackpore 4. Bombay

Codes

(a) 1 and 2 (b) 1 and 3
(c) 2 and 3 (d) 3 and 4

Ans. (b)

Exp. Before the Revolt of 1857, popular Sepoy Mutinies were held a Vellore and Barrackpore.

The Vellore mutiny or Vellore revolution took place on 10th July, 1806 was the first instance of a large scale and violent mutiny by Indian sepoy against the East India Company.

The Barrackpore Mutiny was a rising of native Indian sepoy against their British officers in Barrackpore in November 1824.

29 **Consider the following statements.** *(Chap 13, Class-XII, Old NCERT)*

1. NM Joshi was one of the founders of All India Trade Union Congress (AITUC).
2. All India Trade Union Congress suffered a split in its Nagpur session.
3. NM Lokhande was actively involved in the formation of AITUC.

Which of the statements given above is/are correct?

(a) 1 and 2
(b) 2 and 3
(c) All of these
(d) Only 3

Ans. (c)

Exp. All the statements given above are correct

Narayan Malhar Joshi was one of the founders of AITUC. He was an Indian trade union leader and follower of Gopal Krishna Gokhale. Joshi became involved in labour issues and started the All India Trade Union Congress in 1920 along with Lala Lajpat Rai. In the year 1929, at the 10th Session in Nagpur the split of AITUC took place.The Right-Wing Leaders split away because the Trade Union Congress decided to boycott the Whitley Commission.

Narayan Meghaji Lokhande was actively involved in the formation of AITUC. He was the father of trade union movement in India.He is remembered not only for ameliorating the working conditions of textile mill-hands in the 19th century but also for his courageous initiatives on caste and communal issues.

Chapter 26

Socio-Religious Reform Movements in India

Socio-Religious Reform Movements in India

Social Reform Movements

Brahmo Samaj
- Founded by Raja Ram Mohan Roy in 1828
- Purpose was to purify Hinduism and preach monotheism

Prathana Samaj
- Founded by Atmaram Pandurang with the help of Keshub Chandra Sen in 1867; Main focus on disapproval of caste system

Arya Samaj
- Formally set-up by Swami Dayanand Saraswati at Bombay in 1875
- Focused on reforming Hindu religion and providing education

Ramkrishna Mission
- Founded by Swami Vivekanand on the name of his spiritual Guru Ramakrishna Paramhansa in 1897
- Mainly propagate the Hindu philosophy of Vedanta-Advaita Vedanta and four Yogic ideals-Jnana, Bhakti Karma and Raja Yoga

Young Bengal Movement
- Was an intellectual and radical movement among youths; Led by Henry Vivian Derozio

Theosophical Society
- Founded by Madame HP Blavatsky and Colonel MS Olcott in New York in 1875 In India it gained momentum after emergence of Annie Besant

Religious Reform Movements

Swami Narayana Sect
- Swami Sahajanand was founded Swami Narayan sect in 1822 in Gujarat
- Advocated vegetarianism and advised people to shun liquor and drugs

Deva Samaj
- Founded by Shiv Narain Agnihotri in 1887 at Lahore; Emphasised the worship of Supreme God

Wahabi Movement
- Muslim revivalist; Response to western influences and the degeneration; Led by Syed Ahmad Barelvi

Ahmadiya Movement
- Was launched by Mirza Ghulam Ahmad of Qadiyan in 1889; Opposed Jihad

Deoband Movement
- Founded in 1867 by Muhammad Qasim Nanautavi and Rashid Ahmad Gangohi
- Aim was moral and religious regeneration of the Muslim Community

Nirankari Movement
- Founded by Baba Dayal Das
- Rejected idolatry, eating meat and drinking liquor, worship of one God and nirankar formless

Prominent Social Refomers

Raja Ram Mohan Roy
- Regarded as Father of Indian Renaissance
- Organised a crusade against practice of Sati
- Assisted David Hare informing Hindu College; Wrote 'A Gift to Monotheists'

Swami Dayanand Saraswati

Founded Arya Samaj (1875); Wrote Satyarth Prakash; Gave the slogan ' Back to the Vedas'

Swami Vivekananda
- Original name Narendra Nath Dutta; Combined simple teachings of Shri Ramakrishna with his well-founded modern outlook

Annie Besant
- Laid the foundation of Central Hindu College in Banaras in 1898
- Took enormous efforts towards the cause of the education of women

Ishwar Chandra Vidyasagar
- Played crucial role in enactment of law permitting Widow Remarriage in 1856
- Protested against child marriage and campaigned against polygamy

Balshastri Jambhekar
- Father of Marathi Journalism; Edited first newspaper in Marathi language named Darpan

SOURCE **New NCERT Class VIII** (Civilising the Native, Educating the Nation), **New NCERT Class VIII** (Women, Caste and Reform), **New NCERT Class VIII** (Religious and Social Reform Movements and Cultural Awakening), **Old NCERT Class VIII** (Growth of New India-Religious and Social Reform after 1858)
Tamil Nadu Board Class XII, Unit 4 (Advent of Gandhi and Mass Mobilisation)
Tamil Nadu Board Class XI, Unit 19 (Towards Modernity)

1 **With reference to Raja Ram Mohan Roy, consider the following statements.** *(Chap 7, Class-XII, Old NCERT)*

1. He established Atmiya Sabha as a part of Brahmo Samaj.
2. Brahmo Samaj had a definite view on Karma and transmigration of soul.
3. Radha Kant Deb was an ardent supporter of the Brahmo Samaj.
4. He set up the Hindu College at Calcutta in collaboration with David Hare.

How many of the statements given above is/are correct?

(a) Only one (b) Only two
(c) Only three (d) All of these

Ans. *(a)*

Exp. Only one statement i.e., (4) is correct regarding Raja Ram Mohan Roy.

Raja Ram Mohan Roy collaborated with David Hare to establish the Hindu College in Calcutta in 1817.

Statements (1), (2) and (3) are incorrect because Raja Ram Mohan Roy established the Atmiya Sabha in 1815, which later evolved into the Brahmo Samaj in 1828. So, the Atmiya Sabha was not initially a part of Brahmo Samaj.

Brahmo Samaj, founded by Raja Ram Mohan Roy and Debendranath Tagore, did not have a definite view on Karma and transmigration of the soul. Brahmo Samaj aimed at monotheism, worship of the formless God, and rejection of idol worship, but it did not formulate specific views on Karma and the transmigration of the soul.

Radha Kant Deb was associated with the Tattwabodhini Sabha, not the Brahmo Samaj. He was a critic of Brahmo Samaj's reforms and engaged in theological debates with Roy.

2 **Which of the following statements are correct regarding contributions of Raja Ram Mohan Roy?** *(Chap 7, Class-XII, Old NCERT)*

1. He promoted introduction of English education.
2. He carried out religious reforms in Hinduism.
3. He attacked polygamy and degraded condition of women.

Codes

(a) 1 and 3 (b) 1 and 2 (c) Only 1 (d) All of these

Ans. *(d)*

Exp. All the statements are correct regarding contributions of Raja Ram Mohan Roy.

He is regarded as the first great leader of Modern India. He emphasised on the Western education, as he believed that Western culture can regenerate Indian society.

He carried out religious reforms in Hinduism and opposed idol worship, rigidity of caste and prevalence of meaningless religious rituals. He advocated monotheism and women's right. He condemned the subjugation of women and attacked polygamy and degraded condition women.

3 **Which of the following statements is/are correct regarding Brahmo Samaj?** *(Chap 8, Class-VIII, New NCERT) (IAS Pre 2012)*

1. It opposed idolatry.
2. It denied the need for a priestly class for interpreting the religious texts.
3. It popularised the doctrine that the Vedas are infallible.

Codes

(a) Only 1 (b) 1 and 2 (c) Only 3 (d) 1, 2 and 3

Ans. *(b)*

Exp. Statements (1) and (2) are correct regarding Brahmo Samaj. It was founded by Raja Ram Mohan Roy in 1828. The principles of Brahmo Samaj were as follows

It forbade idol worship and discarded meaningless rites and rituals.

It also forbade its members from attacking any religion.

It denied the need for a priestly class for interpreting the religious texts.

The Samaj actively supported the movement for widow remarriage, abolition of polygamy, women's education, etc.

Statement (3) is incorrect because Brahmo Samaj never popularised the doctrine that Vedas are infallible.

4 **Which Governor-General, described in the passage, reformed the military by prohibiting flogging as a punishment in the British Indian army, effectively controlled organised Thuggee and endeavored to eradicate prevalent superstitious practices such as Sati and widow burning?** *(Chap 8, Class-VIII, New NCERT)*

(a) Lord Warren Hastings (b) Lord Arthur Wellesley
(c) Lord William Bentinck (d) Lord Amherst

Ans. *(c)*

Exp. The Governor-General described in the passage is Lord William Bentinck. Lord William Bentinck played a crucial role in reforming the British Indian army by prohibiting the practice of flogging as a punishment. Flogging was a severe and harsh form of corporal punishment, and its prohibition was a significant step towards humane treatment within the military. In December 1829, Lord William Bentinck, the first Governor-General of British-ruled India, took a decisive step by banning the practice of Sati, eradicated the menace of Thuggee. Bentinck, along with his chief captain William Henry Sleeman, took measures to suppress Thuggee.

5 **Which of the following books were written by the Raja Ram Mohan Roy?** *(Chap 5, Class-XII, Old NCERT)*

1. Percepts of Jesus
2. Satyarth Prakash
3. Gift to Monotheists

Codes

(a) 1 and 3 (b) 2 and 3 (c) Only 3 (d) All of these

Ans. *(a)*

Exp. Among the given options, the book 'Percepts of Jesus' and 'Gift to Monotheists' were written by Raja Ram Mohan Roy.

In 1809, Raja Ram Mohan Roy wrote 'Gift to Monotheists' in Persian, in which he put forward argument against belief in many Gods.

In 1820, he published 'Percepts of Jesus' in which he tried to separate the moral and philosophic message of the New Testament.

The book 'Satyarth Prakash' is written by Dayananda Saraswati.

6 **Consider the following statements.** *(Chap 7, Class-XII, Old NCERT)*

1. Raja Ram Mohan Roy was a pioneer of Indian journalism.
2. He condemned the oppressive practices of Bengal Zamindars.
3. He also advocated for the Indianisation of the superior services.

Which of the statements given above are correct?

(a) 1 and 2
(b) 2 and 3
(c) 1, 2 and 3
(d) 1 and 3

Ans. (c)

Exp. Statements (1), (2) and (3) are correct. Raja Ram Mohan Roy was a pioneer of Indian journalism. He brought out journals in Bengali, Persian, Hindi and English to spread scientific, literary, and political knowledge among the people. He also represented popular demands and grievances before the government through his journals.

He condemned the oppressive practices of Bengal Zamindars, which had reduced the peasants to a miserable condition.

He also raised the demands for the Indianisation of the superior services. Besides it, he also advocated for the separation of the executive and judiciary, trial by jury, and judicial equality between Indians and Europeans.

7 **Which of the following statements is/are correct about Dharma Sabha?** *(Unit 4, Class-XII, Tamil Nadu Board)*

1. It was founded by Radhakanta Deb in Kolkata.
2. It was an orthodox Hindu society, established mainly to counter the ongoing Socio-Religious Reform Movements led by reformers like Henry Derozio and Raja Ram Mohan Roy.
3. The Dharma Sabha Supported the Hindu Widow Remarriage Act, 1656.

Select the correct answers using the codes given below.

(a) 1 and 2 (b) 2 and 3
(c) 1 and 3 (d) All of these

Ans. (a)

Exp. Statements (1) and (2) are correct regarding Dharma Sabha. Radhakanta Deb founded the Dharma Sabha in Calcutta in 1830. Radhakanta Deb was a scholar who was proficient in Sanskrit, Persian and Arabic. The organisation was established to counter the social reform movements led by reformers like Raja Ram Mohan Roy and Henry Derozio.

Statement (3) is incorrect because the Dharma Sabha campaigned against the Hindu Widow Remarriage Act of 1856. The society opposed liberal and radical reforms, such as the abolition of Sati Pratha. The Hindu Widow's Remarriage Act of 1856 stated that all marriages made contrary to the provisions of the section may be declared void by a court of law.

8 **Consider the following pairs.** *(Unit 19, Class-XI, Tamil Nadu Board)*

Organisation	Founded by
1. Dharma Sabha	– Raja Radhakant Deb
2. Tattvabodhini Sabha	– Rabindranath Tagore
3. Brahmo Samaj of India	– Raja Ram Mohan Roy
4. Paramahansa Mandali	– Dadoba Pandurang

How many of the pairs given above is/are correctly matched?

(a) Only one (b) Only two
(c) Only three (d) All of these

Ans. (b)

Exp. Only two pairs i.e., (1) and (4) are correctly matched.

Radhakanta Deb founded the Dharma Sabha in Calcutta in 1830. The organisation was established to oppose the Social Reform Movements led by figures like Raja Ram Mohan Roy and Henry Derozio. The Paramahansa Mandali was founded in 1849 by Dadoba Pandurang, Durgaram Mehtaji and a group of his friends.The group was closely related to the Manav Dharma Sabha, which was established in 1844 in Surat.

Pairs (2) and (3) are incorrectly matched because Debendranath Tagore established the Tattvabodhini Sabha on 6th October, 1839. Keshubsen and his followers broke away from Brahmo Samaj in 1866 and established what was called the 'Brahmo Samaj of India'.

9 **Consider the following statements with respect to Prarthana Samaj.** *(Class-XI, Old NCERT)*

1. It is a Hindu reform society established by Dadoba Pandurang in 1867.
2. It opposed the caste system and introduced widow remarriage and the abolition of child marriage.

Which of the statements given above is/are correct?

(a) Only 1
(b) Only 2
(c) Both 1 and 2
(d) Neither 1 nor 2

Ans. (c)

Exp. Both the statements (1) and (2) are correct. Prarthana Samaj was a social and religious reform movement in Bombay, India, in 1867. The movement was founded by Dadoba Pandurang and his brother Atmaram Pandurang. The movement was influenced by the Brahmo Samaj, a social-religious reform movement founded in 1828 by Raja Ram Mohan Roy. The Prarthana Samaj opposed the caste system and advocated for widow remarriage and the abolition of child marriage. It believed in the spiritual equality of all castes and the existence of one god. They also opposed untouchability, the dowry system and polygamy.

10 Which of the following statements is correct with reference to the Young Bengal Movement?

(Chap 8, Class-VIII, New NCERT)

(a) It was started by Vivian Derozio.
(b) Vivian Derozio was teacher at Sanskrit College in Calcutta.
(c) Participants of this movement supported the orthodox ideas.
(d) None of the above

Ans. (a)

Exp. Statement (a) is correct with reference to the Young Bengal Movement as it was started by Henry Vivian Derozio.

He was a teacher at Hindu College from 1826 to 1831. The participants of this Movement attacked the old and decadent customs, rites and demanded education for masses. They were passionate advocates of women's rights and demanded education for them. They were liberal and opposed the orthodox ideas.

11 Consider the following statements with regard to Ishwar Chandra Vidyasagar.

(Chap 8, Class-VIII, New NCERT)

1. He was born in 1820 in Bengal.
2. He promoted study of Sanskrit to the lower class.
3. He played a key role in the passing of the law which made the marriage of widow legal.

Which of the statements given above is/are correct?

(a) Only 1 (b) 1 and 2
(c) 2 and 3 (d) 1, 2 and 3

Ans. (d)

Exp. Statements (1), (2) and (3) are correct regarding Ishwar Chandra Vidyasagar. Ishwar Chandra Vidyasagar was born in 1820, in Bengal. He was a great scholar and social reformer.

He introduced the study of modern Western thought in the Sanskrit College and admitted students from the so-called lower castes to study Sanskrit. Earlier, Sanskrit was the monopoly of Brahmins and the lower castes were not allowed to study it.

He also played an instrumental role in passing the Widow Remarriage Act in 1856. Because of his constant agitation and advocacy, widow remarriage was made legal.

12 Which of the following belongs to Prarthana Samaj?

(Class-XI, Old NCERT)

1. Dr Atmaram Pandurang
2. Keshab Chandra Sen
3. RG Bhandarkar
4. Mahadev Gobind Ranade
5. NG Chandavarkar
6. P Anandacharlu

Choose the correct answer using the codes given below.

(a) 1, 2, 3 and 5 (b) 1, 2, and 6
(c) 1, 3, 5 and 6 (d) 1, 2, 3, 4, and 5

Ans. (d)

Exp. Dr. Atmaram Pandurang, Keshab Chandra Sen, RG Bhandarkar, Mahadev Gobind Ranade and NG Chandavarkar are associated with Prarthana Samaj. In 1867, Keshab Chandra Sen assisted Atmaram Pandurang in establishing the Prarthana Samaj in Bombay. Mahadev Govind Ranade joined the society in 1870, his efforts helped the society develop a reputation throughout India. RG Bhandarkar and NG Chandavarkar were the additional society head.

Prarthana Samaj (Prayer Society) is a Hindu reform movement that originated in Bombay in 1867. The movement was inspired by the Brahmo Samaj, a similar reform movement in Bengal. The Prarthana Samaj advocated for several social reforms, including opposition to the caste system, introduction of widow remarriage, encouragement of female education and abolition of child marriage.

P. Anandacharlu wasn't associated with the Prarthana Samaj, he was involved in Madras Mahajana Sabha, founded in 1884, this organisation aimed to uplift the social and educational status of Indians in the Madras Presidency.

13 Which of the following statements are correct about Prarthana Samaj? *(Chap 8, Class-VIII, Old NCERT)*

1. It was an offshoot of Arya Samaj of India.
2. It was a reform movement within Hinduism.
3. It was established in the year 1860.
4. It concentrated on social reforms like intercaste marriage, remarriage of widows and upliftment of woman of depressed classes.

Codes

(a) 1 and 3 (b) 1, 2 and 3 (c) 2 and 4 (d) All of these

Ans. (c)

Exp. Statements (2) and (4) are correct about Prarthana Samaj.

Prarthana Samaj was founded by Atmaram Pandurang in 1867. Justice Mahadev Govind Ranade joined this society in 1870. The aim of the society was the promulgation of theistic worship and social reform. Its early goals were opposition of the caste system, introduction of widow remarriage, the encouragement of female education and the abolition of child marriage.

14 Who among the following was responsible for the revival of Vedas?

(Chap 8, Class-VIII, Old NCERT) (UPPSC Pre 1995)

(a) Ramkrishna Paramhansa (b) Ramanuja
(c) Swami Dayananda Saraswati (d) Swami Vivekananda

Ans. (c)

Exp. Swami Dayananda Saraswati was responsible for the revival of Vedas. He gave the slogan of 'Go Back to Vedas' and attributed all the beliefs from the Vedic period. He denied the authenticity of Puranas, as he believed that they were responsible for idolatry in Hinduism. He popularised the doctrine that the Vedas are infallible.

15 Consider the following statements.

(Chap 8, Class-VIII, Old NCERT)

1. Dayananda Saraswati founded the Arya Samaj in 1875.
2. The Arya Samaj repudiated the authority of the caste system.
3. Dayananda Saraswati's real name was Narendra Nath.

Which of the statements given above are correct?

(a) 1, 2 and 3 (b) 1 and 2 (c) 2 and 3 (d) 1 and 3

Ans. (b)

Exp. Statements (1) and (2) are correct.

Dayananda Saraswati founded the Arya Samaj in Bombay in 1875. It supported four Varna system but also believed that it should be based on merit not birth. It believed that Hindu religion gives everyone an equal place in the spiritual and social life. In this way, it repudiated the authority of the caste system.

Statement (3) is incorrect because Dayananda Saraswati's real name was Mool Shankar.

16 Which of the following statements is incorrect with reference to Dayananda Saraswati and Arya Samaj in India? *(Chap 8, Class-VIII, Old NCERT)*

(a) He believed that Vedas were fallible.
(b) He launched Shuddhi Movement.
(c) Arya Samajists opposed child marriage and encouraged remarriage of women.
(d) None of the above

Ans. (a)

Exp. Statement (a) is incorrect regarding Dayananda Saraswati and Arya Samaj because it believed that Vedas were infallible. Dayananda Saraswati looked upon the Vedas as 'India's Rock of Ages'. He believed that the Hindu religion and the Vedas on which it was based were eternal, unalterable, infallible and divine. Therefore, he gave the slogan 'Go Back to the Vedas' and 'the Vedas are the Source of All Knowledge'.

According to him, the later Hindu scriptures such as Puranas were responsible for the evil practice of idol worship and other superstitious beliefs in the Hindu religion.

17 Which of the following pairs are correctly matched?

(Chap 8, Class-VIII, Old NCERT)

Social Reform Movement	Founder
1. Brahmo Samaj	– Swami Brahmanand
2. Dev Samaj	– Pandit Shiv Narayan Agnihotri
3. Arya Samaj	– Swami Dayananda Saraswati
4. Ramkrishna Mission	– Swami Ramkrishna Paramhansa

Codes

(a) 1 and 2 (b) 2 and 3
(c) 3 and 4 (d) 1 and 4

Ans. (b)

Exp. Pairs (2) and (3) are correctly matched.

Dev Samaj was founded in 1887, at Lahore by Pandit Shiv Narayan Agnihotri, an erstwhile founder of Brahmo Samaj.

Arya Samaj was founded by Swami Dayananda Saraswati on 7th April, 1875 in Bombay.

Pairs (1) and (4) are incorrectly matched.

Brahmo Samaj was founded by Raja Ram Mohan Roy in 1828, which is earlier known as Brahmo Sabha.

Ramkrishna Mission was established by Swami Vivekananda in 1897. Swami Vivekananda was the chief disciple of Swami Ramkrishna Paramhansa.

18 Consider the following statements with reference to the Bal Shastri Jambhekar. *(Chap 13, Class-XII, Old NCERT)*

1. He started a weekly newspaper named Darpan.
2. He was first social reformer of Bombay.

Which of the statements given above is/are correct?

(a) Only 1 (b) Only 2
(c) Both 1 and 2 (d) Neither 1 nor 2

Ans. (c)

Exp. Both the statements (1) and (2) are correct with reference to the Bal Shastri Jambhekar.

Bal Shastri Jambhekar was a pioneer of Social reform through journalism in Bombay. He started the weekly newspaper 'Darpan' in 1832. He is known as the Father of Marathi Journalism. In 1840, he started 'Digdarshan' which published articles on science and history.

19 Consider the following statements about Paramahansa Mandali. *(Chap 8, Class-VIII, Old NCERT)*

1. It was founded by Dadoba Pandurang, Mehtaji Durgaram in Maharashtra in 1849.
2. Its founders advocated for the worship of one God and challenged the caste system.
3. Dadoba outlined seven principles in his book Dharma Vivechan, emphasising universal love, moral conduct and accessibility of knowledge.

How many of the statements given above is/are correct?

(a) Only one (b) Only two
(c) All three (d) None of these

Ans. (c)

Exp. All three statements i.e., (1), (2) and (3) are correct. Paramahansa Mandali was founded by Dadoba Pandurang, Mehtaji Durgaram and others in Maharashtra in 1849. It was a socio-religious reform movement. Its founders had a single-god belief and were primarily motivated by caste restrictions. Members ate food prepared by members of low castes during its sessions. In 1848, Dadoba Pandurang wrote down some important ideas in a book called "Dharma Vivechan". These are below

Worship should be limited to God alone.

Love and morality serve as the foundation of true religion.

Everyone should receive the proper education in an equal manner.

There is just one caste of humanity.

Reason should be the foundation of our words and deeds.

Thought freedom should be guaranteed to every person.

There is only one form of spirituality.

20 Which of the statements given below are incorrect about Vivekananda? *(Chap 8, Class-VIII, Old NCERT)*

1. He was guru of Ramakrishna.
2. He died in the year 1910.
3. He promoted Indian Culture.
4. He urged people of India to work for their own salvation.

Codes

(a) 1, 2 and 3 (b) 2, 3 and 4
(c) 1, 3 and 4 (d) 1 and 2

Ans. (d)

Exp. Statements (1) and (2) are incorrect about Swami Vivekananda. He was the chief disciple of the 19th century mystic Ramakrishna Paramhansa and established Ramakrishna Mission in 1897. He died at Belur Math (West Bengal) in 1902.

Statements (3) and (4) are correct as Swami Vivekananda introduced the world to the Indian philosophies of Vedanta and Yoga. He preached 'neo-Vedanta', an interpretation of Hinduism. Similar to Gautama Buddha, he urged people of India to work for their own salvation and reject orthodox religious practices.

21 Consider the following statements regarding Mahadev Govind Ranade. *(Class-XI, Old NCERT) (MPPSC Pre 2012)*

1. He was influenced by Saint Tukaram.
2. He established many institutions.
3. He was a moderate.
4. He promoted adult education and remarriage.

Which of the statements given above is/are correct?

(a) 2 and 3
(b) 1, 2 and 3
(c) 2, 3 and 4
(d) All of the above

Ans. (d)

Exp. All the given statements are correct about Mahadev Govind Ranade. MG Ranade was influenced by Saint Tukaram, while he attended Prarthana Samaj meetings. He used Tukaram's Abhangas and argued that the principal message of Bhagwat Dharma was compassion, love, devotion and humility. He established many institution like Poona Sarvajanik Sabha (1870), Vaktruttvottejak Sabha (1875), etc. MG Ranade was one of the founding members of Indian National Congress. He belonged to the moderate group in Congress. He strenuously advocated widow remarriage and female education. He was one of the founders of the Widow Remarriage Association in 1861.

22 Consider the following passage. *(Chap 8, Class-VIII, Old NCERT)*

Its establishment was inspired from the Brahmo Samaj. It was setup at Madras in the year 1864. It advocated discarding of caste distinction of widow remarriage and girls education. It also condemned the superstitions and rituals of orthodox Hinduism.

Which organisation is being described in the above paragraph?

(a) Brahmo Sabha (b) Justice Movement
(c) Veda Samaj (d) Arya Samaj

Ans. (c)

Exp. The description given in question is about Veda Samaj which was established by Keshab Chandra Sen and K Sridharalu Naidu in 1864. Naidu renamed the Veda Samaj as Brahmo Samaj of Southern India in 1871.

Caste Movement and Organisations

23 Consider the following statements in the context of the Paramhansa Mandali. *(Chap 8, Class-VIII, New NCERT)*

1. It was founded in 1840.
2. Its main objective is to abolish caste system.
3. Its headquarters was in Calcutta.
4. The member of this group believed in violent means.

Which of the statements given above are incorrect?

(a) 1 and 2 (b) 2 and 3
(c) 1 and 3 (d) 1, 3 and 4

Ans. (d)

Exp. Statements (1), (3) and (4) are incorrect in the context of the Paramhansa Mandali.

Paramhansa Mandali was founded by Dadoba Pandurang and Balshastri Jambhekar of Maharashtra in 1849. The principles of the Samaj denied polytheism of popular Hinduism, the caste system and the Brahmanical monopoly of knowledge. Its headquarter was in Bombay.

24 Consider the following literary works. *(Class-XI, Old NCERT)*

1. Tuhfat-ul-Muwahhidin 2. Vedanta Gantha
3. Kenopanishads 4. The Precepts of Jesus

Which of the above-mentioned works are the creations of Raja Ram Mohan Roy?

(a) 1, 2, and 3 (b) 2, 3, and 4
(c) 1 and 3 (d) All of these

Ans. (d)

Exp. All literary works are related to Raja Ram Mohan Roy.

Raja Ram Mohan Roy (1772-1833) wrote Tuhfat-ul-Muwahhidin (A Gift to Monotheists) in 1804. It was originally written in Persian by Shaykh Wali Allah al-Dihlawi. The book was Roy's first work and was written in Persian with an introduction in Arabic. Vedanta Gantha was written by Raja Ram Mohan Roy in 1815. Raja Ram Mohan Roy translated the Kenopanishad into Bengali in 1816.

The Kenopanishad is one of the principal Upanishads, exploring profound spiritual concepts and the nature of reality. Raja Ram Mohan Roy also wrote 'The Precepts of Jesus in 1820'. The book is a collection of teachings and moral principles extracted from the New Testament of the Bible. In it, Roy emphasises monotheism and tries to separate the miracle from philosophical and moral messages.

25 Satya Shodhak Samaj organised *(Chap 8, Class-VIII, Old NCERT) (IAS Pre 2016)*

(a) a movement for the upliftment of tribals in Bihar.
(b) a Temple Entry Movement in Gujarat.
(c) an Anti-Caste Movement in Western India.
(d) a Peasant Movement in Punjab.

Ans. (c)

Exp. The Satya Shodhak Samaj organised an Anti-Caste Movement in Western India. It was founded by Jyotirao Phule in 1873 in Pune, Maharashtra.

The main objective of the group was to liberate the social status of Shudra and untouchable castes. He preached that there is no requirement of intermediary such as priest or a preceptor to offer his prayer to God.

26 Consider the following statements about Arya Samaj. *(Chap 13, Class-XII, Old NCERT)*

1. It emphasised monotheism, the rejection of idol worship and the importance of Vedic education.
2. 'The Suddhi Movement' was started by the Arya Samaj, Its agenda was to end the practice of untouchability by converting people ostracised from other religions to Hinduism.

Which of the statements given above is/are correct?

(A) Only 1 (b) Only 2
(c) Both 1 and 2 (d) Neither 1 nor 2

Ans. (c)

Exp. Both the statements (1) and (2) are correct as the Arya Samaj is an Indian Hindu reform movement that emphasises monotheism, the rejection of idol worship, and the importance of Vedic education. The Arya Samaj's beliefs and practices are based on the belief in the infallible authority of the Vedas. The 'Shuddhi Movement' was started by the Arya Samaj and its founder was Swami Dayanand Saraswati. It had a social reform agenda behind its rational and was aimed at abolishing the practice of untouchability by converting outcasts from other religion to Hinduism.

27 Which of the following pairs is correctly matched? *(Chap 8, Class-VIII, Old NCERT)*

(a) Satnami Movement – Ghasidas
(b) Matua Mahasangha – Haridas Thakur
(c) Self Respect Movement – EV Ramaswamy
(d) All of the above

Ans. (d)

Exp. All the pairs are correctly matched.

The Satnami Movement in Central India was founded by Ghasidas who worked among the leather workers and organised a movement to improve their social status. The Matua Mahasangha was a religious reform movement and a sect formed by Haridas Thakur in East Bengal.

The Self Respect Movement was started by EV Ramaswamy. It is also called the Dravidian Movement.

28 Match List I with List II . *(Class-XI, Old NCERT)*

List I	List II
A. Theosophical Society	1. Hridaynath Kunzru
B. Satya Shodhak Samaj	2. Rama Bai
C. Sewa Samiti	3. Blavatsky
D. Sharda Sadan	4. Jyoti Rao Phule

Codes

	A	B	C	D
(a)	1	2	4	3
(b)	3	4	2	1
(c)	3	4	1	2
(d)	2	4	1	3

Ans. (c)

Exp. The correct matching is A-3, B-4, C-1, D-2.

The **Theosophical Society** was founded by HP Blavatsky and HS Olcott in New York in 1875. Society emphasised the commonality of human culture.

Jyotiba Phule founded **Satya Shodhak** Samaj in Pune, Maharashtra, in 1873. It was a reformational society that promoted education and increased social rights, justice and political access in the deprived sections.

Hridayanath Kunzru founded the **Seva Samiti** in Allahabad in 1914. Kunzru was a member of the Servants of Indian Society and a member of the Constituent Assembly of India.

Pandita Ramabai Sarasvati, an Indian social reformer, established **Sharda Sadan** in 1889. The school was dedicated to young widowed women in Mumbai.

29 Which of the following statements is correct regarding Kandukuri Veerasalingam?
(Chap 8, Class-VIII, Old NCERT)

(a) He started Telugu journal to promote social reform.
(b) He promoted girls education and widow remarriage.
(c) He was influenced by the ideas of the Brahmo Samaj.
(d) All of the above

Ans. (d)

Exp. All the given statements are correct regarding Kandukuri Veerasalingam.

He is considered as the 'Father of Renaissance Movement' in Telugu. He wrote the first novel in Telugu language. He set up schools for the education of girls and women. He also performed the first widow remarriage in Andhra Pradesh. He was influenced by the ideas of the Brahmo Samaj.

30 Consider the following statements with reference to the Dharma Paripalana Yogam.
(Chap 8, Class-VIII, Old NCERT)

1. It was founded by the Narayan Guru in 1903.
2. Through this organisation, Narayan Guru cherished the idea of 'one caste, one religion and one God' for all.

Which of the statements given above is/are incorrect?

(a) Only 1 (b) Only 2
(c) Both 1 and 2 (d) Neither 1 nor 2

Ans. (a)

Exp. Statement (1) is incorrect regarding Dharma Paripalana Yogam.

The Sree Narayana Dharma Paripalana Yogam was founded by Padmanabhan Palpu and other Ezhava leaders of Kerala in 1903 with the guidance and blessings of Sree Narayana Guru. The society worked for the upliftment of lower castes by educating them and opposed Brahmin domination.

31 Consider the following statements with reference to the Self-Respect Movement.
(Chap 8, Class-VIII, New NCERT)

1. Its base was in North-Western India.
2. Its most prominent objective was to fight for the women rights.

Which of the statements given above is/are correct?

(a) Only 1 (b) Only 2
(c) Both 1 and 2 (d) Neither 1 nor 2

Ans. (d)

Exp. Neither statements (1) nor (2) are correct regarding Self-Respect Movement.

It was started by EV Ramaswamy Naicker in Tamil Nadu in 1925. It was an egalitarian movement that propagated the ideologies of breaking down of the Brahmanical hegemony, equal rights of the backward classes and women in the society.

32 During the period of the socio-religious reforms, there were many organisations which opposed the socio-religious reform. Which of the following are such organisations? *(Chap 8, Class-VIII, New NCERT)*

1. Sanatan Dharma Sabha
2. Bharat Dharma Mahamandal
3. Arya Samaj
4. Brahman Sabha

Codes

(a) 1, 2 and 3 (b) 2, 3 and 4 (c) 1, 2 and 4 (d) All of these

Ans. (c)

Exp. Sanatan Dharma Sabha, Bharat Dharma Mahamandal and Brahman Sabha are the organisations that opposed the socio-religious reforms during 19th century.

Arya Samaj did not opposed socio-religious reforms as it was an Indian Hindu Reform Movement that promoted the values and practices mentioned in Vedas. Arya Samaj was founded by Dayananda Saraswati in 1875.

33 Consider the following statements
(Chap 13, Class-XII, Old NCERT) (UPPSC Pre 2019)

Statement-I The Arya Samaj Movement gave self-confidence and self-reliance to the Hindus.

Statement-II The Arya Samaj Movement undermined the belief in superiority of White Race.

Which one of the following is correct in respect of the above statements?

(a) Both Statement-I and Statement-II are correct and Statement-II is the correct explanation for Statement-I.
(b) Both Statement-I and Statement-II are correct and Statement-II is not the correct explanation for Statement-I.
(c) Statement -I is correct, but Statement- II is incorrect
(d) Statement -I is incorrect, but Statement -II is correct

Ans. (b)

Exp. Both Statement-1 and Statement-II are correct and Statement-II is not the correct explanation for Statement-I.

Arya Samaj Movement gave self-confidence and self-reliance to the Hindus. It is a monotheistic Indian Hindu Reform Movement that promoted the values and practices based on the belief in the infallible authority of the Vedas. Dayanand's vision of India included a classless and casteless society, an united India (religiously, socially and nationally) and an India free from foreign rule, with Aryan religion being the common religion of all. Thus, he undermined the belief in superiority of White Race.

34 Consider the following statements.
(Chap 13, Class-XII, Old NCERT)

1. Arya Samaj prevented the conversion of Hindus to other religion.
2. Arya Samajist, Hansraj started the Gurukul near Haridwar in 1902.

Which of the statements given above is/are correct?
(a) Only 1 (b) Only 2
(c) Both 1 and 2 (d) Neither 1 nor 2

Ans. (a)

Exp. Statement (1) is correct as Arya Samaj inculcated a spirit of self-respect and self-reliance. At the same time, one of the Arya Samaj's objectives was to prevent the conversion of Hindus to other religion. However, this crusade against other religion became contributory factor in the growth of communalism in India in the 20th century.

Statement (2) is incorrect because Arya Samajist, Swami Shradhananda started the Gurukul near Haridwar in 1902, to propagate the more traditional ideals of education.

Reforms among Muslims, Parsis and Sikhs

35 Match List I with List II. *(Chap 8, Class-VIII, Old NCERT)*

List I (Movement)	List II (Associated leader)
A. Faraizi Movement	1. Syed Ahmad Khan
B. Deoband Movement	2. Haji Shariatullah
C. Aligarh Movement	3. Muhammad Qasim
D. Tariqa Movement	4. Titu Mir

Codes

	A	B	C	D		A	B	C	D
(a)	1	2	4	3	(b)	3	4	2	1
(c)	3	4	1	2	(d)	2	3	1	4

Ans. (d)

Exp. The correct matching is A-2, B-3, C-1, D-4.

Haji Shariatullah (1781-1840) founded the Faraizi Movement in 1818. The movement's objectives were to revive Islam and improve the condition of Muslim peasants who were opposed by Hindu and British landlords.

Muhammad Qasim Nanotavi and Rashid Ahmed Gangohi founded the Deoband Movement in 1866. The movement's goal was to educate Muslims and abolish British rule to restore the Muslim community. The movement began at the Darul Uloom, an Islamic academic center in Deoband, Saharanpur.

Sir Syed Ahmad Khan (1817-1898) founded the Aligarh Movement in 1875. Khan was a prominent Muslim reformer in the 19th century. He was a vocal opponent of medieval backwardness and a supporter of a logical approach to religion.

Titu Mir was the leader of the Tariqa Movement in West Bengal. The Tariqah-i-Muhammadiya was a Muslim revivalist movement that started in the early 19th century. The movement's goal was to establish the code of life that the Prophet Muhammad advocated.

36 Which reformer does the following passage relate to? *(Chap 8, Class-VIII, Old NCERT)*

"He insisted on the cooperation of the Muslims with the British Government and looked at all political movements with distrust. Thus, when the Indian National Congress was formed, he opposed it. He regarded education alone as the means of national progress."

Codes
(a) Keshab Chandra Sen (b) Lord Macaulay
(c) Sir Syed Ahmad Khan (d) Badruddin Tyabji

Ans. (c)

Exp. The following passage is related to Sir Syed Ahmad Khan. He was one of the greatest Muslim reformers of India. He interpreted Quran in the light of modern rationalism and science. He took up the struggle against fanaticism, ignorance, narrow mindedness and bigotry and laid emphasis on free thinking.

37 Consider the following Assertion (A) and Reason (R) and choose the correct code. *(Chap 8, Class-VIII, Old NCERT)*

Assertion (A) Sir Syed Ahmad Khan discouraged scientific learning among Muslims.

Reason (R) The Mohammedan Literary Society of Calcutta was founded by Nawab Abdul Latif.

Codes
(a) Both A and R are true and R is the correct explanation of A.
(b) Both A and R are true, but R is not the correct explanation of A.
(c) A is true, but R is false.
(d) A is false, but R is true.

Ans. (d)

Exp. Assertion (A) is false, but Reason (R) is true.
Sir Syed Ahmad Khan stressed on the importance of modern scientific education for Muslims to advance their conditions. The Mohammedan Literary Society of Calcutta (Now Kolkata) was founded in 1863, by Nawab Abdul Latif. It promoted Western education among Indian Muslims.

38 Which of the following statements was/were made by Sir Syed Ahmad Khan? *(Chap 8, Class-VIII, Old NCERT) (MPSC Pre 2001)*

1. Unless the modern education and English language are adopted, the progress of Muslims is difficult.
2. Hindus and Muslims are two eyes of an Indian bride.
3. Hindu and Muslim are two separate nations in Hindustan.
4. Muslims should stay away from Indian National Congress.

Codes
(a) 1 and 2 (b) 3 and4 (c) Only 3 (d) All of these

Ans. (d)

Exp. All the given statements were made by Sir Syed Ahmad Khan. Syed Ahmad Khan wanted Muslims to learn Western Science and English to progress and get jobs. He believed that unless the modern education and English language are adopted, the progress of Muslims is difficult. Speaking at a meeting of the Indian Association, he spoke how Hindu and Muslim constitute the two eyes of a beautiful bride. He stated that Muslims and Hindus constituted two separate nations. Syed Ahmad Khan took the reactionary view on Indian politics and launched propaganda against the Congress. He called the Congress a Hindu- dominated organisation and adviced Muslims to stay away from it.

39 Consider the following statements about Rahnumai Mazdayasnan Sabha. *(Chap-10, Class-XII, Old NCERT)*

1. Rahnumai Mazdayasnan Sabha was founded by a group of English-educated Parsis in 1851.
2. Its object was the regeneration of the social condition of the Parsis and the restoration of the Zoroastrian religion to its pristine purity.

Which of the statements given above is/are correct?

(a) Only 1 (b) Only 2
(c) Both 1 and 2 (d) Neither 1 nor 2

Ans. (c)

Exp. Both the statements (1) and (2) are correct.

A group of English-educated Parsis established the Rahnumai Mazdayasnan Sabha (Religious Reform Association) in 1851. The movement's leaders included Naoroji Furdonji, Dadabhai Naoroji, KR Cama and SS Bengalee. The group's goal was to "regeneration of the social conditions of the Parsis and the restoration of the Zoroastrian faith to its pristine purity". The Sabha campaigned for the education of Parsi priests and the spread of Western education among the Parsis, including girls. The Sabha also stood against social consciousness that deterred women and girls from getting educated and orthodoxies regarding their marriages and social position.

40 At which of the following places, Singh Sabha Movement was formed? *(Chap 8, Class-VIII, Old NCERT)*

1. Amritsar 2. Lucknow 3. Lahore 4. Delhi

Codes

(a) 1 and 3 (b) 2 and 3 (c) 2 and 4 (d) 3 and 4

Ans. (a)

Exp. The Sikh reform movement, namely Singh Sabha Movement was started in 1870s. Singh Sabha was formed at Amritsar and Lahore. The two Sabhas were later merged. It played an important role in the spread of education.

41 Consider the following statements. *(Chap 10, Class-XII, Old NCERT)*

1. Akali Movement was started in 1921.
2. Gurdwara Act was enacted in the year 1925 as a result of Akali Movement.
3. Khalsa College in Amritsar was started before the beginning of Akali Movement.

Which of the statements given above is/are correct?

(a) Only 1 (b) 1 and 2
(c) 2 and 3 (d) 1, 2 and 3

Ans. (d)

Exp. All the statements (1), (2) and (3) are correct.

The Akali Movement also called Gurdwara Reform Movement. This campaign brought reform in the Gurdwaras in India during the early 1920s.

This movement led to the introduction of Gurdwara Act in 1925, which placed all the historical Sikh shrines in India under the control of Shiromani Gurdwara Parbandhak Committee.

Khalsa College in Amritsar was founded in 1892.

Women's Education and Other Women Specific Reforms

42 Which of the following pairs is correctly matched? *(Class-XI, Old NCERT)*

	Organisation		Associated leader
(a)	Poona Sarvajanik Sabha	–	Shiv Narayan Agnihotri
(b)	Radha Swami Satsang	–	MG Ranade
(c)	Dev Samaja	–	Shivdayal Sahab
(d)	Asiatic Society of Bengal	–	William Jones

Ans. (d)

Exp. Only pair (d) is correctly matched.

The Asiatic Society of Bengal was founded by Sir William Jones, a British lawyer and Orientalist, 15th January, 1784. The society was established at Fort William in Kolkata to promote Oriental studies.

While The Poona Sarvajanik Sabha was founded in 1870 by Mahadev Govind Ranade, Ganesh Vasudeo Joshi, SH Chiplunkar and their associates. The organisation was a sociopolitical group in British India that acted as a mediator between the government and the people to promote the legal rights of the peasantry.

The Radha Swami Satsang is an esoteric Hindu and Sikh sect founded in 1861 by Shiv Dayal Saheb in Agra, India. The sole purpose of this satsang is to experience the divinity of God who resides in all of us.

The Dev Samaj was founded by Shiv Narayan Agnihotri. The main objective of Dev Samaj were to propagate beauty, truth and goodness in thoughts, action and speech, among all the classes of people, irrespective of their colour, creed, caste or country.

43 Which of the following statements is correct regarding Pandita Ramabai? *(Chap 8, Class-VIII, Old NCERT)*

1. She was a scholar of Sanskrit.
2. She founded a widow's home at Poona to provide shelter to women's.

Codes

(a) Only 1 (b) Only 2
(c) Both 1 and 2 (d) Neither 1 nor 2

Ans. (c)

Exp. Both the statements (1) and (2) are correct regarding Pandita Ramabai.

Pandita Ramabai was a women's rights and education activist. She was a pioneer in the education and emancipation of women in India and a social reformer. She started Sadan for Child in the late 1890's, She founded Muki Mission at Kedgaon village in Pune.

She was the first woman to be awarded the titles of Pandita as a Sanskrit Scholar and Saraswati after being examined by faculty of the University of Calcutta.

44 Who founded the Widow Remarriage Association in the 1850's? *(Chap 5, Class-XII, Old NCERT)*

(a) Iswar Chandra Vidyasagar
(b) Vishnu Shastri Pandit
(c) Mahadev Govinda Ranade
(d) Jyotirao Govindrao Phule

Ans. (b)

Exp. The Widow Remarriage Association was founded by Vishnu Shastri Pandit in 1850, in Bombay. It's aim was to promote Widow Remarriage and to campaign against child marriages.

Cultural Awakening

45 Which social reformer founded the Gujarati weekly 'Satya Prakash' to promote widow remarriage? *(Chap 13, Class-XII, Old NCERT)*

(a) Jaganath Shankar Seth
(b) Bhau Daji
(c) Karsondas Mulji
(d) Vishnu Shastri Pandit

Ans. (c)

Exp. Karsondas Mulji founded the Gujarati weekly 'Satya Prakash' to promote widow remarriage, in 1852. It was later merged with Rast Goftar, another newspaper published in Bombay. Jaganath Seth, Bhau Daji and Vishnu Shastri Pandit are also some of the prominent social reformers who advocated the women's education. Vishnu Shastri pandit founded the Widow Remarriage Association in the 1850s.

46 Consider the following statements with reference to the Tatvabodhini Sabha. *(Chap 5, Class-XII, Old NCERT)*

1. It was founded in the year 1849.
2. It promoted a systematic study of India's past in the Bengali language.

Which of the statements given above is/are incorrect?

(a) Only 1
(b) Only 2
(c) Both 1 and 2
(d) Neither 1 nor 2

Ans. (a)

Exp. Statement (1) is incorrect regarding Tatvabodhini Sabha. Tatvabodhini Sabha was founded by Debendranath Tagore in 1839. The main objective of the Sabha was to promote a more rational and humanist form of Hinduism based on the Vedanta, the Upanishads that form the last part of the Vedas.

47 Consider the subsequent statements with reference to the Theosophical society *(Chap 10, Class-XII, Old NCERT)*

1. Annie Besant founded the Theosophical society in New York City, United States in 1875.
2. It rejected the Hindu beliefs in reincarnation.
3. The Theosophical Movement came to be conflated with the Hindu renaissance.

How many of the statements given above is/are incorrect?

(b) Only one (c) Only two
(c) All three (b) None of these

Ans. (b)

Exp. Only two statements i.e., (1) and (2) are incorrect regarding Theosophical society. Madame HP Blavatsky and Colonel MS Olcott founded the Theosophical Society in New York City in 1875. The society's headquarters were established in Adyar, India in, 1882. Annie Besant (1847-1933) became President of the Theosophical Society in India in 1917, making the movement more popular. The Theosophical Society believes that a special relationship can be established between a person's soul and God through contemplation, prayer and revelation. It accepts the Hindu beliefs in reincarnation and karma and draws inspiration from the philosophy of the Upanishads and Samkhya, yoga and Vedanta schools of thought.

48 Which of the following statements about Theosophical Society are correct? *(Chap 10, Class-XII, Old NCERT)*

1. Its founders were non-Indians.
2. In India, its headquarters was in Calcutta.
3. Its advocates were in favour of the revival of Hinduism.
4. It recognised the doctrine of the transmigration of soul.

Codes

(a) 1, 2 and 3 (b) 2, 3 and 4 (c) 1, 3 and 4 (d) 1 and 2

Ans. (c)

Exp. Statements (1), (3) and (4) are correct about Theosophical Society.

The Theosophical Society was founded by Madam HP Blavatsky and Colonel Olcott in New York, in 1875. The Theosophists respected all religions.

Its advocates were however in favour of the revival of Hinduism and Vedic learning. It recognised the doctrine of Karma and transmigration of soul.

Statement (2) is incorrect because the society has its centre in India in Adyar, near Madras.

Chapter 27

Development of Education and Press During the British Rule

Development of Education and Press During the British Rule

Development of Education

Education Under East India Company

- Warren Hasting set-up Calcutta Madrasa for Muslim law in 1781; Jonathan Duncan started Sanskrit College at Varanasi; Fort William College set-up by Wellesley in 1800 to train Civil Servants of company

Orientalist-Anglicist Controversy

- Ultimately Macaulay's minute settled debate favouring English education for small minorities under Downward Filtration Theory

Wood's Despatch (1854)

- Referred as 'Magna Carta of English Education in India'; Rejected downward filtration theory and favoured mass education
- Hierarchy of education-Vernacular primary schools (villages), Anglo-Vernacular (High School)

Development of Education in Post-Independence Era

- **Radhakrishnan Commission** (1948) Establishment of University Grants Commission (UGC); Central Government got responsibility to promote higher education
- **Kothari Education Commission** (1964-66) Provide free and compulsory education for children between 6 to 14 years; Three language formula

Development of Education Under Crown Rule

Hunter Education Commission (1882-83)

- Established to review the progress of education in country; Transfer of control of primary education to district and municipal boards

Indian University Act (1904)

- Raleigh Commission set-up to suggest measures for improvement of working of universities
- Based on its recommendations, the Indian Universities act was passed

Government Resolution on Education Policy (1913)

- Urged provincial governments to take early steps to provide free elementary education to the poorer and more backward section

Saddler University Commission

- Set-up to study and report on problems of Calcutta University; Three-year degree course in universities

Hartog Committee (1929)

- Recommended selective system of admission to universities; Deserving students (academic course) and vocational courses for average

Sergeant Plan of Education (1944)

- Provided for adequate technical, commercial and arts education and abolition of Intermediate course

Development of Technical Education

- Engineering College at Roorkee (1847); Agriculture College at Pusa

Development of Press

Beginning

- First newspaper Bengal Gazette by James Hickey in 1780; Payam-e-Azadi (1857) by Nana Saheb Peshwa; The Hindu and Swadesamitran by G Subramaniya

Censorship of Press Act, 1799

- Enacted by Lord Wellesley; Imposed wartime press restriction; Relaxed under Lord Hasting

Licensing Regulations, 1823

- Enacted by the John Adams; Press without license became a penal

Metcalfe Act, 1835

- Repealed Licensing Regulation, 1823; Charles Metcalfe named Liberator of the Indian press

Vernacular Press Act, 1878

- Enacted to punish and repress seditious writing; District Magistrate empowered to take undertaking from printer and publisher of any Vernacular newspaper; Magistrate's action was final and no appeal

Indian Press Act, 1910

- Revision of the Vernacular Act empowered the local government to demand a security at registration from printer/ publisher

SOURCE *New NCERT, Class VIII* (*Civilising the 'Native', Educating the Nation*) *NIOS, Module 4 Chap 21* (*Indian National Movement*) *Tamil Nadu Board Class XII, Unit 1* (*Rise of Nationalism in India*)

1 **Which of the following statements are true with reference to Western education introduced by the British?** *(Chap 6, Class-VIII, New NCERT)*

1. It increased the sense of nationalism among the Indians.
2. English was accepted as the language of the entire country.
3. It created an educated middle class.
4. English language was not accepted by all the educated people in the country.

Codes

(a) 1, 2 and 3 (b) 2, 3 and 4 (c) 1 and 2 (d) 3 and 4

Ans. (d)

Exp. Statements (3) and (4) are true about Western education introduced by the British.

Initially, the Western education has created a new educated middle class who favoured British rule and were not in favour of nationalism.

Many of the educated Indians did not accept English as an official language. For instance, Gandhiji openly expressed dissatisfaction over use of English language in his public speech at Banaras Hindu University in 1916.

2 **With the reference to educational institutions during colonial rule in India, consider the following pairs.** *(Chap 6, Class-VIII, New NCERT)*

Institutions		Founders
1. Sanskrit College at Banaras	–	William Jones
2. Calcutta Madarsa	–	Warren Hastings
3. Fort William College	–	Arthur Wellesley

Which of the pairs given above is/are correctly matched?

(a) 1 and 2 (b) Only 2 (c) 1 and 3 (d) Only 3

Ans. (b)

Exp. Pair (2) is correctly matched because Calcutta Madarsa was established by Warren Hastings in 1781.

Pairs (1) and (3) are incorrectly matched because Sanskrit College at Banaras was established by Jonathan Duncan in 1791 and Fort William College was established in 1800 by Richard Wellesley.

3 **With reference to the Fort William College at Calcutta, which of the statements is/are correct?** *(Chap 6, Class-VIII, New NCERT) (UP RO/ARO Pre 2021)*

1. It was founded on 10th June, 1800 AD within the Fort William Complex in Calcutta.
2. The main purpose of establishing this college, was to teach Indian languages to British officers.

Select the correct answer using the codes given below.

(a) Only 1 (b) Only 2
(c) Both 1 and 2 (d) Neither 1 nor 2

Ans. (b)

Exp. Statement (2) is correct about the Fort William College, Calcutta. The main purpose of establishing Fort William College was to provide education in Indian languages to British officers and civil servants. It aimed to train British administrators and officials in the languages and customs of the Indian subcontinent to facilitate better governance and communication between the British rulers and the Indian subjects.

Statement (1) is not correct because Fort William College in Calcutta (now Kolkata) was founded on 10th November, 1800.

It was established by Lord Wellesley, who was the Governor-General of India at the time.

4 **Wellesley established the Fort William College at Calcutta because** *(Chap 6, Class-VIII, New NCERT)*

(a) he was asked by the Board of Directors at London to do so.
(b) he wanted to revive interest in oriental learning in India.
(c) he wanted to provide William Carey and his associates with employment.
(d) he wanted to train British civilians for administrative purpose in India.

Ans. (d)

Exp. Wellesley established the Fort William College at Calcutta because he wanted to train British civilians for administrative purpose in India.

Lord Wellesley was the Governor-General of India between 1798 and 1805. The British territories in India had expanded greatly in the 1800s and there was an urgent need for a more thoroughly organised administration. The organised administration required trained men, who could not only communicate in the local languages but also understand the country and the people they were rapidly gaining control over. Lord Wellesley therefore established the Fort William College at Calcutta to train British officials.

5 **Match the List I with List II and select the correct answer using the codes given below the lists.** *(Chap 21, Module-4, NIOS) MPSC Pre 2016)*

List-I	List-II
A. Warren Hastings	1. Calcutta Madarsa
B. Jonathan Duncan	2. Sanskrit College, Banaras
C. Sir William Jones	3. Bengal Asiatic Society
D. Sir William Wilberforce	4. Evangelical Sect

Codes

	A	B	C	D		A	B	C	D
(a)	1	2	4	3	(b)	3	4	1	2
(c)	1	2	3	4	(d)	4	3	2	1

Ans. (c)

Exp. The correct matching is A-1, B-2, C-3, D-4.

Warren Hastings founded the Calcutta Madarsa in 1781.

In 1791, **Jonathan Duncan** started the Sanskrit College at Banaras for the study of Hindu Law and Philosophy.

William Jones founded Bengal Asiatic Society in 1784.

William Wilberforce was associated with Clapham sect, which is an Evangelical sect. They worked for the liberation of slaves and abolition of slave trade.

6 Regarding Wood's Despatch, which of the following statements are true? *(Chap 6, Class-VIII, New NCERT) (Class-XI, Old NCERT) (IAS Pre 2018)*

1. Grants-in-aid system was introduced.
2. Establishment of universities were recommended.
3. English as a medium of instruction at all levels of education was recommended.

Select the correct answer by using the codes given below.

(a) 1 and 2 (b) 2 and 3 (c) 1 and 3 (d) All of these

Ans. (a)

Exp. Statements (1) and (2) are correct regarding the Wood's Despatch.

In 1854, Charles Wood prepared a despatch on educational system for India. It was considered the 'Magna Carta of English Education in India'. This document was the first comprehensive plan for the spread of education in India.

Some of its provisions included the system of Grants-in-aid to encourage private enterprise.

The despatch recommended the establishment of universities in the three Presidency towns of Calcutta, Bombay and Madras.

Statement (3) is incorrect because it recommended English as the medium of instruction for higher studies and vernaculars at the school level.

7 The Indian Universities Commission was appointed in 1902 by Lord Curzon, its members were *(Unit 1, Class-XII, Tamil Nadu Board) (66th BPSC Pre 2020)*

(a) BG Tilak and Surendranath Banerjee
(b) BK Gokhale and Rasbehari Bose
(c) Syed Hussain Belgrami and Justice Gooroodas Banerjee
(d) Syed Hussain Belgrami and Surendranath Banerjee

Ans. (c)

Exp. The members of the Indian Universities Commission were Syed Hussain Belgrami and Gooroodas Banerjee.

The Indian Universities Commission was a body appointed in 1902 on the instructions of Viceroy of India Lord Curzon intended to make recommendations for reforms in university education in India.

8 Consider the following statements regarding Wood's Dispatch of 1854. *(Class-XI, Old NCERT) (69th BPSC Pre 2023)*

1. It recommended English as the medium of instruction for higher studies.
2. It laid stress on female education and vocational training.
3. It led to the expansion of English education only.

How many of the statements given above is/are correct?

(a) Only one (b) Only two
(c) All three (d) None of these

Ans. (b)

Exp. Only two statements i.e., (1) and (2) are correct with respect to Wood's Dispatch of 1854. It recommended English as the medium of instruction for higher studies and vernacular language at primary or elementary education. It laid stress on female education and vocational training in order to create a wider range of products, as well as to create a healthy market for the purchase of such product.

Statement (3) is incorrect because it led to educational expansion of all subject in vernacular and English language.

9 Consider the following Assertion (A) and Reason (R) and choose the correct code.

Assertion (A) The Asiatic Society of Bengal was established in the period of Warren Hastings and he modestly declined the offer of Presidentship of that learned body in favour of Sir William Jones.

Reason (R) Warren Hastings was himself a great scholar and ardent orientalist who used to encourage the study of Sanskrit, Persian and Arabic. *(Chap 6, Class-VIII, New NCERT) (UPPSC Pre 2019)*

Codes

(a) Both A and R are true and R is the correct explanation of A.
(b) Both A and R are true, but R is not the correct explanation of A.
(c) A is true, but R is false.
(d) R is true, but A is false.

Ans. (b)

Exp. Both Assertion (A) and Reason (R) are true, but Reason (R) is not the correct explanation of Assertion (A). Asiatic Society of Bengal was a scholarly society founded on 15th January, 1784, by Sir William Jones, a British lawyer and orientalist, to encourage oriental studies.

Warren Hastings was himself a great scholar and an ardent orientalist. He took an interest in translating the Bhagavad Gita into English and his efforts led to the first translation appearing in 1785.

10 Arrange the following events in their chronological order and select the correct answer using the codes given below. *(Class-XI, Old NCERT) (MPSC Pre 2010, UPPSC Pre 2018)*

1. Hunter Commission 2. Sadler Commission
3. Wood's Despatch 4. Sargent Plan

Codes

(a) 1, 2, 4, 3 (b) 3, 2, 1, 4 (c) 1, 2, 3, 4 (d) 3, 1, 2, 4

Ans. (d)

Exp. The correct chronological order of the given events is 3, 1, 2, 4.

Sir Charles Wood, the President of the Board of Control of the English East India Company, had an important effect on spreading education in India.

Lord Ripon, the then Governor-General of India appointed the first Indian Education Commission on 3rd February, 1882 under the Chairmanship of Sir William Hunter.

The Government of India appointed the Sadler Commission in, 1917 to study and report on the problems of the Calcutta University.

The Sargent Scheme, formally known as the report of the Sargent Commission on Post-War Education Development in India. It outlined the future development of literacy and education in India.

11 Which of the following was a recommendation of Hunter's Commission? *(Chap 6, Class-VIII, New NCERT) (HPSC Pre 2014)*

(a) Women's education
(b) New regulation for the organised senates system
(c) Gradual withdrawal of state support from higher education
(d) Introduction of civic education at college and university level

***Ans.* (a)**

Exp. Women's education was a recommendation of Hunter's Commission. Major recommendation by the Hunter Commission of 1882 resulted in the following changes in the education system of British India

Preference was given to literate candidates for government jobs in the lower levels. District and municipal boards were entrusted with the management of primary education under the Local Self-Government Act.

12 Which one of the following pair is incorrectly matched? *(Class-XI, Old NCERT)*

Education Commission/Committee		Year
(a) Sadler University Commission	–	1917
(b) Hunter Education Commission	–	1887
(c) The Hartog Committee	–	1929
(d) Indian Universities Act	–	1904

***Ans.* (b)**

Exp. Pair (b) is incorrectly matched because the Hunter Education Commission was a commission appointed by Viceroy Lord Ripon with the goals of investigating complaints about the non-implementation of the Wood's Despatch of 1854, the current status of elementary education in the British territories, and suggesting ways to extend and improve it.

The report of this commission, led by Sir William Wilson Hunter, was submitted in 1882.

13 Which of the following statements are true about the Vernacular Press Act of 1878? *(Class-XI, Old NCERT)*

1. Vernacular newspaper publishers and printers had to give in writing that they will not criticise the government policies.
2. The owners of printing press had no right to go to the court against the action taken by the government.
3. This act was applicable only to the vernacular newspapers.

Codes

(a) 1 and 3 (b) 1 and 2
(c) All of these (d) 2 and 3

***Ans.* (c)**

Exp. All the given statements (1), (2) and (3) are true about Vernacular Press Act of 1878. As per the Act, the District Magistrate was empowered to call upon the printer and publisher of any vernacular newspaper to enter into a bond with government.

The printers and publishers had to give in writing that they will not criticise the government policies. Publisher had to deposit security which could be forfeited if they violated the act and press equipment could be seized if the offence re-occurred. The Magistrate's action was final and the owners of printing press had no right to go to the court against the action taken by the government. This Act was applicable only to the vernacular newspapers.

14 Satyashodhak Samaj acquired a unique rural base in Deccan and Vidarbha due to the important role of the Din Mitra newspaper published from *(Class-XI, Old NCERT) (MPSC Pre 2016)*

(a) Satara (b) Mahad (c) Taravadi (d) Vai

***Ans.* (c)**

Exp. Satyashodhak Samaj acquired a unique rural base in Deccan and Vidarbha due to the important role of the Din Mitra newspaper published from Taravadi. It was published in 1910, under the leadership of Mukundrao Patil. It is popular for the fact that practically the entire Satyashodhak literature is in Marathi and not in English.

15 From the options given below, find the correct combination of the names of editors of the nationalist newspapers 'The Hindu, Kesari, Bengalee, Hindustani and Sudharak'. *(Class-XI, Old NCERT) (64th BPSC Pre 2018)*

(a) Surendranath Banerjee, G Subramania Iyer, Bal Gangadhar Tilak, Ganga Prasad Verma, Gopal Krishna Gokhale
(b) Bal Gangadhar Tilak, G Subramania Iyer, Surendranath Banerjee, Ganga Prasad Verma, Gopal Krishna Gokhale
(c) G Subramania Iyer, Bal Gangadhar Tilak, Ganga Prasad Verma, Gopal Krishna Gokhale, Surendranath Banerjee
(d) G Subramania Iyer, Bal Gangadhar Tilak, Surendranath Banerjee, Ganga Prasad Verma, Gopal Krishna Gokhale
(e) None of the above/More than one of the above editors of the names of editors of the nationalist new paper is.

***Ans.* (d)**

Exp. The correct combination of the names of editors of the nationalist newspapers are G. Subramania Iyer, Bal Gangadhar Tilak, Surendranath Banerjee, Ganga Prasad Verma, Gopal Krishna Gokhale.

The Hindu was started as a weekly in 1878 and became a daily in 1889. G Subramania Iyer was the founder of 'The Hindu'. The Kesari newspaper was started in 1881 in Marathi by Bal Gangadhar Tilak.

The Bengalee was an English newspaper founded in 1862 by Girish Chandra Ghosh in Kolkata. Surendranath Banerjee was its editor. Hindustani newspaper was founded by Ganga Prasad Verma. He was a freedom fighter from Lucknow.

Sudharak was founded by Gopal Ganesh Agarkar in 1888. Gopal Krishna Gokhale was its editor.

Chapter 28

The Revolt of 1857

The Revolt of 1857

Causes of the Revolt

Political
- Ignorance of interest of Kings and Nawabs
- Annexation policy of Doctrine of Lapse by Lord Dalhousie
- Annexation of Awadh on charge of misgovernance

Administrative
- Dissatisfaction of zamindars towards revenue settlement policies of Britishers
- Complex judicial system

Socio-Religious
- Fear due to activities of Christian Missionaries
- Abolition of custom of Sati

Economic
- Economic exploitation of country; Improvisation of peasants, artisans and handicraftsmen
- Rural and agrarian distress

Military
- Dissatisfaction among sepoys regarding pay, allowance and condition of services
- Government Service Entitlement Act making compulsory overseas services

Immediate
- Introduction of enfield rifle whose cartridge was supposedly made of cow and pig fat it hurts the religious sentiments of Hindus and Muslims

Other Aspects of Revolt

Impact of Revolt
- Transferred administration from East India Company to the British Crown
- Governor-General was given the title of Viceroy

Queen's Proclamation at Allahabad
- On 1st November, 1858 rule of East India Company came to an end
- Promised autonomy and respect to native rulers; Share of European in army increased

Views of Historians
- KK Datta consider it mainly a military out break VD Savarkar in his book 'First War of Indian Independence' described it as 'planned war of Indian Independence'
- RC Majumdar called it neither First, nor National, nor a War of Independence

Centers of Revolt

Delhi	General Bakht Khan
Lucknow	Begum Hazrat Mahal
Bihar	Kunwar Singh
Kanpur	Nana Saheb and Tantia Tope
Bareilly	Khan Bahadur Khan
Faizabad	Maulvi Ahmadullah
Jhansi	Rani Lakshmi Bai
Prayagraj	Maulavi Liyaqat Ali

Beginning and Course of Revolt
- On 8th April, 1857, Mangal Pandey hanged to death for attacking his officers in Barrackpore
- Soldiers in Meerut marched to Jail and released imprisoned sepoys and attacked British officials
- Civilians also joined the unrest and captured Delhi
- Delhi was captured by British on 20th September, 1857
- Bahadur Shah taken prisoner and sent to Rangoon

Weakness
- Limited to Northern states; Some classes didn't join; Indian rulers actively helped British officials
- Traditional weapons with the rebels against modernised weapons of Company

Causes of Failure
- Poor organisation and lack of coordination among rebels; Better resource and modern weapons with the Britisher
- Telegraph system provided information about the movement of rebels

Significance
- Hindu- Muslim unity and absence of communal characteristics
- Emergence of new sense of modern nationalism

SOURCE ***New NCERT Class VIII*** *(Ruling the Countryside, When the People Rebel),* ***Old NCERT Class VIII*** *(Revolt against British Rule, British Policies and Administration in India after 1858, Changes in Economic Life, Weaver, Iron Smelter and Factory Owners),* ***New NCERT Class XII*** *(Rebels and the Raj, Colonial Cities,* ***Old NCERT Class XII*** *(The Revolt of 1857, Administrative Changes After 1858, Economic Impact of British Rule),* ***Tamil Nadu Board Class XI, Unit 18*** *(Early Resistance to British Rule)*

1 Which one of the following was not a cause of the Revolt of 1857? *(Chap 5, Class-VIII, Old NCERT)*

(a) The rumour that the British had mixed the bone dust of Cows and pigs into the flour being sold in the market.
(b) The prophecy that British rule would come to an end on the centenary of the Battle of Plassey on 23rd June, 1857.
(c) Popular discontent with British rule.
(d) The prophecy that the end of British rule would lead to the end of the Kali Yuga and the return of Ram Rajya.

Ans. (b)

Exp. The prophecy that British rule would come to an end on the centenary of the Battle of Plassey on 23rd June, 1857 was not a cause of the Revolt of 1857. During the revolt, a number of rumours spreaded, which changed the scenario. These rumours basically stirred people to action.

2. Consider the certain measures of Dalhousie. *(Chap 5, Class-VIII, Old NCERT)*

1. Doctrine of Lapse
2. Fear of loss of religion and caste
3. Abolition of titles and pensions of several rulers
4. Educational reforms

How many of the above measures of Dalhousie were responsible for the Revolt of 1857?

(a) Only one
(b) Only two
(c) Only three
(d) All four

Ans. (c)

Exp. Only three measures i.e. (1), (2) and (3) were responsible for the Revolt of 1857. Certain measures of Dalhousie such as Doctrine of Lapse, fear of loss of religion and caste among natives and abolition of titles and pensions of several rulers were responsible for the Revolt of 1857.

Educational reforms were not responsible for the Revolt of 1857. The following educational reforms during the rule of Lord Dalhousie were included.

In 1854, he received instructions from the President of the Board of Control, Sir Charles Wood, concerning education in India.

3 Consider the following statements. *(Chap 2, Class-XII, New NCERT)*

1. The first British land -revenue settlement 'Summary settlement' was enacted in 1856.
2. The summary settlement removed the Taluqdars wherever possible.
3. Summary settlement undermine the power of Taluqdars.

How many of the statements given above is/are correct?

(a) Only one (b) Only two
(c) All three (d) None

Ans. (c)

Exp. All three statements i.e. (1), (2) and (3) are correct as, after the annexation of Awadh in 1856, the British adopted a new policy on revenue known as the Summary settlement, on the grounds that the Taluqdars were interlopers with no permanent stake in the land, they had kept themselves through the force and fraud. The Taluqdars were at the forefront of a revolt against the British revenues policies because it diminished their power over the peasants.

4 Consider the following statements. *(Chap 8, Class-XII, Old NCERT)*

1. The sepoys of Awadh played a key role in the Revolt of 1857.
2. Indian sepoys formed more than 87% of the British troops in India but were considered inferior to British soldiers.
3. An Indian sepoy was paid less than a European sepoy of the same rank.
4. Sepoys must be ready to serve even in British land across the sea.

How many of the statements given above is/are correct?

(a) Only one (b) Only two
(c) Only three (d) All four

Ans. (d)

Exp. All four statements i.e. (1), (2), (3) and (4) are correct as, the largest numbers of soldiers who participated in the Revolt of 1857 came from Oudh (Awadh). Due to this Awadh was called 'the Nursery of the Bengal Army' large numbers of sepoys belonged to the peasantry class and was treated less than a European sepoy of the same rank. In 1856 Lord Canning issued the General Services Enlistment Act which required that the sepoys must be ready to serve even in British land across the sea.

5 Consider the following statements related to the cause of the 1857 Revolt. *(Chap 5, Class-VIII, Old NCERT)*

1. It was a great disparity in salaries between the Indian and European soldiers.
2. The Indian sepoys were treated with contempt by their European officers.
3. The sepoys were sent to distant parts of the empire but were not paid any extra allowance.

How many of the statements given above is/are correct?

(a) Only one (b) Only two
(c) All three (d) None of these

Ans. (c)

Exp. All three statements i.e. (1), (2) and (3) are correct. Salaries and pensions related issues between the Indian and British soldiers was one of the military causes responsible for the Revolt of 1857. The Indian soldiers in the British army were treated differently from their English counter parts.

The Indian sepoys were not allowed to get their bhattas, if they had actively involved in duties other than their headquarters. As per the Post Office Act of 1854, the privilege of sending letters free of cost to their relatives was stopped.

6 Consider the following statements related to the Revolt of 1857. *(Chap 8, Class-XII, Old NCERT)*

1. Indore troops had joined the Revolt against the wish of their king.
2. Mangal Pandey was executed at Meerut.
3. Tantia Tope was active both at Kanpur and Jhanshi.
4. Sindhia sought refuge from the British at Agra.

How many of the statements given above is/are correct?

(a) Only one (b) Only two (c) Only three (d) All four

Ans. (c)

Exp. Only three statements i.e., (1), (3) and (4) are correct related to the Revolt of 1857.

Indore troops under the leadership of Saadat Khan attacked on British troops. He was not only defeated British but compelling them to flee their base in 1857 Revolt. Tantia Tope was active both at Kanpur and Jhanshi. His guerrilla tactics left the British amazed at his soldiery. Sindhia sought refuge from the British at Agra in 1857 Revolt. Maharaja Jayajirao led his forces to morar to fight rebel army.

Statement (2) is incorrect because Mangal Pandey was executed at Barrackpur Cantonment in West Bengal on 8th April, 1857 not in Meerut.

7 Consider the following statements regarding causes of Revolt of 1857. *(Chap 5, Class-VIII, New NCERT)*

1. Denial of the adoption of child by the childless kings.
2. The British policy of looking down upon Indian subjects.
3. Discriminations among English and Indian soldiers.
4. Social reform and conversion to Christianity.

Which of the statements given above is/are correct?

(a) Only 1 (b) Only 2
(c) 3 and 4 (d) All of these

Ans. (d)

Exp. All of the given statements i.e. (1), (2) (3) and (4) are correct regarding causes of Revolt of 1857. It was caused by the social, political, economic and religious grievances faced by Indians. Some of them are given below

The doctrine of lapse denied political rights to adopted child by childless kings.

Indians at every walk of their life were discriminated and British adopted a policy of looking down on Indian subjects. They were treated as second class citizens.

In military, the Indian soldiers were discriminated and were denied of the privileges, enjoyed by British soldiers.

Social reforms such as prohibition of Sati and freedom to Christian missionaries to convert people further alienated the masses.

8 Which of the following groups did not participated in the Revolt of 1857? *(Unit 18, Class-XI, Tamil Nadu Board)*

1. Agriculture labour
2. Sahukars
3. Farmers
4. Landlords

Codes

(a) Only 1 (b) 1 and 2
(c) Only 2 (d) 2 and 4

Ans. (d)

Exp. Sahukars and landlords did not participate in the Revolt of 1857.

Even though the Revolt of 1857 spread over a vast territory and was widely popular among the people, it could not embrance the entire country or all the groups and classes of Indian society.

Most rulers of the Indian states and landlords, who were selfish to the core and were fearful of British might refused to join in. The Sahukars were the chief targets of the villager's attacks. They were, therefore, naturally hostile to the revolt.

9 Which one of the following statements about the Revolt of 1857 is correct? *(Chap 2, Class-XII, Old NCERT)*

(a) The revolt was carefully organised and planned by the Rajas, Nawabs and Taluqdars
(b) Rumours and prophecies did not play any role in its outbreak and spread
(c) The rebel proclamations in 1857 repeatedly appealed to all sections of the population irrespective of their caste and creed
(d) The British succeeded in quickly and easily controlling the rebels

Ans. (c)

Exp. Statement (c) is correct regarding Revolt of 1857 because the rebel proclamations in 1857 repeatedly appealed to the all sections of the population irrespective of their caste and creed. Many proclamations and notifications were issued by the rebels.

Statements (a), (b) and (d) are incorrect because the revolt was poorly organised and planned by the Rajas, Nawabs and Taluqdars, which was the greatest weakness of the Revolt. Rumours and prophecies played a huge role in inciting the sentiments of masses against the Britishers. Britishers found it very difficult to suppress the revolt due to huge participation of masses.

10 First event relating to the war of independence of 1857 was *(Chap 5, Class-VIII, Old NCERT)*

(a) Kanpur's Revolt and taking over the leadership by Nana Saheb.
(b) Begum Hazrat Mahal's leadership of Awadh.
(c) Marching of sepoys to Delhi's Red Fort.
(d) Revolt by Rani of Jhansi.

Ans. (c)

Exp. The first event relating to the war of independence of 1857 was marching of sepoys to Delhi's Red Fort. On 10th May, 1857, a band of sepoys from Meerut marched to the Red Fort in Delhi. They gathered around the Red Fort and demanded to meet Bahadur Shah Zafar. The emperor was hesitant to challenge the might of the British but the soldiers proclaimed Bahadur Shah as their leader.

11 Which of the following is one of the social reasons for 1857 Revolt? *(Unit 18, Class-XI, Tamil Nadue Board)*

1. The English could not establish any social relationship with the Indians.
2. The racial arrogance of the British created a difference between the rulers and the ruled.

Which of the statements given above is/are correct?

(a) Only 1 (b) Only 2
(c) Both 1 and 2 (d) Neither 1 nor 2

Ans. (c)

Exp. Both the statements (1) and (2) are correct as, economic, political, social, religious and military causes were responsible for the Revolt of 1857 .The British were not very sensitive to the feelings of the vast mass of Indian people. So they could not establish any social relationship with the Indians. They considered that they belonged to a superior race and used to humiliate the Indians.

12 Which of the following is correct in association with Bahadur Shah Zafar? *(Chap 5, Class-VIII, Old NCERT)*

(a) He was taken prisoner in 1857
(b) He was tried and exiled to Bhutan
(c) He died in the year 1865
(d) His elder son was declared as his successor

Ans. (a)

Exp. Statement (a) is incorrect in association with Bahadur Shah Zafar because Emperor Bahadur Shah was found guilty of aiding the Revolt of 1857. He was sentenced to life imprisonment and was deported to Yangon (Rangoon) in Myanmar where he died in 1862. As the punishment, his two sons were shot dead in front of him.

13 Consider the following statements. *(Chap 5, Class-XII Old NCERT)*

1. Introduction of the enfield rifle was the immediate factor for start of the revolt.
2. The revolt broke out in Northern and Central part of India.

Which of the statements given above is / are correct?

(a) Only 1 (b) Only 2
(c) Both 1 and 2 (d) Neither 1 nor 2

Ans. (c)

Exp. Both the statements (1) and (2) are correct. The immediate cause of India's first war of Independence (Revolt of 1857) was usage of cartridges. It was said that the cartridge of the rifle was wrapped in the fat of cow and pig. The cartridge had to be bitten off before loading it into the gun. Thus, both the Hindu and Muslim soldiers were reluctant to use the 'English' rifle. It violated the religious sentiments of the sepoys.

The revolt broke out in Northern and Central part of India.

14 Consider the following pairs. *(Chap 8. Class-XII Old NCERT)*

1. Bakht Khan – Delhi
2. Maulavi Ahmadullah – Awadh
3. Kunwar Singh – Bihar
4. Nana Saheb – Kanpur

How many of the pairs given above is/are correctly matched?

(a) Only one (b) Only two
(c) Only three (d) All four

Ans. (d)

Exp. All four pairs i.e., (1), (2) (3) and (4) are correctly matched.

Bakht Khan was the Commander-in-Chief of the Independent Forces in the region of Delhi during the Indian Rebellion of 1857 against the East India Company.

Maulavi Ahmadullah was a famous freedom fighter and was a leader of the Indian Rebellion of 1857. He was known as the Lighthouse of Rebellion in Awadh region.

Kunwar Singh was a leader and military commander during the Indian Rebellion of 1857. He was the chief organiser of the fight against the British in Bihar.

Nana Saheb was the Peshwa of the Maratha empire, aristocrat and fighter, who led the rebellion in Kanpur during the Revolt of 1857.

15 Consider the following statements about the leaders of Revolt of 1857. *(Chap 5, Class-VIII, Old NCERT)*

1. Tantia Tope was Commander-in-Chief of the army of Nana Saheb.
2. In Bareli (Bareilly), Khan Bahadur Khan led the revolt against the British.

Which of the statements given above is/are correct?

(a) Only 1
(b) Only 2
(c) Both 1 and 2
(d) Neither 1 nor 2

Ans. (c)

Exp. Both the statements (1) and (2) are correct about the leaders of Revolt of 1857.

Tantia Tope was an important figure in the Revolt of 1857. In collaboration with Nana Saheb, he secretly organised an anti-British upsurge in Kanpur. In May, 1857, Tantia became the Commander-in-Chief of the Indian troops stationed at Kanpur.

Khan Bahadur Khan Rohilla, the grandson of Hafiz Rahmat Khan, set up his own government in Bareilly during the Revolt of 1857 against British.

16 Shah Mal was one of the many leaders who played an important part in the Revolt of 1857. Which of the following statements is/are incorrect in his context? *(Chap 5, Class-XII, New NCERT)*

1. Shah Mal mobilised the headmen and cultivators of Chaurasee Des.
2. He took over the bungalow of an English officer, turned it into a 'Hall of Justice'.
3. He was killed in battle in July, 1860.

Codes

(a) Only 1 (b) Only 2
(c) Only 3 (d) All of these

Ans. (c)

Exp. Statement (3) is incorrect in the context of role played by Shah Mal in the Revolt of 1857 because Shah Mal was killed in battle in July, 1857. He lived in Pargana Barout in Uttar Pradesh.

17 Who among the following leaders were successful in escaping to Nepal during the brutal suppression by the British after the outbreak of Revolt of 1857? *(Chap 5, Class-VIII, Old NCERT)*

1. Tantia Tope 2. Hazrat Mahal
3. Kunwar Singh 4. Nana Saheb

Codes

(a) 1 and 3 (b) 2 and 4 (c) 3 and 4 (d) All of these

Ans. (b)

Exp. Among the given leaders of Revolt of 1857, Hazrat Mahal and Nana Saheb were, successful in escaping to Nepal during the brutal suppression by the British after the outbreak of Revolt of 1857.

Begum Hazrat Mahal was the leader of the sepoys at Lucknow. She finally found asylum in Nepal in Hallaur where she died in 1879.

Nana Saheb was Peshwa of the Maratha empire, who led the rebellion in Kanpur during the Revolt of 1857. After the Britishers recaptured Kanpur, Nana Saheb successfully escaped to Nepal.

18 Which of the following statements is/are correct in the context of the leaders of the Revolt of 1857? *(Chap 5, Class-VIII, Old NCERT)*

1. All the leaders coordinated with each other in smooth manner.
2. Rani Lakshmibai was killed in the year 1857.
3. Kunwar Singh was betrayed by a friend to the British was hanged.

Codes

(a) Only 2 (b) 1 and 2 (c) 2 and 3 (d) None

Ans. (d)

Exp. None of the given statement is correct in the context of the leaders of the Revolt of 1857.

There was no coordination or central leadership during the Revolt. The principal rebel leaders were brave and capable, but could not match their British opponents in leadership and coordination.

Rani Lakshmibai died during fight with British military rulers near Gwalior at Kotah-ki-Serai in 1858.

Kunwar Singh was the Zamindar of Jagdishpur of Bihar. He was the leader of Bihar in the Revolt of 1857. In 1858, he succumbed to injuries, which he sustained in the fight against the British on 26th April, 1858. The revolutionary Tantia Tope was betrayed by a friend in the course of Revolt of 1857.

19 Match the following lists correctly and choose the correct code. *(Chap 6, Class-XII, Old NCERT)*

List I (Leaders)	List II (Revolt Centre)
A. Rani Lakshmibai	1. Jhansi
B. Bahadur Shah II	2. Delhi
C. Tantia Tope	3. Kanpur
D. Begum Hazrat Mahal	4. Lucknow

Codes

	A	B	C	D
(a)	1	2	3	4
(b)	1	3	2	4
(c)	4	3	2	1
(d)	1	2	4	3

Ans. (a)

Exp. The correct matching is A-1, B-2, C-3, D-4.

Jhansi The 20 years old Rani Lakshmibai led the rebels when the Britishers refused to accept the claim of her adopted son to the throne of Jhansi.

Delhi The last Mughal Emperor Bahadur Shah Zafar was proclaimed as the leader by the sepoys in Delhi.

Kanpur The Commander-in-Chief of the soldiers in Kanpur was Tantia Tope.

Lucknow It was the capital of Awadh. Begum Hazrat Mahal, one of the begums of the king of Awadh took up the leadership of the revolt.

20 Consider the following statements. *(Chap 5 Class-VIII Old NCERT)*

Statements-I The first War of Independence in 1857 failed to secure freedom from the British.

Statements-II The leadership of Bahadur Shah Zafar did not have popular support and most of the Indian rulers of important states shield away from the struggle.

Which one of the following is correct in respect of the above statements?

(a) Both Statement-I and Statement-II are correct and statement-II is the correct explanation for Statement-I
(b) Both Statement-I and Statement-II are correct and Statement-II is not the correct explanation for Statement-I
(c) Statement-I is correct, but Statement-II is incorrect
(d) Statement-I is incorrect, but Statement-II is correct

Ans. (a)

Exp. Both Statement-I and Statement-II are correct and Statement-II is the correct explanation for Statement-1.

The Revolt of 1857 suffered from a weak leadership. It was not planned and organised. There was a clear lack of unity among the rebels and there was no common purpose among them during the Revolt of 1857.The revolt did not spread to all parts of India instead it was confined to the Northern and Central India. Therefore, it failed to secure freedom from the British Government. The symbolic leadership belonged to the Mughal Emperor, Bahadur Shah Zafar but the real command was in the hands of General Bakht Khan who had led the troops. Emperor was perhaps the weakest link in the chain of leadership of the revolt.

21 Which of the following was the most important weakness of Revolt of 1857? ***(Chap 5, Class-VIII, Old NCERT)***

1. Lack of discipline among rebel sepoys
2. The rebels lacked coordination and union
3. Lack of modern weapons

How many of the statements given above is/are correct?

(a) Only one (b) Only two
(c) All three (d) None of these

Ans. (c)

Exp. All three statements i.e. (1) (2) and (3) are correct regarding weakness of Revolt of 1857.

The rebels had failed because they lacked coordination. There was no proper leadership structure and a coherent strategy. Due to lack of communication facilities, the sepoys of the widely dispersed cantonments could not act simultaneously in a concerted manner. The British soldiers were equipped with latest weapons and used the telegraph and railways to their advantages.

22 Consider the following Assertion (A) and Reason (R) and choose the correct code. ***(Chap 5, Class-VIII, Old NCERT)***

Assertion (A) The Revolt of 1857 failed to secure freedom from British Government.

Reason (R) British introduced many administrative reforms after the Revolt of 1857.

Codes

(a) Both A and R are true and R is the correct explanation of A.
(b) Both A and R are true, but R is not the correct explanation of A.
(c) A is true, but R is false.
(d) A is false, but R is true.

Ans. (b)

Exp. Both Assertion (A) and Reason (R) are true, but Reason (R) is not the correct explanation of Assertion (A). The Revolt of 1857 marked the end of the East India Company's rule in India. India now came under the direct rule of the British crown.

Thus, it failed to secure freedom from the British Government. The Queen's proclamation of 1858, promised to respect the sovereignty of princely states. It also introduced few administrative reforms.

The Governor-General's office was replaced by that of the Viceroy. The rights of Indian rulers were recognised. The ratio of British officers to Indian soldiers increased but the armoury remained in the hands of the Britishers.

23 The Azamgarh proclamation of 25th August, 1857 stressed on, which one of the following issues? ***(Chap 2, Class-XII, New NCERT)***

1. Hindu-Muslim divide
2. Support to the English Government
3. The return of the Badshahi
4. The imposition of heavy *Jumas* (revenue demand)

Select the correct answer using the codes given below.

(a) Only 1 (b) Only 2
(c) Only 3 (d) 1, 2, 3 and 4

Ans. (a)

Exp. Option (1) is correct.

The Azamgarh proclamation of 25th August, 1857 stressed on the issue of Hindu-Muslim divide.

Azamgarh Proclamation was published by Firuz Shah, the grandson of Mughal emperor Bahadur Shah Zafar. It stressed on the need of unity among Hindu and Muslim Communities.

The proclamation appealed to the people that the people belonging to different castes should remain together during this time. Rebels wanted full power to be vested in the hands of the emperor.

24 What was/were the object/objects of Queen Victoria's Proclamation (1858)? ***(Chap 6, Class-VIII, Old NCERT) (IAS Pre 2014)***

1. To disclaim any intention to annex the Indian states.
2. To place the Indian administration under the British crown.
3. To regulate East India Company's trade with India.

Codes

(a) 1 and 2 (b) Only 2
(c) 1 and 3 (d) 1, 2 and 3

Ans. (a)

Exp. Statements (1) and (2) are correct regarding objective of Queen Victoria's Proclamation (1858). This proclamation clarified the intention of British Government towards India. The responsibilities of administration of India was transferred from East India Company to the British crown. The proclamation also stated that the British authorities will not interfere in internal affairs of princely states and will not annex any territories.

Statement (3) is incorrect because the Charter Act of 1833 had already abolished the East India Company's monopoly of trade with India.

25 What changes was/were introduced in the administration after the Revolt of 1857? *(Chap 6, Class-VIII, Old NCERT)*

(a) The Governor-General was also given tittle of Viceroy.
(b) Governor-General's Council was enlarged.
(c) Both (a) and (b)
(d) Neither (a) nor (b)

Ans. (c)

Exp. Both the statements (a) and (b) are correct regarding the changes introduced in the administration after the Revolt of 1857.

The Governor-General was given a new title of Viceroy who was a representative of the crown. Lord Canning was the first Viceroy of India. It created a new office of the Secretary of State for India.

The Secretary of State was vested with complete authority and control over Indian administration. A 15 Member Council of India was established to assist the Secretary of State, which was an advisory body.

26 After the Revolt of 1857, British brought reforms in the provincial administration. Consider the following statements in the context of reforms in the provincial administration. *(Chap 7, Class-XII, Old NCERT)*

1. The system of giving fixed grants to provinces was ended in 1882.
2. The first step in the direction of separating central and provincial finances was taken in 1870 by Lord Mayo.

Which of the statements given above is/are correct?

(a) Only 1 (b) Only 2
(c) Both 1 and 2 (d) Neither 1 nor 2

Ans. (c)

Exp. Both the statements (1) and (2) are correct regarding reforms introduced in provincial administration after the Revolt of 1857.

In 1870, Lord Mayo had taken the first step in the direction of separating central and provincial finances. The provincial governments were granted fixed sums out of central revenues for the administration of certain services.

In 1882, Lord Ripon had brought some changes. The system of giving fixed grants to the provinces was ended and instead a province was to get the entire income within it from certain sources of revenue.

27 The Resolution passed by the Lord Ripon's Government was one of the major administrative changes introduced after the 1858. Which of the following was part of this Resolution? *(Chap 7, Class-XII, Old NCERT)*

1. Rural and urban bodies were promoted.
2. The majority of members of the local bodies were officials of Company.
3. It permitted the election of non-official as chairman of a local body.
4. Elected members were in Minority.

Codes

(a) 1 and 2 (b) 2 and 3 (c) 3 and 4 (d) 1, 3 and 4

Ans. (d)

Exp. Statements (1), (3) and (4) are correct with reference to resolution passed by the Lord Ripon's Government. Lord Ripon is still remembered by the Indians for his attempts to establish local self-government. He sought to remove the obstacles in the sphere of local self-government by his resolution of 1882. In towns, the powers and responsibilities of the Municipalities were enlarged.

The members where to be partly elected and partly nominated. The Chairman was to be a non-official member. The local bodies were kept free from government control.

However, under this resolution on local self-governance, the majority members of the local bodies were officials of Company.

28 After the Revolt of 1857, the British recruited the soldiers from *(Chap 7, Class-XII, Old NCERT) (BPSC Pre 2008)*

(a) Draining of UP and Bihar
(b) Bengalis and Odias from the East
(c) Gurkhas, Sikhs and Pathan in the North
(d) Madras presidency and Marathas

Ans. (c)

Exp. After the Revolt of 1857 in India, the British recruited the soldiers in the British Indian army from Sikh, Gurkha and Pathan communities on a large scale and declared them as martial communities. These communities supported Britishers in suppression of Revolt of 1857.

29 Which of the following were the reasons for the failure of the Revolt of 1857? *(Class-XII, Old NCERT)*

1. The Military superiority of the British.
2. The rebels did not have a unified programme and ideology.
3. There was a lack of support from all the sections of society.

Codes

(a) 1 and 2 (b) 2 and 3
(c) All of these (d) None of these

Ans. (c)

Exp. All of the reasons are correct for failure of the Revolt of 1857. Superior military strength and resources of British East India Company was the cause for failure. They used automated gun, artillery against Indian rebel. Lack of coordinated and unified leadership among Indian were the another important reason for failure. Lack of support from all strata of society, such as urban middle class did not support the revolt. This was among the important reason for failure of revolt.

30 **Consider the following statements.** *(Class-XII, Old NCERT)*

Statement-I 'The 1857 Revolt was a war of fanatic religionists against christians': statement by Sir James Outram.

Statement-II The so called First National war of Independence of 1857 is neither first nor national nor a war of independence : statement by RC Majumdar.

Which one of the following is correct in respect of the above statements?

(a) Both Statement-I and Statement-II are correct and Statement-II is the correct explanation for Statement-I
(b) Both Statement-I and Statement-II are correct and Statement-II is not the correct explanation for Statement-I
(c) Statement-I is correct, but Statement-II is incorrect
(d) Statement-I is incorrect, but Statement-II is correct

Ans. (d)

Exp. Statement-I is incorrect, but Statement-II is correct. 1857 Revolt was a war of fanatic religionists against Christians. This statement was stated by LER Rees.

Dr. RC Majumdar considers the Revolt of 1857 as neither the first nor national nor a war of independence as a large part of the country remained unaffected many section of the people took no part in the upsurge.

31 **Hindu-Muslim unity was the main pillar of the Revolt of 1857. In order to create disunity and rift between both the communities, what measures was/were taken by British?** *(Chap 6, Class-VIII, Old NCERT)*

1. In early years, Muslims were discriminated against in services.
2. They were shown as the oppressor of Muslims.
3. It was propagated that the interest of Hindus will be met only on being loyal to British rule.

How many of the statements given above is/are correct?

(a) Only one (b) Only two
(c) All three (d) None of these

Ans. (b)

Exp. Only two statements i.e. (1) and (3) are correct regarding attempt by the Britishers to create rift and disunity among Hindu and Muslim community in the course of Revolt of 1857. British Government took various measures in order to create disunity among Hindus and Muslims during 1857.

In early years, Muslims were discriminated in services. The Britishers gave preference to Hindu soldiers in recruitment in comparison to Muslim soldiers.

British colonial authorities also propagated through propaganda that the interest of Hindus will be met only on being loyal to British rule.

Statement (2) is incorrect because Muslim community was shown as oppressor of Hindus by the Britishers.

32 **Consider the following statements with reference to the steps taken towards reorganisation of Army after the Revolt of 1857.** *(Chap 8, Class-XII, Old NCERT)*

1. The proportion of Europeans to Indians in the army was raised.
2. The older policy of excluding Indians from the officer corps was abolished.
3. Indian regiments were made a mixture of various castes and groups.

How many of the statements given above is/are correct?

(a) Only one
(b) Only two
(c) All three
(d) None of the above

Ans. (b)

Exp. Only two statements i.e., (1) and (3) are correct regarding reorganisation of Army after the Revolt of 1857. After the Revolt of 1857, Britisher reorganised the Indian Army to mitigate the possibility of further revolt and breaking the unity among sepoys. The proportion of Europeans to Indians in the army was raised and fixed at one to two in the Bengal Army and two to five in the Madras and the Bombay armies.

Indian regiments were made a mixture of various castes and groups, which were so placed as to balance each other.

Statement (2) is incorrect because older policy of excluding Indians from the officer corps was continued. Till 1914, no Indian could rise higher than the rank of a subedar.

33 **Which of the following pairs is/are correctly matched?** *(Chap 6, Class-VIII, Old NCERT)*

1. Indian Council Act	–	1892
2. Queen Victoria's Proclamation	–	1857
3. Charter Act	–	1831

Codes

(a) Only 1
(b) Only 2
(c) Only 3
(d) All of these

Ans. (a)

Exp. Pair (1) is correctly matched. The Indian Council Act, 1892 was passed by the British Parliament. It increased the number of non-official members in Legislative Council. These member were also given rights to ask question on the budget.

Pairs (2) and (3) are incorrectly matched because Queen Victoria's proclamation was read by Viceroy Canning in November, 1858. and the Charter Act was passed in 1833 (not in 1831).

Chapter 29

Indian National Movement : First Phase (1885-1915)

Indian National Movement : First Phase (1885-1915)

Rise of Nationalism and Congress

Socio-Religious Reform Movement
- Steps were taken by Brahmo Samaj
- Paramhans Mandali, Prarthana Samaj and Arya Samaj

Reactionary Policies of Lytton
- Reduction in age limit for Civil Services; Vernacular Act; Arms Act in 1878; Organisation of Delhi Darbar during famine

Ilbert Bill Controversy (1883-84)
- Bill intended to end judicial disqualification on the basis of race differences

Political Association before Congress
- Landholder's society in 1838 by Dwarkanath Tagore
- British Indian Association (1851) by Radhakant Deb
- East India Association (1866) by Dadabhai Naoroji; Indian League (1875) by Sisir Kumar Ghosh
- Bombay Presidency Association (1885) by Badruddin Tyabji, Pherozshah Mehta and KT Telang

Establishment of Congress
- Planned by retired Civil Servants AO Hume
- First session in Bombay in 1885 with WC Bonnerjee as President

Objective of Congress
- Training and organisation of public opinion
- Consolidation of national unity
- Formulation of popular demands

Moderate and Extremist Phase

Moderate Phase (1895-1905)
- **Important Leaders** Dadabhai Naoroji; MG Ranade; Gopal Krishna Gokhale; WC Bonerjee; SN Banerjee; Pherozshah Mehta
- **Methodology** Creation of public opinion
- Used 3 Ps- Petitions, Protests, and Prayers; Publication of newspaper; Organised meetings, resolutions and speeches
- **Demands** Not ask for independence
- Demanded concessions and presented their grievances; Asked for reform in legislature, civil services, removing ban on press, newspaper and speeches

Contribution
- Succeeded in creating awareness
- Trained people in political work
- Economic critique of British rule
- Exposed true character of British rule

Extremist Phase (1905-1919)
- **Important Leaders** Raj Narain Bose; Aswini Kumar Datta; Aurobindo Ghosh; Bipin Chandra Pal; Bal Gangadhar Tilak; Lala Lajpat Rai
- **Establishment of Muslim League** In Dhaka in 1906; Leaders were Salimulla Khan and Aga Khan; First President- Waqar-ul-Mulk Mustaq Hussain
- **Partition of Bengal, 1905** Announced by Curzon; Separated largely Muslim Eastern Areas from the largely Hindu Western areas of Bengal

Movements

Swadeshi and Boycott Movement
- Resolution of Boycott was announced in Calcutta town hall and proclamation of Swadeshi was made
- Partition day (16th October, 1905) was observed as a day of mourning
- Vande Mataram became theme song
- Under the presidentship of Gopal Krishna Gokhale Congress in 1905, Condemned partition and supported anti-partition and Swadeshi movement
- Bengal National College set up in 1906 (Principal - Aurobindo Ghosh)
- National Council of Education set up by Satish Chandra Mukherjee and other Nationalist leaders
- Swadeshi enterprises set up
- Ganpati and Shivaji festival used as a medium of mass education by Tilak

Surat Split (1907)
- Extremist wanted Tilak or Lajpat Rai as President and Nagpur as venue of Congress session
- Moderates chose Rashbehari Ghosh as President and Surat as venue
- Rigid attitude of both sides

First Phase of Revolutionary Activities (1907-1912)
- Inspired by Russian and Irish nationalist
- Focused on individual heroic
- Organised assassinations of unpopular officials
- Conducted dacoities to raise funds

SOURCE *Old NCERT Class VIII (Rise of Nationalism), Old NCERT Class VIII (Struggle for Swaraj), Old NCERT Class X (India's Struggle for Independence), Old NCERT Class XII (Growth of New India-The Nationalist Movement, 1858-1905), Old NCERT Class XII (Struggle for Swaraj-I, 1919-1927), Old NCERT Class XII (Nationalist Movement 1905-1918 : Growth of Militant Nationalism) Tamil Nadu Board Class XII, Unit 1 (Early Resistance to British Rule)*

Pre-Congress Organisations/ Rise of Nationalism

1 Which of the following factor(s) was/were responsible for the rise of nationalism in India?

(Chap 9, Class-XII, Old NCERT)

1. Economic backwardness
2. Influences of Western ideas
3. Discovery of past
4. Development of press

Codes

(a) 1 and 2 (b) 2 and 3 (c) 1, 2 and 3 (d) All of these

Ans. (d)

Exp. All of the given factors were responsible for the rise of nationalism in India. The repressive colonial policies made Indians conscious about their economic backwardness. They in order to counter the arguments put forth by Britishers that ancient Indians were barbaric and uncivilised, started studying their own past and culture.

The resultant was rediscovery of India's glorious past added to this, the influence of Western ideas such as modern concept of nationalism, rule of law etc, and development of Western education and press played a significant role in the rise of nationalism in 19th century.

2 Consider the following statements with reference to the rise of nationalism in India.

(Chap 9, Class-XII, Old NCERT)

1. Modern English education system became medium for spreading nationalist ideas in different linguistic region.
2. The educated Indians were loyal to British throughout the freedom struggle.

Which of the statements given above is/are incorrect?

(a) Only 1 (b) Only 2
(c) Both 1 and 2 (d) Neither 1 nor 2

Ans. (b)

Exp. Statement (2) is incorrect regarding the rise of nationalism in India. The educated Indians were not loyal to British throughout the freedom struggle. They influenced the countrymen to speak against the British rule. They played an important role during the freedom struggle.

3 Consider the following statements.

(Chap 9 , Class-XII, Old NCERT)

1. The Zamindari Association was an association of zamindars in India. It was later renamed to Landholders' Society.
2. The Landholders' Society was limited in its approach as it covered the demand and interests of landlords only.
3. It used constitutional agitation for the redressal of grievances and hence marked the beginning of the organised political struggle.

How many of the statements given above is/are correct?

(a) Only one (b) Only two
(c) All three (d) None of these

Ans. (c)

Exp. All three statements are correct as the first political organisation established in India in 1838 was known as Zamindari Association or Landholders society.It was established in Calcutta to promote and protect the interests of landholders (Zamindars). It used constitutional agitation for the redressal of grievances. The founding members of this organisation were Radhakant Deb and Dwarka Nath Tagore.

4 Consider the following statements about Dadabhai Naoroji.

(Chap 9, Class-XII, Old NCERT)
(Unit 1, Class-XII, Tamil Nadu Board)

1. He wrote a book 'Poverty and Un-British Rule in India.'
2. He worked as a professor of Gujarati in the University College, London.
3. He laid the foundation of woman's education in Bombay.
4. He was elected as a member of British Parliament on the ticket of the Conservative Party.

How many of the statements given above is/are incorrect?

(a) Only one (b) Only two (c) Only three (d) All four

Ans. (a)

Exp. Only statement i.e., (4) is incorrect about Dadabhai Naoroji. Dadabhai Naoroji was elected as a member of the British Parliament on the ticket of the Liberal Party. He was elected as the Member of Parliament (MP) for the Finsbury Central constituency in London. He won the seat in the 1892 general election, becoming the first Indian to be elected to the British Parliament.

5 Consider the following statements in the context of Dadabhai Naoroji. *(Chap 9, Class-XII, Old NCERT)*

1. Dadabhai Naoroji was born in 1867.
2. He is popularly known as 'Grand Old Man of India.'
3. He was the first economic thinker of India.

How many of the statements given above is/are correct?

(a) Only one (b) Only two
(c) All three (d) None of these

Ans. (b)

Exp. Only two statements i.e., (2) and (3) are correct regarding Dadabhai Naoroji.

Dadabhai Naoroji was known as the 'Grand Old Man of India.' He was the first economic thinker of India. His book 'Poverty and Un-British Rule in India', highlighted the economic exploitation of India. He also theorised the concept of 'Drain of Wealth'.

Statement (1) is incorrect because Dadabhai Naoroji was born in 1825 not in 1867.

6 **Which of the following factors contributed to the emergence and growth of pre-Congress nationalist organisations?** *(Chap 9 , Class-XII, Old NCERT)*

1. Discontent with discriminatory policies like the Arms Act and Vernacular Press Act.
2. Increased awareness of India's glorious past and cultural heritage.
3. Western education exposing Indians to ideas of liberty and self-government.
4. Formation of social reform movements like Brahmo Samaj and Arya Samaj.

How many of the statements given above is/are incorrect?

(a) Only one (b) Only two
(c) Only three (d) All four

***Ans.* (d)**

Exp. All four statements i.e., (1), (2), (3) and (4) are correct with reference to factors contributed to the emergence and growth of pre-Congress nationalist organisations.

Discontent with discriminatory policies acts like the Arms Act and Vernacular Press Act restricted rights and freedoms, fuelling resentment against British rule.

Awareness of India's past Rediscovering India's rich history and cultural heritage instilled pride and challenged the narrative of British superiority.

Western education exposure to ideas of individual liberty, constitutionalism, and nationalism inspired Indians to demand similar rights.

Social reform movements groups like Brahmo Samaj and Arya Samaj fostered unity and challenged social injustices, contributing to the awakening of national consciousness.

7 **Consider the following statements with reference to British India Association.** *(Chap 12, Class-XII, Old NCERT)*

1. It was established after the merger of Landholder's society with Bengal British Indian society in 1851.
2. It worked towards protection of interest of small farmers.

Which of the statements given above is/are correct?

(a) Only 1 (b) Only 2
(c) Both 1 and 2 (d) Neither 1 nor 2

***Ans.* (a)**

Exp. Statement (1) is correct with reference to British India Association as 'British India Association' was established in 1851 after the merger of Landholders' Society with Bengal British Indian Society. Radhakanta Deb was its first President while Debendranath Tagore was its General Secretary.

Statement (2) is incorrect because it favoured and worked towards protection of interest of zamindars.

8 **Consider the following statements with reference to Surendranath Banerjee.** *(Chap 12, Class-XII, Old NCERT)*

1. He was dismissed by the British from the Indian Civil Service.
2. He was associated with the Landholders' Society.

Which of the statements given above is/are correct?

(a) Only 1 (b) Only 2
(c) Both 1 and 2 (d) Neither 1 nor 2

***Ans.* (a)**

Exp. Statement (1) is correct with reference to Surendranath Banerjee as Surendranath Banerjee was unjustly turned out of the Indian Civil Service as his superiors could not tolerate the presence of an independent minded Indian in the rank of this service.

Statement (2) is incorrect as Surendranath Banerjee was associated with Indian Association of Calcutta.

9 **Consider the following statements.** *(Chap 12, Class-XII, Old NCERT)*

1. The All India National Conference at Calcutta was organised in December 1883.
2. The Indian National Conference merged with the Indian National Congress in 1886.

Which of the statements given above is/are correct?

(a) Only 1 (b) Only 2
(c) Both 1 and 2 (d) Neither 1 nor 2

***Ans.* (c)**

Exp. Both the statements (1) and (2) are correct.

The All India National Conference at Calcutta was organised in December 1883. It was sponsored by Indian Association and was attended by several leaders from outside Bengal. It adopted a programme very similar to the one adopted by the Indian National Congress with which it merged in 1886.

10 **Consider the following statements.** *(Chap 9, Class-XII , Old NCERT)*

1. He was one of the founders of the Bombay Presidency Association as also the Indian National Congress.
2. From about the middle of the 1890s till his death in 1915 he was a dominant figure in the Indian National Congress and was often accused of exercising autocratic authority over it.

To whom does above statements refer to?

(a) Pherozeshah Mehta (b) Bal Gangadhar Tilak
(c) Gopal Krishna Gokhale (d) Madan Mohan Malaviya

***Ans.* (a)**

Exp. Bombay Presidency Association was founded in 1885 by Pherozeshah Mehta, Badruddin Tyabji and KT Telang. It was formed in opposition to the Ilbert Bill and Lytton's other reactionary policies. The main objective of this organisation was to mobilise public opinions on issues faced by Indians.

11 **Arrange the establishment of the following in a chronological order (starting with the earliest).** *(Chap 9, Class-XII, Old NCERT)*

1. The East India Association
2. The Poona Sarvajanik Sabha
3. Indian Association
4. The Bombay Presidency Association

Codes

(a) 1, 2, 3, 4 (b) 1, 3, 2, 4
(c) 2, 3, 4, 1 (d) 3, 2, 1, 4

Ans. (a)

Exp. The correct chronological order is 1, 2, 3, 4. Dadabhai Naoroji started the East India Association in London in 1867.

Poona Sarvajanik Sabha was started in 1870 by Mahadev Govind Ranade and his associates in Pune.

Indian Association was formed in 1876 by Surendranath Banerjee and Anand Mohan Bose.

Bombay Presidency Association was started in 1885 by Pherozshah Mehta, Badruddin Tyabji and KT Telang.

12. **Consider the following pairs.** *(Chap 9, Class-XII, Old NCERT)*

1. East India Association – Raja Ram Mohan Roy
2. Poona Sarvajanik Sabha – KT Telang
3. Madras Mahajan Sabha – Anand Charlu

How many of the pairs given above is/are correctly matched?

(a) Only one (b) Only two
(c) All three (d) None of these

Ans. (a)

Exp. Only one pair i.e., (3) is correctly matched. Madras Mahajan Sabha was formed by G. Subramaniam, P Anand Charlu and V Raghava Chari. It raised the concerns and grievances faced by Indians to the British authorities.

The East India Association was formed by Dada Bhai Naoroji in 1867 and Poona Sarvajanik Sabha was established by Mahadev Govind Ranade.

13 **Consider the following statements.** *(Chap 9, Class-VIII, Old NCERT)*

1. In 1878, Arms Act was enacted which banned arm owning right of Indians.
2. Government brought 'Ilbert Bill' in 1883.

Which of the statements given above is/are correct?

(a) Only 1
(b) Only 2
(c) Both 1 and 2
(d) Neither 1 nor 2

Ans. (c)

Exp. Both the statements (1) and (2) are correct.

In 1878, the Arms Act was passed, under which Indians were not allowed to possess arms. It was promulgated during the reign of Viceroy Lord Lytton.

Government brought Ilbert Bill in 1883 with the main objective to allow Indian judges to try cases in session courts involving Britishers. It was promulgated during the reign of Viceroy Lord Ripon.

Indian National Congress

14 **Consider the following statements.** *(Chap 9, Class-XII, Old NCERT)*

1. First session of the Indian National Congress was held under the presidency of WC Banerjee.
2. Lord Dufferein was the Viceroy of British India at the time of first session of the Congress.
3. George Yule was the first Englishman to become the president of INC.

How many of the statements given above is/are correct?

(a) Only one (b) Only two
(c) All three (d) None of these

Ans. (c)

Exp. All three statements i.e., (1), (2) and (3) are correct as Womesh Chandra Banerjee was the President of the first session of the Indian National Congress. This session was held from 28th to 31st December, 1885 in Bombay. It was attended by 72 delegates from all over India.

The first session of Congress was held in Bombay at Gokuldas Tejpal Sanskrit Pathshala in 1885. It was earlier named as Indian National Union, however on the advice of Dadabhai Naoroji, the organisation was renamed as 'Indian National Congress'. George Yule was a Scottish merchant in England and India who served as the fourth President of the Indian National Congress in 1888 at Allahabad session.

15 **Consider the following statements about Indian National Congress.** *(Chap 9, Class-XII, Old NCERT)*

1. The first session was scheduled to be held in Poona, but due to a Plague outbreak it was shifted to Bombay.
2. The first session was held at Gokuldas Tejpal Sanskrit College, Bombay.
3. There were 72 delegates in the first session.

How many of the statements given above is/are correct?

(a) Only one (b) Only two
(c) All three (d) None of these

Ans. (c)

Exp. All three statements i.e. (1), (2) and (3) are correct as in March 1885, it was decided that a Conference of the Indian Nation Union would be convened at Poona but venue had to be shifted to Bombay because of Plague outbreak in Poona.

The first meeting was held on Monday 28th December, 1885 in Gokuldas Tejpal Sanskrit College, Bombay. It was attended by 72 delegates from all over India.

16 **Consider the following statements.**

(Chap 12, Class-XII, Old NCERT)

1. The Indian National Congress was established by retired civil servant AO Hume.
2. George Yule was the General Secretary of the Congress in 1885.

Which of the statements given above is/are correct?

(a) Only 1 (b) Only 2
(c) Both 1 and 2 (d) Neither 1 nor 2

Ans. (a)

Exp. Statement (1) is correct as, the Indian National Congress was established by retired Civil Servant AO Hume in 1885. Its objective was to create a platform for dialogue between educated Indians and British colonial authorities.

Statement (2) is incorrect because AO Hume was the General Secretary of the Congress in 1885. George Yule was the first European to be elected as President of the Indian National Congress.

17 **Consider the following statements.**

(Chap 12, Class-XII, Old NCERT)

1. The first woman President of the Indian National Congress was Sarojini Naidu.
2. The first Muslim President of the Indian National Congress was Badruddin Tyabji.

Which of the statements given above is/are correct?

(a) Only 1 (b) Only 2
(c) Both 1 and 2 (d) Neither 1 nor 2

Ans. (b)

Exp. Statement (2) is correct as Badruddin Tyabji presided over the third session of the Indian National Congress in 1887, at Madras. He became the first Muslim President of Indian National Congress.

Statement (1) is incorrect because the first woman President of the Indian National Congress was Annie Besant in Calcutta Session of Indian National Congress in 1917. She was a reputed theosophist, women's rights activist, writer and orator. Sarojini Naidu was the first Indian woman to preside over the session of Indian National Congress.

18 **Which of the following statements is/are correct in the context of Indian National Congress?**

(Chap 9, Class-VIII, Old NCERT)

1. In 1890, Kadambini Ganguli, the first woman graduate of Calcutta University addressed the Congress session.
2. Dadabhai Naoroji never held post of Congress President.

Which of the statements given above is/are correct?

(a) Only 1
(b) Only 2
(c) Both 1 and 2
(d) Neither 1 nor 2

Ans. (a)

Exp. Statement (1) is correct in the context of Indian National Congress. In 1890, session of Indian National Congress was held in Calcutta. It was presided by Pheroz Shah Mehta. At this conference, Kadambini Ganguli, the first woman graduate of the Calcutta University, addressed the Congress session.

Statement (2) is incorrect because Dadabhai Naoroji presided over the Calcutta Session (1886), Lahore Session (1893), Calcutta Session (1906) of the Congress.

19 **Regarding the Indian National Congress (INC), consider the following statements.**

(Chap 9, Class-VIII, Old NCERT

1. The Safety Valve Theory regarding the formation of INC emerged from a biography of AO Hume written by Wedderburn.
2. Since its inception, INC took up social reforms as a part of its agenda.
3. In the initial years of INC formation, the INC president belonged to the same region where the session was being held.

How many of the statements given above is/are correct?

(a) Only one (b) Only two
(c) All three (d) None of these

Ans. (a)

Exp. Only one statement i.e., (1) is correct as the Safety Valve Theory of INC formation proposes that AO Hume formed the Congress with the idea that it would prove to be a safety valve for releasing the growing discontent of the Indians.

It was first mentioned in William Wedderburn's biography of AO Hume published in 1913.

Statements (2) and (3) are incorrect because the main aim of the Indian National Congress in the initial stage was to found a democratic, nationalist movement and politicise and politically educate people. Initially, Congress did not take up questions of social reform.

At its second session, the President of the Congress, Dadabhai Naoroji, laid down this rule and said that A National Congress must confine itself to questions in which the entire nation has direct participation. INC followed a convention that the President should belong to a region other than where the Congress session was being held.

20 **Which of the following leaders presided over the session of the Indian National Congress?**

(Chap 9, Class-VIII, Old NCERT)

1. AO Hume 2. Badruddin Tyabji
3. Romesh Chandra Dutt 4. Vijaylakshmi Pandit
5. Gopal Krishna Gokhale

Codes

(a) 1, 2 and 3 (b) 2, 3 and 4
(c) 2, 3 and 5 (d) 3, 4 and 5

Ans. (c)

Exp. The correct answer is 2, 3 and 5. Badruddin Tyabji was the first Muslim President of Indian National Congress. He presided over Madras Session in 1887.

Romesh Chandra Dutt presided over the Lucknow Session in 1899.

Gopal Krishna Gokhale presided over the Banaras Session in 1905.

21 **Match the following lists correctly and choose the correct code.** *(Chap 12, Class-XII, Old NCERT)*

List I (Congress Session)	List II (Year)
A. Surat	1. 1906
B. Allahabad	2. 1910
C. Calcutta	3. 1905
D. Banaras	4. 1907

Codes

	A	B	C	D		A	B	C	D
(a)	4	2	1	3	(b)	2	1	4	3
(c)	2	1	3	4	(d)	4	1	3	2

Ans. (a)

Exp. The correct matching is A-4, B-2, C-1, D-3.

Indian National Congress (INC) session of 1907 was presided by Rash Bihari Bose in **Surat**.

Allahabad session of INC 1910 was presided by William Wedderburn.

Calcutta session of INC 1906 was presided by Dadabhai Naoroji.

Banaras session of INC 1905 was presided by Gopal Krishna Gokhale.

22 **Consider the following statements about the early nationalists.** *(Chap 9, Class-XII, Old NCERT)*

1. They aroused national feeling.
2. They emphasised on the national unity.
3. They equally gave importance to the social reforms.

Which of the statements given above is/are correct?

(a) 1 and 3 (b) 1 and 2 (c) 1, 2 and 3 (d) 2 and 3

Ans. (c)

Exp. All the statements (1), (2) and (3) are correct regarding early nationalists. The early nationalists aroused the feeling of one nation. They trained Indians in the art of political work. They brought out the true nature of the British rule in India. They were successful in bringing about certain reforms from the British Government. Besides political reform, the early nationalists also favoured social reforms in India.

23 **Consider the following statements.** *(Chap 12, Class-XII, Old NCERT)*

1. During the late 19th century, the Indian National Congress was the only channel through which, the stream of nationalism flowed.
2. Constitutional agitation was the main method adopted by moderate leaders of the Congress.

Which of the statements given above is/are correct?

(a) Only 1 (b) Only 2
(c) Both 1 and 2 (d) Neither 1 nor 2

Ans. (b)

Exp. Statement (2) is correct as the early nationalists (moderates) relied on constitutional and peaceful methods to achieve their aims. They made use of petitions, prayers and protests to achieve their objectives.

Statement (1) is incorrect as during the late 19th century, besides Indian National Congress, provincial conferences, provincial and local associations and nationalist newspapers were the other prominent organs of growing nationalist movement.

24 **Consider the following statements about the moderate leaders of the Indian National Congress.** *(Chap 9, Class-XII, Old NCERT)*

1. They criticised the British for drain of wealth from India.
2. They advocated boycott of foreign goods.
3. They ignored the issue of exploitation of Indian rural people by the zamindars.
4. They did not comprehended the vital role played by India in the imperial economy of Britain.

How many of the statements given above is/are incorrect?

(a) Only one (b) Only two
(c) Only three (d) All four

Ans. (a)

Exp. Only one statement i.e., (4) is incorrect regarding moderate leaders of the Indian National Congress.

The moderate leaders of the Indian National Congress comprehended the vital role played by India in the imperial economy of Britain.

According to them, the policies of Britain curbed the growth of Indian economy and was responsible for widespread poverty and hunger. However, it immensly benefitted the British economy.

25 **Who among the following were moderates?** *(Chap 10, Class-VIII, Old NCERT)*

1. GK Gokhale
2. Dadabhai Naoroji
3. Pherozeshah Mehta
4. Aurobindo Ghosh
5. BG Tilak
6. Bipin Chandra Pal

Codes

(a) 1, 2, 3, 4 and 6 (b) 1, 2 and 3
(c) 4, 5 and 6 (d) 1, 2, 3 and 4

Ans. (b)

Exp. GK Gokhale, Dadabhai Naoroji, Pherozshah Mehta, WC Banerjee, G Subramaniya Iyyer, Madan Mohan Malaviya and Surendranath Banerjee are few of the moderate leaders of Indian National Congress (INC).

Bal Gangadhar Tilak, Bipin Chandra Pal and Aurobindo Ghosh were extremist leaders of the Indian National Congress.

26 Consider the following statements with reference to the Indian National Congress.

(Chap 9, Class-VIII, Old NCERT)

1. The time period of Congress from 1885-1905 was known as an era of moderates.
2. British officials considered Congress as an organisation of masses.
3. Lala Lajpat Rai and Bipin Chandra Pal supported the policy of Petition and Prayers.

How many of the statements given above is/are correct?

(a) Only one (b) Only two
(c) All three (d) None of these

***Ans.* (a)**

Exp. Only one statement i.e., (1) is correct with reference to the Indian National Congress (INC). The time period from 1885 to 1905 of INS can be called the 'Moderate Phase'. The leaders of this phase are called moderates.

Statements (2) and (3) are incorrect because British official considered Congress as an organisation of middle class.

Viceroy, Lord Duffer in denounced the Congress as 'Microscopic Minority'.

Lala Lajpat Rai and Bipin Chandra Pal belonged to the Extremist Phase of Indian National Congress, which focused on mass mobilisation of masses.

27. Consider the following in the context of initial phase of the Indian Freedom Struggle.

(Chap 9, Class-VIII, Old NCERT)

1. One section of the Congress supported the radical ideologies and it came to known as Extremist.
2. The international events at the end of 19th and beginning of 20th century inspired the Indian Freedom Struggle.

Which of the statements given above is/are correct?

(a) Only 1 (b) Only 2
(c) Both 1 and 2 (d) Neither 1 nor 2

***Ans.* (c)**

Exp. Both the statements (1) and (2) are correct in the context of initial phase of the Indian Freedom Struggle. In the beginning of the 20th century, a different group emerged which had a rather aggressive approach against the British Empire. This group was called the Extremist and did not believe in the peaceful stance of the moderate leaders. The international events at the end of 19th and beginning of 20th century such as Boers war, Irish struggle, etc, inspired the Indian Freedom Struggle.

28 Consider the following statements.

(Unit 1, Class-XII, Tamil Nadu Board)

Statement-I In 1907, Congress's Annual Session was presided by Rash Behari Ghosh.

Statement-II In this session, Congress got divided into two groups (moderates and extremists).

Which one of the following is correct in respect of the above statements?

(a) Both Statement-I and Statement-II are correct and Statement-II is the correct explanation for Statement-I.
(b) Both Statement-I and Statement-II are correct and Statement-II is not the correct explanation for Statement-I.
(c) Statement-I is correct but Statement-II is incorrect.
(d) Statement-I is incorrect but Statement-II is correct.

***Ans.* (b)**

Exp. Both Statement-I and Statement-II are correct and Statement-II is not the correct explanation for Statement-I.

The 1907 session of the Indian National Congress was presided over by Rash Behari Ghosh. It was the session that witnessed the division of the Congress into two major factions, the moderates and the extremists.

The President of the 1916 Congress Session was Ambika Charan Mazumdar, moderates and extremists got united in this session.

29 Consider the following statements about the Indian National Congress. ***(Class-XII, Old NCERT)***

1. Sarojini Naidu was the first woman to be the President of the Congress.
2. CR Das was in prison when he functioned as the President of the Congress.
3. The first Britisher to become the President of the Congress was Alan Octavian Hume.
4. Alfred Webb was the President of the Congress in 1894.

How many of the statements given above is/are correct?

(a) Only one (b) Only two
(c) Only three (d) All four

***Ans.* (b)**

Exp. Only two statements i.e., (2) and (4) are correct. In 1921, Ahmedabad became the host of the annual session of the Indian National Congress for the second time since 1902. The session was presided over by Hakim Ajmal Khan, who acted on behalf of Chittaranjan Das. Alfred Webb was the President of the Congress in 1894.

Statements (1) and (3) are incorrect because Annie Besant was the first woman to be the President of the Congress. George Yule was the first British President of the Indian National Congress (INC).

30 Consider the following statements with reference to Bal Gangadhar Tilak. ***(Chap 14, Class-XII, Old NCERT)***

1. He edited the Kesari newspaper.
2. He commenced the beginning of Shivaji festival.
3. In the year 1896-97, he started No-tax Campaign.

How many of the statements given above is/are correct?

(a) Only one (b) Only two
(c) All three (d) None of these

***Ans.* (c)**

Exp. All three statements i.e., (1), (2) and (3) are correct regarding Bal Gangadhar Tilak.

Kesari was a Marathi newspaper founded by Lokmanya Bal Gangadhar Tilak in 1881. He used to run his two newspapers, Kesari in Marathi and Mahratta in English. He started public celebration of Ganesh Chaturthi in 1893 to arouse public sentiments against Britishers. He also commenced Shivaji festival for political unification of masses. During 1896-1897, Tilak initiated a 'No-tax Campaign' in Maharashtra. He asked the famine-stricken peasants of Maharashtra to withhold payment of land revenue if their crops had failed.

31 Consider the following statements with reference to the Calcutta session of Indian National Congress 1906. *(Chap 14, Class-XII, Old NCERT)*

1. It was presided by Gopal Krishna Gokhale.
2. Self -government or 'Swaraj' was declared goal of Indian National Congress.

Which of the statements given above is/are correct?

(a) Only 1 (b) Only 2
(c) Both 1 and 2 (d) Neither 1 nor 2

Ans. (b)

Exp. Statement (2) is correct as in Calcutta session of Indian National Congress in 1906, the debates and disagreements between the moderate and the militant nationalists were settle through declaration of Self-government or 'Swaraj' as the goal of Congress. Statement (1) is incorrect as Dadabhai Naoroji was the President of Calcutta session of Indian National Congress in 1906.

32 Match the following lists correctly and choose the correct code. *(Chap 11, Class-XII, Old NCERT)*

List I (Leaders of Swadeshi Movement)	List II (Place)
A. Chidambaram Pillai	1. Punjab
B. Hari Sarvottama Rao	2. Andhra Pradesh
C. Lala Lajpat Rai	3. Delhi
D. Syed Haidar Raza	4. Madras

Codes

	A	B	C	D		A	B	C	D
(a)	4	2	1	3	(b)	2	1	4	3
(c)	2	1	3	4	(d)	4	1	3	2

Ans. (a)

Exp. The correct matching is A-4, B-2, C-1, D-3.

Chidambaram Pillai was a prominent nationalist leader from Madras. He organised Swadeshi Movement in Madras province.

Hari Sarvottama Rao was the main leader of Swadeshi Movement in Andhra Pradesh.

Lala Lajpat Rai organised Swadeshi and Boycott Movement in Punjab.

Syed Haidar Raza was the main leader of Anti-Partition or Swadeshi and Boycott Movement in Delhi.

33 Which of the following programmes were launched by the nationalist against the partition of Bengal? *(Chap 9, Class-VIII, New NCERT)*

1. Boycott
2. Swadeshi
3. Non-Cooperation
4. National Education

Codes

(a) 1, 2 and 3 (b) 2, 3 and 4
(c) 1, 3 and 4 (d) 1, 2 and 4

Ans. (d)

Exp. Statements (1), (2) and (4) are correct. The Boycott of British goods, Swadeshi Movement and the promotion of National education were launched by Indian nationalists in response to the partition of Bengal in 1905. To protest the partition and show their unity against British policies, Indian nationalists initiated the Swadeshi Movement. The Swadeshi Movement aimed at Boycotting British goods and promoting the use of Indian-made products. Nationalists emphasised the need for a system of education that celebrated Indian traditions, culture and history. The idea was to create a generation of educated Indians who were proud of their heritage and culture and were actively engaged in the struggle for independence.

34 Which statements is/are correct with reference to Civil Administration, 1905? *(Class-XII, Old NCERT)*

1. Lord Curzon decided to rearrange the provincial boundaries.
2. A new province named East Bengal and Assam was created.

Codes

(a) Only 1 (b) Only 2
(c) Both 1 and 2 (d) Neither 1 nor 2

Ans. (c)

Exp. Both the statements are correct with reference to Civil Administration, 1905. The first Partition of Bengal was a territorial reorganisation of the Bengal Presidency. The reorganisation separated the largely Muslim Eastern areas from the largely Hindu Western areas.

East Bengal, because of isolation and poor communications, had been neglected in favour of West Bengal and Bihar.

Curzon choose to unite Assam, with 15 districts of East Bengal and thus, forming a new Province. The capital was Dacca (now Dhaka, Bangladesh) and the people were mainly Muslim.

35 Consider the following statements. *(Chap 11, Class-XII, Old NCERT)*

1. The objective behind the Partition of Bengal, 1905 was to ensure governance.
2. Partition of Bengal began a transformation of the Indian National Congress from a middle-class pressure group into a Nationwide Mass Movement.
3. Partition of Bengal suppressed the rising sentiments of the nationalism.

How many of the statements given above is/are correct?

(a) Only one (b) Only two
(c) All three (d) None of these

Ans. (a)

Exp. Only one statement i.e., (2) is correct as the Partition of Bengal transformed the Indian National Congress from a middle-class pressure group into a Nationwide Mass Movement.

Statements (1) and (3) are incorrect because even though Bengal was partitioned on the pretext of ensuring governance, the reality was to weaken the national movements. The Bengal partition did not suppress the rising sentiments of the nationalism. It became a cause for Nationwide Mass Movement.

36 Consider the following statements with reference to the Partition of Bengal. *(Chap 9, Class-VIII, Old NCERT)*

1. Muslim League supported the Partition of Bengal.
2. In the decade of the Partition of Bengal, Muslim League demanded for the separate electorate by the government.

Which of the statements given above is/are correct?

(a) Only 1 (b) Only 2
(c) Both 1 and 2 (d) Neither 1 nor 2

Ans. (c)

Exp. Both the statements (1) and (2) are correct regarding the Partition of Bengal.

The Partition of Bengal was supported by the Muslims of East Bengal and their support was motivated by the poor economic conditions in East Bengal. In 1906, the Muslim League demanded separate electorate.

37 Which of the following programmes were organised by the Nationalist against the Partition of Bengal? *(Class-XII, Old NCERT)*

1. Boycott
2. Indigenous
3. Arayagha
4. National Education

Codes

(a) 1, 2 and 3 (b) 2, 3 and 4 (c) 1, 3 and 4 (d) 1, 2 and 4

Ans. (d)

Exp. Boycott, Indigenous and National Education programmes were organised by the Nationalist against the Partition of Bengal. Among the movements various forms of a struggle was taken boycott and burning of foreign clothes, picketing of shops selling foreign goods that encountered the greatest visible success on the practical and popular level. In the field of National Education, this emphasis on self-reliance was most evident. The National College of Bengal was founded as its principal with Aurobindo. Numerous national schools have been established throughout the country in a short period of time. The National Education Council was established in August, 1906.

38 Consider the following statements with reference to Swadeshi Movement. *(Chap 9, Class-VIII, Old NCERT)*

1. It encouraged the idea of Swadeshi enterprise.
2. The national education was promoted as a part of Swadeshi Movement.

Which of the statements given above is/are correct?

(a) Only 1
(b) Only 2
(c) Both 1 and 2
(d) Neither 1 nor 2

Ans. (c)

Exp. Both the statements (1) and (2) are correct with reference to Swadeshi Movement.

After the Partition of Bengal, Swadeshi Movement was formally started from Town Hall Calcutta on 7th August, 1905 to curb import of foreign goods by relying on domestic production. It also promoted the idea of Swadeshi enterprises and national education.

National education was also promoted in the Swadeshi Movement. In 1906, the National Council of Education was set up to organise National Education System. For technical education, Bengal Institute of Technology was established.

39 Consider the following statements. *(Chap 9, Class-VIII, New NCERT) (IAS Pre 2023)*

Statement-II 7th August is declared as the National Handloom Day.

Statement-II It was in 1905 that the Swadeshi Movement was launched on the same day.

Which one of the following is correct in respect of the above statements?

(a) Both Statement-I and Statement-II are correct and Statement-II is the correct explanation for Statement-I.
(b) Both Statement I and Statement-II are correct and Statement-II is not the correct explanation for Statement-I.
(c) Statement-I is correct, but Statement-II is incorrect.
(d) Statement-I is incorrect, but Statement-II is correct.

Ans. (a)

Exp. Both Statement- I and Statement-II are correct and Statement-II is the correct explanation for Statement-I. 7th August is celebrated as the National Handloom Day in India. It is a day dedicated to honouring the handloom weaving community and highlighting the significant contribution of the handloom sector to the socio-economic development of the country.

The Swadeshi Movement, which aimed to promote indigenous industries and revive domestic products, was indeed launched on 7th August, 1905. This movement included support for handloom weavers as part of its borader objectives.

40 With reference to the period of Extremist Nationalist Movement in India with its spirit of Swadeshi, which one of the following statements is not correct? *(Class-XII, Old NCERT)*

(a) Liyakat Hussain led the Muslim peasants of Barisal in their agitations.
(b) In 1889, the scheme of National Education was formulated by Satish Chandra Mukherjee.
(c) The Bengal National College was founded in 1906, with Aurobindo as the Principal.
(d) Tagore preached the cult of Atmashakti, the main plank of which was social and economic regeneration of the villages.

Ans. (a)

Exp. Statement (a) is not correct because Barisal Movement was not led by Liyakat Hussain. Barisal agitation of 1913 was led by Trailokyanath Chakraborty and Pratul Chandra Ganguly to incite rebellion against British Raj.

41 Consider the following statements. *(Chap 11, Class-XII, Old NCERT)*

Statement-I Partition of Bengal in 1905 brought to an end of moderates' role in the Indian Freedom Movement.

Statement-II The Surat session of Indian National Congress separated the extremists from the moderates.

Which one of the following is correct in respect of the above statements?

(a) Both Statement-I and Statement-II are correct and Statement-II is the correct explanation for Statement-I.
(b) Both Statement I and Statement-II are correct and Statement- II is not the correct explanation for Statement-I.
(c) Statement-I is correct, but Statement-II is incorrect.
(d) Statement-I is incorrect, but Statement-II is correct.

Ans. (d)

Exp. Statement-I is incorrect but, statement-II is correct. The role of moderates continued even after the Partition of Bengal in 1905.

Extremists and moderates separated at Surat session in 1907 but reunited at 1916 session at Lucknow.

42 Which one of the following defines extremist ideology during the early phase of Indian freedom movement? *(Class-XII, Old NCERT)*

(a) Stimulating the production of indigenous articles by giving them preference over imported commodities.
(b) Obtaining self-government by aggressive means in place of petitions and constitutional ways.
(c) Providing national education according to the requirements of the country.
(d) Organising coups against the British empire through military revolt.

Ans. (b)

Exp. Extremist ideology was to obtain self-government by aggressive means in place of petitions and constitutional ways. An extremist ideology refers to a set of beliefs or principles that advocate for radical and often uncompromising approaches to achieve certain goals or objectives.

43 Consider the following statements behind the main reason for the first split in the Indian National Congress. *(Chap 9, Class-VIII, Old NCERT)*

1. Introduction of Communalism into Indian politics by Lord Minto.
2. The moderates were opposed to the use of boycott.
3. Foundation of Muslim League.
4. Aurobindo Ghosh's inability to be elected as the President of the Indian National Congress.

How many of the statements given above is/are correct?

(a) Only one (b) Only two
(c) Only three (d) All four

Ans. (a)

Exp. Only one statement i.e., (2) is correct. The main reason for the first split (Surat split) of the Congress was that the moderates were opposed to the use of boycott. According to them, it involved the use of force and thereby unsuitable as political strategy to fight against Britishers.

Whereas, boycott was the main strategy advocated by the extremist section led by Bal Gangadhar Tilak. Also, the extremists had lack of faith in the capacity of the moderates to negotiate with the British Government.

44 Consider the following statements with reference to the Morley Minto Reform. *(Chap 11, Class-XII, Old NCERT)*

1. It introduced separate electorate in Indian politics.
2. It covered the Muslims, Sikhs, and Schedule Caste.

Which of the statements given above is/are incorrect?

(a) Only 1 (b) Only 2
(c) Both 1 and 2 (d) Neither 1 nor 2

Ans. (b)

Exp. Statement (2) is incorrect with reference to the Morley Minto Reform because the separate electorate for Sikhs, Christians and Anglo-Indians was expanded by Montague-Chelmsford reforms of 1919. It first time introduced the separate electorate for Muslims for election to the Central council.

45 Consider the following statements with reference to Delhi Darbar of 1911. *(Chap 9, Class-VIII, Old NCERT)*

1. The Partition of Bengal was annulled.
2. The capital of British India was transferred from Calcutta to Delhi.
3. Congress participated in the Delhi Darbar.

How many of the statements given above is/are incorrect?
(a) Only one (b) Only two
(c) All three (d) None of these

Ans. (a)

Exp. Only one statement i.e., (3) is incorrect with reference to Delhi Darbar of 1911 because the Congress passed a resolution condemning the pomp and show of this Darbar at the cost of the poor Indians.

It was organised in 1911 under the Viceroyship of Lord Hardinge to commemorate the coronation of king George V in Britain. In this Darbar, two key decisions were taken

(i) Transfer of capital of India from Calcutta to Delhi.
(ii) Annulment of Partition of Bengal.

Revolutionary Movements/Activities

46 Consider the following statements with reference to the revolutionary movements/activities.

(Chap 11, Class-XII, Old NCERT)

1. Chapekar brothers established the Abhinav Bharat Society.
2. In 1897, the Chapekar brothers assassinated two unpopular British officials at Poona.

Which of the statements given above is/are correct?
(a) Only 1 (b) Only 2
(c) Both 1 and 2 (d) Neither 1 nor 2

Ans. (b)

Exp. Statement (2) is correct with reference to the revolutionary movement as the Chapekar brothers–Damodar Hari Chapekar and Balkrishna Hari Chapekar assassinated. British official WC Rand and his military escort Lieutenant Ayerst at Pune in 1897.

Statement (1) is incorrect as Abhinav Bharat Society was established by Savarkar brothers in 1904.

47 Consider the following statements.

(Chap 11, Class-XII, Old NCERT)

1. Yuganter served as a mouthpiece of the militant Nationalist.
2. The Yuganter (Jugantar) party was colonial Bengal's most powerful revolutionary terrorist organisation.
3. It was operating in Bengal for independence.

How many of the statements given above is/are correct?
(a) Only one (b) Only two (c) All three (d) None of these

Ans. (b)

Exp. Only two statements i.e., (1) and (3) are correct. Yuganter served as a mouthpiece of the militant Nationalist. The Jugantar party was established in April 1906 by leaders like Aurobindo Ghopsh, his brother Barin Ghosh, Hemchandra Kanungo, and Upen Banerjee, along with 21 revolutionaries. It was one of the two main secret revolutionary trends operating in Bengal for Indian independence .

48 With reference to Indian Revolutionary movement, consider the following statements.

(Chap 14, Class-XII, Old NCERT)

1. Revolutionary movement started as a consequence of British policies.
2. Khudiram Bose and Prafulla Chaki threw bomb at judge in Delhi.
3. Shyamji Krishnavarma carried out revolutionary activities in London.

How many of the statements given above is/are incorrect?
(a) Only one (b) Only two
(c) All three (d) None of these

Ans. (a)

Exp. Only one statement i.e., (2) is incorrect with reference to Indian Revolutionary movement. Khudiram Bose in April 1908, alongwith his fellow revolutionary Prafulla Chaki threw bomb on a carriage in Muzaffarpur, with an intention of assassinating the Chief Presidency Magistrate, Douglas Kingsford.

49 Consider the following freedom fighters.

(Chap 9, Class-VIII, Old NCERT) (IAS Pre 2022)

1. Barindra Kumar Ghosh
2. Jogesht Chandra Chatterjee
3. Rash Behari Bose

Who of the above was/were actively associated with the Ghadar Party?
(a) 1 and 2 (b) Only 2 (c) 1 and 3 (d) Only 3

Ans. (d)

Exp. Rash Behari Bose was actively associated with the Ghadar Party. Indian reevolutionaries in the United States of America and Canada had established the Ghadar (Rebellion) Party in 1913. While most of the members of the party were Sikh peasants and soliders, their leaders were mostly educated Hindus or Muslims. Ras Behari Bose, Raja Mahendra Pratap, Lala Hardayat, Abdul Rahim, Maulana Abidullah Sindhi, Champak Raman Pillai, Sardar Singh Rana and Madam Cama were some of the prominent Indians Ghadar Leaders who carried on revolutionary activities and propaganda outside India.

Barindra Kumar Ghosh was founding member of Jugantar (weekly Bengali). It was a revolutionary outfit in Bengal.

Jogesh Chandra Chatterjee, initially joined Anushilan Samiti of Bengal, later he became the part of Hindustan Republican Association (HRA).

50 Consider the following statements.

(Chap 14, Class-XII, Old NCERT)

1. Anushilan Samiti was an organisation that existed in Bengal.
2. It was two parts were the Dhaka Anushilan Samiti and the Jugantar Group centered.
3. In 1905, the Samiti Published 'Bhavani Mandir'.

How many of the statements given above is/are correct?
(a) Onle one
(b) Only two
(c) All three
(d) None of the above

Ans. (c)

Exp. All three statements i.e., (1), (2) and (3) are correct as the 'Anushilan Samiti' was a revolutionary organisation existed in Bengal. It was established in 1907 in Calcutta under the leadership of Paramnath Mitra. Its two parts were the Dhaka Anushilan samiti centered in Dhaka and the Jugantar Group centered at Calcutta. The Samiti was inspired by the thoughts, Speeches and writings of Swamivivekanand and influenced by Bankim Chandra Chatterjee's Anandmath. In 1905, the Samiti published 'Bhavani Mandir'.

51 Given below is a list of organisations. *(Chap 11, Class-XII, Old NCERT)*

1. Abhinav Bharat
2. Anushilan Samiti
3. New Nationalist Party
4. Indian Patriot Association

Select those, engaged in revolutionary activities, using the codes given below.
(a) 1, 2 and 3 (b) 2, 3 and 4
(c) 1 and 2 (d) 1, 2 and 4

Ans. (c)

Exp. Among the given options (1) and (2) i.e., Abhinav Bharat and Anushilan Samiti was engaged in revolutionary activities. Abhinav Bharat Society was a secret society founded by Vinayak Damodar Savarkar and his brother Ganesh Damodar Savarkar in 1904.
Anushilan Samiti was founded by Paramnath Mitra and Barindra Kumar Ghosh in 1907. It supported revolutionary violence as the means for ending British rule in India.

52 Consider the following statements with reference to the early phase of revolutionary movement in India? *(Chap 10, Class-VIII, Old NCERT)*

1. The headquarters of Ghadar movement was in Lahore.
2. A Provisional Government of India was formed in Kabul.

Which of the statements given above is/are incorrect?
(a) Only 1 (b) Only 2
(c) Both 1 and 2 (d) Neither 1 nor 2

Ans. (a)

Exp. Statement (1) is incorrect with reference to the early phase of revolutionary movement in India as the Ghadar Party had its headquarters in San Francisco, California.

53 Consider the following statements regarding Ghadar Party. *(Chap 9, Class-VIII, Old NCERT)*

1. The party was formed by Indian migrants in US and Canada.
2. The party started a newspaper named Ghadar.
3. It was founded by Sohan Singh Bhakna and Lala Hardayal.

How many of the statements given above is/are correct?
(a) Only one (b) Only two
(c) All three (d) None of these

Ans. (c)

Exp. All three statements i.e., (1), (2) and (3) are correct as Ghadar Party was founded by Sohan Singh Bhakna along with Lal Hardayal in 1913. It was an international political movement consisting of emigrant Indians to overthrow British rule in India. The Name Ghadar Party was adopted after the launch of its Journal Ghadar in 1913.

54 Consider the following statements in the context of revolutionaries in 20th century. *(Chap 9, Class-VIII, Old NCERT)*

1. In 1912, revolutionaries threw bomb at Viceroy Hardinge.
2. Viceroy Hardinge was killed in this attack.
3. Ghadar Movement was started in 1913.

Which of the statements given above is/are correct?
(a) Only 1 (b) Only 2 (c) 1 and 3 (d) 1, 2 and 3

Ans. (c)

Exp. Statements (1) and (3) are correct in the context of revolutionaries in 20th century.
In 1912, revolutionaries made an attempt to assassinate the then Viceroy of India, Lord Hardinge by throwing bomb in Chandni Chowk in Delhi.
Ghadar Movement was started in 1913 in San Francisco by Lala Hardayal and Sohan Singh Bhakna.
Statement (2) is incorrect because Viceroy Hardinge suffered several injuries due to the bomb attack, but he was not killed.

55 Consider the following statements. *(Chap 11, Class-XII, New NCERT)*

1. Akhil Bharat Hindu Mahasabha is a Hindu Nationalist Political Party in India.
2. The organisation was originally called Sarvadeshik Hindu Sabha ('Pan-Country Hindu Assembly').
3. Damodar Savarkar was associated with Hindu Mahasabha.

How many of the statements given above is/are correct?
(a) Only one (b) Only two
(c) All three (d) None of these

Ans. (c)

Exp. All three statements are correct regarding Hindu Mahasabha as it is a non-secular party, established in 1915 by Madan Mohan Malviya for safeguarding issues of Hindus. During the World War II, the Mahasabha supported the British War effort and briefly entered coalitions with the Muslim League in provincial and central councils. It emerged as a distinct party under the leadership of Vinayak Damodar Savarkar.

Formation of Muslim League

56 Consider the following statements.

(Chap 16, Class-X, Old NCERT)

1. The AIML (The All India Muslim League) was the first Muslim Political Party of India.
2. It was formed under the leadership of Agha Khan.
3. Muslim League supported the partition of Bengal.

How many of the statements given above is/are correct?

(a) Only one (b) Only two (c) All three (d) None of these

Ans. (c)

Exp. All three statements are correct as the All India Muslim League was a political party founded in 1906 with the aim of representing the interest of All India Muslim League in a country made up of mostly Hindus. The Muslim League supported the partition of Bengal and demanded special safeguard for the Muslims in government service.

57 Consider the following statements.

(Chap 16, Class-X, Old NCERT)

1. Nawab Salimullah was the first President of Muslim League.
2. The AIML was essentially a party of educated elite Muslims.
3. Muhammad Ali Jinnah joined the league in 1913.

How many of the statements is/are correct?

(a) Only one
(b) Only two
(c) All three
(d) None of the above

Ans. (c)

Exp. All three statements are correct as the first Honourary President of the League was Sir Sultan Muhammad Shah (Aghaa Khan III). The AIML was essentially a party of educated elite Muslims, at least in the beginning. The party's chief aim was to promote and secure civil rights for Muslims. Muhammad Ali Jinnah joined the league in 1913.

58 Consider the following pairs.

(Chap 16, Class-X, Old NCERT)

Journal/ Newspaper		Author/ Editor
1. Comrade	–	Muhammad Ali Jauhar
2. Al Hilal	–	Abul Kalam Azad
3. Kesari	–	Muhammad Ali Jinnah

How many of the pairs given above is/are correctly matched?

(a) Only one pairs (b) Only two pairs
(c) All three pairs (d) None of these

Ans. (b)

Exp. Only two pairs i.e., (1) and (2) are correctly matched.

Comrade was a weekly English newspaper, published and edited by Muhammad Ali Jauhar between 1911 and 1914. Al-Hilal was a weekly Urdu-language newspaper established by the Indian Muslim Independence activist Maulana Abul Kalam Azad.

Pair (3) is not correctly matched because Kesari was a Marathi newspaper founded in 1881 by Lokmanya Bal Gangadhar Tilak.

Chapter 30

Indian National Movement : Second Phase (1915-1935)

Indian National Movement : Second Phase (1915-1935)

Lucknow Pact (1916)
- Finalised at Lucknow Session of Congress presided by Ambika Charan Majumdar
- Extremist led by Tilak readmitted in Congress
- Muslim League and Congress put forth a joint demand
- Assisted by Annie Besant and Tilak
- Acceptance of separate electorates gave tactical acceptance of two-nation theory

Home Rule League Movement
- Indian response to First World War
- Inspired by Irish Home Rule League
- Main objective was self-rule
- Two separate leagues- Tilak's league covered Maharashtra (except Bombay), Karnataka, Central Province and Berar
- And Annie Besant's league had 200 branched and covered rest of India

Gandhian Era
- Gandhiji Activism in South Africa: Set up Natal Indian Congress (1894) and newspaper Indian Opinion
- Led Satyagraha against Registration Certificate
- Campaign against restrictions on Indian Migration and Campaigned against poll tax and invalidation of Indian Marriages

Gandhi's Arrival in India
- In 1915
- Sought guidance from Gopal Krishna Gokhale

Champaran Satyagraha, 1917
- First Civil Disobedience movement in India; Invited by Rajkumar Shukla
- Led peasants and opposed Tinkathia system
- Agitation against high rents and illegal dues by cultivation of Indigo

Ahmedabad Mill Strike, 1918
- First Hunger strike in Indian National movement
- Dispute between cotton mill owners and workers over issue discontinuation of plague bonus
- Gandhiji demanded for a 35 % hike and took a fast unto death

Kheda Satyagraha, 1918
- First Non-Cooperation Movement by Gandhiji
- Opposed imposition of land revenue despite crop failure

Rowlatt Act, 1919
- Authorised the Government to imprison any person without trial and conviction in a court of law
- Officially called the Anarchial and Revolutionary Crimes Act; Mass protest was organised by the Gandhiji

Jallianwala Bagh Massacre, 1919
- Protest against Rowlatt Act was organised in Amritsar
- Brig-Gen Reginald Dyer ordered fire on unarmed peaceful protest
- Rabindranath returned Knighthood
- Gandhi surrendered his title of 'Kaiser-e- Hind'

Nehru Report, 1928
- Prepared by a committee headed by Motilal Nehru; Done in response to challenge posed by Simon Commission and Lord Birkenhand; Recommended-dominion status

Karachi Session of the Congress in 1931
- Endorsed Gandhi-Irwin pact
- Presided by Vallabhbhai Patel
- Resolution of Fundamental Rights and National Economic Programmed was adopted

Poona Pact, 1932
- Against provision of Separate electorate to depressed classes under Communal Award; Abandoned this idea but seats increased to 18% of total in Central legislature

Round Table Conferences (1930-32)
- Three conferences organised in England to discuss Constitutional reforms
- Congress (Gandhiji) participated in second conference (1931)

Hindustan Republic Association
- Founded in Kanpur by Ramprasad Bismil, Jogesh Chandra Chatterjee and Sachin Sanyal

Hindustan Socialist Republic Association
- Formed under the leadership of Chandrashekar Azad
- Saunders was assassinated (1927) by Bhagat Singh to avenge the death of Lajpat Rai

SOURCE **Old NCERT Class VIII** (*Struggle for Swaraj*), **Old NCERT Class VIII** (*Nationalist Movement from 1923 to 1939*), **Old NCERT Class VIII** (*The Making of the National Movement : 1870s-1947*), **Old NCERT Class X** (*India's Struggle for Independence*), **New NCERT Class XII** (*Understanding Partition : Politics, Memories, Experiences*), **New NCERT Class XII** (*Mahatma Gandhi and the Nationalist Movement : Civil Disobedience and Beyond*), **Old NCERT Class XII** (*Struggle for Swaraj I, 1919-1927*), **Old NCERT Class XII** (*Struggle for Swaraj I 1927-1947*) **Tamil Nadu Board Class XII, Unit-3** (*Impact of World War I on Indian Freedom Movement*) **NIOS, Module-4, Chap 20** (*Nationalism*)

1 **Consider the following statements.**

(Chap 10, Class-VIII, Old NCERT)

1. Gandhiji actively fought for the Indians in the South Africa.
2. He returned to India in 1915.
3. Rowlatt Satyagraha was his first movement in India.

Which of the statements given above is/are correct?

(a) Only 1 (b) 1 and 2
(c) 2 and 3 (d) 1, 2 and 3

Ans. (b)

Exp. Statements (1) and (2) are correct.

Gandhiji actively fought for the Indians in the South Africa. In 1906-1907, Mahatma Gandhi started a Satyagraha in South Africa against the compulsory registration and passes for Indians. In 1910, he announced Satyagraha against emigration and restriction in Natal (South Africa). On 9th January, 1915, Mahatma Gandhi returned to India from South Africa.

Statement (3) is incorrect because Champaran Satyagraha (1917) was his first movement in India. He had started Rowlatt Satyagraha in 1919.

2 **Which of the following were the causes behind the launch of 'Non-Cooperation Movement'?**

(Chap 20, Module-4, NIOS)

1. Jallianwala Bagh Massacre
2. Resentment with Rowlatt Act
3. Khilafat Movement
4. Montagu-Chelmsford Reforms

Select the correct answer using the codes given below.

(a) 1, 2 and 3
(b) 2, 3 and 4
(c) 1, 3 and 4
(d) 1, 2, 3 and 4

Ans. (d)

Exp. The Non-Cooperation Movement was a response to the Jallianwala Bagh Massacre, Resentment towards the Rowlatt Act, the Khilafat Movement and dissatisfaction with the Montagu-Chelmsford Reforms. Together, these factors led to a united effort by Indians to resist British rule through non-violent means. Firstly, the tragic incident known as the Jallianwala Bagh Massacre in 1919 had a big impact.

The Rowlatt Act, which came into effect in 1919. This law allowed the British Government to arrest and detain people without a trial.

The Khilafat Movement, began in 1919, was also a factor. This movement was a response to the mistreatment of the Ottoman Empire by the Allies after World War I.

The Montagu-Chelmsford Reforms of 1919, though introducing some changes, fell short of Indian expectations for self-governance.

3 **Which of the following was/were the recommendations of the Simon Commission set up in 1927?** *(Chap 11, Class-VIII, Old NCERT)*

1. Establish representative government in the provinces.
2. Provincial Legislative Council members should be increased.
3. The Governor should have discretionary power in administrative power and internal securities.

Select the correct answer using the codes given below.

(a) 1 and 2 (b) 2 and 3
(c) 1, 2 and 3 (d) None of these

Ans. (c)

Exp. All three statements (1), (2) and (3) are correct regarding the recommendations of the Simon Commission.

The important recommendations were the Abolition of dyarchy, establishment of representative governments in the provinces, Governor should have discretionary power in administrative power and internal securities, provincial Legislative Council members should be increased, retention of separate communal electorates until communal tensions had died down and Government of India's complete control over the High Court. The Simon Commission, also known as the India Statutory Commission, was established in 1927 to recommend constitutional reforms in India. The commission's report was published in 1930.

4 **Consider the following statements.**

(Chap 12, Class-XII, Old NCERT)

1. Dr. Rajendra Prasad persuaded Mahatma Gandhi to come to Champaran to investigate the problem of peasants.
2. Mahatma Gandhi was appointed as a member of Inquiry Commission after Champaran Satyagraha.

Which of the statements given above is/are correct?

(a) Only 1 (b) Only 2
(c) Both 1 and 2 (d) Neither 1 nor 2

Ans. (b)

Exp. Statement (2) is correct because in June 1917, the Government appointed an Inquiry commission with Gandhiji as one of the members.

Statement (1) is incorrect because Raj Kumar Shukla and Sant Raut, a moneylender who owned some land, persuaded Gandhi to go to Champaran and thus, the Champaran Satyagraha began.

5 **Arrange the following events in chronological order.**

(Chap 11, Class-VIII, Old NCERT)

1. Komagata Maru incident
2. Kheda Satyagraha
3. Kakori Conspiracy
4. Non-Cooperation Movement

Select the correct answer using the codes given below.

(a) 3-4-1-2 (b) 3-1-2-4 (c) 1-2-4-3 (d) 3-2-4-1

Ans. (c)

Exp. The correct chronological order is 1-2-4-3. Komagata Maru Incident took place in 1914. The Kheda Satyagraha(1918) was a protest against the British Government's decision to impose taxes on the peasants of Kheda district in Gujarat during a severe famine. The Non-Cooperation Movement was started on 1st August, 1920 by the Indian National Congress (INC) under the leadership of Mahatma Gandhi. The movement was launched with the aim of obtaining self-governance. However, Gandhi decided to end the campaign in February, 1922 after the Chauri Chaura tragedy. The Kakori Train Robbery took place on 8th August, 1925.

6 Consider the following statements. *(Chap 9, Class-VIII, New NCERT)*

1. The Lucknow Pact of 1916 promoted the spirit of unity between the Indian National Congress and the All India Muslim League.
2. Tilak was opposed to the signing of Lucknow Pact.

Which of the statements given above is/are correct?

(a) Only 1 (b) Only 2
(c) Both 1 and 2 (d) Neither 1 nor 2

Ans. (a)

Exp. Statement (1) is correct as the Lucknow Pact was an agreement reached between the Indian National Congress and the All India Muslim League (AIML) at a joint session of both the parties held in Lucknow in December, 1916. It promoted the spirit of unity between the two major political parties in India.

Statement (2) is incorrect because Tilak was not opposed to the signing of Lucknow Pact. He along with Mohammad Jinnah played an important role in signing of the pact.

7 Which of the following statements is/are correct about Morley-Minto? *(Chap 12, Class-XII, Old NCERT)*

1. It considerably increased the size of the Legislative Councils, both central and provincial.
2. It provided for the first time, the association of Indians with the Executive Councils of the Viceroy and Governors.

Select the correct answer using the codes given below.

(a) Only 1 (b) Only 2
(c) Both 1 and 2 (d) Neither 1 nor 2

Ans. (c)

Exp. Both the statements (1) and (2) are correct. The Act of 1909 is also known as Morley-Minto Reforms (Lord Morley was the then Secretary of State for India and Lord Minto was the then Viceroy of India). The Morley-Minto Reforms significantly expanded the size of both central and provincial Legislative Councils. More Indian representatives were allowed to participate in these Councils, providing them with a platform to voice their concerns and contribute to decision-making. For the first time, the reforms allowed Indians to be associated with the Executive Councils of the Viceroy (the highest-ranking British official in India) and Governors of provinces. This association meant that Indians could now have a say in the formulation and execution of administrative policies.

8 Which of the following statements regarding Home Rule League in India are correct? *(Chap 16, Class-X, Old NCERT)*

1. The movement was led by the moderate Congress leaders.
2. There were two Home Rule Leagues.
3. The movement became strong, because other mass agitations could not be launched by the Congress during the World War.
4. The government was non-reactive to the movement.

Select the correct answer using the codes given below.

(a) 1, 2 and 3 (b) 1, 3 and 4 (c) 1 and 4 (d) 2 and 3

Ans. (d)

Exp. Statements (2) and (3) are correct regarding Home Rule League in India. Tilak founded the first Home Rule League at the Bombay Provincial Congress at Belgaum in April 1916, then after this Annie Besant founded second League at Adyar, Madras in September 1916. The movement became strong as other mass agitations could not be launched by the Congress during World War I. Statements (1) and (4) are incorrect because both Tilak and Besant belonged to the extremists group.

This movement created a stir within the country. This movement led to the Montagu declaration for responsible government in India.

9 With reference to Montagu-Chelmsford Reform, consider the following statements. *(Chap 16, Class-X, Old NCERT)*

1. In the provinces, Dyarchy was introduced.
2. There were elected majorities in the Legislative Assemblies.
3. All Provincial subjects were given in hands of Legislative Assembly.

How many of the statements given above is/are incorrect?

(a) Only one (b) Only two
(c) Only three (d) None of these

Ans. (a)

Exp. Only one statement i.e., (3) is incorrect with reference of Montagu-Chelmsford Reforms, because under Montagu-Chelmsford Reforms, Provincial subjects were divided into two lists-reserved and transferred. The Montagu–Chelmsford Reforms or more briefly known as the Mont–Ford Reforms, were introduced by the colonial government to introduce self-governing institutions gradually in British India.

- The Imperial Legislative Council was now to consist of two houses: the Central Legislative Assembly and the Council of State.
- The provinces were to follow the Dual Government System or Dyarchy.

10 Consider the following statements about the Swadeshi Movement. *(Chap 12, Class-XII, Old NCERT)*

1. The protests against the partition began in 1903 but gained momentum and better organisation after the official announcement and implementation in 1905.
2. It was an anti-partition movement by the moderate leaders like Surendranath Banerjee and Krishna Kumar Mitra.
3. Surendranath Banerjee and Ramendra, Sundar Trivedi called for celebrating Raksha-Bandhan and Arandhan on the day of implementation of partition.

How many of the statements given above is/are correct?

(a) Only one (b) Only two
(c) All three (d) None of these

***Ans.* (b)**

Exp. Only two statements i.e., (1) and (2) are correct regarding the Swadeshi Movement. Before the official announcement and implementation of the partition of Bengal, there was growing discontentment among Indians. However, the Swadeshi Movement gained momentum and better organisation after the official announcement of the partition in 1905. The Swadeshi Movement was an anti-partition movement.

Moderate leaders like Surendranath Banerjee and Krishna Kumar Mitra actively participated in this movement.

Statement (3) is incorrect because Rabindranath Tagore and Ramendra Sundar Trivedi further supported the cause by calling for the observance of Raksha-Bandhan and Arandhan on the day of the partition's implementation, not Surendranath Banerjee.

11 Consider the following statements with respect to the Rowlatt Act. *(Class-XII, Old NCERT)*

1. It was passed by the government under the period of Lord Chelmsford.
2. The seeds of the Rowlatt Act were sown in 1915 when the repressive Defense of India Act was imposed to curb anti-colonial activities during World War I.
3. It was enacted on the recommendations of the Sedition Committee under Sir Sydney Rowlatt.
4. The first major public protest by Mahatma Gandhi against this unjust law was organised on 30th March, 1919.

How many of the statements given above is/are correct?

(a) Only one (b) Only two
(c) Only three (d) All four

***Ans.* (d)**

Exp. All four statements i.e., (1), (2), (3) and (4) are correct regarding the Rowlatt Act.

The Rawlatt Act was passed during the period of Lord Chelmsford was served as a Viceroy of India from 1916 to 1921. The origins of the Rowlatt Act can be traced back to the Defense of India Act (1915). During World War I, the British colonial authorities imposed the Defense of India Act to suppress anti-colonial activities.

The Rowlatt Act was enacted on the recommendations of the Sedition Committee under Sir Sydney Rowlatt. The committee evaluated the links between political terrorism in India and proposed measures to address perceived threats. Mahatma Gandhi played a pivotal role in opposing the Rowlatt Act. On 30th March, 1919, he organised a major public protest against this unjust law.

12 Consider the following statements about Champaran Satyagraha. *(Chap 12, Class-XII, Old NCERT)*

1. European planters plan to grow indigo on 3/20 part of the total land is the primary reason behind Champaran Satyagraha.
2. Mahatma Gandhi was invited by Dr. Rajendra Prasad to visit Champaran district.
3. One reason for this movement was that the price paid to the ryots was decided based on the area of the land and not on the quantity of crop production.

How many of the statements given above is/are correct?

(a) Only one (b) Only two
(c) All three (d) None of these

***Ans.* (b)**

Exp. Only two statements i.e., (1) and (3) are correct regarding Champaran Satyagraha.

The Champaran Satyagraha was triggered by the exploitation of farmers by European indigo planters. European planters forced Indian tenant farmers to cultivate a portion (usually 3/20 part) of their land with indigo. One of the key reasons for Champaran Satyagraha was that the price paid to the ryots (tenant farmers) for indigo cultivation was determined based on the area of land they cultivated. The quantity of crop production was not considered, leading to unfair compensation for their labour.

Statement (2) is incorrect because Rajkumar Shukla, a farmer of the Champaran invited Mahatma Gandhi to visit the Champaran district in Bihar. Dr. Rajendra Prasad participated in Champaran Satyagraha along with Mahatma Gandhi, JB Kriplani, Majharul Haque and other prominent leaders.

13 **Consider the following Assertion (A) and Reason (R) and choose the correct code.**
(Chap 9, Class-VIII, New NCERT)

Assertion (A) Rabindranath Tagore relinquished the knighthood.

Reason (R) He did so to support Khilafat Movement.

Codes

(a) Both A and R are true and R is the correct explanation of A
(b) Both A and R are true, but R is not the correct explanation of A
(c) A is true, but R is false
(d) A is false, but R is true

Ans. (c)

Exp. Assertion (A) is true, but Reason (R) is false Rabindranath Tagore relinquished his knighthood, awarded the British in protest of Jallianwala Bagh massacre. This massacre took place on 13th April , 1919, in Amritsar, when crowd in Jallianwala Bagh was fired upon by British Indian Army.

In his letter to the Viceroy, he declared that the time has come when badges of honour make our shame glaring in their incongruous context of humiliation.

14 **Arrange the following events in chronological order.**
(Chap 12, Class-XII, Old NCERT)

1. The Rowlatt Act passed
2. Jallianwala Bagh Massacre
3. Non-Cooperation Movement
4. Khilafat Movement

Select the correct answer using the codes given below.

(a) 3-4-1-2 (b) 3-1-2-4
(c) 1-2-4-3 (d) 3-2-4-1

Ans. (c)

Exp. The correct chronological order is 1-2-4-3.
The Imperial Legislative Council, British India's Parliament, passed the Rowlatt act on 18th March, 1919. The act gave the government the power to detain and imprison people without trial.

The Jallianwala Bagh Massacre took place on 13th April, 1919 in Amritsar. It occurred on Baisakhi Day when a large crowd gathered at Jallianwala Bagh to peacefully protest against the repressive measures of the British.

The Khilafat Movement began in 1919. It was a political campaign launched by Indian Muslims in British India to protest British policies towards Turkey and the dismantling of the Ottoman empire after World War I.

The Non-Cooperation Movement was launched by Gandhi on 1st August, 1920. It was the first mass political movement under Gandhiji. The movement aimed to obtain self-governance.

15 **Consider the following statements about Abdul Ghaffar Khan.** *(Chap-12, Class-XII, Old NCERT)*

1. Abdul Ghaffar Khan had started educational and social reform work deriving inspiration from the Deoband Muslim nationalist group and Khilafat Movement.
2. He started the first Pushto political monthly Pakhtun in 1928.
3. He attended the Lahore Congress Session along with a large contingent of Pathans.

Which of the statements given above is/are correct?

(a) 1 and 2 (b) 2 and 3
(c) 1 and 3 (d) 1, 2 and 3

Ans. (d)

Exp. Statements (1), (2) and (3) are correct. Abdul Ghaffar Khan, the son of a prosperous village chief near Peshawar, initiated educational and social reform efforts among his Pathan community in 1912. His inspiration evolved successively from the Deoband Muslim nationalist group, the Khilafat Movement and the modernistic reforms of Amir Amanullah, the Afghan king whose progressive policies led to his overthrow in 1928. By the mid-1920s, Abdul Ghaffar Khan became known as 'Badshah Khan'. In May 1928, he established the first Pushto political monthly, Pakhtun. Additionally, he formed the volunteer brigade Khudai Khidmatgar. Abdul Ghaffar Khan, along with a significant contingent of Pathans who were members of Khudai Khidmatgar, participated in the Lahore Congress.

16 **Select the correct sequence of the following events by using the codes given below.**
(Chap 12, Class-XII, Old NCERT)

1. Jallianwala Bagh Massacre
2. Dr. Satya Pal's incarceration
3. All-India Khilafat Conference, 1919

Codes

(a) 2, 1, 3 (b) 1, 2, 3
(c) 2, 3, 1 (d) 3, 2, 1

Ans. (a)

Exp. The correct sequence of the given events is 2, 1 and 3.

On 10th April, 1919, two leaders of the Congress, Dr. Satya Pal and Dr. Saifuddin Kitchlew, were arrested at Amritsar.

The Jallianwala Bagh Massacre, also known as the Amritsar Massacre, took place on 13th April, 1919.

In November 1919, a Joint Conference of the Muslims and Hindus known as Khilafat Conference was called at Delhi in pursuance of the Muslim League President, Fazl-ul-Haq.

17 Which of the following statements about Mahatma Gandhi are true? *(Chap 12, Class-XII, Old NCERT)* *(UPPSC Pre 2010)*

1. He received his early education in Rajkot.
2. He married Kasturba at the age of 13th.
3. He studied law at the Inner temple, London.
4. He was most influenced by Ruskin's book 'Unto This Last'.

Codes

(a) 1and 2
(c) 1,3 and 4
(b) 1, 2 and 3
(d) All of the above

Ans. (d)

Exp. All of the given statements are true regarding Mahatma Gandhi. He was born on 2nd October, 1869 in Porbandar, Gujarat. When Gandhiji was nine years old, he went to a local school at Rajkot. At the age of 13, Mahatma Gandhi was married to Kasturba. In the year 1888, he left for London to study law. He joined there Inner temple and he was most influenced by John Ruskin's book 'Unto This Last'.

18 Consider the following statements regarding the Non-Cooperation Movement. *(Chap 12, Class-XII, Old NCERT)*

1. Congress organised a mass movement for the first time.
2. Growth of Hindu-Muslim Unity.
3. Many national education institutions such as Kashi Vidyapith came into existence.
4. British Government's willingness to grant political concessions to Indians.

Which of the statements given above is/are correct?

(a) 1, 2, 3 and 4
(b) 1, 2 and 3
(c) 1 and 3
(d) 3 and 4

Ans. (b)

Exp. Statements (1), (2) and (3) are correct regarding Non-Cooperation Movement. It was first mass movement organised by the Congress under the leadership of Mahatma Gandhi. Along with this movement, Khilafat movement was also launched by Indian Muslims. Both these movements converged with each other and reflected the growth of Hindu-Muslim Unity. Under this movement, Gandhi urged for boycott of English education, therefore many universities such as Kashi Vidyapith and Bihar Vidyapith were opened by nationalists.

Statement (4) is incorrect because this movement was ruthlessly suppressed by Colonial authorities. Many political leaders including Gandhiji was imprisoned. They didn't show any willingness to grant political concessions to Indians.

19 During Non-Cooperation Movement, protest and campaign were held across the country. One such protest among them was popular Moplah Rebellion. It was held in which of the following regions? *(Chap 10, Class-VIII, Old NCERT)*

(a) Maharashtra (b) Kerala
(c) Bengal (d) United Province

Ans. (b)

Exp. The Moplah Rebellion held in Kerala. It happened from 20th August, 1921 to 1922 in the Malabar region of Kerala, India. The Moplah or Malabar Rebellion of 1921 was a series of riots by the Mappila Muslims of Kerala against the oppressive policies of Britishers. The popular uprising was also against Hindu landlords.

20 Which one of the following is a very significant aspect of the Champaran Satyagraha? *(Chap 12, Class-XII, Old NCERT)* *(UPPSC Pre 2018)*

(a) Active all India participation of lawyers, students and women in the national movement.
(b) Active involvement of Dalit and Tribal communities of India in the national movement.
(c) Joining of peasants unrest to India's National Movement.
(d) Drastic decrease in the cultivation of plantation crops and commercial crops.

Ans. (c)

Exp. Joining of peasants unrest to India's National Movement is a very significant aspect of the Champaran Satyagraha. The Champaran Peasant Movement was launched in 1917. The issue was indigo cultivation under the Tinkathia system. Gandhiji tried to convince the authorities to end the system. Demand was accepted and 25% compensation was given. It was the first Satyagraha, taken up by Gandhiji in India.

21 Consider the reason for Mahatma Gandhi to organise a Satyagraha on behalf of the peasant of Kheda. *(Chap 12, Class-XII, Old NCERT) (IAS Pre 2011)*

1. The administration did not suspend the land revenue collection inspite of a drought.
2. The administration proposed to introduce Permanent Settlement in Gujarat.

Which of the statements given above is/are correct?

(a) Only 1 (b) Only 2
(c) Both 1 and 2 (d) Neither 1 nor 2

Ans. (a)

Exp. Statement (1) is correct as the administration did not suspend the land revenue collection inspite of a drought was the reason for Mahatma Gandhi to organise a Satyagraha on behalf of the peasants of Kheda. As per law, the farmers were entitled to remission if the produce was less than a quarter of the normal output. Gandhi started Satyagraha and later the government accepted the demand of the Satyagraha and exempted the payment of land revenue.

Statement (2) is incorrect because Permanent Settlement system was introduced by Lord Cornwallis through the Permanent Settlement Act, 1793. It covered areas of Bengal, Bihar and Odisha. The administration did not propose to introduce Permanent Settlement in Gujarat.

22 For which of the following reasons Swaraj Party founded in India? *(Chap 12, Class-XII, Old NCERT)*

1. Withdrawal of Non-Cooperation Movement by Mahatma Gandhi.
2. Entering in the Council and show the hollowness of the Government of India's Act of 1919.
3. Repression by the British Government.
4. To occupy the political privileges.

Codes

(a) Only 1 (b) 1 and 2
(c) 1, 2 and 3 (d) 1, 3 and 4

Ans. (b)

Exp. Statements (1) and (2) are correct because Swaraj Party was founded in India by CR Das and Motilal Nehru after the Chauri-Chaura incident when, Mahatma Gandhi withdrew the Non-Cooperation Movement in 1922. The failure of the Congress to express the drawbacks of Government of India's Act of 1919 is the another major reason behind the establishment of Swaraj Party. Therefore, these leaders felt that by actively participating in assembly they can expose the hollowness of the Government of India's Act of 1919.

Statements (3) and (4) are incorrect because the Swaraj Party was formed in 1923 with the aim of self-government and political freedom for the Indian people from the British Raj. Neither, repression by the British Government nor lust for political privileges was the motive behind formation of Swaraj Party.

23 Which of the following statements is/are true about the Simon Commission? *(Chap 9, Class-VIII, New NCERT)*

1. It was constituted in 1927.
2. It was headed by Sir John Simon.
3. It consists of two Indian members.

Codes

(a) 1 and 2 (b) Only 2
(c) 2 and 3 (d) All of these

Ans. (a)

Exp. Statements (1) and (2) are true about the Simon Commission because this commission was constituted under the leadership of Sir John Simon in 1927 to look into the functioning of the constitutional system in India and suggest changes.

Statement (3) is incorrect because it was officially known as 'Indian Statutory Commission' and consists of four conservative, two labourites and one liberal member from the British Parliament. No Indian was a part of Simon Commission.

24 What was the main reason behind the Constitution of Simon Commission? *(Chap 11, Class-VIII, Old NCERT)*

(a) To analyse the working style Government in India.
(b) To study the constitutional reforms in India.
(c) Suggest ways for controlling nationalism in India.
(d) To suggest ways for increasing revenue.

Ans. (b)

Exp. The main reason behind the Constitution of Simon Commission was to study the constitutional reforms in India. Simon Commission was formed to analyse the working of the Government of India Act, 1919 and suggest further constitutional and administrative reforms within the British Colonial Rule of India. Congress decided to boycott the Simon Commission because no Indian was included in it.

25 Which of the following statements is/are correct regarding the Nehru Report? *(Chap 13, Class-XII, New NCERT)*

1. Its chief architect was Motilal Nehru.
2. It was passed by All Party Convention in 1928 held at Calcutta.
3. It demanded for complete Swaraj for India.

Codes

(a) Only 1 (b) 2 and 3
(c) 1 and 2 (d) All of these

Ans. (a)

Exp. Statement (1) is correct regarding the Nehru Report as the Nehru Report 1928 was a report by a committee headed by Pt. Motilal Nehru.

Statements (2) and (3) are incorrect as on 12th February, 1928, All Parties Conference was called at Delhi. It was attended by the representatives of 29 organisations in response to the appointment of Simon Commission and challenge given by Lord Birkenhead secretary of state for India. It was presided over by MA Ansari.

Also the Nehru Report demanded for dominion status for India.

26 Consider the following statements. *(Chap 12, Class-XII, Old NCERT) (UP UDA/LDA 2010)*

Statement-I Mahatma Gandhi postponed the Non-Cooperation Movement in 1922.

Statement-II The postponement was opposed by CR Das and Motilal Nehru.

Which one of the following is correct in respect of the above statements?

(a) Both Statement-I and Statement-II are correct and Statement-II is the correct explanation for Statement-I
(b) Both Statement-I and Statement-II are correct and Statement-II is not the correct explanation for Statement-I
(c) Statement-I is correct but Statement-II is incorrect
(d) Statement-I is incorrect but Statement-II is correct

Ans. (b)

Exp. Both Statement-I and Statement-II are correct and Statement-II is not the correct explanation for Statement-I. Mahatma Gandhi decide to suspend the Non-Cooperation Movement, which he had initiated, following the violent incident known as the Chauri-Chaura Incident. The Chauri-Chaura incident involved a clash between protesters and the police in Chauri-Chaura, a town in Uttar Pradesh, India, On 5th February, 1922.

27 The Lahore Session of the Indian National Congress is very important in history because *(Chap 13, Class-XII, New NCERT)*

1. the Congress passed a resolution demanding complete independence.
2. the rift between the extremists and moderates was resolved in that session.
3. a resolution was passed rejecting the Two-Nation Theory in that session.

Which one of the following is correct in respect of the above statements?

(a) Only 1 (b) 2 and 3
(c) 1 and 3 (d) None of these

Ans. (a)

Exp. Statement (1) is correct with reference to the importance of the Lahore Session in history as the Indian National Congress on 19th December, 1929, passed the historic 'Poorna Swaraj' – which means total independence resolution at its Lahore Session.

A public announcement was made on 26th January, 1930, a day which the Congress Party selected for the Indians to celebrate as 'Independence Day'.

Statements (2) and (3) are incorrect because the rift between the extremists and moderates was resolved in Lucknow Session of Indian National Congress (1916).

The resolution was passed rejecting the Two-Nation Theory in Lahore Session of Indian National Congress (1940).

28 Consider the following Assertion (A) and Reason (R) and choose the correct code. *(Chap 15, Class-XII, Old NCERT) (UPPSC Pre 2003)*

Assertion (A) The salt agitation was launched by Mahatma Gandhi in 1930.

Reason (R) Mahatma Gandhi's object was to make salt available free to the poor.

Codes

(a) Both A and R are true and R is the correct explanation of A.
(b) Both A and R are true, but R is not the correct explanation of A.
(c) A is true, but R is false.
(d) A is false, but R is true.

Ans. (b)

Exp. Both Assertion (A) and Reason (R) are true, but Reason (R) is not the correct explanation of Assertion (A). The salt agitation was launched by Mahatma Gandhi from Dandi on 12th March, 1930 as a Civil Disobedience Movement. Gandhi and his followers made salt in violation of the salt laws. This act was a symbol of the Indian people's refusal to live under British made laws and therefore under British rule. Thus, Gandhi's object was not only to make salt available free to the poor, but also to symbolically oppose the unjust British rule.

29 Indicate true sequence of events concerning the postponement of Non-Cooperation Movement. *(Chap 12, Class-XII, Old NCERT)* *(40th BPSC Pre 1995)*

1. Police firing in Chauri-Chaura.
2. Police station set fired by violent crowd.
3. Postponement of movement by Gandhiji.
4. Arresting of Gandhiji.

Which one of the following is correct in respect of the above statements?

(a) 1, 2, 3 and 4 (b) 2, 1, 3 and 4
(c) 4, 1, 2 and 3 (d) 2,1,4 and 3

Ans. (a)

Exp. The correct chronological sequence is 1,2,3 and 4. On 5th February, 1922 of Chauri Chaura in Uttar Pradesh a Procession of Peasant was organised. The Police fired at the peasant. In relation the angry peasanks attacked and burnt the Police killing 22 Policemen. Gandhi was upset and suspended the Non-cooperation movement immediately. After postponement, Mahatma Gandhi was arrested.

30 During the Indian Freedom struggle, consider the following statements with reference to the Home Rule Movement. *(Chap 12, Class-XII, Old NCERT)*

1. During this movement, Tilak linked the question of Swaraj with the demand for the establishment of linguistic states and providing education in the vernacular languages.
2. At Allahabad, Jawaharlal Nehru joined Annie Besant's Home Rule League.

Which of the statements given above is/are correct?

(a) Only 1 (b) Only 2
(c) Both 1 and 2 (d) Neither 1 nor 2

Ans. (c)

Exp. Both the statements (1) and (2) are correct with reference to the Home Rule Movement during the Indian Freedom struggle. In 1914, Annie Besant choose to expand her activities by establishing a movement for Home Rule, inspired by the Irish Home Rule League. During the Bombay Provincial Conference held in Belgaum in April, 1916, Tilak established the Home Rule League. Tilak linked the idea of Swaraj with the demand for Education in Vernacular language and the formation of Linguistic state.

League was able to spread political and cultural consciousness to more regions in the country. By September, 1916, Annie Besant declared the formation of her Home Rule League, appointing George Arundale, a follower from her Theosophical community, as the Organising Secretary. The growth of Annie Besant's League membership occurred at a slower pace compared to Tilak's. Apart from her existing Theosophical followers, several others, including Jawaharlal Nehru in Allahabad and B. Chakravarti and J. Banerjee in Calcutta, joined the Home Rule League.

31 Consider the following statements with reference to the participation of women's in Civil Disobedience Movement. *(Chap 9, Class-VIII, New NCERT)*

1. Sarojini Naidu was an important leader in Dandi March.
2. Ambabai from Karnataka actively participated in this movement.

Which of the statements given above is/are correct?

(a) Only 1
(b) Only 2
(c) Both 1 and 2
(d) Neither 1 nor 2

Ans. (c)

Exp. Both the statements (1) and (2) are correct with reference to the participation of women's in Civil Disobedience Movement. In Civil Disobedience Movement, thousands of women also participated, people boycotted foreign materials like clothes, Liquor shops were also picketed.

On 21st May, 1930, Sarojini Naidu led a protest against the Dharsana Salt Works by non-violent protestors. Ambabai from Karnataka, also actively participated in this movement.

32 During the Indian freedom struggle, the Khudai Khidmatgars, also known as Red Shirts, called for *(Chap 13, Class-XII, Old NCERT) (IAS Pre 2002)*

(a) the Union of Pashtun tribal areas in North-West with the Afghanistan.
(b) the adoption of terrorist tactics and methods for terrorising and finally ousting the colonial rulers.
(c) the adoption of communist revolutionary ideology for political and social reform.
(d) the Pathan regional nationalist unity and a struggle against colonialism.

Ans. (d)

Exp. During the Indian freedom struggle, the Khudai Khidmatgars called for the Pathan regional nationalist unity and a struggle against colonialism. They were also known as Red shirts and was a volunter organisation founded by Khan Abdul Ghaffar Khan.

Khudai Khidmatgar literally translates as the servants of God, represented a non-violent freedom struggle against the British Empire by the Pashtuns (also known as Pathans, Pakhtuns or Afghans) of the North-West Frontier Province.

33 What was the objective of organising Round Table Conference in London? *(Chap 13, Class-VIII, Old NCERT)*

1. Discussion on self-rule
2. To discuss Simon Commission Report
3. Constitutional reforms

Codes

(a) Only 1
(b) 2 and 3
(c) Only 3
(d) All of these

Ans. (b)

Exp. The main objective of organising Round Table Conference in London were to discuss Simon Commission Report and to further constitutional reforms in India.

Round Table Conference (1930-1932), in Indian history was a series of meetings in three sessions called by the British Government to consider the future Constitution of India.

The conference resulted from a review of the Government of India Act of 1919, undertaken in 1927 by the Simon Commission, whose report was published in 1930. The conference was held in London.

34 The Trade Disputes Act of 1929, provide for *(Chap 12, Class-XII, Old NCERT) (IAS Pre 2013)*

(a) the participation of workers in the management of industries.
(b) arbitary power to the management to quell industrial disputes.
(c) an intervention was the British court in the event of trade disputes.
(d) a system of tribunals and a ban on strikes.

Ans. (d)

Exp. The Trade Disputes Act of 1929, provide for a system of tribunals and a ban on strikes.The main aim of act was to lay down the procedures for the establishment of courts of inquiry and Boards of Conciliation. It also prohibited strikes or lock-outs without notice in public utility services.

35 Who among the following revolutionaries were hanged in the famous Kakori Conspiracy Case? *(Chap 12, Class-XII, Old NCERT) (HPSC Pre 2021)*

1. Ram Prasad Bismil
2. Rajendra Lahiri
3. Asfaqullah Khan
4. Bhagat Singh
5. Thakur Roshan Singh
6. Chandra Shekhar Azad

Codes

(a) 1, 2, 3 and 4
(b) 1, 2, 3 and 5
(c) 1, 3, 4 and 5
(d) All of the above

Ans. (b)

Exp. Ram Prasad Bismil, Ashfaqullah Khan, Thakur Roshan Singh and Rajendra Lahiri were hanged in the famous Kakori Conspiracy Case. On 9th August, 1925, members of the Hindustan Republican Association (HRA), robbed a train at Kakori station near Lucknow in Uttar Pradesh. The mastermind of the action was Ram Prasad Bismil. The other key players in this audacious attack on the British establishment, were Ashfaqullah Khan, Chandra Shekhar Azad, Rajendra Lahiri and Roshan Singh.

36 Match the following lists and choose the correct codes. *(Chap 13, Class-XII, Old NCERT)*

List I (Act/Event)	List II (Year)
A. Rowlatt Act	1. 1922
B. Salt March	2. 1931
C. Chauri Chaura Incident	3. 1930
D. Second Round Table Conference	4. 1919

Codes

	A	B	C	D		A	B	C	D
(a)	4	3	1	2	(b)	3	1	4	2
(c)	4	3	2	1	(d)	3	4	2	1

Ans. (a)

Exp. The correct matching is A-4, B-3, C-1, D-2.

The Rowlatt Act (famously known as the Black Act) refers to the draconian law passed by the British Government in March 1919 to curb civil liberties.

The Salt March, which took place from March to April 1930, in India, was an act of civil disobedience led by Mahatma Gandhi.

The Chauri Chaura Incident took place on 4th February, 1922 at Chauri Chaura in the Gorakhpur district of the United Provinces.

The Second Round Table Conference was held in London from 7th September, 1931 to 1st December, 1931 with the participation of Gandhi and the Indian National Congress.

37 Consider the following statements.

Statement-I Protest, led by Lala Lajpat Rai, was organised in Lahore in 1928, against Simon Commission.

Statement-II Simon Commission did not have a single Indian member in it. *(Class-XII, Old NCERT)* *(HPSC Pre 2021, MPPSC Pre 2008)*

Which one of the following is correct in respect of the above statements?

(a) Both Statement-I and Statement-II are correct and Statement-II is the correct explanation for Statement-I.

(b) Both Statement-I and Statement-II are correct and Statement-II is not the correct explanation for Statement-I.

(c) Statement-I is correct, but Statement-II is incorrect.

(d) Statement-I is incorrect, but Statement-II is correct.

Ans. (a)

Exp. Both Statement-I and Statement-II are correct and Statement-II is the correct explanation for statement -I. Lala Lajpat Rai died on 17th November, 1928, after suffering grievous injuries during a Lathi Charge carried out by the police, when Simon Commission visited, where on, 30th October, 1928, Lala Lajpat Rai led the protest against the commission in a peaceful manner but police responded with violence.

38 The Karachi resolution of Congress in 1931 advocated, which of the following issues? *(Chap 13, Class-XII, Old NCERT)*

(a) State shall not own or control key industries and services.

(b) State shall handover the key industries and services to the Indian business groups.

(c) State should allow the Indian business group to invert 50% of the capital.

(d) State should own or control key industries and services.

Ans. (d)

Exp. The Karachi resolution of Congress in 1931 advocated state ownership of key industries and services such as mines and transport. Beside this, Congress Party also pushed for following reforms

Basic civil rights. Equality before law.

Elections based on Universal Adult Franchise.

Free and compulsory primary education.

Better living conditions for workers.

39 Who amongst the following was responsible for the formation of the Independence of India League in 1928? *(Chap 12, Class-XII, Old NCERT) (UP Lower 2008)*

1. Jawaharlal Nehru
2. Subhash Chandra Bose
3. Acharya Narendra Dev
4. Jayaprakash Narayan

Select the correct answer by using the codes given below.

(a) 1, 2 and 3 (b) 2, 3 and 4 (c) 1 and 2 (d) 3 and 4

Ans. (c)

Exp. Jawaharlal Nehru and Subhash Chandra Bose were responsible for the formation of the Independence of India League in 1928. Srinivasa Iyengar was its first President. The Independence for India League was founded in opposition to the Nehru Report. It was founded with purpose to articulate for complete independence ahead of Dominion Status. Independence League played an important role to unite progressive powers against the British rule.

40 Consider the following statements. *(Chap 11, Class-VIII, Old NCERT)*

1. In 1932, British Government announced separate electorate for untouchable caste.
2. Indian leaders welcomed this decision.
3. Giving separate electorate was part of the policy of 'Divide and Rule'.

Which of the statements given above is/are correct?

(a) Only 1 (b) Only 2 (c) 1 and 3 (d) 1, 2 and 3

Ans. (c)

Exp. Statements (1) and (3) are correct.

The Communal Award was announced by the British Prime Minister Ramsay MacDonald on 16th August, 1932. Also known as the MacDonald Award, it was announced after the Round Table Conference (1930–1932) and extended the separate electorate to depressed Classes (now known as the Scheduled Caste) and other minorities. It was part of British Policy of 'Divide and Rule'.

Statement (2) is incorrect because it was declared by Gandhi for more than once that the separate electorate for the depressed class was an attempt to divide and detach the depressed classes from the main body of Hindus.

41 Which of the following movements drew women out from the seclusion of home? ***(Class-XII, Old NCERT)***

1. Swadeshi Movement
2. Home Rule Movement
3. Non-Cooperation Movement
4. Civil Disobedience Movement

Select the correct answer by using the codes given below.

(a) 1 and 3 (b) 2 and 4 (c) 3 and 4 (d) 1, 2, 3 and 4

Ans. (d)

Exp. All of these movements drew women out from the seclusion of home. Swadeshi Movement was launched in 1905 against the partition of Bengal. Men and Women rallied together in the movement. Home Rule Movement launched in 1916. Many women joined the Home Rule Movement.

Annie Besant once said, Home Rule became tenfold more affective with the involvement of women. In Non-Cooperation Movement women came out in large numbers in 1920 on the call of Gandhiji.

They took to streets picketing liquor shops and holding dharnas. Civil Disobedience Movement (1930) saw a large scale women participation. Sarojini Naidu, Amrita Kaur, Kamladevi Chattopadhyay were some of the women leaders.

42 Consider the following statements with reference to the State's People Struggle.

(Chap 13, Class-XII, Old NCERT)

1. All-India States Peoples' Conference was formed in the year 1927.
2. Jawaharlal Nehru presided over the conference of Praja Mandal in the year 1928.

Which of the statements given above is/are correct?

(a) Only 1

(b) Only 2

(c) Both 1 and 2

(d) Neither 1 nor 2

Ans. (a)

Exp. Statement (1) is correct with reference to the State's People Struggle.

The All-India States People's Conference was a conglomeration of political movements in the Princely states of the British Raj, which were variously called Praja Mandals or Lok Parishads.

The first session of the organisation was held in Bombay, in December 1927.

Statement (2) is incorrect because Jawaharlal Nehru presided over the conference of Praja Mandal in 1939.

43 Which of the following is correct in the context of the States People's Struggle?

(Chap 13, Class-XII, Old NCERT)

(a) At Tripuri Session Congress decided to take active part in the States People Congress.

(b) British used Princes to prevent the growth of national unity.

(c) Both a and b

(d) Neither a nor b

Ans. (c)

Exp. Both the statements (a) and (b) are correct regarding states people's struggle. At Tripuri session, Congress decided to take active part in the state's people Congress. This session was presided by Subhash Chandra Bose (and later after dispute by Rajendra Prasad).

The Indian National Congress supported the states people's struggle and urged the princes to introduce democratic representative government and grant fundamental civil rights.

Ever since the formation of Indian National Congress, the British colonial authorities used princes to counter-balance and to prevent the growth of national unity.

44 Consider the following statements about Salt March.

(Chap 9, Class-VIII, New NCERT)

(UPPSC Pre 2012)

1. The Salt March was deliberately ignored by the European media.
2. The Salt March was widely covered by the American and European press.
3. The Salt March was the first nationalist activity in which women participated in large numbers.
4. The Salt March impressed upon the British urgent need to devolve more power to Indians.

Which of the statements given above is/are correct?

(a) 1, 2 and 4 (b) 2, 3 and 4 (c) 3 and 4 (d) 2 and 3

Ans. (b)

Exp. Statements (2), (3) and (4) are correct about Salt March. The Dandi March, also called Salt Satyagraha led by Mahatma Gandhi from 12th March, 1930-6th April, 1930. Salt March was covered widely by the American and European press at that time. The march also led to global attention towards the Indian Independence Movement. The Salt March was the first nationalist activity in which women participated in large numbers.

The Salt March impressed upon the British, the urgent need to devolve more power to Indians. Thousands of people broke the Salt law and other colonial rules to protest against the British Government.

Statement (1) is incorrect because the Salt March was not deliberately ignored by the European media.

45 With reference to the Indian Freedom Struggle, the decade of 1920s is popularly known for 'Growth of Communalism'. *(Chap 13, Class-XII, Old NCERT)*

1. Socio-economic backwardness
2. British policy of divide and rule
3. Side-effect of militant nationalism

Which one of the above is/are correct reason for this growth?

(a) 1, 2 and 3 (b) 2 and 3 (c) 1 and 3 (d) 1 and 2

Ans. (a)

Exp. All the statements (1), (2) and (3) are correct regarding 'Growth of Communalism' in decade of 1920s. During the British rule, the widespread poverty and socio-economic backwardness created limited growth opportunities for masses. They started competing for the limited resource. It gradually, bolstered the hatred towards other religious groups.

Britishers also added fuel to the fire by introducing divisionary politics such as separate electorates for minorities. During 1920s, militant nationalist used Hindu symbolism to unite the masses against Britishers. It however allured the masses form nationalist struggle.

46 Consider the following statements with reference to the demand of Pakistan. *(Chap 14, Class-XII, New NCERT)*

1. Choudhry Rahmat Ali coined the term Pak-stan.
2. Idea of Pakistan as a separate state was coined for Muslims belonging to Punjab, Afghan, Kashmir, Sindh and Baluchistan.

Which of the statements given above is/are correct?

(a) Only 1
(b) Only 2
(c) Both 1 and 2
(d) Neither 1 nor 2

Ans. (c)

Exp. Both the statements (1) and (2) are correct regarding the demand of Pakistan.

On 28th January, 1933, Choudhry Rehmat Ali voiced his ideas on 'Pak-stan'. By the end of 1933, the word 'Pakistan' became common vocabulary where an 'I' was added to ease pronunciation. He coined the word 'Pakistan' for 30 million Muslims who live in the five Northern units of India–Punjab, North-West Frontier Province, Kashmir, Sindh and Baluchistan.

47 Arrange the following events in chronological order. *(Chap 9, Class-VIII, New NCERT) (UPPSC Mains 2009)*

1. Karachi Session of Indian National Congress
2. Execution of Rajguru
3. Gandhi-Irwin Pact

Select the correct answer using the codes given below.

(a) 3, 2, 1 (b) 1, 2, 3 (c) 2, 3, 1 (d) 1, 3, 2

Ans. (a)

Exp. The correct chronological order of the given events is 3, 2, 1. Gandhi-Irwin Pact, agreement signed on 5th March, 1931, between Mohandas Karamchand Gandhi and Lord Irwin, British Viceroy (1926-1931) of India before the Second Round Table Conference.

Shivaram Hari Rajguru was an Indian revolutionary from Maharashtra. In 23rd March, 1931, he was hanged by the British Government along with his associates Bhagat Singh and Sukhdev Thapar.

The Gandhi-Irwin Pact was endorsed by the Congress in the Karachi Session of 1931, that was held from 26th-31st March, 1931. The Karachi Session was presided by Sardar Patel. Gandhi was nominated to represent Congress in the Second Round Table Conference.

48 Consider the following statements regarding Nehru Report. *(Class-XII, Old NCERT)*

1. Tej Bahadur Sapru participated in drafting this report.
2. It accepted the principle of separate communal electorates.
3. It defined the Dominion status as the form of government desired by India.

Which of the statements given above is/are correct?

(a) Only 1 (b) 2 and 3 (c) 1 and 3 (d) 1, 2 and 3

Ans. (c)

Exp. Statements (1) and (3) are correct regarding Nehru Report. The Nehru Report, named after its principal author Motilal Nehru, was finalised during the All-Parties Conference held in February, May and August 1928. Motilal Nehru served as the Chairman of the Committee, which included notable members such as Sir Ali Imam, Tej Bahadur Sapru and Subash Chandra Bose. Later, MR Jayakar and Annie Besant joined the Committee, with Jawaharlal Nehru appointed as the secretary. The report, shaped by this committee, defined Dominion Status as the preferred form of government for India. Notably, it rejected the previous constitutional reforms based on the principle of separate communal electorates. While seats were to be reserved for Muslims in the centre and in provinces where they were a minority, no reservations were proposed in provinces where they constituted a numerical majority.

49 Consider the following statements with reference to the MN Roy. *(Chap 13, Class-XII, Old NCERT)*

1. He was a communist leader.
2. He became the first Indian to be elected to the leadership of the Communist International.

Which of the statements given above is/are correct?

(a) Only 1 (b) Only 2
(c) Both 1 and 2 (d) Neither 1 nor 2

Ans. (c)

Exp. Both the statements (1) and (2) are correct regarding MN Roy.

Manabendra Nath Roy was an Indian revolutionary, radical activist and political theorist, as well as a noted philosopher in the 20th century.

Roy was a founder of the Mexican Communist Party and the Communist Party of India. He was also the first Indian to be elected to the leadership of Communist International.

50 Which one of the following is correct in the context of growth of socialist idea in Congress? *(Chap 13, Class-XII, Old NCERT)*

(a) Congress Socialist Party was formed in 1934.
(b) Jawaharlal Nehru was founding member of this Party.
(c) Jayaprakash Narayan was not associated with the Congress Socialist Party.
(d) None of the above

Ans. (a)

Exp. Statement (a) is correct regarding the growth of socialist idea in Congress. Congress Socialist Party or (CSP) was a left-wing group within the Congress. It was formed with Acharya Narendra Deva as President and Jayaprakash Narayan as General Secretary in 1934.

Revolutionary Activities

51 Consider the following statements with reference to the Revolutionary nationalists. *(Chap 9, Class-VIII, New NCERT)*

1. Hindustan Socialist Republican Association (HSRA) in 1924 at Ferozeshah Kotla in Delhi.
2. Bhagat Singh, Azad and Rajguru assassinated Saunders in 1928.
3. Bhagat Singh and Rajguru threw a bomb in the Central Legislative Assembly.

Which of the statements given above is/are correct?

(a) Only 1
(b) Only 2
(c) 2 and 3
(d) 1, 2 and 3

Ans. (b)

Exp. Statement (2) is correct with reference to the Revolutionary nationalists as on 17th December, 1927, the revolutionaries Bhagat Singh and Shivaram Rajguru shot and killed Assistant Superintendent of police John Saunders.

Statements (1) and (3) are incorrect because Hindustan Socialist Republican Association (HSRA) was a revolutionary organisation, also known as Hindustan Socialist Republican Army established in 1928 at Feroz Shah Kotla in New Delhi by Chandrasekhar Azad, Bhagat Singh, Sukhdev and others.

On 8th April, 1929, Bhagat Singh and BK Dutt threw a bomb in the Central Legislative Assembly, as a protest against the passage of the Public Safety Bill and the Trade Disputes Bill.

52 Which of the following statements is/are correct with reference to Punjab Naujawan Sabha? *(Chap 13, Class-XII, Old NCERT)*

(a) It was established in 1926.
(b) Mahatma Gandhi played key role in its foundation.
(c) Both a and b
(d) Neither a nor b

Ans. (a)

Exp. Statement (a) is correct with reference to Naujawan Bharat Sabha. It was founded by Bhagat Singh in 1926. Members from the Hindu, Muslim and Sikh communities were there in the organisation. The public meeting of the association was reduced after the killing of JP Saunders in 1928. In 1929, the association was banned.

53 Which of the following statements about Bhagat Singh is/are not true? *(Chap 13, Class-XII, Old NCERT)*

1. Bhagat Singh was influenced by socialist idea.
2. He was a member of the Hindustan Socialist Republican Association.
3. Bhagat Singh threw a bomb in the Central Legislative Assembly in 1929 with the objective to kill as many people as possible.

Codes

(a) 1 and 3 (b) 2 and 3 (c) Only 2 (d) Only 3

Ans. (d)

Exp. Statement (3) is not true about Bhagat Singh.

On 8th April, 1929, Bhagat Singh and BK Dutt threw a bomb in the Central Legislative Assembly, as a protest against the passage of the Public Safety Bill and the Trade Disputes Bill which would reduce the civil liberties of citizens in general and workers in particular.

The objective of the attack was to get arrested and to use the trial court as a forum to propagate their agenda so that people would become familiar with their movement and ideology.

54 Match List I with List II. *(Chap 13, Class-XII, Old NCERT)*

	List I		List II
A.	Howrah Conspiracy Case	1.	Master Ami Chand (Amir Chand)
B.	Lahore Conspiracy Case	2.	Aurobindo Ghosh
C	Delhi Conspiracy Case	3.	Jatindra Nath Mukherjee
D.	Alipore Conspiracy Case	4.	Rajguru

Codes

	A	B	C	D
(a)	4	3	2	1
(b)	1	2	4	3
(c)	3	4	1	2
(d)	2	3	4	1

Ans. (c)

Exp. The correct matching is A-3, B-4, C-1, D-2.

The **Howrah-Sibpur Conspiracy Case** refers to the arrest and trials of 47 Indian nationalists of the Anushilan Samiti for murder of Inspector Shamsul Alam on 24th January, 1910 in Calcutta. Of the accused, Jatindra Nath Mukherjee and Narendra Nath Bhattacharya were among those convicted and sentenced to one year imprisonment.

During the Anti-Simon Commission protests to avenge the killing of Lala Lajpat Rai, Bhagat Singh, Rajguru, Jai Gopal and Sukhdev shot on the DSP-JP Saunders. They were tried in the **Lahore Conspiracy Case.**

Delhi Conspiracy Case was an assassination attempt on Lord Hardinge, the then Viceroy of India.

The revolutionaries were led by Rash Behari Bose, organised by Basant Kumar Biswas, Amir Chand and Avadh Behari.

A homemade bomb was thrown into the Viceroy's howdah (elephant-carriage), during a ceremonial procession in Delhi.

The **Alipore Conspiracy Case** Trial refers to an attempt to murder the district judge of Muzaffapur Aurobindo Ghosh was defended by Chittaranjan Das in the Alipore bomb case. It took place in the year 1908.

55 Match List I with List. *(Chap 13, Class-XII, Old, NCERT)*

List I	List II
A. Chittagong Armoury Raid	1. Surya Sen
B. Abhinav Bharat	2. Guru Ram Singh
C. Anushilan Samiti	3. Vinayak Damodar
D. Kuka Movement	4. Barindra Kumar Ghosh

Codes

	A	B	C	D		A	B	C	D
(a)	4	3	2	1	(b)	1	2	4	3
(c)	3	4	1	2	(d)	1	3	4	2

Ans. (d)

Exp. The correct matching is A-1, B-3, C-4, D-2.

The **Chittagong Armoury Raid** was an attempt by armed Indian independence fighters led by Surya Sen to raid the Chittagong armoury of police and auxiliary forces in British India's Bengal Presidency (Now Bangladesh).

Abhinav Bharat was named after the Abhinav Bharat Society, an organisation founded by Vinayak Damodar in 1904. The organisation believed in armed revolution.

Anushilan Samiti was a revolutionary organisation in Bengal established in 1902. Barindra Kumar Ghosh was the chief of this organisation.

Kuka Movement was led by Kuka Sikhs, also known as the Namdhari Sikhs, under the leadership of Baba Ram Singh.

Chapter 31

Indian National Movement : Third Phase (1935-1947)

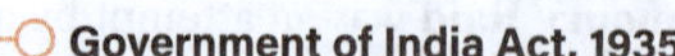

Indian National Movement : Third Phase (1935-1947)

Government of India Act, 1935

- Promulgated in the backdrop of Three Round Table Conferences (1931-32)

Provincial Election

- In Lucknow and Faizpur session Congress decided to contest the election
- Election held in February 1937
- Congress ministries formed in 7 out of 11 provinces; Had coalition government in two provinces
- Non-Congress ministries in Bengal and Punjab

Tripuri Session and Forward Bloc

- Tripuri Session of INC presided over by Subhash Chandra Bose
- Forward Bloc led by Subhash Chandra Bose (President)

August Offer, 1940

- Promised Dominion status, expansion of Viceroy's executive council with majority Indians
- Setting Constituent Assembly after the war

Response

Congress rejected as there was no offer to form National Government

Individual Satyagraha

- Launched by Gandhiji to show that nationalist patience was not due to weakness
- Express people's feeling that they are not interested in the war
- Planned Delhi Chalo movement Vinoba Bhave was the first and JL Nehru was the second Satyagrahi

Cripps Mission, 1942

- Sent because of the imminent threat of India's invasion and to seek its support for war
- Proposed- dominion status, freedom to opt out of Commonwealth
- Constitutional Assembly consisted solely of Indian after the war
- No Separate Constitution for Provinces

Quit India Movement

- Launched after failure of Cripps mission
- Quit India Resolution passed on 8th August, 1942 at Bombay
- Gandhiji gave the slogan, "Do or Die

Indian National Army (INA)

- First created by Mohan Singh by enlisting retreating Soldiers from Malaya and Prisoners of war from Japan
- Rash Behari Bose had created Indian Independence League (IIL) in Tokyo
- INA functioned under this league

Rajgopalachari Formula, 1944

- Formulated for Congress and Muslim League Cooperation
- League was to cooperate with Congress to form Provisional government at the Centre Approval of plebiscite for the Muslim majority areas to form separate state

Desai Liaqat Pact, 1945

- Called for equal number of representatives for both the Muslim League and Congress in the Central Executive and 20% reserved seats for minorities

Wavell Plan, 1945 (Shimla)

- Proposed equal representation to Hindu and Muslim
- With exception of Governor-General and Commander-in-Chief all other members of Executive Council to be Indian

Cabinet Mission, 1946

- Divided India subcontinent in three major groups of Provinces
- Rejected demand of full-fledged Pakistan

Mountbatten Plan (3nd June, 1947)

- India would be spilt into 2 Nations
- Gave autonomy and Sovereignty to both units

SOURCE **New NCERT Class VIII** *(How, When and Where),* **New NCERT Class VIII** *(The Making of the National Movement : 1870s-1947),* **Old NCERT Class VIII** *(Nationalist Movement from 1923 to 1939),* **Old NCERT Class X** *(India's Struggle for Independence),* **New NCERT Class XII** *(Understanding Partition: Politics, Memories, Experiences),* **New NCERT Class XII** *(Mahatma Gandhi and the Nationalist Movement: Civil Disobedience and Beyond),* **Old NCERT Class-XII** *(Struggle for Swaraj II 1927-1947),* **NIOS, Module-4,** *(Indian National Movement)*

1 Consider the following statements with reference to the Government of India Act 1935.

(Chap 13, Class-XII, Old NCERT)

1. It provided for establishment of All India Federation.
2. It was implemented in the year 1936.

Which of the statements given above is/are incorrect?

(a) Only 1 (b) Only 2
(c) Both 1 and 2 (d) Neither 1 nor 2

Ans. (b)

Exp. Statement (2) is incorrect with reference to the Government of India Act, 1935 as this Act was passed by the British Parliament in 1935 and came into effect in 1937. Some of the key features of the Act were

The creation of a 'Federation of India' that consisted of two levels; a Central Executive and Parliament and below it, provinces and princely states.

Dyarchy was introduced at the central level, key subjects like defence and foreign affairs were under the direct control of the Governor-General.

Three subject list were introduced – Federal list, Provincial list and Concurrent list.

2 Consider the following Assertion (A) and Reason (R) and choose the correct code.

(Chap 13, Class-XII, Old NCERT) (IAS Pre 2008)

Assertion (A) The Congress Ministries in all the provinces resigned in the year 1939.

Reason (R) The Congress did not accept the decision of the Viceroy to declare war against Germany in the context of the Second World War.

Codes

(a) Both A and R is true and R is the correct explanation of A.
(b) Both A and R is true, but R is not the correct explanation of A.
(c) A is true, but R is false.
(d) A is false, but R is true.

Ans. (a)

Exp. Both Assertion (A) and Reason (R) is true and Reason (R) is the correct explanation of Assertion (A).

The Congress Ministries in all the provinces resigned in the year 1939. The Second World War broke out in September 1939, when Nazi Germany attacked Poland. The Government of India also joined the war without consulting the National Congress or the elected members of Central Legislature. They demanded that India must declared free before it could actively participate in the war. The British Government refused to accept this demand, and the Congress ordered its ministers to resign.

3 In which of the following states, Congress did not win an absolute majority in the elections for the legislative assemblies, which were held under the 1935 Act?

(Chap 11, Class-VIII, Old NCERT) (UPPSC Mains 2004)

(a) Madras (b) Bihar (c) Orissa (d) Bengal

Ans. (d)

Exp. Among the given options, Congress did not win an absolute majority in the elections for the legislative assembly in Bengal. In Bengal, Congress was the largest Party but the Krishak Praja Party of A.K. Fazlul Huq was able to form a coalition government. Provincial elections were held in British India in 1936-37 as mandated by the Government of India Act, 1935.

The Indian National Congress emerged in power in eight of the provinces i.e. Madras, Central Provinces, Bihar, Orissa, United Provinces, Bombay Presidency, Assam, and North-West Frontier Province.

4 Consider the following statements.

Statement-I Indian National Congress had collaborated/assisted British in Second World War.

Statement-II Because they were expecting complete independence. *(Chap 13, Class-XII, Old NCERT)*

(UPPSC Pre 1992)

Which one of the following is correct in respect of the above statements?

(a) Both Statement-I and Statement-II are correct and Statement-II is the correct explanation for Statement-I.
(b) Both Statement-I and Statement-II are correct and Statement-II is not the correct explanation for Statement I.
(c) Statement-I is correct, but Statement-II is incorrect.
(d) Statement-I is incorrect, but Statement-II is correct.

Ans. (b)

Exp. Both Statement-I and Statement-II are correct and Statement-II is not the correct explanation for Statement-I. Initially, the Indian National Congress refused to let the British Government use Indian men, money and material in the war. The Congress declared that the country was prepared to cooperate with the British for World War Second. They could be used only on the condition of granting the right of self-determination to the Indians. But the British Government refused to accept this and the Congress Ministries resigned.

5 Consider the following reports connected with Muslim grievances in the Congress administered provinces. *(Chap 13, Class-XII, Old NCERT) (UP Lower 2013)*

1. Pirpur Report
2. Shareef Report
3. Muslim sufferings under Congress rule

Select the correct chronological order of the reports by using the codes given below.

(a) 1, 2 and 3 (b) 2, 1 and 3 (c) 3, 1 and 2 (d) 1, 3 and 2

Ans. (a)

Exp. The correct chronological order of the reports is 1, 2 and 3. In 1938, Pirpur report brought out by the league listed cruelties suffered by Muslims in the Congress ruled provinces. It tried to project a pro-Hindu stance and anti-Muslim bias in them. This report became an important document used to demand and justify the partition of the country.

Shareef Report, 1938, documenting pro-Hindu and anti-Muslim bias under Congress Governments.

In 1938 and 1939, the Muslim League tried to bring light to the grievances of Muslims and Muslim groups in Indian states run by Congress Governments; the effort led to documents like the Pirpur Report, 1938, Muslim sufferings under the Congress rule by AK Fazlul Haque.

6 Consider the following statements with reference to the Individual Satyagraha. *(Chap 13, Class-XII, Old NCERT)*

1. It was launched during Civil Disobedience Movement.
2. Through this movement Gandhiji want to use the opportunity of Second World War for snatching independence.

Which of the statements given above is/are incorrect?

(a) Only 1 (b) Only 2
(c) Both 1 and 2 (d) Neither 1 nor 2

Ans. (c)

Exp. Both the statements (1) and (2) are incorrect with reference to Individual Satyagraha. Individual Satyagarha was the resultant of August offer. The aim of Individual Satyagraha was to affirm the Right to Speech. Another objective of Individual Satyagraha was to publish this message to the whole world that India is not supporting Second World War.

7 Which of the following statement about Cripps Mission is incorrect? *(Chap 13, Class-XII, Old NCERT)*

(a) In March, 1942 Cripps persuaded war cabinet to agree to a draft declaration.
(b) Jawaharlal Nehru and Sardar Patel represented Congress to negotiate with the mission.
(c) It was not accepted by the Congress.
(d) The mission offered formation of Constitution making body after the war.

Ans. (b)

Exp. Statement (b) is incorrect about Cripps Mission as Maulana Abul Kalam Azad (not Jawaharlal Nehru and Sardar Patel) represented Congress to negotiate with Cripps Mission.

This mission was sent by the British Government in 1942 to secure full cooperation of India, in Second World-War. It offered formation of an Indian Union with a dominion status and a body charged with the task of making Constitution for India will be setup.

It was rejected by the Congress.

8 Consider the following statements.

Statement-I The Congress Ministries in all the provinces resigned in the year 1939.

Statement-II The Congress did not accept the decision of the Viceroy to declare war against Germany in the context of the Second World War.

(Chap-13, Class-XII, Old NCERT), (IAS Pre 2008)

Which one of the following is correct in respect of the above statements?

(a) Both Statement-I and Statement-II are correct and Statement-II is the correct explanation for Statement-I.
(b) Both Statement-I and Statement-II are correct and Statement-II is not the correct explanation for Statement-I.
(c) Statement-I is correct but Statement-II is incorrect.
(d) Statement-I is incorrect but Statement-II is correct.

Ans. (b)

Exp. Both Statement-I and Statement-II are correct and Statement-II is not the correct explanation for Statement-I. All Congress Ministries resigned in October, 1939 when World War Second started in 1939, the British were fighting against the axis powers. The viceroy of India announced India's involvement without consisting its representation political leaders. Congress asked for transfer of power in repayment of their cooperation in war, which the British Government denied. As a result Congress Ministries resigned.

9 Consider the following statements about Quit India Movement. *(Chap 9, Class-VIII, New NCERT)*

1. It was launched in the year 1942.
2. Mahatma gave the slogan 'Do or Die' in this movement.
3. Communications and railway lines were dismantled.

Which of the statements given above is/are correct?

(a) Only 1 (b) 1 and 2
(c) 2 and 3 (d) 1, 2 and 3

Ans. (d)

Exp. All the given statements (1), (2) and (3) are correct. Quit India Movement launched in 1942, was the most powerful mass movement launched in India. Under Mahatma Gandhi's leadership, people across India came together to uproot British imperialism.

In 1942, in a fiery speech in Mumbai, Mahatma Gandhi gave a 'Do or Die' call to the people of India in a final push to make the British quit. Disruption of communication and railway lines and formation of parallel government was the feature of Quit India Movement.

10 Given below is a list of places. In these which of parallel government was/were established during 'Quit India Movement'? *(Chap 13, Class-XII, Old NCERT) (UPPSC Mains 2002)*

1. Balia 2. Satara 3. Hazaribagh 4. Meerut
5. Agra

Codes

(a) 1 and 2 (b) 1, 2 and 3 (c) 2, 3 and 5 (d) 2, 3 and 4

Ans. (a)

Exp. Among the given places the parallel governments was established during 'Quit India Movement' at Balia and Satara. Parallel governments were established at many places such as

Balia (in August 1942 for a week) — under Chittu Pandey. He got many Congress leaders released.

Tamluk (Midnapore, from December, 1942 to September 1944)—which undertook cyclone relief work, sanctioned grants to schools, supplied paddy from the rich to the poor, organised Bidyut Bahinis etc.

Satara (mid-1943 to 1945)—named 'Prati Sarkar', was organised under leaders like YB Chavan, Nana Patil, etc. Village libraries and Nyayadan Mandals were organised, prohibition campaigns were carried on and 'Gandhi marriages' were organised.

11 Consider the following statements with reference to the Subhash Chandra Bose.

(Chap 9, Class-VIII, New NCERT)

1. In 1941, he left country to head towards Germany.
2. He raised the Azad Hind Fauj.

Which of the statements given above is/are correct?

(a) Only 1
(b) Only 2
(c) Both 1 and 2
(d) Neither 1 nor 2

Ans. (c)

Exp. Both the statements (1) and (2) are correct regarding Subhash Chandra Bose. In January 1941, Subhash Chandra Bose secretly left his Calcutta home, went to Singapore, *via* Germany, and raised the Azad Hind Fauj or the Indian National Army (INA). Subhash Chandra Bose became the Commander-in-Chief of the Indian National Army from 1943 to 1945.

12 With reference to the proposals of Cripps Mission, consider the following statements.

(Chap 3, Class-VII, Old NCERT)
(IAS Pre 2023)

1. The Constituent Assembly would have members nominated by the Provincial Assemblies as well as the Princely States.
2. Any Province, which is not prepared to accept the new Constitution would have the right to sign a separate agreement with Britain regarding its future status.

Which of the statements given above is/are correct?

(a) Only 1 (b) Only 2
(c) Both 1 and 2 (d) Neither 1 nor 2

Ans. (a)

Exp. Statement (2) is the correct answer with reference to the proposals of Cripps Mission.

In March 1942, a mission headed by Stafford Cripps was sent to India with Constitutional proposals to seek Indian support for the war. The British Government would accept the new Constitution subject to two conditions : (i) any province not willing to join the Union could have a separate Constitution and form a separate Union and (ii) the new Constitution-making body and the British Government would negotiate a treaty to effect the transfer of power and to safeguard racial and religious minorities.

13 Which of the following is not correctly matched?

(Chap 16, Class-X, Old NCERT)

Events	Years
(a) Quit India Movement	– 1942
(b) Cabinet Mission Plan	– 1946
(c) Provincial Government of India	– 1943
(d) Individual Satyagraha	– 1943

Ans. (d)

Exp. Pair (d) is not correctly matched because Indian National Congress launched Individual Satyagraha under the leadership of Gandhiji in the year 1940. It was direct result of August Offer, which was rejected by Congress. The aim of Individual Satyagraha was to give another opportunity to the British Government to accept demands of Congress peacefully.

14 Identify the famous Indian National Army officers who were put on trial in Red Fort at Delhi.

(Chap 13, Class-XII, Old NCERT)

1. Nawaz Khan
2. Gurbaksh Singh Dhillon
3. Laxmi Sehgal
4. Prem Sahgal

Codes

(a) 1 and 2 (b) 2 and 3 (c) 1 and 3 (d) 1, 2 and 4

Ans. (d)

Exp. All the given officers of Indian National Army except Laxmi Sehgal were put on trial in Red Fort at Delhi. The Indian National Army trials (also known as the INA trials and the Red Fort trials) was the British Indian trial by court-martial of a number of officers of the Indian National Army (INA) between November 1945 and May 1946, on various charges of treason, torture, murder and abetment to murder, during the Second World War.

In total, approximately ten court-martials were held. The first of these was the joint court-martial of Colonel Prem Sahgal, Colonel Gurbaksh Singh Dhillon and Major-General Shah Nawaz Khan.

15 'Quit India Movement' was the reaction of

(Chap 13, Class-XII, Old NCERT), (UK UDA/LDA 2003)

1. the disappointment of Indians against Cripps Mission.
2. the threat of Japanese attack on India.
3. to provoke countrymen to adopt violent means by Gandhiji's articles.
4. due to passing the proposal of August, 1942 by AICC.

Codes

(a) 1 and 2 (b) 1, 2 and 4
(c) 2, 3 and 4 (d) All of these

Ans. (b)

Exp. Options (1), (2) and (4) were the reaction of 'Quit India Movement'. By the middle of 1942, Japanese troops were approaching the borders of India. Pressure was mounting from China, the United States and Britain to solve the issue of the future status of India before the end of the war. In March, 1942, the Prime Minister dispatched Sir Stafford Cripps, member of the War Cabinet, to India to discuss the British Government's Draft Declaration. The draft granted India Dominion status after the war but otherwise conceded few changes to the British Government Act of 1935. The failure of the Cripps Mission further estranged the Congress and the British Government.

Statement (3) is incorrect because Gandhiji did not mentioned violent activity in his article. He gave the slogan 'Do or Die' through the paper.

16 **Match List I with List II.**

(Chap 21, Class-XII, NIOS) (UPPSC Pre 2008)

List I	List II
A. Simon Commission	1. 1885
B. Quit India Movement	2. 1942
C. Formation of INC	3. 1927
D. Morley-Minto Reform	4. 1909

Codes

	A	B	C	D		A	B	C	D
(a)	4	3	2	1	(b)	1	2	4	3
(c)	3	2	1	4	(d)	2	3	4	1

Ans. (c)

Exp. The correct matching is A-3, B-2, C-1, D-4.

Simon Commission came to India in 1927. The aim of this commission was to examine the Government of India Act of 1919.

Quit India Movement was launched on 9th August, 1942. It was launched after the failure of Cripps Mission.

Indian National Congress was formed in December, 1885. AO Hume was the founder of Congress.

Morley-Minto Reforms were announced in 1909. This act introduced separate electorate on the basis of religion. Therefore, Minto came to be known as the Father of Communal Electorate in India.

17 **Match List I and List II.**

(Class-XII, Old NCERT) (Tamil Nadu PCS Pre 2022)

List-I	List-II
(a) Resignation of Congress Ministers	1. 1943
(b) Neil Statue Satyagraha	2. 1942
(c) Quit India Resolution	3. 1927
(d) Provincial Government of Free India	4. 1939

Codes

	A	B	C	D		A	B	C	D
(a)	4	3	2	1	(b)	1	2	4	3
(c)	3	2	1	4	(d)	2	3	4	1

Ans. (a)

Exp. The correct matching is A-4, B-3, C-2, D-1.

Resignation of Congress Ministers in 1939 in provinces. It was happened because Viceroy linlithgow announced participation of India in World War-II without consulting INC.

Neil Statue Satyagraha was an agitation in 1927. It was related to removal of the statue of Colonel James. Neil situated at mount road in Madras.

Quit India Resolution was passed by Congress Committee in 1942. It was started due to failure of Cripps Mission.

Provincial Government of Free India was established in 1943. It was established in-exile in Singapore by Indian in exile headed by Subhas Chandra Bose.

18 **Which of the following is/are correct with reference to the Cabinet Mission?**

(Chap 14, Class-XII, New NCERT) (IAS Pre 2015)

1. It recommended a Federal Government.
2. It enlarged the powers of the Indian courts.
3. It provided for more Indians in ICS.

Codes

(a) Only 1 (b) 2 and 3
(c) 1 and 3 (d) None of these

Ans. (a)

Exp. Option (1) is correct regarding Cabinet Mission. The Cabinet Mission of 1946 proposed for the establishment of a Federal Government. It also suggested that Constituent Assembly will be formed of the representatives of the Provincial Assemblies and the Princely States.

Each province had to be allotted a total number of seats in proportion to its population. The Constituent Assembly had to comprise 293 members from the British Provinces and 93 members from the Princely States and a from Chief Commissioner's Province.

19 **Consider the following statements with respect to Cabinet Mission Plan.** *(Chap 14, Class-XII, New NCERT)*

1. The Cabinet Mission Plan recommended a two-tier confederation.
2. It recommended for grouping of existing provincial assemblies into three section while electing Constituent Assembly.
3. Initially, all the major parties accepted this plan.

Which of the statements given above is/are correct?

(a) Only 1 (b) 1 and 2 (c) 2 and 3 (d) 1, 2 and 3

Ans. (c)

Exp. Statements (2) and (3) are correct regarding Cabinet Mission Plan. Cabinet Mission was formed by the initiative of British Prime Minister Clement Atlee in 1946.

It recommended the existing provincial assemblies being grouped into three sections while electing the Constituent Assembly.

Initially, all the major parties accepted this plan. But the agreement was short lived because it was based on mutually opposed interpretations of the plan and Muslim league withdrew its acceptance of the long term plan on 29th July, 1946 and gave a call of direct action.

Statement (1) is not correct as it recommended a three-tier confederation of India.

20 **Consider the following statements.**

(Chap 2, Class-X, New NCERT)

Statement-I As a result of Quit India Movement, British and Muslims came closer to each other due to similar hatred against Congress.

Statement-II Jinnah had worked as staunch ally of the British Government and asked the Muslims to stay away from Congress's Movement of 1942.

Which of the following is correct in respect of the above statements?

(a) Both Statement-I and Statement-II are correct and Statement-II is the correct explanation for Statement-I.
(b) Both Statement-I and Statement-II are correct and Statement-II is not the correct explanation for Statement I.
(c) Statement-I is correct, but Statement-II is incorrect.
(d) Statement-I is incorrect, but Statement-II is correct.

Ans. (a)

Exp. Both Statement-I and Statement-II are correct and Statement-II is the correct explanation for Statement-I.

The Quit India Movement was launched after the failure of the Cripps Mission when it failed to solve the constitutional deadlock. The Quit India Movement marked the culmination of Indian National Movement. As a result of Quit India Movement, British and Muslims came closer to each other due to similar hatred against Congress. Meanwhile, Jinnah had worked as staunch ally of the British Government and asked the Muslims to stay away from Congress's Movement of 1942.

21 **Match the following lists and choose the correct code.**

(Chap-13, Class-VII, Old NCERT)

List I (Movement/Events)	List II (Year)
A. Individual Satyagraha	1. 1942
B. Declaration of Indian Independence	2. 1947
C. Arrival of Cripps Commission	3. 1938
D. National Planning Committee	4. 1940

Codes

	A	B	C	D		A	B	C	D
(a)	4	2	1	3	(b)	2	1	4	3
(c)	2	1	3	4	(d)	4	1	3	2

Ans. (a)

Exp. The correct matching is A-4, B-2, C-1, D-3.

Individual Satyagraha was launched by Indian National Congress under the leadership of Gandhiji in the year 1940.

Indian Independence was declared On 15th June, 1947, the British House of Commons passed the Indian Independence Act, or Mountbatten Plan, which divided India into two dominions, India and Pakistan.

Cripps Mission arrived in India in 1942 in which he proposed India to be given dominion status after war.

The National Planning Committee was set up by SC Bose in 1938.

22 **Consider the following statements with reference to the Clement Attlee's announcement.**

(Chap 16, Class-X, Old NCERT)

1. He declared that British would quit India by June 1948.
2. He announced this declaration in the year 1946.

Which of the statements given above is/are correct?

(a) Only 1
(b) Only 2
(c) Both 1 and 2
(d) Neither 1 nor 2

Ans. (a)

Exp. Statement (1) is correct regarding Clement Attlee's announcement. The Prime Minister of Britain, Clement Attlee declared on 20th February, 1947 in the House of Commons that the British would quit India after transferring power into the responsible hand not later than June 1948.

23 **Which party gave a call for 'Direct Action' and which date was chosen as the 'Direct Action Day'?**

(Chap 13, Class-XII, Old NCERT)

(a) Muslim League; 16th August, 1946
(b) Indian National Congress; 8th August, 1942
(c) The Hindu Mahasabha; 3rd June, 1946
(d) Indian National Army; 18th August, 1945

Ans. (a)

Exp. In 1946, Muhammad Ali Jinnah of Muslim League party declared 16th August as 'Direct Action Day' and called for Muslims all over the country to 'suspend all business'. This was to put pressure on the British Government to relent to the Muslim League's demand of dividing the country based on religion, thereby allowing the creation of Muslim dominated Pakistan.

24 **Which of the following statements about India's independence is/are correct?**

(Chap 13, Class-XII, Old NCERT)

1. The formal transfer of power on 15th August, 1947 heralding India's Independence was announced by Lord Mountbatten.
2. Mahatma Gandhi was not present at the festivities in the Capital on 15th August, 1947.

Codes

(a) Only 1
(b) Only 2
(c) Both 1 and 2
(d) Neither 1 nor 2

Ans. (c)

Exp. Both the statements (1) and (2) are correct regarding India's Independence.

The transfer of power was officially announced by Lord Mountbatten on 15th August, 1947. Mahatma Gandhi was not present at the festivities in the Capital on 15th August, 1947 as he was in Bengal among the people. He was already in distress due to the partition and riots which were happening in the state among the different communities. He stayed in the state to save thousands of people from being slaughtered in the name of religion.

Chapter 32

Governors, Governor-General and Viceroys

Governors, Governor-Generals and Viceroys

Governors and Governor-Generals of Bengal

Governor of Bengal (1757-74)

- **Robert Clive** (1757-60 and 1765-74) Became Governor after Victory at Battle of Plassey; Dual government in Bengal

Later Governors

- Henry Vanisttart led British forces in Battle of Buxar
- Under Governorship of John Cartier first famine of modern India occurred in 1770

Governor- Generals of Bengal (1773-1833)

- **Warren Hastings** (1773-84) Board of Revenue established in Calcutta to supervise the collection of revenue
- **Lord Cornwallis** (1786-93)
  - Started the Civil Services for administration of British India
  - Introduced Zamindari system in 1793
- **Lord Wellesley** (1793-98)
  - First subsidiary alliance with Nizam of Hyderabad
- **Sir George Barlow** (1805-07)
  - Vellore mutiny of Sepoys in 1806
- **Lord Minto I** (1807-13); Treaty of Amritsar with Ranjit Singh in 1809
- **Lord Hastings** (1813-23)
  - Treaty of Sagauli with Gorkhas in 1816
  - Fought Third Maratha war wherein Maratha power was finally crushed

Governor-Generals of India

- **Lord Amhrest** (1823-28)
  - Fought First Burmese war in 1824 and first Barrackpore Mutiny took

Governor-Generals of India

- **Lord William Bentinck** (1828-35)
  - Father of Modern Western Education in India
- **Sir Charles Metcalfe** (1834-36)
  - Known for freeing the Press
- **Lord Auckland** (1836-42)
  - First Afghan war in which British suffered heavy losses
  - Tripartite treaty between Shah Shuja, Ranjit Singh and British for Afghanistan Sher Shah Suri Marg was renamed as Grand Trunk road

Lord Ellenborough (1842-44)

- Sindh was annexed in 1843 in the leadership of Charles Napier; Indian Slavery Act, 1843 abolished slavery in India

Lord Hardings I (1844-56)

- Fought Anglo- Sikh war and concluded it with Treaty of Lahore in 1846; Steps to abolish female infanticide and human sacrifice

Lord Dalhousie (1848-56)

- Wood's Education Dispatch; First railway line connecting Bombay to Thane; Started electronic telegraph

Viceroys

Lord Canning (1856-62)

- Last Governor-General and first Viceroy of India; Revolt of 1857

Lord Mayo (1869- 72)

- System of state railway
- First Census of India in 1872

Lord Lytton (1876-80)

- Organised Delhi Darbar in 1877
- Passage of Vernacular Press Act

Lord Ripon (1880-84)

- Repealed Vernacular Press Act
- Introduced First Factory Act

Lord Curzon (1899-05)

- Planned partition of Bengal
- Established Indian University commission

Lord Minto II (1905-10)

- Muslim League was formed; Swadeshi movement and Surat split in Congress

Lord Irwin (1926-31)

- Arrival of Simon Commission
- Publication of Nehru report

Lord Mountbatten (1947-48)

- Announced Mountbatten plan directing partition of India

C. Rajagopalachari (1948-50)

- First Indian Governor- General
- Constitution was adopted on 26th November, 1949

SOURCE New NCERT Class VIII *(How, When and Where)*, Old NCERT Class X *(India's Struggle for Independence)*, New NCERT Class VIII *(The Making of the National Movement 1870-1947)*, Old NCERT Class XII *(The Structure of Government and the Economic Policies of the British Empire in India, 1757-1857)* Tamil Nadu Board Class-XI, Unit 17 *(Effects of British Rule)*

1 **Given below are two statement, one is labelled as Assertion (A) and the other is labelled as Reason (R).** *(Unit 17, Class-XI, Tamil Nadu Board) (Haryana PCS Pre 2023)*

Assertion (A) The 'Doctrine of Lapse' formulated by Governor-General Dalhousie disregarded the right of an adopted heir to the throne and the state automatically lapsed into British dominion if the ruler died without any biological natural heir.

Reason (R) The Doctrine of Lapse was one part of Dalhousie's programme of bringing a unified India under strict control by doing away with alternative sovereignties held by Indian rulers and princes.

In the light of the above statements, choose the most appropriate answer from the options given below.

(a) Both A and R are true and R is the correct explanation of A.
(b) Both A and R are true, but R is not the correct explanation of A.
(c) A is true, but R is false.
(d) A is false, but R is true.

Ans. (a)

Exp. Both Assertion (A) and Reason (R) are true and Reason (R) is the correct explanation of Assertion (A). The Doctrine of Lapse was applied to those Princely States in which ruler was either 'manifestly incompetent or died without a male heir'. It was a strategy of Lord Dalhousie's programme of bringing a unified India under strict control by doing away with alternative sovereignties held by Indian rulers and princes.

2 **Which one of the following is incorrect in the context of Lord Clive?** *(Chap 1, Class-VIII, New NCERT)*

(a) He was appointed as the Governor-General of Bengal in 1765.
(b) He led British in Battle of Plassey.
(c) Both a and b
(d) Neither a nor b

Ans. (a)

Exp. Statement (a) is incorrect in the context of Lord Clive because Robert Clive was the first Governor of Bengal during 1757-1760. During his reign, the East India Company won the Battle of Plassey and Battle of Buxar, which ultimately paved the way for British conquest of India. He was re-appointed as Governor of Bengal in 1765. The office of Governor-General of Bengal was created in 1774 and Warren Hasting became the first Governor-General of Bengal.

3 **Which reforms were made by Lord Dalhousie for the decentralisation of the army? Which of the following statements is incorrect in this respect?** *(Unit 17, Class-XI, Tamil Nadu Board) (MPSC Pre 2012)*

(a) Bengal Army was shifted to Meerut.
(b) The war weapons were brought from Calcutta to Meerut.
(c) Established the main centre at Shimla.
(d) He trusted the Indian Army.

Ans. (d)

Exp. Statement (d) is incorrect about Lord Dalhousie because he did not trust the Indian Army. Infact, he foresaw the danger of greater numerical increase of the Indian Army.

He shifted Bengal Army to Meerut. The weapons used in war were brought from Calcutta to Meerut. He also established the main centre of army at Shimla. He proposed reduction of the strength of the Indians in the army. He reformed the military system and wanted to maintain balance between the British and the Indian troops.

4 **Given below are two statements, one is labelled as Assertion (A) and the other is labelled as Reason (R).** *(Chap 9, Class-XII, Old NCERT) (Haryana PCS Pre 2023)*

Assertion (A) Indian National Congress was started by AO Hume under the official direction, guidance and advice of Lord Dufferin, the Viceroy.

Reason (R) The Indian National Congress was to provide a mild, safe, peaceful and constitutional outlet or safety value for rising discontent among the masses.

In the light of the above statements, choose the correct answer from the options given below.

(a) Both A and R are true and R is the correct explanation of A.
(b) Both A and R are true, but R is not the correct explanation of A.
(c) A is true, but R is false.
(d) A is false, but R is true.

Ans. (a)

Exp. Assertion (A) and Reason (R) are true and Reason (R) is the correct explanation of Assertion (A).

Indian National Congress was founded by AO Hume under the official direction, guidance and advice of Lord Dufferin. It was established in 1885. AO. Hume founded the Congress with the expectation that it would function as 'Safety Valve' for the escalating discontent among Indian. It provided a mild, safe, peaceful and constitutional outlet or safety value for rising discontent among the masses.

5 **By which one of the following Acts was the Governor-General of Bengal designated as the Governor-General of India?** *(Class-XII, Old NCERT) (IAS Pre 2023)*

(a) The Regulating Act
(b) The Pitt's India Act
(c) The Charter Act of 1793
(d) The Charter Act of 1833

Ans. (d)

Exp. By the Charter Act of 1833, the Governor-General of Bengal designated as the Governor-General of India. The Charter Act of 1833 was a significant constitutional instrument defining the scope and authority of the East India Company. The liberal and utilitarian philosophy of Bentham was made popular by the provisions of this Act. The Governor-General of Fort William was hereafter called the Governor-General of India. Lord Bentinck was the first 'Governor-General of India'. A Law Member was appointed to the Governor-General's Council. TB Macaulay was the first Law Member of the Governor-General-in-Council.

6 Consider the following statements.

(Chap 1, Class-VIII, New NCERT)

1. Charles Cornwallis was the Governor-General of India in 1793.
2. During his tenure many reforms were introduced.
3. Mahalwari system was implemented during his reign.

Which of the statements given above is/are correct?

(a) Only 1 (b) 1 and 2
(c) 2 and 3 (d) 1, 2 and 3

Ans. (b)

Exp. Statements (1) and (2) are correct.

Charles Cornwallis was the Governor-General of India from 1786 to 1793.

His tenure was marked by several constitutional as well as administrative reforms. Notable among them include - Introduction of Permanent Settlement and Cornwallis code in 1793. He also initiated police reforms in India.

Statement (3) is incorrect because Mahalwari system was introduced by Holt Mackenzie in 1822.

7 Match List I with List II and select the correct answer by using the codes given below the lists.

(Class-XII, Old NCERT) (UPPSC Pre 1994)

List I	List II
A. Clive	1. Removal of Press Restriction
B. Bentinck	2. Partition of Bengal
C. Charles Metcalfe	3. Dual Government in Bengal
D. Curzon	4. English Education

Codes

	A	B	C	D		A	B	C	D
(a)	3	4	1	2	(b)	4	1	3	2
(c)	2	4	3	1	(d)	3	2	1	4

Ans. (a)

Exp. The correct matching is A-3, B-4, C-1, D-2.

Lord Clive introduced system of Dual Government in Bengal in 1765. Under this system, the administration of Bengal was divided into two parts Diwani and Nizamat.

During **William Bentinck**'s reign English education was introduced in India. The English Education Act 1835 was a Legislative Act which provided fund for spending on education and literature in India.

Charles Metcalfe removed the Press Restriction. Sir Charles Metcalfe passed the Press Act in 1835 to restore press freedom. He repealed the obnoxious 1823 ordinance earned him 'liberator of the Indian press'.

Lord Curzon was behind the partition of Bengal. Partition was announced on 16th July, 1905 by Lord Curzon. The partition divides the province between West Bengal, whose majority was Hindu and East Bengal whose majority was Muslim.

8 Consider the following statements.

(Class-XII, Old NCERT) (IAS Pre 2007)

1. Robert Clive was the first Governor-General of Bengal.
2. William Bentinck was the first Governor-General of India.

Which of the statements given above is/are correct?

(a) Only 1 (b) Only 2
(c) Both 1 and 2 (d) Neither 1 nor 2

Ans. (b)

Exp. Statement (2) is correct as William Bentinck was the first Governor-General of India. He served as the Governor-General of India from 1828-1835. He was credited with major social and educational reforms in India including abolition of Sati and suppressing female infanticide.

Statement (1) is incorrect because the first Governor-General of Bengal was Warren Hastings with tenure of office from 1772-1785. The post of Governor-General of Bengal was created in 1773. Robert Clive was an British Military commander who led the victory for Britain in the Battle of Plassey.

9 Lord Dalhousie planned for the construction of a network of railways in India in order to

(Chap 3, Class-XII, Old NCERT)

(a) easily procure and export raw material for the interest of India for export.
(b) provide a profitable channel of investment for British capital.
(c) Both a and b
(d) provide cheap and easy means of transport in India.

Ans. (c)

Exp. Both statements (a) and (b) are correct regarding motive behind construction of a network of railways in India by Lord Dalhousie.

The railway network was planned by Lord Dalhousie primarily with a view to link India's raw material producing areas in the interior with the ports of export. With an annual guaranteed return it was also intended to provide a profitable channel of investment for British capital.

10 Consider the following statements with reference to the development of means of transport.

(Chap 3, Class-XII, Old NCERT)

1. Work on the Grand Trunk Road from Calcutta to Delhi was begun in 1839.
2. The contribution of Indian capital in construction of the Railway was negligible.

Which of the statements given above is/are correct?

(a) Only 1 (b) Only 2
(c) Both 1 and 2 (d) Neither 1 nor 2

Ans. (c)

Exp. Both the statements (1) and (2) are correct regarding development of means of transport.

Work on the Grand Trunk road from Calcutta to Delhi was begun in 1839 and completed in 1850's.

The entire amount of over 350 crores of rupees invested on Railways was provided by British investors, Indian capital contributing only a negligible share of it.

11 In the Government of India Act 1919, the functions of Provincial Government were divided into 'Reserved' and 'Transferred' subject. Which of the following were treated as 'Reserved' subjects?
(Chap 16, Class-X, Old NCERT) (IAS Pre 2022)

1. Administration of Justice
2. Local Self-Government
3. Land Revenue
4. Police

Select the correct answer using the code given below.

(a) 1, 2 and 3 (b) 2, 3 and 4
(c) 1, 3 and 4 (d) 1, 2 and 4

Ans. (c)

Exp. Options (1), (3) and (4) are correct. Under the Government of India Act 1919, subjects were divided into two lists reserved which included subjects such as law and order, finance, land revenue, irrigation, administration of justice, police etc. The reserved subjects were to be administered by the Governor through his Executive Council of bureaucrats, and the transferred subjects were to be administered by ministers nominated from among the elected members of the Legislative Council.

Statements (2) incorrect because Local Self-Government was a transferred subject under the Government of India Act, 1919. Another transferred subjects such as education, health, industry, agriculture, excise, etc.

12 Who among the following decided that Bahadur Shah Zafar would be last Mughal King and after his death none of his descendants would be recognised as kings? *(Chap 1, Class-VIII, New NCERT)*

(a) Lord Canning (b) Lord John Lawrence
(c) Lord Dalhousie (d) Lord William Bentinck

Ans. (a)

Exp. In 1856, Lord Canning decided that Bahadur Shah Zafar would be the last Mughal king and after his death, none of his descendants would be recognised as a ruler. They would just be called Prinees. This disrespectful behaviour towards the Mughal Emperor is also one of the political reasons for the Revolt of 1857. Lord Canning become the first Viceroy of India and served from year 1858-1862.

13 Which one of the following pairs is not correctly matched? *(Class-XII, Old NCERT)*
(UP UDA/LDA 2010)

(a) Hector Munro – Battle of Buxar
(b) Lord Hastings – Anglo-Nepal War
(c) Lord Wellesley – Fourth Anglo-Mysore War
(d) Lord Cornwallis – Third Anglo-Maratha War

Ans. (d)

Exp. Pair (d) is not correctly matched because Lord Hasting was the Governor-General of Bengal, who led the East India Company against Maratha. The Third Anglo-Maratha War (1817–1819) was the final and decisive conflict between the English East India Company and the Maratha Empire in India.

The war left the company in control of most of India. It began with an invasion of Maratha territory by British East India Company troops. The troops were led by Governor-General Hastings.

14 Subsidiary Alliance was a system devised by Lord Wellesley in 1798. All those entered into such an alliance with the British had to accept certain term and conditions. *(Class-XII, Old NCERT)*
(Haryana PCS Pre 2023)

1. The British would be responsible for protecting their ally from external and internal threats to their power.
2. In the territory of the ally, a British armed contingent would he stationed and ally would provide resources for their maintenance.
3. The ally would enter into agreements with other rulers or engage in warfare only with the permission of the British.
4. Ally may walk away with the alliance anytime at the disagreement.

Choose the correct answer from the options given below.

(a) Only 1 (b) 1 and 2 (c) 1, 2 and 3 (d) 2, 3 and 4

Ans. (c)

Exp. Statements (1), (2) and (3) are correct with respect to Subsidiary Alliance which was introduced by Lord Wellesley in 1798. Under this system, an Indian ruler who formed a treaty with the company in question would be provided with protecting against any external attacks. The British would be responsible for protecting their ally from external and internal threats to their power. In the territory of the ally a British armed contingent would be stationed and ally would provide resources for their maintenance.

The ally would enter into agreements with other rulers or engage in warfare only with the permission of the British.

Statement (4) is incorrect because there were no provision for ally state to walk away with the alliance at anytime.

15 **Consider the following statements with reference to the Lord Dufferin.** *(Chap 16, Class-X, Old NCERT)*

1. Congress was formed, during his reign.
2. He referred Congress as representing a microscopic minority.

Which of the statements given above is/are correct?

(a) Only 1 (b) Only 2
(c) Both 1 and 2 (d) Neither 1 nor 2

Ans. (c)

Exp. Both the statements (1) and (2) are correct regarding Viceroy, Lord Dufferin.

The Indian National Congress (INC) was formed in 1885 by AO Hume during the reign of Lord Dufferin. The first session of the INC took place at Gokuldas Tejpal Sanskrit college at Bombay. Lord Dufferin referred Congress as representing a microscopic minority.

16 **Which one among the following statements is true about Lord Curzon?** *(Chap 16, Class-X, Old NCERT)*

(a) He had full sympathy for the Congress.
(b) He introduced the subsidiary alliance.
(c) He succeeded Lord Canning as the Viceroy of India.
(d) He announced Partition of Bengal.

Ans. (d)

Exp. Statement (d) is true about Lord Curzon.

Lord Curzon was the Viceroy of India from 1899 to 1905. The partition of Bengal province came into effect during his viceroyalty on 16th October, 1905.

From starting, he was hostile to the Congress and envisioned its downfall by following a (reward and penalty) towards moderates and extremists.

Subsidiary alliance was introduced by Lord Wellesley under, which Indian kingdoms were forced to surrender their authority to the English. Lord Elgin (1862-1863) succeeded Lord Canning as the Viceroy of India.

17 **Consider the following Assertion (A) and Reason (R) and choose the correct code.** *(Chap 16, Class-X, New NCERT)*

Assertion (A) Curzon came to India as the new Viceroy in the year 1899.

Reason (R) He was successful in assisting peaceful demise of the Congress.

Codes

(a) Both A and R are true and R is the correct explanation of A.
(b) Both A and R are true, but R is not the correct explanation of A.
(c) A is true, but R is false.
(d) A is false, but R is true.

Ans. (c)

Exp. Assertion (A) is true, but Reason (R) is false. Lord Curzon became the Viceroy of India in 1899. One of the stated goal of the Lord Curzon was to assist the peaceful demise of the Indian National Congress.

However, the repeated attempts of Curzon to sow the seeds of discontent between the moderates and extremist faction of the Congress and governs India on the principle of divide and rule through partition of Bengal, were not successful in assisting peaceful demise of the Congress.

18 **Arrange the following in the correct chronology (From earliest to last).** *(Chap 1, Class-VIII, New NCERT)*

1. Ripon 2. Lytton
3. Curzon 4. Canning
5. Dalhousie

Codes

(a) 3, 4, 2, 1 and 5 (b) 5, 4, 2, 1 and 3
(c) 5, 2, 1, 3 and 4 (d) 2, 1, 3, 4, and 5

Ans. (b)

Exp. The correct chronology of Viceroy or Governor-General of India is 5, 4, 2, 1 and 3.

Lord Dalhousie was Governor-General from 1848 to 1856. During his reign, railways, telegraph system and Public Works Department were introduced in India.

Lord Canning was the first Viceroy of India from1856 to 1862. During his reign, the Revolt of 1857 happened.

Lord Lytton was the Viceroy of India form 1876 to 1880. His reign was characterised by Indo-Afghan wars and appointment of Hunter Commission for Education.

Lord Ripon was the viceroy of Indian from 1880 to 1884. Lord Ripon was known as the Father of Local Self-Government.

Lord Curzon was the Viceroy of India from 1899 to 1905. Partition of Bengal was announced under his reign.

19 **Consider the following statements with reference to the Shimla Conference.** *(Chap 16, Class-X, Old NCERT)*

1. It was presided by the Governor-General Lord Minto II.
2. It was held in the year 1907.

Which of the statements given above is/are incorrect?

(a) Only 1 (b) Only 2
(c) Both 1 and 2 (d) Neither 1 nor 2

Ans. (b)

Exp. Statement (2) is incorrect with reference to the Shimla Conference. It was held in 1906. It was a gathering of 35 prominent Indian Muslim leaders led by Aga Khan III at the Viceregal lodge in Shimla and it was precided by Lord Minto II. The Deputation aimed to convince Lord Minto for granting Muslims greater representation in politics.

20 **Who was the Governor-General of India, when the Council Act, 1909 was enacted to consolidate the moderate nationalist?** *(Chap 16, Class-X, Old NCERT)*

(a) Lord Minto II
(b) Lord Hardinge II
(c) Lord Lansdowne
(d) Lord Irwin

Ans. (a)

Exp. Lord Minto II was the Governor-General of India, when the Council Act, 1909 was enacted. The Indian Council Act, 1909 or Morley-Minto Reforms was passed in an attempt to widen the scope of Legislative Councils and placate the demands of moderates in Indian National Congress. It introduced separate and discriminatory electorate.

21 Identify the Governor-General/Viceroy, who was/were attacked with the intension of being killed? *(Chap 16, Class-X, Old NCERT)*

1. Lord Reading
2. Lord Minto
3. Lord Dufferin
4. Lord Hardinge

Codes

(a) 1 and 2 (b) 2 and 3
(c) 1 and 3 (d) 2 and 4

Ans. (d)

Exp. Lord Minto and Lord Hardinge were attacked with the intension to kill.

Lord Minto was the Governor-General of India from 1905 to 1910. He was attacked on 16th November, 1909 in Ahmedabad, by a Gujarati extremist, Mohanlal Pandya.

Lord Hardinge was the Governor-General of India from 1910 to 1916. He was attacked Delhi in 1912, while carrying out royal procession on occasion of transfer of capital from Calcutta to Delhi.

22 Name the Viceroy during whose tenure a system called dyarchy was introduced in provinces as a step towards Constitutional reforms. *(Chap 16, Class-X, Old NCERT)*

(a) Lord Linlithgow (b) Lord Lytton
(c) Lord Ripon (d) Lord Chelmsford

Ans. (d)

Exp. The system of Dyarchy was introduced during the tenure of Lord Chelmsford in 1919. Under this system, the provincial subjects were divided into two parts–transferred and reserved. The transferred subjects were to be administered by the Governor with the aid of ministers responsible to the Legislative Council.

The reserved subjects were to be administered by the Governor and his Executive Council without being responsible to the Legislative Council.

23 Which of the following statements is/are correct with reference to Lord Irwin? *(Chap 16, Class-X, Old NCERT)*

(a) Gandhi-Irwin Pact was signed, during his reign.
(b) As per Gandhi-Irwin Pact, Civil Disobedience Movement was called off.
(c) He was succeeded by the Lord Willingdon.
(d) All of the above

Ans. (d)

Exp. All of the given statements are correct regarding Lord Irwin.

The Gandhi-Irwin Pact was a political agreement signed by Mahatma Gandhi and Lord Irwin, Viceroy of India on 5th March, 1931. As per the Pact, the Civil Disobedience Movement in India was called off. Lord Irwin was succeeded by Lord Willingdon (1931-1936).

24 Wellesley established the Fort William College at Calcutta because *(Class-XII, Old NCERT) (IAS Pre 2020)*

(a) he was asked by the Board of Directors at London to do so.
(b) he wanted to revive interest in oriental learning in India.
(c) he wanted to provide William Carey and his associates with employment.
(d) he wanted to train British civilians for administrative purpose in India.

Ans. (d)

Exp. Wellesley established the Fort William College at Calcutta because he wanted to train British civilians for administrative purpose in India.

He established Fort William College in 1800 to train British civilians in the context of Indian local language, history, culture and local laws in order to effectively govern the British empire in India.

25 Which statements are correct in connection with Lord Cornwallis? *(Class-XII, Old NCERT) (CGPSC Pre 2014)*

1. Cleansing of administration.
2. Modernisation of the police system.
3. Established police stations at every 20 miles.
4. Appointed Indians on higher posts.

Codes

(a) 1 and 2 (b) 1, 2 and 3
(c) 2, 3 and 4 (d) 3 and 4

Ans. (b)

Exp. Statements (1), (2) and (3) are correct about Lord Cornwallis.

Cornwallis, aimed at cleaning the administration. He abolished the vicious system of paying small salaries. Cornwallis inaugurated the policy of making appointments mainly on the basis of merit thereby laying foundation of the Indian Civil Services.

He was associated with modernisation of police system. In the Regulations of 1791, the powers and jurisdiction of the Police Superintendent were defined.

Each district was divided into thanas/police stations. Every thana covered an area of 20 square miles.

Statement (4) is incorrect because he appointed only englishmen to posts of responsibility. These posts were not allowed for Indians.

Chapter 33

India After Independence

India after Independence

Challenges for Newly Independent India

- Incoming of 8 million refugees from Pakistan
- Negotiation with more than 500 princely states; Choice of apt political system for new nation
- Overcoming colonial legacy
- Impoverishment of masses

Integration of Princely States

- Indian Independent Act of 1947 ended British Paramountcy on India states and Princely states were given choice of either merging with India or Pakistan or remain Independent
- By the 15th August, 1947 majority of states get merged with India. Junagarh, Hyderabad and Kashmir retained their autonomy

Junagarh

- Had Hindu majority but ruled by Muslim Nawab, Mahawat Khan
- Nawab announced merger of Junagarh into Pakistan
- Resistance of people and later Plebiscite
- Majority voted for merger with India

Kashmir

- Majority population was Muslim but ruled by Hindu king
- Decided neither to integrate with Pakistan nor with India
- Pakistan attacked Kashmir and its ruler Hari Singh requested Indian Military for help and integrated its state with India
- In 1954 Constituent Assembly of Jammu and Kashmir confirmed integration of Kashmir with India

Hyderabad

- Biggest Princely state in India. Nawab Mir Usman Ali Khan wanted to integrate with Pakistan but the majority of population was Hindu; Signed a standstill agreement to retain same status as it had before 15th August, 1947
- But started building military strength and weaponising its army
- By military action in September 1948, It was integrated into India

Integration of European Colonies

- After Independence, Portuguese had Goa, Daman and Diu, Dadra and Nagar Haveli and French colonies included Pondicherry, Karikal, Yanam, Mahe and Chandranagar
- In 1954 through a treaty all the French colonies liberated
- In 1961 Daman and Diu and Goa were merged into the Republic of India after attaining Independence from Portuguese rule

Formation of States and Linguistic Problem

- Before Independence Congress promised formation of Linguistic state
- After Independence both Nehru and Patel were against creation of Linguistic states; Potti Sriramulu went on hunger strike demanding the formation of Andhra state
- His death led to formation of new state of Andhra Pradesh
- In 1956 State Reorganisation Commission recommended reorganisation of states based on linguistic criteria; In 1960, Bombay divided into separate state for Marathi and Gujarat speakers
- In 1966 state of Punjab divided into Punjab and Haryana

Tribal Integration and National Consolidation

- Manipur was monarchy and it merged into India in September, 1949
- In 1972 Meghalaya was made another state
- Mizoram became a full state in 1987
- In Jharkhand, Jharkhand Mukti Morcha and Shibu Soren led the demand and got statehood in 2000

Foreign Policy

- PM Jawaharlal Nehru also served as Foreign Minister of newly Independent India

Non-Alignment Movement (NAM)

- India pursued non-alignment with leaders of Egypt, Yugoslavia, Indonesia and Ghana
- Afro- Asian conference in Bandung in 1955 led to establishment of NAM
- It played an active role in mediating between the American and Soviet alliances
- This aim is derived from the Directive Principles of State Policy

Panchsheel Agreement

- Signed between India and China in 1954 over the issue of Tibet
- Main points- peaceful co-existence
- Mutual respect for each other's territorial integrity and Sovereignty
- Mutual non-interference
- Mutual non-aggression
- Equality and mutual benefit

SOURCE New NCERT Class VIII *(India after Independence)*, New NCERT Class XII *(Understanding Partition)*, Old NCERT Class XII *(Struggle for Swarajya)*

1 **Consider the following statements.**

(Chap 13, Class- XII, Old NCERT)

1. The first independence day of India was celebrated on 15th August, 1947.
2. On 14th August, 1947, Jawaharlal Nehru delivered his famous speech in the Constituent Assembly.

Which of the statements given above is/are correct?

(a) Only 1 (b) Only 2
(c) Both 1 and 2 (d) Neither 1 nor 2

Ans. (c)

Exp. Both the statements (1) and (2) are correct. After years of struggle, India celebrated its first independence on 15th August, 1947. The announcement that India and Pakistan will be free was made on 3rd June, 1947.

In a memorable address to the Constituent Assembly on the night of 14th August, 1947 Jawaharlal Nehru giving expression to the feeling of people, said " Long year ago we made a tryst with destiny, and the times comes when we shall redeem our pledge".

2 **Which three states delayed their accession to India even after the merger of other Princely States?**

(Chap 14, Class-XII, New NCERT) (UPPSC Pre 1998)

(a) Junagarh, Mysore, Jammu and Kashmir
(b) Junagarh, Hyderabad, Jammu and Kashmir
(c) Udaipur, Kapurthala, Jammu and Kashmir
(d) Hyderabad, Udaipur, Travancore

Ans. (b)

Exp. Junagarh, Hyderabad, Jammu and Kashmir delayed their accession to India even after the merger of other Princely States. Although, the states were free to choose whether they wished to accede to India or Pakistan.

Junagarh, on 26th October, the Nawab and his family fled to Pakistan following clashes with Indian troops.

Hyderabad, on 13th September, 1948, the Indian Army was sent into Hyderabad under 'Operation Polo'.

Jammu and Kashmir, on 26th October, 1947, Hari Singh the Maharaja of Jammu and Kashmir, signed off the Instrument of Accession in which Jammu and Kashmir agreed that state would become a part of India.

3 **Consider the following statements.**

(Chap 13, Class-XII, Old NCERT) (CGPSC Pre 2007)

1. In July, 1952, JB Kripalani formed the Kisan Mazdoor Praja Party.
2. PG Ghosh and T Prakasam were associated with the Kisan Mazdoor Praja Party.

Select the correct answer by using the codes given below.

(a) Statement 1 is true, but statement 2 is false.
(b) Statement 1 is false, but statement 2 is true.
(c) Both statements 1 and 2 are true.
(d) Both statements 1 and 2 are false.

Ans. (b)

Exp. Statement (1) is false, but statement (2) is true. Jivatram Bhagwandas Kripalani or JB Kripalani cstablished the Kisan Mazdoor Praja Party in June, 1951. The party was formed mostly with Indian National Congress dissidents.

4 **Who among the following was the founder of 'Hind Mazdoor Sabha' established in the year 1948?**

(Chap 13, Class-XII, Old NCERT) (IAS Pre 2018)

(a) B Krishna Pillai, EMS Namboodiripad and KC George
(b) Jayaprakash Narayan, Deendayal Upadhyay and MN Roy
(c) CP Ramaswamy Iyer, K Kamaraj and Veeresalingam Pantulu
(d) Ashok Mehta, TS Ramanujam and GG Mehta

Ans. (d)

Exp. The 'Hind Mazdoor Sabha' was founded in Howrah in West Bengal on 29th December, 1948 by Basawon Singh (Sinha), Ashok Mehta, RS Ruikar, Maniben Kara, Shibnath Banerjee, RA Khedgikar, TS Ramanujam, VS Mathur and GG Mehta.

5 **Gandhiji suggested to Mountbatten that**

(Chap 14, Class-XII, Old NCERT) (IAS Pre 2000)

(a) postpone granting of Independence.
(b) invite Jinnah to form Government.
(c) invite Nehru and Jinnah to form the Government together.
(d) invite the army to take over for some time.

Ans. (b)

Exp. Gandhiji suggested to Mountbatten that, he must invite Jinnah to form Government.

Mahatma Gandhi violently opposed the idea of partition of India and fought hard to convince political leaders from both Indian National Congress and Muslim league that Hindus and Muslim can leave in harmony.

6 **Consider the following statements.**

(Chap 12, Class-XII, New NCERT) (Unit 8, Class-XII, Tamil Nadu Board) (IAS Pre 2007)

1. Jawaharlal Nehru was the Prime Minister of India in his fourth term at the time of his death.
2. Jawaharlal Nehru was elected as Rae Bareilly's MP.
3. The first non-Congress Prime Minister of India was appointed to the post in the year 1977.

Which of the statements given above is/are correct?

(a) 1 and 2 (b) Only 3
(c) Only 1 (d) 1 and 3

Ans. (d)

Exp. Statements (1) and (3) are correct.

Jawaharlal Nehru was the Prime Minister of India in his fourth term at the time of his death. The first non-Congress Prime Minister of India was appointed to the post in the year 1977 led by Morarji Desai, who served as the fourth Prime Minister of India between 24th July, 1977 to 28th July, 1979.

Statement (2) is incorrect because Jawaharlal Nehru was elected from Phulpur constituency in Uttar Pradesh as MP.

7 The demand for the Tebhaga Peasant Movement in Bengal was for

(Chap 13, Class- XII, Old NCERT) (IAS Pre 2013)

1. the reduction of the share of the landlords from one-half of the crop to one-third.
2. the grant of ownership of land to peasants as they were the actual cultivators of the land.
3. the uprooting of Zamindari system and the end of serfdom.
4. writing off all peasant debts.

How many statements given above is/are correct?

(a) Only one (b) Only two
(c) Only three (d) All of these

Ans. (a)

Exp. Only one statement i.e., (1) is correct. The demand for the Tebhaga Peasant Movement in Bengal was for the reduction of the share of the landlords from one-half of the crop to one-third. This peasant movement was launched in the Bengal region in 1946-1947 against the oppressive jotedars.

8 In the Interim government, Rajendra Prasad held the portfolio of

(Chap 13, Class-XII, Old NCERT) (IAS Pre 2006)

1. Defence
2. Security and Commonwealth Affairs
3. Food and Agriculture

How many terms given above is/are correct?

(a) Only one
(b) Only two
(c) All three
(d) None of the above

Ans. (a)

Exp. Only one term i.e., (3) is correct. In the Interim government, Rajendra Prasad held the portfolio of Food and Agriculture.

He also served as the President of the Constituent Assembly and after Independence held the position of first President of the Republic of India.

9 "Can you show me one free country where there are separate electorates..... the British element is gone, but they have left mischief behind."

Who among the following said the above mentioned statement in the Constituent Assembly debates?

(Chap 14, Class-XII, New NCERT) (UPPSC Pre 2021)

(a) Somnath Lahiri
(b) Jawaharlal Nehru
(c) Sardar Vallabhbhai Patel
(d) NG Ranga

Ans. (c)

Exp. Sardar Vallabhbhai Patel said the give statement in the context of demands of separate electorates for Muslims in Constituent Assembly. He along with Govind Ballabh Pant vehemently opposed the demand of separate electorates. They believed it was the root cause of rise of communalism and partition of India.

Indian Paintings

Indian Paintings

Origin
- Flourished in India from pre-historic times
- Bhimbetka and Lakhudiyar rock painting have earliest pre-historic paintings in India
- Miniature painting is small sized colourful paintings with complex and gentle brush work

Development
- **Pre-historic Rock Painting**
  - Done on rock shelters and walls of caves
  - Depicts early life and activities of human society
- **Bhimbetka Cave Painting**
  - Discovered in 1957-58 by VS Wakankar
- **Lakhudiyar**
  - Located in Almora district in Uttarakhand
  - 3 categories of paintings- white, black and red ochre
- **Jogimara Cave**
  - Located in Surguja district of Chhattisgarh
  - Dated back to around 200 BC
- **Ajanta Cave** Painting In Aurangabad district of Maharashtra; Discovered by John Smith
- **Ellora Cave**
  - Located in Chhatrapati Sambhaji Nagar district of Maharashtra
  - Contains Buddhist, Brahmanical and Jain caves
- **Bagh Cave** Located in Dhar district of Madhya Pradesh; Built in the 5th to 6th century AD
- **Badami Cave**
  - Located in state of Karnataka; Chalukyan king Mangalesh a patronised the excavation of the Badami caves
- **Sittanavasal**
  - Also known as Arivar Koil; located in Tamil Nadu
  - Magnificent mural painting dating back to Pallava era of 6th century AD to Pandyan era of 9th century AD
- **Chola Art**
  - Found in the Natyakuran of Brihadeeswara temples of Thanjavur
  - Used murals or tempera technique
- **Pala**
  - Patronised by Pala rulers of Bengal and Bihar during 9th till 12th century AD earliest miniature painting in manuscripts
- **Vijayanagra**
  - Painting at Trichy, done in the 14th century represents earliest phase of the Vijayanagra style

Living Art traditions of India
- **Mithila Painting**
  - Also called Madhubani painting
  - Characterised by bright colours
- **Warli Painting**
  - Developed around the coast of Western Ghats; Themes portrayed acts of hunting, fishing, etc
- **Gond Painting**
  - Colourful depiction of animals, humans and flora
  - Portrayed Krishna with his cows surrounded by Gopi
- **Pata Painting**
  - Done on fabric, palm leaf or paper is also known as Pachedi, Phad, etc
- **Kalamkari Painting**
  - Ancient style of hand painting done on cotton or silk fabric with a pen

Babur
Baburnama mentions two famous artists Bihzad and Shah Muzaffar

Humayun
Invited two Persian artists- Mir Sayyaid Ali and Abd Us Samad to carry out royal paintings

Akbar
Illustration of various epics like Hamza Nama; Govardhan and Miskin were popular for visuals of court scenes

Jahangir
Employed Aqa Riza and Abul Hasan; Incorporated European style of paintings into Indian art

Rajasthani Schools of Painting
- **Mewar School**
  - Flourished under the rule of Jagat Singh I
  - Sahibdin painted Yuddha Kanda of Ramayana Bundi School
- **Bundi School**
  - Begin during the reign of Rao Bhoj Singh
  - Popular for its unblemished colour sense
  - Baramasa is a popular theme
- **Bikaner School**
  - Influenced by the Mughal elegance and subdued colour palette
- **Kishangarh School**
  - Distinguished by their eyebrows, lotus petals shaped eyes, having dropping eyelids
- **Jodhpur School**
  - Flourished under Maharaja Jaswant Singh

SOURCE ***New NCERT Fine Arts Class XI*** *(Pre historic Rock Paintings),* ***Old NCERT Class X*** *(The Heritage of India),* ***New NCERT Fine Arts Class XI*** *(Post-Mauryan Trends in Indian Arts and Architecture),* ***New NCERT Fine Arts Class XI*** *(Later Mural Traditions),* ***New NCERT Fine Arts Class XII*** *(The Mughal School of Miniature Painting, the Manuscript Painting Tradition, the Rajasthani School of Painting, the Deccani School of Painting, the Pahari School of Painting, the Bengal School and Cultural Nationalism, the Living Art Traditions of India)*

1 What is the similarity between the Pre-historic sites of Kupgallu, Piklihal and Tekkalkota in Karnataka? *(Chap 1, Class-XI, New NCERT Fine Arts)*

(a) They contain paintings belonging to Neolithic period.
(b) They are the only sites in India where fossils of Homo-erectus have been discovered.
(c) They give the first evidence of use of microliths in India.
(d) They contains only specimen of rock paintings belonging to Lower Palaeolithic age in India.

Ans. (a)

Exp. The similarity between the Pre-historic sites of Kupgallu, Piklihal and Tekkalkota in Karnataka is that they contain paintings belonging to Neolithic period. Three types of paintings have been reported from here i.e., paintings in white, paintings in red ochre over a white background and paintings in red ochre. The subjects depicted in these paintings include bulls, elephants, sambhars, gazelles, sheep, goats, horses, stylised humans, tridents etc.

2 Consider the following statements with reference to the Pre-historic paintings at Lakhudiyar cave in Uttarakhand. *(Chap 1, Class-XI, New NCERT Fine Arts)*

1. Human figures in these paintings are represented in stick-like forms.
2. A long-snouted animal, a fox and a multiple legged lizard are the main animal motifs.
3. The paintings at Lakhudiyar can be divided into three categories: man, animal and geometric patterns in black, white and green ochre.

Which of the statements given above is/are correct?

(a) 1 and 2 (b) 2 and 3 (c) 1 and 3 (d) All of these

Ans. (a)

Exp. Statements (1) and (2) are correct with reference to the Pre-historic paintings at Lakhudiyar cave in Uttarakhand. The Lakhudiyar caves are located in Kumaon hills of Uttarakhand and contain Pre-historic paintings. Humans are represented in stick-like forms. A long-snouted animal, a fox and a multiple legged lizard are the main animal motifs. One of the interesting scenes depicted in this painting is of hand-linked dancing human figures.

Statement (3) is incorrect because the Pre-historic paintings at Lakhudiyar can be divided into three categories: man, animal and geometric patterns in black, white and red (not green) ochre.

3 Which method was used for executing the painting on the walls and ceilings in Cave no. 3 and Cave no. 4 of the Bagh caves in Madhya Pradesh? *(Chap 2, Class-XII, New NCERT)*

(a) Fresco technique
(b) Tempera method
(c) Encaustic painting
(d) Oil painting

Ans. (b)

Exp. The paintings on the walls and ceilings in Cave no. 3 and Cave no. 4 of the Bagh caves were executed using the tempera method, which involves the use of a permanent fast-drying painting medium. This technique was commonly employed for creating durable and long-lasting artworks, and it was particularly well-suited for the cave environment.

4 With reference to the Pre-historic paintings at Bhimbetka, which of the following statements are correct? *(Chap 1, Class-XI, New NCERT Fine Arts)*

1. The caves of Bhimbetka were discovered in 1957–58 by eminent archaeologist VS Wakankar.
2. The largest number of paintings at Bhimbetka belongs to the Mesolithic age.
3. The Human figurines in these paintings are depicted as hunting wild animals.

Codes

(a) 1 and 2 (b) 2 and 3
(c) 1 and 3 (d) All of these

Ans. (d)

Exp. All the given statements (1), (2) and (3) are correct regarding Pre-historic paintings at Bhimbetka. It is a Pre-historic site located in the Vindhyan ranges of Madhya Pradesh. It contains about eight hundred rock shelters, five hundred of which bear paintings. It contains paintings belonging to all the Pre-historical phases but the largest number of paintings at this site belongs to the Mesolithic age.

These caves were discovered in 1957–58 by eminent archaeologist VS Wakankar. Elaborate themes depicting the lives of ancient human such as group hunting, dancing and other household scenes are illustrated at Bhimbetka.

5 Which among the following sites contains Pre-historic paintings? *(Chap 1, Class-XI, New NCERT Fine Arts)*

1. Mirzapur 2. Pahargarh
3. Vettavalam 4. Langhanaj

Codes

(a) 1, 2 and 3 (b) 2, 3 and 4
(c) 1, 3 and 4 (d) 1, 2 and 4

Ans. (a)

Exp. Among the given options, Mirzapur, Pahargarh and Vettavalam are sites, which contain Pre-historic paintings. Langhanaj is a Mesolithic site found near Sabarmati river basin in Gujarat. It was discovered by HD Sonkalia.

Mirzapur located in Maikal hills of Uttar Pradesh contains Pre-historic paintings belonging to Upper Paleolithic and Mesolithic age. It has also been discovered from Pahargarh caves in Madhya Pradesh and at Vettavalam in Tamil Nadu among others.

Langhanaj is a Mesolithic site located in Gujarat. It doesn't contain pre-historic paintings.

6 **Consider the following statements regarding Pre-historic paintings.**

(Chap 1, Class-XI, New NCERT Fine Arts)

1. These paintings were done on the walls of caves which also served as the habitation sites for the Pre-historic man.
2. Since, they used rocks of minerals such as haematite, limestone and chalcedony for obtaining colour, these paintings have survived thousands of years.
3. These pictures depict, in a dramatic way, both men and animals engaged in the struggle for survival.

Which of the statements given above is/are incorrect?

(a) 1 and 2 (b) 2 and 3 (c) Only 2 (d) Only 3

Ans. (c)

Exp. Statement (2) is incorrect regarding Pre-historic paintings as these paintings have survived thousands of years not because of use of haematite, limestone and chalcedony but due to chemical reaction of the oxides present on the surface of the rocks.

7 **Kalamkari painting refers to**

(Chap 6, Class-XI, New NCERT), (UPPSC Pre 2015)

(a) a hand-painted cotton textile in South India.
(b) a handmade drawing on bamboo handicrafts in North-East India.
(c) a block-painted woollen cloth in Western Himalayan region of India.
(d) a hand-painted decorative silk cloth in North-Western India.

Ans. (a)

Exp. Kalamkari or Qalamkari is a type of hand-painted or block-printed cotton textile, produced in South India (Andhra Pradesh). Its name originates in the Persian, which is derived from the words Qalam (pen) and Kari (craftmanship), meaning 'drawing with a pen'.

To create design contours in Kalamkari paintings, artists use a bamboo or date palm stick pointed at one end with a bundle of fine hair attached to this pointed end to serve as the brush or pen.

8 **Consider the following famous names.**

(Chap 2, Class-XII, New NCERT), (IAS Pre 2009)

1. Amrita Shergill 2. Bikash Bhattacharjee
3. NS Bendre 4. Subodh Gupta

Who among the above is/are famous as an artist(s)?

(a) Only 1 (b) 1 and 4
(c) 2, 3 and 4 (d) All of these

Ans. (d)

Exp. All of these mentioned above are the famous artists.

Amrita Shergill was a Hungarian-Punjabi Indian painter. She has been called 'one of the greatest avantgarde women artists of the early 20th century' and a 'pioneer' in modern Indian art. Her famous work includes Klara Szepessy, 1932, Hungarian Gypsy Girl, 1932 and Group of Three Girls, 1935.

Bikash Bhattacharjee was an Indian painter from Kolkata in West Bengal. Through his paintings, he depicted the life of the average middle class Bengali.

Narayan Shridhar Bendre was a 20th century Indian artist. He made a name for himself as a landscape artist. Hairdo (1949), The Sunflower (1955), Monkey (1957) are some of his notable works.

Subodh Gupta was an Indian contemporary artist based in New Delhi. My Mother and Me (1997), Very Hungry God (2006), What does the vessel contain, That the river does not (2012) are some of his famous works.

9 **With respect to Mughal paintings, consider the following statements.**

(Chap 3, Class-XII, New NCERT Fine Arts) (JKPSC Pre 2023)

1. Daswant and Basawan were two famous painters of Jahangir's court.
2. Mughal paintings reached a climax under Jahangir.
3. Aurangzeb's lack of interest in paintings led to a dispersal of artists of different places.

Which of the statements given above is/are correct?

(a) 1 and 2 (b) 2 and 3
(c) 1 and 3 (d) 1, 2 and 3

Ans. (b)

Exp. Statements (2) and (3) are correct with respect to Mughal paintings. Jahangir had a deep interest in painting art and under him, Mughal painting achieved its zenith. During his tenure, the Persian and Indian style of painting was fully synthesised.

The golden age of the Mughal art started their slow decline during reign of Aurangzeb. He was more conservation and less interested in art for cultural growth of empire.

Statement (1) is not correct because Daswant and Basawan were the two famous painters of Akbar's court.

10 **The Ajanta painting contains one of the richest specimens of mural paintings in India. The themes of these paintings are mainly derived from**

(Chap 4, Class-XI, New NCERT Fine Arts)

1. Avadana 2. Jatakas
3. Bhagwati Sutra 4. Life of Buddha

Codes

(a) 1, 2 and 3 (b) 2, 3 and 4
(c) 1, 3 and 4 (d) 1, 2 and 4

Ans. (d)

Exp. The themes of Ajanta paintings are mainly derived from Buddhism and its texts such as Avadana and Jatakas. The life of Buddha is also illustrated through the beautiful imagery created by the Ajanta paintings.

Some paintings such as Simhala Avadana, Mahajanaka Jataka and Vidhurpundita Jataka cover the entire wall of the cave. Ajanta caves is located in Aurangabad district of Maharashtra and contains twenty-nine caves.

The Bhagwati Sutra is one of the sacred books in Jainism.

11 Consider the following statements regarding Ajanta paintings. *(Chap 4, Class-XI, New NCERT Fine Arts)*

1. They used the technique of outward projection.
2. Lines are clearly defined and are very rhythmic.
3. It contains paintings belonging to both Buddhism and Jainism.
4. The figures in these paintings are heavy like the sculptures of Western India.

How many of the statements given above is/are incorrect?

(a) Only one (b) Only two
(c) All four (d) None of these

Ans. (a)

Exp. Only one statement i.e., (3) is incorrect regarding Ajanta paintings as Ajanta caves contain paintings belonging to Buddhism alone. The themes of Ajanta paintings are mainly derived from Buddhism and its texts such as Avadanas and Jatakas.

Ajanta caves are located in Aurangabad district of Maharashtra and contain twenty-nine caves enriched with richest specimen of Mural painting in India. The chief characteristic of these paintings are regular use of technique of outward projection, clearly defined and rhythmic line and merger of body colour with outer line. Additionally, the figures in these paintings are heavy and follow sculptural tradition of the Western India.

12 Which among the following cave sites contains the paintings of Tara, Avalokiteshvara, Manushi Buddhas and Amitabha? *(Chap 4, Class-XI, New NCERT Fine Arts)*

(a) Bagh
(b) Bhimbetka
(c) Ellora
(d) Nagarjuna

Ans. (c)

Exp. Among the given options, the cave sites of Ellora contain the paintings of Tara, Avalokiteshvara, Manushi Buddhas and Amitabha. Ellora caves located in Aurangabad district of Maharashtra. It contains paintings dating from the fifth century AD onwards to the eleventh century AD.

13 Which of the following pairs is matched incorrectly? *(Chap 4, Class-XI, New NCERT Fine Arts)*

Paintings		Caves
(a) Buddha, Yashodhara and Rahul	–	Ajanta
(b) Kalyanasundara	–	Bhimbetka
(c) Rang Mahal	–	Bagh
(d) Queen and attendants	–	Badami

Ans. (b)

Exp. Pair (b) is matched incorrectly because the painting of Kalyanasundara (a form of God Shiva) is depicted in Ellora Caves. It also contains painting profusely depicting other Shavite themes such as Ravana shaking Mount Kailash and Andhakasurvadha.

14 The rich specimens of mural paintings have been found in three palaces- Dutch Palace, Krishnapuram Palace and Padmanabhapuram Palace. They are located in which of the following states of India? *(Chap 5, Class-XI, New NCERT Fine Arts)*

(a) Andhra Pradesh
(b) Maharashtra
(c) Kerala
(d) Karnataka

Ans. (c)

Exp. The Dutch Palace, Krishnapuram Palace and Padmanabhapuram Palace is located in Kerala. It contains rich specimens of the mural paintings. Mural painting in Kerala evolved during the period from the 16th to the 18th century by adopting stylistic elements from Nayaka and Vijayanagara schools.

15 Which of the following pairs is/are correctly matched? *(Chap 8, Class-XII, New NCERT) (IAS Pre 2009)*

	Traditions		States
1.	Gatka, a traditional Marshal art	–	Kerala
2.	Madhubani is a traditional painting	–	Bihar
3.	Singhey Khababs, Sindhu Darshan Festival	–	Jammu and Kashmir

Codes

(a) 1 and 2 (b) Only 3
(c) 2 and 3 (d) All of these

Ans. (c)

Exp. Pairs (2) and (3) are correctly matched.

Madhubani painting is also called Mithila painting is a style of Indian painting. Practiced in the Mithila region of Bihar and the adjoining parts of Terai in Nepal.

Singhey Khababs, Sindhu Darshan Festival is a celebration of river Sindhu or Indus one of the world's longest river, which gave India its name.

Pair (1) is not correctly matched because Gatka is a Punjabi traditional combat training.

16 Consider the following statements with reference to the Badami Cave paintings. *(Chap 5, Class-XI, New NCERT Fine Arts)*

1. The painters evolved a language taking clues from contemporary traditions, like Kathakali and Kalam Ezhuthu.
2. The Chalukya king, Mangalesha, patronised the excavation of the Badami caves which contains a beautiful image of God Vishnu.
3. The mural paintings developed under the Chalukyas represents extension of the tradition of mural painting from Ajanta to Badami in South India.

Which of the statements given above are correct?

(a) 1 and 2 (b) 2 and 3
(c) 1 and 3 (d) All of these

Ans. (b)

Exp. Statements (2) and (3) are correct regarding Badami cave paintings. Badami was the capital of the early Chalukyan dynasty, which ruled the region from 543 to 598 AD. The caves at Badami and Aihole contains richest specimen of Chalukya paintings and represents extension of the tradition of mural paintings from Ajanta to Badami in South India. The Chalukya king, Mangalesha, patronised the excavation of the Badami caves. He was the younger son of the Chalukya king, Pulakeshin I, and the brother of Kirtivarman I.

The Cave No. 4 is related with Vaishnavism and is also called as Vishnu cave.

Statement (1) is incorrect because mural paintings at Kerala evolved by taking clues from the contemporary traditions of the state like Kathakali and Kalam Ezhuthu.

17 With reference to Vijayanagara paintings, which of the following statements is/are correct? *(Chap 5, Class-XI, New NCERT Fine Arts)*

1. The paintings at Tirupparankunram, near Trichy, done in the 14th century AD represent the early phase of the Vijayanagara style.
2. In Hampi, the Virupaksha temple has paintings on the ceiling of its *mandapa* narrating events from dynastic history and episodes from the Ramayana and the Mahabharata.
3. The Vijayanagara paintings heavily borrowed elements from the Nayaka school of Paintings.

Codes

(a) 1 and 2 (b) 2 and 3
(c) 1 and 3 (d) All of these

***Ans.* (a)**

Exp. Statements (1) and (2) are correct with reference to Vijayanagara paintings.

The paintings at Tirupparankunram, near Trichy, done in the 14th century AD represent the early phase of the Vijayanagara style. In Hampi, the Virupaksha temple has paintings on the ceiling of its *mandapa* narrating events from dynastic history and episodes from the Ramayana and the Mahabharata.

Another panel of the same temple depicts Vidyaranya, the spiritual teacher of Bukkaraya Harsha, being carried in a palanquin in a procession.

Statement (3) is incorrect because Nayaka dynasty flourished in the 17th and 18th centuries AD and borrowed the elements of Vijayanagara paintings.

18 Consider the following statements with reference to the South Indian mural paintings. *(Chap 5, Class-XI, New NCERT Fine Arts)*

1. Paintings at the Kanchipuram temple were patronised by the Pallava king, Rajasimha.
2. The mural paintings of Chola times depict different aspect of Shiva including that of Nataraja.
3. Among the Southern kingdoms, Pandyas didn't patronised mural paintings.

Which of the statements given above is/are incorrect?

(a) 1 and 2 (b) 2 and 3 (c) Only 2 (d) Only 3

***Ans.* (d)**

Exp. Statement (3) is incorrect with reference to South Indian mural paintings because Pandyas were also great patron of architecture and paintings. Tirumalaipuram caves and Jaina caves at Sittanavasal are some of the surviving examples of mural painting during the reign of Pandya rulers.

19 Match the following lists correctly and choose the correct code. *(Chap 5, Class-XI, New NCERT Fine Arts)*

List I (Temples/ Caves)	List II (Paintings)
A. Kanchipuram	1. Somaskanda
B. Krishna temple, Pundareekapuram	2. Dakshinamurthy
C. Lepakshi	3. Krishna playing flute accompanied by Gopika
D. Sittanavasal	4. Dancing figures of celestial nymphs

Codes

	A	B	C	D		A	B	C	D
(a)	1	3	2	4	(b)	2	1	4	3
(c)	3	4	1	2	(d)	4	2	1	3

***Ans.* (a)**

Exp. The correct matching is A-1, B-3, C-2, D-4.

The **Kanchipuram** temple was constructed during the reign of Pallava ruler, Rajasimha. It contained mural painting on the pillars of the temple which depicts Somaskanda.

Krishna temple, Pundareekapuram at Kottayam in Kerala contains richest specimen of Kerala mural painting. It illustrates Krishna playing flute accompanied by Gopika.

The **Lepakshi** temple constructed during the reign of Vijayanagara empire at Hindupur in Andhra Pradesh. It contains mural painting of Dakshinamurthy (a form of Shiva).

The **Sittanavasal** cave contains paintings engraved during the reign of Pandya dynasty. One of the paintings at Sittanavasal depicts dancing figures of celestial nymphs.

20 Which Mughal ruler established *karkhanas* for painting? *(Chap 3, Class-XII, New NCERT Fine Arts)* *(BPSC Pre 2020)*

(a) Akbar (b) Jahangir (c) Shah Jahan (d) Humayun

***Ans.* (a)**

Exp. The Mughal Emperor, Akbar had established *karkhanas* for painting. He had laid great emphasis on illustration of manuscripts.

Akbar was great patron of art and is considered as the pioneer of the miniature painting in the Mughal empire. It was under his patronage that several seminal projects of translation and illustration of manuscripts were carried out such as Baburnama, Akbarnama, Hamzanama, etc.

21 Identify the ruler on the basis of given description.

(Chap 3, Class-XII, New NCERT Fine Arts)

"He had proclaimed that he could distinguish between the works of each noted painter even if a painting was product of joint work".

(a) Shah Jahan (b) Akbar
(c) Jahangir (d) Sher Shah Suri

Ans. (c)

Exp. The given description highlights the artistic taste of the Mughal Emperor, Jahangir. His reign is considered as the 'golden period of Mughal painting'. Under his patronage, the Mughal painting achieved naturalism and scientific accuracy of the highest degree. He employed Aqa Riza, a well-known Iranian painter and his son Abul Hasan to achieve unparalleled sophistication in painting. In his memoirs, Tuzuk-i-Jahangiri, he proclaimed that "he could distinguish between the works of each noted painter even if a painting was a product of joint work".

22 Who among the following Mughal Emperors shifted emphasis from illustrated manuscripts to album and individual portrait?

(Chap 3, Class-XII, New NCERT Fine Arts) (IAS (Pre) 2019)

(a) Humayun (b) Akbar (c) Jahangir (d) Shah Jahan

Ans. (c)

Exp. Among the given options, the Mughal Emperor, Jahangir shifted emphasis from illustrated manuscripts to album and individual portrait . His period is also referred as golden period of Mughal paintings. The Mughal Emperor, Akbar encouraged creation of illustrated manuscripts.

23 Consider the following statements with reference to the Mughal paintings.

(Chap 3, Class-XII, New NCERT Fine Arts)

1. During the reign of Akbar, painting was organised in one of imperial establishments and was used for communicating ideas about the Kingdom and the power of Kings.
2. Mughal painting reached a climax under Jahangir who popularised the portrait paintings and paintings of animals.
3. Under Jahangir, European painting was introduced at the court by the Danish priests. It led to incorporation of principal of fore-shortening techniques in the painting.

Which of the statements given above is/are incorrect?

(a) 1 and 2 (b) 2 and 3 (c) Only 2 (d) Only 3

Ans. (d)

Exp. Statement (3) is incorrect with reference to the Mughal paintings because during the reign of Akbar, European painting was introduced at the court of Mughals by the Portuguese priests. It led to incorporation of principal of fore-shortening techniques in the Mughal painting.

24 Match the following lists correctly and choose the correct code. *(Chap 3, Class-XII, New NCERT Fine Arts)*

List I (Famous painters)	List II (Mughal rulers)
A. Mir Sayyid Ali and Abd al-Samad	1. Jahangir
B. Govardhan and Miskin	2. Akbar
C. Aqa Riza and Abul Hasan	3. Humayun

Codes

	A	B	C		A	B	C
(a)	1	3	2	(b)	2	1	3
(c)	3	2	1	(d)	1	2	3

Ans. (c)

Exp. The correct matching is A-3, B-2, C-1.

The famous painters, **Mir Sayyid Ali and Abd-al-Samad** were associated with Humayun. Both of these artists were originally from Persia and were invited by Humayun who established a workshop for painting and calligraphy.

Govardhan and **Miskin** were famous painters of the reign of Akbar. They were celebrated for their visuals of court scenes. Baswan and Daswant were other famous painters during the reign of Akbar.

Jahangir employed **Aqa Riza**, a well-known Iranian painter and his son **Abul Hasan** to achieve unparalleled sophistication in painting.

25 Consider the following statements.

(Chap 3, Class-XII, New NCERT Fine Arts)

1. Mughal painting is the style of miniature painting which is known for its sophisticated techniques and diverse range of subjects and themes.
2. Humayun started the project of illustration of Hamzanama that was continued by his son and successor Akbar.
3. Mughal paintings during the reign of Jahangir were characterised by minute details and refined rendering of lavish court scenes.
4. After coronation of Aurangzeb, the imperial *karkhana* was immediately shut down and all the artists migrated to the regional kingdoms.

Which of the statements given above are incorrect?

(a) Only 4 (b) 2, 3 and 4 (c) 1, 3 and 4 (d) Only 1

Ans. (a)

Exp. Statement (4) is incorrect because the imperial *karkhana* where manuscripts were produced was not immediately shut down after the accession of Aurangzeb.

26 Which one of the following books contains illustrative paintings of recipes with a section on hunting, methods for preparation of medicines, cosmetics, perfumes and directions on their use?

(Chap 1, Class-XII, New NCERT Fine Arts)

(a) Nimat Khana (b) Rasamanjari
(c) Kitab-e- Nauras (d) Chachnama

Ans. (a)

Exp. Among the given options, Nimat Khana contains illustrative paintings of recipes with a section on hunting, methods for preparation of medicines, cosmetics, perfumes and directions on their use. It was painted at Mandu (in Madhya Pradesh) during the reign of Nasir Shah Khalji (1500–1510 AD).

27 By the 16th century, Rajput style of painting became popular in the Western India. It illustrated themes depicted in which of the following ancient texts? *(Chap 2, Class-XII, New NCERT Fine Arts)*

1. Gita Govinda by Jayadeva
2. Rasamanjari by Bhanudatta
3. Rasikapriya by Keshav Das
4. Kavipriya by Rashkan

Codes

(a) 1, 2 and 3 (b) 2, 3 and 4 (c) 1, 3 and 4 (d) 1, 2 and 4

Ans. (a)

Exp. The Rajput style of painting, which became popular in the Western India by the 16th century illustrated themes depicted in - Gita Govinda by Jayadeva, Rasamanjari by Bhanudatta, Rasikapriya and Kavipriya by Keshav Das and Bihari Satsai by Bihari Lal among others.

Besides these, Bardic legends and other romantic tales, such as Dhola-Maru, Sohni-Mahiwal, Mrigavati, Chaurpanchashika and Laur Chanda were also used as themes in Rajput style of painting. Themes were also drawn from the religious texts such as Ramayana, Bhagvata Purana, Mahabharata, Devi Mahatmya, etc.

28 Match the following. *(Chap 3, Class-XII, New NCERT) (Telangana PCS Pre 2023)*

	List I (Painters)		List II (Mughal rulers)
A.	Mir Sayyid Ali	1.	Humayun
B.	Daswant	2.	Akbar
C.	Ustad Mansur	3.	Jahangir
D.	Mir Hashim	4	Shah Jahan

Codes

	A	B	C	D		A	B	C	D
(a)	1	2	3	4	(b)	2	4	1	3
(c)	1	3	2	4	(d)	3	1	4	2

Ans. (a)

Exp. The correct matching is A-1, B-2, C-3, D-4.

Mir Sayyid Ali was court painter of Humayun. He was famous for art of portraiture. He was the Persian miniature painter before working under Mughal dynasty in India.

Daswant was court painter in Akbar's court. He was leading figure, illustration of Jaipur painting.

Ustad Mansur was court poet of Jahangir. He was the leading nature painter at the court.

Mir Hashim was court poet in Shah Jahan's court. He was famous for pencil sketching.

29 Match the following lists correctly and choose the correct code. *(Chap 2, Class-XII, New NCERT Fine Arts)*

	List I (School of Paintings)		List II (Features)
A.	Kishangarh	1.	Professional studios called Mandi were established in the supervision of master artists.
B.	Bikaner	2.	Portrayed the theme of divine lovers Radha and Krishna, in courtly surroundings.
C.	Jaipur	3.	Hunting scenes and depiction of flora and fauna with picturesque landscape.
D.	Bundi	4.	Paintings were made and stored at Surat Khana.

Codes

	A	B	C	D
(a)	1	3	2	4
(b)	2	1	4	3
(c)	3	4	1	2
(d)	4	2	1	3

Ans. (b)

Exp. The correct matching is A-2, B-1, C-4, D-3.

The **Kishangarh** school of painting portrayed the theme of divine lovers Radha and Krishna, in courtly surroundings. Nihal Chand was the most celebrated artist of this school who painted 'Bani Thani'.

The **Bikaner** school of painting was characterised by the establishment of professional studios called 'Mandi' where a group of artists worked under the supervision of a master artist.

In **Jaipur** School, paintings were made and stored at Surat Khana. This school flourished under the reign of Sawai Jai Singh.

The **Bundi** school of painting was characterised by hunting scenes and depiction of flora and fauna with picturesque landscape.

30 The famous miniature painting of 'yogini' is associated with, which of the following schools of painting? *(Chap 4, Class-XII, New NCERT Fine Arts)*

(a) Ahmadnagar school of painting
(b) Golconda school of painting
(c) Vijayanagara school of painting
(d) Bijapur school of painting

Ans. (d)

Exp. The famous miniature painting of 'yogini' is associated with Bijapur school of painting. The school of Bijapur was patronised by Ali Adil Shah I (1558–1580 AD) and his successor Ibrahim II (1580–1627 AD), both patrons of art and literature.

Paintings from Bijapur in the sixteenth century have a richly illustrated encyclopaedia known as the Nujum al-Ulum.

31 **With reference to the Deccani School of Painting, which of the following statements are correct?**

(Chap 4, Class-XII, New NCERT Fine Arts)

1. The earliest examples of Deccani painting are in a volume of poems, celebrating the reign of Hussain Nizam Shah I of Ahmadnagar.
2. Gold was lavishly used in the Golconda school of painting.
3. Bijapur's art became popular as Dutch merchants carried the portraits of sultans in the late seventeenth century to Europe.

Codes

(a) 1 and 2 (b) 2 and 3 (c) 1 and 3 (d) All of these

Ans. (a)

Exp. Statements (1) and (2) are correct with reference to Deccani School of Painting.

The earliest examples of Deccani painting are in a volume of poems, celebrating the reign of Hussain Nizam Shah I of Ahmadnagar. It contains 12 miniature paintings illustrating battle, court and marriage scene.

The Golconda school of painting was characterised by the lavish use of Gold.

Famous paintings of this school include Diwan of Hafiz, Poet in a Garden, portrait of Muhammad Qutb Shah among others.

Statement (3) is incorrect because Golconda's art (not Bijapur) became popular as Dutch merchants carried the portraits of sultans in the late seventeenth century to Europe.

32 **Consider the following statements with reference to folk paintings of India.** *(Chap 6, Class XII, New NCERT) (CGPSC Pre 2021)*

Statement (1) Theme of Pattachitra painting is Jagannath and influenced by Vaishnava sect.

Statement (2) Manjusha paintings are made on jute and paper cans.

Statement (3) Pithora paintings are made by some tribes of Gujarat and Madhya Pradesh.

Select the correct answer using the codes given below.

(a) Statements 1 and 2 are true.
(b) Statements 2 and 3 are true.
(c) Statements 1 and 3 are true.
(d) All statements are true.

Ans. (d)

Exp. All the given statements are true.

Pattachitra is a picture painted on a piece of cloth. This form of art is closely related to the cult of Shri Jagannath in Puri and Vaishnava sect. It is believed to have originated in the 12th century. Some themes depicted through these paintings are Thia Badia, Dashavatara Patti and Panchamukhi.

Manjusha art is the folk art of the Ang region (Bhagalpur, Bihar). It is based on folklore of 'Bihula-Bishari'. It contains only three colours namely pink, green and yellow. They are made on bamboo, jute and paper.

Pithora painting is a tribal painting of India that belongs to the Rathwas, Bhilals, Nayaks and Tadi tribes, residing in and around Chhota Udaipur and Kawat in Eastern Gujarat and parts of Western Madhya Pradesh.

33 **Consider the following statements with reference to Pahari School of Painting.**

(Chap 5, Class-XII, New NCERT Fine Arts)

1. God Rama giving away the possession of Ayodhya and Ram and Laxman following sage Vishwamitra to the forest is among the most famous painting of Basholi school of painting.
2. Pandit Seu and his sons Manak and Nainsukh were the most famous painter of Guler school of painting.
3. The Kangra style of painting is marked by delicacy of line, brilliance of colour and minuteness of decorative details.

Which of the statement(s) given above is/are correct?

(a) 1 and 2 (b) 2 and 3
(c) 1 and 3 (d) All of the above

Ans. (d)

Exp. All of the given statements (1), (2) and (3) are correct regarding Pahari School of Painting. God Rama giving away the possession of Ayodhya and Ram and Laxman following sage Vishwamitra to the forest is among the most famous painting of Basholi school of painting.

During the reign of the King Kirpal Pal (1678 to 1695 AD) Basholi developed a distinctive and magnificent style of painting.

Pandit Seu and his sons Manak and Nainsukh were the most famous painter of Guler school of painting which flourished under the reign of Raja Govardhan Chand.

The Kangra school of painting which developed under the reign of Raja Sansar Chand is marked by delicacy of line, brilliance of colour and minuteness of decorative details.

34 **Who among the following established the 'Indian Society of Oriental Art'?**

(Chap 6, Class-XII, New NCERT Fine Arts) (UPPSC Pre 2015)

(a) Nihar Ranjan Ray
(b) Narendra Mohan Mukherjee
(c) Abanindranath Tagore
(d) Barindra Kumar Ghosh

Ans. (c)

Exp. Abanindranath Tagore founded the 'Indian Society of Oriental Art' in 1907. This school supported the Swadeshi values in Indian art and aspired to create a new type of painting that was Indian not only in subject matter but also in style. Abanindranath Tagore along with EB Havell were critical of colonial Art Schools and the manner in which European taste in art was being imposed on Indians.

35 The Paintings of Abanindranath Tagore have been classified as

(Chap 6, Class-XII, New NCERT Fine Arts) (IAS Pre 1999)

(a) realistic (b) socialistic
(c) revivalistic (d) impressionistic

Ans. (c)

Exp. The paintings of Abanindranath Tagore have been classified as revivalistic. He is considered as the founder of modern Indian painting.

He criticised the European artists for imposing the ideas and style of Western painting to India.

He supported the growth of indigenous style of paintings.

36 Whcih of the following pair is matched correctly?

(Chap 6, Class-XII, New NCERT Fine Arts)

Famous Painters of Modern India		Paintings
(a) Kshitindranath Majumdar	–	City in the Night
(b) Abdul Rehman Chughtai	–	Rasa-Lila
(c) Gaganendranath Tagore	–	Rama Vanquishing the Pride of the Ocean
(d) Raja Ravi Varma	–	Radhika

Ans. (d)

Exp. Pair (d) is matched correctly as the modern Indian painter Raja Ravi Varma was associated with Puranic painting, 'Rama Vanquishing the Pride of the Ocean'. He was one of the first Indian painters to use oil paint and master the art of lithographic reproduction for mythological subject.

While pairs (a), (b) and (c) are matched incorrectly.

The modern Indian painter **Kshitindranath Majumdar** was associated with watercolour painting Rasa-Lila which portrays the divine life of God Shri Krishna.

The modern Indian painter **Abdul Rehman Chughtai** was associated with the wash and tempera painting Radhika. He was a descendant of Ustad Ahmed, the chief architect of Shah Jahan.

The modern Indian painter **Gaganendranath Tagore** was associated with watercolour painting 'City in the Night'. He was one of the earlier Indian painters, who made use of language and syntax of Cubism to render his ideas.

37 'Madhubani' painting is related to which state?

(Chap 8, Class-XII, New NCERT Fine Arts) (MPPSC Pre 2013)

(a) Uttar Pradesh (b) Bihar
(c) Kerala (d) Tamil Nadu

Ans. (b)

Exp. 'Madhubani' painting is related to Bihar. Also referred as mithila painting, this unique style of painting is practised by the women. It is characterised by use of geometric patterns, colourful motifs and intense emotions. The themes of Madhubani paintings usually include natural elements like fish, birds, animals, turtle, sun, moon, etc.

38 Given below are two statements one is labelled as Assertion (A) and the other is labelled as Reason (R).

(Chap 8, Class-XII, New NCERT)
(Chap 14, Module-2, NIOS) (HPSC Pre 2021)

Assertion (A) Daswant painter had committed suicide out of madness.

Reason (R) The manuscript of Daswant's work Khandan-e-Taimuria is preserved in Khuda Baksh Oriented Public Library, Patna.

In the light of the above statements, choose the most appropriate answer from the options given below.

(a) Both A and R are correct and R is the correct explanation of A.
(b) Both A and R are correct and R is not the correct explanation of A.
(c) A is correct, but R is not correct.
(d) A is not correct, but R is correct.

Ans. (b)

Exp. Both Assertion (A) and Reason (R) is correct, but Reason (R) is not the correct explanation of Assertion (A). Daswant painter had committed suicide out of madness.

The manuscript of Daswant's work Khandan-e-Taimuria is preserved in Khuda Baksh Oriented Public Library, Patna.

39 Match the following lists correctly and choose the correct code. *(Chap 8, Class-XII, New NCERT Fine Arts)*

List I (Folk Paintings)	List II (Associated States)
A. Warli painting	1. Bihar
B. Mithila painting	2. Maharashtra
C. Sawara painting	3. Odisha
D. Pata Chitra painting	4. Madhya Pradesh

Select the correct matching wring the codes given below.

	A	B	C	D		A	B	C	D
(a)	1	3	2	4	(b)	2	1	4	3
(c)	3	4	1	2	(d)	2	4	1	3

Ans. (b)

Exp. The correct matching is A-2, B-1, C-4, D-3.

Warli is folk painting of Maharashtra. It is practised by Warli tribes living in the Konkan areas of Maharashtra.

Mithila painting is a folk painting performed by women of the Mithila region of the Bihar. It is also known as Madhubani painting.

Sawara painting is practised by tribals of Madhya Pradesh, Jharkhand and Odisha.

Pata Chitra painting is practised by the artists from Odisha.

Pata Chitras are done on small strips of cotton cloth, which is prepared by coating the cloth with soft white stone powder and glue made from tamarind seeds.

Chapter 35

Sculpture Art of India

Sculpture Art of India

Art forms of Harappan Civilization
Stone statue of Priest king: Made of steatite and was found in Mohenjodaro; Draped in Shawl; Wears an armlet in rightarm; Short beard; Half closed elongated eyes

Dancing girl
World's first bronze sculpture of a dancing girl; Found in Mohenjo-Daro; Wears bangles on left arm; An armlet or bangle adorn her right arm; Full of expression and bodily vigor and conveys a lot of

Male Torso
Found from Harappa; Made of red limestone; Indicated that the people of Indus Valley Civilisation knew to make such sculptures that can bend their neck and

Mother Goddess
Adorned with necklaces hanging over and wearing a loin cloth and girdle

Terracotta
Figures of a male in a yogic posture; Figurines of bearded males with coiled hair; Figurines of toy carts with wheels, whistles, rattles, birds and animals

Seals
Thousands of seals made of steatite found; Engraved in a pictographic script; Most remarkable seal- Pashupati seal

Pottery
Plain pottery more common than painted ware; Black painted ware has a fine coating of red slip on which geometric and animal design were drawn;

Mauryan Pillars
Stone pillars erected by Ashoka found in the entire Mauryan empire; Top portion of the pillar was carved with capital figures, the bull, lion, elephant; Carved out of single rock-cut pillars thus displaying the carver's skills; finest specimen- lion capital at Sarnath

Gandhar a School of Art
Flourished in modern day Pakistan and Afghanistan; Important center of Mahayana Buddhism due to its strategic location imbibed all kinds of foreign influences like Persian, Greek, Roman, Saka and Kushana

Mathura School
Flourished in Mathura during the reign of Kushana between first-third century AD

Indian Bronze Sculptures
Bronze sculpture and statuettes of Buddhist, Hindu and Jain icons made from lost-wax technique; Jain tirthankara images discovered from Chausa, Bihar belonging to Kushana period; At Nalanda a school of bronze-casting emerged during the rule of Pala dynasty; In Pallava period icon of Shiva seated in ardhaparyanka asana

Lost-Wax Technique
Also prevalent in Indus Valley culture; Technique used for making objects of metal; Involves several different steps and made by hand

Nataraja
Dancing figure of Shiva as Nataraja was evolved and fully developed during the Chola period; Bronze image of Nataraja in Chatura-tandava pose; Three- eyed and four armed Shiva is dancing with his right foot places on the demon of ignorance, Apasmara

Portrait of Krishnadeva Raya
During the 16th century at Tirupati, life-size standing portrait statues were cast in bronze, depicting Krishnadevaraya with his two queens, Tirumalamba and Chinnadevi

Avalokitesvara
Four-armed Avalokitesvara images have been sculpture in tribhanga posture; Images of Tara seated on the throne and her right hand in the Abhaya-mudra

SOURCE *New NCERT Fine Arts Class XI* (Arts of Mauryan Period), *New NCERT Fine Arts Class XI* (Post-Mauryan Trends in Indian Arts and Architecture), *New NCERT Fine Arts Class XI* (Indian Bronze Sculpture), *New NCERT Class-XII Fine Arts* (The Bengal School and Cultural Nationalism), *New NCERT Class-XII Fine Arts* (The Modern Indian Art), *New NCERT Class-XII Fine Arts* (The Living Art Traditions of India, Fine Arts)

1 **Consider the following statements with reference to the Mauryan sculpture.**

(Chap 3, Class-XI, New NCERT Fine Arts)

1. The Lion capital discovered from Sarnath is the finest example of sculpture from the Mauryan period.
2. One of the distinguishing elements in all the images sculpted in the Mauryan age is their polished surface.
3. Large number of images of Buddha and Bodhisattva were sculpted in the North-Western part of Indian subcontinent during the age of Maurya.

Which of the statements given above are correct?

(a) 1 and 3 (b) 1 and 2 (c) 2 and 3 (d) 1, 2 and 3

Ans. (b)

Exp. Statements (1) and (2) are correct regarding Mauryan sculpture. The reign of Mauryan Empire saw earliest development of Indian sculptural tradition. The Lion capital discovered from Sarnath is the finest example of sculpture from the Mauryan period.

The life-size standing image of a Yakshini near modern Patna is another good example of the sculptural tradition of the Mauryan period. One of the distinguishing elements in all the images sculpted in the Mauryan age, is their polished surface.

Statement (3) is incorrect as images of Buddha and Bodhisattva in India were sculpted only after advent of Mahayana sect of Buddhism in first century AD.

2 **Which among the following pairs is incorrectly matched?** *(Chap 3, Class-XI, New NCERT Fine Arts)*

	Sculpture Artists from Ancient India	Inscriptions
(a)	Kanha	Pitalkhora
(b)	Balaka	Kondane caves
(c)	Nihal Chand	Lomas Rishi cave
(d)	All of the above	

Ans. (c)

Exp. Pair (c) is incorrectly matched because Nihal Chand was the famous painter, associated with Kishangarh School of painting in 18th century AD. He is not an inscription artist. The name of the sculpture artist Kanha and his disciple Balaka is mentioned in Pitalkhora and Kondane caves respectively. In ancient India, sculptures were commissioned by the rulers, common people as well-by guilds (associations of traders/merchants).

3 **A fine sculpture of an elephant had been discovered from Dhauli. It also contains edicts of the Mauryan Emperor, Ashoka. It is present in which of the following present day state of India?**

(Chap 3, Class-XI, New NCERT Fine Arts)

(a) Madhya Pradesh (b) Bihar
(c) Odisha (d) Rajasthan

Ans. (c)

Exp. The sculpture of an elephant discovered at Dhauli is located in Odisha. It also contains edicts of the Mauryan Emperor, Ashoka.

This sculpture is a beautiful example of modelling in round with linear rhythm. In 1837, it was discovered by an art-historian Markham Kittoe.

4 **Consider the following statements regarding art of sculptural tradition in Post-Mauryan age.**

(Chap 4, Class-XI, New NCERT Fine Arts)

1. The sculpture narrating Queen Mayadevi's (mother of Siddhartha Gautam) dream is beautifully carved in the *torana* of Sarnath Stupa.
2. The pictorial representation of sculptures at Bharhut depicts stiffness in the body whereas it is absent in the sculptures at Sanchi.
3. The visit of Ashoka to the Ramgrama Stupa is carved with considerable details in the Sanchi Stupa.

Which of the statements given above are correct?

(a) 1 and 3 (b) 1 and 2
(c) 2 and 3 (d) 1, 2 and 3

Ans. (c)

Exp. Statements (2) and (3) are correct regarding art of sculptural tradition in Post-Mauryan age. The main difference between pictorial representation of sculptures at Bharhut and Sanchi is that in Bharhut, it depicts stiffness in the body.

The sculptural tradition at Sanchi shows more advancement in carving technique and better modelling technique. Sanchi Stupa-1 contains elaborated historical narratives in which events associated with Buddhism are depicted. Notable among them are–Ashoka visit to Ramgrama stupa, Seige of Kushinara and Buddha's visit to Kapilavastu.

Statement (1) is incorrect as the sculpture narrating Queen Mayadevi's (mother of Siddhartha Gautam) dream is beautifully carved in the **torana** of Sanchi (not Sarnath) Stupa.

5 **The name of the preaching mudra associated with Buddha first sermon at Sarnath in Gandhara style sculpture is**

(Chap 10, Class-XI, Old NCERT) (JPSC Pre 2008)

(a) Abhaya
(b) Dhyana
(c) Dharmachakra
(d) Bhumisparsha

Ans. (c)

Exp. The name of the preaching mudra associated with Buddha's first sermon at Sarnath in Gandhara style sculpture is Dharmachakra. Dharmachakra mudra symbolises one of the most important moments in the life of Buddha, the occasion when he preached to his companions the first sermon after his enlightenment in the Deer Park at Sarnath.

6 With reference to the difference between Mathura and Sarnath school of art, which of the following statements are correct?

(Chap 4, Class-XI, New NCERT Fine Arts)

1. Buddha images in Sarnath have plain transparent drapery covering both shoulders whereas in Mathura it continues to depict folds of the drapery in the sculpture of the Buddha.
2. The Mathura School of Art was patronised by the rulers of Gupta dynasty whereas Sarnath School of Art flourished under the reign of Kushans.
3. In Sarnath, the halo around the head of Buddha has very little ornamentation whereas in Mathura halo around the head of Buddha is profusely decorated.

Codes

(a) 1 and 3 (b) 1 and 2 (c) 2 and 3 (d) 1, 2 and 3

Ans. (a)

Exp. Statements (1) and (3) are correct with reference to the difference between Mathura and Sarnath school of art. The Sarnath school of art flourished under the reign of Gupta rulers. It carried forward the sculptural traditions of Mathura and Gandhara in the Eastern India. However, some minute difference is observed between the Sarnath and Mathura school of Art. Buddha images in Sarnath have plain transparent drapery covering both shoulders whereas in Mathura, it continues to depict folds of the drapery in the sculpture of the Buddha.

Secondly, the halo around the head of Buddha has very little ornamentation whereas in Mathura halo around the head of Buddha is profusely decorated.

Statement (2) is incorrect as Mathura school of Art was a patronised by the Kushana rulers whereas the Sarnath school flourished under the reign of Guptas.

7 Consider the following statements with reference to the Amravati school of Art.

(Chap 4, Class-XI, New NCERT Fine Arts)

1. Sculptural forms created in Amravati school are characterised by intense emotions.
2. Narratives are profusely depicted which include events from the life of the Buddha and the Jataka stories.
3. It was patronised by the Pallava rulers.

Which of the statements given above are correct?

(a) 1 and 3 (b) 1 and 2 (c) 2 and 3 (d) 1, 2 and 3

Ans. (b)

Exp. Statements (1) and (2) are correct with reference to the Amravati school of Art. In Southern India, the Amravati was centre of sculptural tradition. At Amravati, the events from the life of the Buddha and the Jataka stories are depicted. Sculptures at Amravati school was characterised by intense emotions, **tribhanga** posture and complex overlapping in order to create a three dimensional effect.

Statement (3) is incorrect as this school flourished under the reign of Satavahana rulers (not Pallava).

8 Which of the following pair is matched correctly?

(Chap 4, Class-XI, New NCERT Fine Arts)

Sculptures		Places
(a) Depiction of Ruru Jataka	–	Mathura
(b) Buddha's visit to Kapilavastu	–	Bharhut
(c) Jain Tirthankaras images	–	Sanchi
(d) Bodies shown with three bents	–	Amravati

Ans. (d)

Exp. Pair (d) is matched correctly as the sculptures at Amravati shows bodies with three bents (tribhanga) and was characterised by the intense emotions.

Pairs (a), (b) and (c) are matched incorrelty.

The sculpture depicting event from Ruru Jataka has been discovered from Bharhut Stupa.

The Buddha visit to Kapilavastu has been illustrated through sculpture in Sanchi Stupa- I.

The images of Jain Tirthankaras along with their Shashan Devi have been discovered from Mathura.

9 Which among the following is the oldest Bronze sculpture discovered from the Indian subcontinent?

(Chap 7, Class-XI, New NCERT Fine Arts)

(a) Dancing girl from Mohenjodaro
(b) Pashupati from Harappa
(c) Venus figurine from Belan Valley
(d) Humped bull from Bhimbetka

Ans. (a)

Exp. The Dancing girl from Mohenjodaro is the oldest Bronze sculpture discovered from the Indian subcontinent. The bronze girl was made using the lost-wax casting technique and shows the expertise of the people in making bronze works during that time. The 'Indus dancing girl' represents a 'stylistically poised female figure performing a dance'.

10 With reference to the cultural history of India, sculptures of Jaina Tirthankara have been discovered from which of the following places?

(Chap 7, Class-XI, New NCERT Fine Arts)

1. Akota near Vadodara 2. Chausa in Bihar
3. Hansi in Haryana 4. Chirand in Bihar

Codes

(a) 1, 3 and 4 (b) 1, 2 and 3 (c) 2, 3 and 4 (d) All of these

Ans. (b)

Exp. Among the given options, (1), (2) and (3) are correct regarding discovery of sculptures of Jaina Tirthankara in India.

The sculptures of Jaina Tirthankara have been discovered from Akota near Vadodara, Chausa in Bihar and Hansi in Haryana. It has also been discovered in Mathura, which was the centre of school of art under the Kushans. Chirand is located near the confluence of Ganga and Son in Bihar.

It is a neolithic site from where large number of bone artefacts have been discovered. No sculpture of Jaina Tirthankara has been discovered from Chirand.

11 Half Shiva and Half Parvati in Ardhanarishvara idol are *(Chap 4, Class-XI, Art and Culture NCERT Part-1)* *(UPPSC Pre 1997)*

(a) Yoga of men and women (b) Yoga of God and Goddess
(c) Yoga of God and Shakti (d) None of these

Ans. (c)

Exp. Half Shiva and Half Parvati in Ardhanarishvara idol are yoga of God and Shakti. The Ardhanarishvara is a form of Shiva combined with his consort Parvati Ardhanarishvara is depicted as half male and half female, equally split down the middle.

The earliest Ardhanarishvara images are dated to the Kushana period, starting from the first century AD. Ardhanarishvara represents the synthesis of masculine and feminine energies of the universe (Purusha and Prakriti) and illustrates how Shakti, the female principle of God, is inseparable from (or the same as, according to some interpretations) Shiva, the male principle of God and vice-versa.

12 Which stone is used for the sculpture of Mathura? *(Chap 4, Class-XI, New NCERT) (CGPSC Pre 2013)*

(a) Marble (b) Black Stone (c) Red Sandstone (d) Granite

Ans. (c)

Exp. Red Sandstone is used for the sculpture of Mathura. Mathura School of Art flourished in Mathura, Uttar Pradesh during the reign of Kushana Emperor Kanishka in the first century AD. The sculptures made in this school of arts is less spiritual. Mathura art includes both standing and seated statues of the Buddha.

13 With reference to the Bronze sculpture of Shiva as Nataraja, which of the following statements are correct? *(Chap 7, Class-XI, New NCERT Fine Arts)*

1. In this Chola masterpiece, Shiva is depicted in dancing posture symbolising the end of cosmic world.
2. In this sculpture, Shiva has been shown balancing himself on his right leg and suppressing the apasmara, the demon of ignorance or forgetfulness, with the foot of the same leg.
3. He, in the upper left hand, holds the damaru his favourite musical instrument to keep on the beat **tala** (rhythm).

Codes

(a) 1 and 3 (b) 1 and 2 (c) 2 and 3 (d) 1,2 and 3

Ans. (b)

Exp. Statements (1) and (2) are correct regarding the Bronze sculpture of Shiva as Nataraja. This sculpture is the richest specimen of artistic advancement reached under the Chola Empire. In this sculpture, Shiva is depicted in dancing posture symbolising the end of cosmic world. Further, he has been shown balancing himself on his right leg and suppressing the apasmara, the demon of ignorance or forgetfulness, with the foot of the same leg.

Statement (3) is incorrect as in this sculpture, Shiva is seen holding his favourite musical instrument, damru in his upper right hand to keep on the beat tala (rhythm).

14 Consider the following pairs. *(Chap 7, Class-XI, New NCERT Fine Arts)*

	Jaina Tirthankara		Associated Yakshinis or Shasanadevis
1.	Adinath	–	Chakreshvari
2.	Neminath	–	Ambika
3.	Mahavira	–	Lopamudra

How many of the pairs given above is/are incorrectly matched?

(a) Only one (b) Only two
(c) All three (d) None of these

Ans. (a)

Exp. Only one pair i.e., (3) is incorrectly matched as Shasanadevis associated Yakshini of Mahavira is Siddhayavani Devi. The concept of Yaksha and Yakhsini is integral to all three ancient Indian religions (Hinduism, Buddhism and Jainism).

15 Match the following lists correctly and choose the correct code. *(Chap 7, Class-XI, New NCERT Fine Arts)*

List I (Sculptures)	List II (Places)
A. Kalyanasundara murti	1. Kurkihar near Nalanda
B. King, Krishnadevaraya with his two queens, Tirumalamba and Chinnadevi	2. Himachal Pradesh
C. A four-armed Avalokitesvara	3. Thanjavur
D. Mahishasuramardini Durga	4. Tirupati

Codes

	A	B	C	D		A	B	C	D
(a)	1	2	3	4	(b)	3	4	1	2
(c)	2	3	1	4	(d)	4	3	1	2

Ans. (b)

Exp. The correct matching is A-3, B-4, C-1, D-2.

The **Kalyanasundara murti** is depicted in Kalyanasundara temple at Thanjavur. This sculpture is highly remarkable for the manner in which Panigrahana (ceremony of marriage) is represented by two separate statuettes.

The sculpture depicting **King, Krishnadevaraya with his two queens, Tirumalamba and Chinna Devi** has been found at Tirupati. It is life-size standing portrait statues cast in bronze.

The sculpture of a **four-armed Avalokitesvara** has been discovered from Kurkihar near Nalanda. It is one of the richest specimens of the Pala sculpture.

The sculpture of **Mahishasuramardini Durga** has been discovered from Himachal Pradesh. The sculptures of Narasimha avatar of God Vishnu has also been discovered from Himachal Pradesh.

16 **Consider the following statements.**

(Chap 7, Class-XI, New NCERT Fine Arts)

1. During the Gupta and Post-Gupta many standing Buddha images with right hand in abhaya mudra were cast in North India, particularly in Uttar Pradesh and Bihar.
2. Vakataka bronze images of the Buddha from Phophnar, Maharashtra shows influence of Mathura school of Art.
3. In Buddhist centres like Nalanda, a school of bronze casting emerged around the ninth century during the rule of the Pala Dynasty in Bihar and Bengal regions.

Which of the statements given above are correct?

(a) 1 and 3
(b) 1 and 2
(c) 2 and 3
(d) 1, 2 and 3

Ans. (a)

Exp. Statements (1) and (3) are correct as during the Gupta and Post-Gupta, many standing Buddha images with right hand in abhaya mudra were cast in North India, particularly in Uttar Pradesh and Bihar.

Notable examples of this sculpture include images of Buddha at Dhaneshwar Khera (Uttar Pradesh) and Sultanganj (Bihar). It was patronised by the Gupta and Pala rulers.

In Buddhist centres like Nalanda, a school of bronze casting emerged around the ninth century during the rule of the Pala Dynasty in Bihar and Bengal regions.

Statement (2) is incorrect as Vakataka bronze images of the Buddha from Phophnar, Maharashtra, are contemporary with the Gupta period bronze. They show the influence of the Amaravati style of art.

17 **Gandhara style of art is a synthesis of**

(Chap 4, Class-XI, New NCERT)
(UPPSC Pre 1996, RAS/RTS Pre 2009)

(a) Indian and Persian art (b) Indian and Chinese art
(c) Indian and Turkish-Afghani art
(d) Indian and Greek art

Ans. (d)

Exp. Gandhara style of art is a synthesis of Indian and Greek art. The Gandhara school of Art evolved during the reign of Kushana Emperor Kanishka.

The Gandhara school of Art arose from the fusion of these Greco-Roman and Indian ideas, as well as the influence of other foreign traditions such as those from China and Iran The main theme of the Gandhara school of Art was Lord Buddha and the Bodhisattvas because it was closely associated with Mahayana Buddhism.

18 **Half Shiva and half Parvati in Ardhanarishvara idol are**

(Chap 7, Class-XI, New NCERT Fine Art)

(a) Yoga of men and women (b) Yoga of God and Goddess
(c) Yoga of God and Shakti (d) None of the above

Ans. (c)

Half Shiva and half Parvati in Ardhanarishvara idol are yoga of God and Shakti. The Ardhanarishvara is a form of Shiva combined with his consort Parvati. Ardhanarishvara is depicted as half male and half female, equally split down the middle. The earliest Ardhanarishvara images are dated to the Kushana period, starting from the first century AD. Ardhanarishvara represents the synthesis of masculine and feminine energies of the universe (Purusha and Prakriti) and illustrates how Shakti, the female principle of God, is inseparable from (or the same as, according to some interpretations) Shiva, the male principle of God and *vice-versa*.

Chapter 36

Indian Architecture: Styles and Development

Indian Architecture : Styles and Development

Harappan Architecture

- **The Great Bath**
  - Found in Mohenjodaro (a large rectangular tank in a courtyard surrounded by a corridor on all four sides)

Mauryan Architecture

- **Rock Cut Monuments**
  - Rock-Cut elephant cave at Dhauli is a monument with linear rhythm
  - Rock-cut cave carved at Barabar hills known as Lomas Rishi cave
- **Pillars**
  - Built by Ashoka
  - Mauryan art
  - Made up of spotted red and white sandstone; Palace of Chandragupta Maurya fine example of stone art; Pillar had three parts- prop under the foundation, shaft or the column and the capital
- **Stupas**
  - Built of huge mounds of mud,
  - Enclosed in the carefully burnt small standard bricks
  - Contains Buddha's burial mounds and places of major event of his life Consists of a cylindrical drum and a circular anda with a Harmika and Chhatra on the top
  - Greatest example- Sanchi Stupa
- **Viharas**
  - Excavated in all the cave site of Ajanta and Ellora
  - Plan consists of a Veranda, a hall and cells around the walls of hall

Styles of Temple Architecture

- **Nagara**
  - Became popular in Northern India
  - Entire temple built on stone platform; Does not have elaborate Boundary walls or gateways
  - Garbhagriha located directly under the tallest tower
- **Temples**
  - Dashavatar Vishnu temple in Deogarh; Lakshmana temple in Khajuraho; Chausath Yogini and Kandariya Mahadeva temple built by Chandela king; Sun temple at Modhera built by Raja Bhimdeva I of Solanki dynasty
- **Dravida**
  - Enclosed within a compound wall
  - Front wall has an entrance gateway in its center known as Gopuram
  - Word Shikara is used only for the crowning elements at the top of temples
  - Equivalent to the Amlak and Kalasha of North India temples; Large water reservoir or a temple tank within the complex
- **Temples**
  - Shor temple, Mahabalipuram ; Brihadeeshwara temple, Thanjavur (reign of Chola)

Vesara Temple Style

- Hybridised style containing elements from both Nagara and Dravida
- **Temples**
  - Kailashnath temple at Ellora, Virupaksha temple at Hampi.

Forms of Arts

- **Pallava Art** Shows the transition from rock-cut architecture to the stone-built temples; Introduced by Mahendravarman I; five Rathas (Panchapandava rathas) Signifies five different style of temple architecture
- **Chalukyan Art** Structural temple at Aihole, Badami and Pattadakal; Paintings in Badami cave temple and in Ajanta cave
- **Rashtrakuta Art** Rashtrakuta dynasty were Great patrons of art and architecture; Prominent monuments- Ellora and Elephanta caves
- **Buddhist and Jaina Architectural Development** Mahabodhi temple at Bodhgaya was first constructed during the reign of Ashoka
- **Indo-Islamic Architecture** Had Saracenic, Persian and Turkish influences; Had distinct style in Jaunpur and Bengal; Gujarat borrowed elements from regional temple traditions

Mughal Architecture

- **Babur** Constructed mosque at Rohilakhand and Panipat
- **Humayun** Built the fifth Delhi- Din Panah city
- **Akbar** Mausoleum of Humayun; Fortress- palace in Agra; Newly constructed city of Fatehpur Sikri became capital of the empire
- **Jahangir** Mausoleums of Akbar in Sikandara near Agra has features of Buddhist architecture
- **Shahjahan** Constructed Taj Mahal, a huge white marble building of simple, symmetrical plan

SOURCE Old NCERT Class X (The Heritage of India) **New NCERT Fine Arts ClassXI** (Post-Mauryan Trends in Indian, Art and Architecture), New NCERT Fine Arts Class XI (Some Aspects of Indo-Islamic Architecture), **New NCERT Fine Arts Class XI** (Temple Architecture and Sculpture), NIOS Module-1 Chap 1 (Understanding Indian History)

1 Which of the following is/are famous for Sun temple(s)? *(Chap 1, Module -1, NIOS), (IAS Pre 2017)*

1. Arasavalli 2. Amarkantak 3. Omkareshwar

Codes

(a) Only 1 (b) 2 and 3 (c) 1 and 3 (d) 1, 2 and 3

Ans. (a)

Exp. Arasavalli temple is famous for Sun temples. The temple was built in seventh century AD by king Devendra Varma, a ruler of Kalinga. This temple is considered one of the oldest Sun temples in India.

2 Ellora cave temples are related to *(Chap 4, Class-XI, New NCERT Fine Arts), (UP Lower 2002), (UPPSC Mains 2002, 2006) (JPSC Pre 2008)*

1. Hinduism 2. Buddhism 3. Jainism

Choose the correct answer from the codes given below.

(a) Only 1 (b) Only 2 (c) 1 and 2 (d) 1, 2 and 3

Ans. (d)

Exp. Ellora cave temples are related to three major religions, Buddhism, Jainism and Hinduism.

17 caves out of these 34 are themed around Hinduism.12 caves depict the themes of Buddhists and 5 caves are of Jain Faith. The Rashtrakuta dynasty and Kalachuris constructed part of the Hindu and Buddhist caves of Ellora and the Yadava dynasty constructed a number of the Jain caves.

3 Given below are two statements. *(Chap 6, Class-XI, New NCERT Fine Arts), (Haryana PCS Pre 2021)*

Statement (1) The temples of Virupaksha and Pampadevi were built by choosing a beautiful place like Vijayanagara.

Statement (2) The Vijayanagara rulers adopted the earlier traditions, innovated them and developed them further.

In the light of the above statements, choose the correct answer from the options given below.

(a) Both statements 1 and 2 are true.
(b) Both statements 1 and 2 are false.
(c) Statement 1 is true, but statement 2 is false.
(d) Statement 1 is false, but statement 2 is true.

Ans. (a)

Exp. Both the statements (1) and (2) are true.

The temples of Virupaksha and Pampadevi were built by choosing a beautiful place like Vijayanagara. It is presently located in Hampi in the Vijayanagara district of Karnataka in India. It is dedicated to Sri Virupaksha, a form of Shiva. It is located on the bank of the Tungabhadra river. The Vijayanagara rulers adopted the earlier traditions innovated them and developed them further. Most of beautification had been done during Krishnadevaraya such as carving pillar, addition of Kalyana Mandapa, an open pavilion, these were the important structure which were added by their kings.

4 Consider the following statements with reference to Chaitya and Vihara. *(Chap 4, Class-XI, New NCERT Fine Arts)*

1. Chaitya was the place of residence for the Buddhist monks whereas Vihara was place where monks meditated.
2. The Chaitya hall at Bhaja is in Maharashtra.

Which of the statements given above is/are correct?

(a) Only 1 (b) Only 2
(c) Both 1 and 2 (d) Neither 1 nor 2

Ans. (b)

Exp. Statement (2) is correct with reference to Chaitya and Vihara. The Chaitya hall at Bhaja is in Pune, Maharashtra. It contains 22 rock cut caves belonging to Hinayana sect of Buddhism. Other notable Buddhist rock cut cave sites of Maharashtra include Ajanta, Pitalkhora, Ellora, Nashik, Junnar, Karla and Kanheri.

Statement (1) is incorrect because Chaitya is a prayer hall where Buddhist monks meditated whereas the dwelling place of monks is called Vihara.

5 Which of the following monuments were associated with the Mauryan Period? *(Chap 4, Class-XI, New NCERT Fine Arts)*

1. Ramapurva Bull 2. Great Bath
3. Sanchi Stupa 4. Amravati Stupa

How many of the monuments given above is/are associated with Mauryan period?

(a) Only one (b) Only two
(c) Only three (d) All of these

Ans. (b)

Exp. Only two monuments i.e., (1) and (3) are associated with the Mauryan period. The construction of Rampurva Bull and Sanchi Stupa was done in the Mauryan age. Rampurva Bull is a sandstone pillar erected by the Mauryan Emperor, Ashoka in Rampurva, Bihar. It is now shifted to Rashtrapati Bhavan in New Delhi. Sanchi Stupa was originally commissioned by the Mauryan Emperor Ashoka in third century BC. It was built over the relics of Buddha.

The Great Bath is an architectural specimen of the Indus Valley period whereas Amravati Stupa was constructed during the reign of Satavahana rulers in Andhra Pradesh.

6 With reference to ancient India, consider the following statements. *(Chap 4, Class-XI, NCERT Fine Arts), (IAS Pre 2023)*

1. The concept of Stupa is Buddhist in origin.
2. Stupa was generally a repository of Relice.
3. Stupa was a votive and commemorative structure in Buddhist tradition.

How many of the statements given above is/are correct?

(a) Only one (b) Only two
(c) All three (d) None

Ans. (b)

Exp. Only two statements i.e., (2) and (3) are correct with reference to ancient India.

Stupa was generally a repository of relice. Relics are objects asssociated with the Buddha, such as his physical remains, personal belongings, or items used by him. They are consiered sacred and hold great spiritual significance in Buddhism.

Stupa was votive and commemorative structure in Buddhist tradition. Stupas are often built as acts of devotion and as offerings to the Buddha or other enlightened beings. Stupas are also constructed to commemorate significant events, individuals or historical sites. For example, stupas might be built to mark the birthplace, enlightenment site, or the site of the Buddha's parinirvan (passing away).

Statement 1 is incorrect. Stupa is a pre-Buddhist tumuli in which sramans were buried in a seated position called chaitya. The term 'stupa' comes form the Sanskrit word 'stup,' which means 'healp' or 'pile'.

7 Which of the following statements are correct with reference to the Sanchi Stupa?

(Chap 4, Class-XI, New NCERT Fine Arts)

1. It has four beautifully decorated *toranas* depicting various events from the life of the Buddha and the Jatakas.
2. It was constructed during the reign of Mauryas and is characterised by more advanced carving technique than Bharhut.
3. Two of its toranas (gateways) were destroyed on the orders of Pushyamitra Shunga.

Codes

(a) 1 and 2 (b) 2 and 3
(c) 1 and 3 (d) All of these

Ans. (a)

Exp. Statements (1) and (2) are correct regarding Sanchi Stupa. This stupa constructed during the reign of Mauryan Emperor Ashoka has four beautifully decorated toranas (gateways) depicting various events from the life of the Buddha and the Jatakas. Compared to the Bharhut Stupa which was also constructed during the reign of Mauryas, the sculptures at Sanchi depicts more advanced carving techniques.

Statement (3) is incorrect because toranas contain sculptures belonging to the reign of Pushyamitra Shunga. It was not destroyed on the orders of Pushyamitra Shunga.

8 Consider the following statements with reference to the Amravati Stupa.

(Chap 4, Class-XI, New NCERT Fine Arts)

1. It is located in present day Indian state of Andhra Pradesh and was patronised by the Satavahana rulers.
2. Like the Sanchi Stupa, the Amravati Stupa also has Pradakshina Patha enclosed within a *vedika* on which many narrative sculptures are depicted.
3. Unlike the Sanchi Stupa, the *torana* of the Amravati Stupa has been preserved.

How many of the above statements is/are correct with reference to the Amravati Stupa?

(a) Only one (b) Only two
(c) All three (d) None of these

Ans. (b)

Exp. Only two statements i.e. (1) and (2) are correct regarding Amravati Stupa. This stupa has a mahachaitya hall in Amravati, in modern Indian state of Andhra Pradesh. It was patronised by Satavahana rulers.

Similar to the Sanchi Stupa, the Amravati Stupa also has Pradakshina Patha enclosed within a vedika on which many narrative sculptures are depicted. However, sculptures present in this stupa are characterised by intense emotions and more bodily movement.

Statement (3) is incorrect as the torana of the Amravati Stupa has been destroyed because of the neglect of local rulers and British authorities.

9 With reference to the Ajanta Caves, which of the following statements are correct?

(Chap 4, Class-XI, New NCERT Fine Arts)

1. It has 29 caves and is located in Aurangabad district of Maharashtra.
2. Ajanta is the only surviving example of painting of the first century BC and the fifth century AD.
3. Artistic development of the Ajanta caves was patronised by the Rashtrakuta rulers.

How many of the statements given above is/are correct?

(a) Only one (b) Only two (c) All three (d) None of these

Ans. (b)

Exp. Only two statements i.e. (1) and (2) are correct regarding Ajanta Caves. It contains 29 caves adorned with beautiful paintings associated with Buddhism and is located in Aurangabad district of Maharashtra. It has large Chaitya Viharas and is decorated with sculptures and paintings. Ajanta is the only surviving example of painting of the first century BC and the fifth century AD.

Statement (3) is incorrect because artistic development of the Ajanta caves was patronised by the rulers of Vakataka dynasty. Rashtrakuta were patrons of rock-cut structural temple of Ellora.

10 Consider the following statements with reference to Ellora Caves. ***(Chap 4, Class-XI, New NCERT Fine Arts)***

1. It is a unique art-historical site in the country as it has monasteries associated with the three religions (Buddhism, Jainism and Hinduism) dating from the fifth century AD onwards to the 11th century AD.
2. As the caves were not plastered before painting, nothing visible is left.
3. Ajanta also has excavated double-storeyed caves but at Ellora, the triple storey is a unique achievement.

Which of the statements given above is/ are incorrect?

(a) 1 and 2 (b) 2 and 3
(c) Only 2 (d) Only 3

Ans. (c)

Exp. Statement (2) is incorrect with reference to Ellora Caves because many paintings at Ellora including that related with Vajrayana Buddhism like Tara, Mahamayuri, Akshobhya and of God Vishnu and Shiva is still visible in Ellora. Further in Mural painting (as in Ellora), rocks are firstly plastered before painting.

11 Consider the following pairs.

(Chap 14, Class-X, Old NCERT), (IAS Pre 1997)

Site		Well known for
1. Besnagar	–	Shaivite cave shrine
2. Bhaja	–	Buddhist cave shrine
3. Sithannavasal	–	Jain cave shrine

How many of the pairs given above is/are correctly matched?

(a) Only one (b) Only two
(c) All three (d) None of these

Ans. (b)

Exp. Only two pairs i.e. (2) and (3) are correctly matched. Bhaja caves is a group of 22 rock cut caves built during the second century BC. This cave is also known as Bhaje caves and is located in Pune district, near Lonavala Maharashtra. The Caves belong to the Hinayana Buddhism sect in Maharashtra. The cave consists of numerouse stupas and the most prominent excavation is chaitya griha-cave XII.

Sithannavasal caves located in Pudukottai district of Modern Tamil Nadu belong to Jainism. In ancient days, the Jain Monks used to live in caves and hillocks so as to perform their ascetic life. They polished the hill for the prupose of poojas and penance in the open shelter.

Pair (1) is incorrectly matched becasue Besnagar also knwon as Vidisha is a town located in modern Madhya Pradesh. On the outskirts of Besnagar (Vidisha), stands the quaint Heliodourus Pillar dedicated to the God Vishnu, set up by a Greek named Heliodorus who is said to have adopted Hinduism and became a disciple of Lord Vishnu. Today, the pillar is worshipped by the local as 'Khamba Baba' and so the Besnagar site is well known for Vaishnavite sect not Shaivite sect.

12 Match List I with List II and select the correct answer by using the codes given below the lists.

(Chap 14, Class-X, Old NCERT), (IAS Pre 1997)

List I	List II
A. Gupta	1. Badami
B. Chandela	2. Panamalai
C. Chalukya	3. Khajuraho
D. Pallava	4. Deogarh

Codes

	A	B	C	D		A	B	C	D
(a)	4	3	1	2	(b)	4	2	3	1
(c)	2	3	4	1	(d)	3	4	1	2

Ans. (a)

Exp. The correct matching is A-4, B-3, C-1, D-2.

One of the finest Gupta style of architecture can be observed in Deogarh temple, also known as Dashavatara temple. It is a stone temple located in Jhansi district of Uttar Pradesh.

Khajuraho temple, dedicated to Hinduism and Jainism, was constructed between 885 AD and 100 AD by Chandela dynasty. It is located in Madhya Pradesh.

Badami cave is the example of Chalukyan architecture style. Mangalesha, the Chalukyan king was responsible for its completion. These are Brahminical and Jain caves.

Panamalai is the Pallava's architecture. It is located in Villupuram district of Tamil Nadu.

13 Which one of the following was made earliest, with reference to the art and archaeological history of India? *(Chap 14, Class-X, Old NCERT) (IAS (Pre) 2015)*

(a) Lingaraja temple at Bhubaneswar
(b) Rock-cut elephant at Dhauli
(c) Rock-cut monuments at Mahabalipuram
(d) Varaha image at Udayagiri

Ans. (b)

Exp. Among the given monuments, the Rock-cut elephant at Dhauli was made earliest with reference to the art and archaeological history of India. It was constructed during the reign of emperor Ashoka in the second century BC at Brahmagiri hills near Bhubaneswar.

The Varaha image at Udayagiri was constructed in fourth or fifth century AD under the patronage of Gupta rulers. Lingaraja temple at Bhubaneswar was constructed in 11th century AD during the reign of Jajati Keshari. Rock-cut monuments at Mahabalipuram was constructed during the reign of Pallava rulers in sixth and seventh century AD.

14 With reference to Buddhist history, tradition and culture in India, consider the following pairs.

Famous Shrines	Locations
1. Tabo Monastery and temple complex	Spiti Valley
2. Lhotsava Lhakhang temple, Nako	Zanskar Valley
3. Alchi temple complex	Ladakh

Which of the pairs given above is/are correctly matched? *(Chap 4, Class-XI, New NCERT Fine Arts), (IAS Pre 2014)*

(a) Only 1 (b) 2 and 3
(c) 1 and 3 (d) All of these

Ans. (c)

Exp. Pairs (1) and (3) are correctly matched as Tabo Monastery and temple complex are located in Spiti valley. Tabo is noted for being the oldest continuously operating Buddhist enclave in both India and the Himalayas. It was built by the Buddhist king Yeshe-O, which was later renovated by the royal priest, Jangchub-O.

Alchi Monastery is located in Alchi village in Ladakh. It comes under the Ladakh Autonomous Hill Development Council. It is said to be the oldest and most famous monastery administered by the Likir Monastery.

Pair (2) is incorrectly matched because Lhotsava Lhakhang temple, Nako is located in Himachal Pradesh.

15 The main architectural features of the temples of which of the following regions is characterised in the three orders–Rekhapida, Pidhadeul and Khakra?

(Chap 6, Class-XI, New NCERT Fine Arts)

(a) Odisha (b) Assam
(c) Gujarat (d) Rajasthan

Ans. (a)

Exp. The main architectural features of Odisha temples are classified in three orders, i.e., Rekhapida, Pidhadeul and Khakra. It constitutes a distinct sub-style within the Nagara order.

Notable examples of temples constructed on this architectural style include Sun temple at Konark, Jagannath temple at Puri and Lingaraja temple at Bhubaneswar.

16 Among the given elements, which one is integral feature of the South Indian temples and it is generally not seen in the North Indian temples?

(Chap 14, Class-X, Old NCERT)

1. Gopurams
2. Shikhara
3. Garbhagriha

Codes

(a) Only 1 (b) Only 2
(c) Both 1 and 2 (d) Neither 1 nor 2

Ans. (a)

Exp. Among the given options, Gopurams are integral feature of South Indian temples and it is generally not seen in the North Indian temples. In temples constructed in Dravida style, front wall has an entrance gateway in its centre, which is known as a Gopuram. The shape of the main temple tower known as Vimana in Tamil Nadu is like a stepped pyramid that rises up geometrically rather than the curving Shikhara of North India. In the South Indian temple, the word 'Shikhara' is used only for the crowning element at the top of the temple. Whereas, Shikhara in Nagara style means the main tower over the room of the deity.

Garbhagriha, the room containing main deity constitutes an important element in all the three temple building styles of India.

17 Match List I with List II and select the correct answer from the codes given below the lists.

(Chap 14, Class-X, Old NCERT), (UPPSC Mains 2013)

List I (Gupta temples)	**List II** (Locations)
A. Brick-built temple	1. Eran
B. Dashavatara temple	2. Deogarh
C. Shiva temple	3. Bhitargaon
D. Vishnu temple	4. Bhumara

Codes

	A	B	C	D		A	B	C	D
(a)	4	2	1	3	(b)	3	2	4	1
(c)	2	1	3	4	(d)	1	3	2	4

Ans. (b)

Exp. The correct matching is A-3, B-2, C-4, D-1.

The temple at Bhitargaon in Kanpur (Uttar Pradesh) is one of the earliest surviving **Brick-built temples** of India. It was built in the fifth century AD during the Gupta empire.

Dashavatara temple is a sixth century Vishnu temple located in Deogarh, Uttar Pradesh. It has a simple, one cell square plan and is one of the earliest Hindu stone temples.

Bhumara temple of Shiva is a fifth or sixth century of Gupta Era Hindu stone temple site dedicated to Shiva near Satna, in the Indian State of Madhya Pradesh.

The **Vishnu temple** is located in Eran, Madhya Pradesh. It has a damaged colossal statue of Vishnu that is 13.17 feet high. This temple is mostly ruined, but shows signs of having a sanctum, a mandapa and all the elements of a Hindu temple.

18 With reference to the Indian history of art and culture, consider the following pairs.

(Chap 4, Class-XI, New NCERT Fine Arts), (IAS Pre 2014)

	Famous works of sculptures	Sites
1.	A grand image of Buddha's Mahaparinirvana with a numerous celestial musicians above and the sorrowful figures of his followers below.	– Ajanta
2.	A huge image of Varaha Avatar (boar incarnation) of Vishnu, as he rescues Goddess Earth from the deep and shaotic waters, sculpted on rock.	– Mount Abu
3.	'Arjuna's Penance' 'Descent of the Ganga' sculpted on the surface of huge boulders.	– Mahabalipuram

Which of the pairs given above is/are correctly matched?

(a) 1 and 2 (b) Only 3
(c) 1 and 3 (d) All of these

Ans. (c)

Exp. Pairs (1) and (3) are correctly matched as in cave 26 of Ajanta caves, Buddha is lying on his right side. The sculpture has a length of 7 metres. The panel below the sculpture shows Buddha's disciples and celestial figures float above. This is one of the grandest and most sensitive depiction in all of Buddhist art.

'Descent of the Ganga' also known as 'Arjuna's Penance' is located in Mahabalipuram. It is a huge rock relief carved on pink granite. It contains different stories of Mahabharata in the form of sculptures.

Pair (2) is incorrectly matched because Varaha Avatar can be found in Udayagiri cave no 5. It has the narrative of Vishnu in his Varaha or man-boar avatar rescuing Goddess Earth in crisis.

19 **Consider the following statements with reference to the art and culture in Gupta Period.**

(Chap 14, Class-X, Old NCERT)

1. The construction of Hindu temple began in this period.
2. Paintings and sculptures at Ajanta caves were patronised by Gupta rulers.

Which of the statements given above is/are correct?

(a) Only 1 (b) Only 2
(c) Both 1 and 2 (d) Neither 1 nor 2

Ans. (a)

Exp. Statement (1) is correct with reference to the art and culture in Gupta Period. The construction of Hindu temple began during the Gupta period. Parvati temple of Nachna Kuthara and Vishnu temple of Tigawa Jabalpur are some of the earliest temples constructed in North India under the reign of Gupta rulers. The Gupta era in India marked the beginning of the free standing temple architecture.

Statement (2) is incorrect becasue paintings and sculptures at Ajanta caves were patronised by Vakataka rulers who were contemporary of Gupta rulers in Deccan.

20 **Match the following lists correctly and choose the correct code.** *(Chap 14, Class-X, Old NCERT)*

List I (Temples)	List II (Associated Dynasties)
A. Kailashnath	1. Chandela
B. Brihadeshwara	2. Rashtrakuta
C. Khajuraho	3. Vijayanagara
D. Lepakshi	4. Chola

Codes

	A	B	C	D		A	B	C	D
(a)	1	2	3	4	(b)	2	4	1	3
(c)	2	3	4	1	(d)	4	3	1	2

Ans. (b)

Exp. The correct matching is A-2, B-4, C-1, D-3.
The **Kailashnath** temple at Ellora was built in Dravida style by Krishna III ruler of Rashtrakuta dynasty.

Brihadeshwar temple constructed around 1009 AD by Rajaraja Chola is one of the best examples of temple constructed in Dravida style of architecture.

The temples of **Khajuraho** were constructed by the Chandela rulers in Nagara style of temple architecture.

The **Lepakshi** temple was built by the brothers Viranna and Virupanna. It is dedicated to Veerabhadra and is an example of the Vijayanagara architectural style.

21 **Pietra dura is related to which of the following?**

(Chap 4, Class-X, Old NCERT) (BPSC Pre 2020)

(a) Decorating the walls with floral designs made of semi-precious stones
(b) Building sloping walls in minars
(c) Use of arch in construction
(d) Use of marble in buildings

Ans. (a)

Exp. Pietra dura is related to decorating the walls with floral designs made of semi-precious stones. It became an essential element of medieval architecture under the Mughal empire. It was used by the Shah Jahan in the construction of Red Fort at Delhi.

22 **With reference to the Lingaraja temple, which of the following statements are correct?**

(Chap 14, Class-X, Old NCERT)

1. It is constructed in Nagara style of temple architecture and is located in Odisha.
2. It is dedicated to the Hindu God Shiva.
3. Twelve pairs of enormous wheels sculpted with spokes are present in this temple.

How many of the statements given above is/are correct?

(a) Only one (b) Only two
(c) All three (d) None of these

Ans. (b)

Exp. Only two statements i.e. (1) and (2) are correct with reference to the Lingaraja temple. The Lingaraja temple of Bhubaneswar, Odisha was constructed in Nagara style of temple architecture. It was built by King Jajati Keshari in the 10th century AD and completed by King Lalatendu Keshari in the 11th century AD.

Statement (3) is incorrect because twelve pairs of enormous wheels sculpted with spokes are present in Sun temple at Konark.

23 **Consider the following statements with reference to the Vijayanagara School of architecture.**

(Chap 6, Class-XI, New NCERT Fine Arts)

1. Vijayanagara architecture was synthesises of the centuries-old Dravida temple architecture with Islamic styles demonstrated by the neighbouring sultanates.
2. With its seat at Hampi, the rulers of Vijayanagara built beautiful temples such as Hazara Rama and Virupaksha temple.

3. The Italian traveller Marco Polo gave an illustrative account of Vijayanagara architecture.

Which of the statements given above are correct?

(a) 1 and 2 (b) 2 and 3
(c) 1 and 3 (d) All of these

Ans. (a)

Exp. Statements (1) and (2) are correct regarding Vijayanagara school of architecture. Vijayanagara architecture was synthesises of the centuries-old Dravida temple architecture with Islamic styles demonstrated by the neighbouring sultanates.

Its capital was Hampi which itself contained beautiful temples constructed by its rulers. Notable among them is Hazara Rama temple and Virupaksha temple constructed during the reign of Deva Raya II.

Statement (3) is incorrect because Marco Polo visited parts of Southern India during the 12th century AD. Hence, he didn't gave an illustrative account of Vijayanagara architecture.

24 With reference to the Kailashnath temple at Ellora, which of the following statements are correct? *(Chap 6, Class-XI, New NCERT Fine Arts)*

1. This temple was constructed by the Rashtrakuta rulers in Dravida style.
2. It is built on the monolith rock with a *vimana* rising to thirty metres.
3. Unlike the temples in South India, there is no evidence of sculpture at this temple.

Codes

(a) 1 and 2 (b) 2 and 3 (c) 1 and 3 (d) All of these

Ans. (a)

Exp. Statements (1) and (2) are correct regarding Kailashnath temple at Ellora. This temple is dedicated to God Shiva and was constructed by Krishna III of Rashtrakuta dynasty. It is one of the magnificent styles of temple constructed in Dravida style. It was built on the monolith rock with a vimana rising to thirty metres. It is located in Ellora cave in Maharashtra.

Statement (3) is incorrect becuase kailashnath temple is adorned by beautiful sculptures.

25 Consider the following statements with reference to the Vesara style of temple architecture. *(Chap 6, Class-XI, New NCERT Fine Arts)*

1. This style of temple building was prevalent in Deccan and is characterised by the synthesis of Nagara and Dravida style of temple building.
2. This style was popularised by the Chalukya rulers of Karnataka.
3. The most prominent example of this temple is the Lad Khan temple at Aihole in Karnataka.

Which of the statements given above is/are incorrect?

(a) 1 and 2 (b) 2 and 3
(c) Only 2 (d) Only 3

Ans. (d)

Exp. Statement (3) is incorrect regarding Vesara style of temple architecture because Lad Khan temple is one of the oldest temples in the Aihole temple complex. It is constructed in Panchayatana style of architecture. Notable examples of temple constructed in Vesara style include Kallesvara temple at Kukkanur and Ramalingesvara temple at Gudur.

26 Which one of the following monuments had been constructed entirely of marble with reference to medieval architecture? *(Chap 14, Class-X, Old NCERT)*

(a) Jama Masjid of Fatehpur Sikri
(b) Moti Masjid of Agra Fort
(c) Qila-e-Kuhana mosque
(d) Jama Masjid at Delhi

Ans. (b)

Exp. Among the given options, Moti Masjid (mosque) has been constructed entirely of marble. This mosque is under the compound of Red Fort in Delhi. It was built by the Mughal Emperor Aurangzeb from 1659-1660 AD.

27 Identify the region after reading the given passage. *(Chap 14, Class-X, Old NCERT)*

The oblong shape of structures and the peculiar style of roof constructions were some of the distinctive features of this regional architecture. Adina mosque and the tomb of Jalal-ud-din Muhammad Shah belong to this region.

(a) Gujarat (b) Mandu (c) Jaunpur (d) Bengal

Ans. (d)

Exp. The given description highlights the style of architecture prevalent in Bengal in medieval times. This style was characterised by oblong shape of structures and the peculiar style of roof constructions. Adina mosque and the tomb of Jalal-ud-din Muhammad Shah at Pandua and the Dakhil Darwaza and Tantipara mosque at Gaur are some of the notable examples of this style of medieval architecture.

28 With the arrivals of Turks and other Muslims from the Persia, Arabia and Central Asia new architectural style developed in Indian subcontinent. The main architectural feature(s) of this new style were *(Chap 14, Class-X, Old NCERT)*

1. Mehrab
2. Minaret
3. Domes
4. Calligraphic printing

Codes

(a) 1 and 2 (b) 2 and 3
(c) 1 and 3 (d) All of these

Ans. (d)

Exp. The main architectural features of Indo-Islamic style, which was introduced in India after the arrival of Turks and other Muslim invaders from the Persia, Arabia and Central Asia are Mehrab, Minaret, Domes and

Calligraphic printing. The hybridisation of these elements along with the earlier architectural.elements prevalent in ancient India resulted into a new and unique style of architecture.

29 Consider the following statements with reference to the architectural development in the Deccan. *(Chap 14, Class-X, Old NCERT)*

1. The Jama Masjid of Gulbarga is the only mosque in India to have a covered courtyard.
2. The madrasa of Mahmud Gawan is located at Bidar.

Which of the statement(s) given above is/are correct?

(a) Only 1 (b) Only 2
(c) Both 1 and 2 (d) Neither 1 nor 2

Ans. (c)

Exp. Both the statements (1) and (2) are correct regarding architectural development in Deccan in the medieval phase. The founder of Bahamani kingdom Alauddin Hasan Bahmani Shah constructed Jama Masjid at Gulbarga in 14th century AD. It is the only mosque in India to have a covered courtyard. The Madrasa of Mahmud Gawan is located at Bidar. It was built in 15th century AD. Mahmud Gawan was the Prime Minister of the Sultanate of Bahamani.

30 Match the following lists correctly and choose the correct code. *(Chap 14, Class-X, Old NCERT)*

List I (Monuments)	List II (Associated Rulers)
A. Tomb of Salim Chisti	1. Ahmed Shah
B. Alai Darwaza	2. Akbar
C. Teen Darwaza	3. Alauddin Khilji
D. Quwwat-ul-Islam mosque	4. Qutb-ud-din Aibak

Codes

	A	B	C	D
(a)	1	2	3	4
(b)	2	3	1	4
(c)	2	3	4	1
(d)	4	3	1	2

Ans. (b)

Exp. The correct matching is A-2, B-3, C-1, D-4.

Tomb of Salim Chisti was built by Mughal Emperor, Akbar in Fatehpur Sikri near Agra.

Alai Darwaza was built by ruler of Delhi Sultanate, Alauddin Khilji in Delhi near Qutub Minar.

Teen Darwaza was built by Ahmed Shah the Sultan of Gujarat in Ahmedabad.

Quwwat-ul-Islam mosque was built in Delhi by the first ruler of Delhi Sultanate, Qutb-ud-din Aibak.

31 Arrange the given monuments created during the medieval period in the chronological order. *(Chap 14, Class-X, Old NCERT)*

1. Atala Mosque at Jaunpur
2. Buland Darwaza
3. Taj Mahal
4. Badshahi Mosque at Lahore
5. Mausoleum of Sher Shah at Sasaram

Codes

(a) 1, 2, 4, 5, 3 (b) 1, 5, 2, 3, 4
(c) 1, 2, 3, 4, 5 (d) 5, 4, 3, 1, 2

Ans. (b)

Exp. The correct chronological order of the given medieval monuments is 1, 5, 2, 3, 4.

Atala Mosque at Jaunpur was constructed during the reign of Ibrahim Shah of Sharqi dynasty in 1408 AD.

The Mausoleum of Sher Shah at Sasaram was constructed in 1545 AD by Sher Shah Suri and his son Islam Shah.

Buland Darwaza was constructed at Fatehpur Sikri by the Mughal Emperor Akbar in 1575 AD to commemorate his victory over Gujarat.

Taj Mahal was constructed in Agra during the reign of Mughal Emperor, Shah Jahan in 1632 AD.

Badhshahi Mosque at Lahore was constructed at Lahore during the reign of Mughal Emperor, Aurangzeb in 1673 AD.

32 The medieval Gujarat school of architecture borrowed, which of the following elements from regional temple traditions? *(Chap 8, Class-XI, New NCERT)*

1. Toranas
2. Lintels in Mihrabs
3. Carvings of bell and chain motifs
4. Double dome

Codes

(a) 1, 3 and 4 (b) 1, 2 and 3
(c) 2, 3 and 4 (d) All of these

Ans. (b)

Exp. The medieval Gujarat school of architecture borrowed the elements of constructing and decorating toranas (gateways), lintels in Mihrabs and carving of bell and chain motifs from regional temple traditions. Notable examples of monuments constructed on this style include-Teen Darwaza, Tomb of Ahmed Shah, Rani Sipri Mosque among others.

The feature of double dome was introduced in India by Lodi (Afghan) rulers in India.

33 Match the following lists correctly and choose the correct code. *(Chap 14, Class-X, Old NCERT)*

List I (Monuments)	List II (Places)
A. Tomb of Itmad-ud-Daula	1. Mandu
B. Chand Minar	2. Agra
C. Jahaz Mahal	3. Jaipur
D. Amer Fort	4. Daultabad

Codes

	A	B	C	D
(a)	1	2	3	4
(b)	3	4	1	2
(c)	2	4	1	3
(d)	4	3	1	2

Ans. (c)

Exp. The correct matching is A-2, B-4, C-1, D-3.

Tomb of Itmad-ud-Daula is located in Agra. It was built during the reign of Mughal Emperor, Jahangir.

Chand Minar is located in Daultabad. Built in the 15th century, it is a 110- feet-high tapering tower divided into four storeys.

Jahaz Mahal is located in Mandu. It was built by rulers of Malwa, Akbar II and Bahadur Shah II.

Amer Fort is located in Jaipur. It was built by Sawai Jai Singh of Jaipur.

34 Consider the following statements with reference to Indo-Islamic architecture. *(Chap 14, Class-X, Old NCERT)*

1. Muslims, forbidden to replicate living forms on any surface, developed their religious art and architecture consisting of the arts of arabesque, geometrical patterns and calligraphy on plaster and stone.
2. The walls in all buildings were extremely thick and were largely constructed of rubble masonry, which was easily available.
3. Tombs were largely built on a simple square or rectangular plan and were meant to provide temporary accommodation to Indian and foreign travellers and pilgrims.

How many of the statements given above is/are incorrect?

(a) Only one (b) Only two
(c) All three (d) None of these

Ans. (a)

Exp. Only one statement (3) is incorrect with reference to Indo-Islamic architecture because tombs in Islamic architecture are monumental structures over graves of rulers or famous personalities. Sarais were constructed to provide temporary accommodation to Indian and foreign travellers and pilgrims.

35 With reference to the Mughal architecture, which of the following statements are correct? *(Chap 8, Class-XI, New NCERT Fine Arts)*

1. Unlike the Persians' use of bricks and glazed tiles, the Mughal builders used stone and marble in the construction of tomb.
2. It began with the advent of Shah Jahan whose reign is also referred as the golden age of Mughal architecture.
3. Two significant features of the Mughal architecture are the large gateways and the placement of the building in the midst of park.

How many of the statements given above is/are correct?

(a) Only one
(b) Only two
(c) All three
(d) None of the above

Ans. (b)

Exp. Only two statements i.e. (1) and (3) are correct regarding Mughal architecture.

They introduced some Persian elements in Indian architecture however, unlike the Persians' use of bricks and glazed tiles, the Mughal builders used stone and marble in the construction of tomb.

Two significant features of the Mughal architecture are the large gateways and the placement of the building in the midst of park (*Charbagh* style).

Statement (2) is incorrect because Mughal architecture formally began under the reign of Akbar under whom magnificent buildings of Fatehpur Sikri were constructed.

The tomb of Humayun was also constructed during the reign of Akbar.

Chapter 37

Music, Dance and Theatre Craft

Music, Dance and Theatre Craft

Music

Introduction

- History of Indian music and dance is traced from the Vedic age
- Sama Veda contained the Shlokas related to music
- Detailed information is also found in Bharatmuni's Natyashashtra

Indian Classical Music

- Broadly two traditions,
- The Hindustani form prevalent in North India and Carnatic music from

Hindustani Classical Music

- Traced back to Delhi sultanate and to Amir Khusrau; He invented Sitar and the Tabla and introduced new ragas; Gharana transmitted musical knowledge and style across generation

Dhrupad

- Traditionally performed by men with a Tanpura and Pakhawaj; Lyrics sung are in medieval form of Hindi; Sung in four styles- Bansi Gaurhar, Dagur, Kandhar, Nauhar; Famous vocalists- Uday Bhawalkar, Pandit Ritwik Sanyal

Khayal

- Consists of about 4-8 lines of lyrics set to a tune; Theme is romantic in nature; Uses taan in the compositions; Modern day vocalists are- late Bhimsen Joshi, Nagaraja Havaldar

Dhamar

- Similar to Dhrupad but chiefly associated with festival of Holi; Composed in praise of Lord Krishna

Tarana

- Songs used to convey a feel of joy and are usually performed towards the end of a concert

Thumri

- Informal vocal form; begun with the court of Nawab Wajid Ali Shah

Carnatic Music

- Attributed collectively to Shyam Shastri, Thyagaraja and Muthuswami Dikshitar; Thyagaraja reversed both as a saint and an artist; Main compositions are known as Kriti; Carnatic alapana is similar to alap in Hindustani classical music

Gharana of Classical Music

Gwalior Gharana

- Oldest among all the Khayal gayaki
- Founders are-Ustad Hassu Khan Ustad Haddu Khan, Ustad Nathu Khan
- Prominent exponents are- Bal Krishna, Ealchal Karanjikar, Vishnu Digambar Paluskar, Pandit Omkarnath Thakur

Agra Gharana

- Placed great importance on developing forcefulness and depth in the voice
- Founders are- Haji Sujan Khan, Ustad Ghagghe, Khuda Baksh; Prominent exponents- Faiyaz Khan, Latafat Hussain Khan and Dinkar Kaikini

Kirana Gharana

- In this style, Swara is used to create an emotional mood by means of elongation and use of Kanas
- Founder are- Abdul Karim Khan and Abdul Wahid Khan
- Prominent exponents- Hirabhai Barodakar, Begum Akhtar, Bhimsen Joshi, Gangubhai Hangal

Jaipur Gharana

- Complex and melodic form arising out of involutedly and undulating phrases that comprises the piece
- Founded by Ustad Alladiya Khan
- Prominent exponents- Mallikarjun Mansur, Kesarbhai Kerkar, Kishori Amonkar, Shruti Sadolikar

Mewati Gharana

- Gave importance to developing the mood of the raga through the notes forming

Theatre Craft and Dance

Classical Dance Form of India

- **Bharatanatyam** (Tamil Nadu)
  - Performed by the women
  - Known for its beautiful body movements and gestures
- **Kathak** (Uttar Pradesh)
  - Comes from the word 'Katha' which means story
- **Kathakali** (Kerala)
  - Includes intriguing face movements and the heavy costumes
  - Face masks and paints
  - Music includes only vocals called soppanam
- **Odissi** (Assam)
  - Developed in temples
  - Considered oldest dance form which included more than 50 intriguing mudras
- **Manipuri**
  - Performed to narrate the romantic relationship between the Hindu gods Radha and Krishna
- **Tribal Dance**
  - Muria dance performed by Muria tribe of North Bastar
  - Saila dance form of Chhattisgarh
- **Theatre Crafts**
  - Important theatre forms in India
  - Koodiyattam (Kerala); Jatra (Bengal/Bihar/Odisha); Yakshagana (Karnataka); Swang (Haryana/Rajasthan/UP); Bhand Pather (Kashmir); Tamasha /Maharashtra)

SOURCE *Old NCERT Class X (The Heritage of India)*, *NIOS Module-6B, Chap 29 (Contemporary Cultural Situation)*

1 **Match the following lists correctly and choose the correct codes.** *(Chap 14, Class-X, Old NCERT)* *(Chap 29, Module-6B, NIOS)*

List I (Treatise on Music)	List II (Authors)
A. Natyashastra	1. Bharata
B. Brihaddesi	2. Matanga
C. Sangeet Ratnakar	3. Sarangdeva
D. Kitab-e-Nauras	4. Ibrahim Adil Shah II

Codes

	A	B	C	D		A	B	C	D
(a)	1	3	4	2	(b)	1	2	3	4
(c)	3	4	1	2	(d)	4	2	1	3

Ans. (b)

Exp. The correct matching is A-1, B-2, C-3, D-4.

Natyashastra was composed by the sage Bharata in Sanskrit. Written around 200 BC, it is considered as the earliest treatise which deals with all aspect of Visual arts such as music, drama, dance, etc.

Brihaddesi is ancient treatise on Music, composed in Sanskrit by sage Matanga. It gives an elaborate account of different ragas.

Sangeet Ratnakar was composed in 13th century AD by Sarangdeva. It is considered as one of the most authentic works on Indian music.

Kitab-e-Nauras was written by the ruler of Adil Shahi dynasty, Ibrahim Adil Shah II in Dakhini language. It contains songs in praise of Hindu deities and Muslim saints.

2 **Match List I with List II and select the correct answer by using the codes given below the lists.** *(Chap 14, Class-X, Old NCERT)*

List I	List II
A. Ravi Shankar	1. Shehnai
B. Hariprasad Chaurasia	2. Tabla
C. Zakir Hussain	3. Sitar
D. Bismillah Khan	4. Flute

Codes

	A	B	C	D		A	B	C	D
(a)	1	2	3	4	(b)	3	4	2	1
(c)	4	3	2	1	(d)	2	4	1	3

Ans. (b)

Exp. The correct matching is A-3, B-4, C-2, D-1.

Ravi Shankar was an Indian sitarist and composer. As a sitar maestro, he became the world's best known exponent of North Indian classical music in the second half of the 20th century.

Hariprasad Chaurasia is an Indian music director and classical flutist, who plays the flute in the Hindustani classical tradition.

Zakir Hussain is an Indian tabla player, composer and music producer. He is widely considered as one of the greatest tabla player of all time.

Bismillah Khan popular shehnai player. He was awarded Bharat Ratna in 2001. He became third classical musician of India after Ms. Subbalakshmi and Ravi Shankar to be awarded by the Bharat Ratna.

3 **Consider the following dance form of India.** *(Chap 14, Class-X, Old NCERT)*

1. Kathakali
2. Kuchipudi
3. Bharatnatyam
4. Kalbelia

How many of the above is/are not a classical dance form?

(a) Only one (b) Only two
(c) Only three (d) None of these

Ans. (a)

Exp. Only one option i.e. (4), Kalbelia is not a classical dance form of India. It is a folk dance from Rajasthan, which is performed by tribes of snake charmers. The Sangeet Natak Academy had accorded the status of Classical dance to these eight Indian dance forms i.e.,.

1. Kathakali (Kerala)
2. Kuchipudi (Andhra Pradesh)
3. Bharatnatyam (Tamil Nadu)
4. Manipuri (Manipur)
5. Mohiniyattam (Kerala)
6. Odissi (Odisha)
7. Sattriya (Assam)
8. Kathak (Northern India)

4 **Consider the following statements.** *(Chap 14, Class-X, Old NCERT)*

1. Amir Khusrau originated Qawwali and Khayal style of music.
2. He is also credited with invention of musical instruments.
3. He was patronised by the Mughal rulers.

Which of the statements given above are correct?

(a) 1 and 3 (b) 1 and 2
(c) 2 and 3 (d) 1, 2 and 3

Ans. (b)

Exp. Statements (1) and (2) are correct. Amir Khusrau originated Qawwali and Khayal style of Hindustani music. He is also credited with invention of musical instruments such as Sitar and Tabla. Ashiqa, Nuh Sipihr and Qiranal – Sadayan were some of the literary creation of Amir Khusrau.

Statement (3) is incorrect because Amir Khusrau was patronised by Delhi Sultanate ruler, Alauddin Khilji. He was also a disciple of Nizamuddin Auliya and had believed to have seen the reign of seven sultans of Delhi Sultanate.

5 **Who among the following were prominent figures of the Carnatic music?** *(Chap 14, Class-X, Old NCERT)*

1. Purandaradasa
2. Tyagaraja
3. Syamasastri
4. Mutthuswami Dikshitar

Codes

(a) 1 and 2 (b) 2, 3 and 4
(c) 3 and 4 (d) All of these

Ans. (d)

Exp. Purandaradasa, Tyagaraja, Syamasastri and Mutthuswami Dikshitar were prominent figures of Carnatic music. Purandaradasa was a 15th century AD musician and philosopher from Karnataka. He was also known as the Sangeeta Pitamah of Carnatic music.

He laid out the basic rules for teaching Carnatic music. Tyagaraja, Syamasastri and Mutthuswami Dikshitar are considered as trinity of Carnatic music. They brought monumental change in the Carnatic music in 18th century AD.

6 **Consider the following Assertion (A) and Reason (R) and choose the correct code.** *(Chap 14, Class-X, Old NCERT)*

Assertion (A) Most of the words and themes of Classical music has been derived from Hindu mythology.

Reason (R) Music was not the part of original Islamic traditions.

Codes

(a) Both A and R are true and R is the correct explanation of A.
(b) Both A and R are true but R is not the correct explanation of A.
(c) A is true, but R is false.
(d) A is false, but R is true.

Ans. (b)

Exp. Both Assertion (A) and Reason (R) are true but Reason (R) is not the correct explanation of Assertion (A). Both the style of Indian Classical music viz. Hindustani and Carnatic music is heavily influenced by Hindu mythology and philosophy. The themes, words, ragas etc., are derived from ancient Indian tradition. Music was not the part of original Islamic traditions. Many conservative accounts of early Islamic traditions prohibit music.

7 **Consider the following Assertion (A) and Reason (R) and choose the correct code.** *(Chap 14, Class-X, Old NCERT)*

Assertion (A) The popular image of Shiva in the form of Nataraja symbolises the influence of dance on the life of the Indian people.

Reason (R) Dance in India is treated as a medium for expression of emotions and storytelling.

Codes

(a) Both A and R are true and R is the correct explanation of A.
(b) Both A and R are true, but R is not the correct explanation of A.
(c) A is true, but R is false.
(d) A is false, but R is true.

Ans. (b)

Exp. Both Assertion (A) and Reason (R) are true, but Reason (R) is not the correct explanation of Assertion (A). The popular image of Shiva in the form of Nataraja symbolises the influence of dance on the life of the Indian people.

Unlike the West, where dance is seen as method of recreation, it is embedded in culture of India.

Shiva in Nataraja form is associated with the end of cosmic world and is beautifully depicted in sculpture created during the reign of Imperial Cholas.

While dance in India is treated as a medium of expression of emotions and storytelling.

The nine rasas such as lasya, karuna is illustrated through Indian classical dances. Further, the art of storytelling such as kandas (chapters) of Hindu Epics is well developed in Indian Classical dance.

Chapter 38

Indian Language, Literature and Philosophy

Indian Language, Literature and Philosophy

Indian Languages

Indo-Aryan
- Spoken by around 70 % of the population of the country
- Sanskrit, Hindi, Bengali, Punjabi, Gujarati etc. are part of this family

Dravidian
- Second largest family of languages in India
- Consists of South Indian languages like Tamil, Kannada, Malayalam and Telugu

Austric
- Oldest and most indigenous language in the language family of India
- Speakers concentrated in the hilly and tribal areas of Central and Eastern India
- Languages Santhali, Nicobarese, Khond

Sino-Indian
- Language spoken in the North-East and northern parts of India
- **Includes** Naga, Bodo, Tibetan, Ladakhi
- **Other Linguistic Family** Fifth family of language spoken in South Andaman is Ongan (language -onge and Jarawa); Almost extinct linguistic Family- Andamanese

Role of Sanskrit
- Belonged to the Indo
- European group of language
- Scientific grammar compiled by Panini in 4th century BC
- Language of religion, philosophy and learning

Indian Literatures

Jain Literature
- Written in Prakrit and were finally compiled in 6th century AD in Vallabhi Gujarat; Important works known as Angas, Upangas, Prakirnas, Chhedab sutras and Malasutras

Buddhist Literature
- Written in Pali language; Divided into the canonical and the non-canonical
- Canonical literature- Tripatika (Vinaya, Sutta and Abhidhamma Pitaka)

Sangam Literature
Poets, bards, writers and authors came from various parts of South India to Madurai were called Sangam as

Brahmi Script
Originator of most of the present Indian script including Devanagri, Bengali, Tamil and Malayalam

Kharosthi Script
- Written from right to left
- Used in Gandhara culture of North-Western India

Nagri Script
- Eastern version of Gupta script
- Early form of Devanagri script

Literature in Medieval Period
- Somadeva's Katha Sarit Sagara is a collection of India legends, fairy tales and folk tales with multiple layer of story within a story
- Kalhana's Rajatarangini related to Kashmir is first systematically written history book

Development of Indian Philosophy

Nyaya
- Follows a scientific and a rational approach
Founded by sage Gautama; Believes that gaining knowledge through the five senses is the sole way of attaining liberation from cycle of Birth and death

Sankhya
- Oldest of all philosophies
- Founded by Kapila
- Dualistic philosophy with Purusha (soul) and Prakriti(nature) in it

Yoga
- Expounded by Patanjali
- Accepts the Sankhya psychology and metaphysics, but is more theistic, with the addition of a divine entity to Sankhya's 25 elements of reality

Vaisheshika
- Founded by Kannada in 6th century BC
- Atomist and pluralist in nature; Basis of the school's philosophy is that all objects in the physical universe are reducible to a finite number of atoms

Purva Mimansa
- Believes in complete authority of vedas; Based on sage Jaimini's mimamsa sutras; Emphasises the power of Yajnas and mantra in sustaining the activities of the universe

Uttar Mimamsa (Vedanta)
- It is a monistic school of philosophy that believes that the world is unreal and only reality is Brahman

SOURCE **Old NCERT Class-X** (The Heritage of India), **Tamil Nadu Board, Class-XI, Unit 9** (Cultural Development in South India)

1 Consider the following sttements.

Statement (1) Shwetambara Dharmasutra consists of twelve Angas.

Statement (2) Compilation of these Angas according to Shwetambara tradition was done in a Dharma assembly held at Vallabhi.

(Unit 3, Class-XI, Tamil Nadu Board) (CGPSC Pre 2021)

Codes

(a) Statement 1 and Statement 2 are true.
(b) Statement 1 is false, but Statement 2 is true.
(c) Statement 1 and Statement 2 are false.
(d) Statement 1 is true, but Statement 2 is false.

Ans. (a)

Exp. Both the Statement 1 and Statement 2 are true as in 512 AD, the Shwetambara held another Council at Vallabhi. The Shwetambaras recompiled the Agamas and recorded them as written manuscripts under the leadership of Acharya Shraman Devardhigani along with other 500 Jain scholars. In this Vallabhi Council, twelve Angas were composed.

2 Which of the following pairs of writers and books in Ancient India is incorrectly matched?

(Unit 8, Class-XI, Tamil Nadu Board) (MPSC Pre 2021)

(a) Mricchakatika – Shudraka
(b) Raghuvansham – Kalidasa
(c) Buddhacharita – Ashvaghosha
(d) Kadambari – Harshavardhana

Ans. (d)

Exp. Pair (d) is incorrectly matched because Banabhatta is the author of Kadambari.

He was the court poet of Harsha, He wrote Harsha biography called Harshacharita.

3 In the context of Indian languages.

(Chap 14, Class-X, Old NCERT)

1. Tamil is the oldest Dravidian language.
2. Buddhist literature was written in Pali language.
3. Languages of Northern India belong to Indo-European group.

Which of the statements given above is/are correct?

(a) Only 1 (b) 2 and 3 (c) 3 and 1 (d) All of these

Ans. (d)

Exp. All statements are correct in the context of Indian languages. Tamil which is spoken in the Tamil Nadu is the oldest Dravidian language. This language and its literature developed alongside the Sangam Age. The other Dravidian language developed in the first millennium of the Christian era. Buddha, in order to reach the masses and better spread the newly formed doctrine of Buddhism, choose the Pali language which was the language of the commoner in the sixth century BC in Bihar and Eastern Uttar Pradesh.

The languages of North India (Hindi, Bengali, Gujarati etc) belong to Indo-European group of languages.

4 With reference to the language development in India, which of the following statements is/are incorrect?

(Chap 14, Class-X, Old NCERT)

1. Prakrit was language spoken by people belonging to higher classes.
2. Sanskrit was dominant language during the Gupta period.

Codes

(a) Only 1 (b) Only 2
(c) Both 1 and 2 (d) Neither 1 nor 2

Ans. (a)

Exp. Statement (1) is incorrect with reference to the language development in India as Prakrit language in the ancient India was spoken by the common people in the areas adjoining modern day territories of Bihar and Uttar Pradesh. As, it was associated with the common people, Mahavira preached the doctrine of Jainism in Prakrit.

5 Which one of the following pairs of authors of different language and their works on theme of Mahabharata is correctly matched?

(Unit 9, Calss-XI, Tamil Nadu Board) (IAS Pre 1997)

(a) Sarala Dasa – Bengali
(b) Kanshi Ram – Odia
(c) Tikkana – Marathi
(d) Pampa – Kannada

Ans. (d)

Exp. Pair (d) is correctly matched as Pampa authored on various works on theme of Mahabharata in Kannada language. Pampa, also known as Adikavi, was a Kannada language Jain poet. He was court poet of Chalukyan king Arikasari II. He is best known for his epics Vikramarjuna Vijaya or Pampa Bharata and Adi Purana.

Pairs (a), (b) and (c) are incorrectly matched because Sarala Dasa was a 15th century poet and a scholar of Odia literature. Kanshi Ram was an Indian Bengali poet. He was an important poet in Medieval Bengali literature. Tikkana was a 13th century Telugu poet. He was the second poet of the 'Trinity of Poets' that translated Mahabharata into Telugu.

6 Arrange the following languages in the chronological order. ***(Chap 14, Class-X, Old NCERT)***

1. Prakrit 2. Sanskrit
3. Urdu 4. Apabhramshas

Codes

(a) 1, 2 ,4, 3 (b) 2, 1, 4, 3
(c) 3, 1, 4, 2 (d) 4, 1, 3, 2

Ans. (b)

Exp. The correct chronological order of the given languages is Sanskrit < Prakrit < Apabhramshas<Urdu.

Among the Indo-European languages, Sanskrit was first developed and used in India. It was introduced in India with the arrival of Indo-Aryans in the 15th century BC.

Prakrit was one of the local dialects used in Indian subcontinent from the seventh and sixth centuries BC. It was spoken by commoners and used by Jaina monks as well as by Ashoka to propagate his message of Dhamma through inscriptions.

Apabhramshas was formalised form of Prakrit language developed during the Gupta age. It formed the basis of modern Indian languages which developed in the various regions of India during the medieval period.

Urdu language was developed during the age of Delhi Sultanate. It is a synthesis of the Hindi and the Persian language. Gradually, in medieval period, it became common language of towns in all over India.

7 Consider the following statements with reference to the development of Urdu language.

(Chap 14, Class-X, Old NCERT)

1. It was developed during the reign of Delhi Sultanate.
2. Its vocabulary is drawn from Hindi and Persian language.
3. It served as the court language for majority of the rulers of the Delhi Sultanate.

Which of the statements given above is/are incorrect?

(a) 1 and 3 (b) Only 3 (c) Only 2 (d) 1 and 4

Ans. (b)

Exp. Statement (3) in incorrect with reference to the development of Urdu language as during the reign of Delhi Sultanate, Persian served as the court language for the majority of rulers. Official documents (such as land records) and literature developed in this language.

8 Which among the following ancient treatise are in the form of dialogues and express the highest thoughts in simple and beautiful imagery?

(Chap 14, Class-X, Old NCERT)

(a) Brahmanas (b) Aranyakas
(c) Upanishads (d) Manusmriti

Ans. (c)

Exp. Among the given options, the ancient treatise, Upanishads are in the form of dialogues and express the highest thoughts in simple and beautiful imagery. It was compiled towards the end of the Vedic period in 600 BC in Panchala and Videha kingdoms. It dealt with the questions like the origin of universe, birth and death, the material and spiritual world, nature of knowledge and many other questions. The earliest Upanishads are Brihad- Aranyaka and Chanddogya Upanishad.

9 Which among the following path(s) is/are suggested in Bhagvad Gita for attaining salvation?

(Chap 14, Class-X, Old NCERT)

(a) Gyan (b) Bhakti
(c) Karma (d) All of these

Ans. (d)

Exp. Gyan, Bhakti and Karma are the three paths suggested in Bhagvad Gita for attaining salvation. Bhagvad Gita is a part of ancient Indian epic, the Mahabharata and contains dialogues between the God Krishna and Arjuna.

These three paths as elaborated in Bhagvad Gita later developed in different schools of Indian philosophy. Mahabharata was compiled by Vyasa and reflects the state of affairs from the tenth century BC to the fourteenth century BC.

10 Which one of the following explains the practice of Vattakirutal as mentioned in Sangam poems?

(Class-XII, Old NCERT) (IAS Pre 2023)

(a) Kings employing women bodyguards
(b) Learned persons assembling in royal courts to discuss religious and philosophical matters
(c) Young girls keeping watch over agricultural fields and driving away birds and animals
(d) A king defeated in a battle committing ritual suicide by starving himself to death

Ans. (d)

Exp. A king defeated in a battle committing ritual suicide by starving himself to death explains the practice of 'Vattakirutal' as mentioned in Sangam poems.

Vattakirutal also Vadakiruthal and Vadakiruttal, was a Tamil ritual of fasting till death. It was especially widespread during the Sangam age. The Tamil kings, in order to save their honour, and prestige, were prepared to meet their death facing North.

'Vatakkirutta' and never would they turn their back in battle.

11 Kumarasambhava, Raghuvamsa, Meghduta are among greatest literary works of Gupta period. These were written by *(Chap 14, Class-X, Old NCERT)*

(a) Vishnu Sharma
(b) Sudraka
(c) Kalidasa
(d) Amoghvarsha

Ans. (c)

Exp. Kumarasambhava, Raghuvamsa, Meghduta were compiled by Kalidasa. He was among the nine luminaries (*navratna*) of the Gupta Emperor, Chandragupta II. Kalidasa composed poems and drama in Sanskrit and his works are unrivalled for their poetry and style.

He also wrote Abhijnanashakuntalam which is considered to be one of the best hundred literary works in the World.

Vishnu Sharma wrote ancient book of fables the Panchatantra. Another poet of the Gupta age, Shudraka compiled Mrichchhakatika and the Buddhist monk, Ashvaghosha wrote Buddhacharita in Post-Mauryan age.

12 With the reference to ancient Indian History consider the following pairs. *(Class-XII, Old NCERT)*

	Literary work		Author
1.	Devichandragupta	–	Bilhana
2.	Hammira-Mahakavya	–	Nayachandra Suri
3.	Minda-Panha	–	Nagarjuna
4.	Nitivakyamrita	–	Somadeva Suri

How many of the pairs given above is/are correctly matched?

(a) Only one (b) Only two (c) Only three (d) All four

Ans. (c)

Exp. Only three pairs i.e. (2) (3) and (4) are correctly matched. Hammira Mahakavya is a 15th century Indian Sanskrit epic poem written by the Jain scholar Nayachandra Suri. It is a legendary biography of the 12th century Chahamana King Hammira.

The Milinda Panha (also known as the "Questions of King Milinda" or The Debate of King Milinda) is a famous Pali Buddhist text written by Nagasena (also known as Nagarjuna) that is considered part of the Thervada Buddhist tradition. It is a dialogue between the Indo-Greek King Menander I (known as Milinda in Pali) and the Buddhist monk Nagasena.

Somadeva Suri was a South Indian Jain monk of the 10th century CE. Somadeva Suri also wrote the Nitivakyamrtam Nectar of the Science of Polity, a treatise on statecraft. The text of the Nitivakyamrtam mentions that Somadeva was also the author of a literary work called Yashastilaka.

Pair (1) is incorrectly matched because Devi-Chandraguptam is the Sanskrit play of Vishakhadeva (Vishakhadatta). Its the story of Gupta King Ramagupta who decides to surrender his queen Dhruvadevi to a Shaka invader but his younger brother Chandragupta enters the enemy camp disguised a queen and kills the enemy.

13 Match the following lists correctly and choose the correct code. *(Chap 14, Class-X, Old NCERT)*

List I (Literature written in Ancient India)	List II (Authors)
A. Daskumaracharita	1. Dandin
B. Kirtarjuniya	2. Bharavi
C. Utter-Ramacharita	3. Bhavabhuti
D. Buddhacharita	4. Ashvaghosha

Codes

	A	B	C	D		A	B	C	D
(a)	1	2	3	4	(b)	2	1	4	3
(c)	3	4	1	2	(d)	2	1	3	4

Ans. (a)

Exp. The correct matching is A-1, B-2, C-3, D-4.

Daskumaracharita was compiled by Dandin in the seventh to eighth centuries AD. It deals with the tale of ten princes.

Kirtarjuniya was compiled by Bharavi in sixth century AD. It is an epic poem describing the confrontation between Arjuna and God Shiva.

Utter-Ramacharita was compiled by Bhavabhuti. It is a Sanskrit play illustrating the later life of the God Rama.

Buddhacharita was compiled by Ashvaghosha in the first century AD. It gives biographical account of Gautama Buddha in Sanskrit.

14 The world's second tallest statue in sitting pose of Ramanuja was inaugurated by the Prime Minister of India at Hyderabad recently. Which one of the following statements correctly represents the teachings of Ramanuja? *(Class-XII, Old NCERT) (IAS Pre 2022)*

(a) The best means of salvation was devotion
(b) Vedas are eternal, self-existent and wholly authoritative
(c) Logical arguments were essential means for the highest bliss.
(d) Salvation was to be obtained through meditation

Ans. (a)

Exp. The world's second tallest statue in sitting pose of Ramanuja was inaugurated by the Prime Minister of India at Hyderabad recently. The best means of salvation was devotion correctly represents the teachings of Ramanuja. Philosopher and social reformer, Saint Ramanujacharya born in 1017 in Sriperumbudur in Tamil Nadu, travelled across India, advocating equality and social justice. He advocated universal salvation through devotion to God, compassion, humility, equality and mutual respect, which is known as Sriv Vaishnavam Sampradaya. Ramanuja revived the Bhakti movement, and his preachings inspired other Bhakti schools of thought. He is considered to be the inspiration for poets like Annamacharya, Bhakti Ramdas, Thyagaraja, Kabir and Meerabai.

15 Which among the following work written in Hindi marks the beginning of the Bardic literature? *(Chap 14, Class-X, Old NCERT)*

1. Panchantantra by Vishnu Sharma
2. Kathasarit Sagar by Bilhana
3. Prithviraj Raso by Chand Bardai
4. Daskumaracharita by Dandin

Codes

(a) Only 1 (b) Only 2 (c) Only 3 (d) Only 4

Ans. (c)

Exp. Option (3) is correct. Prithviraj Raso written by Chand Bardai in Hindi marks the beginning of the Bardic literature. It deals with the heroic deeds of the Chahamana King, Prithviraj Chauhan. Chand Bardai was the court poet of Prithviraj Chauhan who was defeated by Muhammad Ghori in the Second Battle of Tarain in 1192. AD.

16 Consider the following statements with reference to the literature in India. *(Chap 14, Class-X, Old NCERT)*

1. Nalayira –Divyaprabhandham is related with the Nayanars.
2. Nripatunga wrote a great work of poetry in Kannada called the Kavirajamarga.

3. Pampa, Ponna and Kamban are known as three jewels of early Kannada literature.

Which of the statements given above is/are incorrect?

(a) 1 and 2 (b) 1 and 3
(c) 2 and 3 (d) None of these

Ans. (b)

Exp. Statements (1) and (3) are incorrect with reference to the literature in India.

Nalayira- Divyaprabhandham contains hymns related with Alvars (not Nayanars). The Alvars were Bhakti saints of Tamil Nadu who were devotees of God Vishnu. Pampa, Ponna and Ranna (not Kamban) are known as three jewels of early Kannada literature. Kamban was a medieval Tamil poet and the author of the Ramavataram, the Tamil version of Ramayana.

17 Match the following lists correctly and choose the correct code. *(Chap 14, Class-X, Old NCERT)*

List I (Literature written in Medieval India)	List II (Authors)
A. Chandayana	1. Zia-ud-Din Barani
B. Tarikh-i- Firuzshahi	2. Mulla Daud
C. Alha Udal	3. Allasani Peddana
D. Manucharita	4. Jagnayak

Codes

	A	B	C	D		A	B	C	D
(a)	1	2	3	4	(b)	2	1	4	3
(c)	3	4	1	2	(d)	2	1	3	4

Ans. (b)

Exp. The correct matching is A-2, B-1, C-4, D-3.

Chandayana was written by the Sufi saint Mulla Daud in Awadhi language in 14th century AD. It is a love story of Norak and Chanda.

Tarikh-i-Firuzshahi was written by Zia-ud-Din Barani in 14th century AD. It is commentary on the political events of Delhi Sultanate from the reign of Ghiyasuddin Balban to Firoz Shah Tughlaq.

Alha Udal was written in Hindi by Jagnayak. It consists of a number of ballads describing the brave acts of two brothers Alha and Udal of Mahoba who resisted the attack of Prithiviraj Chauhan.

Manucharita was written in Telugu by Allasani Peddana in 16th century AD. He was one of the *Asthadiggaja* in the court of Krishnadeva Raya.

18 Which one of the following pairs is not correctly matched? *(Chap 14, Class-X, Old NCERT) (RAS/RTS Pre 2021)*

	Books		Authors
(a)	Nagdaman	–	Sayanji Jhula
(b)	Ranmal Chhand	–	Shridhar Vyas
(c)	Bhasha Bhushan	–	Maharaja Jaswant Singh
(d)	Neh Tarang	–	Sawai Pratap Singh

Ans. (d)

Exp. Pair (d) is not correctly matched because the author of Neh Tarang is Rao Buddha Singh not Sawai Pratap Singh. It is spiritual poetic epic in which the story of Lord Krishna and Radha have been depicted.

19 Consider the following texts and arrange them in chronological order. *(Chap 14, Class-X, Old NCERT) (UPPSC Pre 2020)*

1. Fatawa-i-Jahandari
2. Prithviraja-Raso
3. Kitab-ul-Hind
4. Tabaqat-i-Nasiri

Codes

(a) 2, 3, 4, 1 (b) 3, 1, 2, 4 (c) 4, 3, 1, 2 (d) 3, 2, 4, 1

Ans. (d)

Exp. The correct chronological order of the above texts is 3, 2, 4, 1

Kitab-ul-Hind was written by Al-Biruni in the year 1030. AD. It was in Arabic language.

Prithviraja-Raso was written by Chand Bardai in 1235 AD. It is based on the life of Prithviraj III.

Tabaqat-i-Nasiri was written by Minhaj-i-Siraj in 1260 AD. Written in Persian.

Fatawa-i-jahandari was written by Ziyauddin Barani in 1357 AD.

20 Which of the following works was/were written by the Amir Khusrau? *(Chap 14, Class-X, Old NCERT)*

1. Ashiqa
2. Nuh Sipihr
3. Qiranal-Sadayan
4. Fatawa-i- Jahandari

Codes

(a) 1 and 2 (b) 2 and 3
(c) 1, 2 and 3 (d) All of these

Ans. (c)

Exp. Ashiqa, Nuh Sipihr and Qiranal-Sadayan were some of the literary creations of Amir Khusrau. He was also a disciple of Nizamuddin Auliya and believed to have seen the reign of seven sultans of Delhi Sultanate. He also invented the musical instrument, sitar and Ghazal style of Hindustani music. While Fatawa-i- Jahandari was written by Zia-ud-Din Barani.

21 Consider the following statements with reference to the Amir Khusrau. *(Chap 14, Class-X, Old NCERT)*

1. He praised India as the Earthly Paradise.
2. He considered Persian as a mother tongue.
3. He composed verses in Hindi and Persian language.

Which of the statements given above is incorrect?

(a) Only 1 (b) Only 2 (c) Only 3 (d) None of these

Ans. (b)

Exp. Statement (2) is incorrect with reference to the Amir Khusrau. Amir Khusrau took great pride in his being an Indian and considered Hindavi (the Hindi spoken in region of Delhi) as his mother tongue. He also believed that in many respects the essence of Hinduism resembled Islam.

NCERT MCQ

Practice Set (1-3)

Indian History

Scan the QR Code given below to get the PDF of these Practice Sets.